PHILIP'S

STREET ATLAS
Edinburgh
and East Central Scotland

First published in 1995 by

Philip's, a division of
Octopus Publishing Group Ltd
2–4 Heron Quays, London E14 4JP

Second colour edition 2002
First impression 2002

ISBN 0-540-08178-7 (pocket)
© Philip's 2002

 Ordnance Survey®

This product includes mapping data licensed
from Ordnance Survey® with the permission
of the Controller of Her Majesty's Stationery
Office. © Crown copyright 2002. All rights
reserved. Licence number 100011710

Printed and bound in Spain
by Cayfosa-Quebecor

Contents

III   **Key to map symbols**

IV   **Key to map pages**

VI   **Route planning**

VIII   **Administrative and Postcode boundaries**

1   **Street maps** at 2½ inches to 1 mile

232   **Street map of Edinburgh city centre** at 5 inches to 1 mile

234   **Index** of towns and villages

235   **Index** of streets, hospitals, industrial estates, railway stations, schools, shopping centres and universities and places of interest

Digital Data

The exceptionally high-quality mapping found in this atlas is available as digital data in TIFF format, which is easily convertible to other bitmapped (raster) image formats.

The index is also available in digital form as a standard database table. It contains all the details found in the printed index together with the National Grid reference for the map square in which each entry is named.

For further information and to discuss your requirements, please contact Philip's on 020 7531 8439 or ruth.king@philips-maps.co.uk

Key to map symbols

III

(22a)	**Motorway** with junction number	Walsall	**Railway station**
	Primary route – dual/single carriageway		**Private railway station**
	A road – dual/single carriageway	South Shields	**Metro station**
	B road – dual/single carriageway		**Tram stop, tram stop under construction**
	Minor road – dual/single carriageway		**Bus, coach station**
	Other minor road – dual/single carriageway		**Ambulance station**
	Tunnel, covered road		**Coastguard station**
	Road under construction		**Fire station**
	Pedestrianised area		**Police station**
DY7	**Postcode boundaries**		**Accident and Emergency entrance to hospital**
	County and unitary authority boundaries	H	**Hospital**
	Railway, railway under construction	+	**Place of worship**
	Tramway, tramway under construction	i	**Information Centre** (open all year)
	Miniature railway	P	**Parking**
	Rural track, private road or narrow road in urban area	P&R	**Park and Ride**
	Gate or obstruction to traffic (restrictions may not apply at all times or to all vehicles)	PO	**Post Office**
	Path, bridleway, byway open to all traffic, road used as a public path	X	**Camping site**
58			**Caravan site**
230	**Adjoining page indicators**		**Picnic site**
241		Prim Sch	**Important buildings, schools, colleges, universities and hospitals**
	The map area within the pink band is shown at a larger scale on the page indicated by the red block and arrow	River Medway	**Water name**

Acad	**Academy**	Mkt	**Market**
Allot Gdns	**Allotments**	Meml	**Memorial**
Cemy	**Cemetery**	Mon	**Monument**
C Ctr	**Civic Centre**	Mus	**Museum**
CH	**Club House**	Obsy	**Observatory**
Coll	**College**	Pal	**Royal Palace**
Crem	**Crematorium**	PH	**Public House**
Ent	**Enterprise**	Recn Gd	**Recreation Ground**
Ex H	**Exhibition Hall**	Resr	**Reservoir**
Ind Est	**Industrial Estate**	Ret Pk	**Retail Park**
IRB Sta	**Inshore Rescue Boat Station**	Sch	**School**
		Sh Ctr	**Shopping Centre**
Inst	**Institute**	TH	**Town Hall/House**
Ct	**Law Court**	Trad Est	**Trading Estate**
L Ctr	**Leisure Centre**	Univ	**University**
LC	**Level Crossing**	Wks	**Works**
Liby	**Library**	YH	**Youth Hostel**

River, stream

Lock, weir

Water

Tidal water

Woods

Built up area

Church   **Non-Roman antiquity**

ROMAN FORT   **Roman antiquity**

■ The small numbers around the edges of the maps identify the 1 kilometre National Grid lines

■ The dark grey border on the inside edge of some pages indicates that the mapping does not continue onto the adjacent page

The scale of the maps on the pages numbered in blue is 3.92 cm to 1 km • 2½ inches to 1 mile • 1: 25344

0	¼	½	¾	1 mile
0	250 m	500 m	750 m	1 kilometre

The scale of the maps on pages numbered in red is 7.84 cm to 1 km • 5 inches to 1 mile • 1: 12672

0	220 yards	440 yards	660 yards	½ mile
0	125 m	250 m	375 m	½ kilometre

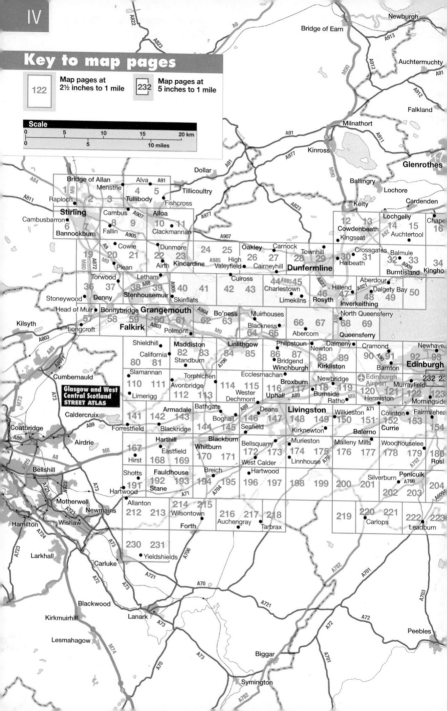

St Andrews

Cupar

Ladybank

A92

A916

A914

A91

A917

A915

Crail

Kilrenny

Anstruther Easter

Anstruther Wester

Pittenweem

St Monans

Kennoway

A911

Leven

Methil

Earlsferry

Buckhaven

A915

A955

Dysart

Kirkcaldy

17
18

A921

35

51	Dirleton		North Berwick		
	52	53	54	55	56
Gullane Hill	Gullane		Kingston		Scoughall
	Aberlady	Fenton Barns	Whitekirk		76	77	78	79
Craigielaw	72	73	74	75	Tyninghame	Dunbar
	70	71	Drem	East Fortune	West Barns	Bellhaven
		Ballencrieff				

Dirleton A198

North Berwick

Gullane

Kingston

Scoughall

Aberlady

Fenton Barns

Whitekirk

Tyninghame

Dunbar

Craigielaw

Drem

East Fortune

West Barns

Bellhaven

Ballencrieff

Leith		Cockenzie and Port Seton	Longniddry	Athelstaneford	East Linton	Broxburn		108	109
94	95	96	97	98	99	100	101	102	103	104	105	106	107	Skateraw
Portobello		Prestonpans	Tranent		Traprain	Stenton	Pitcox	Spott	Innerwick

Leith

94 95

A199

Cockenzie and Port Seton

96 97

Longniddry

98 99

Prestonpans

Athelstaneford

100 101

A1

East Linton

102 103

Traprain

104 105

Stenton

Pitcox

Broxburn

106 107

Spott

A1

108 109

Skateraw

Innerwick

Portobello

124 125 126 127

Musselburgh

Tranent

128 129

Macmerry

130 131

A6093

Haddington

132 133

Papple

134 135

Halls

136 137 138 139

140

Cove

Craigmillar

Whitecraig

Wallyford

Elphinstone

Samuelston

Garvald

Oldhamstocks

Cockburnspath

Gilmerton

155 156 157

Danderhall

A6124

Ormiston

Cousland

158 159

160 161

East Saltoun

162 163

Gifford

Carfrae

164 165 166

Danskine

Dalkeith

Loanhead

181

Mayfield

Bonnyrigg
and Lasswade

182 183

A7

Pathhead

184 185

Crichton

West Peaston

186 187

Humbie

Gilchriston

188 189

Longyester

190

Carrington

205 206

Gorebridge

207

North
Middleton

208 209

Borthwick

Tynehead

210 211

A68

224 225 226 227

Falahill

Gilston

228 229

Duns

A6105

A1

A1107

A6112

A6112

Lauder

A697

A6089

A6105

A697

A68

A7

Coldstream

Innerleithen

A72

Galashiels

A6091

Melrose

Earlston

A68

A6105

A697

A698

Kelso

A6105

Route planning

Scale

0 1 2 3 4 5 6 7 8 km
0 1 2 3 4 5 miles

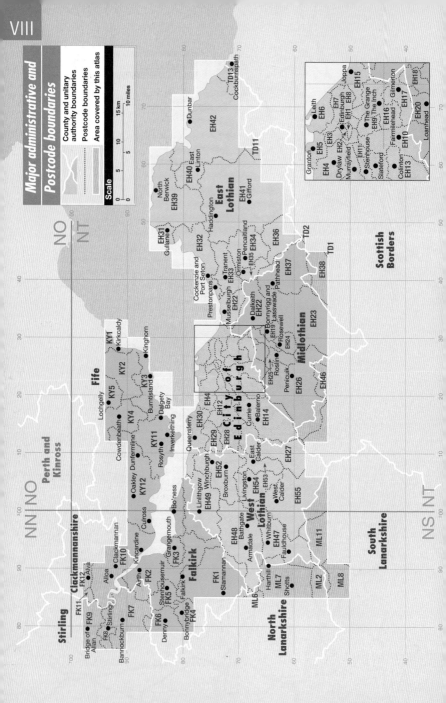

Major administrative and Postcode boundaries

County and unitary authority boundaries
Postcode boundaries
Area covered by this atlas

Scale
0   5   10   15 km
0   5   10 miles

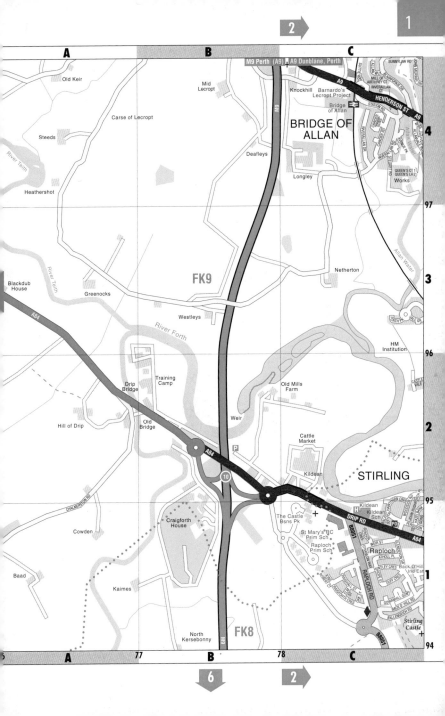

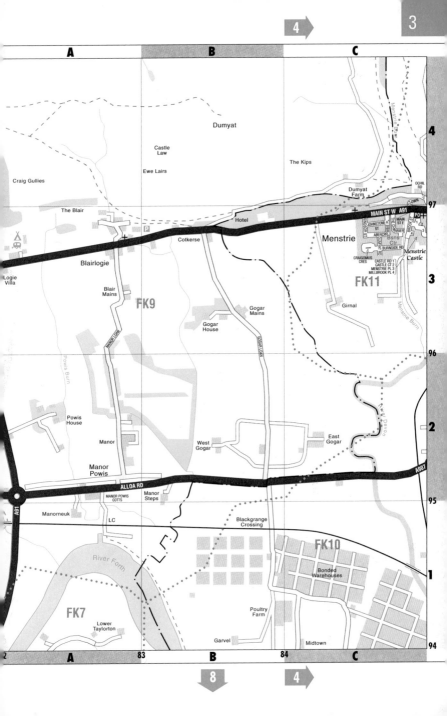

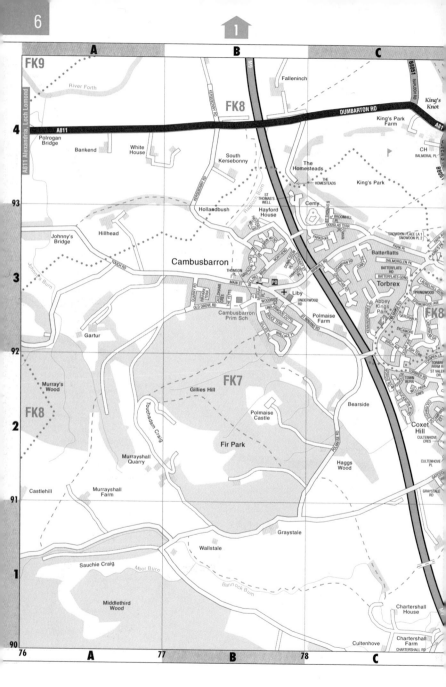

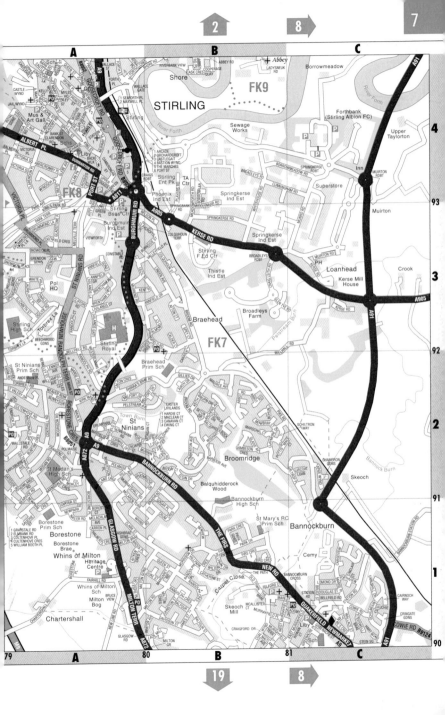

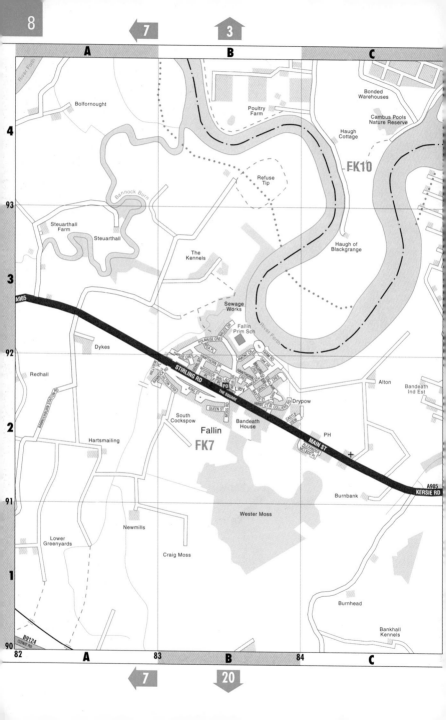

A   **B**   **C**

River Forth

Bolfornought

Poultry
Farm

Bonded
Warehouses

Cambus Pools
Nature Reserve

Haugh
Cottage

4

FK10

Bannock Burn

Refuse
Tip

93

Steuarthall
Farm

Steuarthall

The
Kennels

Haugh of
Blackrange

3

A905

River Forth

Sewage
Works

Fallin
Prim Sch

92

Dykes

POLMAISE CRES

BRIDGE DR

HAMONT CRES

FARM RD

Redhall

DARDIE CRES

HAWTHORN

WOODSIDE

HILLVIEW

HAWTHORN

BRUCE CRES

OAK RD

Alton

Bandeath
Ind Est

STIRLING RD

WALLACE

BANNOCKBURN STATION RD

KING ST

THE SQUARE

PO

Liby

HIRST CT

CASTLE CRES

Drypow

QUEEN ST

MOSS RD

COLLIERS

2

South
Cockspow

Fallin

FK7

Bandeath
House

CASTLE
VIEW

PH

Hartsmailing

MAIN ST

ALEXANDER
MCKENZIE PL

+

A905
KERSIE RD

91

Burnbank

Newmills

Wester Moss

Lower
Greenyards

Craig Moss

1

Burnhead

B9124
COWIE RD

Bankhall
Kennels

90
82   **A**   **83**   **B**   **84**   **C**

4 **10**

A B C

Cambus Farm
Arnsbrae
Gean House

PH
DEVON PL
Cambus

D'URRAR DR
Alloa Acad
Claremont Prim Sch

STIRLING RD

PO

A907

ALLOA

4

Orchard Farm
Orchard House

FK10

THE PAVILIONS

Smart Village Bsns Campus

LC

A907

Pier

SMITHFIELD LOAN

93

Works

FORBES ST

3

Bandeath Ind Est

Tullibody Inch

Longcarse

Works

CARPENTERS WYND
CALEDONIAN RD

KELLIEBANK
CRAIGWARD

KELLIEBANK
DOWNS CRES

Longcarse Reach

92

Rhind

Inch

Throsk House

Works

Pier

South Alloa

2

Throsk

River Forth

KERSIE RD

Kersie Mains

KERSIE TERR

FK7

91

Mains of Throsk

Poppletrees

Kersie Bridge

KERSIE RD

South Mains

Willowbank

Meadowfield

South Kersie

1

FK2

A905

90

35 A **86** B **87** C

21 **10**

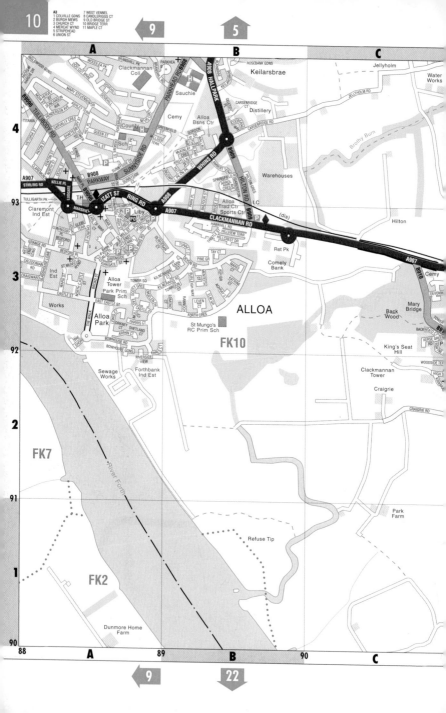

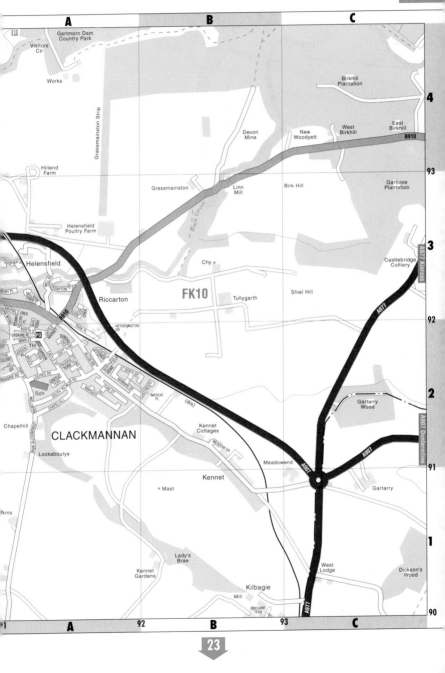

4

93

3

92

2

91

1

90

Gartmorn Dam Country Park
Visitors Ctr
P
Works

Grassmainston Strip

Birkhill Plantation

Devon Mine
New Woodyett
West Birkhill
East Birkhill
B910

Hillend Farm

Grassmainston
Linn Mill
Birk Hill
Gartlove Plantation

Helensfield Poultry Farm

Black Devon

Helensfield

Riccarton

FK10

Chy

Tullygarth
Shiel Hill

B910

Castlebridge Colliery

A977 Kinross

HETHERINGTON DR

PARK PL

MAIN ST
TH
PO
Sch

ST SERFS GR

MERCAT PL

(dis)

A977

Chapelhill

CLACKMANNAN

Lookaboutye

Kennet Cottages

MEADOW GR

Gartarry Wood

Meadowend

A907

A907

A907 Dunfermline

Kennet

Mast

Gartarry

Arns

Lady's Brae

Kennet Gardens

West Lodge

Dickson's Wood

Kilbagie
Mill

ORCHARD TERR

A977

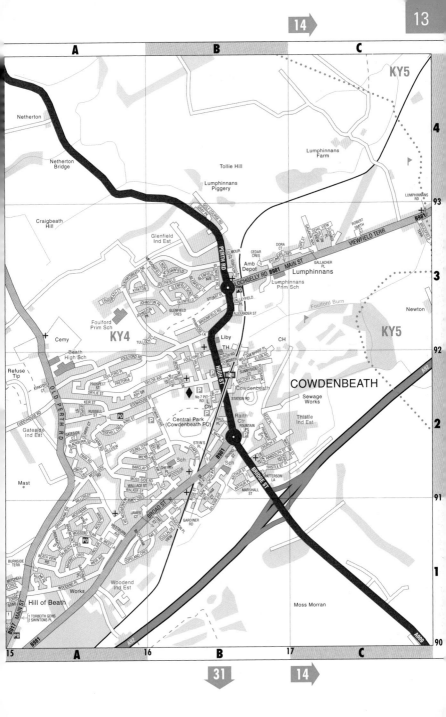

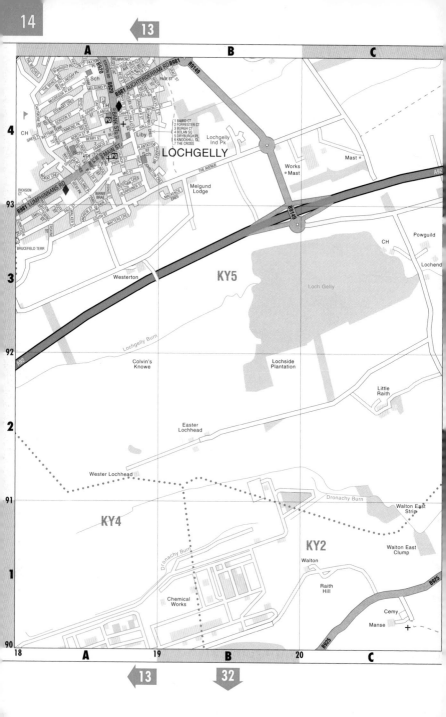

A   B   C

B920

DRUMMOND

B9149

B981 AUCHTERDERRAN RD B981

PAGE ST

4

1 BAIRD CT
2 FORRESTER CT
3 BURGH CT
4 BOLAN SQ
5 DRYBURGH PL
6 KNOCKHILL PL
7 THE CROSS

Lochgelly
Ind Pk

CH

Liby

Sch

PO

LOCHGELLY

Works
Mast

Mast

A92

Powguild

CH

Lochend

93

Melgund
Lodge

MACKENZIE CRES

B9149

DICKSON CT

B981 LUMPHINNANS RD

BRUCEFIELD TERR

3

Westerton

KY5

Loch Gelly

92

Lochgelly Burn

Colvin's
Knowe

Lochside
Plantation

Little
Raith

2

Easter
Lochhead

Wester Lochhead

91

Dronachy Burn

Walton East
Strip

KY4

Walton East
Clump

KY2

Dronachy Burn

Walton

B925

1

Chemical
Works

Raith
Hill

Cemy

Manse

B925

90

18   A   19   B   20   C

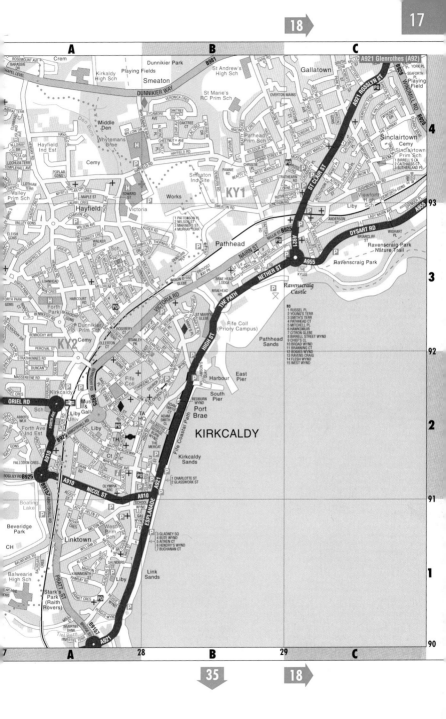

A955 Leven
Colliery
Blair
Point

BORELAND
RD

B923

A955

KY1

Randolph
Ind Est

NORMAND RD

STEWART ST

File Coastal Path

4

Dysart
1 LOUGHBOROUGH RD
2 WEST PORT
3 ST SERF'S PL
4 WEST QUALITY ST
5 EAST QUALITY ST
6 ORCHARD PL
7 ORCHARD LA
8 FITZROY ST
9 McDOUALL STUART PL
10 VICTORIA ST

93

A955

Mus

DYSART RD

RECTORY LA

B923

Ravenscraig
Park

Panhall

3

92

2

91

1

90

30   A   31   B   32   C

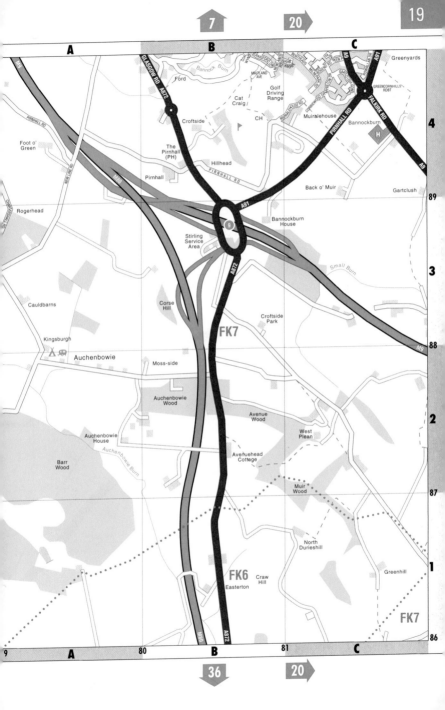

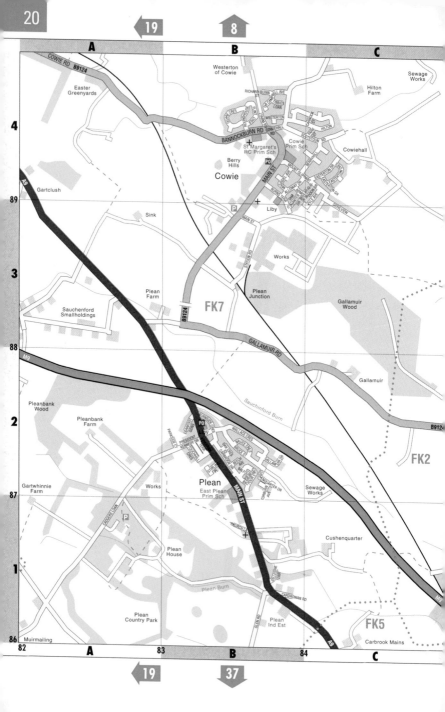

A   B   C

9   22

A806

4

Easter Moss

FK7

Windmill
(disused)

Dunmore Moss

Moss
Wood

89

Hillhead

Darnbogue

Dunmore Wood

FAIRFIELDS

3

Carnock
House

North
Doll

88

Castleton

Whitehill

Tower

FK2

South
Doll

2

Avenue
Plantation

Bullions

B9124

Powbridge

Davidscraig
Wood

Pow Burn

87

Pleanmill

Powdrake
Farm

Powside

Bridge-end

Tramways

1

Sauchinford Burn

Pow Burn

Letham
Moss

FK5

Mossneuk

Rosehill

Pow Burn

86

85   A   86   B   87   C

38   22

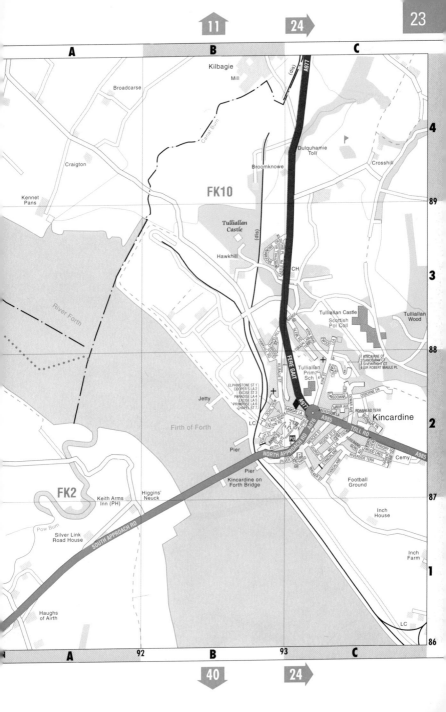

A
B
C

4
89
3
88
2
87
1
86

Kilbagie
Mill
Broadcarse
Canal Burn
Dulquhamie Toll
Broomknowe
Crosshill
Craigton
FK10
Kennet Pans
Tulliallan Castle (dis)
Hawkhill
CH
Tulliallan Castle
Scottish Pol Coll
Tulliallan Wood
River Forth
FERE GAIT
1 KINCAIRNE CT
2 SANDHAVEN CT
3 SILVERWRIGHT CT
4 SIR ROBERT MAULE PL
Tulliallan Prim Sch
ELPHINSTONE ST 1
COOPER'S LA 2
EXCISE ST 3
PARADISE LA 4
EXCISE LA 5
PRIMROSE LA 6
CHAPEL ST 7
Jetty
RAMSAY LA
ANDERSON LA
ROANHEAD TERR
WAR AVE
OSBORNE DR
Kincardine
Firth of Forth
LC
LIBY
TOLL RD
A985
Pier
PO
P
A985
NORTH APPROACH RD
Cemy
Pier
Kincardine on Forth Bridge
RIVERSIDE TERR
FK2
Higgins' Neuck
Football Ground
Keith Arms Inn (PH)
Inch House
Silver Link Road House
Pow Burn
SOUTH APPROACH RD
Inch Farm
Haughs of Airth
LC

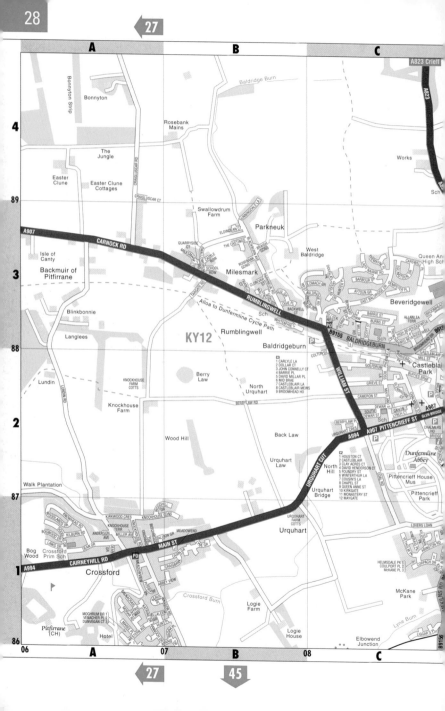

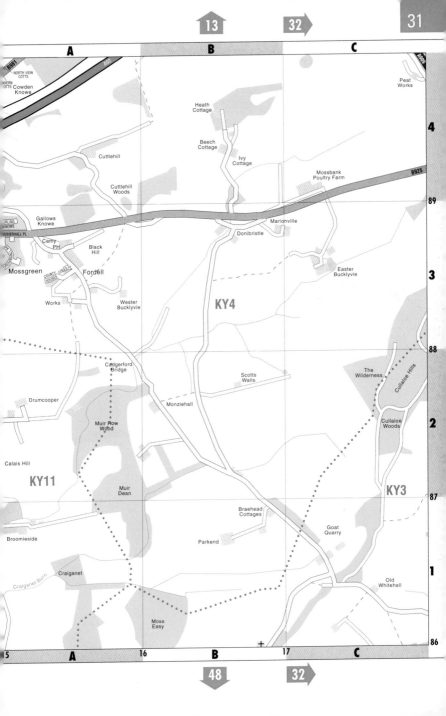

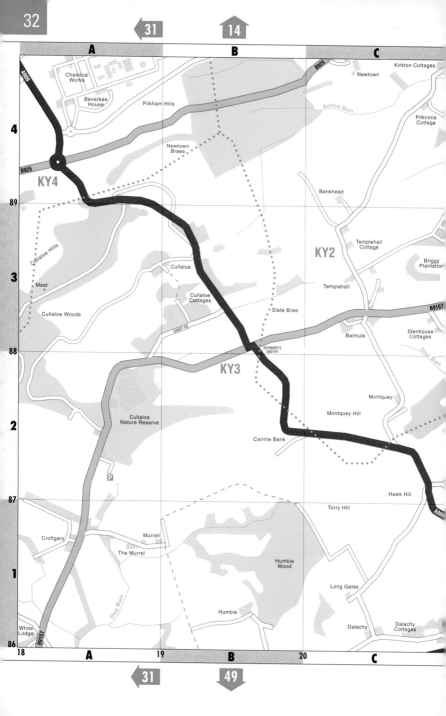

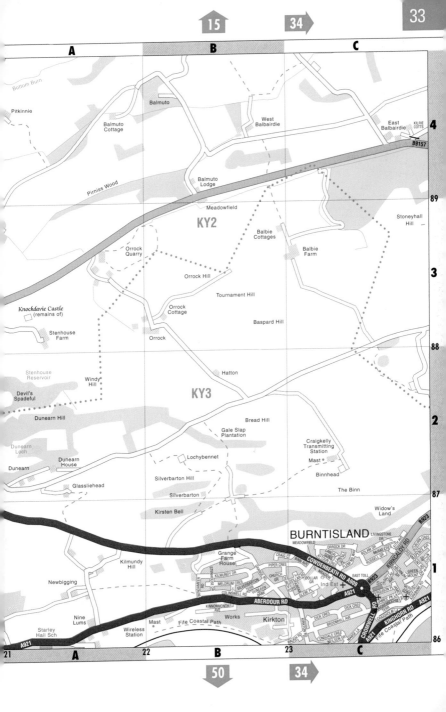

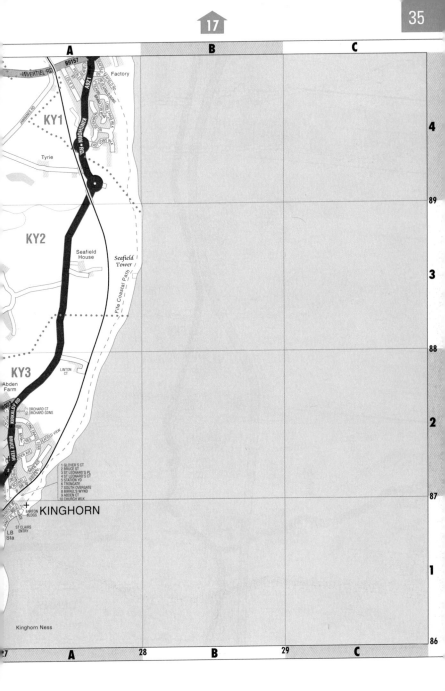

A B C

4

89

3

88

2

87

1

86

INVERTIEL RD
B0157
Factory

KY1

Tyrie

KINGHORN RD
A921

KY2

Seafield House
Seafield Tower

Fife Coastal Path

KY3

LINTON CT

Abden Farm

KIRKALDY RD

BRUCE TERR

1 ORCHARD CT
2 ORCHARD GDNS

1 GLOVER S CT
2 BRUCE ST
3 ST LEONARD'S PL
4 ST LEONARD'S CT
5 STATION YD
6 TRONGATE
7 SOUTH OVERGATE
8 BIRREL'S WYND
9 ABDEN CT
10 CHURCH WLK

KINGHORN
BARTON BLDGS
ST CLAIRS ENTRY
LB Sta

Kinghorn Ness

27 A 28 B 29 C

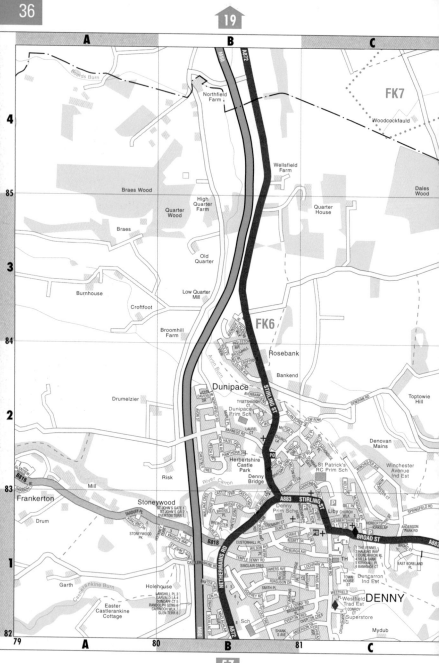

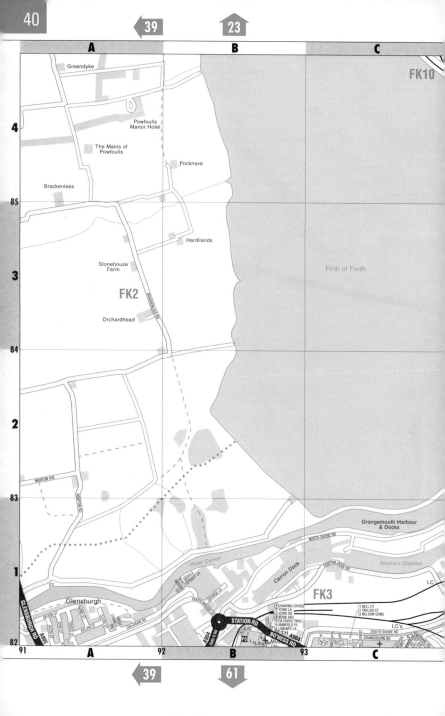

A **B** **C**

FK10

Greendyke

Powfoulis
Manor Hotel

4

The Mains of
Powfoulis

Pocknave

Brackenlees

85

Hardilands

Firth of Forth

Stonehouse
Farm

3

FK2

BRACKENLEES RD

Orchardhead

84

2

NEWTON AVE

83

Grangemouth Harbour
& Docks

NORTH SHORE RD

Western Channel

River Carron

Carron Dock

CENTRAL DOCK RD

LC

1

FK3

1 BELL CT
2 TAYLOR CT
3 NELSON GDNS

GLENSBURGH RD

A905

Glensburgh

DEVON ST

KELVIN ST

KINGS ST

TEES ST

PARK ST

AVON ST

DALDRAIN RD

NEWTON RD

SOUTH BRIDGE ST

DORSET LA

GRANGE LA

SOUTH BRIDGE ST

STATION RD

BO'NESS RD

A904

A904

1 CHARING CROSS
2 YORK LA
3 YORK SQ
4 YORK ARC
5 LA PORTE PREC
6 ANNFIELD PL
7 LIBRARY LA

SOUTH SHORE RD

GRANGEBURN RD

LC's

PO

82

91 **A** 92 **B** 93 **C**

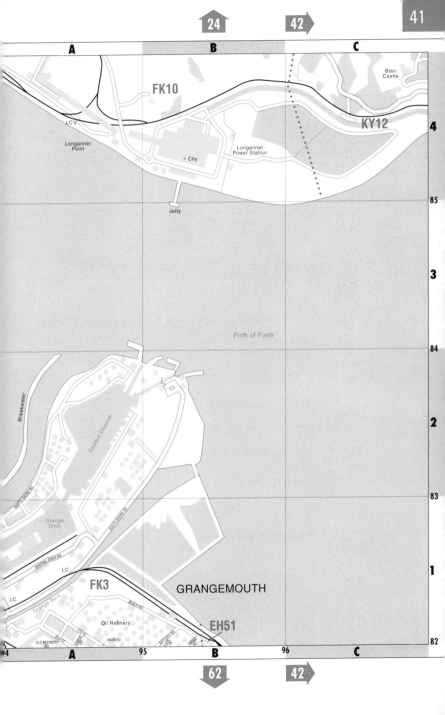

A   B   C

FK10

KY12

Blair
Castle

LC's

Longannet
Point

Longannet
Power Station

Chy

4

85

Jetty

3

84

Firth of Forth

Breakwater

Eastern Channel

2

83

NORTH SHORE RD

SOUTH SHORE RD

Grange
Dock

CENTRAL DOCK RD

LC

1

LC

FK3

Grange Burn

BEACH RD

GRANGEMOUTH

EH51

Oil Refinery

OLD REFINERY RD

MAIN RD

BATTERY RD

82

94   A   95   B   96   C

A **B** **C**

Mus
Dunimarle
Castle
BALSOWNIE W
Sch
Palace Mus
KY12
L.C
P
PH
PO
Sch
Blairburn
CULROSS

1 TANHOUSE BRAE
2 MID CSWY
3 LITTLE CSWY
4 LITTLE SANDHAVEN
5 BACK ST
6 BLACKADDER HAVEN

4

85

3

84

Firth of Forth

2

83

1

West Pier

82
97 **A** 98 **B** 99 **C**

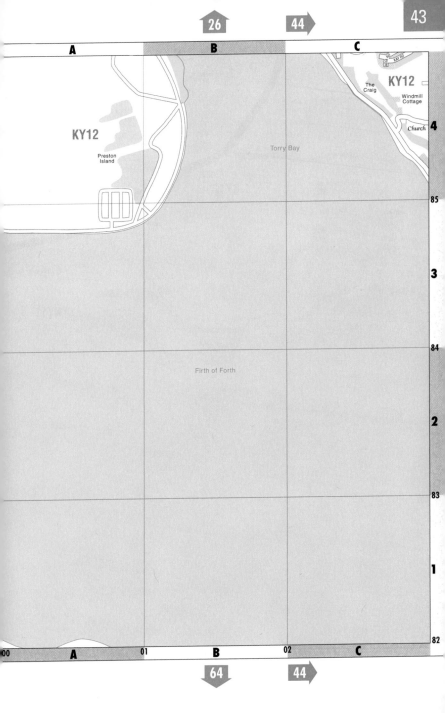

A
B
C

KY12

The Craig

Windmill Cottage

KY12

KAY RD

Church

4

Preston Island

KY12

Torry Bay

85

3

84

Firth of Forth

2

83

1

82

A

B

C

Muirside
Cottage

Muirside

Mire End

Bankhead

4

KY11

CRAIGWELL PATH

Crombie

Crombie
Prim Sch

Shoreside

Bullions Farm
Cottages

KY12

MAIN RD

85

Stripeside

Bullions

Crombie
Farm

Waukmill
Cottages

+

Kiln
Hill

A985

Crombie
Point

3

Crombie
Pier

Waukmill

CAMP RD

ORDNANCE RD

KY11

Kinniny Braes

Ironmill
Bay

84

Crombie
Pier

2

Jetty

Firth of Forth

83

1

82

03

A

04

B

05

C

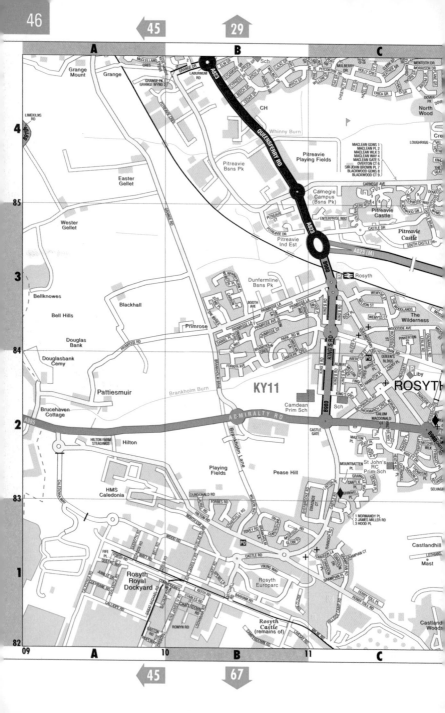

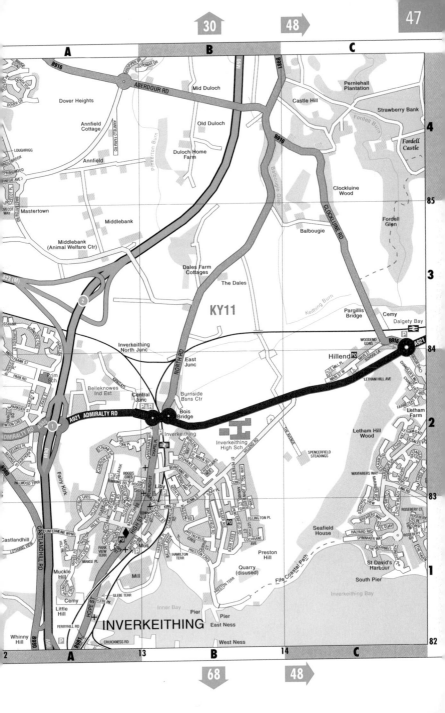

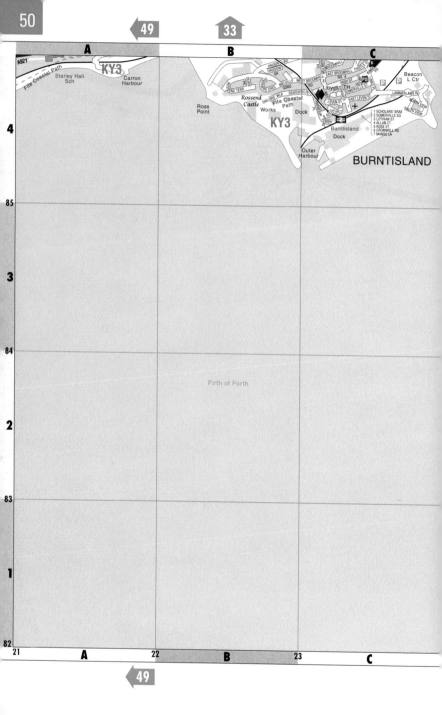

A921

KY3

Fife Coastal Path

Starley Hall
Sch

Carron
Harbour

A

B

Ross
Point

Rossend
Castle

Fife Coastal
Path

Works

Dock

KY3

Burntisland
Dock

1 SCHOLARS' BRAE
2 SOMERVILLE SQ
3 LOTHIAN ST
4 ALLAN CT
5 ROSE ST
6 CROMWELL RD
7 MANSE LA

C

Beacon
L Ctr

P

P

LAMMERLAWS RD

SOUTH VIEW

NORTH VIEW

BROOMHILL

EAST BROOMHILL
RD

WEST BROOMHILL
RD

HIGH ST

SOMERVILLE ST

EAST LEVEN ST

Liby

TH

Outer
Harbour

BURNTISLAND

4

85

3

84

Firth of Forth

2

83

1

82

21

A

22

B

23

C

49

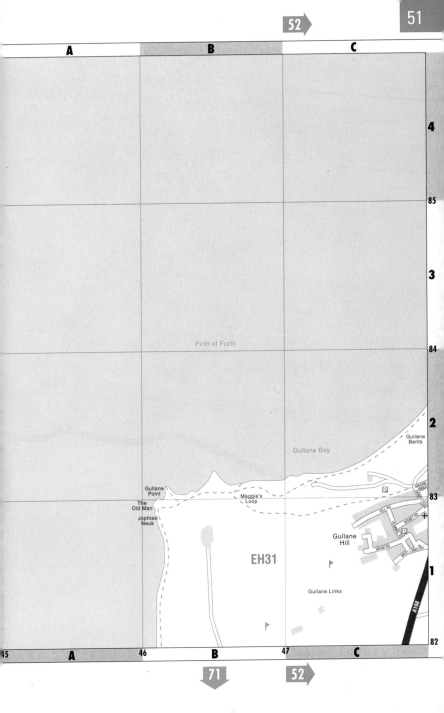

2

Gullane
Bents

Firth of Forth

Gullane Bay

P

MARINE
AVENUE

83

Gullane
Point

Maggie's
Loop

The
Old Man

Jophies
Neuk

P

HILL RD

BISSET RD

HUMBIE RD

GOOSE GREEN RD

Gullane
Hill

WHIM RD

WEST LINKS RD

EH31

1

Gullane Links

A198

82

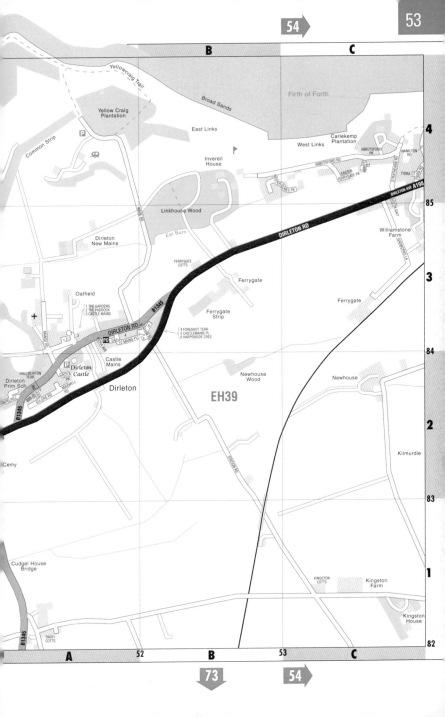

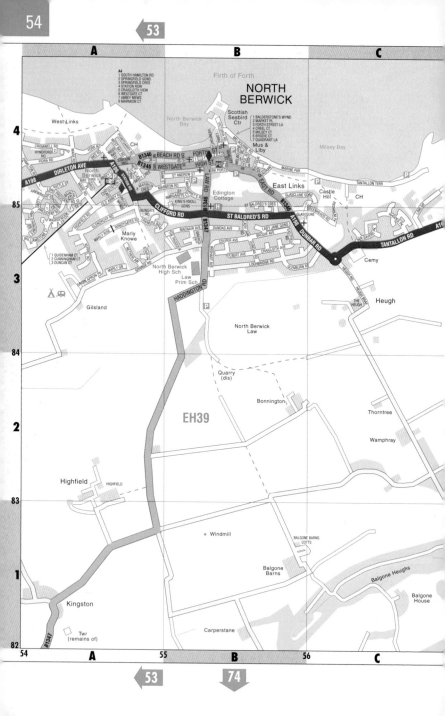

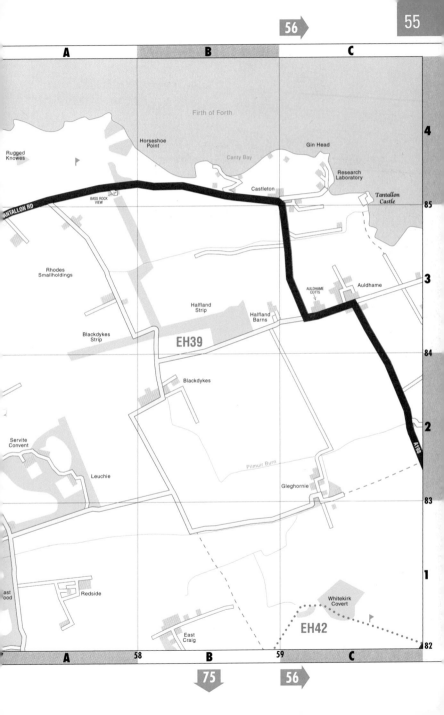

A

B

C

Firth of Forth

Rugged
Knowes

Horseshoe
Point

Canty Bay

Gin Head

4

Castleton

Research
Laboratory

Tantallon
Castle

TANTALLON RD

BASS ROCK
VIEW

85

Rhodes
Smallholdings

AULDHAME
COTTS

Auldhame

3

Halfland
Strip

Halfland
Barns

Blackdykes
Strip

EH39

84

Blackdykes

Servite
Convent

Leuchie

Pilmuir Burn

Gleghornie

83

2

A198

1

ast
ood

Redside

Whitekirk
Covert

EH42

East
Craig

82

A

58

B

59

C

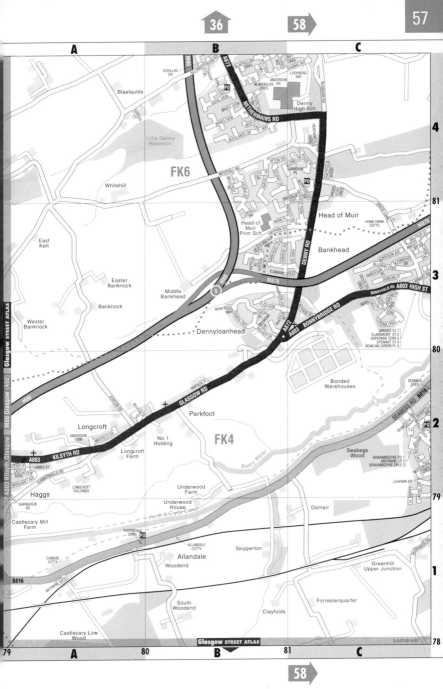

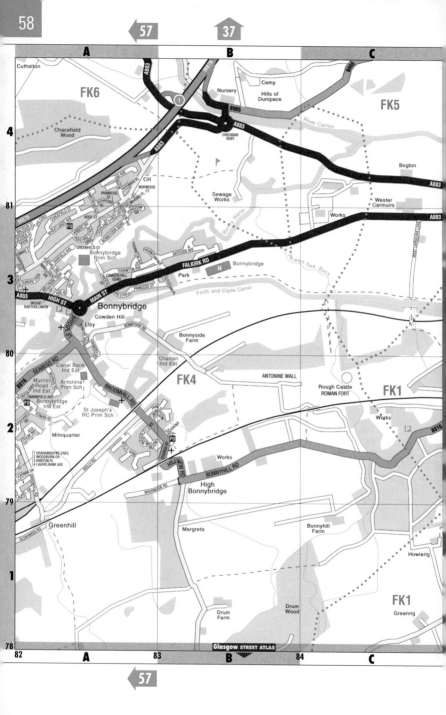

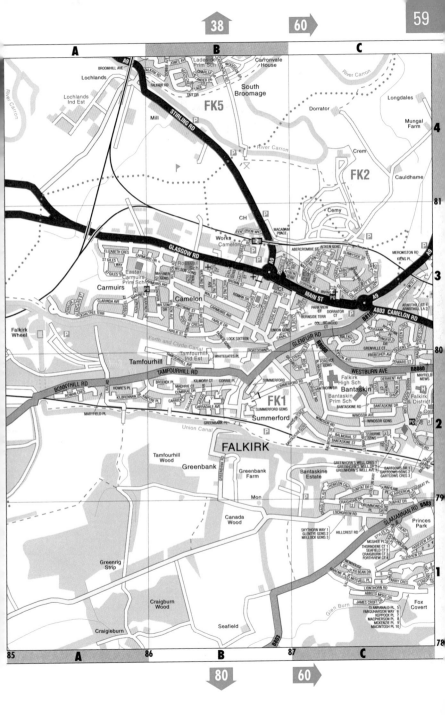

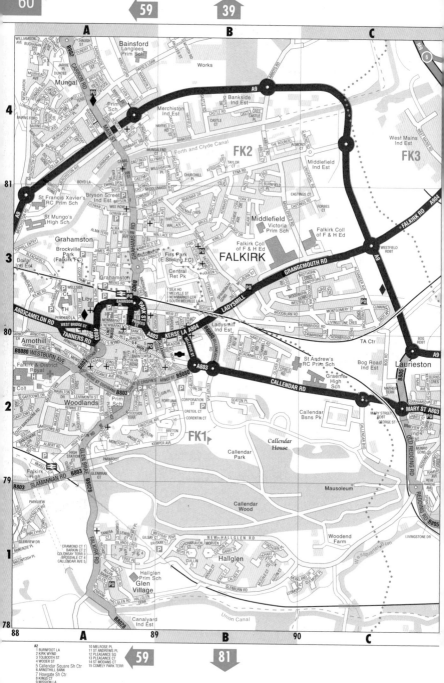

A2
1 BURNFOOT LA
2 KIRK WYND
3 TOLBOOTH ST
4 WOOER ST
5 Callendar Square Sh Ctr
6 ARNOTHILL BANK
7 Howgate Sh Ctr
8 KINGS CT
9 MISSION LA
10 MELROSE PL
11 ST ANDREWS PL
12 PLEASANCE SQ
13 PLEASANCE CT
14 ST MODANS CT
15 COMELY PARK TERR

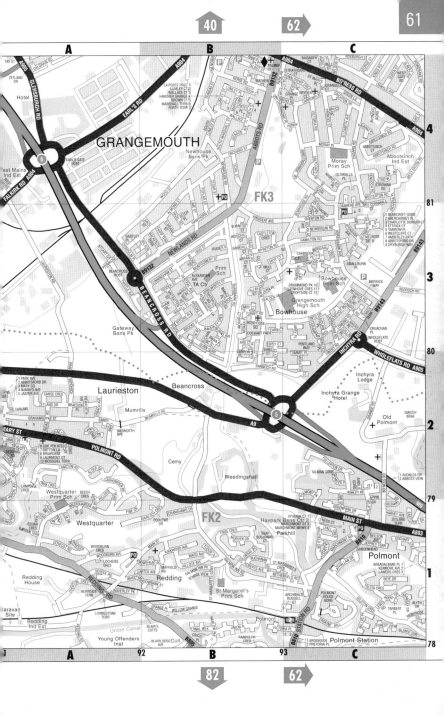

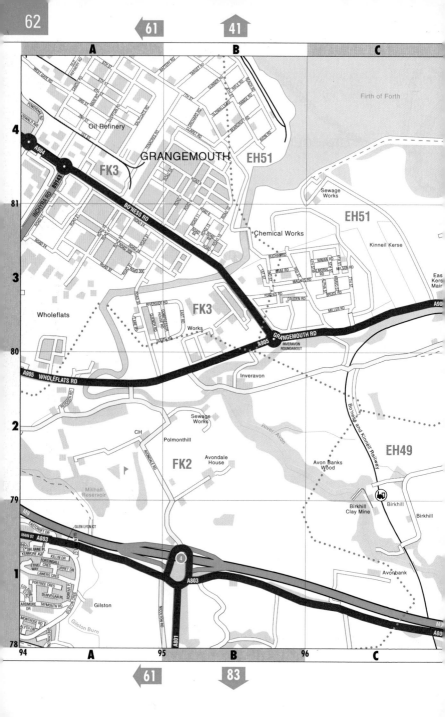

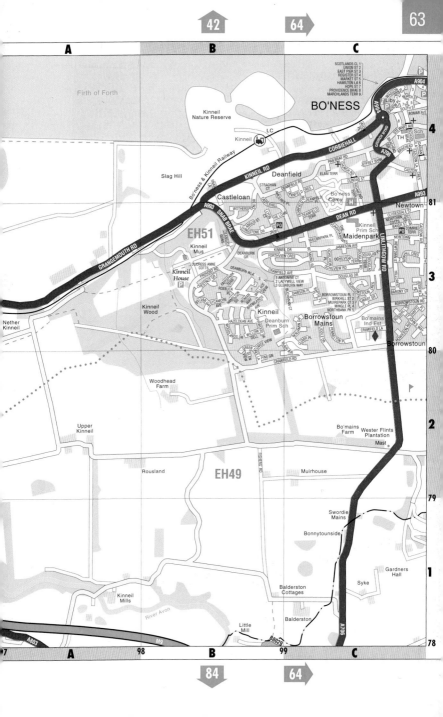

A B C

4

81

3

Carras
Gate

Shore
Woods

The
Fishery

Stacks
Cottages

EH51

Stacks

Firth of Forth

Blackness
Bay

Blackness
Castle

Black Ness

Pier

WEST
TERR

Hotel
B903

NOBIRROM
TERR

Blackness

80

Blackness
House

Hope Park
Lodge

ST NINIANS WAY

Burnshot

Wester
Burnshot

Blackness
Prim Sch

Black Burn

B9109

2

Dyland
Cottages

A903

WOODLEA
COTTS

CHAMPANY
HOLDINGS

CAULDCOATS
HOLDINGS

EH49

MANNERSTON
HOLDINGS

79

Mannerston

MANNERSTON
HOLDINGS

Binns Hill

Twr

EH30

1

A904

Paddockhall

PADDOCKHALL
COTTS

The Binns

The Binns

Garden
House

M9

MERRYLEES

B9109

West Lodge

A904

M9

78

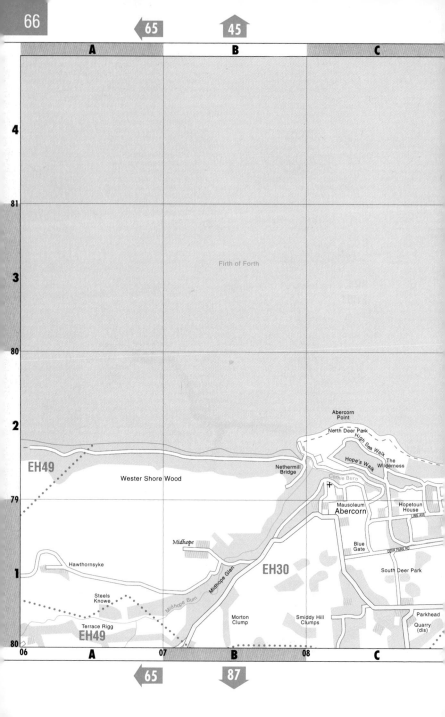

A **B** **C**

4

81

Firth of Forth

3

80

2

Abercorn
Point

North Deer Park

High Sea Walk

EH49

Hope's Walk

The
Wilderness

Nethermill
Bridge

Wester Shore Wood

Cornie Burn

79

Mausoleum

Hopetoun
House

Abercorn

LIME AVE

Midhope

Blue
Gate

DEER PARK RD

1

Hawthornsyke

Midhope Glen

EH30

South Deer Park

Steels
Knowe

Midhope Burn

Parkhead

Morton
Clump

Smiddy Hill
Clumps

Quarry
(dis)

Terrace Rigg

EH49

80

06 **A** **07** **B** **08** **C**

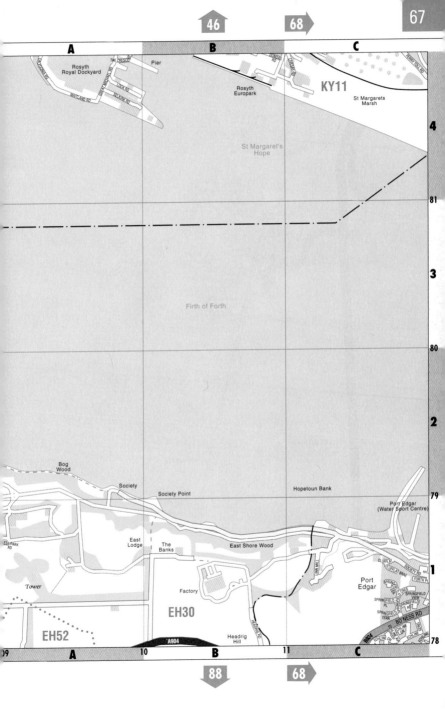

A
B
C

Rosyth
Royal Dockyard
CALDERYA RD
MAITLAND RD
THE CRESCENT
DOCK RD
BRICK RACHEL RD
SELKIRK RD
Pier

Rosyth
Europark

KY11
St Margarets
Marsh

4

St Margaret's
Hope

81

Firth of Forth

3

80

2

Bog
Wood

Society

Society Point

Hopetoun Bank

79

Port Edgar
(Water Sport Centre)

East
Lodge

The
Banks

East Shore Wood

BEG PARK
RD

Tower

EH30

Factory

Port
Edgar
CLUB LA
UPHALL BRAE
SOCIETY PL
FORTH PL
SPRING
SPRINGFIELD
PL.
SPRINGFIELD
TER
SPRINGFIELD
BO NESS RD

EH52

A904

Headrig
Hill

HOPE LN
ECHLINE DR
ECHLINE GN

78

09
A
10
B
11
C

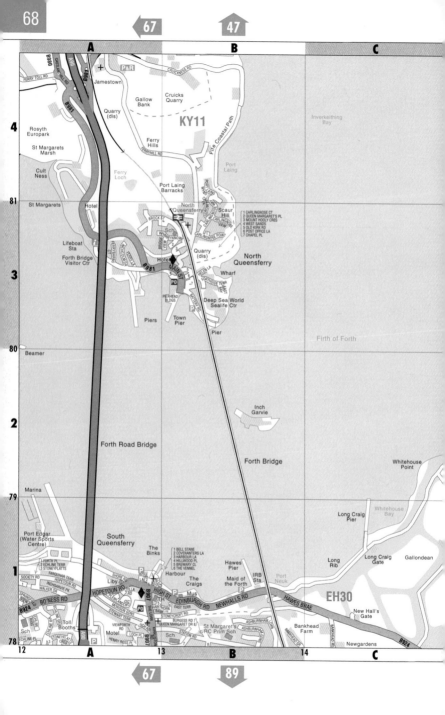

Firth of Forth

Hound
Point

Peatdraught
Bay

The
Warrens

Fishery
Cottage

EH30

euchold

Leuchold Wood

Castle Craig
Clump

Castle
Craig

Midlothian
Clump

Crow
Thickets

Barnbougle
Castle

Mons Hill

New England

Dalmeny Park

Peacock Ride

Livingston
Clump

Dalmeny
House

Firth of Forth

Craigielaw Point

Green Craig

EH32

Green Craig (Hotel)

Harestane Wood

Gosford Bay

Tollbar Strip

A198

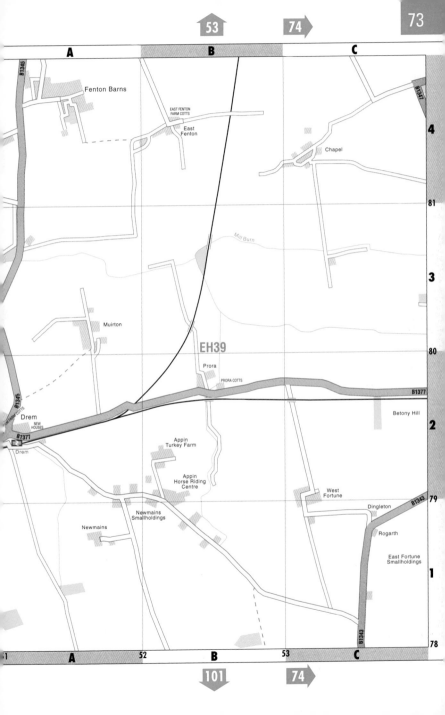

A B C

B1345

Fenton Barns

EAST FENTON
FARM COTTS

East
Fenton

B1347

Chapel

4

81

Mill Burn

3

Muirton

EH39

80

Prora

PRORA COTTS

B1377

B1345

Betony Hill

Drem
NEW HOUSES

2

B1371

Drem

Appin
Turkey Farm

Appin
Horse Riding
Centre

West
Fortune

Dingleton

B1343

79

Newmains
Smallholdings

Rogarth

Newmains

East Fortune
Smallholdings

1

B1343

78

A 52 B 53 C

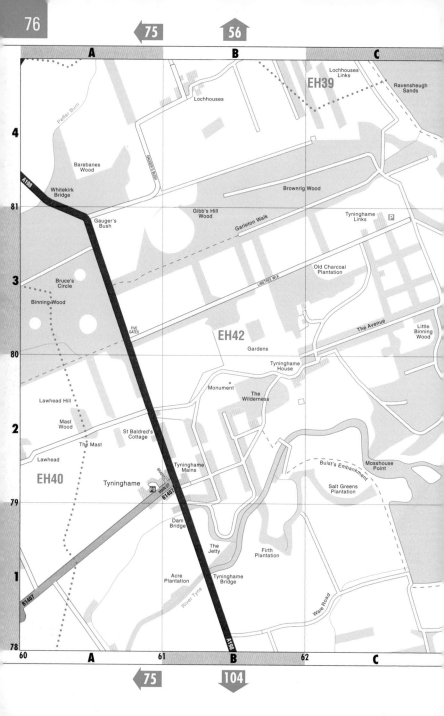

A | B | C

4

81

3

80

2

79

1

78

Frances Craig

Bathan's Sands

St Baldred's
Cradle

Links
Wood

Tyne Sands

Belhaven
Bay

John Muir
Country Park

Fir Links
Wood

Sandy
Hirst

Heckies Hole

Hedderwick
Sands

Hedderwick Hill
Plantation

Young's
Knowe

Hedderwick
Hill

Hedderwick Hill
Cottages

East Links
Family Pk

EH42

Hedderwick Hill
Stables

Hedderwick Burn

Windmill
(dis)

Bjelside

West Barns

PH

1 SPRINGFIELD TERR
2 SPRINGFIELD
3 SCHOOL BRAE
4 THE GREEN
5 STRATHEARN CT

EDINBURGH RD   A1087

Sch

PO

A1087   B6370

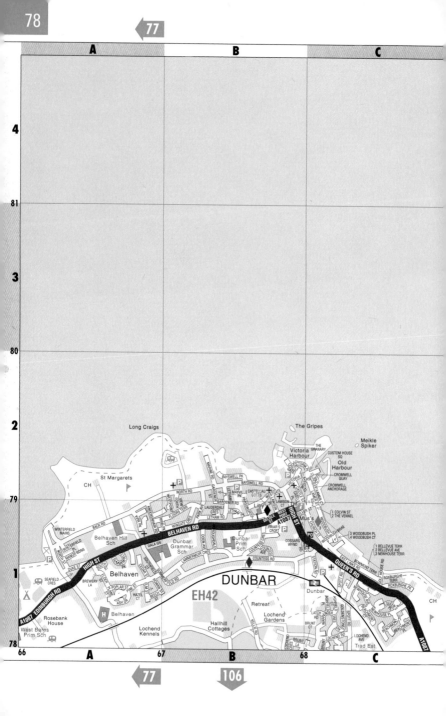

A   B   C

4

81

3

80

2

Long Craigs

The Gripes

St Margarets

Victoria
Harbour

THE
GRANARY

CUSTOM HOUSE
SQ

Meikle
Spiker

Old
Harbour

CH

CROMWELL
QUAY

CROMWELL
ANCHORAGE

79

NORTH RD

BAYSWELL RD

MAYVILLE

CASTELLAU
COTTS

Lin

1 COLVIN ST
2 THE VENNEL

WINTERFIELD
MAINS

BELHAVEN RD

LAUDERDALE
CRES

GARDENER RD

LETHAM RD

Lawson

Mus's

3 WOODBUSH PL
4 WOODBUSH CT

Belhaven Hill
Sch

Dunbar
Grammar
Sch

Dunbar
Prim
Sch

FRIAR'S
CROFT

P

PO

1 BELLEVUE TERR
2 BELLEVUE AVE
3 NEWHOUSE TERR

GALA GN

COSSARS
WYND

ROXBURGHE
TERR

HIGH ST

Belhaven

HAREMOOR CRES

COUNTESS RD

DUNBAR

Dunbar

QUEEN'S RD

ROXBURGHE PL

1

SEAFIELD
CRES

BREWERY
LA

POPLAR ST

EH42

Retreat

CH

A1087 EDINBURGH RD

Rosebank
House

ASH GR

Belhaven

H

Lochend
Gardens

BRUNT
CT

West Barns
Prim Sch

Lochend
Kennels

Hallhill
Cottages

LOCHEND

LOCHEND
AVE

A1087

Trad Est

78

66   A   67   B   68   C

West Links

Sports & Social
Centre

Fluke
Dub

EH42

Lawrie's
Den

The
Vaults

Vaults Wood

Mill Stone
Neuk

B803

Kilbean
Wood

Glenrig

4

Mast

Wester
Strip

Westerglen
Farm

Easter
Strip

Auchengean
Wood

Westerglen
Transmitting
Station

Masts

77

Auchengean

Rottenstocks

3

Barleyside

76

Greencraig

FK1

Darnrig
Moss

2

Masonfield

Works

High
Stanerigg

Darnrigg

75

Lochend

1

Strathavon

Nappyfaulds
House

74

B803

Dyke

85   A   86   B   87   C

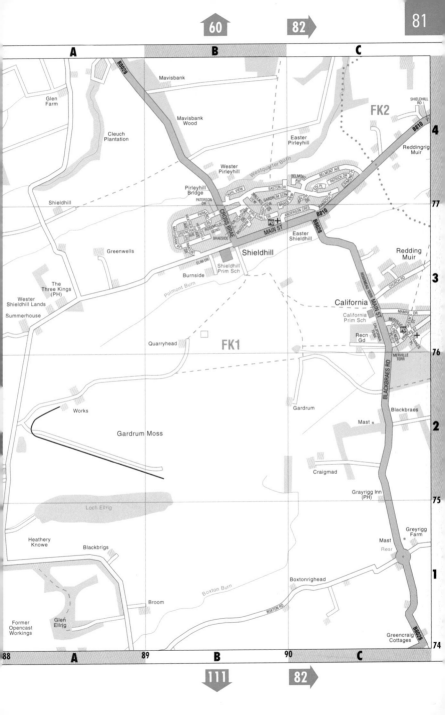

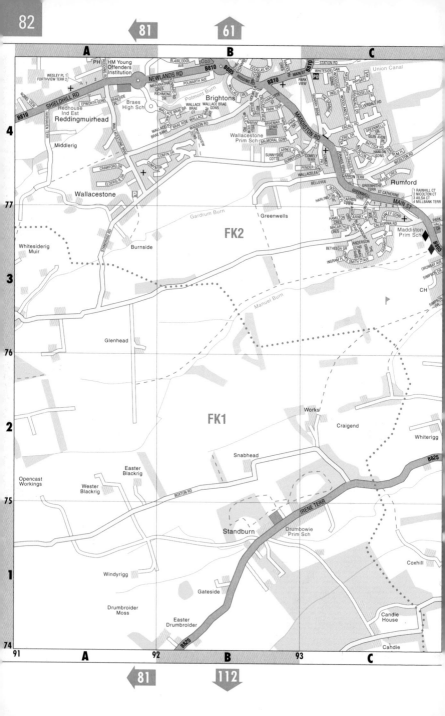

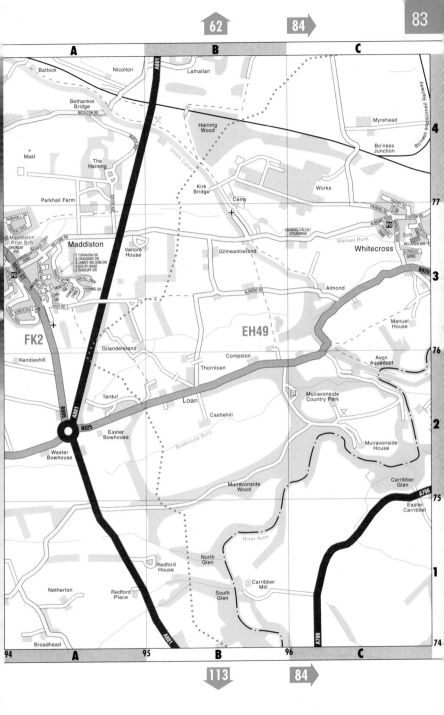

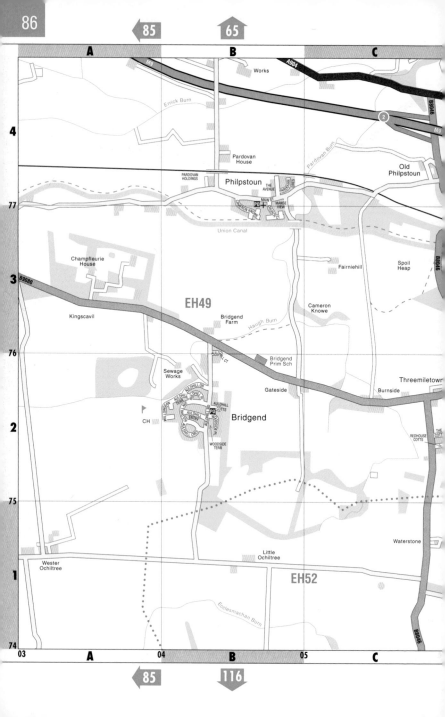

A
B
C

EH30

Philpstoun House

Hopetoun Wood

Woodville

The Manse

A904

B9080

Whitequarries Ind Est

Abercorn Prim Sch

4

Woodend

East Philpstoun

Galascrook

EH49

Duntarvie

77

Philpstoun Mill

Bailies Muir

Philpstoun Muir

Craigton

Fawnspark

Craigton House

3

M9

Union Canal

The Den

EH52

Mounthooly

Myre

76

B9080

Trinlaymire

2

Garage

BENNETT WOOD TERR 1
MIDHOPE PL 2
CRAIGTON CT 3

AULDGATHIE PL

Lampinsdub

TIPPET KNOWES CT

MAIN ST B9080

B2288

75

DUNN PL

TIPPET KNOWES RD

SYCAMORE GR

Glendevon

Winchburgh Prim Sch

CHESTNUT GR

ABERCORN PL

CRAIGTON PL

GLENDEVON PL

GLENDEVON COTTS

Holy Family RC Prim Sch

Winchburgh

NIDDRY RD

Tippet Knowes

Millcraig

Cemy

1

OLD GLENDEVON FARM COTTS

Niddry Burn

Kirklands

B8020

Niddry

Faucheldean

74

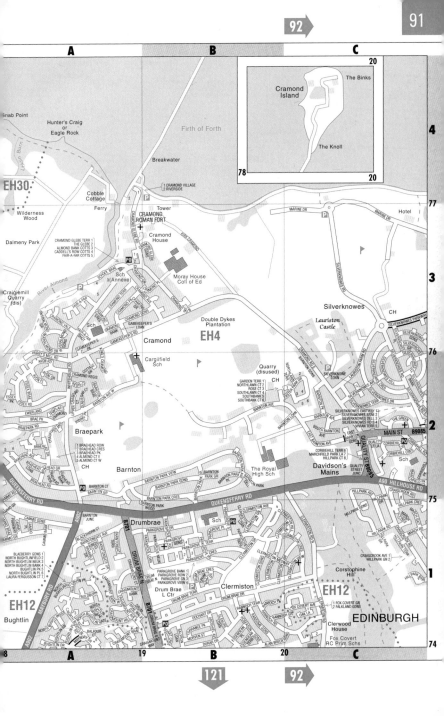

91

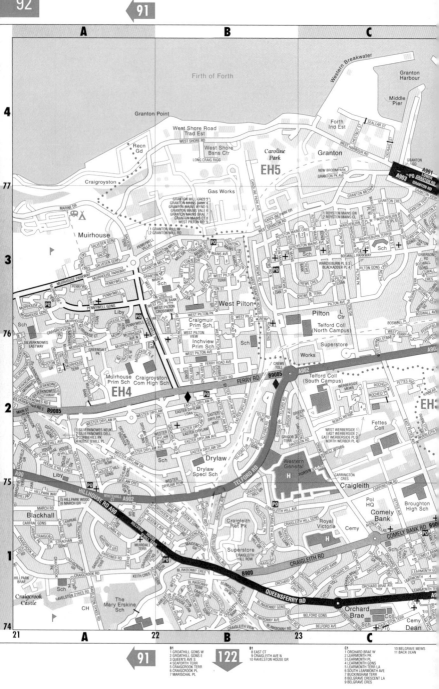

91
122

B1
1 GROATHILL GDNS W
2 GROATHILL GDNS E
3 QUEEN'S AVE S
4 SEAFORTH TERR
5 CRAIGCROOK TERR
6 CRAIGCROOK PL
7 MARISCHAL PL

B1
8 EAST CT
9 CRAIGLEITH AVE N
10 RAVELSTON HOUSE GR

C1
1 ORCHARD BRAE W
2 LEARMONTH PK
3 LEARMONTH PL
4 LEARMONTH GDNS
5 LEARMONTH TERR LA
6 SOUTH LEARMONTH AVE
7 BUCKINGHAM TERR
8 BELGRAVE CRESCENT LA
9 BELGRAVE CRES

10 BELGRAVE MEWS
11 BACK DEAN

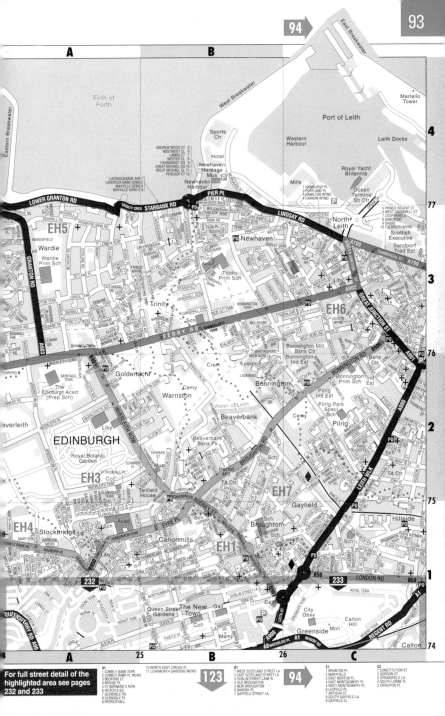

A B

Firth of Forth

East Breakwater

West Breakwater

Martello Tower

Port of Leith

Leith Docks

4

Sports Ctr

Western Harbour

Hotel
Newhaven Heritage Mus

Royal Yacht Britannia

Ocean Terminal Sh Ctr

ANDREW WOOD CT 5
WESTMOST CL 6
LAMBS CT 7
WESTER CL 8
FISHMARKET SQ 9
GREAT MICHAEL CL 10
GREAT MICHAEL CL 11
PEACOCK CT 12

LAVEROCKBANK AVE 1
LAVEROCK BANK GDNS 2
MAYVILLE GDNS 3
MAYVILLE GDNS E 4

Newhaven Harbour

Mills

1 HAMBURG PL
2 PORTLAND PL
3 HAMILTON WYND
4 CANNON WYND

5 PRINCE REGENT ST
6 WEST CROMWELL ST
7 COUPERFIELD
8 SANDPORT
9 SHORE
10 TOLBOOTH WYND

Scottish Executive

Sandport Trad Est

LOWER GRANTON RD
STARBANK RD
TRINITY CRES
PIER PL
LINDSAY RD

North Leith

77

A199

A199

EH5

Wardie

Wardie Prim Sch

Newhaven

PO

Trinity Acad

Trinity Prim Sch

Liby

3

A902

GREAT JUNCTION ST

Trinity

EH6

A900

76

FERRY RD
CHANCELOT TERR

Bonnington Mill Bsns Ctr
Bonnington Ind Est

Bonnington RD

B900

Goldenacre

Cem

Bonnington

Bonnington Prim Sch

Ind Est

The Edinburgh Acad (Prep Sch)

Warriston

Cemy

Water of Leith

Beaverbank

Pilrig Ind Est

Pilrig Park Specl Sch

Pilrig

2

EDINBURGH

Royal Botanic Garden

Liby

Beaverbank Bsns Pk

LEITH WLK

A900

TA Ctr

Heriot Hill

Mus

TA Ctr

EH3

Coll

Tanfield House

EH7

Gayfield

75

EH4

Stockbridge

EYRE PL

Acad

Henderson Row

Canonmills

EH1

Broughton

Hillside

232

Liby

233

LONDON RD

B50

1

PO

The New Town

Queen Street Gardens

Gall

City Obsy

Royal Terr

B50

QUEENSFERRY RD A90

Moray Pl

Heriot Row

Coll

Mem

Liby

A900

WATERLOO PL

A1

Calton Hill

Mon

Greenside

REGENT RD

Calton

74

A B C

25 26

A1
1 COMELY BANK TERR
2 COMELY BANK PL MEWS
3 BEDFORD CT
4 BRIDGE PL
5 ST BERNARD'S ROW
6 VEITCH'S SQ
7 GLENOGLE RD
8 GLENOGLE PL
9 PATRIOTHALL
10 NORTH EAST CIRCUS PL
11 LEARMONTH GARDENS MEWS

B1
1 WEST SCOTLAND STREET LA
2 EAST SCOTLAND STREET LA
3 DUBLIN STREET LANE N
4 OLD BROUGHTON
5 NEW BROUGHTON
6 BARONY PL
7 GAYFIELD STREET LA

C1
1 BRUNTON PL
2 MARYFIELD
3 EAST NORTON PL
4 EAST MONTGOMERY PL
5 WEST MONTGOMERY PL
6 LEOPOLD PL
7 ANTIGUA ST
8 SOUTH GAYFIELD LA
9 GAYFIELD CL

C2
1 CONSTITUTION ST
2 GORDON ST
3 SPRINGFIELD LA
4 SOUTH LORNE PL
5 CRIGHTON PL

A B C

4

77

Firth of Forth

Works
Port of Leith

Docks
East Sands
of Leith

CONSTITUTION
PL

COMMERCIAL
ST

Leith

3

1 BURGESS ST
2 WATERS CL
3 BROAD WYND
4 CHAPEL LA
5 CARPET LA
6 SEAPORT ST
7 QUEEN CHARLOTTE LA

LC

SALAMANDER ST

EH6

ALBERT RD

BALTIC ST
NEW BELL'S CT

76

South Leith
COCHRANE PL 1
GEM PL 2
FINGZIES PL 3
ROSEVALE PL 4
NOBLE PL 5
LINDEAN PL 7

St Mary's (Leith)
RC Prim Sch

Sch
Coll
HERMITAGE PL

Leith
Links

GLADSTONE

Sewage
Works

LC

SEAFIELD RD

Seafield

Seafield

CLAREMONT GDNS

Cemy
Crem

Claremont
Park

2

Thornotreeside
Ind Est

HALMYRE

Leith
Acad

Recn
Gd

WOODVILLE TERR 1
WOODBINE TERR 2
HERMITAGE PARK LA

Hermitage

Quarryholes

PO

H

Eastern
General

SEAFIELD RD

PO

Ind Est

EH15

DALMENY
ST

Cemy

Easter Rd Stad
(Hibernian FC)

Lochend

EDINBURGH

Restalrig

EH7 Craigentinny

CH

75

Albion
Bsns Ctr

John Cotton
Bsns Ctr

Drum

Meadow
Bank
Sh Pk

Meadowbank

St Ninian's
RC Prim Sch

Craigentinny
Prim Sch

CRAIGENTINNY RD

PO

EDINA PL
ROSSIE PL
BOTHW

1

A1

Abbeyhill

DALZIEL PL

LONDON RD

Meadowbank
Sports Ctr

Chapel

RESTALRIG AVE

PORTOBELLO RD

Piershill

A1140

INCHVIEW TERR A1140

MOIRA TERR

STANLEY ST 14

CLOCKMILL

EH8 Parsons
Green

QUEEN'S DR

PIERSHILL

MOLESELEY PL

PO

A1140

BARONSCOURT TERR

Jock's
Lodge

Cemy

Piershill

74

27 A 28 B 29 C

| | A | B | C |

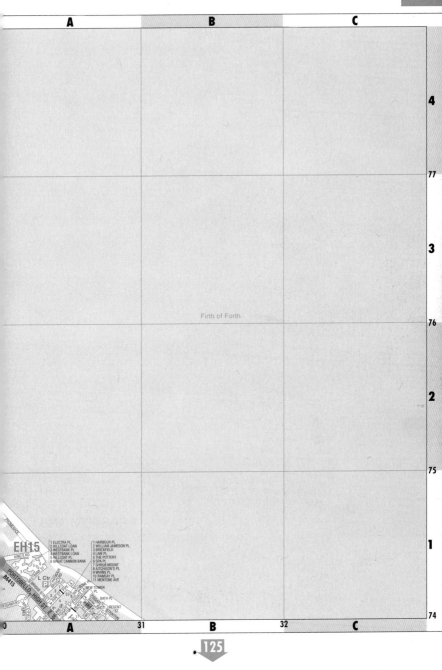

Firth of Forth

EH15

PROMENADE
KING'S RD
PORTOBELLO HIGH ST
B6415
L Ctr
P
NEW TOWER PL
BATH PL
Sch
REGENT ST

1 ELECTRA PL
2 HILLCOAT LOAN
3 WESTBANK PL
4 HILLCOAT PL
5 WESTBANK LOAN
6 GREAT CANNON BANK

1 HARBOUR PL
2 WILLIAM JAMESON PL
3 BRICKFIELD
4 LAW PL
5 THE POTTERY
6 SPA PL
7 SHRUB MOUNT
8 AITCHISON'S PL
9 WHINS PL
10 RAMSAY PL
11 MENTONE AVE

30 · 31 · 32

4 · 77 · 3 · 76 · 2 · 75 · 1 · 74

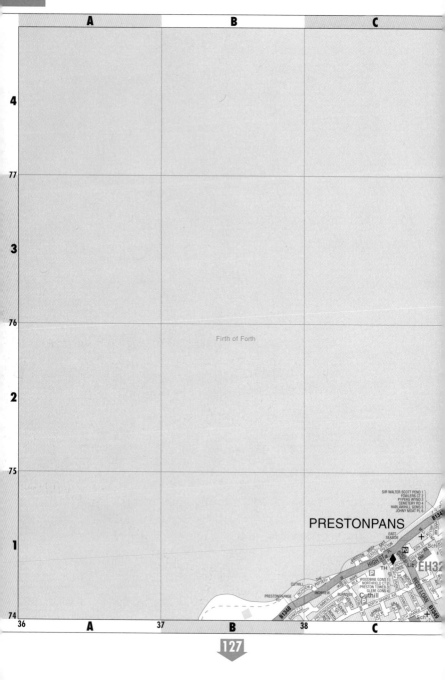

Firth of Forth

SIR WALTER SCOTT PEND 1
FOWLERS CT 2
PYPERS WYND 3
CEMETERY RD 4
HARLAWHILL GDNS 5
JOHNY MOAT PL 6

PRESTONPANS

EAST
SEABIDE

B1348

HIGH ST

EH32

WOODBINE GDNS 1
NORTHFIELD CT 2
PRESTON TOWER 3
GLEBE GDNS 4

Cuthill

CUTHILL

THE
POTTERY

PRESTONGRANGE
RD

B1348

97
70

A

B

C

4

Firth of Forth

77

Eventyr

A198

B1348

Fernyness
Wood

LYARS RD

3

CH

Liby

CHURCH
GDNS

Sch

WEMYSS
TERR

B1377

Longniddry

Seton Sands

P

P

PO

MAIN ST

A198

Longniddry

Longniddry
FARM COTTS

76

B1348

Longniddry Dean

Lorne
Bridge

Longniddry
Farm

B6363

2

EH32

Seton Dean

SETON
MAINS

Cantyhall
Bridge

Cantyhall

Canty Burn

Redcoll

St Germains
Crossing

75

A198

LC

Chesterhall

THE
STEADING

St Germains

St Germains
Farm

Southfield

B6363

1

Opencast
Workings

EH33

74

42

A

43

B

44

C

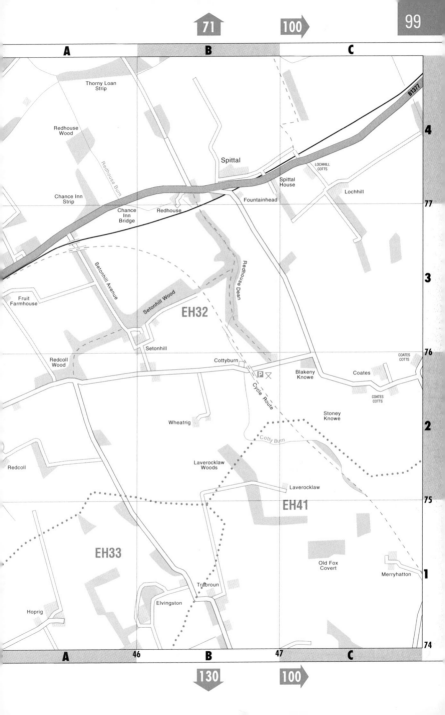

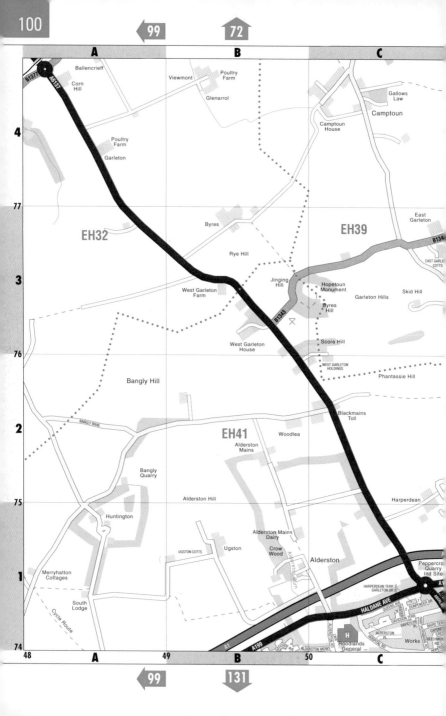

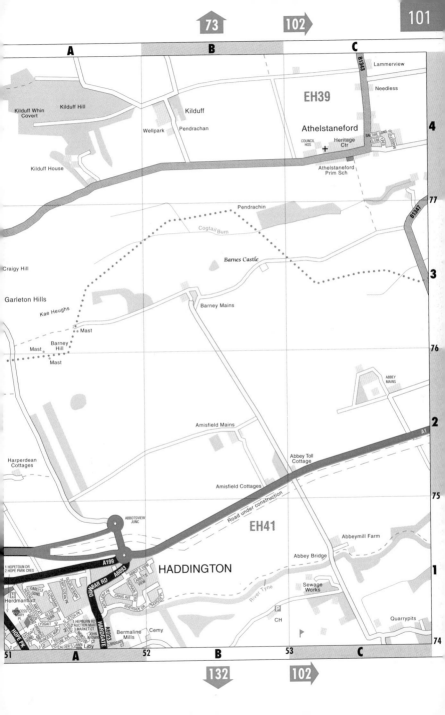

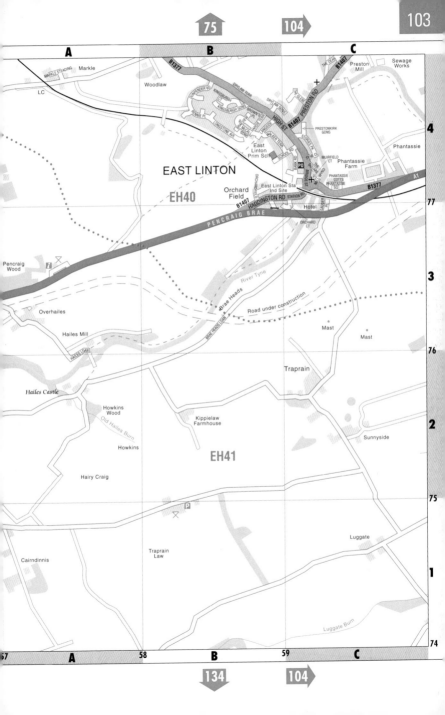

A **B** **C**

Markle Steading
Markle

Woodlaw

B1377

Preston Mill

Sewage Works

LC

The Dean
B1407
B1407

Preston

Kingsburgh
Kingsburgh Gdns
Brown St
Commander Rd
Lennie Pl
Lindsay Cres
Balfour St
High St
B1407
Preston Rd

4

East Linton Prim Sch

Prestonkirk Gdns

Muirfield Ct

Phantassie

EAST LINTON

Orchard Road
Abbey Rd
Gordon Rd
PO
The Square
Bridge End
Station Rd

Phantassie Farm

EH40

Orchard Field
East Linton Sta Ind Site

Phantassie Cotts
Phantassie

A1

B1377

B1407
Hotel

77

PENCRAIG BRAE

Haddington Rd
Orchard Ct

Pencraig Wood

ℹ

River Tyne

3

Overhailes

Brae Heads

Road under construction

Mast

Hailes Mill

Brae Heads Cott

Mast

76

Hailes Loan

Traprain

Hailes Castle

Howkins Wood

Kippielaw Farmhouse

Old Hailes Burn

Sunnyside

2

Howkins

EH41

Hairy Craig

75

P

Luggate

Cairndinnis

Traprain Law

1

Luggate Burn

74

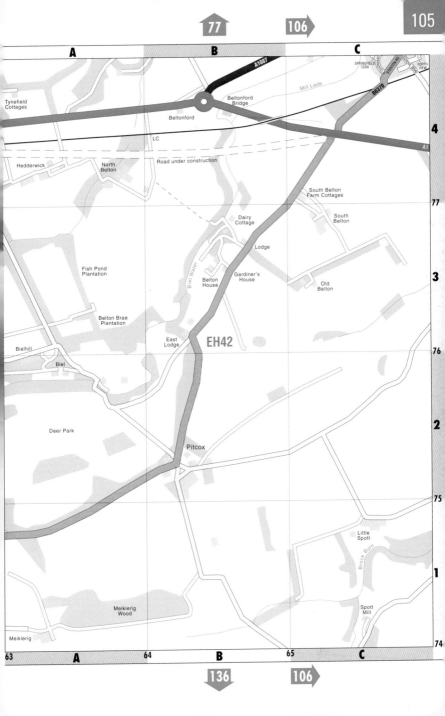

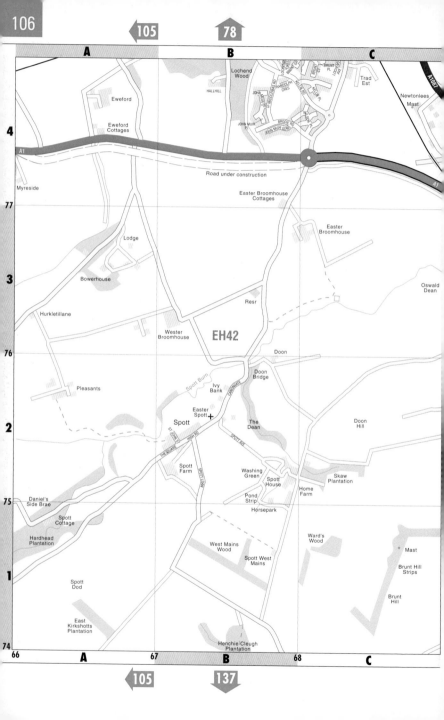

A   B   C

4

A1

77

Myreside

Eweford

Eweford
Cottages

Lochend
Wood

HALLHILL

RANDOLPH
CRES

Trad
Est

Newtonlees
Mast

JOHN MUIR
PL

JOHN MUIR GDNS

BROUGE RD

A1087

Road under construction

Easter Broomhouse
Cottages

Easter
Broomhouse

3

Lodge

Bowerhouse

Hurkletillane

Wester
Broomhouse

Resr

EH42

Oswald
Dean

76

Spott Burn

Pleasants

Ivy
Bank

Doon

CADGERGATE

Doon
Bridge

2

Easter
Spott

Spott

LOW RD

ST JOHN PL

The
Dean

SPOTT AVE

Doon
Hill

Doon
Dean

Skaw
Plantation

75

Daniel's
Side Brae

Hardhead
Plantation

Spott
Cottage

THE SQUARE

SPOTT LOAN

Spott
Farm

Washing
Green

Spott
House

Pond
Strip

Horsepark

Home
Farm

Ward's
Wood

Mast

Brunt Hill
Strips

1

Spott
Dod

West Mains
Wood

Spott West
Mains

Brunt
Hill

East
Kirkshotts
Plantation

Henchie Cleugh
Plantation

74

66   A   67   B   68   C

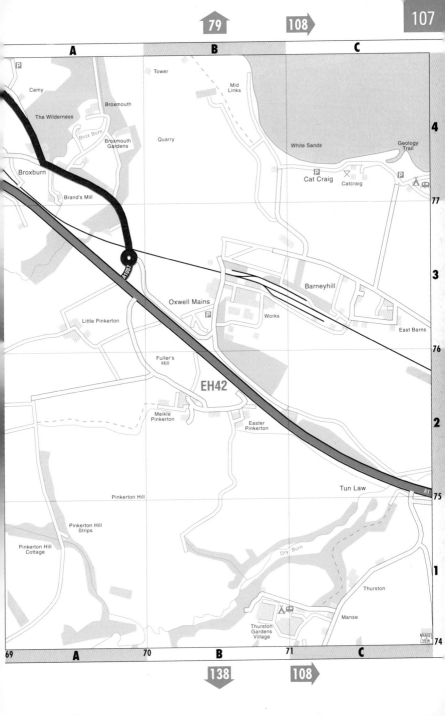

A B C

P

Cemy

Broxmouth

The Wilderness

Brox Burn

Broxmouth Gardens

Broxburn

Brand's Mill

Tower

Quarry

Mid Links

White Sands

Cat Craig

Catcraig

P

Geology Trail

P

A1087

Little Pinkerton

Oxwell Mains

Works

Barneyhill

East Barns

Fuller's Hill

EH42

Meikle Pinkerton

Easter Pinkerton

Pinkerton Hill

Tun Law

A1

Pinkerton Hill Strips

Pinkerton Hill Cottage

Dry Burn

Thurston

Manse

Thurston Gardens Village

MANSE VIEW

4

77

3

76

2

75

1

74

A   B   C

4

Barns Ness

P
Barnsness
Lighthouse

77

3

76

Dryburn
Bridge
Dry Burn

Chapel Point

War Meml

Skateraw Harbour

Quarry

2

P

EH42

Skateraw

Torness
Power Sta

75
A1

Skateraw
Gate

Visitor
Ctr

1

Innerwick
Prim Sch

Corsick Hill

Crowhill

Thornton
Mill

Thornton Burn

Thorntonloch
Bridge

74
72   A   73   B   74   C

Innerwick

Torness Point

Thorntonloch

Mast

EH42

A B C

Wester Jaw

B803

River Avon

Redbra

Wester Loanrigg

BALMULZIER RD

Balmulzier

Loanrigg

4

MANSE PL

MOSSCASTLE RD

THORNDENE TERR

PH

Slamannan Prim Sch

Liby

Hillhead

73

Blinkbonnie

BANK ST

AVONBRIDGE RD

Peatrigend

Crossburn

RUVIKBONNIE TERR

AIR GOWANLEA DR

B803

B8022

Balquhatstone House

Crosshill

B8022

Cullloch Burn

Slamannan

Wester Arnloss

Wester Crosshill

Crosshill

3

Balcastle House

LINTVIEW

North Arnloss

Binniehill Farm

STATION RD

Balquhatstone Mains

Binniehill

FK1

BINNIEHILL RD

72

South Arnloss

2

Salterhill Farm

B825

Easter Drumclair

THOMPSON PL

Low Limerigg

CARRON TERR

Loch House

71

SLAMANNAN RD

Limerigg

Little Black Loch

High Limerigg

Limerigg Prim Sch

B8022

Blackloch

Barnsmuir

1

LOCHSIDE RD

B825

CALDERCRUIX RD

Black Loch

Holehousemuir

Stoneridge

70

85 A 86 B 87 C

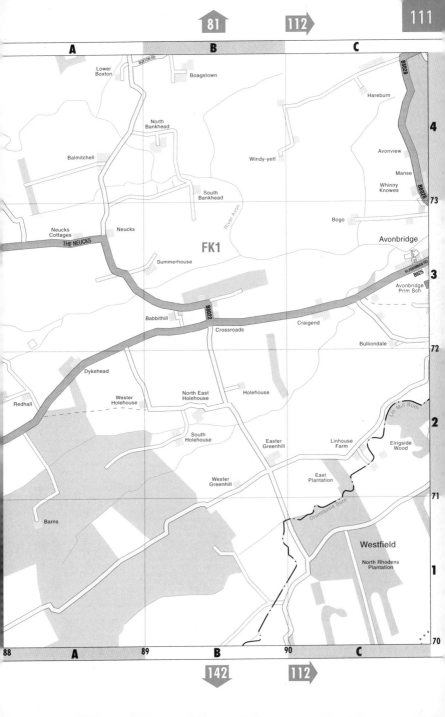

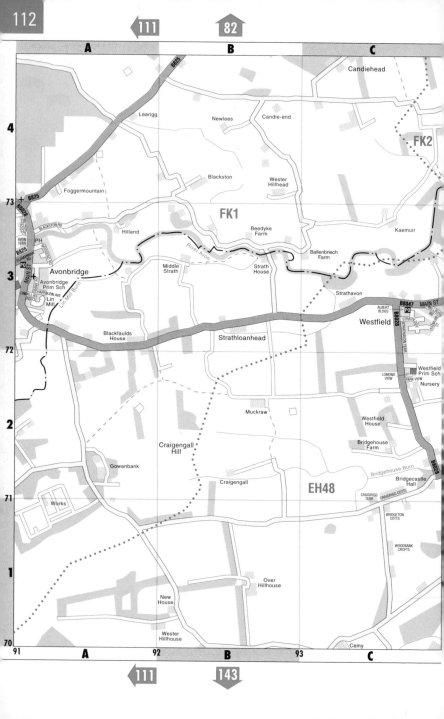

A   **B**   **C**

4

Candiehead

Learigg

Newlees   Candie-end

FK2

Blackston   Wester Hillhead

73   B825

FK1

Foggermountain

Beedyke Farm   Kaemuir

Hillend   River Avon   Ballenbriech Farm

AVON TERR   PH

Avonbridge   Middle Strath   Strath House

B825   MAIN ST   PO

3   Avonbridge Prim Sch   Strathavon

Lin Mill   Lin Mill Burn   ALBERT BLDGS   B8047   MAIN ST   PO

Blackfaulds House   Strathloanhead   **Westfield**   STRATHAVON TERR   B8028

72   Westfield Prim Sch

LOMOND VIEW   PARK VIEW   Nursery

Muckraw   Westfield House

2   Craigengall Hill   Bridgehouse Farm

Gowanbank   Bridgehouse Burn

Craigengall   **EH48**   Bridgecastle Hall

71   CRAIGRIGG TERR   CRAIGRIGG COTTS

Works   BRIDGETON COTTS

WOODBANK CROFTS

1   Over Hillhouse

New House

Wester Hillhouse   Cemy

70   Avonbridge

91   **A**   92   **B**   93   **C**

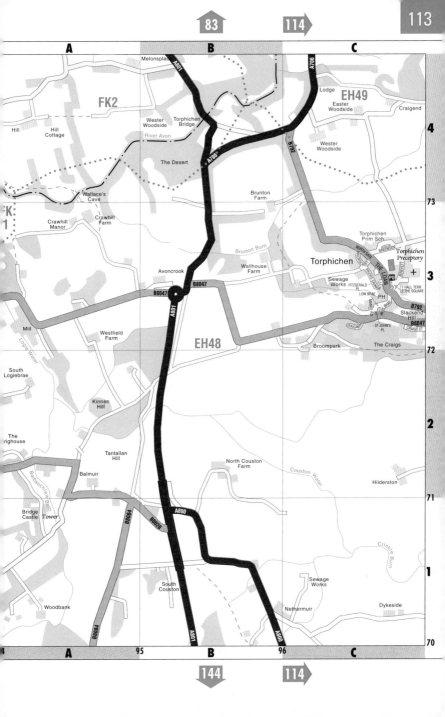

A   B   C

Beecraigs Country Park

Beecraigs

Riccarton Hills

EH49

Beecraigs Hill

Longmuir Plantation

Beecraigs Wood

4

North Mains Hill

North Mains

73

Mains Burn

The Weirds   Castle Strip

Baresheil Knowe

South Mains

Bankhead

Mid Tartraven   Mill Hill Plantation

3

Tartraven

EH48

The Wilderness

Rigghead Plantation

Binnyside Strips

EH52

72

Blackcraig

Bangour Reservoir

Quarter Strip

Boat House

2

Old Wood   The Gullet

Brox Burn

Quarter

Bangour Knowes

71

Linen Faulds

H

Bangour Village

1

Drumcrosshall

Byres

EH54   A89

Drumcross

Wester Dechmont

A89   M8

70

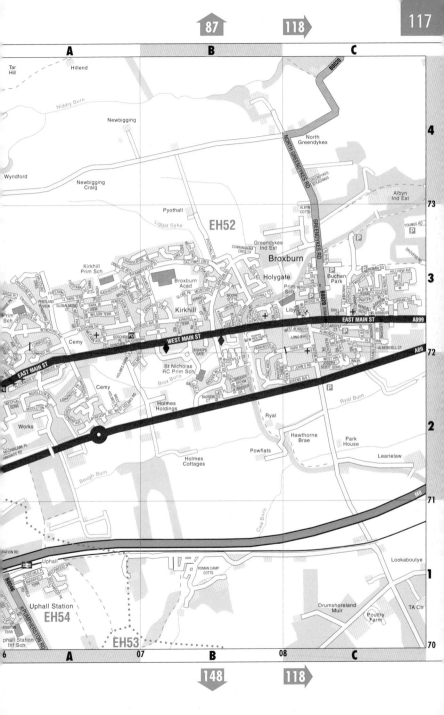

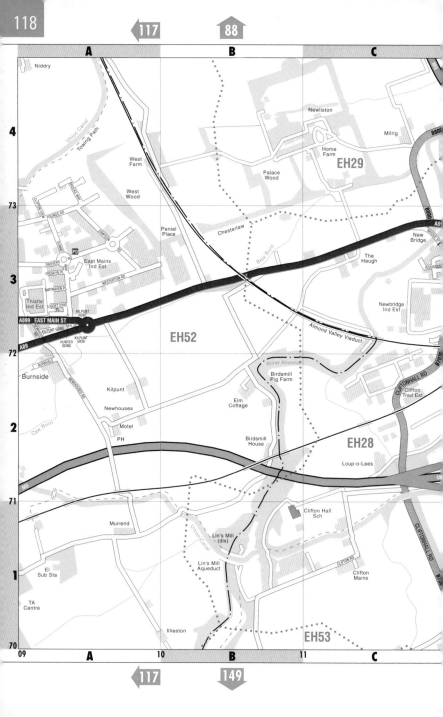

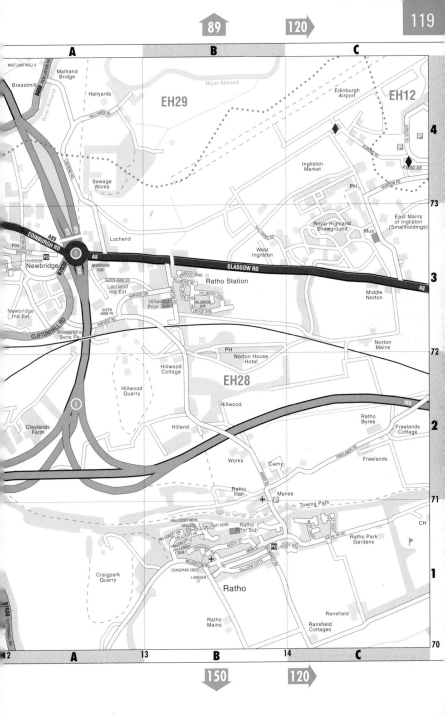

MAITLAND HOG LA

Breastmill

Maitland
Bridge

Hallyards

River Almond

EH29

River Almond

Edinburgh
Airport

EH12

HALLYARDS RD

LOCHEND RD

Sewage
Works

Ingliston
Market

PH

FAIRVIEW RD

East Mains
of Ingliston
(Smallholdings)

Royal Highland
Showground

Mus

West
Ingliston

GLASGOW RD

A8

Ratho Station

Middle
Norton

Norton
Mains

Norton House
Hotel

EH28

M8

Hillwood

Hillend

Ratho
Byres

Freelands
Cottage

Claylands
Farm

FREELANDS RD

Freelands

Works

Cemy

Ratho
Hall

Manse

Towing Path

CH

Union Canal

Ratho
Prim Sch

Ratho Park
Gardens

Craigpark
Quarry

Ratho

Ransfield

Ratho
Mains

Ransfield
Cottages

EDINBURGH RD

A89

M9

Newbridge

PH

P

Riverside

PARKSIDE

NEWBRIDGE
RDBT

Lochend
Ind Est

Newbridge
Ind Est

CLIFTONHALL RD

Alexandra
Bsns Pk

QUEEN ANNE DR

HARVEST DR

Hillwood
Prim Sch

QUEEN
ANNE RD

HARVEST RD

Hillwood
Cottage

Hillwood
Quarry

Lochend

West
Ingliston

HILLWOOD GDNS

HILLWOOD RD

HILLWOOD CERES

HILLWOOD TERR

HILLWOOD
AVE

HILLWOOD RISE

HALLCROFT NEUK

HALLCROFT GDNS

HALLCROFT DR

HALLCROFT PK

HALLCROFT CL

HALLCROFT
RISE

CRAIGPARK AVE

NORTH ST

MAIN ST

WILKIESTON RD

CRAIGPARK CRES

LUMSDEN CT

HILLVIEW COTTS

P

PO

UPDALE SIDE

RATHO PK RD

4

73

3

72

2

71

1

70

12   A   13   B   14   C

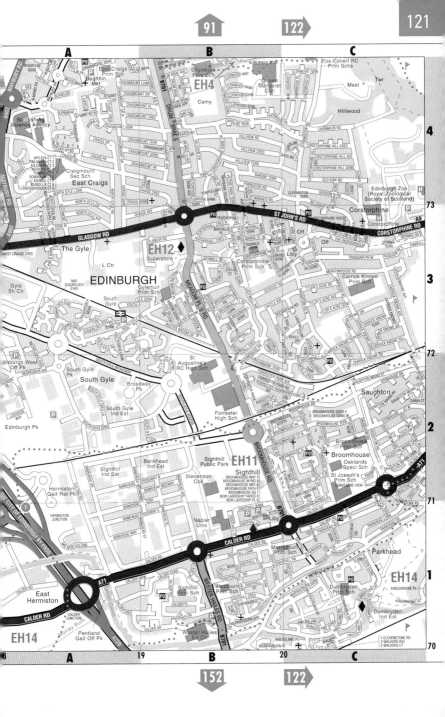

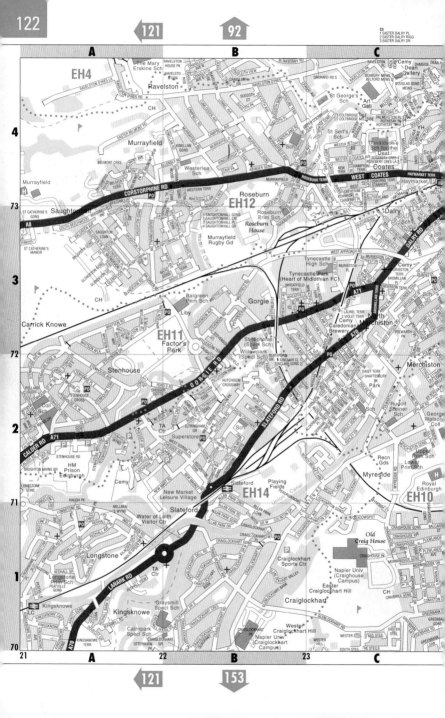

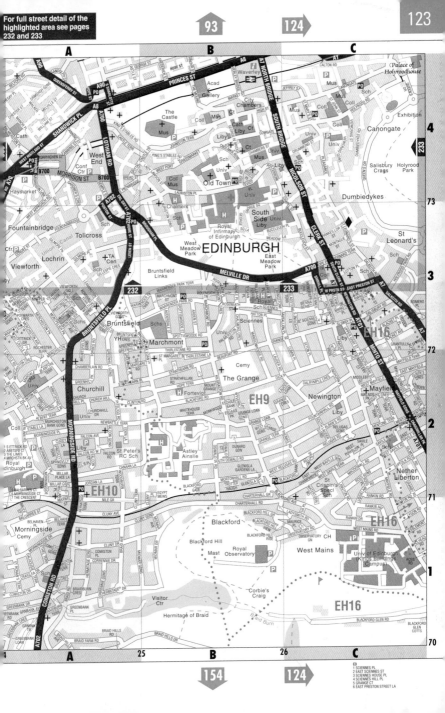

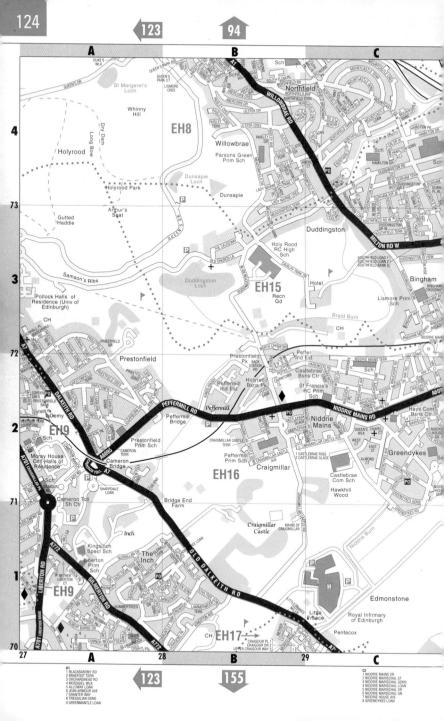

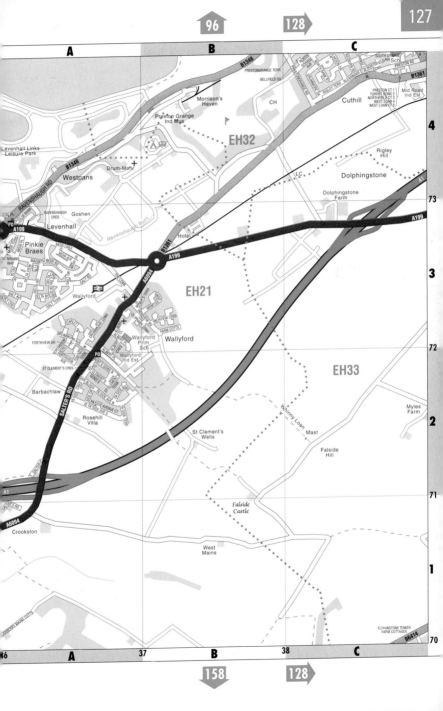

A B C

4

3

2

1

73

72

71

70

EH32

EH21

EH33

B1348
PRESTONGRANGE TERR
BELLFIELD SQ
B1361
Morrison's
Haven
CH
Cuthill
PRESTON CT 1
TURRET GDNS 2
NORTHFIELD CT 3
WEST LOAN 4
WEST LOAN CT 5
RIGLEY TERR
ALEXANDER DR
SOUTH GRANGE
AVE
NORTH GRANGE
PRESTON RD
Mid Road
Ind Est

Preston Grange
Ind Mus
Rigley
Hill

Levenhall Links
Leisure Park
Dolphingstone
LC
A1

B1348
Drum-Mohr
Westpans
Dolphingstone
Farm
73

RAVENSHAUGH RD
RAVENSHAUGH
CRES
Goshen
PO
A199
Levenhall
Hotel
A199
A199

Pinkie
Braes
ST NINIANS
WAY
MAGRE RD
MOIR CRES
MOIR AVE
B1361
A6094
A199

SALT AVE
DELTA AVE
GALT TERR
Wallyford
SCREW CRES
FARM COTTS
FORTHVIEW DR
Wallyford
Prim Sch
3

PO
Wallyford
Ind Est
ST CLEMENT'S CRES

Barbachlaw
Myles
Farm

Rosehill
Villa
St Clement's
Wells
Whinny Loan
Mast
Falside
Hill

SALTER'S RD
Falside
Castle

A1
A6094
Crookston
West
Mains

JEFFREST MAINS COTTS
ELPHINSTONE TOWER
FARM COTTAGES
B6414

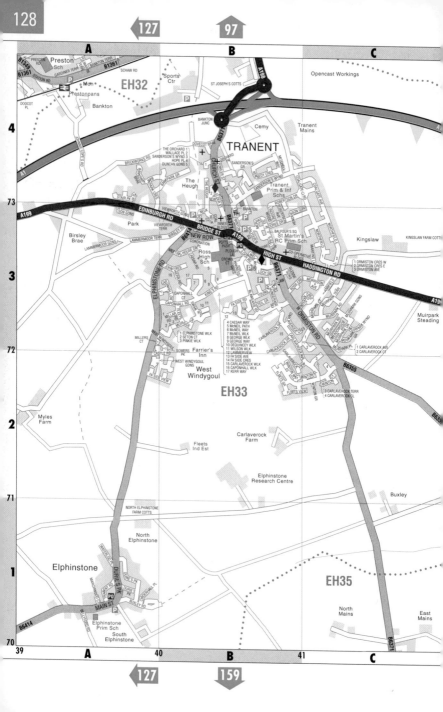

A **B** **C**

Preston Sch
B1348
B1361
SCHAW RD
B1361
GARDINER TERR
SEATON RD
BANKTON TERR
HOPE PL
DOVECOT PL
Mon
Prestonpans
Bankton

EH32

Sports Ctr

St JOSEPH'S COTTS

Opencast Workings

4

BANKTON JUNC

Cemy
Tranent Mains

TRANENT

THE ORCHARD 1
WALLACE PL 2
SANDERSON'S WYND 3
HOPE PL 4
DUNCAN GDNS 5

BRICKWORKS RD
DUNCAN GDNS
PARK VW

STAIR PK
VIEWFORTH GDNS

SANDERSON'S GR
HARDY CRES

Tranent Prim & Inf Schs

73

A199

Edinburgh Rd

EDINBURGH RD

Park

Birsley Brae

LAMMERMOOR TERR

VIEWFORTH

BRIDGE ST
NEW ROW

Bankton

St Martin's RC Prim Sch
BALFOUR'S SQ

Kingslaw

KINGSLAW FARM COTTS

Lammermoor Gdns

A199
CORONATION

Ross High Sch

HIGH ST

HADDINGTON RD

1 ORMISTON CRES W
2 ORMISTON CRES E
3 ORMISTON AVE

3

A199

Muirpark Steading

Millers Ct

CAPONHALL

CAPONHALL RD

Farrier's Inn

West Windygoul Gdns

1 ELPHINSTONE WLK
2 SETON CT
3 PINKIE WLK

4 CAESAR WAY
5 McNEIL PATH
6 McNEIL WAY
7 McNEIL WLK
8 GEORGE WLK
9 GEORGE WAY
10 DEQUINCEY WLK
11 WILSON WLK
12 LAMMERVIEW
13 FA'SIDE AVE
14 FA'SIDE WLK
15 CARLAVEROCK CRES
16 CAPONHALL WLK
17 KERR WAY

1 CARLAVEROCK AVE
2 CARLAVEROCK CT

72

West Windygoul

EH33

FLEETS VIEW

3 CARLAVEROCK TERR
4 CARLAVEROCK CL

B6355

B6355

Myles Farm

Fleets Ind Est

Carlaverock Farm

2

Elphinstone Research Centre

Buxley

71

NORTH ELPHINSTONE FARM COTTS

North Elphinstone

EH35

1

Elphinstone

DURIE ST

MARCHWOOD

MAIN ST

BUXLEY RD

CADGERHALL PL

South Elphinstone

Elphinstone Prim Sch

North Mains

East Mains

B6371

B6414

70

39 **A** **40** **B** **41** **C**

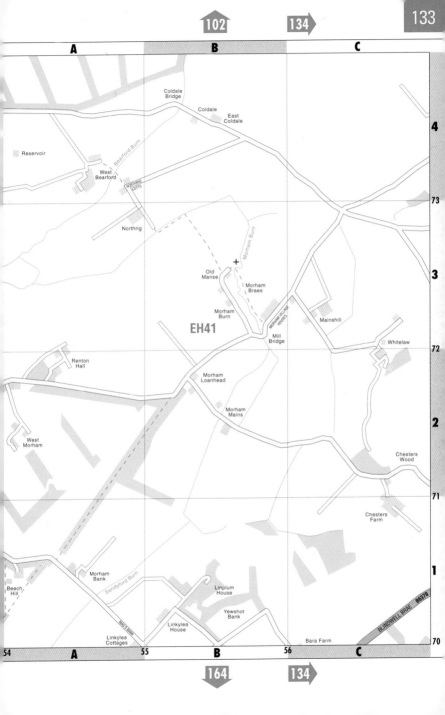

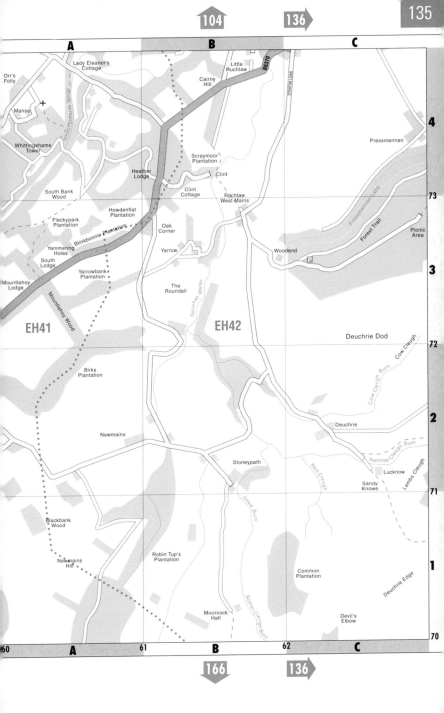

A **B** **C**

4

Bennet's Burn

Ford

Burnhead
Wood

Frizzels
Wood

Ice
Cleugh

Pressmennan
Wood

Channel
Wood

CHANNEL BRAE

73

The
Sneep

Pathhead

Halls

Staneshal
Wood

Cauld Burn

Gallows
Law

Gairy Burn

3

Well Hill

Rottenraw Burn

EH42

72

Hartside

Deuchrie
Wood

Hartside
Law

Rammer
Wood

Hartside Burn

Lint Burn

Sleepy
Knowe

Mearns Cleugh

Herring Road

2

Halls Edge

Lothian Edge

Ox Cleugh

Redscar Burn

Rammer Cleugh

Rammer
Dodd

Herring Road

Rammer Cleugh Burn

Wester Hartside
Edge

71

Crow
Cleugh

Rammer Moss

1

Mossy Burn

Lodge Burn

Watch
Law

70

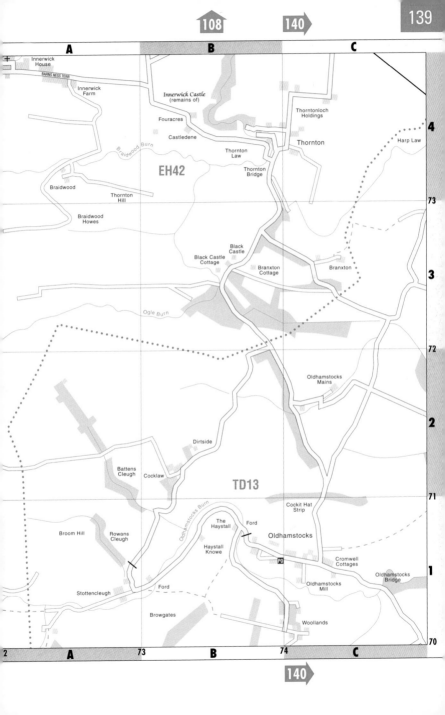

A | B | C

EH42

A1

4

73 Lawfield

Bilsdean Creek

Birnieknowes

The Linn

Gutcher's Hole

3 Bilsdean

Clay Knowe

Broomward

Bilsdean Bridge

Dunglass Old Bridge

Dunglass Bridge

Rams Heugh

Braid Law

Gallows Law Plantation

TD13

Dunglass New Bridge

Dunglass Viaduct

Castle Dyke Cottage

Dunglass Mains

72 Gallows Law

Dunglass Church

Deanberry Hole

COASTGUARD COTTS

Cove

Bilsdean Banks

Bilsdean Burn

Dunglass

Forth Brae

Killflat Wood

WEB EM

Cats Hole Plantation

Rules Law

2 Closehead

Gowdies Well

Belvidere Wood

Dunglass Burn

Eildbalks Wood

Pathhead

LADY HALL RD

Cockburnspath

Southern Upland Way

Cati Heugh

Dean Mill Bog

Cockburnspath Prim Sch

Hotel

A1

Springfield

71

PO

Chapelhill Cotts

Braeside Cottage

Kirklands

Dovecot Hall

Cockburnspath Burn

Sand Pit

Chapelhill

1

Hazeldean Burn

Berwick Burn

Neuk / Farm

Kinegar Strip

70

75 A 76 B 77 C

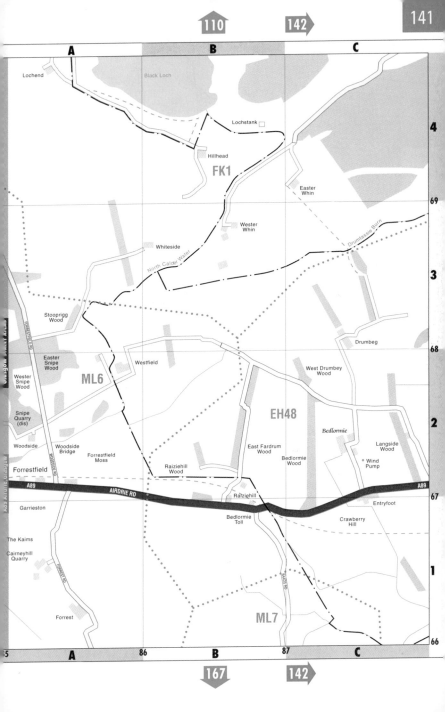

110
142

A   B   C

Lochend

Black Loch

Lochstank

Hillhead

FK1

Easter
Whin

4

69

Wester
Whin

Whiteside

North Calder Water

Drumtassie Burn

3

Stooprigg
Wood

Drumbeg

68

Easter
Snipe
Wood

Westfield

West Drumbey
Wood

ML6

Wester
Snipe
Wood

EH48

Bedlormie

Langside
Wood

Snipe
Quarry
(dis)

East Fardrum
Wood

Bedlormie
Wood

Wind
Pump

2

Woodside

Woodside
Bridge

Forrestfield
Moss

Raiziehill
Wood

Forrestfield

Forrestfield

A89   AIRDRIE RD

Raiziehill

Entryfoot

67

Garrieston

Bedlormie
Toll

Crawberry
Hill

A89

The Kaims

Cairneyhill
Quarry

1

Forrest

ML7

66

A   86   B   87   C

167
142

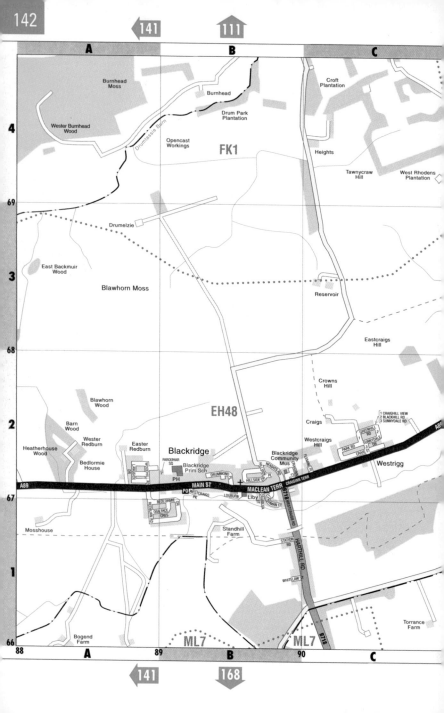

141
111

A   **B**   **C**

Burnhead
Moss

Burnhead

Croft
Plantation

Drum Park
Plantation

Wester Burnhead
Wood

Opencast
Workings

FK1

Heights

4

Drumtassie Burn

Tawnycraw
Hill

West Rhodens
Plantation

69

Drumelzie

East Backmuir
Wood

Reservoir

Blawhorn Moss

3

Eastcraigs
Hill

68

Crowns
Hill

Blawhorn
Wood

EH48

Craigs

1 CRAIGHILL VIEW
2 BLACKHILL RD
3 SUNNYDALE RD

Barn
Wood

Westcraigs
Hill

GREENHILL
RD

PARK RD

SUNNYDALE
DR

2

Heatherhouse
Wood

Wester
Redburn

Easter
Redburn

Blackridge

Blackridge
Community
Mus

CRAIG ST

Westrigg

Bedlormie
House

FARQUHAR
SQ

Blackridge
Prim Sch

DRUMMOND

HEIGHTS RD

PL

CRAIGINN TERR

PH

HILLSIDE CT

A89

MAIN ST

MACLEAN TERR

B718

67

PO

WESTCRAIGS
PL

LOUBURN

Liby

CRAIGEND RD

BEDLORMIE
DR

Mosshouse

DYKEFACE
CRES

Standhill
Farm

STATION
RD

WHITELAW ST

HARTHILL RD

1

Bogend
Farm

Torrance
Farm

B718

66

88   **A**   89   **B**   90   **C**

ML7   **ML7**

141
168

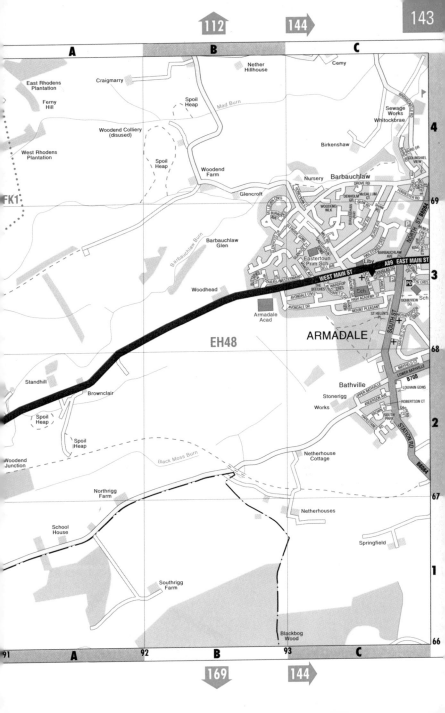

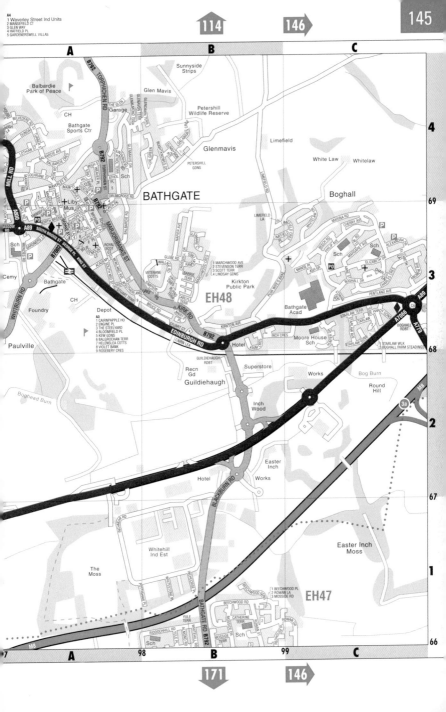

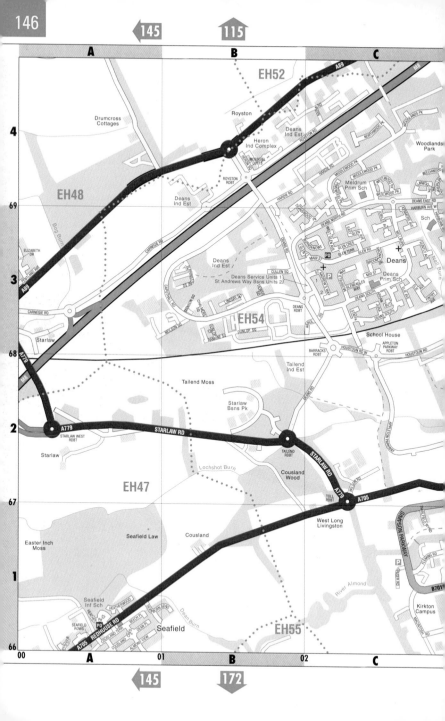

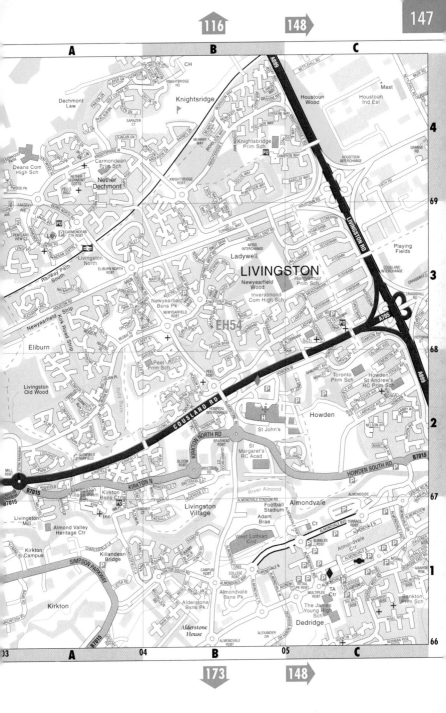

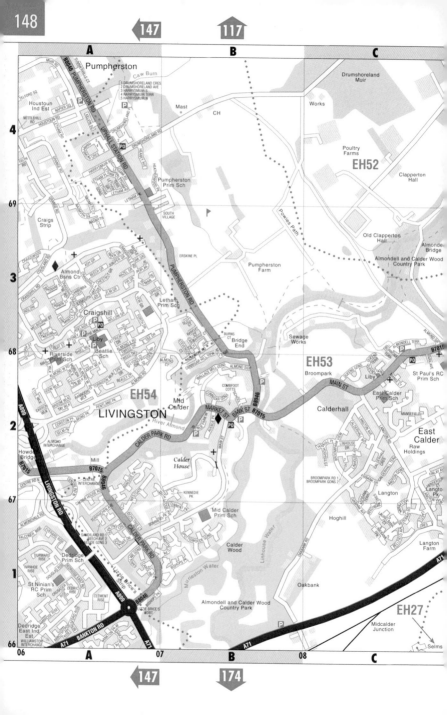

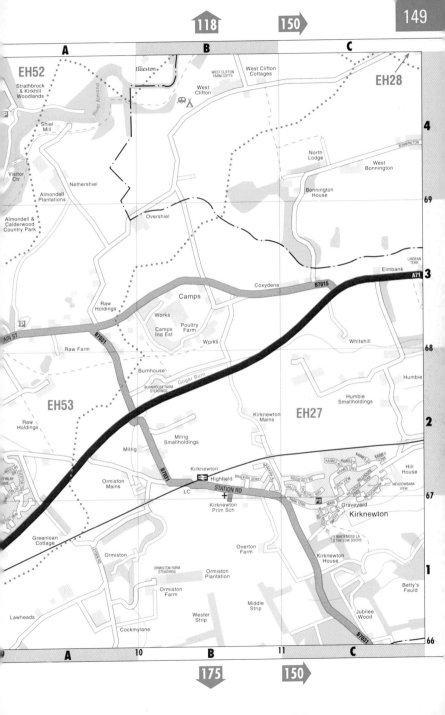

EH52

Strathbrock
& Kirkhill
Woodlands

Illieston

WEST CLIFTON
FARM COTTS

West Clifton
Cottages

West
Clifton

EH28

River Almond

Shiel
Mill

P

Visitor
Ctr

Nethershiel

Almondell
Plantations

Almondell &
Calderwood
Country Park

Overshiel

North
Lodge

West
Bonnington

BONNINGTON

Bonnington
House

4

69

LINDEAN
TERR

Elmbank

A71

Coxydene

B7015

Camps

Raw
Holdings

Works

Poultry
Farm

Camps Ind Est

Works

P

AIN ST

B7031

Raw Farm

Burnhouse

BURNHOUSE FARM
STEADINGS

Gogar Burn

Whitehill

Humbie

Humbie
Smallholdings

68

EH53

Raw
Holdings

Milrig
Smallholdings

Milrig

Kirknewton
Mains

EH27

2

B7031

Kirknewton

Highfield

BRAEKIRK GDNS

BASKIRK LE

ROUGE HILL RD

HALLCRAIG

CHURCHILL WAY

KAIMES

KAIMES

KAIMES

KAIMES GDNS

KAIMES CRES

HILDEMORE

HILDEMORE

HILDEMORE TERR

Hill
House

MEADOWBANK
VIEW

67

LC

Ormiston Mains

STATION RD

Kirknewton
Prim Sch

PARK TERR

FOSTY VIEW

MAIN ST

PO

Graveyard

Kirknewton

Greenloan
Cottage

Ormiston

Overton
Farm

1 WHITEMOSS LA
2 THE LOW DOORS

Kirknewton
House

Betty's
Fauld

1

LESSEN RD

ORMISTON FARM
STEADINGS

Ormiston
Plantation

Middle
Strip

Jubilee
Wood

B7031

Lawheads

Ormiston
Farm

Cockmylane

Wester
Strip

66

149
119

A
B
C

EH28

Tormain

Cup & Ring
marked Rocks

4

Bonnington
Mains

Craw
Hill

Ratho Park
Hotel

St
Mary's
Hall

69

Hatton
Bridge

Entry
Head

Dalmahoy
Stables

Hillview

Hatton
House

Hatton
Mains

BRIDGE END
COTTS

Wilkieston

Hatton
Sports Club

Dalmahoy
Country Club

Orchardfield

CH

3

A71

PO

ORCHARDFIELD
TERR

Orchardfield

Burnwynd

EH27

Linburn

Spittalton
Wood

68

Kinrura

Dalmahoy
Mains

Ravelri
Junctio

Waterloo
Tower

Haggs
Farm

Long
Dalmahoy

2

LONG DALMAHOY RD.

Dalmahoy Hill
Plantation

Easter
Newton

67

Ravelrig
Quarries
(dis)

The
Dean

Dalmahoy
Hill

1

A7

Kaimes
Hill

EH14

Kaimes

Kaimes
Quarry

Burial
Ground
Wood

Kaimes
Wood

A70

GLENBROOK RD.

66

12
A
13
B
14
C

149
176

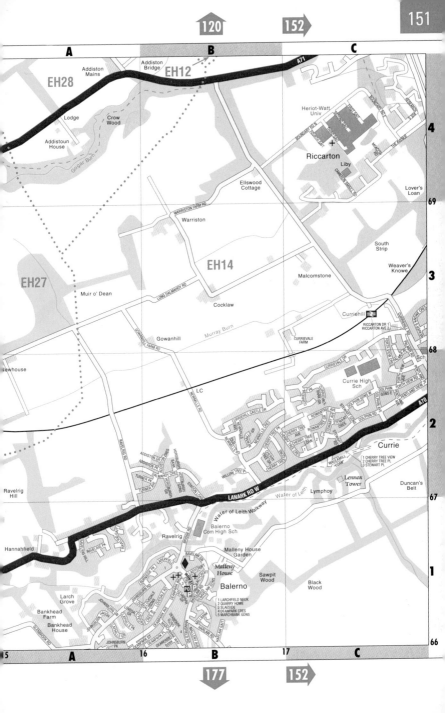

120
152
177
152

A   B   C

A71

EH28

Addiston
Mains

Addiston
Bridge

EH12

Lodge

Crow
Wood

Addistoun
House

Gogar Burn

Heriot-Watt
Univ

BOUNDARY RD

ROWAN TREE AVE

THE AVENUE

Riccarton

Liby

CAMERON SMAIL RD

Lover's
Loan

4

Ellswood
Cottage

69

WARRISTON FARM RD

Warriston

EH14

EH27

Muir o' Dean

Malcomstone

South
Strip

Weaver's
Knowe

3

LONG DALMAHOY RD

Cocklaw

Curriehill

RICCARTON DR 1
RICCARTON AVE 2

Gowanhill

Murray Burn

DOLPHIN FARM RD

CURRIEVALE
FARM

Sch

68

ewhouse

CURRIE LAW

Currie High
Sch

DOLPHIN
GDNS E

PENTLAND VIEW

A70

LC

NEWMILLS RD

CURRIEHILL CASTLE DR

Currie

1 CHERRY TREE VIEW
2 CHERRY TREE PL
3 STEWART PL

Ravelrig
Hill

Ravelrig

Lennox
Tower

Lymphoy

Duncan's
Belt

2

LANARK RD W

Water of Leith

Water of Leith Walkway

67

Hannahfield

Water of Leith Walkway

Balerno
Com High Sch

Malleny House
Garden

Ravelrig

Malleny
House

Sawpit
Wood

Black
Wood

1

Larch
Grove

PO
P

Balerno

1 LARCHFIELD NEUK
2 QUARRY HOWE
3 SLAESIDE
4 DEANPARK CRES
5 MARCHBANK GDNS

Bankhead
Farm

Bankhead
House

JOHNSBURN
PK

66

5   A   16   B   17   C

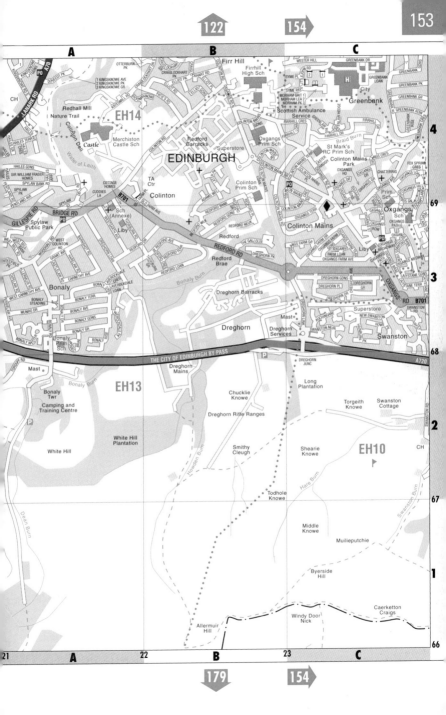

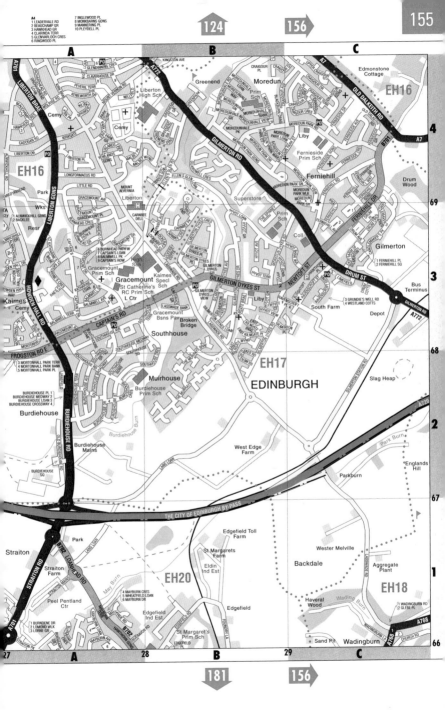

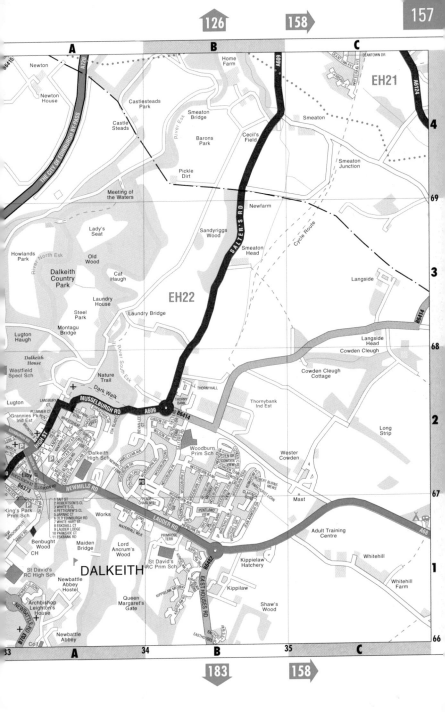

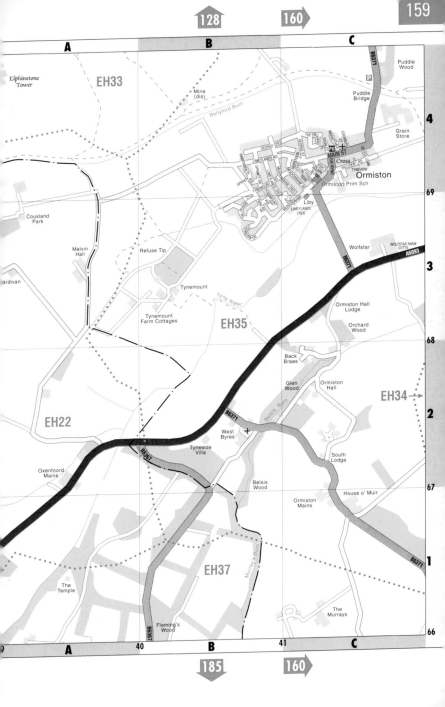

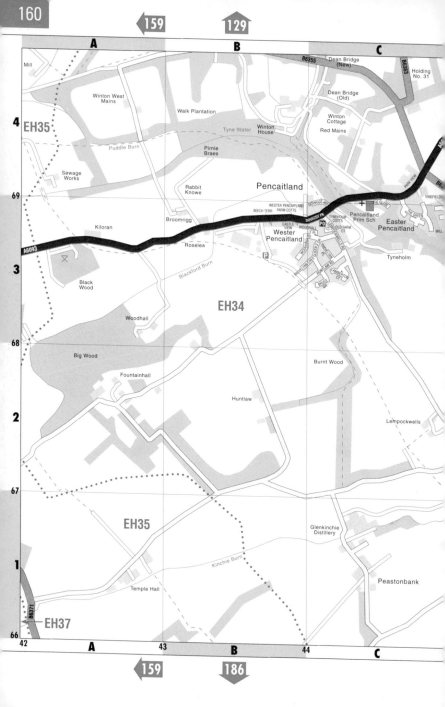

159
129

A
B
C

Mill

B6355
Dean Bridge (New)

B6363
Holding No. 31

Winton West Mains

Walk Plantation

Dean Bridge (Old)

Winton Cottage

4

EH35

Tyne Water

Winton House

Red Mains

Puddle Burn

Pirnie Braes

69

Rabbit Knowe

Pencaitland

Sewage Works

WESTER PENCAITLAND FARM COTTS

Broomrigg

BEECH TERR

DOVECOT PK

WOODHALL

Pencaitland Prim Sch

Easter Pencaitland

Kiloran

CASTLE VIEW

PO

OLD FARM CT

THE GLEBE

VINEFIELDS

MILL

Roselea

Wester Pencaitland

A6093

Blackford Burn

P

TYNEHOLM GREEN RD

TYNEHOLM CT

BRUCE WK

Tyneholm

3

Black Wood

EH34

Woodhall

68

Big Wood

Burnt Wood

Fountainhall

2

Huntlaw

Lempockwells

67

EH35

Glenkinchie Distillery

1

Kinchie Burn

Peastonbank

Temple Hall

B6371

EH37

66

42
A
43
B
44
C

159
186

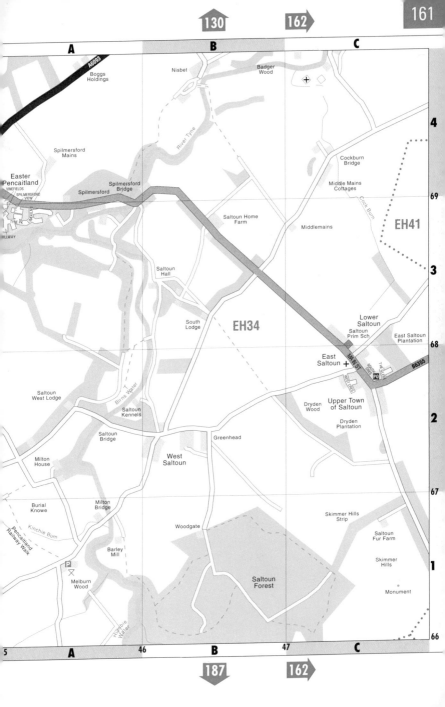

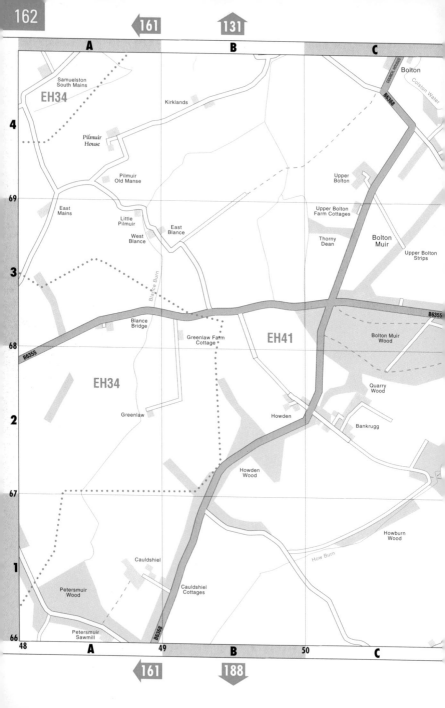

Gowks Hill

Clacherdean Wood

Brounshill

Playmuir Wood

Dalgowrie Brae

Colstoun Old Mill

Crown Wood

Myreside

4

Haydean

Eaglescairnie

Ewelie Wood

South Lodge

Colstoun Water

69

Hay Dean

Home Farm

Slateford

Eaglescairnie Mains

Sandyford Burn

Beugh Banks

Fawn Wood

The Common

Sewage Works

Gifford Vale

3

Heather Wood

Beugh Burn

Membland

Inglisfield

Bell's Wood

Broadwoodside

Speedy Wood

G MILL
STATION RD
Hotel
TH
THE SQUARE
LILLIES LA
B6369
B6355

Bolton Muir Wood

EH41

Newhall Burn

Holynbank

Yester Prim Sch

Lady's Wood

68

Pyotshaw

Speedy Burn

Craises Roundall

Gifford Bank

Gifford

Port Wood

Newhall Port

Blawearie Wood

CH

Broad Wood

Carter's Haugh

Gifford Water

Beechbank Wood

2

Trafalgar

Meg's Bridge

Bents Wood

Baillie's Hag Wood

Newhall Wood

67

Well Hag Wood

Foxes Wood

Bankhead Bridge

Bankhead Wood

Woodhead

Yester Mains

Skedsbush Bridge

Smithy Cottage

Saugh Wood

1

Knawe Burn

Dean Wood

Bonny Wood

Wester Wood

Redshill

Scarhill Wood

66

Green Wood

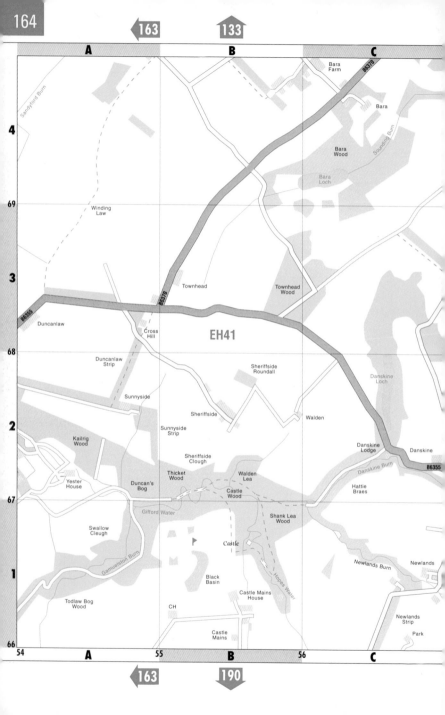

A B C

4

69

3

68

2

67

1

66

54 55 56

Sandyford Burn

Winding Law

B6355

Duncanlaw

Duncanlaw Strip

Cross Hill

Townhead

B6370

EH41

Sheriffside Roundall

Sunnyside

Sheriffside

Sunnyside Strip

Sheriffside Clough

Walden

Kailrig Wood

Thicket Wood

Walden Lea

Yester House

Duncan's Bog

Castle Wood

Gifford Water

Shank Lea Wood

Swallow Cleugh

Gamuelston Burn

Castle

Hopes Water

Black Basin

Castle Mains House

Newlands Burn

Danskine Loch

Danskine Lodge

Danskine

Danskine Burn

B6355

Hattie Braes

Newlands

Newlands Strip

Park

Todlaw Bog Wood

CH

Castle Mains

Bara Farm

B6370

Bara

Bara Wood

Soundrig Burn

Bara Loch

Townhead Wood

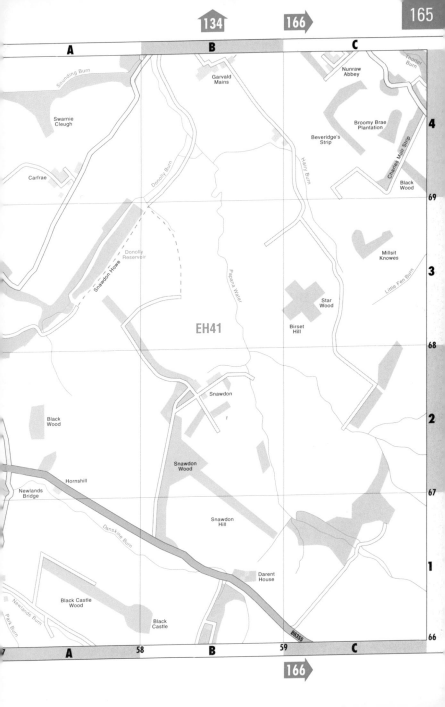

A   B   C

Sounding Burn

Garvald
Mains

Nunraw
Abbey

Thortel
Burn

Swarnie
Cleugh

Broomy Brae
Plantation

Beveridge's
Strip

4

Carfrae

Donolly Burn

Hairy Burn

Charles Muir Strip

Black
Wood

69

Snawdon Howe

Donolly
Reservoir

Millsit
Knowes

Little Fen Burn

3

Papana Water

EH41

Star
Wood

Birset
Hill

68

Snawdon

Black
Wood

2

Snawdon
Wood

Hornshill

67

Newlands
Bridge

Danskine Burn

Snawdon
Hill

Newlands Burn

Black Castle
Wood

Snawdon
Hill

Darent
House

1

Park Burn

Black
Castle

B6355

66

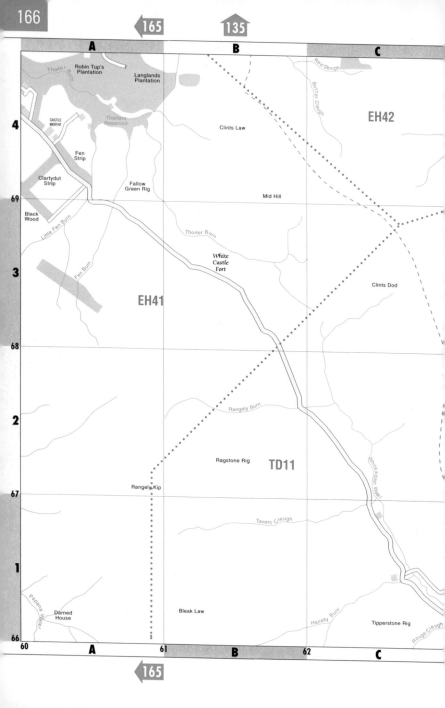

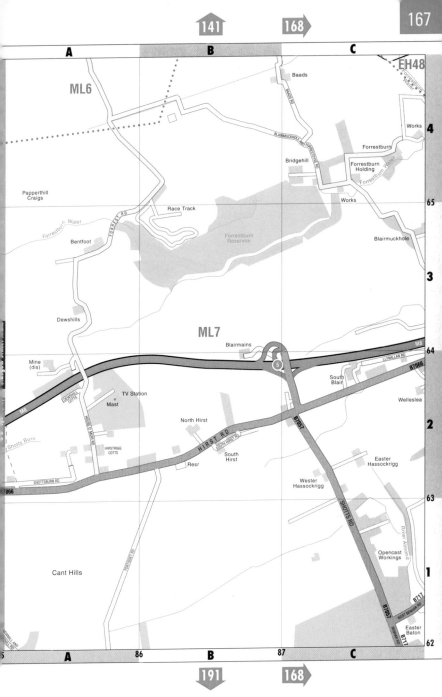

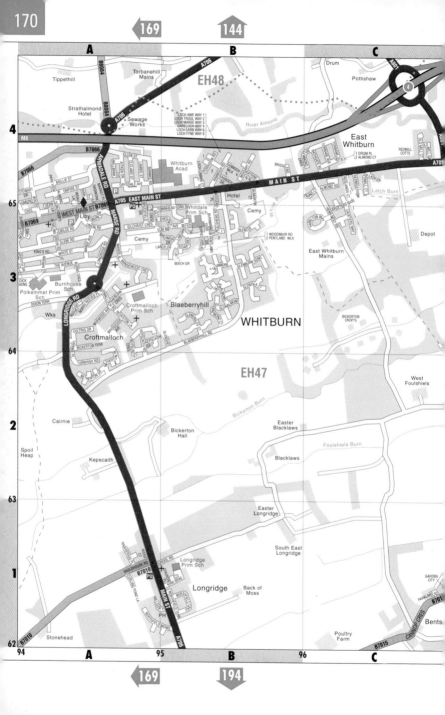

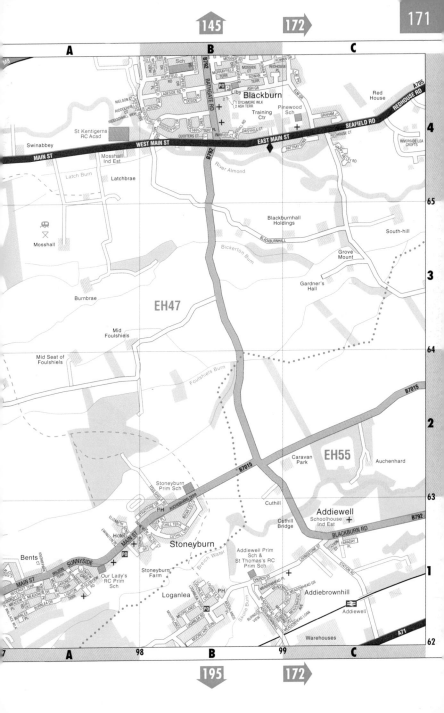

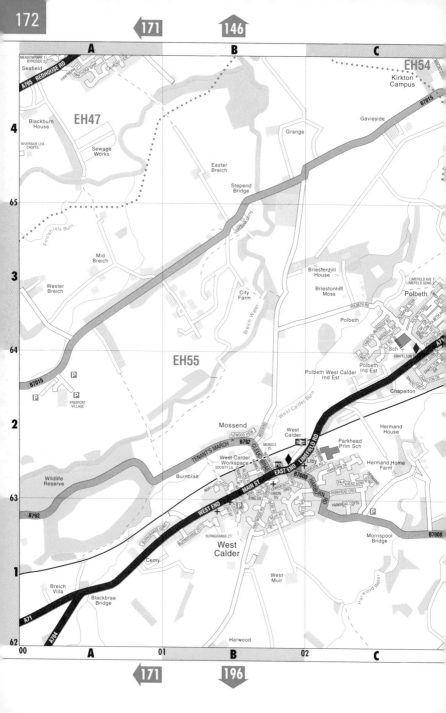

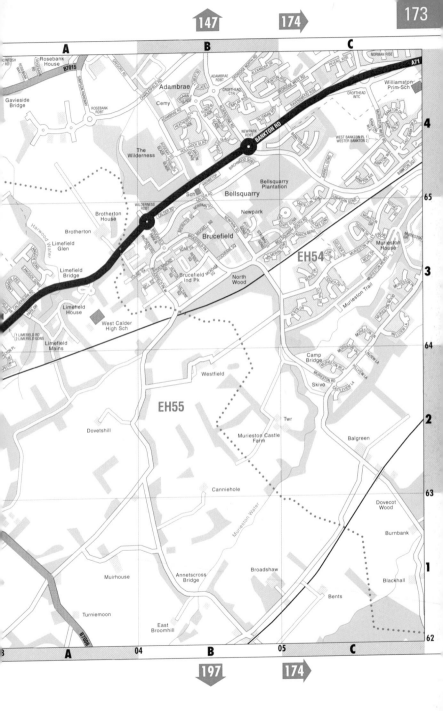

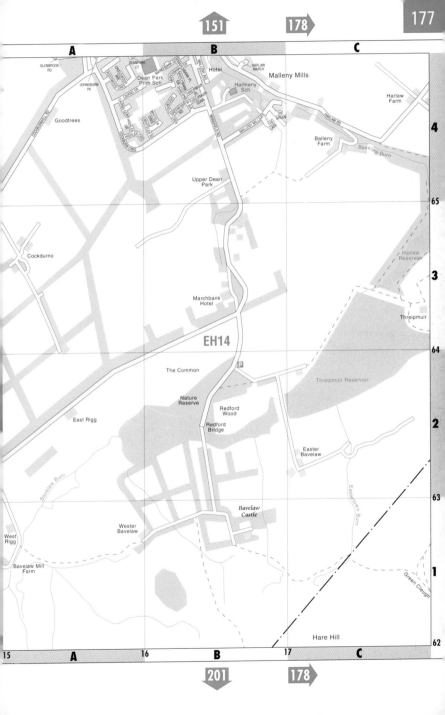

A B C

GLENBROOK RD
Goodtrees
JOHNSBURN PK
DEANPARK CT
Dean Park Prim. Sch
Hotel
HARLAW MARCH
Malleny Mills
Harmeny Sch
Harlaw Farm
THE GREEN
THE LADE
HARLAW RD
Balleny Farm
Bavelaw Burn

Upper Dean Park

Cockdurno

Marchbank Hotel

Harlaw Reservoir

Threipmuir

EH14

The Common

Threipmuir Reservoir

Nature Reserve
Redford Wood
East Rigg
Redford Bridge

Easter Bavelaw

Bavelaw Burn

Bavelaw Castle

Easterton Burn

Wester Bavelaw

West Rigg

Bavelaw Mill Farm

Green Cleugh

Hare Hill

4

65

3

64

2

63

1

62

15 A 16 B 17 C

A **B** **C**

Bonaly
Country Park

Whiteside
Plantations

Bonaly
Resr

Kinleith Burn

EH13

4

Cock
Rig

Malleny Rifle Range
(dis)

Harbour
Hill

Harlaw House
Ranger Ctr

65

Harlaw
Reservoir

Craigentarrie

3

EH14

Bell's
Hill

Threipmuir Reservoir

64

King's
Hill

White Cleugh Burn

2

White Cleugh Burn

White Cleugh

EH26

Logan
Cottage

Black Hill

Logan
House

63

Logan Burn

Gask Hill

1

Howlet's
House

Flesh Cleugh

Green
Cleugh

Loganlea
Reservoir

62

The
Pinnacle

The
Howe

18 **A** **19** **B** **20** **C**

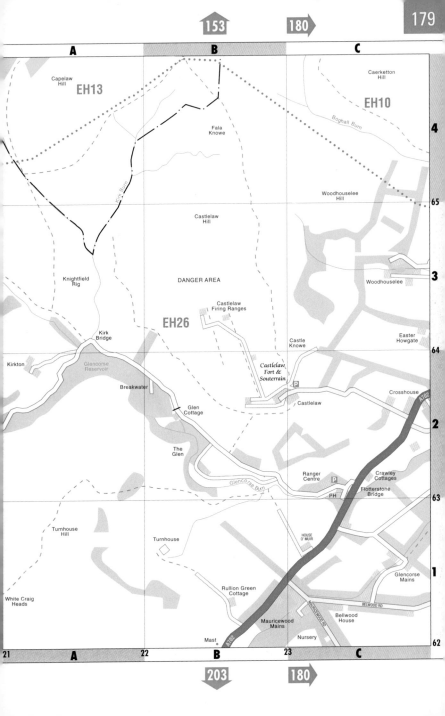

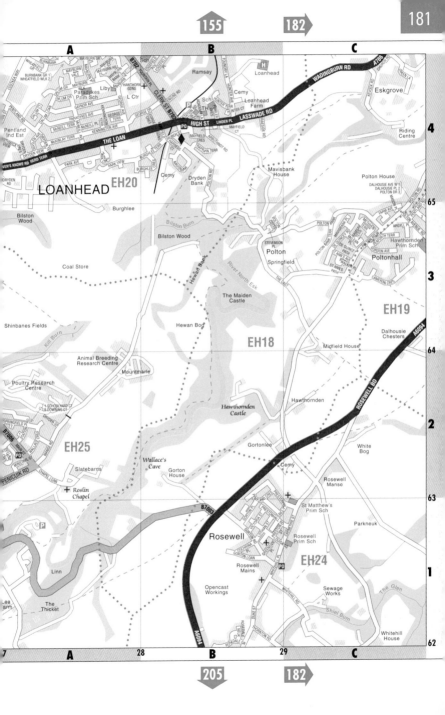

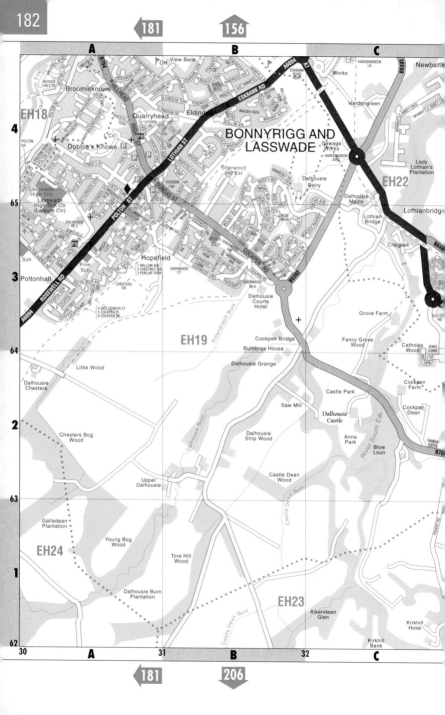

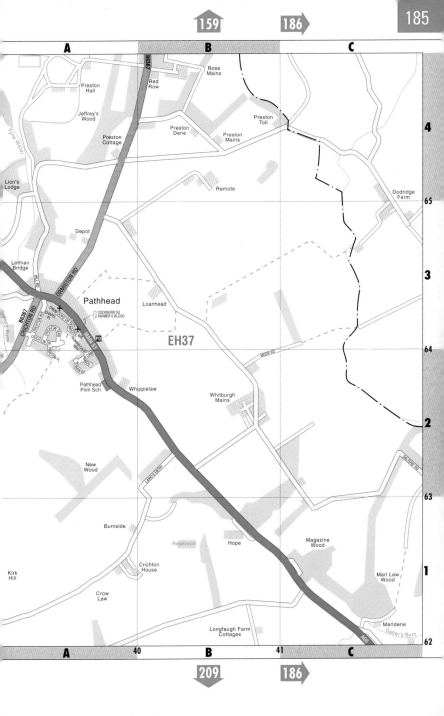

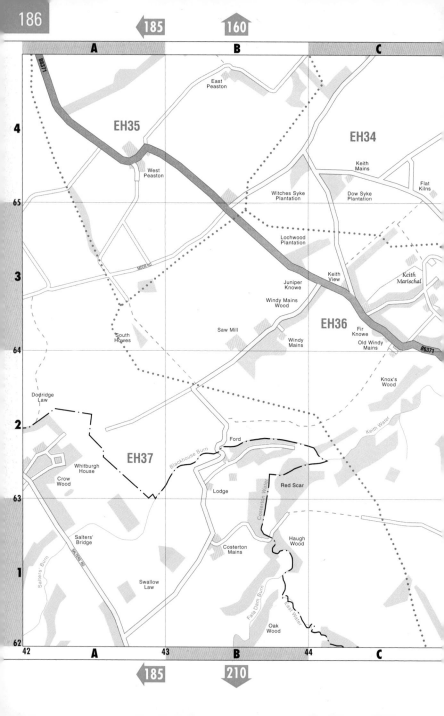

185
160

A   B   C

4

EH35

EH34

East Peaston

West Peaston

Keith
Mains

Flat
Kilns

65

Witches Syke
Plantation

Dow Syke
Plantation

MOOR RD

Lochwood
Plantation

3

Keith
View

Keith
Marischal

Juniper
Knowe

Windy Mains
Wood

South
Howes

Saw Mill

EH36

Fir
Knowe

Old Windy
Mains

B6371

64

Windy
Mains

Knox's
Wood

Keith Water

Dodridge
Law

2

Ford

Whitburgh
House

EH37

Blackhouse Burn

Red Scar

Crow
Wood

Lodge

Costerton Water

63

Salters'
Bridge

Haugh
Wood

SALTERS RD

Costerton
Mains

Salters' Burn

1

Swallow
Law

Fala Dam Burn

East Water

Oak
Wood

62

42   A   43   B   44   C

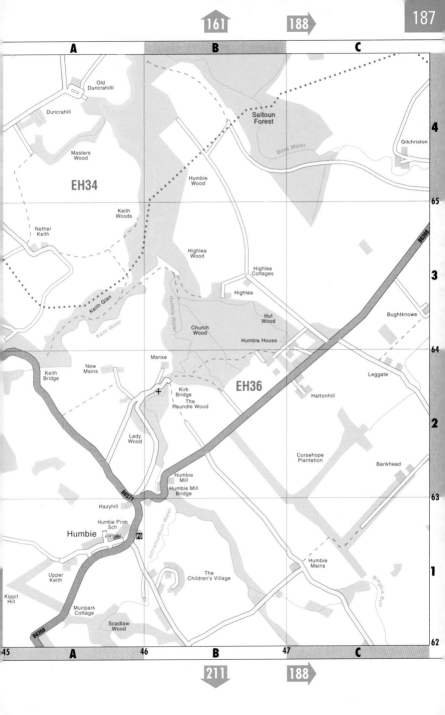

A B C

Old
Duncrahilll

Duncrahill

Masters
Wood

EH34

Keith
Woods

Nether
Keith

Keith Glen

Keith Water

Keith
Bridge

New
Mains

Manse

Keith
Bridge

Lady
Wood

Hazyhill

Humbie Prim
Sch

Humbie

KIRKPITHILL

PO

Upper
Keith

Kippit
Hill

Muirpark
Cottage

Scadlaw
Wood

B6368

B6371

Saltoun
Forest

Birns Water

Gilchriston

Humbie
Wood

4

65

Highlea
Wood

Highlea
Cottages

Highlea

3

Hut
Wood

Bughtknowe

B6368

Church
Wood

Humble House

Humble Water

64

Kirk
Bridge
The
Roundle Wood

EH36

Leggate

Hattonhill

2

Corsehope
Plantation

Bankhead

Humbie
Mill

Humbie Mill
Bridge

63

Johnstounburn Water

The
Children's Village

Humbie
Mains

Bleegie Burn

1

B6368

62

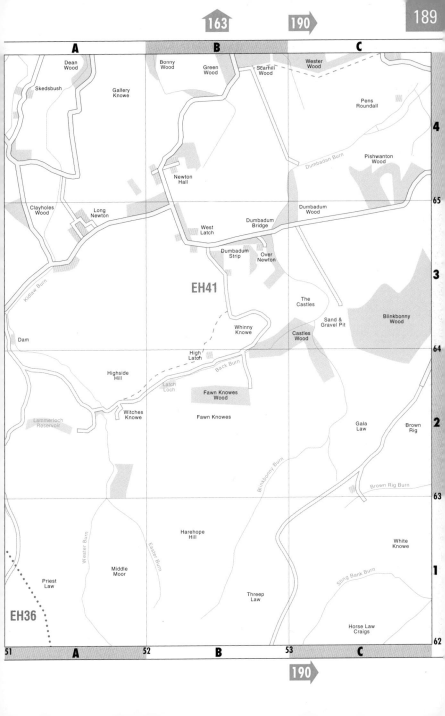

A B C

4

Dean Wood
Skedsbush
Gallery Knowe

Bonny Wood
Green Wood
Scarhill Wood
Wester Wood

Pens Roundall

Dumbadan Burn
Pishwanton Wood

Newton Hall

65

Clayholes Wood
Long Newton

West Latch
Dumbadum Bridge
Dumbadum Wood

3

EH41

Dumbadum Strip
Over Newton

Kidlaw Burn

The Castles

Blinkbonny Wood

Dam

Whinny Knowe

Sand & Gravel Pit
Castles Wood

64

High Latch
Back Burn

Highside Hill
Latch Loch

Fawn Knowes Wood

2

Lammerloch Reservoir
Witches Knowe

Fawn Knowes

Gala Law
Brown Rig

Blinkbonny Burn

63

Brown Rig Burn

Wester Burn
Easter Burn

Harehope Hill

White Knowe

1

Priest Law

Middle Moor

Threep Law

Sting Bank Burn

EH36

Horse Law Craigs

62

51 A 52 B 53 C

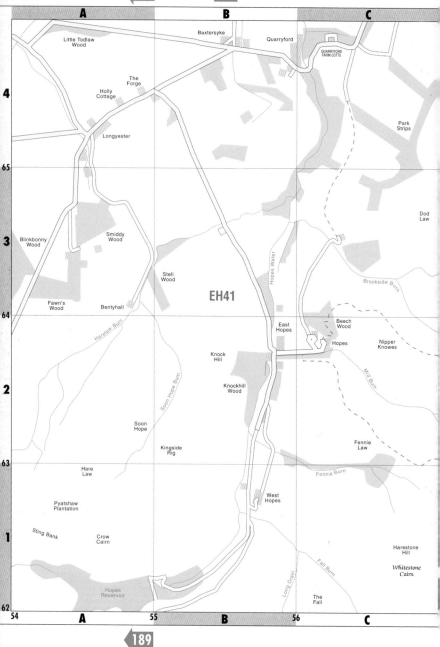

189

164

A   B   C

Little Todlaw
Wood

Baxtersyke

Quarryford

QUARRYFORD
FARM COTTS

The
Forge

4

Holly
Cottage

Park
Strips

Longyester

65

Dod
Law

3

Blinkbonny
Wood

Smiddy
Wood

Hopes Water

Brookside Burn

Stell
Wood

EH41

Fawn's
Wood

Bentyhall

Beech
Wood

64

Haraelaw Burn

East
Hopes

Hopes

Nipper
Knowes

Knock
Hill

2

Soon Hope Burn

Knockhill
Wood

Mid Burn

Soon
Hope

Kingside
Rig

Fennie
Law

63

Hare
Law

Fennie Burn

Pyatshaw
Plantation

West
Hopes

1

Sting Bank

Crow
Cairn

Long Grain

Fall Burn

Harestone
Hill

Whitestone
Cairn

Hopes
Reservoir

The
Fall

62

54   A   55   B   56   C

189

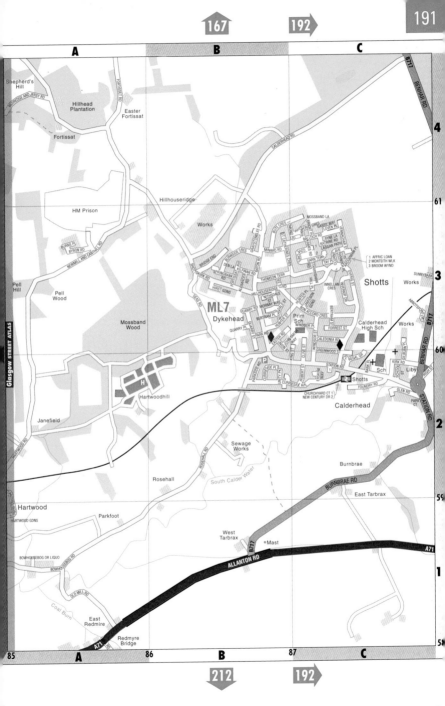

A   B   C

Glasgow Street Atlas

Shepherd's Hill

Hillhead Plantation

Easter Fortissat

Fortissat

HM Prison

Hillhouseridge

Works

Pell Hill

Pell Wood

Mossband Wood

Hartwoodhill

Janefield

Hartwood

HARTWOOD GDNS

Parkfoot

Rosehall

South Calder Water

Sewage Works

Burnbrae

East Tarbrax

BURNBRAE RD

West Tarbrax

Mast

ALLANTON RD

A71

East Redmire

Redmyre Bridge

Coal Burn

OLD MILL RD

BOWHOUSEBOG OR LIQUO

BOWHOUSE

ML7

Dykehead

Shotts

Calderhead High Sch

Works

Works

Calderhead

Prim Sch

SUNNYBANK

1 AFFRIC LOAN
2 MONTEITH WLK
3 BROOM WYND

MOSSBAND LA

Liby

Sch

Shotts

CHURCHYARD CT 1
NEW CENTURY DR 2

STATION RD

BENHAR RD

B717

PARK CT

GLEN RD

FOUNDRY RD

4

61

3

60

2

59

1

5

191 168

A B C

Fauldhouse

4

B717

61

BENHAR RD

CH

South Calder Water

Starryshaw
Farm

3

B717

Spoil
Heap

Stanebent

Cairneyhead

ML7

Stanebent

60

STABLE RD

Stane
Prim Sch

Torbothie

CEMETERY RD

1 ETIVE WLK
2 EG WAY
3 GAIP WYND
4 BOWMORE WLK
5 TORRIN LOAN
6 SPRINGHILL VIEW
7 DORNIE WYND
8 MORAR WAY
9 COIRE LOAN
10 SUNA PATH
11 SALEN LOAN

NEVIS PL

Cemy

EH47

2

B7010

MAIN ST

CHARLOTTE ST

TULLOCH RD

APPIN TERR

LOCHURD

LANSDOWNE CRES

LAGGAN AVE

Stane

SANDYVALE
PL

BLINNY CT 1
TARBRAX PATH 2

B7010 SPRINGHILL RD Springhill

B7010

59

BELMONT DRIVE

ELMWOOD RD

LARCHFIELD PATH

NORTHFIELD AVE

Works

Springhill

SPRINGHILL AND LEADLOCH RD

Knowton
Farm

NETHER FAULDHOUSE RD B715

B7010

A71

1

Works

Lingore Linn

A71

58

88 A 89 B 90 C

191 213

A   B   C

EH47

MOORELAND
GDNS

Hotel

Nether
Longford

West Mains
Cottages

A71

A704

Newhouse

East
White Sykes

4

Nether Longford Moss

Longford Burn

61

Rusha

Longford

Spoil
Heap

Poultry
Farm

Longhill Burn

Longford
Bridge

3

Pateshill Cottage

EH55

60

Works

2

Pate's Hill

Woodmuir Plantation

59

Harwood Water

ML11

1

58

A   B   C

98   99

7

A   B   C

A704

Cow
Hill

Cairnview
Mains

4

Little
Harwood

Hartwood

West
Mains

Hartwood
Bridge

Hartwood
Mains

Harwood Water

61

Mossend

Mid
Hartwood

LOWLANDS
CROFTS

3

WEST HARWOOD
CROFTS

West
Harwood

EH55

60

Bog Burn

Baadsmill

Baad's Mill
Bridge

Vain Syke

2

Adie's Syke

Coal Burn

59

1

Pearie
Law

Cobbinshaw
Reservoir

Benry
Bog

Benry
Bridge

58

00   A   01   B   02   C

173
198

A
B
C

B7008
West Broomhill
Tor Whitie
Harburn
Torphin Bridge
Lodge
Coalheughead Farm
CH
Over Williamston
4
Broadmeadow
East Torphin
Haymains
Whistle Lodge
West Torphin
LC
61
Dog Bush Knowe
Harburn House
Bents Burn
3
Black Burn
Harburnhead
EH55
Camilty Moss
60
Tip
Camp Wood
Camilty Plantation
Camilty Hill
EH27
2
Castle Greg ROMAN FORTLET
59
Crosswood Burn
A70
P
Crosswood Bridge
Shear Bridge
Harburnhead Hill
1
B7008
A70
Otter Burn
58

A
B
C

03
04
05
A70

218
198

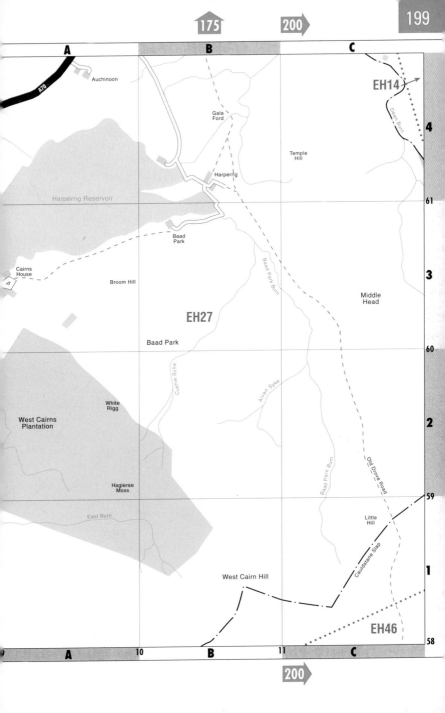

EH14

A70
Auchinoon

Gala
Ford

Temple
Hill

Harperrig Reservoir

Harperrig

4

61

Baad
Park

Dean Burn

Cairns
House

Broom Hill

Baad Park Burn

Middle
Head

3

EH27

Baad Park

60

Cushie Syke

Aiven Syke

White
Rigg

West Cairns
Plantation

2

Hagierae
Moss

Baad Park Burn

Old Drove Road

59

East Burn

Little
Hill

Cauldstane Slap

West Cairn Hill

1

EH46

58

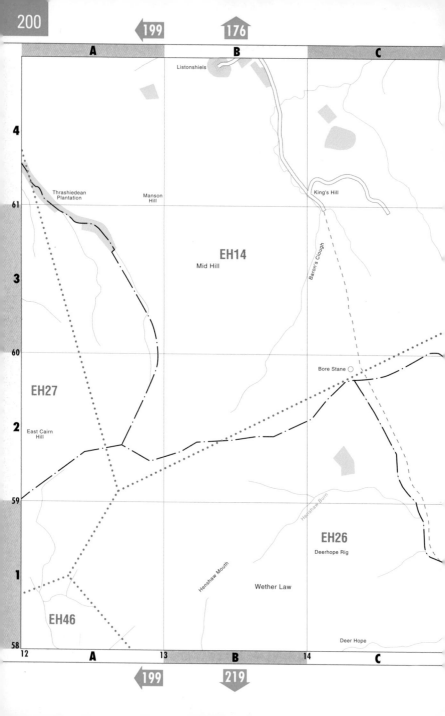

A B C

Listonshiels

4

Thrashiedean
Plantation

Manson
Hill

King's Hill

61

EH14

Mid Hill

Baron's Clough

3

60

Bore Stane ○

EH27

2

East Cairn
Hill

Henshaw Mouth

Wether Law

EH26

Deerhope Rig

59

Hopishaw Burn

1

EH46

Deer Hope

58

12 A 13 B 14 C

A
B
C

Rowantree Burn

EH14

Pentland Hills
Regional Park

Logan Burn

4

61

West Kip

3

Kitchen Moss

Eastside Burn

60

Cap Law

Green Law

2

EH26

Font Stone

Cock Rig

Gutterford Burn

59

Spittal Hill

Monks Burn

Greystone Head

Scroggy Hill

1

North Esk
Reservoir

58

EH14

A **B** **C**

Carnethy
Hill

Crooked Rig

Lover's
Loup

4

Grain Burn

Scald Law

61

East Kip

Grain Hill

Silverburn Quarry
(Whinstone)

A76

3

Kipps
Wood

South
Black Hill

HOPECARN RD

BIGGAR RD

Silver Burn

Eastside

HOPELANDS RD

EH26

Silverburn

60

Westside

Long
Knowe

Eastside Burn

Camp Hill

Troughmoss
Wood

A76

2

Braid Law
Plantation

Braid Law

Eight Mile
Burn

Braidwood
Bridge

Braidwood Burn

Quarrel Burn

Dean
Bridge

59

Braidwood

Corton Burn

Quarrel Burn
Reservoir

Quarrel
Haugh

Matthew's Linn

Pillar
Knowe

1

Joppa Burn

Walstone

A766

Brunston
Cottage

Brunstane

Laughatlothie
Wood

Joppa
Wood

A702

Walstone
Muir

58

18 **A** **19** **B** **20** **C**

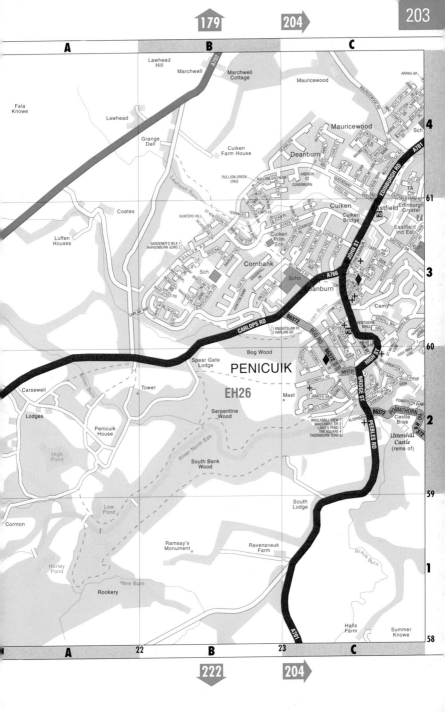

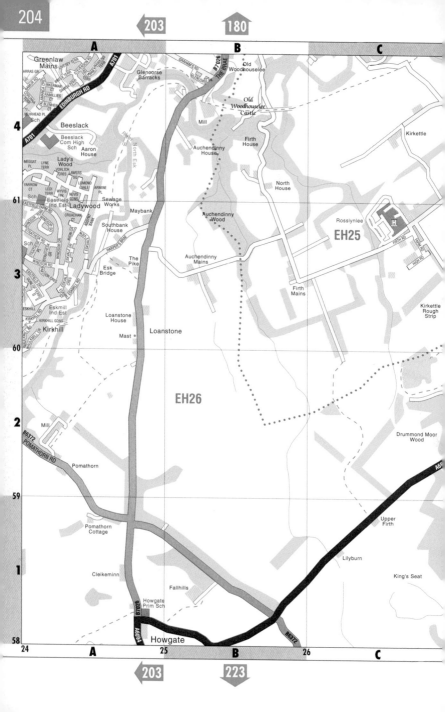

Greenlaw
Mains

ARRAS GR

Glencorse
Barracks

Old
Woodhouselee

B7026 THE BRAE

Beeslack
Beeslack
Com High
Sch

Aaron
House

Old
Woodhouselee
Castle

Kirkettle

Mill

Firth
House

4

A701

EDINBURGH RD

A701

MEGGAT
PL

LYNE
TERR

Lady's
Wood

VORLICH
CRES

JAWERS
SQ

ARMINE
PL

Auchendinny
House

North
House

North Esk

YARROW
CT

LEDI
TERR

WYVIS
PL

NEVIS
DALE

LOMOND
DALE

Sch

Eastfield
Ind Est

Ladywood

Sewage
Works

Maybank

Auchendinny
Wood

Rosslynlee

EH25

H

FIRTH RD

61

Sch

CRUACHAN
CT

Southbank
House

HARPER BRAE

3

Sch

WINDSOR RD

The
Pike

Esk
Bridge

Auchendinny
Mains

Firth
Mains

Kirkettle
Rough
Strip

Eskmill
Ind Est

Kirkhill

KIRKHILL GDNS

Loanstone
House

Mast

Loanstone

60

EH26

2

B6372

POMATHORN RD

Mill

Drummond Moor
Wood

Pomathorn

A6

59

Pomathorn
Cottage

Upper
Firth

1

Cleikeminn

Lilyburn

King's Seat

Fallhills

Howgate
Prim Sch

B7026

A6094

B6372

58

Howgate

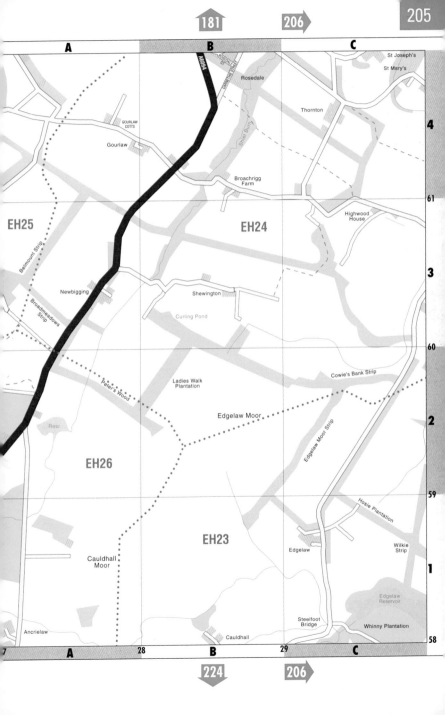

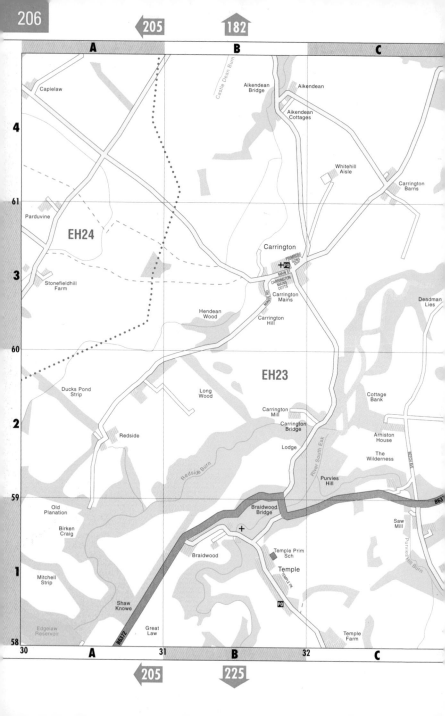

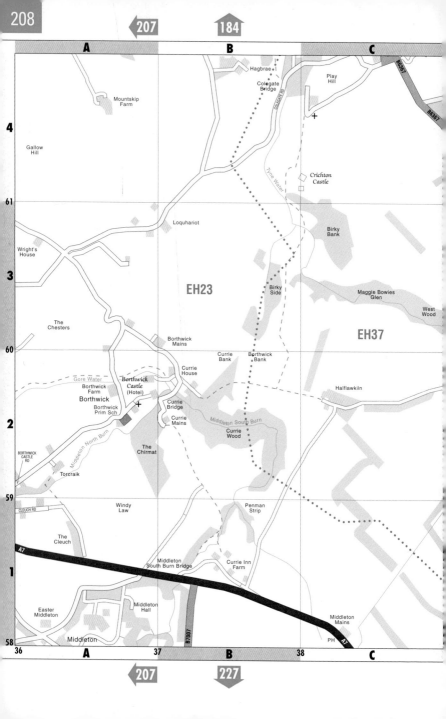

A B C

4

Mountskip Farm

Gallow Hill

Hagbrae
Colegate Bridge

Play Hill

COLEGATE RD

B6367

B6367

Tyne Water

Crichton Castle

61

Loquhariot

Wright's House

Birky Bank

3

EH23

The Chesters

Borthwick Mains

Birky Side

Maggie Bowies Glen

West Wood

EH37

60

Gore Water

Currie Bank

Borthwick Bank

Borthwick Farm

Currie House

Borthwick

Borthwick Castle (Hotel)

Currie Bridge

Halflawkiln

Borthwick Prim Sch

Currie Mains

Middleton South Burn

BORTHWICK CASTLE RD

Middleton North Burn

The Chirmat

Currie Wood

2

Torcraik

59

CLEUCH RD

Windy Law

Penman Strip

The Cleuch

A7

1

Middleton South Burn Bridge

Currie Inn Farm

Easter Middleton

Middleton Hall

Middleton Mains

PH

A7

Middleton

B7007

58

36 A 37 B 38 C

A   B   C

Old Crichton
Dean

A68

Longfaugh

B6458

Harle
Rigging

4

Kiln Wood

Salters' Burn

Saughland

61

3

King's
Knowe

Heathery
Strip

EH37

60

Mains
Wood

2

Tyne Water

Blackcastle

Tynehead

B6458

Tynehead Station
(dis)

Mutual
Wood

Cakemuir
Castle

Cakemuir Burn

59

1

EH23

B6367

58

9   A   40   B   41   C

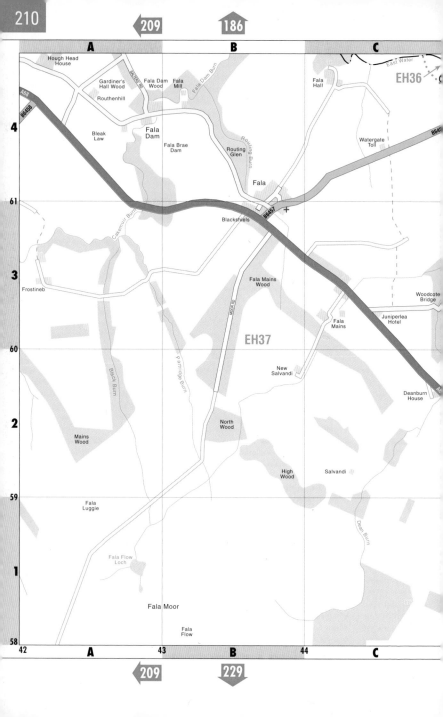

A **B** **C**

Hough Head House

Gardiner's Hall Wood

Fala Dam Wood

Fala Mill

Fala Dam Burn

Fala Hall

EH36

East Water

B658

A68

Routhenhill

Bleak Law

Fala Dam

Fala Brae Dam

Routing Glen

Routing Burn

Fala

Watergate Toll

B64

4

61

Cakemuir Burn

Blackshiels

B6457

Fala Mains Wood

Frostineb

EH37

Fala Mains

Juniperlea Hotel

Woodcote Bridge

3

B6368 RD

New Salvandi

Deanburn House

60

Partridge Burn

Black Burn

North Wood

2

Mains Wood

High Wood

Salvandi

Fala Luggie

59

Fala Flow Loch

Owan Burn

1

Fala Moor

Fala Flow

58

42 **A** **43** **B** **44** **C**

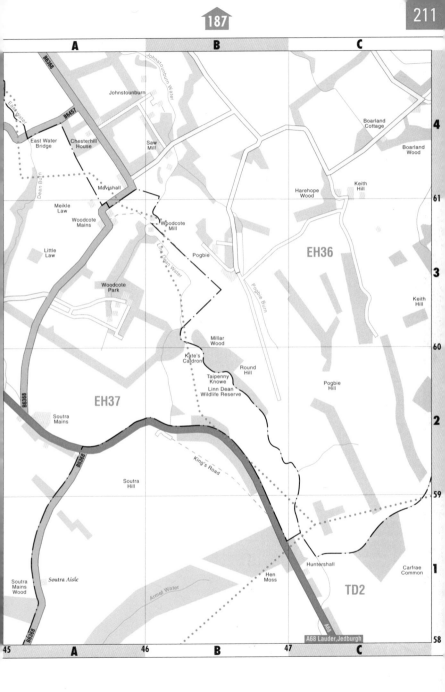

A   B   C

B6368

B6457

Johnstounburn Water

East Water

Johnstounburn

Boarland Cottage

East Water Bridge

Chesterhill House

Saw Mill

Boarland Wood

Dean Burn

Malvishall

Harehope Wood

Keith Hill

61

Meikle Law

Woodcote Mains

Woodcote Mill

The Dean Water

Woodcote Mill

Little Law

Pogbie

EH36

Woodcote Park

Pogbie Burn

Keith Hill

3

Millar Wood

60

Kate's Caldron

B6368

EH37

Taipenny Knowe

Round Hill

Linn Dean Wildlife Reserve

Pogbie Hill

Soutra Mains

2

B6368

King's Road

Soutra Hill

59

Huntershall

Carfrae Common

1

Soutra Mains Wood

Soutra Aisle

Hen Moss

TD2

Armet Water

A68

58

A68 Lauder, Jedburgh

45   A   46   B   47   C

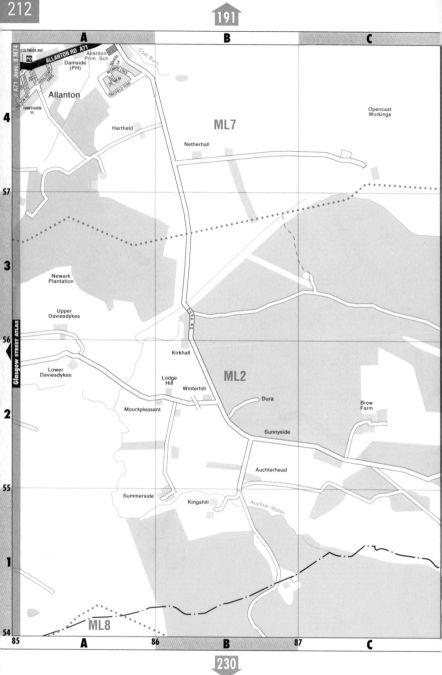

A   **B**   **C**

COLTNESS AVE

ALLANTON RD A71

Allanton
Prim Sch

Damside
(PH)

HAWTHORN
PL

Allanton

Coal Burn

4

Opencast
Workings

Hartfield

ML7

Netherhall

57

3

Newark
Plantation

Upper
Daviesdykes

LEA RD

56

Kirkhall

Lower
Daviesdykes

ML2

Lodge
Hill

Winterhill

Dura

2

Mountpleasant

Sunnyside

Brow
Farm

Auchterhead

55

Summerside

Kingshill

Auchter Water

1

54

ML8

85   **A**   **86**   **B**   **87**   **C**

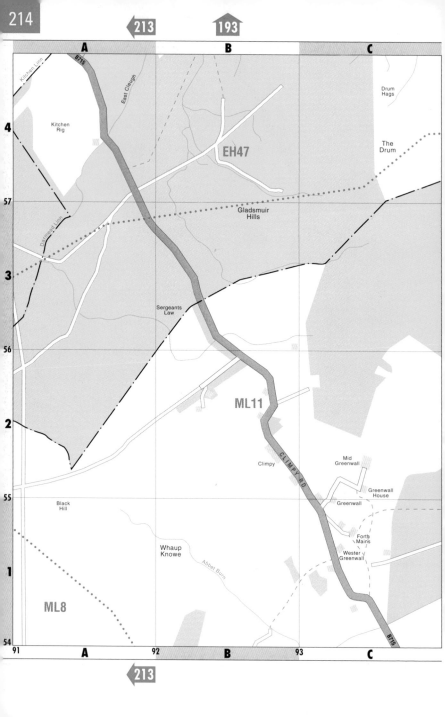

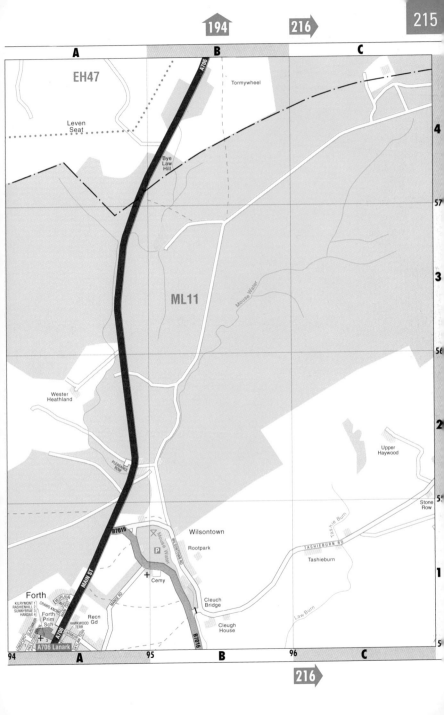

A B C

EH47

Tormywheel

Leven
Seat

Bye
Law
Hill

4

57

ML11

Mouse Water

3

56

Wester
Heathland

2

Upper
Haywood

PLEASANCE
ROW

Stone
Row

55

B7016

Wilsontown

P

Mouse Water

INGERSTON RD

Rootpark

Tashie Burn

TASHIEBURN RD

Tashieburn

1

MAIN ST

Cemy

Cleuch
Bridge

Forth

KILRYMONT 1
RASHIEHILL 2
SUNNYBRAE 3
HANDAX 4

CRAWS KNOWE

Forth
Prim
Sch

Recn
Gd

HAWKWOOD
TERR

Cleugh
House

Law Burn

A706
A706 Lanark

A B C

94 95 96

A   B   C

Hendry's
Corse

4

57

Wormlaw Burn

Worm Law

3

Mosshat Burn

EH55

Mountainblaw
Farm

56

Easter
Mosshat

ML11

2

Burnfoot Poultry
Farm

Wester Mosshat

MOSSHAT RD

Bughtknowes

Old Manse

Burnfoot

Drippool Water

TASHIEBURN RD

55

Crooklands

Lawhead
View

Pentland View

Haywood

Greenbank

Memorial

1

Auchengray Inn
(PH)

Mid
Auchengray

AUCHENGRAY RD

54

Auchengray

Hillhead of
Auchengray

97   A   98   B   99   C

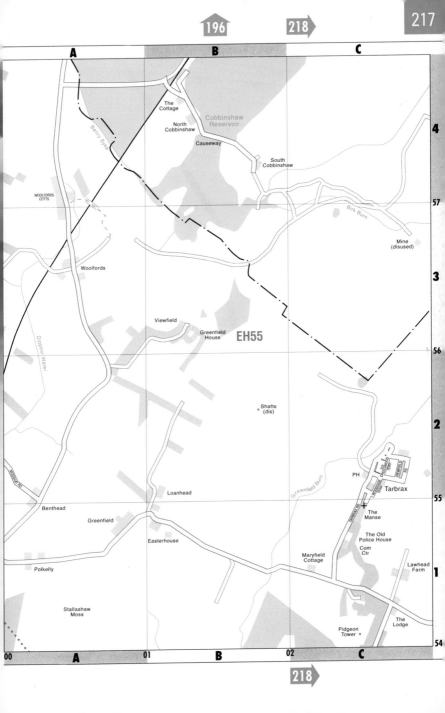

A

B

C

The Cottage

North Cobbinshaw

Cobbinshaw Reservoir

Causeway

South Cobbinshaw

4

Berry Syke

WOOLFORDS COTTS

Birk Burn

57

Woolfords

Mine (disused)

Dippool Water

Viewfield

Greenfield House

EH55

3

56

Shafts (dis)

2

PH

Greenhead Burn

Tarbrax

Benthead

Loanhead

55

Greenfield

The Manse

Easterhouse

The Old Police House

Com Ctr

Polkelly

Maryfield Cottage

Lawhead Farm

1

Stallashaw Moss

Pidgeon Tower

The Lodge

54

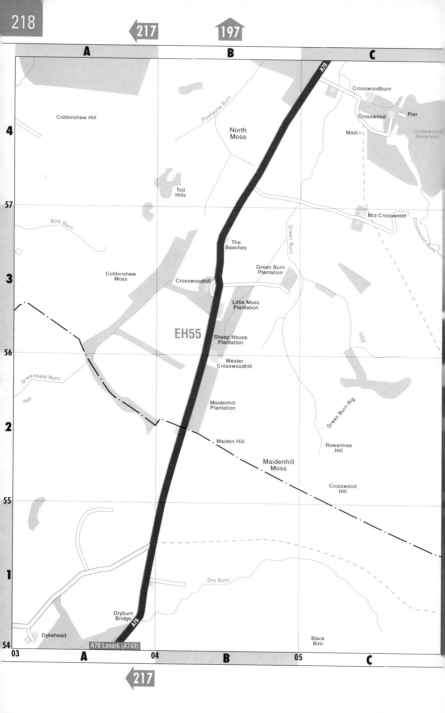

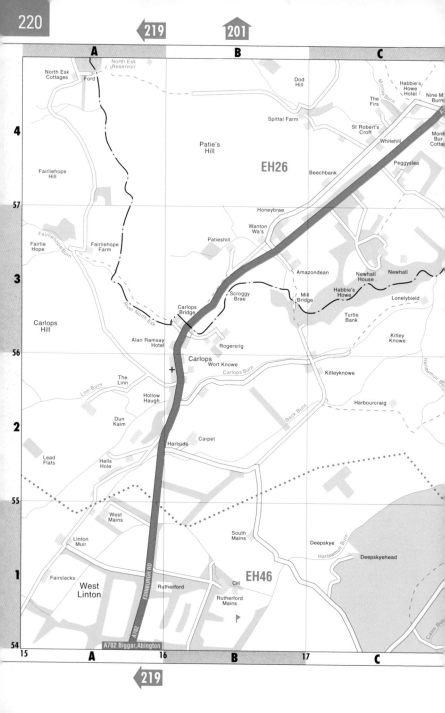

202
222

A

B

C

4

57

3

56

2

55

1

54

Walstone Moss

Saw Mill

Walstone Muir

The Gawk Stone

River North Esk

Auchencorth

Marfield

Hare Moss

The Steele

Marfield Loch

Pillars

EH26

The Steele

Auchencorth Moss

Harlawmuir

Harlawmuir Burn

Harlaw Muir

Monks Burn

A702

Cairn Burn

Tower

P

Deepsyke Forest Wlk

Deepsyke Forest

EH46

8

19

A

B

20

C

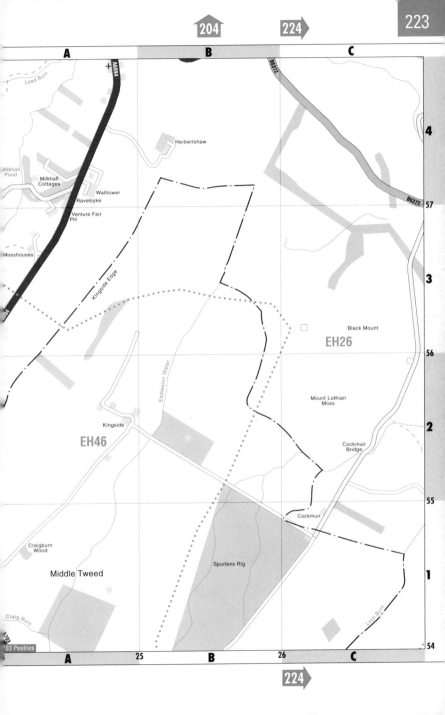

A B C

4

Lead Burn

A6094

Herbertshaw

Milkhall Pond

Milkhall Cottages

Walltower

Ravelsyke

Venture Fair PH

B6372

B6372

57

Mosshouses

Kingside Edge

3

Black Mount

EH26

56

Eddleston Water

Mount Lothian Moss

Kingside

EH46

2

Cockmuir Bridge

55

Cockmuir

Craigburn Wood

Middle Tweed

Spurlens Rig

1

Craig Burn

Loan Burn

54

A
B
C

Rocks
Wood

B3372

Temple
Farm

Walcot Burn

Well
Wood

4

River South Esk

Saw
Mill

Rosebery
Farm

Rosebery

Mill
Wood

Pikeham
Wood

Fountain
Strip

Dove
Wood

Broadhead
Wood

Outerston

Millbank
Cottage

57

Rosebery
Filters

Yorkston

Rosebery
Resr

3

EH23

56

2

River South Esk

Cockmoor
Wood

Howburn

Gladhouse
Mains

55

Blackburn Strip

1

Yorkston
Moss

P

Gladhouse

P

Gladhouse
Resr

Black Burn

54

A
31
B
32
C

A **B** **C**

4

Castleton Burn

Halkerston Glen

Comm Hill

Hurcheon Hill

South Strip

Outerston

Esperston

57

Esperston Law

3

Allanshaw Wood

Rippy Bog

Middleton South Burn

Middleton North Burn

Chester Hill

EH23

Sowburnrig

56

Outerston Hill

Lass Law

2

Latch Burn

55

B7007

Wull Muir

1

B7007

EH3

33 **A** 34 **B** 35 **C**

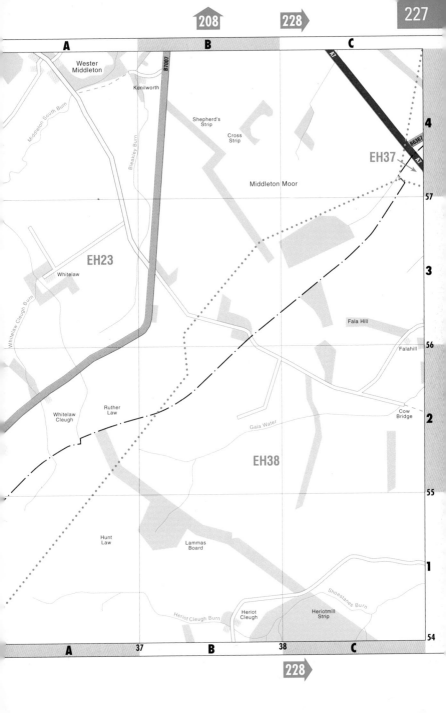

227
209

A   **B**   **C**

Cowbraehill

Cakemuir
Hill

EH37

Cakemuir
Edge

4

B6367

A7

57

Cakemuir Burn

Sandy
Knowe

3

Falahill

56

FALAHILL
COTTS

Nettlingflat

EH38

2

Gala Water

55

Hangingshaw
Hill

Heriot

SHOESTANES TERR
SHOESTANES RD

Shoestanes

1

HERIOT WAY
B709

Shoestanes Burn

Heriot
House

A7

Crookston North
Mains Hill

54

Sandyknowe

B709

A7 Galashiels

39   **A**   40   **B**   41   **C**

EH37

EH38

A

B

C

Master Cleugh Burn

Brothersheils Burn

Makimrich Wood

Brotherstone Hill

Upper Brotherstone

Brothershiels

Gilston Peel

Gilston

Gilston Cottages

Brotherstone Wood

Armet Water

Long Cleugh

Stobbindean Burn

Stobbin Dean

Nether Brotherstone

B6368

TD1

Radio Mast

Hartside Hill

B6368

4

57

3

56

2

55

1

54

A

43

B

44

C

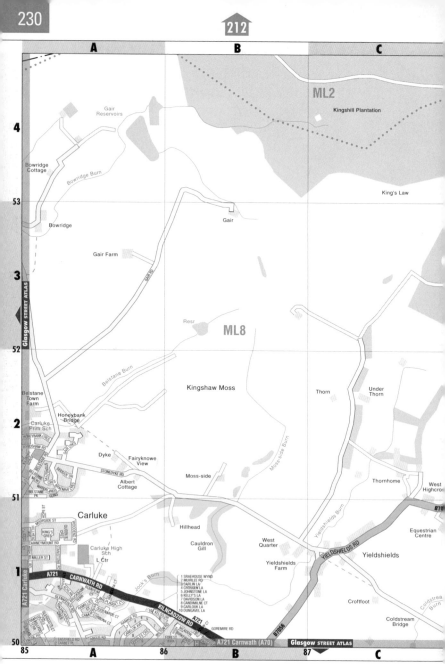

ML2

Kingshill Plantation

Gair Reservoirs

Bowridge Cottage

Bowridge Burn

King's Law

Bowridge

Gair

Gair Farm

ML8

Resr

Glasgow STREET ATLAS

Belstane Burn

Kingshaw Moss

Thorn

Under Thorn

Belstane Town Farm

Honeybank Bridge

Carluke Prim Sch

HONEYBANK CRES

CARLDUB S

Dyke

Fairyknowe View

STONEDYKE RD

Moss-side

Moss-side Burn

Thornhome

West Highcros

Albert Cottage

51

BELSTANE

MAR

BELSTANE PK

Yieldshields Burn

B870

Carluke

MOORSIDE ST

KING'S CRES

Hillhead

Cauldron Gill

West Quarter

Yieldshields

Equestrian Centre

CARNIEMOUNT RD

Carluke High Sch L Ctr

MILLER ST

Jock's Burn

1 SRAEHOUSE WYND
2 MUIRLEE RD
3 CARLIN LA
4 CROSSBER LA
5 JOHNSTONE LA
6 KELLY'S LA
7 DAVIDSON LA
8 CANDIMILNE CT
9 CARLOUK LA
10 DUNGAVEL LA

YIELDSHIELDS RD

Yieldshields Farm

A721 Carluke

A721

CARNWATH RD

KILNCADZOW RD

A721

Croftfoot

Coldstream Burn

GOREMIRE RD

B7056

A721 Carnwath (A70)

Glasgow Street Atlas

Coldstream Bridge

50

85

A

86

B

87

C

A   B   C

ML2

Black Law

4

53

Birniehall

Forth

Netherton Burn

3

Thornmuir

Springfield
Reservoir

52

ML8

Hill of
Westerhouse

Middlehope
Farm

Easterseat

B7056

Knowehead

Middlehouse

Springfield

2

YIELDSHIELDS RD

Netherton Burn

Westerhouse

Damhead

51

East
Highcross

Coldstream Burn

Candymill Burn

1

Mid
Coldstream

Craigend

ML11

50

88   A   89   B   90   C

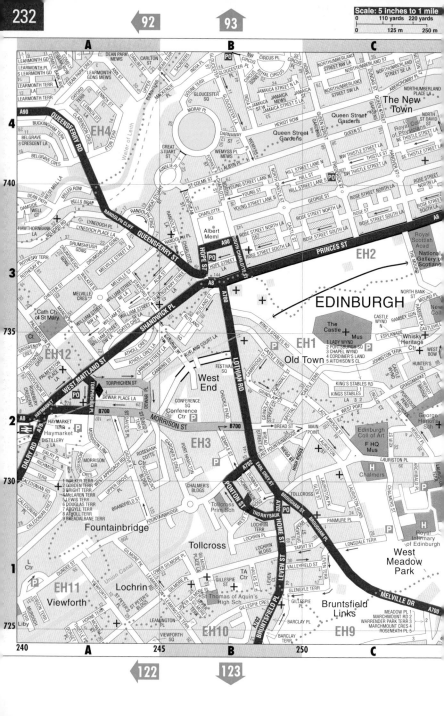

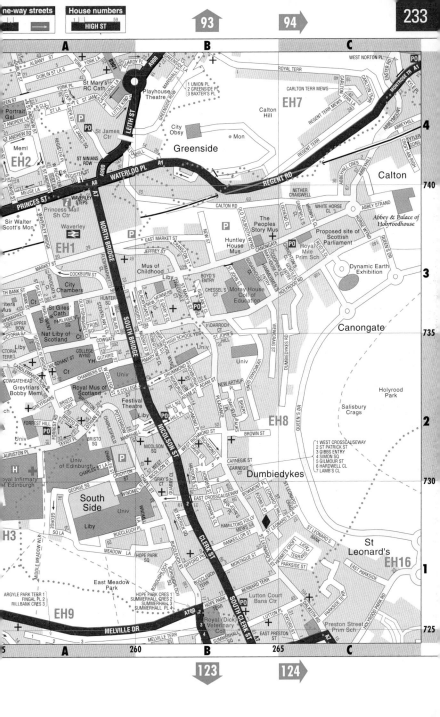

Index

Church Rd **6** Beckenham BR2..........**53** C6

Place name	**Location number**	**Locality, town or village**	**Postcode district**	**Page and grid square**
May be abbreviated on the map	Present when a number indicates the place's position in a crowded area of mapping	Shown when more than one place has the same name	District for the indexed place	Page number and grid reference for the standard mapping

Public and commercial buildings are highlighted in magenta. Places of interest are highlighted in blue with a star ★

Abbreviations used in the index

Acad	**Academy**	Comm	**Common**	Gd	**Ground**	L	**Leisure**	Prom	**Promenade**
App	**Approach**	Cott	**Cottage**	Gdn	**Garden**	La	**Lane**	Rd	**Road**
Arc	**Arcade**	Cres	**Crescent**	Gn	**Green**	Liby	**Library**	Recn	**Recreation**
Ave	**Avenue**	Cswy	**Causeway**	Gr	**Grove**	Mdw	**Meadow**	Ret	**Retail**
Bglw	**Bungalow**	Ct	**Court**	H	**Hall**	Meml	**Memorial**	Sh	**Shopping**
Bldg	**Building**	Ctr	**Centre**	Ho	**House**	Mkt	**Market**	Sq	**Square**
Bsns, Bus	**Business**	Ctry	**Country**	Hospl	**Hospital**	Mus	**Museum**	St	**Street**
Bvd	**Boulevard**	Cty	**County**	HQ	**Headquarters**	Orch	**Orchard**	Sta	**Station**
Cath	**Cathedral**	Dr	**Drive**	Hts	**Heights**	Pal	**Palace**	Terr	**Terrace**
Cir	**Circus**	Dro	**Drove**	Ind	**Industrial**	Par	**Parade**	TH	**Town Hall**
Cl	**Close**	Ed	**Education**	Inst	**Institute**	Pas	**Passage**	Univ	**University**
Cnr	**Corner**	Emb	**Embankment**	Int	**International**	Pk	**Park**	Wk, Wlk	**Walk**
Coll	**College**	Est	**Estate**	Intc	**Interchange**	Pl	**Place**	Wr	**Water**
Com	**Community**	Ex	**Exhibition**	Junc	**Junction**	Prec	**Precinct**	Yd	**Yard**

Index of localities, towns and villages

Abercorn 66 C1
Aberdour 49 B4
Aberlady 71 B2
Addiewell 171 C1
Airth 22 B2
Allandale 57 B1
Alloa 10 B3
Alva 5 A3
Armadale 143 C3
Athelstaneford 101 C4
Auchendinny 180 B1
Auchengray 216 C1
Auchtertool 15 A1
Avonbridge 112 A3
Balerno 151 B1
Bannockburn 7 C1
Bathgate 145 B4
Bilston 180 C3
Blackburn 171 B4
Blackness 65 C2
Blackridge 142 B2
Blairhall 26 A4
Bo'ness 63 F4
Bolton 162 C4
Bonnybridge 58 A3
Bonnyrigg and
Lasswade 182 B4
Borthwick 208 A2
Breich 194 C3
Bridge of Allan 2 A4
Bridgend 86 B2
Brightons 82 B4
Broxburn 117 B3
Burntisland 33 C1
Cairneyhill 27 B1
California 81 C3
Cambus 9 A4
Cambusbarron 6 B3
Cardenden 15 B4
Carluke 230 A1
Carnock 27 B3

Carrington 206 B3
Charlestown 45 A2
Clackmannan 11 A2
Cockburnspath 140 C2
Cockenzie and
Port Seton 97 B3
Comrie 26 B4
Cousland 158 B3
Cowdenbeath 13 C2
Cowie 20 B4
Craigiehall 90 B2
Crombie 44 B4
Crossford 28 A1
Crossgates 30 C3
Culross 42 B4
Currie 151 C2
Dalgety Bay 48 B2
Dalkeith 157 A1
Dalmeny 89 C4
Danderhall 156 B4
Dechmont 116 B1
Denny 36 C1
Dirleton 53 A2
Drem 73 A2
Dunbar 78 B1
Dunfermline 29 B3
Dysart 18 A4
East Calder 148 C2
East Fortune 74 A2
East Linton 103 B4
East Saltoun 161 C2
East Whitburn 170 C4
Easthouses 183 B4
Ecclesmachan 116 C4
Edinburgh 123 B3
Edinburgh 232 C3
Elphinstone 128 A1
Fala 210 B4
Falkirk 60 B3
Fallin 8 B2
Fauldhouse 193 C3

Fishcross 5 C2
Fordell 31 A3
Forrestfield 141 A2
Forth 215 A1
Garvald 134 B1
Gifford 163 C2
Gladsmuir 130 A4
Gorebridge 207 B4
Gowkhall 27 C4
Gowkshill 183 A2
Grangemouth 61 B4
Gullane 52 A1
Haddington 132 B4
Haggs 57 A2
Halbeath 30 A3
Harthill 168 A3
Hartwood 191 A1
Heriot 228 B1
High Bonnybridge .. 58 B2
High Valleyfield 26 B3
Hillend 47 C2
Howgate 204 A1
Humbie 187 A1
Innerwick 108 A1
Inverkeithing 47 A1
Kelty 12 B4
Kincardine 23 C2
Kinghorn 35 A1
Kingseat 12 A1
Kirkcaldy 17 B2
Kirkliston 89 A1
Kirknewton 149 C1
Larbert 38 A1
Laurieston 61 A2
Letham 39 B4
Limekilns 45 C2
Linlithgow 85 A3
Livingston 147 B3
Loanhead 181 A4
Lochgelly 14 B4
Longcroft 57 A2

Longniddry 98 C3
Longridge 170 B1
Macmerry 129 B3
Maddiston 83 A3
Mayfield 183 C3
Menstrie 3 C3
Mid Calder 148 B2
Milton Bridge 180 A1
Musselburgh 126 B4
New Winton 129 A2
Newbridge 119 A3
Newcraighall 125 C2
Newmills 26 B1
Newton 88 A4
Newtongrange 183 D3
North Berwick 54 B4
North Middleton .. 207 C2
North Queensferry .. 68 B3
Oakley 26 C4
Ormiston 159 C4
Pathhead 185 A3
Pencaitland 160 B4
Penicuik 203 B2
Philpstoun 86 B4
Plean 20 B2
Polbeth 172 C3
Polmont 61 C1
Prestonpans 96 C1
Pumpherston 148 A4
Queensferry 89 A4
Ratho 119 B1
Ratho Station 119 B3
Redding 61 B1
Reddingmuirhead .. 82 A4
Rosewell 181 B1
Roslin 180 C2
Rosyth 46 C2
Seafield 146 A1
Shieldhill 81 B3
Shotts 191 C3
Silverburn 202 C3

Skinflats 39 C2
Slamannan 110 A3
South Alloa 9 C2
Spittal 99 B4
Spott 106 B2
Standburn 82 B1
Stenhousemuir 38 C2
Stenton 104 C1
Stirling 7 B4
Stoneyburn 171 B1
Straiton 155 A1
Tarbrax 217 C2
Temple 206 B1
Threemiletown 86 C2
Throsk 9 A2
Torphichen 113 C3
Torryburn 26 C1
Torwood 37 C3
Townhill 29 B4
Tranent 128 B4
Tullibody 4 B2
Tyninghame 76 A2
Uphall 116 C2
Uphall Station 117 A1
Walkerburn 82 A4
Wallacestone 127 B3
Wallyford 127 B3
Wellwood 29 A4
West Barns 77 C1
West Calder 172 B1
West Linton 220 A1
Westfield 112 C3
Westquarter 61 A1
Whitburn 170 B3
Whitecraig 126 C1
Whitecross 83 C3
Whitekirk 75 C4
Wilkieston 150 A3
Winchburgh 87 C1

1

1st St Grangemouth FK3 62 A4
Grangemouth FK3 62 B3

2

2nd St
Grangemouth, Chemical Works FK3 62 B3
Grangemouth, Oil Refinery FK3 62 A4

3

3rd St
Grangemouth, Chemical Works EH51 62 B3
Grangemouth, Oil Refinery FK3 62 A4

4

4th St
Grangemouth, Chemical Works EH51 62 C3
Grangemouth, Oil Refinery FK3 62 A4

5

5th St
Grangemouth, Chemical Works EH51 62 C3
Grangemouth, Oil Refinery FK3 62 A4

6

6th St
Grangemouth, Chemical Works EH51 62 C3
Grangemouth, Oil Refinery FK9 41 A1

7

7th St
Grangemouth, Chemical Works EH51 62 C3
Grangemouth, Oil Refinery FK3 62 B4

8

8th St FK3,EH51 62 B4

A

A1 Ind Pk EH15 125 A4
Abbey & Palace of Holyroodhouse* EH8 233 C3
Abbey Craig Ct FK9 2 B2
Abbey Craig Rd FK10 5 A1
Abbey Cres EH39 54 A4
Abbey Ct EH39 54 A4
Abbey Kings Park Hospl FK7 6 C3
Abbey La EH8 94 A1
Abbey Mains EH41 101 C2
Abbey Mews 7 EH39 54 A4
Abbey Mill FK8 7 B4
Abbey Park Pl KY12 29 A2
Abbey Rd Dalkeith EH22 157 A1
Dunbar EH42 78 B1
North Berwick EH39 54 A4
Stirling FK8 2 B1
Abbey Rd Pl FK8 7 B4
Abbey St Edinburgh EH7 94 A1
High Valleyfield KY12 26 A1
Abbey Strand EH8 233 C3
Abbey View
Crossford KY12 28 B1
Dunfermline KY11 29 C1
Abbeycraig Pk FK9 2 B2
Abbeygrange EH22 183 A3
Abbeyhill EH8 233 C4
Abbeyhill Cres EH8 233 C4
Abbeyhill Prim Sch EH7 94 A1
Abbeymount EH8 233 C4
Abbot Rd FK7 7 B2
Abbot St KY12 29 A2
Abbot's View EH41 101 A1
Abbots Cl EH39 53 C4
Abbots Ct FK2 60 B4
Abbots Mill KY2 17 A2
Abbots Moss Dr FK1 59 C1
Abbots Rd Falkirk FK2 60 B4
Grangemouth FK3 61 B4
Abbots View FK2 61 C2
Abbots Wlk KY2 16 C2
Abbotsford Cres
Edinburgh EH10 123 A2
Shotts ML7 191 C3
Abbotsford Ct EH10 123 A2
Abbotsford Dr
Grangemouth FK3 61 C3
Laurieston FK2 61 A2
Abbotsford Gdns FK2 39 A1
Abbotsford Pk
Edinburgh EH10 123 A2
North Berwick EH39 53 C4
Abbotsford Pl FK8 2 B1
Abbotsford Rd EH39 53 C4
Abbotsford Rise EH54 148 A1
Abbotsford St FK2 60 A4
Abbotsgrange Rd FK3 61 C4
Abbotshall Rd KY2,KY1 17 A1
Abbotsinch Ct FK3 61 C4
Abbotsinch Ind Est FK3 61 C4
Abbotsinch Rd FK3 61 C4
Abbotsview Junc EH41 101 A1
Abbott Ho* KY12 29 A2
Abden Ave KY3 35 A2
Abden Ct KY3 35 A2
Abden Pl KY3 35 A2
Abel Pl KY11 29 C2
Abercairney Cres FK1 82 C3
Abercairney Pl FK3 61 C4
Abercorn Ave EH8 124 B4
Abercorn Cres EH8 124 B4
Abercorn Ct EH8 124 B4
Abercorn Dr EH8 124 B4
Abercorn Gdns EH8 94 B1
Abercorn Gr EH8 124 B4
Abercorn Pl EH52 87 C1
Abercorn Prim Sch EH52 87 B4
Abercorn Rd EH8 124 B4
Abercorn Terr EH15 125 B4
Abercrombie Pl FK11 3 C3
Abercrombie St FK1 59 C3
Abercromby Dr FK9 2 A4
Abercromby Pl
Edinburgh EH3 232 C4
Stirling FK8 7 A4
Tullibody FK10 4 A1
Aberdour Castle* KY3 49 B4
Aberdour Cres KY11 29 B1
Aberdour Pl KY11 29 B2
Aberdour Prim Sch KY3 49 B4
Aberdour Rd
Burntisland KY3 33 B1
Dunfermline KY11 29 C1
Inverkeithing KY11 47 B4
Aberdour Sta KY3 49 B4
Aberlady Bay Nature Reserve* EH32 71 A4
Aberlady Prim Sch EH32 71 B2
Aberlady Rd EH41 100 C1
Aberlour St KY11 46 C2
Abinger Gdns EH12 122 B4
Abington Rd KY12 28 C1
Aboyne Ave FK9 2 B2
Aboyne Gdns KY2 16 C4
Academy La EH20 181 B4
Academy Pk EH6 94 A2
Academy Pl FK7 7 C1
Academy Rd Bo'ness EH51 64 A4
Stirling FK8 7 A4
Academy Sq KY11 45 B2
Academy St Alloa FK10 9 C4
Armadale EH48 143 C3
Bathgate EH48 145 A3
Edinburgh EH6 94 A2
Acheson Dr EH32 127 C4
Achray Ct FK10 10 B3
Achray Dr FK9 2 A2
Acklam Path EH20 180 C4
Acorn Cres FK5 38 B1
Acre Rd EH51 64 B3
Acredale Bathgate EH48 145 A3
Linlithgow EH49 85 A3
Acredales EH41 131 C4
Acredales Wlk EH41 131 C4
Adam Cres FK5 38 C1
Adam Pl KY5 14 A4
Adam Smith Cl KY1 17 B2
Adam Smith Ct KY1 17 B2
Adam Sq EH54 173 B3
Adam St FK2 60 B3
Adambrae Rd EH54 173 B4
Adambrae Rdbt EH54 173 B4
Adams Loan FK2 39 A1
Adams Well EH13 153 B4
Adamson Ave KY2 17 A3
Adamson Cres KY12 29 B3
Adamson Pl FK9 2 A2
Adamson Rd KY5 14 A4
Addiebrownhill EH55 171 B1
Addiewell Prim Sch & St Thomas's RC Prim Sch EH55 171 B1
Addiewell Sta EH55 171 C1
Addiston Cres EH14 151 B2
Addiston Farm Rd EH28 120 A1
Addiston Gr EH14 151 B2
Addiston Pk EH14 151 B2
Adelaide St EH54 148 A3
Adelphi Gr 1 EH15 125 A4
Adelphi Pl EH15 125 A4
Adia Rd KY12 26 C1
Admiral Terr EH10 123 A3
Admiralty Rd
Inverkeithing KY11 47 B2
Rosyth KY11 46 B2
Admiralty St EH6 93 C3
Advocate's Cl EH1 233 A3
Affleck Ct EH12 121 A4
Affric Dr FK2 39 B1
Affric Loan ML7 191 C3
Affric Way KY12 28 A1
Afton Ct Dechmont EH52 116 B1
Stirling FK7 7 B3
Afton Dr FK6 57 B4
Afton Gr KY11 29 C3
Afton Pl EH5 93 A3
Afton Terr EH5 93 A3
Agnew Terr EH6 93 B3
Ailsa Ct FK2 82 C4
Ailsa Gr KY2 16 C4
Ainslie Gdns FK2 61 C2
Ainslie Pl EH3 232 B4
Airdrie Rd EH48,ML6 141 A2
Airlie Dr FK2 61 C1
Airth Dr FK7 7 B2
Airth Prim Sch FK2 22 C2
Airthrey Ave FK9 2 A3
Airthrey Dr FK5 39 A2
Airthrey Rd FK9 2 B3
Aitchison Dr FK5 38 A2
Aitchison's Cl EH1 232 C2
Aitchison's Pl EH15 95 A1
Aitken Cres FK7 7 A1
Aitken Ct KY1 17 A1
Aitken Dr Slamannan FK1 110 A3
Whitburn EH47 170 A4
Aitken Gdns FK1 59 C3
Aitken Orr Dr EH52 117 C3
Aitken Rd FK1 59 B3
Aitken St KY1 17 C4
Aitken Terr FK1 59 B3
Akarit Rd FK5 38 C1
Alan Breck Gdns EH4 91 B1
Albany Bsns Ctr KY12 29 A2
Albany Ind Est KY12 29 A2
Albany La EH1 93 B1
Albany St
Dunfermline KY12 29 A2
Edinburgh EH1 233 A4
Albert Ave FK3 61 C4
Albert Bldgs EH48 112 C3
Albert Cl EH21 127 A3
Albert Cres EH21 127 A3
Albert Pl Stirling FK8 7 A4
Wallyford EH21 127 A3
Albert Rd Edinburgh EH6 94 A3
Falkirk FK1 60 A2
Harthill ML7 168 C3
Albert St Edinburgh EH7 93 C2
Rosyth KY11 46 C2
Albert Terr
Edinburgh EH10 123 A2
Musselburgh EH21 126 C3
Alberta Ave EH54 147 C2
Albion Bsns Ctr EH8 94 A1
Albion Pl EH7 94 A1
Albion Rd EH7 94 A1
Albion Terr EH7 94 A1
Albyn Cotts EH52 117 C3
Albyn Dr EH54 173 C3
Albyn Ind Est EH52 117 C4
Albyn Pl Broxburn EH52 117 C3
Edinburgh EH2 232 B4
Albyn Terr EH52 117 C3
Alcorn Rigg EH14 152 C4
Alcorn Sq EH14 152 C4
Alder Gr Dunfermline KY11 29 B1
Westquarter FK2 61 A2
Alderbank
Livingston EH54 147 C3
Penicuik EH26 203 C2
Alderbank Gdns EH11 122 C2
Alderbank Pl EH11 122 C2
Alderbank Terr EH11 122 C2
Alderston Dr KY12 29 B3
Alderston Mdws EH41 100 C1
Alderston Pl EH41 100 C1
Alderston Rd EH41 131 C4
Alderstone Bsns Pk EH54 147 B1
Alderstone Rd
Livingston, Adambrae EH54 173 B4
Livingston, Howden EH54 147 B2
Alemoor Cres EH7 94 A2
Alemoor Pk EH7 94 A2
Alexander Ave Falkirk FK2 60 C3
Grangemouth FK3 61 B3
Alexander Ct FK9 2 C3
Alexander Dr
Bridge of A FK9 2 A4
Edinburgh EH11 122 B3
Livingston EH54 173 B4
Prestonpans EH32 127 C4
Alexander McLeod Pl FK7 8 C2
Alexander Peden Prim Sch ML7 168 C3
Alexander Pk EH52 117 C2
Alexander Pl KY11 46 C2
Alexander Rd ML7 191 B3
Alexander St
Cowdenbeath KY4 13 B3
Dysart KY1 18 A4
Uphall EH52 117 A2
Alexander The Third St KY3 34 C1
Alexandra Bsns Pk EH28 119 A3
Alexandra Dr Alloa FK10 9 C4
Bathgate EH48 145 C3
Alexandra Pl FK8 2 B1
Alexandra St
Dunfermline KY12 29 A3
Kirkcaldy KY1 17 B3
Alford Ave KY2 16 C4
Alfred Pl EH9 123 C2
Alice Cox Wlk KY11 29 B1
Alice Gr KY4 30 C3
Aline Ct KY11 48 A1
Alison Gr KY12 28 A1
Alison St KY1 17 A1
Allan Barr Ct FK1 60 A1
Allan Cres Denny FK6 36 B2
Dunfermline KY11 29 C1
Allan Ct Burntisland KY3 50 C4
Allan Ct *continued*
Grangemouth FK3 40 C1
Allan Park Cres EH14 122 B2
Allan Park Dr EH14 122 B1
Allan Park Gdns EH14 122 B1
Allan Park Loan EH14 122 B1
Allan Park Rd EH14 122 B1
Allan Pk Cowdenbeath KY4 13 A1
Kirkliston EH29 89 A1
Stirling FK8 7 A4
Allan Rd EH47 169 C3
Allan St EH4 93 A1
Allan Terr EH22 157 A2
Allan Wlk FK9 1 C4
Allan's Prim Sch FK8 7 A4
Allanbank Rd FK5 38 B1
Allandale Cotts FK4 57 B1
Allanfield EH7 93 C1
Allanlea Terr KY12 28 C3
Allanton Prim Sch ML7 212 A4
Allanton Rd ML7 191 B1
Allanvale Rd FK9 1 C4
Allanwater Apartments FK9 2 A4
Allanwater Gdns FK9 2 A4
Allanwood Ct FK9 2 A4
Allardice Cres KY2 16 B3
Allen Gr KY12 26 C4
Aller Pl EH54 147 A2
Allermuir Ave EH25 180 C3
Allermuir Rd EH13 153 A3
Allison Pl EH29 89 A1
Alloa Acad FK10 9 C4
Alloa Rd
Clackmannan FK10 11 A2
Falkirk FK2 39 A2
Fishcross FK10 5 B2
Menstrie FK9 3 A2
Stenhousemuir FK5 38 C2
Tullibody FK10 4 B2
Alloa Trad Ctr FK10 10 B4
Alloa Twr* FK10 10 A3
Alloway Cres FK4 57 C3
Alloway Dr Cowie FK7 20 B4
Kirkcaldy KY2 17 A4
Alloway Loan 5 EH16 124 A1
Alloway Wynd FK5 38 B2
Alma La FK2 60 A3
Alma St Falkirk FK2 60 A3
Inverkeithing KY11 47 B2
Alma Terr FK2 60 A3
Almond Ave EH12 119 C4
Almond Bank Cotts EH4 91 A3
Almond Bsns Ctr EH54 148 A3
Almond Court E EH4 91 A2
Almond Court W EH4 91 A2
Almond Cres EH19 182 A3
Almond Ct
East Whitburn EH47 170 C4
Edinburgh EH16 124 C2
Falkirk FK2 60 C4
Livingston EH54 148 B2
Stirling FK7 7 B3
Almond E Rd EH54 148 A3
Almond Gn EH12 121 A4
Almond Gr
East Calder EH53 148 C3
Queensferry EH30 89 B4
Almond Intc EH54 148 A2
Almond Pk EH54 148 A2
Almond Pl KY1 17 B4
Almond Rd
Blackburn EH47 145 B1
Dunfermline KY11 29 C1
Falkirk FK2 60 C4
Livingston EH54 148 A2
Maddiston FK2 83 B3
Newbridge EH28, EH12 119 C4
Almond S Rd EH53 148 B2
Almond Side EH53 148 B2
Almond Sq
East Whitburn EH47 170 C4
Edinburgh EH12 121 A4
Almond St
Grangemouth FK3 61 B3
Whitburn EH47 170 A4
Almond Terr
Harthill ML7 168 B3
Whitecross EH49 83 C3
Almond Valley Heritage Ctr* EH54 147 A1
Almond View EH47 146 A1
Almond W Rd EH54 148 A2
Almondbank Terr EH11 122 C2
Almondell & Calder Wood Ctry Pk* EH 52 148 C3
Almondell & Calderwood Ctry Pk* EH52 149 A3
Almondell Ct EH52 117 C3
Almondell Rd EH52 117 C3
Almondell Terr EH53 148 C3
Almondhill Rd EH29 89 A1
Almondhill Steading EH29 89 A1
Almondside
Kirkliston EH29 89 A1
Livingston EH54 147 C1
Almondvale Ave EH54 147 C1
Almondvale Bsns Pk EH54 147 B1
Almondvale Bvd EH54 147 C1
Almondvale Cres EH54 147 B1
Almondvale Ctr EH54 147 C1
Almondvale Dr EH54 147 C1
Almondvale East Rd EH54 147 C1
Almondvale N
Livingston EH54 147 B1
Almondvale N *continued*
Livingston EH54 147 C1
Almondvale Parkway EH54 147 C1
Almondvale Pl EH54 147 B1
Almondvale Rd EH54 147 C1
Almondvale Rdbt EH54 147 B1
Almondvale S EH54 147 C1
Almondvale Stadium Rd EH54 147 B1
Almondvale W EH54 147 B1
Almondvale Way EH54 147 B1
Almondview EH54 147 C1
Alness Gr KY12 28 C1
Alnwickhill Cres EH16 154 C3
Alnwickhill Ct EH16 154 C3
Alnwickhill Dr EH16 154 C3
Alnwickhill Gdns EH16 154 C3
Alnwickhill Gr EH16 154 C3
Alnwickhill Loan EH16 154 C3
Alnwickhill Pk EH16 155 A3
Alnwickhill Rd EH16 155 A4
Alnwickhill Terr EH16 154 C3
Alnwickhill View EH16 154 C3
Alpha St EH51 62 C3
Alva Acad FK12 5 A4
Alva Glen Nature Trail* FK12 5 A4
Alva Ind Est FK12 5 B3
Alva Pl EH7 94 A1
Alva Prim Sch FK12 5 A3
Alva St EH2 232 A3
Alyth Dr FK2 62 A1
Amberley Path FK3 61 C3
Ambrose Rise EH54 148 A1
Amisfield Pk EH41 132 B4
Amisfield Pl
Haddington EH41 132 B4
Longniddry EH32 98 C3
Amos Path EH20 180 C4
Amulree Pl EH51 63 B4
Ancrum Bank EH22 156 C1
Ancrum Rd EH22 156 C1
Anderson Ave
Armadale EH48 143 C2
Crossford KY12 28 A1
Newtongrange EH22 183 A3
Anderson Cres FK1 81 C3
Anderson Dr
Cowdenbeath KY4 13 A1
Denny FK6 36 C1
Falkirk FK2 39 A1
Anderson Gdns FK2 82 C3
Anderson Gn EH54 147 B4
Anderson La
Kincardine FK10 23 C2
Rosyth KY11 46 B3
Anderson Park Rd FK6 36 C1
Anderson Pl
Edinburgh EH6 93 C3
Stirling FK7 7 A2
Anderson St
Bonnybridge FK4 58 A3
Dysart KY1 18 A4
Kirkcaldy KY1 17 C3
Anderson Terr FK4 57 A2
Andrew Ave EH48 145 C3
Andrew Carnegie Birthplace Mus* KY12 29 A2
Andrew Cres FK5 38 B2
Andrew Ct EH26 203 C4
Andrew Dodd's Ave EH22 183 C4
Andrew Hardie Dr FK10 10 A4
Andrew St KY5 14 A3
Andrew Wood Ct EH6 93 B3
Angle Park Terr EH11 122 C3
Angres Ct EH22 156 B4
Angus Rd ML8 230 A1
Angus St EH51 63 B3
Ann St EH4 232 A4
Annabel Ct KY11 47 B1
Annan Ct FK1 60 B1
Annandale St EH7 93 C1
Annandale Street La EH7 93 C1
Anne Dr Bridge of A FK9 2 A3
Stenhousemuir FK5 38 C2
Anne St Alloa FK10 9 C4
Bathgate EH48 145 C3
Penicuik EH26 203 C4
Annet Rd FK6 57 B3
Annfield Edinburgh EH6 93 B3
Tranent EH33 128 C3
Annfield Ct EH33 129 B3
Annfield Dr FK7 7 B3
Annfield Farm Rd KY11 47 A4
Annfield Gdns FK8 7 A3
Annfield Gr FK8 7 A3
Annfield Pl FK3 61 B4
Annfield St EH6 93 B3
Anson Ave FK1 59 C2
Antigua St 7 EH1 93 C1
Antonine Ct EH51 63 B3
Antonine Gate FK4 57 A1
Antonine Gdns FK1 59 B3
Antonine Gr FK4 57 C2
Antonine Prim Sch FK4 58 A2
Antonine St FK1 59 B3
Antonine Wall* FK4 58 B2
Appin Cres
Dunfermline KY12 29 A2
Kirkcaldy KY2 16 C4
Appin Gr FK2 61 C2
Appin Terr
Edinburgh EH14 122 B2

Appin Terr continued
Shotts ML7 ...192 A2
Appleton Parkway EH54 ...146 C2
Appleton Parkway Rdbt EH54 ...146 C2
Arboretum Ave EH4 ...93 A1
Arboretum Pl EH3 ...93 A2
Arboretum Rd EH3 ...93 A2
Arbroath Cres FK9 ...2 A2
Arbuthnot Rd EH20 ...181 B4
Arbuthnot St FK1 ...59 C3
Arcade FK8 ...7 A4
Archers Ave FK7 ...7 B2
Archers Ct EH31 ...52 A1
Archibald Pl EH3 ...232 C2
Archibald Russell Ct FK2 ...61 C1
Ard Ct FK3 ...61 B3
Ardeer Pl EH11 ...29 B1
Arden St EH9 ...123 B3
Ardgowan Pl ML7 ...191 C3
Ardmillan Pl EH11 ...122 C3
Ardmillan Terr EH11 ...122 C3
Ardmore Dr FK2 ...62 A1
Ardshiel Ave EH4 ...91 B1
Ardvreck Pl FK2 ...39 A2
Argyle Cres EH15 ...125 B4
Argyle Park Terr EH9 ...233 A1
Argyle Pl EH9 ...123 B3
Argyle St EH6 ...93 C3
Argyll Ave Falkirk FK2 ...60 B3
  Stirling FK8 ...2 B1
Argyll Ct ML7 ...168 C3
Argyll Pl Alloa FK10 ...10 B4
  Bonnyrigg & Lasswade EH19 ...181 C3
Argyll St FK10 ...10 B4
Argyll Terr EH11 ...232 A2
Arkaig Dr KY12 ...28 B1
Arkwright Ct EH39 ...54 A4
Armadale Acad EH48 ...143 B3
Armadale Prim Sch EH48 ...143 C3
Armadale Rd EH47 ...170 A4
Armine Pl EH26 ...204 A4
Armour Ave FK7 ...20 B4
Armour Mews FK5 ...38 B2
Arneil Pl FK2 ...82 B4
Arniston Ho* EH23 ...206 C2
Arniston Rd EH23 ...206 C2
Arniston Rd FK1 ...30 A2
Arnot St FK1 ...60 A2
Arnothill FK1 ...60 A2
Arnothill Bank FK1 ...60 A2
Arnothill Ct FK1 ...59 C2
Arnothill Gdns FK1 ...60 A2
Arnothill La FK1 ...59 C2
Arnothill Mews FK1 ...60 A2
Arnott Gdns EH14 ...122 A1
Arnprior Rd EH23 ...207 B4
Arns Gr FK10 ...9 C4
Arnswell FK10 ...5 B1
Arran EH54 ...146 C3
Arran Cres KY2 ...16 C4
Arran Ct Alloa FK10 ...10 A3
  Grangemouth FK3 ...61 B3
Arran Pl EH15 ...125 B4
Arran Terr FK1 ...59 B2
Arras Gr EH26 ...204 A4
Arrol Cres FK10 ...10 B4
Arrol Pl EH30 ...89 B4
Arrol Sq EH54 ...146 C3
Arthur Pl KY4 ...13 B2
Arthur St
  Cowdenbeath KY4 ...13 B2
  Dunfermline KY12 ...29 A3
  Edinburgh EH6 ...93 C2
Arthur Street La EH6 ...93 C2
Arthur View Cres EH22 ...156 A4
Arthur View Terr EH22 ...156 A4
Arthur's Dr FK5 ...38 C1
Artillery Pk EH41 ...101 A1
Ash Braes EH10 ...23 B2
Ash Gr Alloa FK10 ...10 B3
  Bathgate EH48 ...145 C3
  Blackburn EH47 ...171 B4
  Carnock KY12 ...27 C2
  Cowdenbeath KY4 ...13 A2
  Dunfermline KY11 ...46 B4
  Dunbar EH42 ...78 A1
  Livingston EH54 ...148 A3
  Stenhousemuir FK5 ...38 C1
  Westquarter FK2 ...61 A1
Ash La EH20 ...180 C4
Ash Terr Blackburn EH47 ...171 B4
  ...6 C3
Ashbank Ct EH48 ...144 C3
Ashbank Terr EH53 ...148 C2
Ashbrae Gdns FK7 ...7 A3
Ashburnham Gdns EH30 ...68 B1
Ashburnham Loan EH30 ...68 B1
Ashburnham Rd EH30 ...68 B1
Ashfield Ct EH42 ...78 C1
Ashfield Pl EH42 ...78 C1
Ashgrove Mayfield EH22 ...183 C4
  Musselburgh EH21 ...126 C3
Ashgrove Pl EH21 ...126 C3
Ashgrove View EH21 ...126 C3
Ashley Ct EH49 ...144 A4
Ashley Dr EH11 ...122 C2
Ashley Gdns EH11 ...122 C2
Ashley Hall Gdns EH49 ...84 C3
Ashley Pl EH6 ...93 C2
Ashley Rd EH11 ...61 C2

Ashley St FK4 ...57 C3
Ashley Terr Alloa FK10 ...10 A4
  Edinburgh EH11 ...122 C2
Ashton Gr EH16 ...124 A1
Ashville Terr EH6 ...94 A2
Asquith St KY1 ...17 A2
Assembly St EH6 ...94 A3
Assynt Bank EH26 ...204 A3
Astley Ainslie Hospl EH9 ...123 B2
Atheling Gr EH30 ...89 B4
Athelstaneford Prim Sch EH39 ...101 C4
Athol Cres EH3 ...61 A2
Athol Pl Bathgate EH48 ...145 A4
  Dunfermline KY12 ...29 B2
Athol Terr EH48 ...145 A4
Atholl Cres EH3 ...232 A2
Atholl Crescent La EH3 ...232 A2
Atholl Terr
  Edinburgh EH11 ...232 A2
  Kirkcaldy KY2 ...16 B4
Atlas Cres EH48 ...144 C3
Atrium Way FK4 ...58 A2
Attlee Cres EH22 ...183 C3
Auchengray Rd ML11 ...216 C1
Auchenhard Terr EH47 ...171 B1
Auchentyre Pl FK2 ...39 B2
Auchinbaird FK10 ...5 B1
Auchingane EH10 ...153 C3
Auchinleck Ct EH6 ...93 B3
Auchterderran Rd KY5 ...14 A4
Auchtertool Prim Sch KY2 ...15 A1
Auld Brig Rd FK10 ...10 A3
Auld Orch EH19 ...182 B4
Auldcathie Pl EH52 ...87 C2
Auldgate EH29 ...89 A1
Auldhame Cotts EH39 ...55 C3
Auldhill Ave EH49 ...86 B2
Auldhill Cotts EH49 ...86 B2
Auldhill Cres EH49 ...86 B2
Auldhill Ct EH49 ...86 B3
Auldhill Dr EH49 ...86 B3
Auldhill Entry EH49 ...86 B2
Auldhill Pl EH49 ...86 B2
Auldhill Rd EH49 ...86 B2
Auldhill Terr EH49 ...86 B2
Ava St KY1 ...17 A1
Avalon Gdns EH49 ...84 B4
Aven Dr FK2 ...60 C2
Avenue Park W EH53 ...148 B2
Avenue Pk Bridge of a FK9 ...1 C4
  Mid Calder EH53 ...148 B2
Avenue Rd Aberlady EH32 ...72 B2
  Cockenzie & Port Seton EH32 ...97 B2
  Dalkeith EH22 ...156 C1
Avenue The Bridge of a FK9 ...2 A4
  Currie EH14 ...151 C4
  Dalgety Bay KY11 ...47 C2
  Falkirk FK2 ...39 B1
  Gifford EH41 ...163 C2
  Gorebridge EH23 ...183 A1
  Lochgelly KY5 ...14 B4
  Philpstoun EH49 ...86 B4
  Whitburn EH47 ...170 A3
Avenue Villas EH4 ...92 C1
Averton ML11 ...215 A1
Avon Ct FK1 ...60 B1
Avon Dr EH49 ...84 B4
Avon Gr Edinburgh EH4 ...91 A2
  Penicuik EH26 ...204 A3
Avon Pk FK1 ...111 C3
Avon Pl Bo'ness EH51 ...63 C4
  Edinburgh EH4 ...91 A2
  Linlithgow EH49 ...85 A2
Avon Rd Bathgate EH48 ...145 A4
  Grangemouth FK3 ...61 A2
  Whitecross EH49 ...83 C3
Avon St Denny FK6 ...36 B2
  Grangemouth FK3 ...40 A1
Avon Terr FK1 ...112 A3
Avonbank Ave FK1 ...112 A3
Avonbank Gdns FK6 ...36 B2
Avonbridge Prim Sch FK1 ...112 A2
Avonbridge Rd FK1 ...110 A4
Avondale Cres EH48 ...143 C3
Avondale Dr EH48 ...143 C3
Avondale Pl EH3 ...93 A1
Avondale Rd FK2 ...62 A2
Avondale S EH54 ...147 B1
Avondhu Gdns FK3 ...61 C4
Avonlea Dr FK2 ...61 C2
Avonmill Rd EH49 ...84 B4
Avonmill View EH49 ...84 B4
Avonside Dr FK6 ...36 B3
Avontoun Cres EH49 ...84 A3
Avontoun Pk EH49 ...84 A3
Ayres Wynd EH32 ...96 C1
Aytoun Cres KY3 ...33 C1
Aytoun Gr KY12 ...28 C3

B

Baads Rd EH48,ML7 ...141 B1
Baberton Ave EH14 ...152 B3
Baberton Cres EH14 ...152 C3
Baberton Ct EH14 ...152 C3
Baberton Loan EH14 ...152 C3
Baberton Mains EH14 ...152 B4
Baberton Mains Ave EH14 ...152 B4
Baberton Mains Bank EH14 ...152 B4
Baberton Mains Brae EH14 ...152 B4
Baberton Mains Cres EH14 ...152 B4
Baberton Mains Ct EH14 ...152 B4
Baberton Mains Dell EH14 ...152 B4
Baberton Mains Dr EH14 ...152 B4
Baberton Mains Gdns EH14 ...152 B4
Baberton Mains Gn EH14 ...152 B4
Baberton Mains Hill EH14 ...152 B4
Baberton Mains Lea EH14 ...152 B4
Baberton Mains Loan EH14 ...152 C4
Baberton Mains Pk EH14 ...152 B4
Baberton Mains Pl EH14 ...152 B4
Baberton Mains Rise EH14 ...152 B4
Baberton Mains Row EH14 ...152 B4
Baberton Mains Terr EH14 ...152 B4
Baberton Mains View EH14 ...152 C4
Baberton Mains Way EH14 ...152 C4
Baberton Mains Wood EH14 ...152 B4
Baberton Mains Wynd EH14 ...152 B4
Baberton Pk EH14 ...152 B3
Babins Wynd EH41 ...163 C2
Back Cswy KY12 ...42 B4
Back Dean EH4 ...122 C4
Back O' Hill Ind Est FK8 ...2 A1
Back O' Hill Rd FK8 ...2 A1
Back O' Yds KY12 ...47 A1
Back Rd Alva FK12 ...4 C4
  Dunbar EH42 ...78 A1
Back St KY12 ...42 B4
Back Station Rd
  Edinburgh EH24 ...182 C3
  Linlithgow EH49 ...85 A4
Back Wlk FK8 ...7 A3
Backdean Rd EH22 ...156 A4
Backlee EH16 ...155 A3
Backmarch Cres EH21 ...46 C2
Backmarch Rd KY11 ...46 C2
Backwell Ct KY12 ...28 B3
Backwood Ct FK10 ...10 C3
Badallan Pl EH47 ...193 C3
Badger Brook EH52 ...117 B2
Badger Ct EH52 ...117 B2
Badger Gr EH52 ...117 B2
Badger La EH52 ...117 B2
Badger Mdws EH52 ...117 B2
Badger Pk EH52 ...117 B2
Badger Wlk EH52 ...117 B2
Badger Wood EH52 ...116 B1
Baileyfield Cres EH15 ...125 A4
Baileyfield Est EH15 ...125 A4
Baileyfield Rd
  Edinburgh, Northfield EH15 ...94 C1
  Edinburgh, Portobello EH15 ...125 A4
Bailie Gr EH15 ...125 A3
Bailie Path EH15 ...125 A3
Bailie Pl EH15 ...125 A3
Bailie Terr EH15 ...125 A3
Bailielands EH49 ...85 B4
Baillie St EH47 ...170 A4
Baillie Waugh Rd FK7 ...7 B2
Bain Sq EH54 ...147 B1
Bain St KY5 ...14 A4
Baingle Brae FK10 ...4 A2
Baingle Cres FK10 ...4 A2
Bainsford Prim Sch EH22 ...60 A4
Baird Ave EH12 ...122 B3
Baird Ct KY5 ...14 A4
Baird Dr Armadale EH48 ...143 C4
  Edinburgh EH12 ...122 B3
Baird Gdns EH12 ...122 B3
Baird Gr EH12 ...122 B3
Baird Rd Armadale EH48 ...143 C4
  Livingston EH54 ...147 A1
  Ratho EH28 ...119 B2
Baird St FK1 ...59 B3
Baird Terr
  Edinburgh EH12 ...122 B3
  Haddington EH41 ...100 C1
  Harthill ML7 ...168 B3
Baird's Way EH19 ...182 B4
Bairns Ford Ave FK2 ...60 A4
Bairns Ford Ct FK2 ...60 A4
Bairns Ford Dr FK2 ...60 A4
Bakehouse Cl EH8 ...233 B3
Baker St Bo'ness EH51 ...63 C4
  Stirling FK8 ...7 A3
Balbakie Rd ML7 ...168 C3
Balbardie Ave EH48 ...145 A4
Balbardie Cres EH48 ...145 A4
Balbardie Prim Sch EH48 ...145 A4
Balbardie Rd EH48 ...145 A3
Balbirnie Pl EH12 ...122 C4
Balcarres Ct EH10 ...123 A1

Balcarres Pl EH21 ...126 B4
Balcarres Rd EH21 ...126 B4
Balcarres St EH10 ...123 A1
Balcastle Rd FK1 ...110 A3
Balderston Gdns EH16 ...124 A1
Balderstone's Wynd EH39 ...54 B4
Baldridgeburn KY12 ...28 C3
Baldwin Cres KY2 ...17 A3
Balerno Com High Sch EH14 ...151 B1
Balfour Cres Plean FK7 ...20 B2
  Stenhousemuir FK5 ...38 B1
Balfour Ct
  Dunfermline KY12 ...29 B3
  Edinburgh EH6 ...91 A1
Balfour Pl EH6 ...93 C2
Balfour St Alloa FK10 ...10 B4
  Bannockburn FK7 ...7 B1
  Bonnybridge FK4 ...57 C3
  Edinburgh EH6 ...93 C2
Balfour Terr EH26 ...180 A1
Balfour's Sq EH33 ...128 B3
Balfron Loan EH4 ...91 B3
Balgone Barns Cotts EH39 ...54 B1
Balgreen Ave EH12 ...122 A3
Balgreen Gdns EH12 ...122 A3
Balgreen Pk EH12 ...122 A3
Balgreen Prim Sch EH11 ...122 B3
Balgreen Rd EH12 ...122 B3
Balgrochan Terr [8] ...
Baliol St KY3 ...34 A3
Ballantine Pl EH54 ...147 A2
Ballantyne Rd EH6 ...93 C3
Ballast Bank KY11 ...47 B1
Ballater Dr FK9 ...2 A3
Ballencrieff Cotts EH22 ...72 A1
Ballencrieff Mill EH48 ...144 C4
Ballencrieff Toll FK48 ...114 A1
Ballengeich Pass FK8 ...2 A1
Ballengeich Rd FK8 ...1 C1
Ballingry La KY5 ...14 A4
Ballingry St KY5 ...14 A4
Balloch Rd ML7 ...191 C3
Balmoral Dr Falkirk FK1 ...59 C2
  Kirkcaldy KY2 ...16 B3
Balmoral Gdns
  Brightons FK2 ...82 B4
  Livingston EH54 ...173 B3
Balmoral Pl
  Edinburgh EH3 ...93 A1
  Stenhousemuir FK5 ...38 C2
  Stirling FK8 ...2 B1
Balmoral Rd EH51 ...62 C3
Balmoral St FK1 ...59 C2
Balmuir Ave EH48 ...144 C4
Balmuir Rd EH48 ...144 A4
Balmulzier Rd FK1 ...110 A4
Balmwell Ave EH16 ...155 A3
Balmwell Gr EH16 ...155 A3
Balmwell Pk EH16 ...155 A3
Balmwell Terr EH16 ...155 A3
Balnacraig KY12 ...28 A2
Balquhatstone Cres FK1 ...110 A3
Balquhidderock FK7 ...7 B2
Balsusney Rd KY2 ...17 A3
Baltic St EH6 ...94 A3
Balure Cres FK7 ...8 B2
Balvaird Pl KY12 ...28 B3
Balwearie Cres KY2 ...17 A1
Balwearie Gdns KY2 ...16 C1
Balwearie High Sch KY2 ...17 A1
Balwearie Rd KY2 ...17 A1
Banchory Cotts KY2 ...34 C3
Banchory Pl EH54 ...144 A3
Banchory Prim Sch FK10 ...4 B2
Bancroft Ave EH54 ...147 C2
Bandeath Ind Est
  Fallin FK7 ...8 C2
  Throsk FK7 ...9 A3
Bandeath Rd FK7 ...8 C2
Bandon Ave KY1 ...17 C4
Bangholm Ave EH5 ...93 A3
Bangholm Bower Ave EH5 ...93 A3
Bangholm Gr EH5 ...93 B3
Bangholm Loan EH5 ...93 B3
Bangholm Pk EH5 ...93 A3
Bangholm Pl EH5 ...93 A3
Bangholm Rd EH5 ...93 A3
Bangholm Terr EH3 ...93 A2
Bangholm View EH5 ...93 B3
Bangly Brae EH32,EH41 ...100 A2
Bangor Rd EH6 ...93 C3
Bangour Village Hospl EH52 ...116 A1
Bank Pl ML7 ...191 C3
Bank Rd East Linton EH40 ...103 C4
  Harthill ML7 ...168 C3
Bank St Alloa FK10 ...10 A3
  Edinburgh EH1 ...233 A3
  Falkirk FK1 ...60 A3
  Grangemouth FK3 ...40 A1
  Inverkeithing KY11 ...47 B2
  Kincardine FK10 ...23 B2
  Kirkcaldy KY1 ...17 C4
  Lochgelly KY5 ...14 A4
  Mid Calder EH53 ...148 B2
  North Berwick EH39 ...54 B4
  Penicuik EH26 ...203 C2
  Slamannan FK1 ...110 A3

Bank St continued
  Stirling FK8 ...7 A4
  Whitburn EH47 ...170 A4
Bankfoot EH32 ...96 B1
Bankhead Ave EH11 ...121 B2
Bankhead Broadway EH11 ...121 A2
Bankhead Cotts EH40 ...75 B3
Bankhead Cres FK4 ...57 B3
Bankhead Crossway N EH11 ...121 A2
Bankhead Crossway S EH11 ...121 A2
Bankhead Dr EH11 ...121 A2
Bankhead Gr EH30 ...68 B1
Bankhead Ind Est EH11 ...121 A2
Bankhead Medway EH11 ...121 B1
Bankhead Pl EH11 ...121 B2
Bankhead Rd
  Fishcross FK10 ...5 B2
  Queensferry EH30 ...89 C4
Bankhead St EH11 ...121 A1
Bankhead Terr EH11 ...121 A1
Bankhead Way EH11 ...121 A1
Bankhill EH51 ...61 B3
Bankmill View EH26 ...203 C2
Bankpark Brae EH33 ...128 A4
Bankpark Cres EH33 ...128 A4
Bankpark Gr EH33 ...128 B4
Banks View FK2 ...22 C2
Bankside FK2 ...60 B4
Bankside Ct FK6 ...36 C1
Bankside Ind Est EH54 ...60 B4
Bankton Ave EH54 ...173 C4
Bankton Brae EH54 ...173 C4
Bankton Ct
  Livingston EH54 ...174 A4
  Tranent EH33 ...128 A4
Bankton Dr EH54 ...173 C4
Bankton Gdns EH54 ...173 C4
Bankton Glade EH54 ...174 A4
Bankton Gn EH54 ...173 C4
Bankton Gr EH54 ...174 A4
Bankton Junc EH33 ...128 A4
Bankton La EH54 ...173 C4
Bankton Pk E EH54 ...148 A1
Bankton Pk W EH54 ...148 A1
Bankton Rd EH54 ...147 C1
Bankton Sq EH54 ...173 B4
Bankton Sq EH54 ...173 C4
Bankton Terr
  Prestonpans EH32 ...97 A1
  Tranent EH33 ...128 A4
Bankton Way EH54 ...173 C4
Bankton Wlk EH54 ...173 C4
Bankton Wood EH54 ...174 A4
Bannerman Ave KY11 ...47 B2
Bannerman St KY12 ...29 A3
Bannoch Brae KY12 ...29 B2
Bannock Rd FK7 ...8 B2
Bannockburn Cross FK7 ...7 C1
Bannockburn Heritage Ctr* FK7 ...7 C1
Bannockburn High Sch FK7 ...7 B1
Bannockburn Hospl FK7 ...19 C4
Bannockburn Prim Sch FK7 ...7 B1
Bannockburn Rd
  Cowie FK7 ...20 B4
  Stirling FK7 ...7 B2
Bannockburn Station Rd FK7 ...8 A2
Bantaskin Prim Sch FK1 ...59 C2
Bantaskine Dr FK1 ...59 C2
Bantaskine Gdns FK1 ...59 C2
Bantaskine Rd FK1 ...59 C2
Bantaskine St FK1 ...59 C2
Banton Pl FK4 ...57 A4
Baptie Pl EH51 ...63 C3
Barassie Dr KY2 ...17 A4
Barbauchlaw Ave EH48 ...143 C3
Barbour Ave FK7 ...7 B2
Barbour Gr KY12 ...28 C3
Barclay Pl EH10 ...232 B1
Barclay Rd KY3 ...34 C2
Barclay Terr EH10 ...232 B1
Barclay Way EH54 ...147 C4
Barham Rd KY1 ...46 B1
Barkhill Rd EH49 ...84 C3
Barkin Ct FK1 ...60 A1
Barlaw Gdns EH48 ...144 A3
Barleyhill EH51 ...58 A3
Barleyknowe Cres EH23 ...183 B1
Barleyknowe Gdns EH23 ...183 B1
Barleyknowe La EH23 ...183 B1
Barleyknowe Pl EH23 ...183 B1
Barleyknowe Rd EH23 ...183 B1
Barleyknowe St EH23 ...183 B1
Barleyknowe Terr EH23 ...183 B1
Barn Park Cres EH14 ...152 C4
Barn Pk EH14 ...152 C4
Barnbougle Ride EH30 ...90 B4
Barnego Rd FK6 ...36 B2
Barnes Gn EH54 ...147 B4
Barnet Cres KY1 ...17 A1
Barnhill Dr KY11 ...48 B2
Barnhill Pl KY11 ...48 B2
Barnhill Rd KY11 ...48 B2
Barns Ct EH47 ...170 C4
Barns Ness Terr EH42 ...139 A4

Barns Pk KY11 . . . . 48 A1
Barnsdale Rd FK7 . . . . .7 A2
Barnshot Rd EH13 . . . . 153 A3
Barnton Ave EH4 . . . . .91 B2
Barnton Ave W EH4 . . . . . . .91 A2
Barnton Brae EH4 . . . . .91 A2
Barnton Ct EH4 . . . . .91 A2
Barnton Gdns EH4 . . . . .91 C2
Barnton Gr EH4 . . . . .91 A2
Barnton Junc EH4 . . . . .91 A1
Barnton La FK1 . . . . .60 A2
Barnton Loan EH4 . . . . .91 C2
Barnton Park Ave EH4 . . . . .91 B2
Barnton Park Cres EH4 . . . .91 B2
Barnton Park Dell EH4 . . . . .91 B2
Barnton Park Dr EH4 . . . . . .91 B2
Barnton Park Gdns EH4 . . . .91 B2
Barnton Park Gr EH4 . . . . . .91 B2
Barnton Park Pl EH4 . . . . . . .91 B2
Barnton Park View EH4 . . . .91 B2
Barnton Park Wood EH4 . . .91 B1
Barnton Pk EH4 . . . . .91 C2
Barnton St FK8 . . . . .7 A4
Barntongate Ave EH4 . . . . .91 A1
Barntongate Dr EH4 . . . . . . .91 A1
Barntongate Terr EH4 . . . . .91 A1
Barnwell Rd FK7 . . . . .2 B2
Barons Hill Ave EH49 . . . . . .85 A4
Barons Hill Ct EH49 . . . . . . .85 A4
Baronscourt Rd EH8 . . . . . .94 B4
Baronscourt Terr EH8 . . . . 124 B4
Barony Ct EH11 . . . . .63 C3
Barony Pl [3] EH3 . . . . .93 B1
Barony St EH3 . . . . .93 B1
Barony Terr EH12 . . . . 121 B4
Barr Cres KY11 . . . . .47 B1
Barra Pl FK5 . . . . .39 A2
Barracks Rdbt EH54 . . . . . 146 C3
Barracks St EH32 . . . . .97 B2
Barrie Ct EH54 . . . . 148 B3
Barrie Pl
 [4] Dunfermline KY12 . . . .28 C3
 Grangemouth FK3 . . . . . . .61 B3
Barrie Rd FK5 . . . . .38 C2
Barrie St KY12 . . . . .28 C3
Barrie Terr EH48 . . . . 145 B3
Barton Bldgs KY3 . . . . .35 A1
Barton Rd KY11 . . . . .46 A1
Barton Terr EH47 . . . . 193 C3
Bass Rock View EH39 . . . . . .54 A4
Bastion Wynd FK8 . . . . .7 A4
Bath Pl EH15 . . . . .95 A1
Bath St EH6 . . . . .94 A3
Bath St EH15 . . . . 125 A4
Bath Street La EH15 . . . . . 125 A4
Bathfield EH6 . . . . .93 C3
Bathgate Acad EH48 . . . . . 145 C3
Bathgate Rd
 Blackburn EH47 . . . . 171 B4
 East Whitburn EH47 . . . . . .191 B1
Bathgate Sports Ctr *
 EH48 . . . . 145 A4
Bathgate Sta EH48 . . . . . . 145 A3
Bathville Bsns Ctr EH48 . . 144 A3
Baton Rd ML7 . . . . 191 B3
Batterflats Gdns FK7 . . . . . .6 C3
Batterflats Ho FK7 . . . . .6 C3
Battery Rd
 Grangemouth FK3 . . . . . . .62 B4
 North Queensferry KY11 . . . .68 B3
Battock Rd FK2 . . . . .82 C4
Bavelaw Cres EH26 . . . . . . 203 B3
Bavelaw Gdns EH14 . . . . . 151 B1
Bavelaw Grn EH14 . . . . . . 151 B1
Bavelaw Rd EH14 . . . . 151 B1
Baxter Cres FK6 . . . . .36 B1
Baxter St FK7 . . . . .8 A2
Baxter's Pl EH1 . . . . 233 B4
Baxter's Wynd FK1 . . . . . . .60 A2
Bay View EH32 . . . . .97 B2
Bayne Gdns EH49 . . . . .84 A3
Bayne St FK8 . . . . .2 A4
Bayswell Pk EH42 . . . . .78 B2
Bayswell Rd EH42 . . . . .78 B2
Beach La
 [3] Edinburgh EH15 . . . . 125 A4
 Edinburgh EH15 . . . . .95 A1
 Musselburgh EH21 . . . . . .126 A4
Beach Rd
 Grangemouth FK9 . . . . . . .41 A1
 North Berwick EH39 . . . . . .54 A4
Beachmont Ct EH42 . . . . . .78 C1
Beachmont Pl EH42 . . . . . . .78 C1
Beaconcroft FK9 . . . . .2 B4
Beaconhurst Sch FK9 . . . . . .2 B2
Bean Row FK1 . . . . .60 A2
Beancross Prim Sch FK3 . . .61 B3
Beancross Rd FK3 . . . . .61 B3
Beancross Rdbt FK3 . . . . . .61 C3
Bearcroft Gdns FK3 . . . . . . .61 C4
Bearcroft Rd FK3,EH51 . . . . .62 B4
Bearford Pl EH41 . . . . 132 B4
Bearside Rd FK7 . . . . .7 A2
Beath High Sch KY4 . . . . . . .13 A2
Beath View KY11 . . . . .29 C2
Beath View Rd KY4 . . . . .13 A1
Beatlie Rd EH52 . . . . 115 A2
Beatlie Sch EH54 . . . . 148 A3
Beaton Ave FK7 . . . . .2 A1
Beattie Ave FK8 . . . . .2 A1
Beatty Cres KY11 . . . . .17 B4
Beatty Ct KY11 . . . . .17 B4
Beatty Pl KY12 . . . . .29 B3
Beauchamp Gr [2] EH16 . .155 A4
Beauchamp Rd EH16 . . . . 155 A4
Beauclerc St KY2 . . . . .16 B3
Beaufort Cres KY2 . . . . .16 B3
Beaufort Dr FK2 . . . . .39 A2

Beaufort Rd EH9 . . . . 123 B2
Beauly Ct Falkirk FK1 . . . . . .60 B1
Beauly Ct
 Grangemouth FK3 . . . . . . .61 B2
Beauly Dr EH54 . . . . 148 A2
Beauly Pl KY2 . . . . .16 C4
Beaumont Dr FK2 . . . . .39 A1
Beaverbank Bsns Pk EH7 . .93 B2
Beaverbank Pl EH7 . . . . . . .93 B2
Beaverhall Rd EH7 . . . . .93 B2
Beck Cres KY12 . . . . .29 B3
Beda Pl FK7 . . . . .2 A1
Bedford Ct Alloa FK10 . . . . .10 A3
 [3] Edinburgh EH4 . . . . . .93 A1
Bedford St EH4 . . . . .93 A1
Bedford Terr EH15 . . . . . . 125 B4
Bedlormie Dr EH48 . . . . . . 142 B1
Beech Ave
 Carrington EH23 . . . . 206 C2
 Dalgety Bay KY3, KY11 . . . .48 C3
 Mid Calder EH53 . . . . . . .148 A1
 Plean FK7 . . . . .20 B2
Beech Cres Denny FK6 . . . . .36 B2
 Larbert FK5 . . . . .59 B4
 Westquarter FK2 . . . . .61 A2
Beech Gr
 Dunfermline KY11 . . . . . . .46 B4
 Livingston EH54 . . . . .148 A3
 Whitburn EH47 . . . . .170 B3
Beech Gr Ave EH22 . . . . . . 156 C1
Beech La KY9 . . . . .2 A2
Beech Loan EH19 . . . . 182 A3
Beech Pl Grangemouth FK3 . .61 B3
 Livingston EH54 . . . . .147 B2
 Seafield EH47 . . . . .146 A1
Beech Rd EH48 . . . . 145 C3
Beech St EH42 . . . . .78 A1
Beech Terr EH14 . . . . 160 B3
Beech Way KY11 . . . . .48 A3
Beechbank Cres EH53 . . . . 148 C1
Beeches The
 Armadale EH48 . . . . 143 C3
 Dalgety Bay KY11 . . . . . . .48 B2
 Gullane EH31 . . . . .52 A2
 Lochgelly KY5 . . . . .14 A4
 Newtongrange EH22 . . . . .183 A4
Beechgrove Rd EH22 . . . . . 183 C2
Beechmount Cres EH12 . . . 122 A4
Beechmount Ct ML7 . . . . . 192 A1
Beechmount Pk EH12 . . . . 122 A3
Beechwood Alloa FK10 . . . . .5 A4
 Crossford KY12 . . . . .28 A1
 Linlithgow EH49 . . . . .85 A3
Beechwood Gdns
 Blackburn EH47 . . . . 145 B1
 Stirling FK8 . . . . .7 A3
Beechwood Gr EH54 . . . . . 117 A1
Beechwood Mains
 EH12 . . . . 122 A4
Beechwood Pk
 Livingston EH54 . . . . 146 C4
 Newtongrange EH22 . . . . .183 A3
 Uphall Sta EH54 . . . . .117 A1
Beechwood Pl EH47 . . . . . . 145 B1
Beechwood Rd
 Blackburn EH47 . . . . 145 B1
 Haddington EH41 . . . . . . .131 C4
Beechwood Terr EH6 . . . . . .94 A2
Beecraigs Ctry Pk *
 EH49 . . . . .85 A1
Beeslack Com High Sch
 EH26 . . . . 204 A4
Begbie Pl EH14 . . . . 144 B1
Begg Ave FK1 . . . . .59 C2
Beldorney Pl KY12 . . . . .29 B3
Belford Ave EH4 . . . . .92 C1
Belford Gdns EH4 . . . . .92 C1
Belford Pk EH4 . . . . 122 C4
Belford Pl EH4 . . . . 122 C4
Belford Rd EH4 . . . . 122 C4
Belford Terr EH4 . . . . 122 C4
Belgrave Cres EH4 . . . . .93 A1
Belgrave Crescent La
 EH4 . . . . .232 A4
Belgrave Gdns EH12 . . . . . 121 C4
Belgrave Mews [10] EH4 . . .92 C1
Belgrave Pl EH4 . . . . .92 C1
Belgrave Rd EH12 . . . . 121 C3
Belhaven Hill Sch EH42 . . . .78 A1
Belhaven Hospl EH42 . . . . .78 A1
Belhaven Pl EH10 . . . . 123 A1
Belhaven Rd EH42 . . . . .78 B1
Belhaven Terr EH10 . . . . . . 123 A1
Bell Ct FK3 . . . . .40 B1
Bell Pl EH3 . . . . .93 A1
Bell Rd KY11 . . . . .46 A1
Bell Sq EH54 . . . . 173 B3
Bell Stane EH30 . . . . .68 A1
Bell's Mills Terr EH52 . . . . 207 C1
Bell's Wills EH4 . . . . 122 C4
Bell's Wynd FK1 . . . . .60 A2
Bellamond Cres EH47 . . . . 164 B4
Belleknowes Ind Est
 KY11 . . . . .47 A2
Bellenden Gdns EH16 . . . . 124 B1
Bellerophon Dr EH26 . . . . . 203 C2
Bellevue Brightons EH42 . . . .82 C4
 Edinburgh EH7 . . . . .93 B1
Bellevue Ave EH42 . . . . .78 C1
Bellevue Cres EH3 . . . . .93 B1
Bellevue Gdns EH7 . . . . .93 B2
Bellevue Gr EH7 . . . . .93 B1
Bellevue Pl EH7 . . . . .93 B1
Bellevue Rd St Edinburgh EH7 .93 B1
 Falkirk FK1 . . . . .60 B2

Bellevue Terr
 Dunbar EH42 . . . . .78 C1
 Edinburgh EH7 . . . . .93 B1
Bellfield Ave
 Dalkeith EH22 . . . . 156 C1
 East Calder EH53 . . . . . . .148 C1
 Musselburgh EH21 . . . . . .126 A3
Bellfield Cres KY1 . . . . .18 A4
Bellfield Ct EH21 . . . . 126 A3
Bellfield La EH15 . . . . 125 A4
Bellfield Rd
 Bannockburn FK7 . . . . .7 C1
 Stirling FK8 . . . . .7 A3
Bellfield Sq EH32 . . . . 127 C4
Bellfield St EH15 . . . . 125 A4
Bellfield Terr EH15 . . . . . . 125 A4
Bellfield View EH19 . . . . . . 182 B4
Bellhouse Rd KY3 . . . . .49 A4
Bellman Way KY11 . . . . .48 A3
Bellman's Rd EH26 . . . . . . 203 C3
Bellona Terr EH47 . . . . 193 C3
Bells Brae EH4 . . . . 232 A3
Bells Burn Ave EH49 . . . . . . .85 B4
Bellsdyke Hospl FK5 . . . . . .38 B3
Bellsdyke Rd FK5 . . . . .38 A2
Bellsdyke Rdbt FK5 . . . . . . .38 A2
Bellsmains EH23 . . . . 207 B3
Bellsmeadow Rd FK1 . . . . . .60 B2
Bellsquarry Prim Sch
 EH54 . . . . 173 B4
Bellsquarry South Rd
 EH54 . . . . 173 C3
Bellyeoman La KY12 . . . . . . .29 B3
Bellyeoman Prim Sch
 KY12 . . . . .29 B3
Bellyeoman Rd KY12 . . . . . .29 B3
Bellyford Rd EH33 . . . . 128 A1
Belmont Ave
 Bonnybridge FK4 . . . . .57 B3
 Edinburgh EH12 . . . . .121 C4
 Shieldhill FK1 . . . . .81 C4
Belmont Cres EH12 . . . . . . 122 A4
Belmont Dr ML7 . . . . 192 A1
Belmont Gdns EH12 . . . . . 122 A4
Belmont Pk EH12 . . . . 122 A4
Belmont Rd FK1 . . . . 152 B3
Belmont St FK1 . . . . .60 B2
Belmont Terr EH12 . . . . . . 122 A4
Belmont View EH12 . . . . . . 122 A4
Belstane Mews ML8 . . . . . . .30 A2
Belstane Pk ML8 . . . . .30 A2
Belstane Rd ML8 . . . . .30 A2
Belsyde Ct EH49 . . . . .84 B3
Belvedere La EH48 . . . . . . 144 C4
Belvedere Pk EH6 . . . . .93 B3
Belvedere Pl EH48 . . . . . . 144 C4
Belvedere Rd EH48 . . . . . . 144 C4
Belwood Cres EH26 . . . . . . 180 A1
Belwood Rd EH26 . . . . 179 C1
Ben Alder Pl KY2 . . . . .16 C3
Ben Ledi Rd KY2 . . . . .16 B3
Ben Lomond Dr FK9 . . . . .2 A2
Ben Lomond View KY12 . . . .27 A3
Ben Nevis Pl KY2 . . . . .16 C3
Ben Sayers Pk EH39 . . . . . .54 C3
Benarty St KY2 . . . . .16 B3
Bendachin Dr KY12 . . . . . . .29 C3
Bendameer Rd KY3 . . . . . . .33 B1
Benhar Prim Sch ML7 . . . . 167 C1
Benhar Rd Harthill ML7 . . . 167 C1
 Shotts ML7 . . . . .192 A2
Benington Dr EH51 . . . . .63 C3
Bennet Wood Terr EH52 . . 207 C2
Bennie Terr EH47 . . . . 110 A4
Bennochy Ave KY2 . . . . .17 A3
Bennochy Ct KY2 . . . . .17 A3
Bennochy Gdns KY2 . . . . . .17 A3
Bennochy Gr KY2 . . . . .17 A3
Bennochy Rd KY2 . . . . .16 C3
Bennochy View KY2 . . . . . . .17 A3
Bentheads FK7 . . . . .19 C4
Benview FK7 . . . . .7 B1
Benview Terr EH10 . . . . .55 B3
Beresford Ave EH5 . . . . .93 B3
Beresford Gdns EH5 . . . . . .93 B3
Beresford Pl EH5 . . . . .93 A3
Beresford Rise EH54 . . . . . 148 A1
Beresford Terr EH5 . . . . .93 B3
Berkeley St FK7 . . . . .7 A2
Bernard Shaw St KY12 . . . . .28 C3
Bernard St EH6 . . . . .94 A3
Bernard Terr EH8 . . . . 233 B1
Bernard's Smithy KY3 . . . . . .32 B4
Berry St KY5 . . . . .14 A4
Berryhill FK7 . . . . .20 C4
Berryhill Cres FK3 . . . . .61 C3
Berryhill Pl ML7 . . . . 192 A1
Berrylaw Pl KY12 . . . . .28 B2
Berrylaw Rd KY12 . . . . .28 B2
Bertram St EH48 . . . . 168 B3
Bertram St Harthill ML7 . . . 168 B3
 Shotts ML7 . . . . .191 C3
Bervie Dr EH54 . . . . 173 C3
Berwick Pl Dysart KY1 . . . . .18 A4
 Kirkcaldy KY1 . . . . .18 B4
Bethesda Gr FK2 . . . . .82 C3
Beulah EH21 . . . . 126 A3
Bevan Dr KY11 . . . . .17 B4
Bevan Pl KY11 . . . . .46 C2
Bevan Rd EH22 . . . . 183 A3
Bevan-lee Ct EH22 . . . . . . 157 A2
Beveridge Ave EH22 . . . . . 183 B3
Beveridge Cl EH22 . . . . . . 183 B3
Beveridge Rd KY1 . . . . .17 A2
Beveridge Sq EH54 . . . . . . 147 C1
Beveridge St KY11 . . . . .29 B1

Bickerton Crofts EH47 . . . . 170 C3
Bickerton Terr EH47 . . . . . . 170 A3
Bickram Cres KY12 . . . . .26 A4
Bielside Gdns EH42 . . . . . . .77 C1
Biggar Rd
 Edinburgh EH10 . . . . 154 A2
 Silverburn EH26 . . . . .202 C3
Biggin Wa's KY11 . . . . .17 C4
Bingham Ave EH15 . . . . . . 124 C3
Bingham Broadway
 EH15 . . . . 125 A3
Bingham Cres EH15 . . . . . 125 A3
Bingham Crossway
 EH15 . . . . 124 C3
Bingham Dr EH15 . . . . 125 A3
Bingham Medway EH15 . . . 124 C3
Bingham Pl EH15 . . . . 124 C3
Bingham Way EH15 . . . . . . 124 C3
Binn Ave KY3 . . . . .33 C1
Binnie Pl FK2 . . . . .39 C1
Binniehill Rd FK1 . . . . 110 A3
Binning Rd KY11 . . . . .47 A2
Binning Wood Rd EH42 . . . . .75 C4
Binny Pk EH52 . . . . 116 C4
Birch Ave FK8 . . . . .6 C3
Birch Cres EH20 . . . . 180 C4
Birch Ct Edinburgh EH4 . . . .91 A1
 Livingston EH54 . . . . .147 B1
Birch Gr KY11 . . . . .46 B4
Birchbank KY4 . . . . .13 A1
Birchwood EH10 . . . . .5 B1
Birchwood Gdns EH54 . . . . 173 B4
Birk Hedges EH41 . . . . 130 C3
Birkdale Dr EH52 . . . . 115 A4
Birkdale Pk EH48 . . . . 143 A3
Birkenshaw Way EH48 . . . . 143 C3
Birkenside EH23 . . . . 207 B3
Birkfield Loan ML8 . . . . . . 230 B1
Birkfield Pl ML8 . . . . 230 B1

Blackridge Com Mus *
 EH48 . . . . 142 B2
Blackridge Prim Sch
 EH48 . . . . 142 B2
Blackston Rd FK1 . . . . 112 A3
Blackthorn Ct EH4 . . . . .91 A1
Blackwood Cres EH9 . . . . . 123 C3
Blackwood Ct KY11 . . . . . . .46 C4
Blackwood Gdns KY11 . . . . .46 C4
Blackwood Gn KY11 . . . . . . .46 C4
Blackwood Way KY11 . . . . . .46 C4
Blaeberry Gdns EH4 . . . . . . .91 A1
Blaeberryhill Rd EH47 . . . . 170 B3
Blaefaulds Cres FK6 . . . . . .57 B4
Blair Ave EH51 . . . . .63 C3
Blair Dr Dunfermline KY12 . . .29 A3
 Kelty KY4 . . . . .12 B2
Blair Pl KY2 . . . . .16 B3
Blair St Edinburgh EH1 . . . 233 A3
 Kelty KY4 . . . . .12 B2
Blair Terr FK5 . . . . .39 A2
Blair's Cotts FK2 . . . . .61 B1
Blairdenon Cres FK1 . . . . . .59 C2
Blairdenon Dr FK10 . . . . . . .5 A1
Blairdenon Rd FK12 . . . . . . .4 C3
Blairforkie Dr FK9 . . . . .1 C1
Blairhall Prim Sch KY12 . . . .26 A4
Blairlodge Ave FK2 . . . . .82 A4
Blairmore Rd KY2 . . . . .16 B4
Blairmuckhole & Forrestdyke
 Rd ML7 . . . . 167 C4
Blair Terr FK5 . . . . 117 C3
Blairwood Wlk KY12 . . . . . .26 A4
Blake St KY11 . . . . .29 B1
Blamey Cres KY4 . . . . .13 A1
Blandfield EH7 . . . . .93 B2
Blantyre Terr EH10 . . . . . . 123 A2
Blawearie Rd EH33 . . . . . . 128 B3
Bleachfield Edinburgh EH6 . .93 B2
 Falkirk FK2 . . . . .60 A3
Bleachfield Ct EH12 . . . . . . .29 C2
Blenheim Cre
 Carluke ML8 . . . . 230 A1
 Penicuik EH26 . . . . .204 A4
Blenheim Pl FK5 . . . . .38 C3
Blindwell Brae EH41 . . . . . 133 C1
Blindwells FK12 . . . . .4 C3
Blinkbonnie Terr FK1 . . . . . 110 A3
Blinkbonny Ave EH4 . . . . . .92 B1
Blinkbonny Cres EH4 . . . . . .92 B1
Blinkbonny Gdns EH4 . . . . .92 B1
Blinkbonny Gr EH4 . . . . . . .92 B1
Blinkbonny Gr W EH4 . . . . .92 B1
Blinkbonny Rd
 Currie EH14 . . . . 152 A2
 Falkirk FK1 . . . . .59 C2
Blinkbonny Terr EH4 . . . . . .92 B1
Blinny Ct ML7 . . . . 192 A2
Bloom St EH20 . . . . 147 B4
Bloom Pl EH54 . . . . 147 A1
Bloom Rdbt EH54 . . . . 147 B2
Bloomfield Pl [4] EH48 . . . . 144 B3
Bluebell Glade EH54 . . . . . 173 B4
Blyth Rd EH52 . . . . 117 B2
Blyth St KY12 . . . . .17 C4
Bo'mains Ind Est EH51 . . . .63 C3
Bo'mains Rd EH51 . . . .
Bo'ness & Kinneil Rly *
 EH51 . . . . .63 B4
Bo'ness Acad EH51 . . . . . . .63 C4
Bo'ness Hospl EH51 . . . . . .63 C4
Bo'ness Public Sch (Prim)
 EH51 . . . . .63 C4
Bo'ness Rd
 Grangemouth FK3, EH51 . . . .62 A3
 Polmont FK2 . . . . .61 C2
 Queensferry EH30 . . . . . . .67 A1
Bo'ness Sta * EH51 . . . . . . .64 A4
Boat Gn EH3 . . . . .93 B2
Bobbin Wynd FK7 . . . . .6 B3
Bog Rd Laurieston FK2 . . . . .60 C2
 Penicuik EH26 . . . . .203 C3
 Whitburn EH47 . . . . .170 A4
Bog Rdbt FK2 . . . . .60 C2
Bog Road Ind Est FK2 . . . . .60 C2
Bog The EH51 . . . . .44 A4
Bogend Rd
 Bannockburn FK7 . . . . .19 C1
 Larbert FK5 . . . . .38 A4
 Torwood FK5 . . . . .37 C4
Boghall Dr EH48 . . . . 145 C3
Boghall Farm Steadings
 EH48 . . . . 145 C3
Boghall Prim Sch EH48 . . . 145 C3
Boghall Rdbt EH48 . . . . . . 145 C3
Boghead Cres EH48 . . . . . 144 C3
Bogies Wynd [12] KY1 . . . . 17 B3
Boglily Rd KY2 . . . . .16 B2
Bogpark Rd EH21 . . . . 125 C3
Bogsmill Rd EH14 . . . . 122 A1
Bogwood Ct EH22 . . . . 183 B4
Bogwood Dr EH22 . . . . 183 B4
Bogwood Rd EH22 . . . . 183 C3
Bohun Ct FK7 . . . . .7 C3
Bolam Dr KY3 . . . . .33 C1
Bolam Sq KY3 . . . . .33 C1
Bomar Ave EH51 . . . . .63 A4
Bon Accord Cres ML7 . . . . 191 C3
Bonaly Ave EH13 . . . . 153 A3
Bonaly Brae EH13 . . . . 153 A3
Bonaly Cres EH13 . . . . 153 A3
Bonaly Ctry Pk * EH13 . . . 152 C1
Bonaly Dr EH13 . . . . 153 A3
Bonaly Gdns EH13 . . . . . . 153 A3
Bonaly Gr EH13 . . . . 153 A3

Bickram Cres KY12 . . . . .26 A4
Birkhill Cres EH51 . . . . .63 C3
Birkhill Rd FK7 . . . . .6 C3
Birkhill St EH51 . . . . .63 C3
Birkhill Sta * EH49 . . . . .62 B2
Birnam Ct FK2 . . . . .39 B1
Birnam Rd KY2 . . . . .16 C4
Birnie Brae KY5 . . . . .14 A4
Birnie St KY5 . . . . .14 A4
Birnie Well Rd FK1 . . . . 110 A3
Birniehill Cres EH48 . . . . . . 144 C2
Birniehill Cres EH48 . . . . . . 144 C2
Birniehill Rd EH48 . . . . 144 C2
Birniehill Terr EH48 . . . . . . 144 C2
Birrel's Wynd KY3 . . . . .32 A3
Birrell Gdns EH54 . . . . .29 B1
Birrell Gdns EH54 . . . . 173 C4
Birrell's La KY1 . . . . .17 C4
Birrell Street Wynd [8]
 KY1 . . . . .17 B3
Bishops Gate EH22 . . . . . . 117 B3
Bishops Pk
 Livingston EH53 . . . . 148 A1
 Mid Calder EH53 . . . . . . .148 B1
Black Craigs KY12 . . . . .16 B4
Blackadder Haven KY12 . . . .42 B4
Blackadder Pl EH4 . . . . .92 C3
Blackbarony Rd [1]
 EH16 . . . . 124 A1
Blackbraes Rd FK1 . . . . . . .83 B3
Blackburn Acad KY12 . . . . . .28 B3
Blackburn Crag EH47 . . . . . 171 B1
Blackburn Dr KY4 . . . . .13 A2
Blackburn Prim Sch
 EH47 . . . . 145 B1
Blackburn Rd
 Addiewell EH55 . . . . 171 C1
 Bathgate EH47 . . . . .145 B1
Blackburnhall EH47 . . . . . . 171 B3
Blackchapel Cl EH15 . . . . . 125 A2
Blackchapel Rd EH15 . . . . . 125 A2
Blackcot Ave EH22 . . . . . . 183 B3
Blackcot Dr EH22 . . . . 183 B3
Blackcot Pl EH22 . . . . 183 B3
Blackcot Rd EH22 . . . . 183 B3
Blacket Ave EH9 . . . . 123 C2
Blacket Pl EH9 . . . . 123 C2
Blackfaulds Ct EH47 . . . . . 193 C3
Blackfaulds Dr EH47 . . . . . 193 C3
Blackfaulds Pl EH47 . . . . . 193 C3
Blackford Ave EH9 . . . . 123 B2
Blackford Bank EH9 . . . . . . 123 B2
Blackford Gate EH9 . . . . . . 123 B2
Blackford Glen Cotts
 EH16 . . . . 123 C1
Blackford Glen Rd
 EH16 . . . . 123 C1
Blackford Hill Gr EH9 . . . . 123 B1
Blackford Hill Rise EH9 . . . 123 B1
Blackford Hill View EH9 . . . 123 B1
Blackford Rd EH9 . . . . 123 B2
Blackfriars St EH1 . . . . 233 B3
Blackhall Prim Sch KY12 . . .28 B3
Blackhall St ML7 . . . . 192 A2
Blackie Rd EH6 . . . . .94 B3
Blackmill Cres ML7 . . . . . . .39 A2
Blackmuir Pl FK10 . . . . .4 B2
Blackness Castle * EH49 . . . .45 B2
Blackness Prim Sch
 EH49 . . . . .65 B2
Blackness Rd EH49 . . . . . . .85 A4

Bonaly Prim Sch EH13 . .153 A3
Bonaly Prim Sch (Annexe) EH13 . . . . .153 A3
Bonaly Rd EH13 . . . . .153 A3
Bonaly Rise EH13 . . . . . . .153 A3
Bonaly Steading EH13 . .153 A3
Bonaly Terr EH13 . . . . . . .153 A3
Bonaly Wester EH13 . . . .153 A3
Bonar Pl EH6 . . . . .93 B3
Bond St FK10 . . . . .4 A1
Bonhard Ct EH51 . . . . .64 A3
Bonhard Way EH51 . . . . . . .64 A3
Bonnar St KY12 . . . . .29 A2
Bonnington EH27 . . . . . . .150 A4
Bonnington Ave EH6 . . . . .93 B3
Bonnington Bsns Ctr EH6 . . . . .93 C2
Bonnington Gr EH6 . . . . . .93 B3
Bonnington Ind Est EH6 . .93 C2
Bonnington Mill Bsns Ctr EH6 . . . . .93 C3
Bonnington Prim Sch EH6 . . . . .93 C2
Bonnington Rd
Edinburgh EH6 . . . . .93 C2
Wilkieston EH27 . . . . .150 A3
Bonnington Road La EH6 .93 C2
Bonnington Terr EH6 . . . . .93 B3
Bonnybank Ct EH23 . . . . .207 B4
Bonnybank Rd EH23 . . . .207 B4
Bonnybridge Hospl FK4 . .58 B3
Bonnybridge Ind Est FK4 .58 A2
Bonnybridge Prim Sch FK4 . . . . .58 A3
Bonnybridge Rd FK4 . . . . .57 C3
Bonnyfield Rd FK4 . . . . . .57 C3
Bonnyhaugh EH6 . . . . .93 B2
Bonnyhaugh La EH6 . . . . . .93 B2
Bonnyhill Rd Falkirk FK1 . .59 A2
High Bonnybridge FK4 . . . . . .58 B2
Bonnymuir Cres FK4 . . . . .57 C3
Bonnyrigg Prim Sch EH19 . . . . .182 B3
Bonnyrigg Rd EH22 . . . . .156 C1
Bonnyside Rd FK4 . . . . . . .58 A3
Bonnyton Pl KY11 . . . . .29 B2
Bonnytoun Ave EH49 . . . . .85 B4
Bonnytoun Terr EH49 . . . . .85 B4
Bonnyvale Pl FK4 . . . . .57 C3
Bonnyview Gdns FK4 . . . . .58 A3
Bonnywood Ave FK4 . . . . .58 A4
Booth Ave KY11 . . . . .46 B3
Booth Pl FK1 . . . . .60 A2
Boothacre La EH6 . . . . .94 B2
Boreland Pk KY11 . . . . .47 B2
Boreland Rd Dysart KY1 . . .18 A4
Inverkeithing KY11 . . . . .47 B2
Borestone Cres FK7 . . . . . . .7 A2
Borestone Ct FK7 . . . . .7 A1
Borestone Pl FK7 . . . . .7 A1
Borestone Prim Sch FK7 . .7 A1
Boroughdales EH42 . . . . . .78 B1
Boroughloch EH8 . . . . . . .233 B1
Boroughloch Sq EH8 . . . .233 B1
Boroughmuir High Sch EH10 . . . . .123 A3
Boroughmuir High Sch (Annexe) EH11 . . . . .122 C3
Boroughmuir High Sch Annexe EH10 . . . . .123 A3
Borrowlea Rd FK7 . . . . .7 B4
Borrowmeadow Rd FK7 . . . .7 C4
Borrowstoun Cres EH51 . .63 C3
Borrowstoun Pl EH51 . . . .63 C3
Borrowstoun Rd EH51 . . . .64 A3
Borthwick Castle Pl EH23 . . . . .207 C2
Borthwick Castle Rd EH23 . . . . .207 C1
Borthwick Castle Terr EH23 . . . . .207 C2
Borthwick Pl EH12 . . . . . .122 C4
Borthwick Prim Sch EH23 . . . . .208 A2
Borthwick View EH20 . . . .181 A4
Boswall Ave EH5 . . . . .92 C3
Boswall Cres EH5 . . . . .92 C3
Boswall Dr EH5 . . . . .93 A3
Boswall Gdns EH5 . . . . .92 C3
Boswall Gn EH5 . . . . .93 A3
Boswall Gr EH5 . . . . .92 C3
Boswall Loan EH5 . . . . .92 C3
Boswall Parkway EH5 . . . . .92 C3
Boswall Pl EH5 . . . . .92 C3
Boswall Quadrant EH5 . . . .92 C3
Boswall Rd EH5 . . . . .93 A3
Boswall Sq EH5 . . . . .92 C3
Boswall Terr EH5 . . . . .92 C3
Boswell Dr Kinghorn KY3 . .35 A2
Oakley KY12 . . . . .26 C3
Boswell Rd KY5 . . . . .14 A4
Bothkennar Prim Sch FK2 . . . . .39 C2
Bothkennar Rd FK2 . . . . . . .39 C2
Bothwell Ct KY11 . . . . .29 A1
Bothwell Gdns KY11,KY12 .29 A1
Bothwell St
Dunfermline KY11 . . . . .29 A1
Edinburgh EH7 . . . . .94 A1
Boundary Rd E EH14 . . . .151 C4
Boundary Rd N EH14 . . . .151 C4
Boundary St EH51 . . . . .64 A4
Bouprie Rise KY11 . . . . . . .48 A2
Bourtree Gr KY12 . . . . .26 B4
Bow Butts KY12 . . . . .29 A1
Bow St FK8 . . . . .7 A4
Bowhill Ct EH31 . . . . .52 A1
Bowhill Terr EH5 . . . . .93 A3
Bowhouse Dr KY1 . . . . .35 A4
Bowhouse Gdns FK10 . . . .10 A3
Bowhouse Prim Sch FK3 .61 C3
Bowhouse Rd Alloa FK10 . .10 A3
Grangemouth FK3 . . . . .61 C3
Bowhouse Sq FK3 . . . . .61 B3
Bowhousebog or Liquo ML7 . . . . .191 A1
Bowhousebog Rd ML7 . .191 A1
Bowling Green Pl FK4 . . . .57 C3
Bowling Green Rd
Kirkliston EH29 . . . . .89 A1
Whitburn EH47 . . . . .170 A3
Bowling Green St KY4 . . . .13 B2
Bowling Green The EH6 . .93 C3
Bowmont Pl EH8 . . . . .233 B1
Bowmont Terr EH42 . . . . . .78 C1
Bowmore Wlk ML7 . . . . . .192 A2
Bowyett EH48 . . . . .113 C3
Boxton Rd FK1 . . . . .82 B2
Boyd La FK2 . . . . .60 A3
Boyd Pl KY5 . . . . .14 A4
Boyd St Falkirk FK2 . . . . . . .60 A3
Laurieston FK2 . . . . .61 A2
Boyd's Entry EH1 . . . . . . .233 B3
Boyd-Orr Dr EH26 . . . . . .203 C4
Brackenlees Rd FK2 . . . . . .40 A3
Brackensbrae EH52 . . . . .117 A3
Bracklinn Brae KY12 . . . . .28 C3
Bradbury St FK2 . . . . .39 A1
Brae Head Lodge KY1 . . . .17 B3
Brae Heads Loan EH40, EH41 . . . . .103 B3
Brae Pk EH4 . . . . .91 A2
Brae Rd FK3,EH51 . . . . .62 B3
Brae The Bannockburn FK7 . . .7 B1
Cambusbarron FK7 . . . . .6 B3
Penicuik EH26 . . . . .180 B1
Braeburn Dr EH14 . . . . . .152 A2
Braefoot EH42 . . . . .76 B2
Braefoot Gr KY11 . . . . .48 A1
Braefoot Rd EH51 . . . . .64 A3
Braefoot Terr 2 EH16 . . .124 A1
Braehead Alloa FK10 . . . . . . .4 B1
Alva FK12 . . . . .5 A4
Bo'ness EH51 . . . . .63 C4
Braehead Ave
Edinburgh EH4 . . . . .91 A2
Linlithgow EH49 . . . . .84 C3
Tullibody FK10 . . . . .4 B1
Braehead Bank EH4 . . . . . .91 A2
Braehead Bsns Units EH49 . . . . .84 C3
Braehead Cres EH4 . . . . . .91 A2
Braehead Dr
Edinburgh EH4 . . . . .91 A2
Linlithgow EH49 . . . . .84 C3
Braehead Gr Bo'ness EH51 63 C4
Edinburgh EH4 . . . . .91 A2
Braehead Ho KY1 . . . . .17 B3
Braehead Loan EH4 . . . . . .91 A2
Braehead Pk
Edinburgh EH4 . . . . .91 A2
Linlithgow EH49 . . . . .84 C3
Braehead Pl EH49 . . . . .84 C3
Braehead Prim Sch FK7 . . .7 B2
Braehead Rd
Edinburgh EH4 . . . . .91 A2
Linlithgow EH49 . . . . .84 C3
Stirling FK7 . . . . .7 B2
Braehead Rdbt EH54 . . . .147 B2
Braehead Row EH4 . . . . . . .91 A2
Braehead Terr EH49 . . . . . .84 C3
Braehead View EH4 . . . . . .91 A2
Braekirk Ave EH27 . . . . . .149 B1
Braekirk Gdns EH27 . . . . .149 B2
Braemar Cres
Carluke ML8 . . . . .230 A2
Falkirk FK2 . . . . .60 B3
Braemar Dr Falkirk FK2 . . . .60 B3
Halbeath KY11 . . . . .30 A2
Braemar Gdns
Brightons FK2 . . . . .82 B4
Denny FK6 . . . . .36 B2
Halbeath KY11 . . . . .30 A2
Braemar Pl FK5 . . . . .39 A2
Braemount KY4 . . . . .13 A1
Braepark Rd EH4 . . . . .91 A2
Braes High Sch FK2 . . . . . .82 A4
Braes The Lochgelly KY5 . . . .14 A4
Tullibody FK10 . . . . .4 B2
Braes View Denny FK6 . . . . .57 B4
Shieldhill FK1 . . . . .81 C4
Braeside Alloa FK10 . . . . .5 B1
Shieldhill FK1 . . . . .81 B3
Braeside Cres EH47 . . . . .193 B3
Braeside Gdns EH53 . . . . .148 A1
Braeside Pk EH53 . . . . . . .148 A2
Braeside Pl
Laurieston FK2 . . . . .61 A2
Redding FK2 . . . . .61 A1
Reddingmuirhead FK2 . . . . . .82 A4
Braeside Rd
Gorebridge EH37 . . . . .207 B4
Loanhead EH20 . . . . .181 B4
Braeside Rd N EH23 . . . . .207 B4
Braeside Rd S EH23 . . . . .207 B4
Braeview
East Linton EH40 . . . . .103 B4
Laurieston FK2 . . . . .60 C2
Stenhousemuir FK5 . . . . .38 B1
Braewell Gdns EH49 . . . . . .84 B4
Braid Ave EH10 . . . . .123 A1
Braid Cres EH10 . . . . .123 A1
Braid Farm Rd EH10 . . . . .123 A1
Braid Gn EH54 . . . . .147 B4
Braid Hills App EH10 . . . .154 A4
Braid Hills Ave EH10 . . . .123 A1
Braid Hills Cres EH10 . . . .154 A4
Braid Hills Dr EH16 . . . . .154 B4
Braid Hills Rd EH10 . . . . .154 A4
Braid Mount EH10 . . . . . .154 A4
Braid Mount Crest EH10 . . . . .154 A4
Braid Mount Rise EH10 .154 A4
Braid Mount View EH10 .154 A4
Braidburn Cres EH10 . . . .123 A1
Braidburn Terr EH10 . . . .123 A1
Braidlaw Pk EH26 . . . . . . .203 B3
Braigh Gdns KY12 . . . . .28 B3
Bramble Dr EH4 . . . . .91 A1
Bramble Glade EH54 . . . . .173 B4
Bramdean Gr EH10 . . . . . .154 A4
Bramdean Pl EH10 . . . . . .154 A4
Bramdean Rise EH10 . . . . .154 A4
Bramdean View EH10 . . . .154 A4
Brand Dr EH15 . . . . .125 A4
Brand Gdns EH15 . . . . . . .125 B4
Brandfield St EH3 . . . . . .232 A1
Brandon St EH3 . . . . .93 B1
Brandon Terr EH3 . . . . .93 B2
Brands Row KY4 . . . . .30 C4
Brandy Riggs KY12 . . . . . . .27 B1
Brandy Wells KY12 . . . . . . .27 B1
Brandyhill FK10 . . . . .5 C2
Brankholm Brae KY11 . . . .46 B2
Brankholm Cres KY11 . . . .46 B3
Brankholm La KY11 . . . . . .46 B1
Branning Ct 11 KY1 . . . . . .17 B3
Branshill Pk FK10 . . . . .10 A4
Branshill Rd FK10 . . . . .10 A4
Branxton Wynd KY1 . . . . . .35 A4
Bravo St EH51 . . . . .62 C3
Bread St EH3 . . . . .232 B2
Bread Street La EH3 . . . .232 B2
Breadalbane Pl FK2 . . . . . .61 C1
Breadalbane St EH6 . . . . . .93 C2
Breadalbane Terr EH11 . .232 A2
Breakers Way KY11 . . . . . .47 C1
Brechin Dr FK2 . . . . .62 A1
Breck Terr EH26 . . . . .204 A4
Breich Sta EH55 . . . . .194 B3
Breich Terr EH55 . . . . .194 C3
Brentham Ave FK8 . . . . .7 A3
Brentham Cres FK8 . . . . . . .7 A3
Breslin Terr ML7 . . . . .168 B3
Breton Ct FK1 . . . . .60 B2
Brewery Cl EH30 . . . . .68 A1
Brewery La EH42 . . . . .78 A1
Brewery Pk EH41 . . . . . . .132 A4
Brewlands Ave EH51 . . . . .63 B3
Brewster Pl FK6 . . . . .36 B1
Brewster Sq EH54 . . . . . . .173 B3
Briar Brae FK2 . . . . .82 B4
Briar Cotts EH47 . . . . .171 B1
Briar Pl KY11 . . . . .29 B2
Briarbank Terr EH11 . . . .122 C2
Briarcliff St KY1 . . . . .17 C3
Briardene FK2 . . . . .61 A2
Briarhill Ave KY11 . . . . . . .48 A2
Briars Rd FK10 . . . . .4 C1
Brickfield EH15 . . . . .95 A1
Brickworks Rd EH33 . . . . .128 A4
Bridge Cres FK6 . . . . .36 B1
Bridge End
East Whitburn EH47 . . . . . .170 B4
Edinburgh EH16 . . . . .124 A2
Shotts ML7 . . . . .191 B3
Bridge End Cotts EH27 . .150 B3
Bridge of Allan Prim Sch FK9 . . . . .2 A3
Bridge of Allan Sta FK9 . . .1 C4
Bridge Pl Broxburn EH52 . .117 C3
Denny FK6 . . . . .36 B1
4 Edinburgh EH3 . . . . .93 A1
Shotts ML7 . . . . .192 A2
Bridge Rd Balerno EH14 . . .151 B1
Edinburgh EH13 . . . . .153 A3
Bridge St Bonnybridge FK4 .58 A3
Cowdenbeath KY4 . . . . .13 B2
Dunfermline KY12 . . . . .28 C2
East Linton EH40 . . . . .103 C4
Edinburgh EH15 . . . . .95 A1
Fauldhouse EH47 . . . . .193 C3
Haddington EH41 . . . . .132 B4
Kincardine FK10 . . . . .23 B2
Kirkcaldy KY1 . . . . .17 A1
Musselburgh EH21 . . . . . . .126 B3
Newbridge EH28 . . . . .119 A3
Penicuik EH26 . . . . .203 C2
Tranent EH33 . . . . .128 B3
Bridge Street La EH15 . . . .95 A1
Bridge Terr 10 FK10 . . . . . .10 A3
Bridge View KY11 . . . . .68 B3
Bridgecastle Rd EH48 . . .143 C4
Bridgehaugh Rd FK9 . . . . . .2 A1
Bridgehill FK1 . . . . .112 A3
Bridgend Ct EH48 . . . . . . .144 C3
Bridgend Pk EH48 . . . . . . .144 C3
Bridgend Pl
Bathgate EH48 . . . . .144 C3
Whitburn EH47 . . . . .170 B4
Bridgend Prim Sch EH49 .86 B2
Bridgend Rd FK1 . . . . .112 A3
Bridgeness Cres EH51 . . . .64 B4
Bridgeness La EH51 . . . . . .64 B4
Bridgeness Rd EH51 . . . . . .64 B4
Bridges The KY11 . . . . .48 A1
Bridges View KY12 . . . . . . .29 C3
Bridgeside Ave EH47 . . . .170 A3
Bridgeton Cotts EH48 . . . .112 C1
Brierbush Cres EH33 . . . .129 B3
Brierbush Rd EH33 . . . . . .129 B3
Briery Bank EH41 . . . . . . .132 B4
Briery Bauks EH8 . . . . . . .233 B2
Brig-O-Doon Gr FK7 . . . . .20 C4
Bright Terr EH11 . . . . .232 A2
Bright's Cres EH9 . . . . . . .123 C2
Brighton Pl EH15 . . . . . . .125 A4
Brighton St EH1 . . . . .233 A2
Brisbane St EH54 . . . . . . .148 A3
Bristo Pl EH1 . . . . .233 A2
Bristo Port EH1 . . . . .233 A2
Bristo Sq EH8 . . . . .233 A2
Britwell Cres EH7 . . . . .94 B1
Brixwold Bank EH19 . . . . .182 B3
Brixwold Dr EH19 . . . . . . .182 B3
Brixwold Neuk EH19 . . . . .182 B3
Brixwold Pk EH19 . . . . . . .182 B3
Brixwold Rise EH19 . . . . .182 B3
Brixwold View EH19 . . . . .182 B3
Broad St Alloa FK10 . . . . . . .10 A3
Cowdenbeath KY4 . . . . .13 B1
Denny FK6 . . . . .36 C1
Stirling FK8 . . . . .7 A4
Broad Wynd
Edinburgh EH6 . . . . .94 A3
10 Kirkcaldy KY1 . . . . .17 B3
Broadgait EH31 . . . . .52 A2
Broadgait Ct EH31 . . . . . . .52 A2
Broadgait Gn EH31 . . . . . . .52 A2
Broadhurst Rd EH22 . . . . .183 B4
Broadleys Rd FK7 . . . . .7 B4
Broadleys Rdbt FK7 . . . . . . .7 B3
Broadside Pl FK6 . . . . .36 B1
Brock Pl FK7 . . . . .7 A1
Brock St KY11 . . . . .68 A3
Brocks Way EH52 . . . . . . .118 A4
Brockville Pk (Falkirk FC) FK1,FK2 . . . . .60 A3
Brockwood Ave EH26 . . . .203 B3
Brodick Gdns KY11 . . . . . . .30 A2
Brodick Pl FK1 . . . . .59 B2
Brodick Rd KY2 . . . . .16 C4
Brodie Ave EH39 . . . . .54 B3
Brodie Ct EH39 . . . . .54 B4
Brodie Rd EH42 . . . . .106 B4
Brodie St FK2 . . . . .60 A4
Brodie Wlk KY11 . . . . .30 A2
Broich The FK12 . . . . .4 C4
Bronte Pl FK5 . . . . .39 A2
Brook St Alva FK10, FK12 . . . .5 A3
Menstrie FK11 . . . . .3 C3
Brookbank Terr ML8 . . . . .230 A1
Brooke La FK3 . . . . .61 B3
Brooke St FK3 . . . . .61 B3
Brookfield Pl FK12 . . . . .5 A3
Brookfield Terr EH25 . . . .180 C3
Brookside FK2 . . . . .61 C1
Broom Ct FK7 . . . . .7 B2
Broom Gr KY11 . . . . .46 C4
Broom Pk E FK11 . . . . .4 A3
Broom Pk W FK11 . . . . .4 A3
Broom Pl KY2 . . . . .16 B4
Broom Rd Kirkcaldy KY2 . . .16 B4
Stirling FK7 . . . . .7 B2
Broom Wlk EH54 . . . . .148 A2
Broom Wynd ML7 . . . . . . .191 C3
Broomage Ave FK5 . . . . . . .38 A2
Broomage Cres FK5 . . . . . .38 A2
Broomage Dr FK5 . . . . .38 A2
Broomage Pk FK5 . . . . .38 B1
Broombank Terr EH12 . . . .121 B2
Broomburn Gr EH12 . . . . .121 C2
Broomfield Cres EH12 . . .121 C2
Broomfield Dr KY12 . . . . . .29 A3
Broomfield Rd KY4 . . . . . . .13 B3
Broomhall Ave EH12 . . . . .121 C2
Broomhall Bank EH12 . . . .121 B3
Broomhall Cres EH12 . . . .121 B3
Broomhall Dr EH12 . . . . . .121 B3
Broomhall Gdns EH12 . . . .121 B3
Broomhall Loan EH12 . . . .121 B3
Broomhall Pk EH12 . . . . . .121 B3
Broomhall Pl EH12 . . . . . .121 B3
Broomhall Rd EH12 . . . . . .121 B3
Broomhall Terr EH12 . . . . .121 B3
Broomhead Dr KY12 . . . . . .28 C3
Broomhead Ho 9 KY12 . . .28 C3
Broomhead Pk KY12 . . . . . .28 C3
Broomhill KY3 . . . . .50 C4
Broomhill Ave
Burntisland KY3 . . . . .33 C1
Larbert FK5 . . . . .38 A1
Penicuik EH26 . . . . .203 C2
Broomhill Dr EH22 . . . . . .156 C1
Broomhill Pk 3 EH22 . . . .156 C1
Broomhill Pl Denny FK6 . . .36 B2
Stirling FK7 . . . . .6 C3
Broomhill Rd
Bonnybridge FK4 . . . . .58 A2
Penicuik EH26 . . . . .203 C2
Broomhill St ML7 . . . . . . .168 B3
Broomhouse Ave EH11 . . .121 B2
Broomhouse Bank EH11 . . . . .121 C2
Broomhouse Cotts EH11 . . . . .121 C2
Broomhouse Cres EH11 .121 C2
Broomhouse Ct EH11 . . .121 C2
Broomhouse Dr EH11 . . .121 C2
Broomhouse Gdns E EH11 . . . . .121 C2
Broomhouse Gdns W EH11 . . . . .121 B2
Broomhouse Gr EH11 . . .121 C2
Broomhouse Loan EH11 .121 C2
Broomhouse Medway EH11 . . . . .121 C2
Broomhouse Mkt EH11 . . .121 C2
Broomhouse Path EH11 .121 C2
Broomhouse Pk EH11 . . .121 C2
Broomhouse Pl N EH11 .121 C2
Broomhouse Pl S EH11 . .121 C2
Broomhouse Prim Sch EH11 . . . . .121 C2
Broomhouse Rd EH11 . . .121 B2
Broomhouse Row EH11 .121 C2
Broomhouse Sq EH11 . . .121 C2
Broomhouse St N EH11 .121 C2
Broomhouse St S EH11 .121 C1
Broomhouse Terr EH11 . .121 C2
Broomhouse Way EH11 .121 C2
Broomhouse Wlk EH11 . .121 C2
Broomhouse Wynd EH11 . . . . .121 C2
Broomieknowe
Bonnyrigg & Lasswade EH18 . . . . .182 A4
Dunfermline KY11 . . . . .29 B2
Tullibody FK10 . . . . .4 B2
Broomieknowe Gdns EH19 . . . . .182 A4
Broomieknowe Pk EH19 . . . . .182 A4
Broomknowe Dr FK10 . . . .23 B3
Broomlea Cres EH12 . . . .121 B3
Broompark Gdns
Denny FK6 . . . . .36 C1
East Calder EH53 . . . . .148 C2
Broompark Rd
East Calder EH53 . . . . .148 C2
Edinburgh EH12 . . . . .121 C3
Broompark View EH53 . . .148 C2
Broomridge Rd FK7 . . . . . . .7 A2
Broomside KY2 . . . . .16 B4
Broomside Pl FK5 . . . . .38 B1
Broomside Rd FK4 . . . . . . .58 A2
Broomside Terr EH12 . . . .121 C3
Broomyknowe EH14 . . . . .153 A4
Broomyknowe Dr EH54 . . .146 C3
Brora Pl KY12 . . . . .28 B1
Brosdale Ct FK1 . . . . .60 A1
Brougham Pl EH3 . . . . . . .232 C1
Brougham St EH3 . . . . . . .232 B1
Broughton High Sch EH4 .92 C1
Broughton Market EH3 . . .93 B1
Broughton Pl EH1 . . . . .93 B1
Broughton Place La EH1 .93 B1
Broughton Prim Sch EH7 .93 B2
Broughton Rd EH7 . . . . . . .93 B2
Broughton St EH1 . . . . .93 B1
Broughton Street La EH1 .93 B1
Brown Ave Alloa FK10 . . . . . .4 C1
Stirling FK9 . . . . .2 A1
Brown Ct FK3 . . . . .61 B4
Brown St Armadale EH48 .143 C2
Edinburgh EH8 . . . . .233 B2
Falkirk FK1 . . . . .59 B3
7 Haddington EH41 . . . . . .132 A4
Shotts ML7 . . . . .192 A2
Whitburn EH47 . . . . .170 A3
Brown's Cl EH8 . . . . .233 C3
Brown's Pl EH40 . . . . .103 B4
Brown's Pl EH1 . . . . .232 C2
Brownrigg Farm Cotts EH39 . . . . .74 B3
Broxburn Acad EH52 . . . .117 B3
Broxburn Prim Sch EH52 . . . . .117 C3
Bruart Ave FK5 . . . . .38 C2
Bruce Cres Falkirk FK2 . . . .39 A2
Plean FK7 . . . . .20 B2
Bruce Dr Fallin FK7 . . . . .8 B3
Stenhousemuir FK5 . . . . .38 C2
Bruce Gate FK2 . . . . .22 B1
Bruce Gdns Brightons FK2 .82 B4
Dalkeith EH22 . . . . .157 A1
Rosyth KY11 . . . . .47 A4
Bruce Gr EH34 . . . . .160 C3
Bruce Pl FK3 . . . . .61 C4
Bruce Rd Bathgate EH48 . .145 B3
Grangemouth EH51 . . . . .62 C3
Bruce St Alloa FK10 . . . . . . .10 B4
Bannockburn FK7 . . . . .7 C1
Clackmannan FK10 . . . . .11 A2
Dunfermline KY12 . . . . .28 C2
Edinburgh EH10 . . . . .123 A1
Falkirk FK2 . . . . .60 B3
Kinghorn KY3 . . . . .35 A2
Plean FK7 . . . . .20 B2
Stirling FK8 . . . . .2 A1
Bruce Terr
Cambusbarron FK7 . . . . .6 B3
Kinghorn KY3 . . . . .35 A2
Bruce View FK7 . . . . .7 A1
Brucefield Ave KY11 . . . . . .29 A1
Brucefield Cres FK10 . . . . .11 A2
Brucefield Dr EH47 . . . . .170 A3
Brucefield Feus KY11 . . . . .29 B2
Brucefield Ind Pk EH54 . .173 B3
Brucefield Pk E EH54 . . .173 B3
Brucefield Pk N EH54 . . .173 B3
Brucefield Pk W EH54 . . .173 B3
Brucefield Terr KY4 . . . . . .13 C3
Brucehaven Cres KY11 . . .45 C2
Brucehaven Rd KY11 . . . . .45 B2
Brunstane Bank EH15 . . .125 B3
Brunstane Cres EH15 . . . .125 B3
Brunstane Dr EH15 . . . . .125 B3
Brunstane Gardens Mews EH15 . . . . .125 B4
Brunstane Gdns
Edinburgh EH15 . . . . .125 B4
Penicuik EH26 . . . . .203 B3
Brunstane Mill Rd EH15 .125 C4
Brunstane Prim Sch EH15 . . . . .125 B3
Brunstane Rd EH15 . . . . .125 B4

Brunstane Road N EH15 ...125 B4
Brunstane Road S EH15 ...125 B3
Brunstane Sta EH15 ......125 B3
Brunswick Rd EH7 ....93 C1
Brunswick St EH7 ....93 C1
Brunswick Street La EH7 .93 C1
Brunswick Terr EH7 ....93 C1
Brunt Gr EH42 ....106 B4
Brunt La EH42 ....78 B1
Brunt Pl EH42 ....106 C4
Brunton Pl █ EH7 ....93 C1
Brunton Terr EH7 ....93 C1
Brunton's Cl EH22 ....157 A2
Bruntsfield Ave EH10 ....123 A3
Bruntsfield Cres EH10 ...123 A3
Bruntsfield Gdns EH10 ..123 A3
Bruntsfield Pl EH10 ......232 B1
Bruntsfield Prim Sch
EH10 ....232 B1
Bruntsfield Terr EH10 ...123 A3
Bryans Ave EH22 ....183 A3
Bryans Prim Sch EH22 ..183 A3
Bryans Rd EH22 ....183 A3
Bryce Ave Edinburgh EH7 .94 C1
Falkirk FK2 ....39 A1
Bryce Cres EH14 ....152 A3
Bryce Gdns EH14 ....152 A3
Bryce Gr EH7 ....94 C1
Bryce Pl EH14 ....152 A3
Bryce Rd EH14 ....152 A3
Bryden Ct FK3 ....61 C4
Bryony The FK10 ....4 A1
Bryson Pl EH48 ....145 A3
Bryson Rd EH11 ....122 C3
Bryson St FK2 ....60 A3
Bryson Street Ind Est
FK2 ....60 A3
Bubbles Rdbt EH54 ......147 C1
Buccleuch Ct EH22 ....156 C2
Buccleuch Pl EH8 ....233 A1
Buccleuch St
Dalkeith EH22 ....157 A2
Edinburgh EH8 ....233 B1
Buccleuch Terr EH8 ......233 B1
Buchan Ct EH52 ....117 C3
Buchan La EH52 ....117 C3
Buchan Pl FK3 ....61 A3
Buchan Rd
Bathgate EH48 ....144 C4
Broxburn EH52 ....117 B3
Grangemouth FK3, EH51 ..62 B3
Buchanan Cres EH54 ....147 A3
Buchanan Ct
Bo'ness EH51 ....43 C2
Falkirk FK1 ....42 A1
Kirkcaldy KY1 ....17 A1
Buchanan Dr FK9 ....2 A2
Buchanan Gdns FK2 ....61 B1
Buchanan St
Dunfermline KY12 ....29 A2
Edinburgh EH6 ....93 C2
Buckie Rd EH22 ....183 C3
Buckingham Terr EH4 ...232 A4
Buckstane Pk EH10 ......154 A4
Buckstone Ave EH10 ....154 A4
Buckstone Bank EH10 ...154 A4
Buckstone Circ EH10 ....154 A4
Buckstone Cl EH10 ....154 B3
Buckstone Cres EH10 ...154 A4
Buckstone Crook EH10 ..154 A3
Buckstone Dell EH10 ....154 A4
Buckstone Dr EH10 ......154 A4
Buckstone Gate EH10 ...154 B3
Buckstone Gdns EH10 ..154 A3
Buckstone Gn EH10 ......154 A4
Buckstone Gr EH10 ......154 A4
Buckstone Hill EH10 .....154 A4
Buckstone Howe EH10 ..154 B3
Buckstone Lea EH10 .....154 B3
Buckstone Loan EH10 ...154 A3
Buckstone Loan E EH10 .154 B3
Buckstone Neuk EH10 ...154 B3
Buckstone Pl EH10 ....154 A3
Buckstone Prim Sch
EH10 ....154 A3
Buckstone Rd EH10 ......154 A3
Buckstone Rise EH10 ....154 B3
Buckstone Row EH10 ....154 B3
Buckstone Shaw EH10 ..154 B3
Buckstone Terr EH10 ....154 A3
Buckstone View EH10 ...154 A4
Buckstone Way EH10 ....154 A4
Buckstone Wood EH10 ..154 A3
Buckstone Wynd EH10 ..154 B3
Buffies Brae KY12 ....28 C2
Bughtknowes Dr EH48 ..183 A4
Bughtlin Dr EH12 ....91 A1
Bughtlin Gdns EH12 .....121 A1
Bughtlin Gn EH12 ....91 A1
Bughtlin Loan EH12 ......121 A1
Bughtlin Mkt EH12 ....121 A1
Bughtlin Pk EH12 ....121 A1
Bughtlin Pl EH12 ....121 A1
Builyeon Rd EH30 ....89 A4
Buller St KY5 ....14 A4
Bullet Loan EH41 ....132 B4
Bulloch Cres FK2 ....36 B1
Bungalows The FK5 ....38 A1
Buntine Cres FK7 ....7 A1
Burbank KY12 ....27 B1
Burder Pk FK2 ....60 A2
Burdiehouse Ave EH17 ..155 A2
Burdiehouse Cres EH17 .155 A2
Burdiehouse Crossway
EH17 ....155 A2
Burdiehouse Dr EH17 ....155 A2
Burdiehouse Loan EH17 .155 A2

Burdiehouse Medway
EH17 ....155 A2
Burdiehouse Prim Sch
EH17 ....155 A2
Burdiehouse Rd EH17 ...155 A2
Burdiehouse Sq EH17 ...155 A2
Burdiehouse St EH17 ....155 A2
Burdiehouse Terr EH17 ..155 A2
Burgess Hill EH49 ....85 A3
Burgess Rd EH30 ....89 B4
Burgess St EH6 ....94 A3
Burgess Terr EH9 ....124 A2
Burgh Ct KY5 ....14 A4
Burgh Mews █ FK10 ....10 B3
Burgh Mills La EH49 ......84 B3
Burgh Rd KY4 ....13 B2
Burghlee Cres EH20 .....181 B4
Burghlee Terr EH20 .....181 B4
Burghmuir Ct EH49 ....85 B4
Burghmuir Ind Est FK8 .....7 A3
Burghmuir Rd FK7 ....7 A3
Burghtoft EH17 ....155 C3
Burleigh Cres EH51 ....47 B2
Burleigh Way EH10 ....10 B3
Burlington St EH6 ....93 C3
Burn Dr FK7 ....7 A2
Burnbank Carnock KY12 ..27 B4
Livingston EH54 ....147 B3
Loanhead EH20 ....181 A4
Burnbank Cres EH20 ....155 A1
Burnbank Gr EH20 ....155 A1
Burnbank Rd Falkirk FK2 ..60 A4
Grangemouth FK3 ....61 B3
Burnbank Terr EH25 .....180 C3
Burnbrae Alloa FK10 ....10 B4
Burney Pl KY11 ....46 C2
Burnfield EH54 ....147 A1
Burnfield Pl FK2 ....60 B4
Burnfoot Ct FK3 ....60 A3
Burnfoot La █ FK1 ....60 A2
Burngrange Cotts EH55 .172 B1
Burngrange Ct EH55 .....172 B1
Burngrange Gdns EH55 .172 B1
Burnhead Cres EH16 ....155 A3
Burnhead Gr EH16 ....155 A3
Burnhead Loan EH16 ...155 A3
Burnhead Path E EH16 ..155 A3
Burnhead Path W EH16 .155 A3
Burnhead Rd FK5 ....38 B2
Burnhouse Dr
Dechmont EH52 ....116 B1
Whitburn EH47 ....169 C3
Burnhouse Farm Steadings
EH7 ....149 B2
Burnhouse Ind Est
EH7 ....150 A1
Burnhouse Rd EH52 .....116 B2
Burnhouse Sch EH47 ....170 A3
Burnlea Dr EH47 ....171 A1
Burnlea Pl EH47 ....171 A1
Burns Ave
Armadale EH48 ....143 C3
Grangemouth FK3 ....61 B3
Stenhousemuir FK5 ....38 B2
Burns Cres Harthill ML7 .168 C3
Laurieston FK2 ....60 B2
Whitburn EH47 ....170 A3
Burns Ct EH54 ....148 B3
Burns Pl ML7 ....191 A3
Burns St Dunfermline KY12 .28 C3
Edinburgh EH6 ....93 C3
High Valleyfield KY12 ......26 A1
Stirling FK8 ....2 A1
Burns Terr
Bathgate EH48 ....145 B3
Cowie FK7 ....7 B1
Burnside Dechmont EH52 .116 A1
Edinburgh EH12 ....121 A4
Haddington EH41 ....131 C4
Prestonpans EH32 ....96 C1
Burnside Ave
Armadale EH48 ....143 B3
Easthouses EH22 ....183 B4
Kinghorn KY3 ....34 C2
Polbeth EH55 ....172 B1
Burnside Bsns Ctr KY11 ..47 B2
Burnside Cres
Clackmannan FK10 ....11 A3
Easthouses EH22 ....183 B4
Fauldhouse EH47 ....193 C3
Plean FK7 ....20 B2
Rosyth KY11 ....47 A3
Shotts ML7 ....191 B3
Burnside Ct EH41 ....134 B1
Burnside Gdns EH49 .....85 C3
Burnside Pk EH14 ....151 B1
Burnside Pl Falkirk FK2 ...47 A2
Rosyth KY11 ....47 A2
Burnside Rd
Bathgate EH48 ....144 C4
Edinburgh EH20 ....120 A4
Gorebridge EH23 ....183 B1
Menstrie FK11 ....3 C3

Burnside Rd continued
Polbeth EH55 ....172 C3
Uphall EH52 ....117 A3
Burnside St Alloa FK10 .....5 B1
Rosyth KY11 ....47 A3
Stirling FK7 ....7 B3
Burnside Terr
Cowdenbeath KY4 ....13 A1
East Calder EH53 ....148 C3
Falkirk FK1 ....59 C3
Fauldhouse EH47 ....193 C3
Oakley KY12 ....27 A4
Polbeth EH55 ....172 C3
Redding FK2 ....61 A1
Burnside View EH55 .....171 B1
Burnsknowe EH54 ....146 C3
Burntisland Prim Sch
KY3 ....33 C1
Burntisland Rd KY3 ....34 C1
Burntisland Sta KY3 ......50 C4
Burnvale EH52 ....118 A2
Livingston EH54 ....147 C2
Burt Ave KY3 ....34 C2
Burt Gr KY11 ....29 C1
Burt St KY12 ....29 A3
Bush St EH21 ....126 A3
Bush Terr EH21 ....126 A3
Bute EH54 ....146 C3
Bute Cres
Dunfermline KY11 ....29 C2
Shotts ML7 ....191 B3
Bute Pl FK3 ....61 B3
Bute St FK2 ....60 A3
Bute Wynd KY1 ....17 A1
Butler's Pl EH54 ....147 A2
Butlerfield Ind Est
EH19 ....183 A2
Butterdean Wood* ....
EH33 ....130 B3
Butteries View EH48 .....143 B3
Butts The EH41 ....132 A4
Buxley Rd EH33 ....128 A1
By-Pass Rd FK47 ....122 C4
Byburn EH52 ....16 C4
Byehope Rd EH52 ....117 A2
Byres The KY11 ....46 B3
Byreside EH47 ....146 A1
Byron Rd ML7 ....191 A3

C

Cables Wynd EH6 ....93 C3
Caddell's Row Cotts
EH4 ....90 A1
Cadell Dr █ FK2 ....39 A3
Cadell Pl
Cockenzie & Port Seton
EH32 ....97 B2
Fauldhouse EH47 ....193 C3
Cadgers Loan FK7 ....20 A1
Cadiz St EH6 ....94 A3
Cadogan Rd EH16 ....155 A4
Cadzow Ave EH55 ....63 A3
Cadzow Cres EH51 ....63 C4
Cadzow La EH51 ....63 C4
Cadzow Pl EH7 ....94 B1
Caerketton Ave EH25 ...180 C3
Caerlaverock Ct EH12 ..121 A4
Caesar Rd EH33 ....128 B3
Caesar Way EH33 ....128 A3
Caird's Row EH21 ....126 A4
Cairn Gr KY12 ....28 B1
Cairn Lea EH48 ....145 A3
Cairn's La EH51 ....64 A4
Cairnbank Gdns EH26 ..203 C2
Cairnbank Rd EH26 ......203 C2
Cairncubie Rd KY12 ....29 B4
Cairneyhill Prim & Com Sch
KY12 ....27 B1
Cairneyhill Rd KY12 ....27 B1
Cairneymount Ave FK2 ...43 A3
Cairneymount Rd ML8 ...230 A1
Cairngorm Cres KY2 ......16 C3
Cairngorm Rd FK3 ....61 A3
Cairnhill Ct ML8 ....230 A1
Cairnie Pl EH47 ....170 A3
Cairnmuir Rd EH12 ......121 C4
Cairnoch Way FK7 ....6 B1
Cairnoch Wlk FK6 ....36 B1
Cairnpapple Henge & Cairn*
EH48 ....114 B2
Cairnpapple Ho █
EH48 ....114 B2
Cairnpark Speci Sch
EH14 ....122 A1
Cairns Dr EH14 ....177 A4
Cairns Gdns EH14 ....177 A4
Cairns St E KY1 ....17 B4
Cairns St W KY1 ....17 B4
Cairns The
Charlestown KY11 ....26 A2
Menstrie FK11 ....4 A3
Cairntows Cl EH16 ....124 B2
Cairnwell Pl
Cairneyhill KY12 ....27 B1
Kirkcaldy KY2 ....16 C4
Caithness Ct EH14 ....
Caithness Pl
Edinburgh EH3 ....93 A3
Kirkcaldy KY1 ....17 C4
Caiyside EH10 ....154 A3
Caiystane Ave EH10 .....154 A3
Caiystane Cres EH10 ....154 A3
Caiystane Dr EH10 ....153 C3
Caiystane Gdns EH10 ...153 C3
Caiystane Hill EH10 ......154 A3
Caiystane Terr EH10 .....154 A3

Caiystane View EH10 ....154 A3
Calais View KY11 ....29 C1
Calaisburn Pl KY11 ....29 C1
Calder Cres
Armadale EH48 ....144 A3
Edinburgh EH11 ....121 A1
Calder Ct Edinburgh EH11 .121 B1
Stirling FK7 ....7 B3
Calder Dr
Edinburgh EH11 ....121 B1
Shotts ML7 ....192 A2
Calder Gdns EH11 ....121 B1
Calder Gr EH11 ....121 A1
Calder House Rd EH53 ..148 A2
Calder Junc EH11 ....121 A2
Calder Park Rd EH53 ....148 A1
Calder Pk EH11 ....121 B1
Calder Pl Dalgety Bay KY11 .48 A2
Edinburgh EH11 ....121 B1
Falkirk FK1 ....60 B1
Calder Rd
Edinburgh, East Hermiston
EH14 ....120 A1
Edinburgh, Sighthill EH11 .121 A1
Livingston EH54 ....173 B3
Calder Rd Gdns EH11 ...122 A2
Calder View EH11 ....121 A1
Calder's Lawn EH41 .....101 A1
Calderburn Rd EH55 ....173 A3
Caldercruix Rd FK1 ....110 A1
Calderhall Ave EH53 ....148 C2
Calderhall Cres EH53 ...148 C2
Calderhall Terr EH53 ....148 C2
Calderhead High Sch
ML7 ....191 C3
Calderhead Rd ML7 .....191 B4
Caledonia Rd Rosyth KY11 .46 A1
Shotts ML7 ....191 B3
Caledonia Way █ EH54 ..146 A2
Caledonian Brewery* ....
EH11 ....122 C3
Caledonian Cres EH11 ..232 A1
Caledonian Ct FK2 ....60 B4
Caledonian Pl EH11 .....232 A1
Caledonian Rd Alloa FK10 ..9 C3
Edinburgh EH11 ....232 A1
Fauldhouse EH47 ....193 B3
Caledonian Terr EH47 ..193 B3
Calgary Ave EH54 ....147 C2
California Prim Sch FK1 .81 C3
California Rd FK2 ....82 C3
California Terr FK1 ....81 C3
Callander Dr FK5 ....59 B4
Callander Pk FK1 ....60 C2
Callander Pl DT13 ....140 C2
Callander St KY11 ....30 A2
Callendar Ave FK1 ....60 A1
Callendar Bsns Pk FK1 ..60 C2
Callendar Ho* FK1 ....60 B2
Callendar Rd FK,FK2 .....60 B2
Callendar Riggs FK1 .....60 B2
Callendar Square 5h Ctr 5
FK1 ....60 B2
Calliope Rd KY11 ....46 A1
Calton Cres FK7 ....7 A2
Calton Hill EH7 ....233 B4
Calton Hill Mon* EH7 ...233 B4
Calton Rd EH8 ....233 B3
Calum Macdonald Ct
KY11 ....46 C2
Cambridge Ave EH6 ......93 C2
Cambridge Gdns EH6 ....93 C2
Cambridge St EH1 ....232 A2
Cambus Pools Nature
Reserve* FK10 ....8 A2
Cambusbarron Prim Sch
FK7 ....6 B3
Cambuskenneth Abbey*
FK9 ....2 C2
Cambusnethan St ▇ EH7 .94 A1
Camdean Cres KY11 ......46 B3
Camdean La KY11 ....46 B3
Camden Hill Gdns FK4 ..58 A3
Camelon Ed Ctr FK1 .....59 C3
Camelon Rd FK1 ....59 C3
Camelon Sta FK1 ....59 B3
Cameron Cres
Bonnyrigg & Lasswade
EH19 ....181 C3
Edinburgh EH16 ....124 A2
Cameron Gr KY11 ....47 A2
Cameron House Ave
EH16 ....124 A2
Cameron Knowe EH49 ...86 B3
Cameron March EH16 ...124 A2
Cameron Pk EH16 ....124 A2
Cameron Pl FK2 ....60 B3
Cameron Smail Rd
EH14 ....151 C4
Cameron St KY12 ....28 C2
Cameron Terr
Edinburgh EH16 ....124 A2
Slamannan FK1 ....110 A2
Cameron Toll EH16 ....124 A2
Cameron Toll Gdns
EH16 ....124 A2
Cameron Toll Sh Ctr
EH16 ....124 A2
Cameron Way EH54 .....147 C4
Cameronian Dr ML8 .....230 A1
Cameronian St █ FK8 .....2 A1
Camilla Gr KY2 ....15 B1
Cammo Bank EH4 ....91 A1
Cammo Brae EH4 ....91 A1
Cammo Gdns EH4 ....91 A1
Cammo Hill EH4 ....90 C1

Cammo Parkway EH4 .....91 A1
Cammo Pl EH4 ....91 A1
Cammo Rd EH4 ....90 C1
Cammo Wlk EH4 ....90 C1
Camp Rd Crombie KY12 ..44 B3
Mayfield EH22 ....183 C4
Camp Wood View EH22 .183 C3
Campbell Ave EH12 ......122 B4
Campbell Cres
Laurieston FK2 ....60 C2
Lochgelly KY5 ....14 A4
Campbell Ct
Longniddry EH32 ....98 B3
Torryburn KY12 ....6 C2
Campbell Dr FK5 ....38 B2
Campbell Park Cres
EH13 ....152 C3
Campbell Park Dr EH13 .152 C3
Campbell Rd
Edinburgh EH12 ....122 B4
Longniddry EH32 ....98 B3
Campbell St KY12 ....29 A2
Campbell's Cl EH8 ....233 C3
Camperdown Rd KY11 ...46 B1
Campfield St FK2 ....60 A3
Campie Ct EH21 ....126 A3
Campie Gdns EH21 ......126 A3
Campie La Prim Sch EH21 .126 A3
Campie Prim Sch EH21 .126 A3
Campie Rd EH21 ....126 A3
Campie Terr EH21 ....39 C1
Camps Ind Est Peart 149 B3
Camps Rd KY12 ....27 B3
Camps Rigg EH54 ....147 A4
Campsie Cres KY2 ....16 C4
Campsie Rd FK1 ....61 C3
Campus Rdbt EH54 ......147 B1
Campview EH22 ....156 A4
Campview Ave EH22 ....156 A4
Campview Cres EH22 ...156 A4
Campview Gdns EH22 ..156 A4
Campview Gr EH22 ......156 A4
Campview Rd EH19 ......182 A3
Campview Terr EH22 ....156 A4
Camps Ave EH10 ....154 A3
Camus Pk EH10 ....154 A3
Canaan La EH10 ....123 A2
Canal Bank Ind Est FK4 ..58 A2
Canal St Falkirk FK1 ....59 B4
Canal Terr EH49 ....85 A3
Canal Wlk FK2 ....61 B1
Canalyard Ind Est FK1 ...60 A1
Canavan Ct FK7 ....7 B2
Canberra St EH54 ....148 A3
Candie Cres FK3 ....61 C3
Candie Rd FK3 ....61 C3
Candimilne Ct ML8 ......230 A1
Candlemaker Row EH1 .233 A2
Candlemaker's Cres
EH17 ....155 C3
Candlemaker's Pk EH17 .155 C3
Candleriggs FK10 ....10 A3
Candleriggs Ct 6 FK10 ..10 A3
Caneluk Ave ML8 ....230 A1
Canmore Dr FK5 ....38 C2
Canmore Gr KY12 ....29 A2
Canmore Prim Sch KY12 .29 C1
Canmore St
Dunfermline KY12 ....29 A2
Kinghorn KY3 ....34 C1
Queensferry EH30 ....89 A4
Canmore Terr KY12 ....29 A2
Canning St EH3 ....232 B2
Canning Street La EH3 ..232 A2
Cannon Wynd EH6 ....93 C3
Cannons Way FK2 ....39 A1
Cannop Cres EH47 ......170 C1
Cannon Byrne Glebe KY1 .17 B3
Canon La EH3 ....93 B1
Canon Lynch Ct KY12 ....28 C2
Canon St EH3 ....93 B1
Canongate EH8 ....233 B3
Canonmills EH3 ....93 B2
Cant Crs EH9 ....123 C1
Cantel Gdns ML7 ....191 A2
Cantlie Pl KY11 ....46 C2
Cantsdam Rd KY4 ....12 C4
Canty Gr EH32 ....98 B2
Caokben Rd EH14 ....153 A3
Caplaw Way EH26 ....203 B3
Caponflat Cres EH41 ....100 C1
Caponhall Ct EH33 ......128 B3
Caponhall Dr EH33 ......128 B3
Caponhall Rd EH33 ......128 B3
Cappers Ct EH48 ....143 C2
Captain's Dr EH16 ....155 A3
Captain's Rd EH16,EH17 .155 A3
Captain's Row EH16 .....155 A3
Caputhall Rd EH54 ......146 B3
Carberry Cl EH21 ....127 A2
Carberry Ct EH21 ....157 C4
Carberry Gr EH21 ....126 C2
Carberry Mains Cotts
EH21 ....127 A1
Carberry Pl EH12 ....122 C4
Carberry Rd EH21 ....126 C2
Carbrook Dr FK7 ....20 B2
Carbrook Pl FK3 ....61 C3
Carbrook Terr FK5 ....38 B2
Carcraig Pl KY11 ....48 A2
Cardross Ave EH52 ......117 A3

Cardross Cres EH52 .....117 B3
Cardross Rd EH52 ....117 B3
Cardrowan Rd FK7 ....20 B1
Carfrae Gdns EH4 ....92 A1
Carfrae Gr EH4 ....92 A1
Carfrae Pk EH4 ....92 A1
Carfrae Rd EH4 ....92 A1
Cargil Terr EH5 ....93 A3
Cargilfield Sch FK4 ......91 A2
Carhowden Rd FK2 ....61 A2
Carlaverock Ave EH33 ...128 B3
Carlaverock Ct EH33 ....128 C3
Carlaverock Cres EH33 ..128 B3
Carlaverock Ct EH33 ....128 C3
Carlaverock Dr EH33 ....128 B3
Carlaverock Ct EH33 ....128 B3
Carlaverock Terr EH33 ..128 C2
Carlaverock View EH33 ..128 B3
Carlaverock Wlk EH33 ...128 B3
Carledubs Ave EH52 .....117 A3
Carledubs Cres EH52 ....117 A3
Carlie Ave FK9 ....2 A3
Carlin Craig KY3 ....34 C1
Carlin Cres KY3 ....34 C1
Carlin La ML8 ....230 A1
Carlingnose Ct KY11 .....68 B3
Carlingnose Pk KY11 .....68 B3
Carlingnose Point KY11 ..68 B3
Carlingnose View KY11 ...68 B3
Carlingnose Way KY11 ....68 B3
Carlops Ave EH26 ....203 C3
Carlops Cres EH26 ......203 C3
Carlops Rd EH26 ....203 B3
Carlouk La ML8 ....230 A1
Carlowrie Ave EH30 ......89 C4
Carlowrie Cres EH30 .....89 C4
Carlowrie Pl EH23 ......207 B4
Carlton St EH4 ....93 A1
Carlton Terr EH7 ....233 C4
Carlton Terrace La EH7 ..233 C4
Carlton Terrace Mews
EH7 ....233 C4
Carluke High Sch ML8 ...230 A1
Carluke Prim Sch ML8 ...230 A2
Carlyle Ct
Haddington EH41 ......132 A4
Livingston EH54 ....148 B3
Carlyle La EH41 ....101 A1
Carlyle La **1** KY12 .....28 C3
Carlyle Pl Edinburgh EH7 .94 A1
Musselburgh EH21 .....126 B3
Carlyle St KY12 ....17 A2
Carlyle St KY12 ....26 A2
Carlyle Terr EH48 ....145 B3
Carmel Ave EH29 ....89 A1
Carmel Rd EH29 ....89 A1
Carmaben EH49 ....85 A3
Carmelite Rd EH30 ....89 A4
Carmichael Ct EH9 ....2 A4
Carmondean Centre Rd
EH54 ....147 A4
Carmondean Ctr Rdbt
EH54 ....147 A3
Carmondean Ctr S
EH54 ....147 A3
Carmondean Prim Sch
EH54 ....147 A4
Carmuir ML11 ....215 A1
Carmuirs Ave FK1 ....59 B3
Carmuirs Dr FK1 ....59 B3
Carmuirs Prim Sch FK1 ..59 B3
Carmuirs St FK1 ....59 B3
Carnaughton Pl FK2 ......59 A2
Carnbee Ave EH16 ......155 B3
Carnbee Cres EH16 .....155 B3
Carnbee Dell EH16 .....155 B3
Carnbee End EH16 ......155 B3
Carnbee Pk EH16 ....155 B3
Carnbee Pl KY12 ....29 B2
Carnegie Ave KY11 ....96 C4
Carnegie Campus (Bsns Pk)
KY11 ....46 C4
Carnegie Ct
Dunfermline KY12 ......29 A2
Edinburgh EH8 ....233 B2
Carnegie Dr
Dunfermline KY12 ......29 A2
Falkirk FK1 ....59 B2
Carnegie Rd EH48,EH54 .146 A3
Carnegie St EH8 ....233 B2
Carneil Rd KY12 ....27 B4
Carneil Terr KY12 ....27 B3
Carnethie St EH24 ......181 C1
Carnethy Ave
Edinburgh EH13 ......153 A3
Penicuik EH26 ....203 C3
Carnethy Cres KY2 ....16 C4
Carnethy Ct EH26 ......203 C3
Carnock Hill KY12 ....27 B4
Carnock Prim Sch KY12 ..27 B4
Carnock Rd KY12 ....28 A3
Carnock St FK7 ....20 C4
Carnwath Rd ML8 ....230 A1
Caroline Cres FK2 ....4 C3
Caroline Gdns
Edinburgh EH12 ....121 C4
Mid Calder EH53 ......148 A1
Caroline Park Ave EH5 ...92 B3
Caroline Park Gr EH5 ....92 B3
Caroline Pk EH53 ....148 A1
Caroline Pl EH12 ....121 C4
Caroline Terr EH12 .....121 B4
Carpenters Wynd EH10 ...9 C2
Carpet La EH6 ....94 A3
Carradale Ave FK1 ....59 B2

Carribber Ave EH49 ......84 A3
Carrick Cres EH22 ......183 B4
Carrick Ct FK7 ....7 B3
Carrick Dr KY11 ....48 A2
Carrick Gdns EH54 .....173 C3
Carrick Gr KY11 ....48 A2
Carrick Knowe Ave
EH12 ....121 C3
Carrick Knowe Dr EH12 .121 C3
Carrick Knowe Gdns
EH12 ....121 C3
Carrick Knowe Gr EH12 .121 C3
Carrick Knowe Hill
EH12 ....121 C3
Carrick Knowe Loan
EH12 ....121 C3
Carrick Knowe Parkway
EH12 ....121 C3
Carrick Knowe Pl EH12 .121 C3
Carrick Knowe Prim Sch
EH12 ....121 C3
Carrick Knowe Rd EH12 .121 C2
Carrick Knowe Terr
EH12 ....121 C3
Carrick Pl Falkirk FK2 .....3 A2
Falkirk, Tamfourhill FK1 .59 B2
Carrickvale Ctr Stevenson
Coll EH11 ....122 A2
Carriden Brae EH51 .....64 B3
Carriden Glade EH51 ....64 B4
Carrington Cres EH4 .....92 C2
Carrington Mains Cotts
EH23 ....206 B3
Carrington Rd EH4 ......92 C1
Carron Ave KY11 ....29 C2
Carron La KY11 ....29 C2
Carron Pl Edinburgh EH6 .94 A2
Grangemouth FK3 ......61 B2
Kirkcaldy KY2 ....16 B4
Stirling FK7 ....7 A3
Carron Prim Sch FK2 ....39 A1
Carron Rd FK2 ....60 A4
Carron Terr FK2 ....82 C4
Carron View FK2 ....82 C4
Carron Wlk EH54 ....148 C2
Carronbank Ave FK2 .....39 A1
Carronbank Cres FK6 ....36 C2
Carronbank Ct FK2 ......39 A1
Carronflats Rd FK3 ......61 C4
Carrongrange Ave FK5 ...38 C1
Carrongrange Gdns FK5 .38 C1
Carrongrange Gr FK5 ....38 C1
Carrongrange Rd FK5 ....38 C1
Carrongrange Sch FK5 ...38 C1
Carrongrove Ave FK2 ....39 A1
Carrongrove Bsns Pk
FK2 ....39 A1
Carrongrove Rd FK2 .....39 A1
Carronhall Ave FK2 ......39 B2
Carronlea Dr FK2 ....39 A1
Carronshore Prim Sch
FK2 ....39 B1
Carronshore Rd FK2 .....39 B1
Carronside Pl FK6 ....36 C2
Carronside St FK2 ....60 A4
Carronvale Ave FK5 ......38 B1
Carronvale Rd FK5 ......38 B1
Carronview FK5 ....38 B1
Carsaig Ct FK9 ....2 A3
Carse Cres FK2 ....61 A2
Carse Knowe EH49 ....85 B4
Carse Terr FK10 ....4 C4
Carse View Airth FK2 ....22 C2
Bo'ness EH51 ....63 B3
Carsebridge Ct FK10 ....10 B4
Carsebridge Rd FK10 ....10 B4
Carseview Bannockburn FK7 .7 C1
Tullibody FK10 ....4 A3
Carson Pl KY11 ....46 B3
Carswell Pl KY12 ....28 C3
Cartmore Rd KY5 ....14 A4
Cask Cres FK8 ....7 A4
Cassel's La EH6 ....93 C2
Casselbank St EH6 ....93 C2
Cast The EH18 ....181 B3
Castellau Cotts EH42 ....78 B1
Castings Ave FK2 ....60 A4
Castings Ct Falkirk FK2 ..60 A4
Falkirk, Middlefield FK2 ..60 C3
Castings Dr FK2 ....60 A3
Castings Rd FK2 ....60 A3
Castings The KY12 ....28 B3
Castlehill Rd KY11 ....47 A1
Castle Ave Airth FK2 ...22 C2
Cockenzie & Port Seton
EH32 ....97 C2
Edinburgh EH12 ....121 B3
Stirling FK8 ....7 A4
Castle Brae KY11 ....46 C3
Castle Bsns Pk The FK9 ...1 C1
Castle Cres Denny FK6 ...36 B1
East Calder EH53 .....148 C1
Falkirk FK2 ....60 B4
Torwood FK5 ....37 C4
Castle Ct Falkirk FK2 ...60 B4
Menstrie FK11 ....3 C3
Stirling FK8 ....7 A4
Castle Dr Airth FK2 .....22 C2
Dunfermline KY11 ....46 C3
Falkirk FK2 ....60 B4
Stenhousemuir FK5 .....38 C1
Castle Gogar* EH12 ....120 B4
Castle Mains EH39 ....53 A3
Castle Mains Pl EH39 ....53 A3
Castle Moffat EH14 .....166 A4

Castle Pk Dirleton EH39 ..53 A2
Kincardine FK10 ....23 B3
Castle Pl Dunbar EH42 ...78 B2
Falkirk FK2 ....60 B4
Gorebridge EH23 ......207 B4
Castle Rd
Cockenzie & Port Seton
EH32 ....97 C2
Falkirk FK2 ....60 B4
Menstrie FK11 ....3 C3
Rosyth KY11 ....46 C1
Stirling FK9 ....2 B2
Tranent EH33 ....128 B3
Winchburgh EH52 ....88 A1
Castle Row KY12 ....28 B3
Castle St Alloa FK10 .....10 A3
Clackmannan FK10 ......11 A2
Dunbar EH42 ....78 B2
Edinburgh EH2 ....232 B3
Castle Terr
Clackmannan FK10 ......11 A2
Cockenzie & Port Seton
EH32 ....97 C2
Denny FK6 ....36 B1
Edinburgh EH2 ....232 B3
Winchburgh EH52 ....88 A1
Castle Vale FK9 ....2 A2
Castle View Aberdour KY3 .49 B4
Airth FK2 ....22 B1
Cockenzie & Port Seton
EH32 ....97 C2
Fallin FK7 ....8 B2
Gorebridge EH23 ......207 B4
Pencaitland EH34 .....160 B3
Castle Wlk EH42 ....97 C2
Castle Wynd FK8 ....7 A4
Castle Wynd N EH1 .....232 C2
Castle Wynd S EH1 .....232 C2
Castleblair **2** KY12 ......28 C3
Castleblair La **7** KY12 ..28 C3
Castleblair Mews 8
KY12 ....28 C3
Castleblair Pk KY12 .....28 C3
Castlebrae Bsns Ctr
EH16 ....124 C2
Castlebrae Com Sch
EH16 ....124 C2
Castlebrae Glade EH16 .124 B2
Castlebrae Rigg EH16 ..124 B2
Castlegait FK8 ....7 A4
Castlehill Bo'ness EH51 ...64 A4
Edinburgh EH1 ....232 C3
Castlehill Ave FK1 ......110 A3
Castlelaurie St FK2 ......60 B4
Castlelaw Cres EH25 ...180 C3
Castlelaw Ct EH26 .....203 C3
**Castlelaw Fort &
Souterrain*** EH26 ....179 B2
Castlelaw Rd EH13 .....153 A3
Castlemains Pl EH39 ....53 B3
Castlemount Terr KY2 ...16 B4
Castlepark Gn EH16 ....124 B2
Castlepark Gdns EH16 ..124 B2
Castlerankine Rd FK6 ...36 B1
Castlerig KY3 ....34 C1
Castleton Cres KY3 ......61 B3
Castleview Dr FK2 ....60 B4
Castleview La EH54 .....173 C2
Castleview Terr FK4 .....57 A2
Cath Church of St Mary*
EH12 ....232 A3
Cathcart Pl EH11 ....122 C3
Cathedral La EH1 ....233 A4
Catherine St FK7 ....7 A3
Catherine Terr EH47 ...145 B1
Cathlaw La EH48 ....114 A3
Catriona Terr EH26 ....180 A1
Cattle Market FK10 ......11 A2
Cauldcoats Holdings
EH49 ....65 A1
Cauldhame Cres FK7 .....6 B3
Causeway The
Bridge of A FK9 ....2 B3
Edinburgh EH15 ....124 B3
Causewayhead Rd FK9 ...2 B2
Causewayside EH9 .....123 C3
Cavalry Park Dr EH15 ..124 B3
Cawder Gdns FK9 ....1 C4
Cawder Rd FK9 ....1 C4
Cawdor Cres KY2 ....16 C3
Cecil St FK7 ....7 A3
Cedar Ave Kirkcaldy KY1 .17 B4
Stirling FK8 ....6 C3
Cedar Cres
Cowdenbeath KY4 ......13 B3
Westquarter FK2 ....61 A1
Whitburn EH47 ....170 B3
Cedar Dr KY12 ....97 B2
Cedar Gr
Dunfermline KY11 ......46 B4
Stenhousemuir FK5 .....38 B1
Cedar Rd EH20 ....180 C4
Cedar St Dunbar EH42 ...78 A3
Grangemouth FK3 ......61 B4
Cedar Wynd ML7 ....192 A2
Cedarbank EH54 ....147 C3
Cedarbank Sch EH54 ...147 C3
Cedars The FK10 ....4 A1
Cedric Rise EH54 ....148 A1
Cemetery Rd
Dalkeith EH22 ....156 C1
Faulldhouse EH47 .....193 B3
Prestonpans EH32 ......96 C1
Shotts ML7 ....192 A2
Central Ave FK3 ....61 B3
Central Bvd FK3 ....38 A2
Central Dock Rd FK3 .....40 C1

Central Dr FK5 ....38 C2
Central Park Ave FK5 ....38 A2
Central Park Bsns Pk
FK5 ....38 A2
Central Pk (Cowdenbeath
FC) KY4 ....13 B2
Central Rd KY12 ....44 B4
Central Ret Pk FK1 ......60 B3
Central Way KY11 ....48 B3
Centre Intc EH54 ....48 B3
Centre Rd N EH54 ......148 A2
Centurion Way FK2 ......59 B3
Chacefield St FK4 ....58 A3
Chacefield Wood FK6 ....57 C4
Chalmers' Bldgs EH3 ...232 B1
Chalmers Bldg EH49 ....84 B4
Chalmers Cres EH9 ....123 B3
Chalmers Ho KY12 ......28 C2
Chalmers Hospl EH3 ...232 C2
Chalmers Sq EH54 .....146 B3
Chalmers St
Dunfermline KY12 ......28 C2
Edinburgh EH3 ....232 C1
Chalmerston Rd FK9 .....1 A2
Chalton Ct FK2 ....2 A4
Chalton Rd FK2 ....2 A4
Chalybeate EH41 ....131 C4
Chamberfield Rd KY12 ...29 B3
Chamberlain Rd EH10 ..123 A2
Chambers Dr FK2 ....39 A1
Chambers St EH1 ....233 A2
Chamfron Gdns FK7 ......7 C2
Champany Holdings
EH49 ....65 A1
Champigny Ct EH21 ....126 C3
Chancelot Cres FK5 .....93 B3
Chancelot Gr EH5 ....93 B3
Chancelot Terr EH6 .....93 B3
Chandler's Rise KY11 ....47 C2
Chandler's Wlk KY11 ....47 C2
Channel Brae EH42 ....136 B4
Chapel Bank EH22 .....158 B3
Chapel Cres FK2 ....39 A2
Chapel Ct EH16 ....124 C2
Chapel Gr KY12 ....38 C2
Chapel Gr KY2 ....16 B4
Chapel La Edinburgh EH6 ..94 A3
Falkirk FK1 ....60 A3
Chapel Level KY2 ....16 C4
Chapel Loan EH25 .....181 A2
Chapel Pl
High Valleyfield KY12 ...26 A1
Inverkeithing KY11 .....47 B2
Kirkcaldy KY2 ....16 B4
North Queensferry KY11 .68 B3
Pathhead EH37 ....185 A3
Chapel Rd KY12 ....16 B4
Chapel St
Cowdenbeath KY4 ......13 B2
Dunfermline KY11 ......28 C2
Edinburgh EH8 ....233 B1
High Valleyfield KY12 ...26 A1
Kincardine FK10 ....23 B3
Lochgelly KY5 ....14 A4
Chapel Villas KY11 ......48 A1
Chapel Wynd EH1 .....232 C2
Chapelhall Gn KY11 .....29 C2
Chapelhill
Clackmannan FK10 ......11 A2
Dirleton EH39 ....53 A2
Kirkcaldy KY2 ....16 B4
Chapelhill St KY11 ......23 B3
Chapelton Ave EH55 ...172 C2
Chapelton Ct EH55 ....172 C2
Chapelton Gdns EH55 ..172 C2
Chapelton Gr EH55 ....172 C2
Chapelton Pl EH55 ....173 A2
Chapelton Terr EH55 ..172 C2
Chapelwell Pl KY11 .....29 C2
Chapman's Brae EH48 .144 C4
Charing Cross FK3 ....40 B1
Charles Ave
Bathgate EH48 ....145 C3
Carluke ML8 ....230 A1
Charles Ct KY11 ....45 C2
Charles Cres FK5 ....59 B4
Charles La EH48 ....145 C3
Charles Rodger Pl FK9 ...2 C4
Charles St Alloa FK10 ....9 C4
Dunfermline KY11 ......29 A1
Edinburgh EH8 ....233 A2
Penicuik EH26 ....203 C4
Shotts ML7 ....192 A2
Stirling FK8 ....7 A3
Charles Street La EH8 ..233 A2
Charles Way KY11 ......45 C2
Charles Way S KY11 .....45 C2
Charlesfield EH48 ......145 C3
Charlesfield La EH41 ...147 A1
Charlesfield Rd EH54 ..173 B4
Charlotte Dundas Ct FK3 .61 C3
Charlotte Hill Ct FK5 ....38 A2
Charlotte La EH2 ....232 B3
Charlotte Sq EH2 ......232 B3
Charlotte St Brightons FK2 .82 B4
Kirkcaldy KY1 ....17 A3
Shotts ML7 ....192 A2
Charter Ct EH25 ....180 C2
Charter The FK11 ....3 C3
Charter St FK7 ....7 A3
Charterhall Gr EH9 ....123 B2
Charterhall Rd EH9 ....123 B1
Charteris Ct EH32 ....98 B3
Charteris Pk EH32 ......98 B3
Charteris Rd EH32 ......98 B3

Chartershall Rd
Bannockburn FK7 ....7 A1
Bannockburn FK7 ....19 A3
Chattan Ave FK9 ....2 A2
Chattan Ind Est FK4 .....58 B2
Chatterrig EH13 ....153 C4
Checkbar Rdbt FK5 ......58 B4
Cherry Ave EH48 ....145 C3
Cherry La EH22 ....183 C3
Cherry Pl KY4 ....13 B2
Cherry Rd EH19 ....13 B3
Cherry Tree Ave EH14 ..151 C2
Cherry Tree Cres EH14 .151 C2
Cherry Tree Gdns EH14 .151 B2
Cherry Tree Gr EH14 ...151 B2
Cherry Tree Loan EH14 .151 C2
Cherry Tree Pk EH14 ...151 B2
Cherry Tree Pl EH14 ...151 C2
Cherry Tree View EH14 .151 C2
Cherrybank KY12 ....29 B3
Cherryton Dr FK10 ......11 A3
Chessel's Ct EH8 ....233 B3
Chesser Ave EH14 .....122 B2
Chesser Cotts EH11 ....122 B2
Chesser Cres EH14 ....122 B2
Chesser Gdns EH14 ...122 A2
Chesser Gr EH14 ......122 A2
Chesser Loan EH14 ....122 A2
Chester Dr EH22 ....183 B3
Chester St EH3 ....232 A3
Chester View EH22 ....183 B3
Chesters (fort) The*
EH39 ....72 C1
Chesters Ct EH19 ......182 A3
Chesters Gr EH19 .....182 A3
Chesters The EH19 ......72 C2
Chesters View EH19 ...182 A3
Chestnut Ave
Kirkcaldy KY1 ....17 B4
Whitburn EH47 ....170 B3
Chestnut Cres FK6 ......36 B2
Chestnut Gr Bo'ness EH51 .63 B3
Bonnyrigg & Lasswade
EH19 ....182 A3
Cockenzie & Port Seton
EH32 ....97 B2
Dunfermline KY11 ......46 C4
Livingston EH54 ....148 A3
Stenhousemuir FK5 .....38 C2
Winchburgh EH52 ....87 C1
Chestnut St EH5 ....92 C4
Cheviot Pl FK3 ....61 C3
Cheviot Rd KY2 ....16 C4
Cheyne St EH4 ....93 A1
Chief's Cl KY1 ....17 B3
Chisholm Ave FK5 ....2 A2
Chisholm Cres KY5 .....14 A4
Chisholm Pl FK3 ....61 A3
Chisholm St KY12 ....29 B4
Chisholm Terr EH26 ...203 C4
Crichton's Cl EH8 ......233 C3
Chrisella Terr FK2 ....83 A3
Christian Cres EH15 ...125 B4
Christian Gr EH15 .....125 A4
Christie Pl KY1 ....17 B4
Christie St KY12 ....29 A3
Christie Terr FK5 ....38 C2
Christiemiller Ave EH7 ..94 C1
Christiemiller Gr EH7 ....94 C1
Christiemiller Pl EH7 ....94 C1
Chuckie Pend EH3 .....232 B2
Church Ct 3 Alloa FK10 .10 A3
Kirkcaldy KY1 ....17 B2
Philpstoun EH49 ....86 C3
Church Gdns EH32 ......98 C3
Church Gr Alloa FK10 .....5 B1
Burntisland KY3 ....33 B1
Church Hill EH10 ......123 A2
Church Hill Pl EH10 ...123 A2
Church La Denny FK6 ...36 B2
Fallin EH21 ....125 C1
California FK1 ....81 C3
North Berwick EH39 ....54 B4
Church St
Addiewell EH55 ....171 B1
Alloa FK10 ....10 A3
Broxburn EH52 ....117 A2
Burntisland KY3 ....33 B1
Cowdenbeath KY4 ......13 B2
Dunbar EH42 ....78 C1
Falkirk FK2 ....39 B1
High Bonnybridge FK4 ..58 B2
Inverkeithing KY11 .....47 B2
Kingseat KY12 ....12 A1
Kirkcaldy KY1 ....17 B3
Limekilns KY11 ....45 B2
Loanhead EH20 ....181 B4
Lochgelly KY5 ....14 A4
Stenhousemuir FK5 .....38 C2
Church Wlk Denny FK6 ..36 C1
Kinghorn KY3 ....35 A2
Church Wynd EH51 ......63 C4

Churchhill Dr EH10 .....123 A2
Churchill Dr FK9 ....2 A3
Churchill Pl Falkirk FK2 ...60 B4
Rosyth KY11 ....46 C2
Churchill St FK10 ....9 C4
Churchill Way EH27 .....149 C2
Churchway EH32 ....98 C3
Churchyard Ct ML7 .....191 C2
Cinderhall Pl EH33 .....128 A1
Circle The EH22 ....156 A4
Circus Gdns EH3 ....232 B4
Circus La EH3 ....93 A1
Circus Pl EH3 ....232 B4
Citadel Pl EH6 ....93 C3
Citadel St EH6 ....93 C3
Citron Glebe 7 KY1 ......17 B3
City Hospl EH14 ....153 C4
City Obsy* EH7 ....233 B4
City Of Edinburgh By-Pass The
Dalkeith EH18, EH22 ......156 B2
Edinburgh EH10 ....154 B2
Whitecraig EH21 ....126 A1
Clackmae Gr EH16 ......154 C4
Clackmae Rd EH16 ......154 C4
Clackmannan Coll of F Ed
FK10 ....10 A4
Clackmannan Prim Sch
FK10 ....11 A2
Clackmannan Rd FK10 ...10 B3
Clackmannan Twr*
FK10 ....10 C2
Clanranald Pl FK1 ....59 C1
Clare Ct EH39 ....54 A4
Clarebank Cres EH6 ......94 A2
Claremont FK10 ....9 C4
Claremont Bank EH7 .....93 B2
Claremont Cres EH7 ......93 B2
Claremont Ct EH7 ....93 B2
Claremont Dr FK9 ....2 B4
Claremont Gdns EH6 .....94 B2
Claremont Gr EH7 ....93 B2
Claremont Ind Est FK10 ..10 A3
Claremont Pk EH6 ....94 A2
Claremont Prim Sch FK10 ..9 C4
Claremont Rd EH6 ....94 A2
Claremont St FK4 ....57 C3
Clarence St EH3 ....93 A1
Clarendon Cres
Edinburgh EH4 ....232 A4
Linlithgow EH49 ....85 A3
Clarendon Pl FK8 ....7 A4
Clarendon Rd
Linlithgow EH49 ....85 A3
Stirling FK8 ....7 A4
Claret Rd
Grangemouth, Bowhouse
FK3 ....61 C3
Grangemouth, Oil Refinery
FK3 ....62 B4
Clarinda Ave FK1 ....59 A3
Clarinda Gdns EH22 .....157 B2
Clarinda Pl FK5 ....38 B2
Clarinda Terr EH16 ......124 A1
Clark Ave Edinburgh EH5 ...93 B3
Linlithgow EH49 ....84 C4
Clark Bldgs EH35 ....159 C4
Clark Pl Edinburgh EH5 ....93 A3
Kirkcaldy KY2 ....17 A3
Clark Rd Edinburgh EH5 ....93 A3
Inverkeithing KY11 ....47 A1
Clark St FK7 ....7 A1
Clarkson Rd EH52 ....117 B3
Claverhouse Dr EH16 ....155 A4
Clay Acres Ct KY12 ....29 A3
Claycrofts Pl FK7 ....7 A3
Clayhills Gr EH14 ....151 A1
Clayhills Pk EH14 ....151 A1
Clayknowes Ave EH21 ...126 A3
Clayknowes Cres EH21 ..126 A3
Clayknowes Ct EH21 ....126 A2
Clayknowes Dr EH21 ....125 C3
Clayknowes Pl 2 EH21 ..126 A3
Clayknowes Way EH21 ..126 A3
Claymore Dr FK7 ....7 B2
Clearburn Cres EH16 ....124 A2
Clearburn Gdns EH16 ...124 A2
Clearburn Rd
Edinburgh EH16 ....124 A2
Gorebridge EH23 ....183 A1
Cleaves The FK10 ....4 A1
Cleekim Dr EH15 ....125 A2
Cleekim Rd EH15 ....125 A2
Cleghorn Dr EH52 ....117 A3
Cleikiminrig EH15 ....125 A2
Cleish Gdns KY2 ....16 C3
Cleish Pl KY11 ....29 C1
Cleish Rd KY11 ....29 C1
Cleland St EH47 ....170 A4
Clement Rise EH54 ......148 A1
Clerics Hill EH29 ....89 A1
Clerk Gr KY11 ....29 C1
Clerk Rd EH26 ....203 B3
Clerk St Edinburgh EH8 ...233 B1
Loanhead EH20 ....181 B4
Clerkington Rd EH41 ....131 C4
Clerkington Wlk EH41 ...131 C4
Clermiston Ave EH4 ......91 B1
Clermiston Cres EH4 .....91 C1
Clermiston Dr EH4 ....91 B1
Clermiston Gdns EH4 .....91 B1
Clermiston Gn EH4 ....91 B1
Clermiston Gr EH4 ....91 B1
Clermiston Hill EH4 ....91 C1
Clermiston Loan EH4 .....91 B1
Clermiston Medway EH4 ..91 B1
Clermiston Pk EH4 ....91 B1
Clermiston Pl EH4 ....91 B1
Clermiston Prim Sch
EH4 ....91 B1
Clermiston Rd EH12 .....121 C4
Clermiston Rd N EH4 ......91 C1
Clermiston View EH4 ......91 C1
Clerwood Bank EH12 ....121 B4
Clerwood Gdns EH12 ....121 B4
Clerwood Gr EH12 ....121 C4
Clerwood Loan EH12 ....121 B4
Clerwood Pk EH12 ....121 B4
Clerwood Pl EH12 ....121 C4
Clerwood Row EH12 .....121 B4
Clerwood Terr EH12 .....121 C4
Clerwood View EH12 ....121 C4
Clerwood Way EH12 .....121 B4
Cleuch Ave FK10 ....4 A1
Cleuch Dr FK12 ....4 C4
Cleuch Rd
North Middleton EH23 ....207 C1
Stirling FK9 ....2 B2
Cleuchbrae EH55 ....172 B2
Cleveland Dr KY11 ....47 A1
Clifford Rd
North Berwick EH39 ....54 B3
Stirling FK8 ....7 A3
Clifton Hall Sch EH28 ....118 B1
Clifton Rd EH28 ....118 C1
Clifton Trad Est EH28 ....118 C2
Clifton View EH52 ....118 A3
Cliftonhall Rd EH28 ......119 A3
Climpy Rd ML11 ....214 B2
Clinkum Bank KY12 ....26 B2
Clinton Rd EH9 ....123 A2
Clive St ML7 ....191 C3
Cloanden Pl KY2 ....17 A2
Clockluine Rd KY11 ....47 C3
Clockmill La EH7,EH8 ......94 A1
Close The KY11 ....46 B1
Clova Dr EH54 ....173 C3
Clovenstone Dr EH14 ....152 C4
Clovenstone Gdns EH14 .152 C4
Clovenstone Pk EH14 ....152 C4
Clovenstone Prim Sch
EH14 ....152 C4
Clovenstone Rd EH14 ....152 C4
Clover Pl EH51 ....63 C3
Cloverbank EH54 ....147 C3
Cloverstone Rdbt EH14 ..152 C4
Cloves The FK11 ....4 A3
Cluanie Ave ML7 ....191 C3
Clufflat EH30 ....67 C1
Clufflat Brae EH30 ....67 C1
Clune Rd KY12 ....27 C4
Clunie Rd KY11 ....29 C2
Clunivar St KY12 ....28 B3
Cluny Ave EH10 ....123 A1
Cluny Dr Edinburgh EH10 .123 A1
Stenhousemuir FK5 ....38 C2
Cluny Gdns EH10 ....123 B1
Cluny Pl EH10 ....123 B2
Cluny Terr EH10 ....123 A1
Clyde Cres
Dunfermline KY11 ....29 C1
Larbert FK5 ....38 A2
Clyde Dr Livingston EH54 .148 A2
Shotts ML7 ....192 A2
Clyde St Falkirk FK1 ....59 C3
Grangemouth FK3 ....40 A1
Clydesdale St EH51 ....63 C3
Clydevale Pl EH54 ....117 A1
Co-Operative Bldgs
EH33 ....128 B3
Coal Neuk EH33 ....128 B3
Coal Neuk Ct EH33 ....128 B3
Coal Rd KY12 ....28 C2
Coal Wynd Bannockburn FK7 .7 B1
Kirkcaldy KY1 ....17 B2
Coalgate FK10 ....10 A3
Coalgate Ave EH33 ....128 C4
Coalgate Rd EH33 ....128 B4
Coalhill EH6 ....93 C3
Coalpots Way FK10 ....5 C2
Coastguard Cotts TD13 ..140 C2
Coates Cotts EH32 ....99 C2
Coates Cres EH3 ....232 A3
Coates Gdns EH12 ....122 C4
Coatfield La EH6 ....94 A3
Cobblebrae Cres FK2 ......39 A1
Cobden Cres EH9 ....123 C2
Cobden Rd EH9 ....123 C2
Cobden St FK12 ....5 A3
Cobden Terr EH11 ....232 A2
Coblecrook Gdns FK12 .....4 C3
Coblecrook La FK12 ....4 C3
Coblecrook Pl FK12 ....4 C3
Coburg St EH6 ....93 C3
Cochran Pl EH7 ....93 B1
Cochran Terr EH7 ....93 B1
Cochrane Ave Falkirk FK2 .60 A2
Inverkeithing KY11 ....47 B1
Cochrane Cres FK12 ....4 C4
Cochrane Pl EH6 ....94 A2
Cochrane Rd KY11 ....46 A1
Cochrane Sq EH54 ....173 B3
Cochrane St
Bathgate EH48 ....145 A4
Falkirk FK1 ....60 A2
Cochrane Way KY11 ....48 A3
Cochrane Wlk KY11 ....29 C2
Cochranes The FK12 ....5 A4
Cochrie Pl FK10 ....4 B1
Cochrina Pl EH24 ....181 B1
Cockburn Cres
Balerno EH14 ....177 A4
Whitecross EH49 ....84 A3
Cockburn Ct EH35 ....159 C4
Cockburn Dr EH35 ....159 B3
Cockburn Sq EH37 ....185 A3
Cockburn St
Edinburgh EH1 ....233 A3
Falkirk FK1 ....60 A2
Cockburnhill Rd EH14 ...177 A4
Cockburnspath Prim Sch
TD13 ....140 C2
Cockenzie Prim Sch
EH32 ....97 B2
Cocklaw St KY4 ....12 B4
Cockles Brae EH41 ....132 C2
Cockmilane Brae EH41 ...132 B3
Cockmylane EH13, EH10 .153 C4
Cockpen Ave EH19 ....182 A3
Cockpen Cres EH19 ....182 A3
Cockpen Dr EH19 ....182 A3
Cockpen Pl EH19 ....182 A3
Cockpen Rd EH19 ....182 B3
Cockpen Terr EH19 ....182 A3
Cockpen View EH19 ......182 A3
Coillesdene Ave EH15 ....125 B4
Coillesdene Cres EH15 ...125 B4
Coillesdene Dr EH15 .....125 B4
Coillesdene Gdns EH15 ..125 B4
Coillesdene Gr EH15 .....125 B4
Coillesdene Loan EH15 ..125 C4
Coillesdene Terr EH15 ...125 B4
Coire Loan ML7 ....192 A2
Coldingham Pl KY12 ....29 B2
Colegate Rd EH37 ....208 B4
Coles Pl KY4 ....31 A3
Colinshiel Ave EH48 ......144 C4
Colinshiel St EH48 ....144 C4
Colinshiel View EH48 ....143 C4
Colinswell Rd KY3 ....33 B1
Colinton Gr EH14 ....122 B1
Colinton Gr W EH14 ......122 B1
Colinton Mains Cres
EH13 ....153 C3
Colinton Mains Dr EH13 .153 B4
Colinton Mains Gdns
EH13 ....153 B4
Colinton Mains Gn
EH13 ....153 B4
Colinton Mains Gr EH13 .153 C4
Colinton Mains Loan
EH13 ....153 B4
Colinton Mains Pl EH13 .153 C4
Colinton Mains Rd
EH13 ....153 B3
Colinton Mains Terr
EH13 ....153 C4
Colinton Prim Sch EH13 .153 B4
Colinton Rd EH10,EH14 ..122 C2
Coll Pl FK3 ....61 B3
College Cres FK2 ....60 B4
College Rdbt EH54 ....147 B1
College Wynd EH1 ....233 A2
Colliers Rd FK7 ....8 B2
Colliery Cres EH22 ....183 A2
Colliery View EH22 ....183 A2
Collingwood Ct FK1 ....59 C3
Collins Cres KY11 ....47 C1
Collins Pl EH3 ....93 A1
Colliston Rd KY12 ....29 B3
Collyland Rd FK10 ....5 B2
Colmestone Gate EH10 ..154 A3
Colonsay Ave FK2 ....61 B1
Colonsay Terr FK1 ....60 A1
Colquhoun St FK7 ....7 B3
Colquhoun Terr FK7 ....7 B3
Colsnaur FK11 ....4 A3
Colstoun Mains Cotts
EH41 ....132 C2
Coltbridge Ave EH12 .....122 B4
Coltbridge Gdns EH12 ...122 C4
Coltbridge Millside
EH12 ....122 C4
Coltbridge Terr EH12 ....122 B4
Coltbridge Vale EH12 ....122 C4
Coltness Ave ML7 ....212 A4
Colton Ct KY12 ....28 C2
Columba Ave EH4 ....92 A1
Columba Rd EH4 ....92 A1
Columbia Ave EH54 ....147 C2
Colville Gdns 1 FK10 ......10 A3
Colvin St EH42 ....78 C1
Combfoot Cotts EH53 ....148 B2
Comely Bank Ave EH4 ......93 A1
Comely Bank Gr EH4 ....92 C1
Comely Bank Pl EH4 ....93 A1
Comely Bank Place Mews 2
EH4 ....93 A1
Comely Bank Rd EH4 ......92 C1
Comely Bank Row EH4 .....93 A1
Comely Bank St EH4 ....92 C1
Comely Bank Terr 1
EH4 ....93 A1
Comely Green Cres 10
EH7 ....94 A1
Comely Green Pl 9 EH7 ..94 A1
Comely Park La KY12 ....29 A2
Comely Park Prim Sch
FK1 ....60 A2
Comely Park Terr 15 FK1 .60 A2
Comely Pk Brightons FK2 ..82 C4
Dunfermline KY12 ....29 A2
Comely Pl FK1 ....60 A2
Comely Terr FK2 ....82 C4
Comiston Dr EH10 ....123 A1
Comiston Gdns EH10 ....123 A1
Comiston Gr EH10 ....154 A4
Comiston Pl EH10 ....123 A1
Comiston Prim Sch
EH13 ....153 C3
Comiston Rd EH10 ....154 A4
Comiston Rise EH10 .....154 A4
Comiston Springs Ave
EH10 ....154 A4
Comiston Terr EH10 .....123 A1
Comiston View EH10 .....154 A4
Commercial Prim Sch
KY11 ....29 B2
Commercial Rd KY11 ......47 B1
Commercial School La
KY12 ....29 A2
Commercial St
Edinburgh EH6 ....93 C3
Kirkcaldy KY1 ....17 B3
Commissioner St EH51 ....64 A4
Commodores Wlk KY11 ...46 B1
Compass Sch The EH41 .131 C4
Compressor House Rd
FK3 ....62 B3
Compton Rd FK3 ....61 B3
Comrie Terr EH51 ....63 C3
Comyn Dr FK2 ....82 B4
Concorde Way KY11 ....47 B2
Coney Pk FK7 ....6 C3
Coneyhill Rd FK9 ....2 A4
Conference Sq EH3 ....232 B2
Conifer Rd EH22 ....183 C4
Coningsby Pl FK10 ....10 A3
Connaught Pl EH6 ....93 B3
Conner Ave FK2 ....60 A4
Conroy Ct FK6 ....36 C1
Considine Gdns 3 EH8 ....94 B1
Considine Terr 2 EH8 .....94 B1
Constable Rd FK7 ....7 A3
Constitution Pl EH6 ....94 A3
Constitution St EH6 ....94 A3
Conway Ct FK1 ....59 C2
Cook Cres EH22 ....183 B3
Cook Pl KY1 ....18 A4
Cook Sq KY5 ....14 A4
Cook St KY1 ....18 A4
Cooper's Cl EH8 ....233 B3
Cooper's La FK10 ....23 C2
Cooperage La FK1,FK2 ....60 A3
Cooperage Quay FK8 ....7 B4
Cooperage Way FK10 ....10 B4
Cope La EH32 ....97 B2
Copeland Cres KY4 ....13 A1
Copland Pl FK12 ....4 C4
Copper Beech Wynd
KY12 ....27 B1
Corbett Pl KY11 ....29 C1
Corbiehall EH51 ....63 C4
Corbiehill Ave EH4 ....92 A2
Corbiehill Cres EH4 ....91 C2
Corbiehill Gdns EH4 ....92 A2
Corbiehill Gr EH4 ....92 A2
Corbiehill Pk EH4 ....92 A2
Corbiehill Pl EH4 ....91 C2
Corbiehill Terr EH4 ....91 C2
Corbieshot EH15 ....125 A3
Corbiewood Dr FK7 ....19 C4
Corbiewynd EH15 ....125 A3
Cordiner's Land EH1 ....232 C2
Corentin Ct FK1 ....60 B2
Cormailin Pl KY12 ....26 A1
Corn Exchange Rd FK8 .....7 A4
Cornbank-St James' Prim
Sch EH26 ....203 B3
Cornfield Pl EH54 ....147 A2
Cornhill Cres FK7 ....7 A2
Cornhill Terr EH6 ....94 A2
Cornton Bsns Pk FK9 ....2 A2
Cornton Cres FK9 ....2 A3
Cornton Prim Sch FK9 ......2 A2
Cornton Rd FK9 ....2 A2
Cornton Vale Cotts FK9 ....2 A2
Cornwall St EH1 ....232 B2
Cornwallis Pl EH3 ....93 B1
Corona Cres FK4 ....57 C3
Coronation Pl
Easthouses EH22 ....183 B4
Skinflats FK2 ....39 C2
Tranent EH33 ....128 B3
Corpach Dr KY12 ....28 C1
Corporation St FK1 ....60 B2
Corrennie Dr EH10 ....123 A1
Corrennie Gdns EH10 ....123 A1
Corrie Ave FK5 ....38 C2
Corrie Ct EH22 ....183 A2
Corrie Pl FK1 ....59 B2
Corruna Ct ML8 ....230 A1
Corslet Cres EH14 ....152 A3
Corslet Pl EH14 ....152 A3
Corslet Rd EH14 ....152 A3
Corston Pk EH54 ....148 A2
Corstorphine Bank Ave
EH12 ....121 B4
Corstorphine Bank Dr
EH12 ....121 B4
Corstorphine Bank Terr
EH12 ....121 B4
Corstorphine High St
EH12 ....121 B3
Corstorphine Hill Ave
EH12 ....121 C4
Corstorphine Hill Cres
EH12 ....121 C4
Corstorphine Hill Gdns
EH12 ....121 C4
Corstorphine Hill Rd
EH12 ....121 C4
Corstorphine Hopl
EH12 ....121 C3
Corstorphine House Ave
EH12 ....121 C3
Corstorphine Park Gdns
EH12 ....121 C3
Corstorphine Prim Sch
EH12 ....121 B3
Corstorphine Rd EH12 ...122 A4
Cortachy Ave FK2 ....39 A2
Cortleferry Dr EH22 ......156 C1
Cortleferry Gr EH22 ......156 C1
Cortleferry Pk 1 EH22 ...156 C1
Cortleferry Terr 2
EH22 ....156 C1
Corunna Pl EH6 ....93 C3
Corunna Terr EH26 ....204 A4
Cossars Wynd EH42 ....78 B1
Costkea Way EH20 ....181 A4
Cotburn Cres KY3 ....33 C1
Cotlands Ave EH32 ....98 B2
Cotlands Pk EH32 ....98 B2
Cotlaws EH29 ....89 A1
Cottage Cres FK1 ....59 C3
Cottage Gn EH4 ....91 A2
Cottage Homes EH13 ....153 A4
Cottage La EH21 ....126 C3
Cottage Pk EH4 ....92 A1
Cotton La FK2 ....61 A2
Cotts The EH49 ....86 C2
Coulport Pl KY12 ....28 C1
Council Hos EH39 ....101 C4
Council Houses EH41 ....162 C4
Countess Ave EH42 ....78 B1
Countess Cres EH42 ....78 B1
Countess Rd EH42 ....78 B1
County Hos KY4 ....31 A3
County Hospl FK10 ....10 A4
County Rd EH32 ....96 C1
County Sq EH32 ....96 C1
Couper Ave EH39 ....54 B3
Couper Gr KY11 ....29 C1
Couper St EH6 ....93 C3
Couperfield EH6 ....93 C3
Court St EH41 ....132 A4
Courthill FK12 ....5 A4
Cousin's La 7 KY12 ....28 C2
Cousland Cres EH47 .....146 A1
Cousland Intc EH54 ......147 C3
Cousland Prim Sch
EH22 ....158 B3
Cousland Rd EH54 ....147 B2
Cousland Terr EH47 ......146 A1
Couston Dr KY11 ....48 A2
Couston Pl KY11 ....48 A2
Couston Rd KY11 ....48 A2
Couston St KY12 ....29 A2
Cove Cres ML7 ....191 C3
Covenanter Rd ML7 ....168 B2
Covenanters La EH30 .....68 A1
Covenanters Rise KY11 ...46 C3
Coville Pl EH3 ....93 A1
Cow Wynd FK1 ....60 A2
Cowan Rd EH11 ....122 C2
Cowan St Bathgate EH48 .145 C3
Bonnybridge FK4 ....58 A3
Cowan Terr EH26 ....203 C4
Cowan's Cl EH8 ....233 B1
Cowane St FK8 ....7 A4
Cowden Cres EH22 ......157 B2
Cowden Gr EH22 ....157 B2
Cowden La EH22 ....157 B2
Cowden Pk EH22 ....157 B2
Cowden Terr EH22 ....157 B2
Cowden View EH22 ......157 B2
Cowdenbeath Prim Sch
KY4 ....13 B2
Cowdenbeath Rd KY3 .....33 C1
Cowdenbeath Sta KY4 ....13 B2
Cowdenhill Rd EH51 ....64 A4
Cowgate EH1 ....233 A2
Cowgatehead EH1 ....233 A2
Cowie Prim Sch FK7 ....20 B4
Cowie Rd Bannockburn FK7 ..7 C1
Cowie FK7 ....20 A4
Cowiehall Rd FK7 ....20 B4
Cowpits Ford Rd EH21 ..126 B2
Cowpits Rd EH21 ....126 B1
Coxfield EH11 ....122 B2
Coxithill Rd FK7 ....7 A2
Cragganmore FK10 ....4 A1
Craig Ave
Haddington EH41 ....101 A1
Whitburn EH47 ....169 C3
Craig Cres FK9 ....2 B2
Craig Ct Bridge of A FK9 ....2 A3
Burntisland KY3 ....33 B1
Craig Leith Rd FK7 ....7 B3
Craig St Blackridge EH48 .142 C2
Rosyth KY11 ....47 A2
Craigallan Pk EH51 ....64 A4
Craigbank Alloa FK10 ....5 B1
Crossford KY12 ....28 B1
Craigbank Prim Sch FK10 ..5 B1
Craigbank Rd FK1 ....112 A3
Craigbeath Ct KY4 ....13 A3
Craigburn Ct FK1 ....59 C1
Craigcrook Ave EH4 ....92 A1
Craigcrook Gdns EH4 ......92 A1
Craigcrook Gr EH4 ....92 A1
Craigcrook Pk EH4 ....92 A1
Craigcrook Pl 6 EH4 ....92 B1
Craigcrook Rd
Edinburgh EH4 ....91 C2
Edinburgh EH4 ....92 A1
Craigcrook Sq EH4 ....92 A1
Craigcrook Terr 5 EH4 ...92 B1
Craigdimas Gr KY11 ....48 A1
Craigearn Ave KY2 ....16 A4
Craigearn Pl KY2 ....16 B4
Craigencalt Farm* KY3 ....34 B2
Craigend Dr FK2 ....83 A3
Craigend Pk EH16 ....124 B1
Craigend Rd FK7 ....7 A2
Craigengar Ave EH52 .....117 A2

Craigentinny Ave EH7 ....94 C1
Craigentinny Ave N EH6 ..94 B2
Craigentinny Cres EH7 ....94 C1
Craigentinny Gr EH7 ......94 C1
Craigentinny Gr EH7 ......94 C1
Craigentinny Prim Sch
EH7 ....94 B1
Craigentinny Rd EH7 ......94 B1
Craigflower Ct KY12 ......26 C1
Craigflower Rd KY12 ......26 C1
Craigford Dr FK7 ....7 B1
Craigforth Cres FK8 ....1 C1
Craighall Ave EH6 ....93 B3
Craighall Bank EH6 ....93 B3
Craighall Cres EH6 ....93 B3
Craighall Gdns EH6 ....93 B3
Craighall Rd EH6 ....93 B3
Craighall St FK8 ....1 C1
Craighall Terr
Edinburgh EH6 ....93 B3
Musselburgh EH21 ....126 C3
Craighill Gdns EH10 ......122 C1
Craighill View EH48 ....142 C2
Craigholm La KY3 ....33 C1
Craighorn FK11 ....4 A3
Craighorn Dr FK1 ....59 C1
Craighorn Rd FK12 ....4 C3
Craighouse Ave EH10 .....122 C1
Craighouse Gdns EH10 ....122 C1
Craighouse Pk EH10 ......122 C1
Craighouse Rd EH10 ......122 C1
Craighouse Terr EH10 ....122 C1
Craigie Ct FK5 ....38 A1
Craigiebield Cres EH23 ...203 C2
Craigielaw Farm Cotts
EH32 ....71 A2
Craigielaw Pk EH32 ....71 A2
Craigievar Ave FK2 ....39 A2
Craigievar Gdns KY2 ......16 C3
Craigievar Sq EH12 ......121 A4
Craigievar Wynd EH12 ...121 A4
Craiginn Ct EH48 ....142 B2
Craiginn Terr EH48 ....142 B2
Craigkennochie Terr
KY3 ....33 C1
Craiglaw EH52 ....116 B1
Craiglea Ct EH48 ....142 B2
Craiglea Dr EH10 ....123 A1
Craiglea Pl EH10 ....122 C1
Craigleith FK10 ....5 C2
Craigleith Ave Falkirk FK1 .59 C1
North Berwick EH39 ......54 B3
Craigleith Ave S EH4 ....122 B4
Craigleith Ave S EH4 .....92 B1
Craigleith Cres EH4 ....92 B1
Craigleith Dr EH4 ....92 B1
Craigleith Gdns EH4 ......92 B1
Craigleith Gr EH4 ....92 B1
Craigleith Hill EH4 ....92 B1
Craigleith Hill Ave EH4 ...92 B1
Craigleith Hill Cres EH4 ..92 B1
Craigleith Hill Gdns EH4 ..92 B1
Craigleith Hill Gn EH4 ....92 B1
Craigleith Hill Gr EH4 .....92 B1
Craigleith Hill Loan EH4 ..92 B1
Craigleith Hill Row EH4 ...92 B1
Craigleith Rd
Edinburgh EH4 ....92 C1
Grangemouth FK3 ....61 B3
Craigleith Ret Pk EH4 ....92 B2
Craigleith Rise EH4 ......122 B4
Craigleith View
Edinburgh EH4 ....122 B4
 North Berwick EH39 .....54 A4
Craiglockhart Ave EH14 ..122 B1
Craiglockhart Bank
EH14 ....122 B1
Craiglockhart Cres
EH14 ....122 B1
Craiglockhart Dell Rd
EH14 ....122 B1
Craiglockhart Dr N
EH14 ....122 B1
Craiglockhart Dr S
EH14 ....122 B1
Craiglockhart Gdns
EH14 ....122 B1
Craiglockhart Gr EH14 ...153 B4
Craiglockhart Loan
EH14 ....122 B1
Craiglockhart Pk EH14 ...122 B1
Craiglockhart Pl EH14 ...122 B1
Craiglockhart Prim Sch
EH11 ....122 C2
Craiglockhart Quadrant
EH14 ....122 B1
Craiglockhart Rd EH14 ...122 B1
Craiglockhart Rd N
EH14 ....122 B1
Craiglockhart Sports Ctr
EH14 ....122 C2
Craiglockhart Terr
EH14 ....122 C2
Craiglockhart View
EH14 ....122 B1
Craigluscar Ct KY12 ......28 A4
Craigluscar Rd KY12 ......28 A4
Craigmillar* EH16 ....124 B1
Craigmillar Castle Ave
EH16 ....124 C2
Craigmillar Castle Gdns
EH16 ....124 B2

Craigmillar Castle Gr
EH16 ....124 B2
Craigmillar Castle Loan
EH16 ....124 C2
Craigmillar Castle Rd
EH16 ....124 B1
Craigmillar Castle Terr
EH16 ....124 B1
Craigmillar Pk EH16 .....124 A2
Craigmillar Pl FK5 ....38 C2
Craigmillar Prim Sch
EH16 ....124 A2
Craigmore Gdns KY12 ....26 C1
Craigmount KY2 ....16 B4
Craigmount App EH12 ...121 B4
Craigmount Ave EH12 ...121 B4
Craigmount Ave N EH4,
EH12 ....91 A1
Craigmount Bank EH4 ....91 A1
Craigmount Bank W EH4 ..91 A1
Craigmount Brae EH12 ...91 A1
Craigmount Cres EH12 ..121 A4
Craigmount Ct EH4 ....91 A1
Craigmount Dr EH12 .....121 A4
Craigmount Gdns EH12 ..121 A4
Craigmount Gr EH12 .....121 A4
Craigmount Gr N EH12 ...121 A4
Craigmount Hill EH4 ......91 A1
Craigmount Loan EH12 ..121 A4
Craigmount Pk EH12 .....121 B4
Craigmount Pl EH12 .....121 B4
Craigmount Sec Sch
EH12 ....121 A4
Craigmount Terr EH12 ...121 A4
Craigmount View EH12 ..121 A4
Craigmount Way EH12 ....91 B1
Craigmyle Pl EH4 ....92 A4
Craigmyle St KY12 ....29 B3
Craigomus Cres FK11 .....3 C1
Craigour Ave EH17 ....155 B4
Craigour Cres EH17 .....155 C4
Craigour Dr EH17 ....155 C4
Craigour Gdns EH17 .....155 C4
Craigour Gn EH17 ....155 B4
Craigour Gr EH17 ....155 C4
Craigour Loan EH17 .....155 C4
Craigour Pl EH17 ....155 C4
Craigour Terr EH17 ......155 C4
Craigpark EH48 ....113 C3
Craigpark Cres EH18 ....219 B1
Craigridge PI KY11 ....48 B3
Craigrie Rd FK10 ....10 C2
Craigrie Terr FK10 ....10 C2
Craigrigg Cotts EH48 ....112 C2
Craigrigg Terr EH48 .....112 C2
Craigroyston Com High Sch
EH4 ....92 A2
Craigroyston Gdns EH4 ..92 A2
Craigroyston Pl EH4 ......92 A3
Craigs Ave EH12 ....113 C3
Craigs Bank EH12 ....121 A4
Craigs Ct EH48 ....121 A4
Craigs Gr EH12 ....121 B4
Craigs Loan EH12 ....121 B4
Craigs Pk EH12 ....121 A4
Craigs Rd EH12 ....121 A4
Craigs Rdbt FK7 ....7 B4
Craigs Terr EH12 ....82 C4
Craigseaton EH52 ....117 A3
Craigshill E EH54 ....148 A3
Craigshill Rd EH54 ......148 A3
Craigshill S EH54 ....148 A3
Craigshill W Rd EH54 ....148 A3
Craigston Dr KY3 ....29 B3
Craigston Pk KY12 ....29 B3
Craigswood EH54 ....148 A3
Craigton Cres FK12 ....4 C3
Craigton Ct EH52 ....87 C1
Craigview EH21 ....13 B1
Craigview Alloa FK10 .....5 B1
Bo'ness EH51 ....64 B4
Craigward FK10 ....10 A3
Craigwell Path KY12 ......44 B4
Crame Terr EH22 ....156 C1
Cramond Bank EH4 ....91 B3
Cramond Bridge Cotts
EH4 ....90 C2
Cramond Brig Toll EH4 ...90 C2
Cramond Cres EH4 ....91 A3
Cramond Ct FK1 ....60 A1
Cramond Gdns
Edinburgh EH4 ....91 A3
Kirkcaldy KY2 ....16 C4
Cramond Glebe Gdns
EH4 ....91 B3
Cramond Glebe Rd EH4 ..91 B3
Cramond Glebe Terr EH4 .91 A3
Cramond Gn EH4 ....91 A3
Cramond Gr EH4 ....91 A3
Cramond Pl
Dalgety Bay KY11 ....48 B2
Edinburgh EH4 ....91 A3
Cramond Prim Sch EH4 ..91 A3
Cramond Prim Sch (Annexe)
EH4 ....91 A3
Cramond Rd N EH4 ......91 A3
Cramond Regis EH4 ......91 A2

Cramond Roman Fort*
EH4 ....91 B3
Cramond Terr EH4 ....91 A3
Cramond Vale EH4 ....91 A3
Cramond Village EH4 ....91 A4
Cranshaws Dr FK2 ....61 B1
Cranston Dr EH22 ....158 B3
Cranston Prim Sch
EH37 ....184 C3
Cranston St
Edinburgh EH8 ....233 B3
Penicuik EH26 ....203 C3
Crarae Ave EH4 ....122 B4
Crathes Ave FK5 ....39 A2
Crathes Gdns EH54 ......173 C3
Crathie Dr FK6 ....36 B2
Craufurdland EH4 ....91 A2
Crawfield Ave EH51 ....63 B3
Crawfield La EH51 ....63 C3
Crawfield Rd EH51 ....63 C2
Crawford Dr FK2 ....82 A4
Crawford Pl KY12 ....29 B4
Crawford Sq FK2 ....22 B2
Crawford Rd EH16 ....124 A2
Crawlees Cres EH22 .....156 C1
Craws Knowe ML11 ......215 A1
Creel Ct EH39 ....54 B4
Creran Dr FK6 ....57 B3
Crescent The
Edinburgh EH10 ....123 A1
Gowkshall EH23 ....183 B2
Rosyth KY11 ....46 A1
Creteil Ct FK1 ....60 B2
Creteil Pl FK1 ....61 B4
Crewe Bank EH5 ....92 C3
Crewe Cres EH5 ....92 B3
Crewe Gr EH5 ....92 C3
Crewe Loan EH5 ....92 B3
Crewe Pl EH5 ....92 B3
Crewe Rd N EH5 ....92 B3
Crewe Rd S EH4 ....92 C2
Crewe Rd W EH5 ....92 C3
Crewe Road Gdns EH5 ...92 B3
Crewe Terr EH5 ....92 C3
Crewe Toll EH4 ....92 B2
Crichton Ave EH37 ......185 A3
Crichton Castle* EH37 ..208 C4
Crichton Dr
Grangemouth FK3 ....61 C4
Pathhead EH37 ....185 A3
Crichton Rd EH37 ....185 A3
Crichton St EH8 ....233 A2
Crichton Terr EH37 ......185 A3
Cricket Pl FK2 ....61 B1
Crighton Pl EH6 ....93 C2
Crimond Pl FK1 ....60 A1
Cringate Gdns FK7 ....7 A2
Crockers Hedges EH41 ..102 B2
Crockett Gdns EH26 .....203 B3
Croft An Righ KY3 ....35 A2
Crofters Gate EH47 ......170 C4
Crofters Way EH47 ......170 C3
Croftfoot Dr EH47 ......194 A3
Croftfoot Pl FK6 ....36 B2
Crofthead Ct FK8 ....2 A1
Crofthead Ctr EH54 .....173 B4
Crofthead Intc EH54 ....173 C4
Crofthead Rd Stirling FK8 .2 A1
Stoneyburn EH47 ....181 A4
Croftmalloch Prim Sch
EH47 ....170 A3
Croftmalloch Rd EH47 ..170 A3
Crofts Rd TD13 ....140 C1
Crofts The EH47 ....104 C1
Croftsacre TD13 ....140 C1
Croftshaw Rd FK12 ....5 A4
Croftside Ct FK13 ....11 A2
Cromar Dr KY12 ....47 B4
Cromarty Pl KY11 ....17 C4
Crombie Prim Sch KY12 ..44 B4
Cromwell Anchorage
EH42 ....78 C2
Cromwell Ct FK1 ....60 B2
Cromwell Pl EH6 ....93 C3
Cromwell Quay EH42 .....78 C2
Cromwell Rd
Burntisland KY3 ....33 C1
Falkirk FK1 ....60 B2
North Berwick EH39 .....54 A4
Rosyth KY11 ....46 C3
Cromwell Rd W FK1 ......60 B2
Cronin Dr EH21 ....126 C2
Crookston Rd EH21 .....126 C2
Crophill FK10 ....4 B1
Crosbies Ct FK8 ....7 A4
Cross Brae FK1 ....81 B3
Cross Cotts EH32 ....97 A1
Cross Loan EH35 ....159 C4
Cross Row KY11 ....45 A2
Cross St Dysart KY1 ......18 A4
Falkirk FK2 ....61 B1
Cross The Linlithgow EH49 .85 A4
Lochgelly KY5 ....14 A3
Cross Way KY11 ....48 B3
Cross Wynd KY12 ....29 A2
Crossen La ML8 ....230 A1
Crossford Prim Sch EH28 .28 A1
Crossgatehead Rd FK2 ...82 B4
Crossgates Prim Sch
KY4 ....30 C3
Crossgreen Dr EH52 ....117 A3
Crossgreen Pl EH52 ....117 A3

Crosshill Dr
Bathgate EH48 ....145 B3
Bo'ness EH51 ....63 C3
Crossroads KY11 ....30 A3
Crossroads EH51 ....30 A3
Crossroads Pl KY11 ......46 C2
Crosswood Ave EH14 ...177 A4
Crosswood Cres EH14 ...177 A4
Crosswood Terr EH55 ...217 C2
Crowhill Rd KY11 ....48 B2
Crown Ct EH33 ....128 B3
Crown Gdns FK10 ....9 C4
Crown Pl EH6 ....93 C2
Crown St EH6 ....93 C2
Crownest Loan FK5 ....38 C1
Cruachan Ave FK9 ....2 A2
Cruachan Ct Falkirk FK1 ..60 B1
Penicuik EH26 ....204 A3
Cruachan Pl FK3 ....61 C3
Cruckburn Wynd FK7 .....6 C2
Cruden Rd EH12 ....62 B3
Cruickness Rd KY11 ......68 B4
Cruickshank Dr FK2 ......62 B3
Cruikshank's Ct FK6 .....36 C1
Crum Cres FK7 ....7 B1
Crusader Dr EH25 ....180 C2
Crusader Rise EH54 .....148 C4
Cuddies La EH13 ....153 A4
Cuddy La EH10 ....123 A2
Cuddyhouse Rd KY4,KY12 .12 B2
Cuffabouts EH51 ....64 B4
Cuguen Pl EH18 ....156 A1
Cuiken Ave EH26 ....203 C3
Cuiken Bank EH26 ......203 B3
Cuiken Terr EH26 ....203 B3
Cuiken Terr EH26 ....203 C3
Cuikenburn EH26 ....203 C4
Cuil Gr KY12 ....30 B3
Cuillin Ct FK1 ....60 B1
Cuillin Pl FK1 ....61 C3
Culduie Circ FK2 ....62 A1
Culfargie St FK2 ....59 A1
Cullaloe Ct KY11 ....49 B4
Cullaloe Nature Reserve*
KY3 ....32 A2
Cullalo View KY4 ....13 B1
Cullen Cres KY2 ....16 C4
Cullen Sq EH54 ....166 B3
Culloch Rd FK4 ....110 A3
Culmore Pl FK1 ....60 C1
Culross Abbey* KY12 ....25 B3
Culross Prim Sch KY12 ..25 A4
Cultenhove Cres
Grangemouth FK3 ....61 C3
Stirling FK7 ....7 A2
Cultenhove Pl FK7 ....7 A2
Cultenhove Rd FK7 ....6 C2
Cultins Rd EH11 ....121 A2
Cultrig Dr EH47 ....170 A3
Cultsykefoot EH47 ......169 C3
Culvain Pl FK1 ....60 B1
Culzean Cres KY2 ....16 B4
Culzean Pl FK5 ....38 C2
Cumberland St EH3 .....93 A1
Cumbernauld Rd FK4 ....57 A2
Cumbrae Ct KY2 ....17 A4
Cumbrae Dr FK1 ....59 B2
Cumbrae Terr KY2 ....17 A4
Cumin Pl EH9 ....123 C2
Cumlodden Ave EH12 ...122 B4
Cumnor Cres EH16 .....124 A1
Cunnigar Gdns EH53 ...148 B2
Cunnigar Hill View
EH53 ....148 B2
Cunningham Cres EH52 .117 B3
Cunningham Ct
Longniddry EH32 ....98 B2
North Berwick EH39 .....54 A3
Cunningham Dr ML7 ....168 B3
Cunningham Gdns FK2 ...60 C3
Cunningham Rd
Rosyth KY11 ....46 B1
Stenhousemuir FK5 ......39 A2
Stirling FK7 ....7 B4
Cunningham St FK2 ......61 B3
Curlew Brae EH54 ....147 B3
Curlew Gdns KY11 ....30 A1
Curling Knowe KY4 ......30 C2
Curling Pk KY4 ....30 C2
Curling Pond La EH47 ...170 A1
Curran Cres EH52 ....117 C3
Currie High Sch EH14 ...151 C2
Currievale Dr EH14 .....151 C2
Currievale Dr S
EH14 ....152 A2
Currierhill Prim Sch
EH14 ....152 A2
Currierhill Rd EH14 .....151 C3
Currievale Farm EH14 ...151 C3
Currievale Park Gr
EH14 ....151 C2
Currievale Pl EH14 ......151 C2
Cushenquarter Dr FK2 ...83 A4
Custom House Sq EH42 ..78 C2
Custonhall Pl FK6 ....36 B1
Cuthill EH32 ....96 B1
Cuthill Cres EH47 ....171 B1
Cuthill Terr EH47 ....171 B1
Cuttyfield Pl FK2 ....39 B2
Cypress Glade EH54 ....173 B4
Cypress Gr KY11 ....46 B4

D

D'arcy Cres EH22 ....183 C4
D'arcy Rd EH22 ....183 C4
D'arcy Terr EH22 ....183 C4
Daiches Braes EH15 .....125 B3
Dairy Cotts EH39 ....53 A1
Daisy Terr EH11 ....122 C2
Daisyhill Ct EH47 ....171 B4
Daisyhill Rd EH47 ......171 B4
Dalbeath Cres KY4 ....13 A1
Dalbeath Gdns KY4 ......12 C1
Dalbeath Way KY12 .....29 C3
Dalderse Ave FK2 ....60 A3
Dalgety Ave EH7 ....94 A1
Dalgety Bay Prim Sch
KY11 ....48 A2
Dalgety Bay Sports & L Ctr*
KY11 ....48 A2
Dalgety Bay Sta KY11 ...47 C3
Dalgety Gdns KY11 ......48 B3
Dalgety House View
KY11 ....48 B3
Dalgety Rd EH7 ....94 A1
Dalgety St EH7 ....94 A1
Dalgleish Ct FK8 ....2 B3
Dalgrain Rd FK3 ....40 A1
Dalhousie Ave EH19 ....182 A3
Dalhousie Ave W EH19 ..182 A3
Dalhousie Cres EH22 ...156 C1
Dalhousie Dr EH19 .....182 A3
Dalhousie Gdns EH19 ...182 A3
Dalhousie Pl EH19 ......182 A3
Dalhousie Rd EH22 .....156 C1
Dalhousie Rd E EH19 ...182 A3
Dalhousie Rd W EH19 ..182 A3
Dalhousie Terr EH10 ...123 A1
Dalkeith Country Pk*
EH22 ....157 A3
Dalkeith Rd EH16 ....157 A2
Dalkeith Rd EH16 ....233 C1
Dalkeith St EH15 ....125 B4
Dallas Ave KY3 ....33 C1
Dallas Dr KY2 ....16 C4
Dalling Ave EH48 ....144 C3
Dalling Rd EH48 ....144 C3
Dalmahoy Cres EH14 ...151 B2
Dalmahoy Rd EH28 .....119 B1
Dalmeny Ho* EH30 ......69 B1
Dalmeny Prim Sch EH30 .89 C4
Dalmeny Rd EH6 ....93 B3
Dalmeny St EH6 ....94 A2
Dalmeny Sta EH30 ......89 B4
Dalmore Dr FK12 ....4 C3
Dalmorglen Pk FK7 ....6 C1
Dalratho Rd FK3 ....61 C4
Dalry Pl EH11 ....232 A2
Dalry Prim Sch EH11 ...122 C3
Dalry Rd EH11 ....122 C4
Dalrymple Cres
Edinburgh EH9 ....123 C2
Musselburgh EH21 ......126 A3
Dalrymple Gdns EH22 ...158 B3
Dalrymple Loan EH21 ...126 B3
Dalton Ct EH22 ....183 C3
Dalum Ct EH20 ....181 A4
Dalum Dr EH20 ....181 A4
Dalum Gr EH20 ....181 A4
Dalum Loan EH20 ....181 A4
Daly Gdns KY12 ....25 C1
Dalziel Ct EH47 ....170 A1
Dalziel Pl EH7 ....94 A1
Damhead Holdings Scheme
Bilston EH10 ....180 B4
Edinburgh EH10 ....154 B1
Damside EH4 ....232 A3
Danderhall Cres EH22 ...156 A4
Danderhall Prim Sch
EH22 ....156 A4
Dania Ct EH11 ....121 C2
Danube St EH4 ....232 A4
Dargai Pl EH22 ....117 A3
Darian La EH51 ....63 C4
Darmeid Pl ML7 ....212 A4
Darnaway St EH3 ....232 B4
Darnell Rd EH5 ....93 A3
Darney Terr KY3 ....34 C1
Darnley St FK8 ....7 A4
Darrach Dr FK2 ....36 A1
Darroch Ct EH8 ....233 B3
Darwin St EH54 ....148 A3
Davaar Dr KY2 ....16 C4
Davaar Pl FK1 ....59 B2
Davenport Pl KY11 ......46 C2
David Henderson Ct
KY12 ....29 A2
David Millar Pl KY12 ...28 C3
David Scott Ave EH22 ..183 C4
David St Dunfermline KY12 .29 A3
Kirkcaldy KY1 ....17 A2
David The First St KY3 ...34 C1
David's Loan FK2 ....39 B1
Davidson Gdns EH4 .....92 A2
Davidson La ML8 ....230 A1
Davidson Pl EH4 ....100 C1
Davidson Rd EH4 ....92 C2
Davidson St EH7 ....7 B1
Davidson Terr EH41 ....100 C1
Davidson Way EH45 ....147 C4
Davidson's Mains Prim Sch
EH4 ....92 C2
Davie St EH8 ....233 B2
Davies Row Denny FK6 ...36 C1

Davies Row continued
Edinburgh EH12 ....**121** B3
Daviot Rd KY12 ....**29** C3
Dawson Ave Alloa FK10 ....**9** C4
Livingston EH54 ....**147** C3
Dawson Pl EH51 ....**63** C3
Dawson St FK2 ....**60** A4
De Quincey Path EH18 ...**181** C3
De Quincey Rd EH18 .....**181** C3
Deacons Ct EH49 ....**85** C3
Dean Acres KY12 ....**26** B4
Dean Bank La EH3 ....**93** A1
Dean Cres FK8 ....**2** B1
Dean Ct EH32 ....**98** B2
Dean Dr KY12 ....**28** A1
Dean East Rd EH54 ....**146** C4
Dean Gallery* EH12 ....**122** C4
Dean Gr KY12 ....**28** A1
Dean Park Cres EH4 ......**232** A4
Dean Park Mews EH4 .....**93** A1
Dean Park Prim Sch
EH14 ....**177** B4
Dean Path EH4 ....**92** C1
Dean Pk Gowkhall KY12 ...**27** C4
Longniddry EH32 ....**98** B2
Newtongrange EH22 ....**183** A3
Dean Pk EH22 ....**183** A3
Dean Pk St EH4 ....**93** A1
Dean Rd Penicuik EH26 ...**203** B3
Seafield EH47 ....**146** A1
Dean Rd Bo'ness EH51 .....**63** C3
Kirkcaldy KY2 ....**17** A2
Longniddry EH32 ....**98** B2
Penicuik EH26 ....**203** B3
Dean Ridge KY12 ....**27** C4
Dean St Edinburgh EH4 ....**93** A1
Whitburn EH47 ....**170** A3
Dean Terr EH4 ....**232** A4
Dean The EH40 ....**75** C1
Deanbank Pl EH23 ....**207** B4
Deanburn EH49 ....**84** C3
Deanburn Gdns EH47 .....**146** A1
Deanburn Pk EH51 ....**63** B3
Deanburn Pk EH49 ....**84** C3
Deanburn Prim Sch
EH51 ....**63** B3
Deanburn Rd EH49 ....**84** C3
Deanburn Wlk EH51 ....**63** B3
Deanery Cl FH7 ....**94** B1
Deanfield Cres EH51 ....**63** C4
Deanfield Dr EH51 ....**63** C4
Deanfield Pl EH51 ....**63** C4
Deanfield Rd EH51 ....**63** B3
Deanfield Terr EH51 ....**63** B3
Deangate Gdns EH51 ......**63** B3
Deanhaugh St EH4 ....**93** A1
Deanpark Ave EH14 ....**151** B1
Deanpark Bank EH14 ......**151** B1
Deanpark Brae EH14 ......**151** B1
Deanpark Cres EH14 ......**151** B1
Deanpark Ct EH14 ....**151** B1
Deanpark Gdns EH14 ......**151** B1
Deanpark Gr EH14 ....**151** B1
Deanpark Pl EH14 ....**151** B1
Deans Com High Sch
EH54 ....**147** A4
Deans Ind Est EH54 ......**146** B3
Deans North Rd
Livingston, Deans EH54 ...**146** C3
Livingston, Nether Dechmont
EH54 ....**147** A3
Deans Prim Sch EH54 ....**146** B3
Deans Rd EH54 ....**146** B3
Deans S EH54 ....**146** C3
Deans Service Units
EH54 ....**116** B1
Deanswood Pk EH54 ......**146** C3
Deantown Ave EH21 ......**157** C4
Deantown Dr EH21 ....**126** C1
Deantown Path EH21 .....**126** C1
Deas Rd
Inverkeithing KY11 ....**47** A1
Shotts ML7 ....**191** B3
Dechmont Inf Sch EH52 ..**116** A1
Dechmont Rd EH52 ....**116** A1
Dechmont Rdbt EH52 ....**116** B1
Dedridge East Ind Est
EH54 ....
Dedridge East Rd EH54 ...**148** A1
Dedridge North Rd
EH54 ....**147** C1
Dedridge Prim Sch
EH54 ....
Dedridge West Rd EH54 ..**173** C4
Dee Dr EH54 ....**148** A3
Dee Pl KY11 ....**29** C1
Dee St ML7 ....**191** B3
Deep Sea World Sealife Ctr*
KY11 ....**68** B3
Deer Park Bsns Campus
EH54 ....**116** B1
Deer Park Dr EH54 ....**116** B1
Deer Park Rd
Abercorn EH30 ....**66** C1
Dechmont EH54 ....**116** B1
Deer Path ML7 ....**168** C3
Deer Pk KY10 ....**1** C1
Deerhill EH52 ....**116** B4
Deerpark Prim Sch FK10 ...**5** C1
Deeside Dr ML8 ....**230** A2
Delisle St EH42 ....**78** B1
Dell Ave EH48 ....**143** C3
Dell Rd EH13 ....**153** A4
Delph Rd KY10 ....**4** B1
Delphwood Cres FK10 .....**4** B1
Delta Ave EH21 ....**127** A3
Delta Cres EH21 ....**127** A3

Delta Dr EH21 ....**127** A3
Delta Gdns EH21 ....**127** A3
Delta Pl EH21 ....**126** B2
Delta Rd EH21 ....**127** A3
Delta View EH21 ....**127** A3
Dempster Pl KY12 ....**28** C3
Den La ML7 ....**191** B3
Den Rd KY2,KY1 ....**17** B3
Dorset Pl EH11 ....**123** A3
Denburn Rd KY1 ....**17** B4
Denend Cres KY2 ....**17** A3
Denham Green Ave EH5 ...**93** A4
Denham Green Pl EH5 .....**93** A3
Denham Green Terr EH5 ...**93** A3
Denholm Ave EH21 ....**125** C2
Denholm Dr EH21 ....**126** A2
Denholm Gr EH48 ....**143** C4
Denholm Rd EH21 ....**125** C3
Denholm Way EH21 ....**125** C3
Denny High Sch FK6 ....**57** C4
Denny Prim Sch FK6 ....**36** B1
Denny Rd Denny FK4, FK6 ..**57** C3
Larbert FK5 ....**38** A1
Denovan Rd FK6 ....**36** C2
Dequincey Wlk EH33 ......**128** B3
Derby St EH6 ....**93** B3
Deroran Pl FK8 ....**6** C3
Derwent Ave FK1 ....**59** C2
Devon Ct FK10 ....**4** A1
Devon Dr FK10 ....**4** A2
Devon Pl Cambus FK10 .....**4** A1
Edinburgh EH12 ....**122** C4
Devon Rd FK10 ....**10** B3
Devon St FK3 ....**40** A1
Devon Terr KY11 ....**29** C1
Devon Village FK10 ....**5** C2
Devonbank FK10 ....**5** C2
Devonway FK10 ....**10** C3
Dewar Ave FK10 ....**23** C2
Dewar Pl EH3 ....**232** A2
Dewar Place La EH3 ......**232** A2
Dewar St EH54 ....**146** B3
Dewar St
Dunfermline KY12 ....**28** C2
Lochgelly KY5 ....**14** A4
Dewshill Cotts ML7 ....**167** A2
Dick Cres KY3 ....**33** C1
Dick Gdns EH47 ....**169** C3
Dick Pl Edinburgh EH9 ....**123** B2
Rosyth KY11 ....**46** C3
Stoneyburn EH47 ....**171** B1
Dick St KY12 ....**29** B3
Dick Terr EH26 ....**203** C3
Dickburn Cres FK4 ....**57** C3
Dickies Wells FK12 ....**5** B4
Dickson Ct
Dunfermline KY12 ....**29** A1
Lochgelly KY5 ....**14** A4
Dickson Dr EH19 ....**182** A4
Dickson St
Dunfermline KY12 ....**29** A1
Edinburgh EH6 ....**93** C2
West Calder EH55 ....**172** B1
Dicksonfield EH7 ....**93** C1
Dinmont Dr EH16 ....**124** A1
Dirleton Ave EH39 ....**54** A4
Dirleton Castle* EH39 .....**53** A2
Dirleton Gdns FK10 ....**9** C4
Dirleton La FK10 ....**9** C4
Dirleton Prim Sch EH39 ...**53** A2
Dirleton Rd Dirleton EH39 ..**53** A3
North Berwick EH39 ....**53** C3
Distillery La EH11 ....**122** C4
Diverswell FK10 ....**5** B1
Dixon Terr EH47 ....**170** A3
Dobbie Ave FK5 ....**38** B1
Dobbie's Rd EH19 ....**182** A4
Dobson's Pl EH41 ....**131** C4
Dobson's View EH41 ......**131** C4
Dobson's Wlk EH41 ....**131** C4
Dochart Cres FK2 ....**61** C1
Dochart Dr EH4 ....**91** B1
Dochart Path FK3 ....**61** B3
Dochart Pl FK1 ....**60** B1
Dock Pl EH6 ....**93** C3
Dock Rd FK3 ....**40** B3
Dock St Bo'ness EH51 ......**63** C3
Edinburgh EH6 ....**93** C3
Falkirk FK2 ....**39** B1
Doctor's Row KY1 ....**17** C4
Dog Well Wynd EH49 ......**85** A4
Dollar Ave FK2 ....**60** A4
Dollar Cres KY2 ....**16** B4
Dollar Ct KY12 ....**28** C3
Dollar Gdns KY2 ....**16** B4
Dollar Gr KY3 ....**33** C3
Dollar Ind Est FK1,FK2 ....**60** A3
Dollar Rd KY3 ....**33** C3
Dolphin Ave EH14 ....**151** C2
Dolphin Gdns E EH14 ....**151** C2
Dolphin Gdns W EH14 ....**151** C2
Dolphin Rd EH14 ....**151** C2
Don Dr EH54 ....**148** A3
Don Rd KY11 ....**29** C1
Don St FK3 ....**40** A1
Donald St KY12 ....**29** A2
Donaldson Ave FK10 ....**4** C1
Donaldson Ct FK10 ....**23** C2
Donaldson Pl FK10 ....**4** C1
Donaldson's Sch for the Deaf
Edinburgh, Coates EH12 ..**122** C4
Edinburgh, Stockbridge EH4 ..**93** A1
Donibristle Gdns KY11 .....**48** A2
Donibristle Ind Pk KY11 ...**48** A2
Donibristle Prim Sch
KY11 ....**48** A1
Doo Dells La KY3 ....**34** C1
Doo'cot Brae FK10 ....**10** A4

Doocot Brae EH51 ....**64** A4
Doocot Pl EH32 ....**128** A4
Doon Ave EH42 ....**78** B1
Doon Wlk EH54 ....**148** A2
Dora Ct KY4 ....**13** B3
Dornie Wynd ML7 ....**192** A2
Dorrator Ct FK1 ....**59** C3
Dorrator Rd FK1 ....**59** C3
Dorset Pl EH11 ....**123** A3
Double Dykes EH21 ......**126** B2
Double Hedges Pk
EH16 ....**124** A1
Double Hedges Rd
EH16 ....**124** A1
Double Row KY11 ....**45** A2
Dougall Ct EH22 ....**183** B3
Dougall Pl EH22 ....**183** B3
Dougall Rd EH22 ....**183** B3
Douglas Ave
Brightons FK2 ....**82** B4
Grangemouth FK3 ....**61** C3
Linlithgow EH49 ....**84** C3
Douglas Cres
Bonnyrigg & Lasswade
EH19 ....**182** A4
Edinburgh EH12 ....**122** C4
Longniddry EH32 ....**98** C3
Douglas Dr Bo'ness EH51 ...**63** C3
Crossford KY12 ....**28** A1
Dunfermline KY12 ....**29** C1
Stirling FK7 ....**7** B2
Douglas Gardens Mews
EH4 ....**122** C4
Douglas Gdns EH4 ....**122** C4
Douglas Pk KY12 ....**29** C1
Douglas Pl Bo'ness EH51 ...**63** C3
Linlithgow EH49 ....**84** C3
Stenhousemuir FK5 ....**38** C2
Douglas Rd Bo'ness EH51 ...**63** C3
Longniddry EH32 ....**98** C3
Rosyth KY11 ....**46** B1
Douglas Sq EH48 ....**143** C3
Douglas St
Bannockburn FK7 ....**7** C1
Dunfermline KY12 ....**29** A2
Kirkcaldy KY1 ....**17** A3
Stirling FK8 ....**2** A1
Douglas Terr
Bo'ness EH51 ....**63** C3
Edinburgh EH11 ....**232** A2
Falkirk FK1 ....**59** C1
Douglas Wynd FK2 ....**117** A3
Doune Cres EH54 ....**39** A2
Doune Pk KY11 ....**48** B2
Doune Terr EH3 ....**232** B4
Dovecot Ct EH14 ....**122** A1
Dovecot Cres KY1 ....**18** A4
Dovecot Gr EH14 ....**122** A1
Dovecot Loan EH14 ....**122** A1
Dovecot Pk Aberdour KY3 ...**49** A3
Edinburgh EH14 ....**122** A1
Linlithgow EH49 ....**85** B4
Pencaitland EH34 ....**160** C3
Dovecot Pl Rosyth KY11 ...**47** A4
Tullibody FK10 ....**4** A2
Dovecot Rd
Edinburgh EH12 ....**121** B3
Tullibody FK10 ....**4** A2
Westquarter FK2 ....**61** A1
Dovecot Way
Pencaitland EH34 ....**160** C4
Rosyth KY11 ....**46** C4
Dovecot Wynd KY11 ....**46** C4
Dovecote Pl EH54 ....**147** B2
Dovehill FK10 ....**10** A4
Dover Dr EH54 ....**147** A4
Dover Hts KY11 ....**47** A4
Dover Pk KY11 ....**47** A4
Dowan Pl FK7 ....**6** B3
Dower Cres EH51 ....**64** A4
Dower Pl FK2 ....**22** B2
Dowie's Mill Cotts EH4 ...**90** C2
Dowie's Mill La EH4 ....**90** C2
Downfield KY4 ....**13** B3
Downfield Pl EH11 ....**122** C3
Downie Gr EH12 ....**121** C3
Downie La EH12 ....**126** B3
Downie Terr EH12 ....**121** C3
Downing Ct EH25 ....**181** A2
Downing Point KY11 ......**48** A1
Downs Cres FK10 ....**9** B2
Dr Campbell Ave FK7 ......**20** B4
Dreghorn Ave EH13 ....**153** C3
Dreghorn Dr EH13 ....**153** C3
Dreghorn Gdns EH13 .....**153** C3
Dreghorn Gr EH13 ....**153** C3
Dreghorn Junc EH10 .....**153** C3
Dreghorn Link EH10,
EH13 ....**153** C3
Dreghorn Loan EH13 .....**153** A3
Dreghorn Pk EH13 ....**153** B3
Dreghorn Pl EH13 ....**153** C3
Drem Farm Cotts EH39 ...**73** A2
Drem Sta EH39 ....**73** A2
Drip Rd FK8,FK9 ....**1** C1
Dronachy Rd KY2 ....**16** C2
Drossie Rd FK1 ....**60** A2
Drove Loan FK4,FK6 ....**57** C4
Drove Loan Cres FK6 ......**57** C4
Drove Rd EH48 ....**143** C4
Droverhall Ave KY4 ....**31** A3
Droverhall Pl KY4 ....**31** A3
Drovers Rd EH52 ....**145** B3
Drum Ave EH17 ....**155** C3
Drum Brae Ave EH12 .....**121** B4
Drum Brae Cres EH4 ......**91** B1
Drum Brae Dr EH4 ....**91** B1
Drum Brae Gdns EH12 ...**121** B4

Drum Brae Gr EH4 ....**91** B1
Drum Brae L Ctr* EH4 ......**91** B1
Drum Brae N EH4 ....**91** A1
Drum Brae Neuk EH12 ...**121** B4
Drum Brae Park App
EH12 ....**121** B4
Drum Brae Pk EH12 ......**121** B4
Drum Brae Pl EH12 ....**121** B4
Drum Brae S EH12 ....**121** B4
Drum Brae Terr EH4 ....**91** B1
Drum Brae Wlk EH4 ....**91** A1
Drum Cotts EH17 ....**155** C3
Drum Farm La EH51 ....**64** B3
Drum Pl
East Whitburn EH47 ....**170** C4
Edinburgh EH17 ....**155** C3
Drum Rd Bo'ness EH51 ......**64** B3
Dunfermline KY11 ....**29** C1
Drum St EH17 ....**155** C3
Drum Terr EH7 ....**94** A1
Drum View Ave EH22 .....**156** A4
Drumacre Rd EH51 ....**64** A3
Drumbowie Prim Sch
FK1 ....**82** B1
Drumbrae Prim Sch
EH4 ....**121** B4
Drumclair Ave FK1 ....**110** A3
Drumcross Rd EH48 ......**145** A4
Drumdryan St EH3 ....**232** B1
Drumlanrig Pl FK5 ....**38** C2
Drummohr Ave EH21 .....**127** A3
Drummohr Gdns EH21 ...**127** A3
Drummond Com High Sch
EH7 ....**93** B1
Drummond La FK2 ....**60** A4
Drummond Pk FK3 ....**61** C3
Drummond Pl
Blackridge EH48 ....**142** B2
Bonnybridge FK4 ....**58** A4
Dunfermline KY12 ....**29** B3
Edinburgh EH3 ....**93** B1
Falkirk FK1 ....**59** C1
Grangemouth FK3 ....**61** C4
Stirling FK8 ....**7** A3
Drummond Place La FK8 ...**7** A3
Drummond Sq
Livingston EH54 ....**173** B3
Lochgelly KY5 ....**14** A4
Drummond St EH8 ....**233** B2
Drummore Dr EH32 ......**127** C4
Drummormie Rd KY12 ....**27** B1
Drumpark Ave EH51 ....**64** A3
Drumpark St FK7 ....**7** A2
West Barns EH42 ....**77** C1
Duke's Wlk EH8 ....**94** A1
Dumbarton Rd
Cambusbarron FK8 ....**6** C1
Stirling FK8 ....**7** A4
Dumbeg Pk EH14 ....**152** B4
Dumbiedykes Rd EH8 ....**233** C2
Dumbryden Dr EH14 .....**121** C1
Dumbryden Gdns EH14 ..**121** C1
Dumbryden Ind Est
EH14 ....**121** C2
Dumbryden Prim Sch
EH14 ....**121** C1
Dumbryden Rd EH14 .....**121** C1
Dumyat Ave FK10 ....**4** A1
Dumyat Dr FK1 ....**59** C2
Dumyat Rd Alva FK12 ......**4** C3
Menstrie FK11 ....**3** C3
Stirling FK9 ....**2** B2
Dumyat Rise FK10 ....**4** C1
Dumyat St FK10 ....**4** C1
Dunard Gdn EH10 ....**123** B2
Dunbar Ave FK5 ....**38** C2
Dunbar Gate FK6 ....**36** C2
Dunbar Gram Sch EH42 ...**78** A1
Dunbar Pl KY12 ....**16** C3
Dunbar Prim Sch EH42 ....**78** B1
Dunbar Rd
Haddington EH41 ....**101** A1
North Berwick EH39 ....**54** C3
Dunbar St EH3 ....**232** B1
Dunbar Sta EH42 ....**78** B3
Dunbar Town House Mus*
EH42 ....**78** B1
Duncairn Ave FK4 ....**57** C3
Duncan Ave FK2 ....**39** A2
Duncan Cres KY11 ....**29** C1
Duncan Ct EH39 ....**54** A3
Duncan Gdns EH33 ......**128** B4
Duncan La EH54 ....**147** A4
Duncan Pl EH6 ....**94** A2
Duncan St
Bonnybridge FK4 ....**57** C3
Edinburgh EH9 ....**123** C2
Kirkcaldy KY2 ....**17** A2
Duncanson Ave FK10 ......**10** A4
Duncanson Dr KY3 ....**34** A1
Duncarron Ind Est FK6 ....**36** C1
Duncarron Pl FK6 ....**36** C1
Duncur Rd EH31 ....**52** B2
Dundaff Ct FK6 ....**36** B2
Dundarroch St FK1 ....**38** A1
Dundas Ave
North Berwick EH39 ....**54** B3
Queensferry EH30 ....**89** B4
Dundas Cotts KY4 ....**57** A1
Dundas Cres
Clackmannan FK10 ....**11** A2
Dalkeith EH22 ....**156** C1
Laurieston FK2 ....**61** A2
Dundas Gdns EH22 ......**183** A1
Dundas Pk EH19 ....**182** B4

Duddingston Loan
EH15 ....**124** C3
Duddingston Mains Cotts
EH15 ....**125** A3
Duddingston Mills EH8 ...**124** C4
Duddingston Park S
EH15 ....**125** A3
Duddingston Pk EH15 ....**125** A4
Duddingston Prim Sch
EH15 ....
Duddingston Rd EH15 ....**124** C4
Duddingston Rd W
EH15 ....**124** C3
Duddingston Rise EH15 ...**124** C3
Duddingston Row EH15 ...**124** C3
Duddingston Sq E EH15 ..**124** C4
Duddingston Sq W
EH15 ....**124** C3
Duddingston View
EH15 ....**124** C3
Duddingston Yds EH15 ...**125** A3
Duddingston Terr EH52 ...**88** A4
Duddington Gdns N
EH15 ....**124** C4
Dudgeon Pl EH29 ....**89** A1
Dudley Ave EH6 ....**93** B3
Dudley Ave S EH6 ....**93** C3
Dudley Bank EH6 ....**93** B3
Dudley Cres EH6 ....**93** B3
Dudley Gdns EH6 ....**93** B3
Dudley Gr EH6 ....**93** B3
Dudley Terr EH6 ....**93** B3
Duff Cres FK8 ....**1** C1
Duff Ct EH39 ....**54** A4
Duff Rd EH11 ....**122** C3
Duff St EH11 ....**122** C3
Duff Street La EH11 ......**122** C3
Duffy Pl KY11 ....**46** C2
Dugald Stewart Ave
EH51 ....**64** A4
Duglas Rise EH54 ....**148** A1
Duke Pl EH6 ....**94** A2
Duke St Alva FK12 ....**5** A4
Bannockburn FK7 ....**7** B1
Clackmannan FK10 ....**11** A2
Dalkeith EH22 ....**157** A2
Denny FK6 ....**36** B2
Dunbar EH42 ....**78** A1
Edinburgh EH6 ....**94** A2
Grangemouth FK3 ....**61** C4
Rosewell EH24 ....**181** B1
West Barns EH42 ....**77** C1
Duke's Wlk EH8 ....**94** A1

Dundas Pl EH29 .... 89 A1
Dundas Rd Dalkeith EH22 .156 C1
  Laurieston EH32 .... 61 A2
  North Berwick EH39 .... 54 B3
  Rosyth KY11 .... 67 B4
  Stirling FK9 .... 2 A2
Dundas St Bathgate EH48 .145 A4
  Bo'ness EH51 .... 63 C4
  Bonnyrigg & Lasswade
  EH19 .... 182 B4
  Edinburgh EH3 .... 93 B1
  Grangemouth FK3 .... 61 A4
  Lochgelly KY5 .... 14 A4
  Townhill KY12 .... 29 B4
Dundee Ct FK2 .... 60 A4
Dundee Pl FK2 .... 60 A4
Dundee St EH11 .... 232 A1
Dundee Terr EH11 .... 122 C3
Dundonald Rd KY11 .... 46 B2
Dundonald St EH3 .... 93 B1
Dundrennan Cotts EH16 .124 B1
Dunearn Bank KY3 .... 33 B1
Dunearn Dr KY2 .... 16 C3
Dunearn Prim Sch KY2 .... 16 C3
Dunedin St EH7 .... 93 B2
Dunfermline Abbey*
  KY12 .... 28 C2
Dunfermline Bsns Ctr
  KY11 .... 29 A1
Dunfermline Bsns Pk
  KY11 .... 29 A1
Dunfermline High Sch
  KY11 .... 29 A1
Dunfermline Mus* KY12 .. 29 A1
Dunfermline Queen Margaret
  Sta KY12 .... 29 C3
Dunfermline Rd
  Crossgates KY4 .... 30 C3
  Limekilns KY11 .... 45 C2
Dunfermline Town Sta
  KY12 .... 29 A2
Dunfermline Wynd KY11 .47 A1
Dungavel La ML8 .... 230 A1
Dunglass Church*
  TD13 .... 140 B2
Dunimarle St KY12 .... 26 A1
Dunipace Cres KY12 .... 29 C3
Dunipace Prim Sch FK6 .. 36 B2
Dunkeld Pl FK2 .... 39 B1
Dunlin Brae EH54 .... 147 B3
Dunlin Dr KY11 .... 30 A2
Dunlop Ct EH54 .... 146 B3
Dunlop Sq EH54 .... 146 B3
Dunlop Terr EH26 .... 204 A3
Dunmar Cres FK10 .... 4 C1
Dunmar Dr FK10 .... 4 C1
Dunn Cres KY11 .... 29 C2
Dunn Pl EH52 .... 87 C1
Dunn St EH52 .... 117 A3
Dunn Terr ML7 .... 168 C3
Dunnet Way EH52 .... 118 A3
Dunnikier Prim Sch KY2 . 17 A3
Dunnikier Way KY11 ...... 17 B3
Dunning Pl FK2 .... 39 B1
Dunnottar Dr FK5 .... 38 C2
Dunnottar Pl KY2 .... 16 C2
Dunollie Ct EH12 .... 121 A4
Dunollie Gdns EH41 ...... 132 B4
Dunpender Dr EH41 .... 100 C1
Dunpender Rd EH40 .... 103 B4
Dunrobin Ave FK5 .... 38 C3
Dunrobin Pl EH3 .... 93 A1
Dunrobin Rd KY2 .... 16 C2
Dunrobin Rd FK1 .... 163 C3
Dunsire St KY1 .... 17 C4
Dunsmuir Ct EH12 .... 121 B3
Dunster Rd FK9 .... 2 B2
Dunure Cres EH54 .... 58 A3
Dunure Pl KY2 .... 16 C2
Dunure St FK4 .... 58 A3
Dunvegan Ave
  Kirkcaldy KY2 .... 16 B3
  Stenhousemuir FK5 .... 38 C2
Dunvegan Ct Alloa FK10 .10 A3
  Crossford KY12 .... 28 A1
  Edinburgh EH4 .... 91 A2
Dunvegan Dr Falkirk FK2 . 39 B1
  Stirling FK9 .... 2 B2
Dunvegan Gdns EH54 ...173 C3
Dunvegan Pl
  Bonnybridge FK4 .... 57 C3
  Polmont FK2 .... 62 A1
Dura Dr ML2,ML7 .... 212 B3
Dura Dr EH4 .... 91 B1
Durham Ave
  Bathgate EH48 .... 144 C3
  Edinburgh EH15 .... 124 C4
Durham Dr
  Bathgate EH48 .... 144 C3
  Edinburgh EH15 .... 125 A3
Durham Gardens N
  EH15 .... 125 A4
Durham Gardens S
  EH15 .... 125 A3
Durham Gr
  Bonnyrigg & Lasswade
  EH19 .... 182 B3
  Edinburgh EH15 .... 125 A4
Durham Pl EH19 .... 182 B3
Durham Pl W EH15 .... 124 C4
Durham Place E EH15 .... 125 A4
Durham Place La EH15 ..125 A4
Durham Rd EH15 .... 125 A4

Durham Road S EH15 ....125 A3
Durham Sq EH15 .... 125 A4
Durham Terr
  Edinburgh EH15 .... 124 C4
  Newmills KY12 .... 26 B1
Durie Pk KY11 .... 50 B4
Durie Pl KY11 .... 29 C2
Durie's Pk EH33 .... 128 A1
Durward Rise EH54 ...... 148 A1
Durward Gr EH16 .... 124 B1
Dyfrig St ML7 .... 191 C3
Dyke Brow ML7 .... 169 A3
Dyke Ct ML7 .... 169 A3
Dyke Rd ML7 .... 169 A3
Dykehead Prim Sch
  ML7 .... 191 C3
Dykes Rd EH26 .... 203 C4
Dykeside Rd EH48 .... 144 C4
Dymond Gr KY1 .... 16 A4
Dynamic Earth Exhibition*
  EH8 .... 233 C3
Dysart Prim Sch KY1 ...18 A4
Dysart Rd KY1 .... 17 C3

E

Eagle Brae EH54 .... 147 B2
Eagle Rock* EH4 .... 91 A4
Earl Grey St EH3 .... 232 B2
Earl Haig Gdns EH5 ...... 93 A3
Earl Of Mar Ct FK10 ..... 10 A3
Earl's Gate Rdbt FK3 .... 61 A4
Earl's Rd FK3 .... 61 A4
Earls Ct FK10 .... 10 A3
Earls Pl EH47 .... 193 C3
Earlsburn Ave FK7 .... 7 A2
Earlshill Dr FK7 .... 7 C1
Earlston Pl 6 EH7 .... 94 A1
Earn Ct Alloa FK10 ...... 10 B3
  Grangemouth FK3 .... 61 B3
Earn Gr KY11 .... 29 C2
Earn Pl FK6 .... 57 B3
Earn Rd KY1 .... 17 B4
Earn Terr ML7 .... 191 C3
East Adam St EH8 .... 233 B2
East Albert Rd KY1 .... 17 B3
East Ave KY12 .... 26 A4
East Baldridge Dr KY12 .28 C3
East Bankton Pl EH54 ...173 C4
East Barnton Ave EH4 ... 91 C2
East Barnton Gdns EH4 .. 91 C2
East Bay KY11 .... 68 B3
East Boreland Pl FK6 ... 36 C1
East Bridge St FK1 .... 60 B2
East Brighton Cres
  EH15 .... 125 A4
East Broomhill Rd KY3 .. 50 C4
East Caiystane Pl EH10 .154 A3
East Caiystane Rd EH10 .154 A3
East Calder Prim Sch
  EH53 .... 144 B1
East Campbell Ct EH32 ..98 B3
East Camus Pl EH10 ..... 154 A3
East Camus Rd EH10 .....154 A3
East Castle Rd EH10 .....123 A3
East Castle St FK10 ...... 10 A3
East Champanyie EH9 ...123 C2
East Clapperfield EH16 .124 A1
East Claremont St EH7 .. 93 B2
East Comiston EH10 ......154 A3
East Craigs Prim Sch
  EH12 .... 121 A4
East Craigs Rigg EH12 ..121 A4
East Croft EH28 .... 119 C1
East Cromwell St EH6 .... 93 C3
East Crosscauseway
  EH8 .... 233 B1
East Ct
  Edinburgh, Greendykes
  EH16 .... 124 C2
  3 Edinburgh, Ravelston
  EH4 .... 92 B1
East Dr Dunfermline KY12 .29 A2
  Stenhousemuir FK5 .... 38 B1
East End EH55 .... 172 B2
East End Park (Dunfermline
  Athletic FC) KY12 ...... 29 A2
East Farm Of Gilmerton
  EH17 .... 155 C3
East Fenton Farm Cotts
  EH39 .... 73 B4
East Fergus Pl KY1 .... 17 A2
East Fettes Ave EH4 ..... 92 C2
East Fountainbridge
  EH3 .... 232 B2
East Garleton Cotts
  EH39 .... 100 C3
East Glen Ave EH54 ......146 C3
East Harbour Rd KY11 ... 45 A2
East Hermitage Pl EH6 .. 94 A2
East Kilngate Pl EH17 ...155 B3
East Kilngate Rigg
  EH17 .... 155 B3
East Kilngate Wynd
  EH17 .... 155 B3
East Leven St KY3 .... 50 C4
East Lillypot EH5 .... 93 A3
East Link Rd FK9 .... 2 B3
East Links Family Pk*
  EH42 .... 77 B1
East Links Rd
  Dunbar EH42 .... 78 C1
  Gullane EH31 .... 52 A1
East Linton Prim Sch
  EH40 .... 103 C4
East Linton Station Ind Site
  EH40 .... 103 C4

East Loan EH32 .... 97 A1
East London St EH7 ...... 93 B1
East Lorimer Pl EH32 .... 97 B2
East Main St
  Armadale EH48 .... 144 A3
  Blackburn EH47 .... 171 B4
  Broxburn EH52 .... 117 C3
  Harthill ML7 .... 168 C3
  Uphall EH52 .... 117 A2
  Whitburn EH47 .... 170 A4
East Mains FK11 .... 4 A3
East Mains Ind Est
  EH52 .... 118 A3
East March St KY1 .... 17 C3
East Market St EH8 ...... 233 B3
East Mayfield EH9 .... 123 C2
East Mill Rd EH47 .... 84 B4
East Montgomery Pl 4
  EH7 .... 93 C1
East Murrayfield EH7 .... 7 C1
East Newington Pl EH9 .123 C3
East Norton Pl 3 EH7 ... 93 C1
East Parkside EH16 ...... 233 C1
East Pier St EH51 .... 63 C4
East Plean Prim Sch FK7 .20 B2
East Port KY12 .... 29 A2
East Port Ave EH41 ...... 132 A3
East Preston St EH8 ..... 233 C1
East Preston Street La 5
  EH8 .... 123 C3
East Quality St KY3 ...... 18 A4
East Queensway EH26 ...203 C3
East Rd Grangemouth FK3 .62 B3
  North Berwick EH39 ...... 54 B4
East Restalrig Terr EH6 .94 A2
East Savile Rd EH16 ..... 123 C1
East Sciennes St 2
  EH9 .... 123 C3
East Scotland Street La 3
  EH3 .... 93 B1
East Seaside EH32 .... 96 C1
East Silvermills La EH3 .. 93 A1
East Stirling St FK12,FK13 . 5 A4
East Suffolk Rd EH16 ....124 A2
East Telferton EH7 .... 94 B1
East Terr EH30 .... 68 B1
East Toll KY3 .... 33 C1
East Trinity Rd EH5 ...... 93 B3
East Vennel FK10 .... 10 A3
East Vows Wlk KY1 .... 35 A4
East Way KY11 .... 48 B3
East Werberside EH4 .... 92 C2
East Werberside Pl EH4 . 92 C2
East Whitefield KY12 .... 29 C3
Eastburn Dr FK1 .... 60 B2
Eastcroft Dr FK2 .... 62 A1
Eastcroft St FK5 .... 38 A1
Easter Bankton EH54 ....174 A4
Easter Belmont Rd
  EH12 .... 122 A4
Easter Carmuirs Prim Sch
  FK1 .... 59 A3
Easter Cornton Rd FK9 ... 2 A2
Easter Currie Cres
  EH14 .... 152 A3
Easter Currie Ct EH14 ...152 A3
Easter Currie Pl EH14 ...152 A3
Easter Currie Terr EH14 .152 A3
Easter Dalry Dr 9 EH11 .122 C3
Easter Dalry Pl 1 EH11 .122 C3
Easter Dalry Rd EH11 ....122 C3
Easter Dalry Rigg 2
  EH11 .... 122 C3
Easter Dalry Wynd
  EH11 .... 122 C3
Easter Drylaw Ave EH4 ..92 B2
Easter Drylaw Bank EH4 . 92 B2
Easter Drylaw Dr EH4 .... 92 B2
Easter Drylaw Gdns EH4 .92 B2
Easter Drylaw Gr EH4 .... 92 B2
Easter Drylaw Loan EH4 .92 B2
Easter Drylaw Pl EH4 .... 92 B2
Easter Drylaw View EH4 .92 B2
Easter Drylaw Way EH4 ..92 B2
Easter Ferrygate Pk
  EH39 .... 53 C4
Easter Haugh EH13 ....153 C4
Easter Haven EH6 .... 94 A2
Easter Liviands FK7 ...... 7 C2
Easter Park Dr EH4 .... 91 C2
Easter Rd Broxburn EH52 .117 C3
  Edinburgh EH6 .... 94 A2
  Shotts ML7 .... 191 B3
Easter Road Stad (Hibernian
  FC) EH7 .... 94 A1
Easter Steil EH10 .... 122 C1
Easter Warriston EH7 .... 93 B2
Easterfield Ct EH54 ......147 B2
Eastern General Hospl
  EH6 .... 94 B2
Eastern Ind Est EH15 ....125 B2
Easterton Cres FK7 ...... 20 C4
Easterton Dr FK7 .... 20 C4
Easterton Gr FK7 .... 20 C4
Eastertoun Gdns EH48 ..143 C3
Eastertoun Prim Sch
  EH48 .... 143 C3
Eastfield EH55 .... 125 C4
Eastfield Cotts EH41 ....144 C1
Eastfield Dr EH26 .... 203 C3
Eastfield Farm Rd EH26 .203 C4
Eastfield Gdns EH15 .....125 C4
Eastfield Ind Est EH26 ..203 C3
Eastfield Park Rd EH26 ..203 C3
Eastfield Pl EH15 .... 125 C4
Eastfield Prim Sch
  EH26 .... 203 C3
Eastfield Rd Carluke ML8 .230 A1

Eastfield Rd continued
  Edinburgh EH28 .... 120 A3
  Fauldhouse EH47 .... 193 C4
  North Berwick EH39 ...... 54 B3
Eastfield View EH47 ..... 193 C4
Easthouses Ct EH22 .....183 B4
Easthouses Ind Est
  EH22 .... 183 B4
Easthouses Pl EH22 ......157 B1
Easthouses Rd
  Dalkeith EH22 .... 157 B1
  Easthouses EH22 .... 157 B1
Easthouses Way EH22 ...157 B1
Easton Ct FK8 .... 2 A1
Easton Dr FK1 .... 81 B4
Easton Rd EH48 .... 144 C4
Eastwood Pk
  Fauldhouse EH47 .... 193 C4
  Livingston EH54 .... 147 A4
Ebenezer Pl FK1 .... 81 C3
Eccles Ct ML7 .... 7 A2
Ecclesmachan Rd EH52 .116 C3
Echline EH30 .... 88 C4
Echline Ave EH30 .... 89 A4
Echline Dr EH30 .... 88 C4
Echline Gdns EH30 .... 67 C1
Echline Gn EH30 .... 68 A1
Echline Gr EH30 .... 68 B1
Echline Pk EH30 .... 88 C4
Echline Prim Sch EH30 .. 68 A1
Echline Rigg EH30 .... 68 A1
Echline Terr EH30 .... 68 B1
Echline View EH30 .... 89 A4
Echobank KY11 .... 47 A1
Eden Dr EH54 .... 148 A2
Eden La EH10 .... 123 A2
Eden Rd Alloa FK10 ...... 9 C4
  Dunfermline KY11 .... 29 C1
Edenhall Bank EH21 .....126 C3
Edenhall Cres EH21 ......126 C3
Edenhall Hospl EH21 ....126 C2
Edenhall Rd EH21 ....126 C3
Edgefield Ind Est EH20 .155 B1
Edgefield Pl EH20 .... 181 B4
Edgefield Rd EH20 .... 155 B1
Edgehead Rd EH37,EH22 .184 B4
Edina Pl EH7 .... 94 A1
Edina St EH7 .... 93 C1
Edinburgh Acad (Prep Sch)
  EH3 .... 93 A1
Edinburgh Acad (UpperSch)
  EH3 .... 93 A1
Edinburgh Butterfly & Insect
  World* EH18 .... 156 B2
Edinburgh Castle* EH1 .232 C3
Edinburgh Crystal*
  EH26 .... 203 C3
Edinburgh Fort Ret Pk
  EH15 .... 125 A2
Edinburgh Pk
  Edinburgh EH12 .... 120 C3
  Edinburgh EH12 .... 121 A2
Edinburgh Rd
  Bathgate EH48 .... 145 B3
  Cockenzie & Port Seton
  EH32 .... 97 A2
  Dalkeith EH22 .... 157 A2
  Harthill ML7 .... 168 B3
  Linlithgow EH49 .... 84 C3
  Musselburgh EH21 .... 126 A3
  Newbridge EH28 .... 119 A3
  Penicuik EH26 .... 204 A4
  Queensferry EH30 .... 68 B4
  Tranent EH33 .... 128 A3
  West Barns EH42 .... 77 C1
  West Linton EH46 .... 220 A1
Edinburgh West Off Pk
  EH12 .... 121 A2
Edinburgh Zoo (Royal
  Zoological Society of
  Scotland)* EH12 .... 121 C4
Edington Cottage Hospl
  EH39 .... 54 B4
Edington Pl KY1 .... 18 A4
Edmonstone Ave EH22 ..156 A4
Edmonstone Dr EH22 ....156 A4
Edmonstone Rd EH22 ....156 B4
Edmonstone Terr EH22 ..156 A4
Edmonton Ave EH54 .....147 C2
Edward Ave
  Stenhousemuir FK5 .... 23 B3
  Stirling FK8 .... 2 B1
Edward Pl FK2 .... 39 C2
Edward Rd FK8 .... 2 A1
Edward St
  Dunfermline KY12 .... 29 A3
  Kirkcaldy KY2 .... 17 A4
Edwards Ct EH41 .... 131 C4
Edzell Way KY11 .... 30 A1
Eglington Pl KY11 .... 47 B1
Eglinton Dr KY12 .... 28 C3
Eglinton Cres EH12 ......122 C4
Egypt Mews EH9 .... 123 B2
Eighth St EH22 .... 183 A3
Eildon St EH3 .... 93 B2
Eildon Terr EH3 .... 93 B2
Elam Terr EH51 .... 63 C4
Elbe St EH6 .... 94 A3
Elcho Ct EH32 .... 98 C3
Elcho Pl EH32 .... 97 B2
Elcho Terr Aberlady EH32 .71 B2
  Edinburgh EH15 .... 125 B4
  Longniddry EH32 .... 98 C3

Elder Pl KY11 .... 46 C3
Elder St Dunbar EH42 .... 78 A1
  Edinburgh EH1 .... 233 A4
  Tranent EH33 .... 128 B4
Elder St E EH1 .... 233 A4
Elderslie Dr FK2 .... 82 A4
Eldin Ind Est EH20 .... 155 B1
Eldin Pl EH18 .... 156 A1
Elindean Ct KY12 .... 28 B3
Elindean Pl EH19 .... 182 A4
Elindean Rd EH19 .... 182 A4
Elindean Terr EH19 ......182 B4
Eldrick Ave EH47 .... 193 C3
Eldrick Cres EH47 .... 193 B3
Eldrick La EH47 .... 193 B3
Eldrick West EH47 .... 193 C3
Electra Pl EH15 .... 95 A1
Elgin Ct KY12 .... 29 A1
Elgin Dr FK7 .... 7 B2
Elgin Pl FK1 .... 60 B2
Elgin Rd KY4 .... 13 B2
Elgin St Dunfermline KY12 .29 A1
  Edinburgh EH7 .... 93 C1
  Kirkcaldy KY2 .... 17 A3
Elgin St N EH7 .... 93 C1
Elgin Terr EH7 .... 93 C1
Eliburn North Rdbt
  EH54 .... 147 A3
Eliburn Rd EH54 .... 147 B2
Eliburn South Rd EH54 .147 B2
Elie Ave EH54 .... 146 C3
Elm Dr FK1 .... 81 B3
Elizabeth Ave
  Grangemouth FK3 .... 61 C4
  Stenhousemuir FK5 .... 38 B1
Elizabeth Cres FK1 ...... 59 A3
Elizabeth Dr EH48 .... 145 C3
Elizabeth Gdns EH47 ....171 A1
Elizabeth La EH48 .... 145 C3
Elizabeth St
  Dunfermline KY11 .... 29 B1
  Stirling FK8 .... 7 A3
Elizafield EH6 .... 93 C2
Ellaleen Gr KY12 .... 28 A3
Ellangowan Terr EH16 ...124 B1
Ellen St EH47 .... 170 A4
Ellen's Glen Loan EH17 .155 B4
Ellen's Glen Rd EH16,
  EH17 .... 155 B4
Ellersly Rd EH12 .... 122 B4
Elliot Gdns EH14 .... 153 B4
Elliot Pk EH14 .... 153 B4
Elliot Rd EH14 .... 153 B4
Elliot St EH7 .... 94 A1
Elliot Rd EH14 .... 153 B4
Elliot St Dunfermline KY11 .29 A1
  Edinburgh EH7 .... 93 C1
Elliot Terr FK2 .... 60 A4
Elliothill St KY11 .... 29 B1
Ellis Pl EH52 .... 117 A3
Ellisland Ave KY2 .... 17 A4
Ellon Pl KY12 .... 29 B3
Ellon Rd KY2 .... 16 B4
Elm Ct FK2 .... 61 A1
Elm Gr Alloa FK10 .... 10 B3
  Blackburn EH47 .... 171 C4
  Dunfermline KY11 .... 46 B4
  Livingston EH54 .... 148 A3
  Stenhousemuir FK5 .... 38 B1
Elm Pk EH47 .... 170 A4
Elm Pl Edinburgh EH6 .... 94 A2
  Kirkcaldy KY2 .... 16 C3
  Mayfield EH22 .... 183 B3
Elm Rd EH48 .... 145 C3
Elm Row
  Bonnyrigg & Lasswade
  EH18 .... 156 A1
  Edinburgh EH7 .... 93 C1
Elm Sq EH47 .... 170 B3
Elm St Dunbar EH42 ...... 78 A1
  Edinburgh EH7 .... 93 C1
Elmbank FK11 .... 4 A3
Elmbank Cres FK4 .... 57 B3
Elmbank Rd FK7 .... 7 A2
Elmbank St FK3 .... 61 B3
Elmfield Ct EH22 .... 157 A2
Elmfield Pk EH22 .... 157 A2
Elmfield Rd EH22 .... 157 A2
Elmwood Pk EH54 .... 146 C4
Elmwood Rd ML7 .... 192 A1
Elmwood Terr EH6 .... 94 A2
Elphinstone Cres FK2 ... 22 C2
Elphinstone Prim Sch
  EH33 .... 128 A1
Elphinstone Rd EH33 ....128 A3
Elphinstone Sq EH54 ....146 B3
Elphinstone St KY10 ..... 23 C2
Elphinstone Tower Farm
  Cotts EH33 .... 127 C1
Elphinstone Wlk EH33 ...128 B3
Eltringham Gdns EH14 ..122 B2
Eltringham Gr EH14 ..... 122 B2
Eltringham Terr EH14 ...122 B2
Emily Ct EH23 .... 183 B1
Emily Pl EH23 .... 183 B1
Empire St EH47 .... 170 A4
Endrick Dr FK6 .... 57 A2
Endrick Pl FK7 .... 7 A2
Engelen Dr FK10 .... 10 A3
Engine La EH48 .... 145 A3
Engine Pl 2 EH48 .... 145 A3
Engine Rd
  Gorebridge EH23 .... 183 A1
  Loanhead EH20 .... 181 B4
Engineering Training Sch
  KY12 .... 17 A2
Ennis Ct EH55 .... 172 C2
Ennis Pk EH55 .... 172 C3
Enterprise Way KY11 .... 46 C3

Eppiestane Rd EH47 .... 170 B3
Epworth Gdns FK2 ....82 A4
Erbach Ave FK2 ....61 A2
Ercall Rd FK2 ....82 C4
Erica Gr KY11 ....46 C4
Ericht Pl ML7 ....191 C3
Eriskay Ct FK1 ....60 B1
Errngath Rd EH51 ....64 A4
Erskine Beveridge Ct
KY11 ....46 A3
Erskine Brae KY12 ....25 B1
Erskine Hill FK2 ....61 C1
Erskine Loan EH31 ....52 A2
Erskine Pl
Clackmannan FK10 ....10 C3
Mid Calder EH53 ....148 B3
Erskine Rd
Broxburn EH52 ....117 B3
Gullane EH31 ....52 A2
Erskine Sq KY11 ....29 B1
Erskine St Alloa FK10 ....10 A4
Alva FK12 ....5 A4
Lochgelly KY5 ....14 A3
Erskine Way
Livingston EH54 ....147 B4
Shotts ML7 ....191 C2
Erskine Wynd KY12 ....27 A4
Esdaile Bank EH9 ....123 B2
Esdaile Pk EH9 ....123 B2
Esk Dr EH54 ....148 A2
Esk Glades EH22 ....157 A2
Esk Pl EH22 ....156 C2
Eskbank Rd
Bonnyrigg & Lasswade
EH19 ....182 B4
Dalkeith EH22 ....156 C1
Eskbank Road Rdbt
EH22 ....156 B1
Eskbank Terr EH22 ....156 C1
Eskdaill Ct EH22 ....157 A2
Eskdaill St EH22 ....157 A2
Eskdale Ct EH19 ....182 A4
Eskdale Dr EH19 ....182 A4
Eskdale Mews EH1 ....126 B3
Eskdale Terr EH19 ....182 A4
Esk Pl EH22 ....156 C2
Eskgrove Dr EH25 ....180 C3
Eskhill EH26 ....203 C3
Eskmill Ind Est EH26 ....204 A3
Eskmill Rd EH26 ....204 A3
Eskside E EH22 ....126 C1
Eskside E EH21 ....126 B3
Eskside W EH21 ....126 B3
Eskvale Cres EH26 ....204 A3
Eskvale Ct EH26 ....204 A3
Eskvale Dr EH26 ....204 A3
Eskvale View EH26 ....204 A3
Eskview Ave EH21 ....126 A3
Eskview Cres EH21 ....126 A3
Eskview Gr
Dalkeith EH22 ....156 C2
Musselburgh EH21 ......126 A3
Eskview Rd
Mayfield EH22 ....183 B3
Musselburgh EH21 ......126 A3
Eskview Terr EH21 ....126 A3
Eskview Villas EH22 .....156 C2
Esmonde Ct KY11 ....46 C1
Esplanade Edinburgh EH1 .232 C3
Kirkcaldy KY1 ....17 B1
Esplanade Terr EH15 ...125 B4
Essendean Pl EH4 ....91 B1
Essendean Terr EH4 ....91 B1
Essex Brae EH4 ....91 A2
Essex Pk EH4 ....91 A2
Essex Rd EH4 ....91 A2
Esslemont Rd EH16 ......124 A1
Estate Ave FK1 ....60 B2
Ethel Terr EH10 ....123 A1
Etive Pl Dalgety Bay KY11 ..48 A1
Stirling FK9 ....2 A2
Etive Way Polmont FK2 ..62 A1
Shotts ML7 ....192 A2
Etive Wlk EH54 ....148 A2
Etna Ct Armadale EH48 ..144 A3
Falkirk FK2 ....60 B4
Etna Rd FK2 ....60 B4
Eton Terr EH4 ....232 A4
Ettrick Cres KY11 ....48 A2
Ettrick Ct Falkirk FK1 .....60 B1
Grangemouth FK3 ....61 C3
Ettrick Dr EH54 ....148 A3
Ettrick Dr EH10 ....123 A3
Ettrick Loan EH10 ....122 C2
Ettrick Rd EH10 ....122 C2
Ettrickdale Pl EH3 ....93 A2
Eva Pl EH9 ....123 C1
Evans Gdns EH19 ....182 B4
Evans St FK5 ....38 B2
Evelyn Terr EH26 ....180 B1
Everard Rise EH54 ....148 A1
Evershed Ct KY11 ....29 C1
Evershed Dr KY11 ....29 C1
Ewart Ave EH48 ....144 A3
Ewart Gr EH51 ....63 C3
Ewerland EH4 ....91 A2
Ewing Ave FK2 ....60 A4
Ewing Ct FK7 ....7 B2
Ewing Dr FK2 ....60 A4
Ewing Pl FK2 ....60 A4
Ewing St Cowdenbeath KY4 ..13 A1
Lochgelly KY5 ....14 A3
Penicuik EH26 ....203 C4
Evington Pl EH47 ....171 A1
Excise La FK10 ....23 C2
Excise St FK10 ....23 C2
Exmouth St EH54 ....148 A3
Eyre Cres EH3 ....93 B1
Eyre Pl EH3 ....93 B1
Eyre Terr EH3 ....93 B1

F

Fa'side Ave EH33 ....128 B3
Fa'side Ave N EH21 ......127 A2
Fa'side Ave S EH21 ......127 A2
Fa'side Avenue Ct EH21 ..127 A2
Fa'side Bldgs EH21 ......127 A2
Fa'side Cres
Tranent EH33 ....128 B3
Wallyford EH21 ....127 A2
Fa'side Gdns EH21 ......127 A2
Fa'side Pk EH21 ....127 A2
Fa'side Rd EH33 ....128 B3
Fa'side Terr EH21 ....127 A2
Fa'side View EH33 ....128 B3
Factory Rd
Bathgate EH48 ....144 C2
Cowdenbeath KY4 ....13 B2
Kirkcaldy KY1 ....17 B3
Fair Isle Prim Sch KY2 ..16 C4
Fair Isle Rd KY2 ....16 C4
Fair Pl KY11 ....47 A2
Fair-A-Far EH4 ....91 A3
Fair-A-Far Cotts EH4 .....91 A3
Fair-A-Far Shot EH4 ......91 A3
Fairbairn Pl EH54 ....147 B2
Fairbairn Rd EH54 ....147 B2
Fairbrae EH11 ....121 C2
Fairfax Ct KY3 ....33 C1
Fairfield Alloa FK10 ....5 B1
Livingston EH54 ....147 A2
Fairfield Ave FK4 ....58 A3
Fairfield Pl FK2 ....60 B3
Fairfield Sch FK10 ....5 A1
Fairfields FK2 ....21 C3
Fairford Gdns EH16 ......124 A1
Fairgreen Pl FK7 ....19 C2
Fairhaven Terr FK2 ....82 A4
Fairhill Rd FK7 ....7 A1
Fairinsfield EH22 ....117 A3
Fairley Ct KY12 ....27 B1
Fairlie Dr FK1 ....59 B3
Fairlie Gdns FK1 ....59 B3
Fairlie St FK1 ....59 B3
Fairmile Ave EH10 ....154 A3
Fairmont Pk EH47 ....169 C3
Fairmount Dr FK10 ....5 A1
Fairspark Terr EH51 ....63 B3
Fairview Rd Bonhill EH19 ..119 C4
Fairway EH41 ....131 C4
Fairway The KY1 ....17 C4
Fairway KY12 ....29 A3
Fairways Ave FK2 ....82 C3
Fairways PH FK4 ....58 A4
Fairy Fa' EH54 ....30 C3
Fairyburn Rd FK10 ....9 C4
Fairykirk Rd KY11 ....47 A2
Faith Mission Coll The
EH17 ....155 C3
Falahill Cotts EH38 ......228 A2
Falcon Ave EH10 ....123 A2
Falcon Brae EH54 ....147 B3
Falcon Ct FK2 ....84 C3
Falcon Dr FK5 ....38 A2
Falcon Gdns EH10 ....123 A2
Falcon Rd EH10 ....123 A2
Falcon Rd W EH10 ....123 A2
Falconer Ct FK7 ....7 B2
Falconer Brae EH54 ......147 C1
Falcons The EH31 ....52 A2
Falkirk & District Royal Infmy
FK1 ....60 A2
Falkirk Coll of F & H Ed
FK2 ....60 C3
Falkirk High Sch FK1 .....59 C2
Falkirk High Sta FK1 ......60 A2
Falkirk Rd
Bannockburn FK7 ....19 C4
Bonnybridge FK4 ....58 B3
Falkirk, FK1, FK3 ....60 A1
Falkirk, Glen Village FK1 ..60 A1
Larbert FK5 ....59 B4
Linlithgow EH49 ....86 C2
Falkirk Wheel* FK1 ....59 A3
Falkland College EH21 ..91 C1
Falkland Pl FK5 ....38 C2
Falla Hill Prim Sch
EH47 ....193 B3
Fallas Pl EH47 ....193 B3
Fallin Prim Sch FK7 ....8 B3
Fallodon Cres KY12 ....17 A2
Falside Cres EH48 ....144 C3
Falside Dr EH48 ....144 C3
Falside Terr EH48 ....144 C3
Faraday Pl EH55 ....171 C1
Farm Ave EH18 ....181 C3
Farm Cotts EH21 ....127 B3
Farm Rd Cowdenbeath KY4 ..13 A2
Cowie FK7 ....20 B4
Crombie KY12 ....48 B3
Fallin FK7 ....8 B3
Roslin EH25 ....7 B3
Farm Row KY12 ....30 A3
Farm St FK1 ....59 A3
Farmer's Bldgs EH37 ..185 A3
Farmstead Rd KY11 ....47 C2
Farne Ct KY11 ....16 C4
Farnell Way KY12 ....29 B3
Farquhar Sq EH48 ....142 B2
Farquhar Terr EH30 ....68 A1
Farquharson Way FK1 ...59 C1
Farrer Gr EH7 ....94 C1
Farrer Terr EH7 ....94 C1

Farrier Ct EH47 ....171 B4
Farteviot Royal Hospl for
Sick Children EH9 ......123 B2
Fauldburn EH12 ....91 A1
Fauldburn Pk EH12 ....91 A1
Fauldhouse Bsns Ctr
EH47 ....193 C3
Fauldhouse Rd EH47 ....170 A1
Fauldhouse Sta EH47 ...193 B3
Featherhall Ave EH12 ...121 B3
Featherhall Cres EH12 ..121 B3
Featherhall Cres N
EH12 ....121 B3
Featherhall Cres S
EH12 ....121 B3
Featherhall Gr EH12 .....121 B3
Featherhall Pl EH12 ......121 B3
Featherhall Rd EH12 .....121 B3
Featherhall Terr EH12 ...121 B3
Fell's Rd EH55 ....172 C3
Fells Rigg EH54 ....147 A4
Fendoch Rd FK6 ....61 C4
Fenton St FK10 ....10 A4
Fentoun Gait EH31 ....52 B1
Fere Gait FK10 ....54 A4
Fereneze Gr EH54 ....147 C2
Fergus Rd KY11 ....29 B1
Fergus Wynd KY1 ....17 A1
Ferguson Ct EH21 ....126 B2
Ferguson Dr Denny FK6 ..36 B1
Falkirk FK2 ....39 A1
Musselburgh EH21 ......126 A2
Ferguson Gdns EH21 ...126 B2
Ferguson Gn EH21 ....126 A2
Ferguson Gr FK4 ....58 A3
Ferguson Pl KY3 ....33 C2
Ferguson St FK8 ....1 C1
Ferguson View EH21 ....126 A2
Ferguson Way
Livingston EH54 ....147 B4
Newtongrange EH22 ....182 C4
Fergusson Rd EH52 ......117 C3
Fern Lea Gr FK2 ....39 B2
Fernbank EH54 ....147 C3
Fernie Pl KY12 ....28 C3
Ferniehill Ave EH17 ......155 C3
Ferniehill Dr EH17 ....155 C3
Ferniehill Gdns EH17 ...155 C3
Ferniehill Gr EH17 ....155 C4
Ferniehill Pl EH17 ....155 C3
Ferniehill Rd EH17 ....155 C3
Ferniehill Sq EH17 ....155 C3
Ferniehill St EH17 ....155 C3
Ferniehill Terr EH17 ......155 C3
Fernieside Ave
Edinburgh EH13 ....152 C2
Edinburgh, Bonaly EH13 ..153 A3
Fernieside Ave EH17 ....155 C4
Fernieside Cres EH17 ...155 C4
Fernieside Dr EH17 ......155 C4
Fernieside Gdns EH17 ..155 C4
Fernieside Gr EH17 ......155 C4
Fernieside Prim Sch
EH17 ....155 C4
Fernlea EH52 ....116 C3
Ferrard Rd KY2 ....16 C2
Ferrier Cres EH48 ....144 A3
Ferris Way KY11 ....48 A2
Ferry Ct FK9 ....2 A2
Ferry La KY11 ....68 A3
Ferry Muir Gait EH30 .....89 A4
Ferry Orch EH30 ....2 B1
Ferry Rd
Edinburgh EH4, EH5 ......92 B2
South Alloa FK7 ....9 C2
Ferry Road Ave EH4 ......92 B2
Ferry Road Dr EH4 ....92 B3
Ferry Road Gdns EH4 ...92 B2
Ferry Road Gr EH4 ....92 B2
Ferry Road Pl EH4 ....92 B2
Ferry Toll Pl KY11 ....46 C1
Ferry Toll Rd KY11 ....46 C1
Ferrybarns Ct KY11 ....68 A3
Ferryburn Gn EH30 ....89 B4
Ferryfield EH5 ....93 A2
Ferrygate Cotts EH39 ....33 B3
Ferryhill Prim Sch EH4 ..92 B2
Ferryhill Rd KY11 ....68 A4
Ferrymuir La EH30 ....89 A4
Ferrymuir Rd EH30 ....89 A4
Festival Sq EH3 ....232 B2
Fetteresk Cotts EH26 ...203 C2
Fettes Ave EH4 ....92 C1
Fettes Coll EH4 ....92 C2
Fettes Rise EH4 ....92 C2
Fiddich Dr EH54 ....173 C3
Fidra Ave EH39 ....53 A3
Fidra Ct EH39 ....53 C4
Fidra Rd EH39 ....54 A4
Fife Coll (Priory Campus)
KY1 ....17 C2
Fife Coll of F & H Ed KY1 ..17 A2
Fife Pl KY11 ....46 A1
Fifth St EH22 ....183 A1
Figgate Bank EH15 ....95 A1
Figgate La EH15 ....95 A1
Figgate St EH15 ....95 A1
Fillyside Ave EH7 ....95 B3
Fillyside Rd EH7 ....95 C3
Fillyside Terr EH7 ....95 B3
Finches The EH52 ....82 A1
Findhorn Pl
Edinburgh EH9 ....123 C2
Falkirk FK1 ....60 B1
Kirkcaldy KY1 ....16 C4

Findlay Ave EH7 ....94 B3
Findlay Cotts EH47 ....94 B2
Findlay Cres KY11 ....46 C2
Findlay Gdns EH7 ....94 B2
Findlay Gr EH7 ....94 B2
Findlay Medway EH7 ......94 B2
Findlay St KY11 ....46 C2
Fingal Pl EH9 ....233 A1
Fingzies Pl EH6 ....94 A2
Finistere Ave FK1 ....60 A2
Finlaggan Ct EH12 ....121 A4
Finlarig Ct FK5 ....38 C2
Finlay Ave EH53 ....148 C2
Finlay Pl EH22 ....183 C3
Fintry Ave EH54 ....148 A2
Fintry Rd FK3 ....61 C3
Fir Gr Dunfermline KY12 ..46 C4
Livingston EH54 ....148 A3
Westquarter FK2 ....61 A1
Fir La FK5 ....38 B3
Firbank Gr EH53 ....148 C2
Firpark Terr FK7 ....6 B3
Firhill Cres EH13 ....153 C4
Firhill Dr EH13 ....153 C4
Firhill High Sch EH14 ...153 B4
Firhill Loan EH13 ....153 C4
Firs Cres FK7 ....7 B1
Firs Entry FK7 ....7 B1
Firs Pk (East Stirlingshire
FC) FK2 ....60 B3
Firs Rd FK10 ....4 B1
Firs St FK2 ....60 B3
Firs The Bannockburn FK7 ..7 B1
Dalgety Bay KY11 ....48 A1
First Gait EH14 ....151 C4
First St EH22 ....183 A2
Firth Cres EH26 ....180 B1
Firth Rd
Auchendinny EH26 ......180 B1
Livingston EH54 ....147 C4
Roslin EH25 ....204 C4
Firwood Dr FK10 ....63 B3
Fishcross Prim Sch FK10 ..5 B2
Fishergate Rd EH32 ....97 C2
Fisherrow Ind Est EH21 ..126 A3
Fishers Rd EH32 ....97 B2
Fishers Wynd EH21 ......126 A3
Fisher's Rd EH51 ....63 B2
Fishmarket Sq EH6 ....93 B4
Fishwives' Cswy EH7,
EH15 ....95 C1
Fitzroy Sq KY1 ....18 A4
Fitzroy St KY1 ....18 A4
Five Gates EH47 ....76 A3
Fivestanks Ct EH52 ......117 A3
Fivestanks Pl EH52 ....117 A3
Flare Rd FK3 ....62 A3
Flax Mill Rd ML7 ....168 C3
Fleets Gr EH33 ....128 B2
Fleets Ind Est EH33 ......128 B2
Fleets Rd EH33 ....128 B3
Fleets View EH33 ....128 B2
Fleming Dr FK5 ....39 A2
Fleming Gdns FK1 ....59 C3
Fleming Pl FK1 ....142 C2
Fleming Rd EH54 ....146 C1
Fleming Way KY3 ....33 C1
Flemington Gdns FK7 ...169 C3
Flesh Wynd KY1 ....17 B3
Fleshmarket Cl EH1 ......233 A3
Fletcher Gr EH26 ....203 C4
Flint Cres FK7 ....20 A4
Floors Pl KY2 ....16 B3
Floors Terr EH47 ....78 B1
Flora Stevenson Prim Sch
EH4 ....92 C1
Florabank Rd EH14 ....101 A1
Flower Pl KY4 ....112 C4
Flower Pl KY4 ....112 C4
Fod St KY11 ....30 A3
Fodbank View KY11 ....29 C2
Follyburn Pl EH54 ....147 A2
Foote Pl FK1 ....46 C2
Foote St KY5 ....14 A3
Forbes Cres FK5 ....38 B1
Forbes Ct FK2 ....60 C3
Forbes Rd
Edinburgh EH10 ....123 A3
Rosyth KY11 ....46 B1
Forbes St Alloa FK10 ......9 C3
Edinburgh EH8 ....233 B1
Forbeslea Gdns KY12 ....27 C4
Forbes Rd EH13 ....153 A1
Ford View EH32 ....98 C2
Ford's Rd EH11 ....122 A2
Fordell Bank KY11 ....48 B2
Fordell Gdns KY11 ....48 B2
Fordell Way KY11 ....48 B2
Fordyce Gdns FK1 ....59 C2
Forebraes FK10 ....10 A4
Foredale Terr EH51 ....64 B4
Foreshot Terr EH34 ......159 A4
Forest Kirk ML8 ....230 B1
Forest Pl KY12 ....29 B4
Forest View KY11 ....61 C1
Forestbank EH54 ....147 C3
Forester's Lea Cres EH22 ..29 C2
Forester's View EH33 ....128 B3
Forfar Pl FK2 ....62 A1
Forgie Cres FK2 ....83 A3
Forglen Rd FK9 ....2 A3
Forglen Rd FK9 ....2 A3
Forker Ave KY11 ....46 B2
Forkneuk Rd EH52 ....116 C2

Forkneuk Steadings
EH52 ....116 C2
Forman Gr KY11 ....29 C1
Forres Dr KY2 ....16 B4
Forres St EH3 ....232 B4
Forrest Hill EH1 ....233 A2
Forrest Pl ML7 ....168 C3
Forrest Rd
Edinburgh EH1 ....233 A2
Forrestfield ML6 ....141 A1
Shotts ML7 ....167 A3
Stirling FK8 ....2 A2
Forrest St ML7 ....191 C3
Forrest Wlk EH52 ....116 C2
Forrester High Sch
EH12 ....121 B2
Forrester Park Ave
EH12 ....121 B2
Forrester Park Dr EH12 ..121 B2
Forrester Park Gdns
EH12 ....121 B2
Forrester Park Gn EH12 ..121 C2
Forrester Park Gr EH12 ..121 B2
Forrester Park Loan
EH12 ....121 B2
Forrester Park Rd EH12 ..121 B2
Forrester Pk EH22 ....22 B2
Forrester Rd
Armadale EH48 ....143 C4
Edinburgh EH12 ....121 B4
Forrestfield Rd ML6 ......141 A3
Forsyth PH FK5 ....39 A2
Fort Ho EH6 ....93 C3
Fort Prim Sch EH6 ....93 C3
Forth Ave Kirkcaldy KY2 ..17 A2
Larbert FK5 ....38 A2
Forth Ave Ind Est KY2 ...17 A2
Forth Bridges Visitors Ctr*
KY11 ....68 A1
Forth Cres Alloa FK10 ....10 B3
Dalgety Bay KY11 ....48 A2
High Valleyfield KY12 .....26 A1
Stirling FK8 ....7 A4
Forth Ct
Cockenzie & Port Seton
EH32 ....97 C2
Dalgety Bay KY11 ....48 A2
Dunfermline KY12 ....29 A1
Stirling FK8 ....2 A1
Forth Dr EH54 ....148 A3
Forth Gdns
Cockenzie & Port Seton
EH32 ....97 C2
Oakley KY12 ....26 C4
Forth Gr EH32 ....97 C2
Forth Ind Est FK5 ....92 C4
Forth Park Dr KY2 ....17 A3
Forth Park Gdns KY2 .....17 A3
Forth Park Maternity Hospl
KY2 ....17 A3
Forth Pk Bridge of A FK9 ..2 A3
Queensferry EH30 ....89 C4
Forth Pl Burntisland KY3 ..50 C4
Queensferry EH30 ....89 C4
Stirling FK8 ....7 A4
Forth Prim Sch ML11 ....215 A1
Forth Rd KY11 ....46 A1
Forth Reach KY11 ....47 C1
Forth St Cambus FK10 ....9 A4
Dunfermline KY12 ....29 A1
Edinburgh EH1 ....93 B1
Falkirk FK1 ....60 B1
Grangemouth FK3 ....61 B4
Kincardine FK10 ....23 B2
North Berwick EH39 ......54 B4
Stirling FK8 ....2 A1
Forth St La EH39 ....54 B4
Forth Terr Dalmeny EH30 ..89 B4
Grangemouth FK3 ....61 B4
Forth Valley Coll of Nursing
& Midwifery FK1 ....60 A2
Forth View
Dalgety Bay KY11 ....48 A2
Inverkeithing KY11 ....47 A1
Kincardine FK10 ....23 B2
Kirknewton EH27 ....149 C2
Stirling FK8 ....2 A1
West Barns EH42 ....77 C1
Forth View Ave EH14 ....151 C2
Forth View Cotts KY12 ..26 C1
Forth View Cres
Currie EH14 ....151 C2
Danderhall EH22 ....156 A4
Forth View Ind Est KY11 ..46 A1
Forth View Rd EH14 .....151 C2
Forth Wynd EH32 ....97 C2
Forthbank (Stirling Albion
FC) FK7 ....7 C4
Forthbank Ind Est KY11 ..10 A2
Forthbank Rd KY11 ....25 C1
Forthside Terr KY11 ....46 B3
Forthvale FK11 ....4 A3
Forthvale Ct FK7 ....2 A1
Forthview FK7 ....7 C1
Forthview Ave EH21 .....127 A2
Forthview Cres
Bo'ness EH51 ....63 B3
Musselburgh EH21 ....127 A3
Forthview Dr EH21 ....127 A3
Forthview Gdns FK2 ......82 B4
Forthview Rd
Edinburgh EH4 ....92 B1
Longniddry EH32 ....98 C3

Forthview Terr
Edinburgh EH4 . . . . .92 A1
Newmills KY12 . . . . .26 B1
Reddingmuirhead FK2 . . . .82 A4
Wallyford EH21 . . . . .127 A2
Forties Rd FK3,EH51 . . . . . .62 B3
Fortingall Cres FK2 . . . . . . .62 A1
Fortissat Ave ML7 . . . . . . .191 B3
Fortisset Rd ML7 . . . . . . .171 B1
Fortuna Ct FK1 . . . . .60 B2
Fortune Ave EH41 . . . . . . .101 A1
Foss's Cl ■ EH41 . . . . . . .132 A4
Foulden Pl KY12 . . . . .29 B2
Foulford Pl KY4 . . . . .13 A2
Foulford Prim Sch KY4 . .13 A3
Foulford Rd KY4 . . . . .13 B2
Foulford St KY4 . . . . .13 B2
Foulis Cres EH14 . . . . .152 C3
Foulshiels Rd EH47 . . . . .171 B1
Foundry La EH20 . . . . . . .155 B1
Foundry Loan FK5 . . . . . . .38 A1
Foundry Rd
Bonnybridge FK4 . . . . .58 A3
Shotts ML7 . . . . .191 C2
Foundry St
Dunfermline KY12 . . . . .29 A2
Falkirk FK2 . . . . .60 A4
Fountain Pl
Cowdenbeath KY4 . . . . .13 B2
Loanhead EH20 . . . . .181 B4
Fountain Rd FK9 . . . . .2 A4
Fountainbridge EH3 . . . . .232 A1
Fountainhall Rd EH9 . . . .123 C2
Fountainhead Rd EH48 . .145 A4
Fountainpark Cres EH11 . .64 B4
Fourth Gait EH14 . . . . . . .151 C4
Fourth St EH22 . . . . .183 A3
Fowler Cres
Loanhead EH20 . . . . .181 B4
Maddiston FK2 . . . . .83 A3
Fowler Pl FK2 . . . . .61 C2
Fowler St EH33 . . . . .128 B4
Fowler Terr EH11 . . . . . . .122 C3
Fowlers Ct EH32 . . . . .96 C1
Fox Covert Ave EH12 . . . . .91 C1
Fox Covert Gr EH12 . . . . . .91 C1
Fox Covert RC Prim Schs
EH12 . . . . .91 C1
Fox Spring Cres EH10 . . .154 A4
Fox Spring Rise EH10 . . .154 A4
Fox St EH6 . . . . .94 A3
Foxknowe Pl EH54 . . . . . .147 A2
Frances View KY1 . . . . .18 A4
Franchi Dr FK5 . . . . .38 C3
Francis Ct KY12 . . . . .28 B3
Francis St KY5 . . . . .14 A4
Frankfield Cres KY11 . . . .48 B2
Frankfield Pl KY11 . . . . . . .48 B2
Frankfield Rd KY11 . . . . . .48 B2
Fraser Ave Edinburgh EH5 .93 A3
Inverkeithing KY11 . . . . . . .47 B1
Fraser Cres EH5 . . . . .93 A3
Fraser Dr KY5 . . . . .14 A4
Fraser Gdns EH5 . . . . .93 A3
Fraser Gr EH5 . . . . .93 A3
Fraser Pl Dysart KY1 . . . . .18 A4
Grangemouth FK3 . . . . .61 B3
Stirling FK9 . . . . .2 A2
Fraser Rd EH54 . . . . .146 C1
Frederick Cres KY11 . . . . .29 A1
Frederick St EH2 . . . . .232 C4
Freeland Ave EH52 . . . . . .117 A3
Freelands Rd
Edinburgh EH28 . . . . .120 A2
Ratho EH28 . . . . .119 C2
Freeport Village EH55 . . . .2 A2
Fremantle St EH4 . . . . . . .148 A3
Freskyn Pl EH52 . . . . .118 A3
Frew Ct KY11 . . . . .29 B1
Friar's Croft EH42 . . . . . . .78 B1
Friars Brae EH49 . . . . .85 A3
Friars Loan EH49 . . . . .85 A3
Friars St FK8 . . . . .7 A4
Friars Way EH49 . . . . .85 A3
Friarton Gdns EH26 . . . . .203 B3
Friendship Gdns FK2 . . . .39 B2
Frobisher Ave FK1 . . . . . . .59 C2
Frogston Ave EH10 . . . . .154 A3
Frogston Brae EH17 . . . .154 C2
Frogston Gdns EH10 . . .154 B3
Frogston Gr EH10 . . . . . .154 B3
Frogston Rd E EH17 . . . .154 C3
Frogston Rd W EH10 . . .154 B3
Frogston Terr EH10 . . . . .154 B3
Fullerton Dr FK2 . . . . .61 C2
Fulmar Brae EH54 . . . . . .147 B3
Fulmar Way FK2 . . . . .62 A1
Furcheons Pk EH8 . . . . . .124 C4
Furnace La EH51 . . . . .64 B4
Furnace Pl KY4 . . . . .13 C3
Furniss Ave KY11 . . . . .46 B3
Fyne La ML7 . . . . .191 C3

G

Gaberston Ave FK10 . . . . . .10 B4
Gagarin Way KY4 . . . . .13 C3
Gair Cres ML8 . . . . .230 A2
Gair Rd ML8 . . . . .230 A3
Gair Wynd ML7 . . . . .192 A2
Gairdoch Dr FK2 . . . . .39 B2
Gairdoch St FK2 . . . . .60 A4
Gairloch Cres FK2 . . . . . . .61 B1
Gala Gn EH42 . . . . .78 A1

Galabraes Cres EH48 . . .145 B4
Galachlawshot EH10 . . . .154 B3
Galachlawside EH10 . . . .154 B3
Galadale EH22 . . . . .183 A3
Galadale Cres EH22 . . . .183 A3
Galadale Dr EH22 . . . . . . .183 A3
Gallacher Pl KY4 . . . . .13 C3
Gallagher Gn EH54 . . . . .147 B4
Gallamuir Dr FK7 . . . . .20 B2
Gallamuir Rd FK7 . . . . .20 B2
Gallolee The EH13 . . . . . .153 B3
Gallow View EH52 . . . . . . .88 A4
Galloway Cres EH52 . . . .117 B3
Galloway Ct FK1,FK2 . . . . .60 A3
Galloway St FK1 . . . . .60 A3
Gallows Loan KY12 . . . . . .29 B2
Gallowsknowe EH49 . . . .84 B4
Galmeilen EH52 . . . . .117 B3
Galt Ave EH21 . . . . .127 A3
Galt Cres EH21 . . . . .127 A3
Galt Dr EH21 . . . . .127 A3
Galt Rd EH21 . . . . .127 A3
Galt Terr EH21 . . . . .127 A3
Gambeson Cres FK7 . . . . .7 A3
Gamekeeper's Loan EH4 .91 A3
Gamekeeper's Pk EH4 . . .91 A3
Gamekeeper's Rd EH4 . . .91 A3
Garbett Rd EH54 . . . . .147 B1
Garden City EH47 . . . . . . .171 A1
Garden Ct KY12 . . . . .29 B4
Garden Pl Cairneyhill KY12 .27 B1
Clackmannan FK10 . . . . . . .11 A2
Livingston EH54 . . . . .147 B2
Townhill KY12 . . . . .29 B4
Garden St FK1 . . . . .60 B3
Garden Terr
Clackmannan FK10 . . . . . . .11 A2
Edinburgh EH4 . . . . .91 C4
Falkirk FK1 . . . . .60 B3
Westquarter FK2 . . . . .61 A1
Gardener Rd EH42 . . . . . . .78 B1
Gardener St EH42 . . . . . . .78 B2
Gardener's Wlk EH26 . . .203 B3
Gardeners Ct KY12 . . . . . .29 A2
Gardeners' St KY12 . . . . . .29 A2
Gardenerswell Villas ■
EH48 . . . . .145 A4
Gardenhead FK2 . . . . .61 C1
Gardens The
Aberlady EH32 . . . . .71 B3
Dirleton EH39 . . . . .53 A3
Gardiner Cres EH32 . . . . .97 A1
Gardiner Gr EH4 . . . . .92 A1
Gardiner Pl
Cowdenbeath KY4 . . . . .13 A1
Newtongrange EH22 . . . . .183 A3
Gardiner Rd
Prestonpans EH32 . . . . .97 A1
Edinburgh EH4 . . . . .92 A1
Gardiner St KY5 . . . . .14 A4
Gardiner Terr
Edinburgh EH4 . . . . .92 A1
Tranent EH33 . . . . .128 A4
Gardiner's Cl EH32 . . . . . .97 B2
Gardner's Cres EH3 . . . .232 B2
Gardner Terr EH41 . . . . . .171 A1
Gardners La EH6 . . . . .81 B4
Gardrum Pl FK2 . . . . .39 B2
Gardrum Gdns FK1 . . . . . .81 B4
Gareloch Way EH47 . . . .170 B4
Garleton Ct EH31 . . . . .52 A1
Garleton Dr EH41 . . . . . . .100 C1
Garngrew Rd FK4 . . . . .57 B4
Garrison Pl FK1 . . . . .60 A3
Garry Pl Falkirk FK1 . . . . . .59 B3
Grangemouth FK3 . . . . .61 C3
Garry St KY5 . . . . .14 A4
Garry Way ML7 . . . . .191 C3
Garry Wlk EH54 . . . . .148 A2
Garscube Terr EH12 . . . .122 B4
Gartclush Gdns FK7 . . . . .19 C4
Gartcows Ave FK1 . . . . . . .60 A2
Gartcows Cres FK1 . . . . . .60 A2
Gartcows Dr FK1 . . . . .60 A2
Gartcows Gdns FK1 . . . . .59 C2
Gartcows Pl FK1 . . . . .60 A2
Gartcows Rd FK1 . . . . .60 A2
Garten Dr ML7 . . . . .192 A2
Garthill Gdns FK1 . . . . . . .60 A2
Garthill La FK1 . . . . .60 A2
Gartmorn Dam Ctry Pk *
FK10 .11 A4
Gartmorn Rd FK10 . . . . .5 B1
Garvald La FK6 . . . . .36 B1
Garvald Rd FK6 . . . . .57 B4
Garvally Cres FK10 . . . . . .10 C4
Garvock Bank KY11 . . . . . .29 C2
Garvock Hill KY12 . . . . .29 B2
Garvock Terr KY12 . . . . . . .29 B2
Gas Wynd KY1 . . . . .17 A1
Gasworks La
North Berwick EH39 . . . . . .53 C3
Falkirk FK1 . . . . .60 B3
Gateside Ave
Bonnybridge FK4 . . . . .58 B3
Haddington EH41 . . . . .100 B1
Gateside Ct KY4 . . . . .13 A2
Gateside Ind Est KY4 . . . .13 A2
Gateside Rd
Haddington EH41 . . . . .131 B4
Kirkliston EH29 . . . . .89 A1
Stirling FK7 . . . . .7 A2
Gauger's Bush EH41 . . . . .76 A4
Gauze Pl EH51 . . . . .64 A3

Gauze Rd EH51 . . . . .64 A3
Gavin Pl EH54 . . . . .147 A3
Gavins Rd FK10 . . . . .4 C1
Gayfield Cl ■ EH1 . . . . . . .93 C1
Gayfield Place La EH1 . . .93 C1
Gayfield Sq EH1 . . . . .93 C1
Gayfield St EH1 . . . . .93 C1
Gayfield Street La ■
EH1 . . . . .93 B1
Gaynor Ave EH20 . . . . . . .181 A4
Gean Rd FK10 . . . . .9 C4
Gelder Dr EH54 . . . . .173 C3
Gellatly Rd KY11 . . . . .29 B1
Gelnorchy Terr EH9 . . . . .123 C2
Gentiles Entry EH8 . . . . .233 C3
George Ave EH20 . . . . . . .181 A4
George Burn Wynd KY1 . .17 B2
George Cres
Loanhead EH20 . . . . .181 A4
Ormiston EH35 . . . . .159 B4
George Dr EH20 . . . . .181 A4
George Heriot's Sch
EH3 .232 C2
George IV Bridge EH1 . . .233 B2
George Laing Ct FK5 . . . .38 C1
George Sq EH8 . . . . .233 A1
George Square La EH8 . .23 A1
George St Alva FK12 . . . . . .5 A3
Armadale EH48 . . . . .143 C3
Bathgate EH48 . . . . .145 A3
Bo'ness EH51 . . . . .63 C3
Cowdenbeath KY4 . . . . .13 B3
Dunfermline KY11 . . . . .29 A1
Edinburgh EH2 . . . . .232 B3
Falkirk FK2 . . . . .60 A3
Grangemouth FK3 . . . . .61 C4
Kincardine FK10 . . . . .23 B3
Kirkcaldy KY2 . . . . .16 B4
Laurieston FK2 . . . . .60 C2
Ormiston EH35 . . . . .159 C4
Stenhousemuir FK5 . . . . . . .38 B2
George Terr EH20 . . . . . . .181 A4
George Watson's Coll
EH10 . . . . .122 C2
George Watson's Coll Lower
Prim Sch EH10 . . . . .122 C2
George Watson's Coll Upper
Prim Sch EH10 . . . . .122 C2
George Way EH33 . . . . . . .128 B3
George Wlk EH33 . . . . . . .128 B3
Gerald Terr FK5 . . . . .38 C2
Gib Gr KY11 . . . . .29 C1
Gibbdun Pl FK6 . . . . .57 C4
Gibbs Entry EH8 . . . . .233 B2
Gibbshill Pl ML7 . . . . .168 B3
Gibraltar Ct EH22 . . . . . . .157 A2
Gibraltar Gdns EH22 . . .157 A2
Gibraltar Terr EH22 . . . . .157 A2
Gibson Dr EH22 . . . . .157 B2
Gibson St FK7 . . . . .93 C2
Gibson Terr EH11 . . . . . . .232 A1
Gisongray St FK2 . . . . .60 A4
Giffard Pk EH8 . . . . .233 B1
Gifford Pk EH8 . . . . .233 B1
Gifford Rd EH41 . . . . .132 B4
Giffordgate EH41 . . . . .132 A4
Gilberstoun EH15 . . . . . . .125 B3
Gilberstoun Brig EH15 . .125 B3
Gilberstoun Loan EH15 . .125 B3
Gilberstoun Pl EH15 . . . .125 B3
Gilberstoun Wynd EH15 .125 B3
Gilbert Ave EH39 . . . . .54 B3
Gilburn Pl Bo'ness EH51 . . .63 B3
Shotts ML7 . . . . .191 C2
Gilchrist Cres EH47 . . . . .170 A3
Gilchrist Dr FK1 . . . . .59 C2
Giles St EH6 . . . . .93 C3
Gilfillan Pl FK2 . . . . .39 B1
Gilfillan Rd KY11 . . . . .29 C1
Gill Pk FK6 . . . . .36 C1
Gill Way KY11 . . . . .29 B1
Gillespie Cres EH10 . . . .232 B1
Gillespie Gr KY12 . . . . . . .26 C4
Gillespie Pl
Bannockburn FK7 . . . . .7 B1
Edinburgh EH11 . . . . .232 B1
Gillespie Rd EH13 . . . . . .152 B3
Gillespie St EH3 . . . . .232 B1
Gillespie Terr FK7 . . . . . . .20 B1
Gillie Ct KY12 . . . . .29 B1
Gillies Dr FK7 . . . . .6 B3
Gillies Hill FK7 . . . . .6 B3
Gillsland Rd EH10 . . . . . . .122 B2
Gilmerton Dykes Ave
EH17 . . . . .155 B3
Gilmerton Dykes Cres
EH17 . . . . .155 B3
Gilmerton Dykes Dr
EH17 . . . . .155 B3
Gilmerton Dykes Gr
EH17 . . . . .155 B3
Gilmerton Dykes Loan
EH17 . . . . .155 B3
Gilmerton Dykes Pl
EH17 . . . . .155 B3
Gilmerton Dykes Rd
EH17 . . . . .155 B3
Gilmerton Dykes St
EH17 . . . . .155 B3
Gilmerton Dykes Terr
EH17 . . . . .155 B3
Gilmerton Dykes View
EH17 . . . . .155 B3
Gilmerton Pl EH17 . . . . . .155 B3
Gilmerton Prim Sch
EH17 . . . . .155 B3

Gilmerton Rd EH17 . . . . .155 B4
Gilmerton Road Rdbt
EH22 . . . . .156 B2
Gilmerton Station Rd
EH17 . . . . .155 C2
Gilmore Pk EH11 . . . . . . .232 A1
Gilmore Pl EH3 . . . . .123 A3
Gilmore Place La EH3 . .232 B1
Gilmour Rd EH16 . . . . . . .123 C2
Gilmour St
Cowdenbeath KY4 . . . . .13 B3
Edinburgh EH8 . . . . .233 B2
Gilsay Ct FK1 . . . . .60 B1
Gilston Cres FK2 . . . . .62 A1
Gipsy La KY11 . . . . .29 C2
Gladney Sq KY1 . . . . .17 A1
Gladsmuir ML11 . . . . .215 A1
Gladsmuir Junc EH33 . . .130 A4
Gladstone Pl
Dunfermline KY12 . . . . .29 A3
Edinburgh EH6 . . . . .94 A2
Stirling FK8 . . . . .2 A1
Gladstone Rd FK5 . . . . . . .38 B2
Gladstone Terr EH9 . . . . .123 C3
Glaive Ave FK7 . . . . .7 B2
Glamis Gdns
Dalgety Bay KY11 . . . . .48 A2
Polmont FK2 . . . . .61 C1
Glamis Pl KY11 . . . . .48 A2
Glamis Rd Kinghorn KY3 . .34 C2
Kirkcaldy KY2 . . . . .16 B4
Glamis Terr KY3 . . . . .34 C2
Glasclune Ct EH39 . . . . . . .54 B4
Glasclune Gdns EH39 . . . .54 B4
Glasgow Rd
Bannockburn FK7 . . . . .19 B4
Bathgate EH48 . . . . .144 B4
Bonnybridge FK4 . . . . .57 B2
Denny FK6 . . . . .36 C1
Edinburgh EH12 . . . . .120 B3
Falkirk FK1 . . . . .59 B3
Ratho Sta EH28 . . . . .119 B3
Stirling FK7 . . . . .7 A1
Glaskhill Terr EH26 . . . . .203 C3
Glass Cres EH52 . . . . .87 C1
Glass Pl EH52 . . . . .87 C1
Glass Rd EH52 . . . . .87 C1
Glassel Park Rd EH32 . . .98 B2
Glasshouse Loan FK10 . .10 A3
Glasswork St KY1 . . . . .17 A2
Glebe Ave Stirling FK8 . . . . .7 A4
Uphall EH52 . . . . .117 A2
Glebe Cres Alva FK12 . . . . .5 A4
Athelstaneford EH39 . . . . .101 C4
Stirling FK8 . . . . .7 A4
Glebe Ct EH47 . . . . .193 B3
Glebe Gdns
Edinburgh EH12 . . . . .121 B3
Prestonpans EH32 . . . . .96 C1
Glebe Gr EH12 . . . . .121 B3
Glebe Pk
Inverkeithing KY11 . . . . . . .47 A1
Kirkcaldy KY1 . . . . .17 B3
Glebe Pl
Bonnyrig & Lasswade
EH18 . . . . .155 C1
Burntisland KY3 . . . . .33 C1
Kinghorn KY3 . . . . .34 C2
Glebe Rd Bathgate EH48 .145 B3
Edinburgh EH12 . . . . .121 B3
Kincardine FK10 . . . . .23 B3
Uphall EH52 . . . . .117 A2
West Calder EH55 . . . . . . .172 B1
Whitburn EH47 . . . . .161 A3
Glebe St Dalkeith EH22 . .157 A2
Denny FK6 . . . . .36 C1
Falkirk FK1 . . . . .60 A3
Glebe The Aberdour KY3 . .49 B4
Alva FK12 . . . . .5 A4
Clackmannan FK10 . . . . . . .11 A2
Dalmeny EH30 . . . . .89 C4
East Linton EH40 . . . . .103 C4
East Saltoun EH34 . . . . . . .161 C2
Edinburgh EH4 . . . . .92 B3
Longniddry EH32 . . . . .98 B4
Linlithgow EH49 . . . . .85 A3
Pencaitland EH34 . . . . .160 C4
West Calder EH55 . . . . . . .172 B1
Gledhill Ave EH51 . . . . . . .64 B3
Glen Albyn Dr KY2 . . . . . . .16 A4
Glen Artney Gr KY11 . . . . .29 B1
Glen Avon Pl FK1 . . . . .59 B3
Glen Beasdale Ct KY11 . .29 B1
Glen Brae FK1 . . . . .60 A2
Glen Bridge KY12 . . . . .28 C2
Glen Bruar Pl KY12 . . . . . .16 A4
Glen Clova Cres KY12 . . .27 B1
Glen Cres Falkirk FK1 . . . . .60 A2
Livingston EH54 . . . . .146 C3
Glen Ct EH54 . . . . .146 B3
Glen Fruin Gr KY12 . . . . . .29 B1
Glen Gdns FK1 . . . . .60 A2
Glen Isla Rd KY2 . . . . .16 B4
Glen Kinchie FK10 . . . . .4 A1
Glen Lyon Ct FK2 . . . . .39 B2
Glen Moriston Dr KY12 . . .27 B1
Glen Nevis Dr KY11 . . . . . .29 B1
Glen Ogle Ct FK2 . . . . .39 B2
Glen Pl EH26 . . . . .203 C3
Glen Rd Armadale EH48 . .143 C3
Livingston EH54 . . . . .146 C3
Denny FK6 . . . . .20 B1
Shotts ML7 . . . . .191 C2

Glen Rd continued
Torwood FK5, FK7 . . . . .37 B4
Glen Shiel Gr KY11 . . . . . .29 B1
Glen St EH3 . . . . .232 C1
Glen Terr Denny FK6 . . . . . .36 B1
Livingston EH54 . . . . .146 C3
Glen The Bathgate EH48 . .145 A4
Tullibody FK10 . . . . .4 B2
Glen Tye Rd FK7 . . . . .7 B3
Glen View Bo'ness EH51 . .63 B2
Glen View Cres EH23 . . . .207 B4
Glen View Gdns EH23 . . .207 B4
Glen View Rd EH23 . . . . . .207 B4
Glen Way ■ EH48 . . . . . . .145 A4
Glenafeoch Rd ML8 . . . . .230 A1
Glenallan Dr EH16 . . . . . .124 A1
Glenallan Loan EH16 . . . .124 A1
Glenalmond EH47 . . . . . . .170 B3
Glenalmond Ct
Broxburn EH52 . . . . .117 A3
Whitburn EH47 . . . . .161 A3
Glenalmond Terr EH48 . .145 A4
Glenard View EH51 . . . . . .64 B3
Glenavon Dr KY12 . . . . . . .27 B1
Glenavon Terr EH48 . . . . .145 A4
Glenbank FK1 . . . . .60 A1
Glenbare Ct EH48 . . . . . . .145 B3
Glenbervie FK5 . . . . .38 B2
Glenbervie Ave FK5 . . . . . .38 B2
Glenbervie Cres FK5 . . . .38 B2
Glenbervie Dr FK5 . . . . . . .38 B2
Glenbervie Gr KY11 . . . . . .29 B1
Glenbervie Rd FK3 . . . . . . .61 C3
Glenbo Dr FK6 . . . . .57 C4
Glenbrae Ct FK1 . . . . .60 A2
Glenbridge Ct KY12 . . . . .28 C2
Glenbrook EH14 . . . . .176 C4
Glenburn Gdns EH47 . . .170 B3
Glenburn Gr KY12 . . . . .26 C4
Glenburn Rd Falkirk FK1 . .60 B1
North Berwick EH39 . . . . . .54 B3
Glencairn Ave EH51 . . . . . .63 B3
Glencairn Cres EH12 . . . .122 C4
Glencairn St EH47 . . . . . . .59 A3
Stirling FK7 . . . . .7 A2
Glencairn Terr EH48 . . . .145 B4
Glen Esk EH47 . . . . .170 B3
Stirling FK8 . . . . .2 A1
Glencorse Pk EH26 . . . . .204 B4
Glencorse Prim Sch
EH26 . . . . .180 A1
Glencoul Ave KY11 . . . . . . .48 A2
Glencross Gdns EH26 . . .203 B3
Glendevon Ave EH12 . . . .122 A3
Glendevon Cotts EH52 . . .87 B1
Glendevon Dr FK3 . . . . .61 C3
Glendevon Gdns EH12 . .122 A3
Glendevon Gr EH12 . . . . .122 A3
Glendevon Pk
Edinburgh EH12 . . . . .122 A3
Winchburgh EH52 . . . . .87 C1
Glendevon Pl EH12 . . . . .122 A3
Glendevon Terr EH12 . . .122 A3
Glendinning Cres EH16 .155 A4
Glendinning Dr EH29 . . . .88 C1
Glendinning Pl EH29 . . . .88 C1
Glendinning Rd EH29 . . . .88 C1
Glendinning Way EH29 . .89 A1
Gleneagles Ct EH47 . . . .170 B3
Gleneagles Way EH54 . .146 C3
Glenesk Cres EH22 . . . . .156 C1
Glenfield Carnock KY12 . . . .27 B3
Livingston EH54 . . . . .147 A2
Glenfield Ave KY4 . . . . .13 B3
Glenfield Cres KY4 . . . . . .13 B3
Glenfield Gdns KY4 . . . . .13 B3
Glenfield Ind Est KY4 . . . .13 B3
Glenfield Rd KY4 . . . . .13 B3
Glenfinlas St EH3 . . . . . . .232 B3
Glenfuir St FK1 . . . . .59 B3
Glenfuir Terr FK1 . . . . .59 C3
Glengarry Cres FK1 . . . . . .59 C1
Glengyle Terr EH3 . . . . . .232 C1
Glenisla Ct EH47 . . . . .170 B3
Glenisla Gardens La
EH9 .123 B2
Glenisla Gdns EH9 . . . . . .123 B2
Glenisla Gr KY11 . . . . .29 B1
Glenkinchie Distillery *
EH34 . . . . .160 C1
Glenlee Ave EH8 . . . . .124 B4
Glenlee Gdns EH8 . . . . . .124 B4
Glenlockhart Bank
EH14 . . . . .122 B1
Glenlockhart Rd EH10 . .122 C1
Glenlockhart Valley
EH14 . . . . .122 B1
Glenmavis Cres ML8 . . . .230 A1
Glenmavis Ct ML8 . . . . . .230 A1
Glenmavis Dr EH48 . . . . .145 A4
Glenmore EH47 . . . . .170 B3
Glenmore Dr FK4 . . . . .57 C3
Glennie Gdns EH33 . . . . .128 B3
Glenochil Pk FK10 . . . . .4 C2
Glenochil Rd FK1 . . . . .4 C2
Glenochil Terr FK10 . . . . . .4 C2
Glenogle Ct EH3 . . . . .93 A1
Glenogle Ho ■ EH3 . . . . . .93 A1
Glenogle Pl ■ EH3 . . . . . . .93 A1
Glenogle Rd EH3 . . . . .93 A1
Glenogle Terr EH3 . . . . . . .93 A2
Glenorchy Rd EH39 . . . . . .54 A3
Glensburgh Rd FK3 . . . . . .61 A4

Glenshee EH47 ... 170 B3
Glenside Ct
 Armadale EH48 ... 143 C3
 Grangemouth FK3 ... 61 B3
Glenside Gdns EH48 ... 143 C3
Glentye Gdns FK1 ... 59 C1
Glenure Loan EH4 ... 91 B1
Glenvarloch Cres **5**
 EH16 ... 155 A4
Glenview Denny FK6 ... 36 A2
 Menstrie FK11 ... 4 A3
 Penicuik EH26 ... 203 C3
Glenview Cres EH47 ... 171 A1
Glenview Dr FK1 ... 59 C1
Glenview Rd FK4 ... 171 A1
Glenwinnel Rd FK12 ... 4 C2
Glenwood Dr EH48 ... 143 B3
Glenyards Rd FK4 ... 58 A1
Gloag Pl EH55 ... 172 B2
Globe Pk FK55 ... 117 B3
Globe Rd KY11 ... 46 B1
Glomach Gr KY12 ... 28 C3
Gloucester La EH3 ... 232 B4
Gloucester Pl EH3 ... 232 B4
Gloucester Sq EH3 ... 232 B4
Gloucester St EH3 ... 232 B4
Glover's Ct KY3 ... 35 A2
Glowrorum Dr FK6 ... 57 C4
Glynwed Ct FK2 ... 60 B4
Godfrey Ave FK6 ... 36 B1
Godfrey Cres FK5 ... 38 B1
Goff Ave EH7 ... 94 C1
Gogar Bridge Rd EH12 ... 120 A4
Gogar Loan FK9 ... 3 B3
Gogar Pl FK7 ... 7 B1
Gogar Rbdt HE12 ... 120 C3
Gogar Station Rd EH12 ... 120 C3
Gogarbank Farm EH12 ... 120 B1
Gogarloch Bank EH12 ... 121 A3
Gogarloch Haugh EH12 ... 121 A3
Gogarloch Muir EH12 ... 121 A3
Gogarloch Rd EH12 ... 121 A3
Gogarloch Syke EH12 ... 121 A3
Gogarstone Rd EH28 ... 120 A3
Goldenacre Terr ... 93 A2
Goldenstones Ave EH42 ... 78 C1
Goldpark Pl EH54 ... 147 A2
Golf Course Rd
 Bonnyrigg & Lasswade
  EH19 ... 182 A4
 Cowdenbeath KY4 ... 13 B3
 Linlithgow EH49 ... 84 C2
 Livingston EH54 ... 147 A4
Golf Ct EH32 ... 71 B2
Golf Dr EH32 ... 97 C2
Golf House Rd EH4 ... 78 C1
Goldfrum St KY12 ... 28 C2
Goodall Cres EH52 ... 116 B1
Goodall Pl FK11 ... 116 A1
Goodall's Pl **9** EH41 ... 132 A4
Goodman Pl FK2 ... 82 C4
Goose Green Ave EH21 ... 126 B4
Goose Green Cres EH21 ... 126 B4
Goose Green Pl EH21 ... 126 B4
Goose Green Rd
 Gullane EH31 ... 52 A1
 Musselburgh EH21 ... 126 B4
Goosecroft Rd FK8 ... 7 A4
Gordon Ave
 Bathgate EH48 ... 145 A3
 Bonnyrigg & Lasswade
  EH19 ... 181 C3
Gordon Cres
 Bridge of A FK9 ... 2 A4
 Stirling FK8 ... 1 C1
Gordon Ct EH52 ... 117 C3
Gordon Dr FK10 ... 10 B4
Gordon Loan EH12 ... 121 C4
Gordon Pl FK11 ... 59 C3
Gordon Rd
 Edinburgh EH12 ... 121 C4
 Rosyth KY11 ... 46 A1
Gordon St
 Cowdenbeath KY4 ... 13 B3
 Easthouses EH22 ... 183 B4
 Edinburgh EH6 ... 94 A2
 Lochgelly KY5 ... 14 A4
Gordon Terr
 Dunfermline KY11 ... 29 A1
 Edinburgh EH16 ... 124 A1
Gordon Way EH54 ... 147 B4
Gore Ave EH23 ... 207 B4
Gorebridge Prim Sch
 EH23 ... 207 B4
Goremire Rd ML8 ... 230 B1
Gorgie Park Cl EH14 ... 122 B2
Gorgie Park Rd
 Edinburgh EH11 ... 122 B3
 Edinburgh EH11 ... 122 B2
Gorgie Rd EH11 ... 122 B2
Gorrie St Denny FK6 ... 36 B1
 Dunfermline KY11 ... 29 B1
Gorsebank EH54 ... 147 C3
Gort Pl FK3 ... 61 B3
Gorton Loan EH12 ... 181 B3
Gorton Pl EH24 ... 181 B3
Gorton Rd EH24 ... 181 B3
Goschen Pl EH52 ... 117 A3
Goschen Terr EH52 ... 117 A3
Gosford Ho* EH32 ... 71 A1
Gosford Pl EH6 ... 93 B3
Gosford Rd
 Cockenzie & Port Seton
  EH32 ... 97 A2
 Kirkcaldy KY2 ... 16 B4
 Longniddry EH32 ... 98 C3
Gosford Wlk EH32 ... 97 B2
Gote La EH30 ... 68 A1

Gourlay Cotts EH24 ... 205 A4
Gourlay St KY2 ... 17 A2
Gourlaybank EH41 ... 101 A1
Gow Cres KY1 ... 17 A2
Gowan Ave FK2 ... 60 A3
Gowan La FK2 ... 60 A3
Gowanbank EH4 ... 147 B3
Gowanbrae EH47 ... 193 C3
Gowanbrae Dr KY12 ... 29 B2
Gowanbrae Pl KY12 ... 29 B2
Gowanbrae Terr KY12 ... 29 B2
Gowanhill Farm Rd
 EH14 ... 151 B3
Gowanhill Gdns FK8 ... 1 C1
Gowanlea Dr FK1 ... 110 A3
Gowan Cl **8** EH41 ... 132 A4
Grace St KY5 ... 14 B4
Gracefield Ct EH21 ... 126 A3
Gracemount Ave EH16 ... 155 A4
Gracemount Bsns Pav
Gracemount Dr EH16 ... 155 A3
Gracemount High Sch
 EH16 ... 155 A3
Gracemount Pl EH16 ... 155 A3
Gracemount Prim Sch
Gracemount Rd EH16 ... 155 A3
Gracemount Sq EH16 ... 155 A3
Gracie Cres FK7 ... 8 B2
Gracie's Wynd EH48 ... 144 A3
Gradlon Pl FK1 ... 60 A2
Graeme High Sch EH41 ... 60 C2
Graeme Pl FK1 ... 60 C2
Graham Ave Larbert FK5 ... 38 A2
 Stirling FK9 ... 2 C3
Graham Cres EH51 ... 64 A4
Graham Ct EH47 ... 171 C4
Graham St Bridge of A FK9 ... 2 A4
 Edinburgh EH6 ... 93 C3
Graham Terr FK2 ... 60 A3
Graham Way EH54 ... 147 B4
Graham's Rd EH26 ... 204 B4
Grahams Rd FK1 ... 60 B3
Grahamsdyke Ave EH51 ... 64 A4
Grahamsdyke Cres EH54 ... 58 A2
Grahamsdyke La EH51 ... 64 A4
Grahamsdyke Pl EH51 ... 64 A4
Grahamsdyke Rd
 Bo'ness EH51 ... 64 B3
 Bonnybridge FK4 ... 58 A2
Grahamsdyke St FK2 ... 61 A2
Grahamsdyke Terr EH51 ... 64 A4
Grahamston Sta FK1 ... 60 A3
Graiglaw Pl EH52 ... 116 B1
Graigleith View FK10 ... 4 B2
Grainger St KY5 ... 14 A4
Grampian Cres EH3 ...
Grange Cotts KY2 ... 34 C3
Grange Cres EH9 ... 123 B2
Grange Cres E EH32 ... 96 C1
Grange Cres W EH32 ... 127 C4
Grange Ct
 5 Edinburgh EH9 ... 123 C3
 North Berwick EH39 ... 53 B3
Grange Dr
 Dunfermline KY12 ... 46 B4
 Falkirk FK2 ... 60 B3
Grange Gdns FK9 ... 2 B2
Grange Gr EH32 ... 96 C1
Grange Knowe EH49 ... 85 B4
Grange La FK1 ... 40 B1
Grange Loan
 Bo'ness EH51 ... 64 A4
 Edinburgh EH9 ... 123 B2
Grange Loan Gdns EH9 ... 123 B2
Grange Pk KY11 ... 46 B4
Grange Pl
 Grangemouth FK3 ... 61 B4
 Redding FK2 ... 61 B4
Grange Prim Sch EH51 ... 64 A4
Grange Rd Alloa FK10 ... 9 C3
 Bridge of A FK9 ... 2 B3
 Broxburn EH52 ... 117 C2
 Burntisland KY3 ... 33 B1
 Dunfermline KY11 ... 29 B1
 Edinburgh EH9 ... 123 B3
 Livingston EH54 ... 148 A4
 North Berwick EH39 ... 54 A3
 Polmont FK2, FK3 ... 61 C4
 Prestonpans EH32 ... 96 C1
Grange Terr Bo'ness EH51 ... 64 A4
 Edinburgh EH9 ... 123 B2
Grange The FK2 ... 82 C4
Grange View EH32 ... 85 B4
Grange Wynd EH21 ... 46 B4
Grangeburn Rd FK3 ... 40 C1
Grangelea Ct FK3 ... 61 C4
Grangemouth High Sch
 FK3 ...
Grangemouth Mus* FK2 ... 40 B1
Grangemouth Rd FK2 ... 60 C2
Grangepans EH51 ... 64 A4
Grangeview FK5 ... 38 C1

Grannies Pk Ind Est
 EH22 ... 157 A2
Grannus Mews EH21 ... 126 B2
Grant Ave EH13 ... 153 A3
Grant Pl FK9 ... 2 A2
Grant St Alloa FK10 ... 9 C3
 West Calder EH55 ... 172 B2
Granton Cres EH5 ... 92 C3
Granton Gdns EH5 ... 92 C3
Granton Gr EH5 ... 92 C3
Granton Mains Ave EH4 ... 92 B3
Granton Mains Bank EH4 ... 92 B3
Granton Mains Brae EH4 ... 92 B3
Granton Mains Ct EH4 ... 92 B3
Granton Mains E EH4 ... 92 B3
Granton Mains Gait EH4 ... 92 B3
Granton Mains Vale EH4 ... 92 B3
Granton Mains Wynd
 EH4 ... 92 B3
Granton Medway EH5 ... 92 B3
Granton Mill Cres EH4 ... 92 B3
Granton Mill Ct EH4 ... 92 A3
Granton Mill March EH4 ... 92 A3
Granton Mill Pk EH4 ... 92 A3
Granton Mill Rd EH4 ... 92 A3
Granton Mill W EH4 ... 92 A3
Granton Park Ave EH5 ... 92 C4
Granton Pl EH5 ... 92 C3
Granton Prim Sch EH5 ... 92 C3
Granton Rd EH5 ... 93 A3
Granton Sq EH5 ... 92 C4
Granton Terr EH5 ... 92 C3
Granton View
 Dalgety Bay KY11 ... 47 C1
 Edinburgh EH5 ... 92 C3
Grants Bank KY12 ... 29 A2
Grantully Pl EH9 ... 123 C2
Granville Terr EH10 ... 123 A3
Granville Way KY11 ... 46 C2
Gray Buchanan Ct FK2 ... 82 B3
Gray Pk KY11 ... 47 B2
Gray Pl KY11 ... 47 B2
Gray St ML7 ... 192 A2
Gray's Loan EH10 ... 122 C2
Graysmill Specl Sch
 EH14 ... 122 B1
Graystale Rd FK7 ... 7 A2
Great Cannon Bank EH15 ... 95 A1
Great Carleton Pl EH16 ... 125 A2
Great Carleton Sq EH16 ... 125 A2
Great Junction St EH6 ... 93 C3
Great Michael Cl EH6 ... 93 B4
Great Michael Rd KY11 ... 46 A1
Great Michael Rise EH6 ... 93 B4
Great Michael Sq EH6 ... 93 B3
Great Stuart St EH3 ... 232 A3
Grebe Gdns KY11 ... 30 A1
Green Apron Pk EH39 ... 54 A2
Green La
 Bonnyrigg & Lasswade
  EH18 ... 181 C4
 Grangemouth FK3 ... 61 B4
Green St Edinburgh EH7 ... 93 B1
 Townhill KY12 ... 29 B4
Green The Alva FK12 ... 5 A4
 Balerno EH14 ... 177 B4
 Bathgate EH48 ... 145 B4
 Edinburgh EH4 ... 92 A2
 Pencaitland EH34 ... 160 C3
 West Barns EH42 ... 77 C1
Green Tree La EH51 ... 63 B3
Greenacre EH14 ... 152 C4
Greenacre Pl KY4 ... 13 A1
Greenacres KY12 ... 12 A1
Greenbank Ave EH10 ... 123 A1
Greenbank Cres EH10 ... 154 A4
Greenbank Dr
 Cowdenbeath KY4 ... 13 A1
 Edinburgh EH10 ... 123 A1
Greenbank Gdns EH10 ... 153 C4
Greenbank Gr EH10 ... 153 C4
Greenbank La EH10 ... 153 C4
Greenbank Loan EH10 ... 122 C1
Greenbank Pk EH10 ... 153 C4
Greenbank Pl
 Edinburgh EH10 ... 123 A1
 Falkirk FK1 ... 59 B2
Greenbank Rd
 Edinburgh EH10 ... 122 C1
 Falkirk FK1 ... 59 B2
Greenbank Rise EH10 ... 153 C4
Greenbank Row EH10 ... 153 C4
Greenbank Terr EH10 ... 123 A1
Greenburn Rd EH47 ... 193 C3
Greencornhills Rdbt FK7 ... 19 C4
Greencraig Ave EH17 ... 155 C3
Greendale Pk EH4 ... 92 A2
Greendykes Ave EH16 ... 124 C2
Greendykes Dr EH16 ... 124 C2
Greendykes Gdns EH16 ... 124 C2
Greendykes Ind Est
 EH52 ... 117 C2
Greendykes Loan **8**
 EH16 ... 124 C2
Greendykes Prim Sch
 EH16 ... 124 C2
Greendykes Rd
 Broxburn EH52 ... 117 C3
 Edinburgh EH16 ... 124 C2
Greendykes Steadings
 EH52 ... 117 C4
Greendykes Terr EH16 ... 124 C2
Gullan's Cl EH1 ... 233 B3

Greenend Dr EH17 ... 155 B4
Greenend Gdns EH17 ... 155 B4
Greenend Pl EH17 ... 155 B4
Greenfield Cres EH14 ... 177 B4
Greenfield Rd EH14 ... 177 B4
Greenfield St Alloa FK10 ... 10 A4
 Bonnybridge FK4 ... 58 A3
Greenhall Rd EH23 ... 183 B1
Greenhead FK12 ... 5 A3
Greenheads Rd EH39 ... 54 C3
Greenhill Ct
 Edinburgh EH10 ... 123 A3
 Fauldhouse EH47 ... 193 C3
Greenhill Gdns EH10 ... 123 A2
Greenhill Pk
 Edinburgh EH10 ... 123 A2
 Penicuik EH26 ... 203 B3
Greenhill Pl EH10 ... 123 A2
Greenhill Rd
 Blackridge EH48 ... 142 C2
 Bonnybridge FK4 ... 58 A2
Greenhill Terr EH10 ... 123 A3
Greenhithe Terr FK2 ... 82 C4
Greenhorn's Well Ave
 FK1 ... 59 C2
Greenhorn's Well Cres
 FK1 ... 59 C2
Greenhorn's Well Dr FK1 ... 59 C2
Greenlaw Gr EH26 ... 180 A1
Greenlaw Hedge EH13 ... 153 C4
Greenlaw Rise EH13 ... 153 C4
Greenloanings KY2 ... 16 B4
Greenmantle Loan **9**
 EH16 ... 124 A1
Greenmount KY4 ... 13 A1
Greenmount Dr
 Burntisland KY3 ... 33 C1
 Shieldhill FK1 ... 81 B3
Greenmount Rd N KY3 ... 33 C1
Greenmount Rd S KY3 ... 34 A1
Greenpark EH17 ... 155 B3
Greenpark Dr FK2 ... 61 C1
Greenrigg Cotts ML7 ... 169 A3
Greenrigg Prim Sch
 ML7 ... 168 C3
Greens The FK2 ... 82 C3
Greenshank Dr KY11 ... 30 A1
Greenside EH48 ... 113 C3
Greenside La EH1 ... 233 B4
Greenside Pl
 Edinburgh EH1 ... 233 B4
 Rosewell EH24 ... 181 B1
Greenside St FK10 ... 10 A3
Greenvale Dr FK2 ... 82 C4
Greenwell St EH47 ... 193 C3
Greenwell Terr FK2 ... 82 C4
Greenwells Dr FK2 ... 82 C4
Greenwood Ave EH14 ... 147 B3
Greenwood Pk EH54 ... 147 B3
Greenwood St ML7 ... 191 C3
Gregory Rd EH54 ... 147 C4
Greig Cres EH48 ... 144 A3
Greig Pl KY5 ... 14 A4
Greig Rd KY11 ... 46 A1
Grendon Ct FK8 ... 7 A3
Grendon Gdns FK8 ... 7 A3
Grenville Ct FK1 ... 59 C2
Grey Craigs KY12 ... 27 B1
Grey School Cnr EH32 ... 96 C1
Greyfriar's Wlk KY11 ... 47 B2
Greyfriars EH1 ... 233 A2
Greyfriars Bobby Meml*
Greygoran FK10 ... 5 B1
Grierson Ave EH5 ... 93 A3
Grierson Cres
 Camelcorn FK7 ... 6 B3
 Edinburgh EH5 ... 93 A3
Grierson Gdns EH5 ... 93 A3
Grierson Rd EH5 ... 92 C3
Grierson Sq EH5 ... 93 A3
Grierson Villas EH5 ... 93 A3
Grieve Ct EH26 ... 203 C4
Grieve St
 Dunfermline KY12 ... 28 C2
 Kirkcaldy KY2 ... 17 A3
Griffith St FH47 ... 170 A1
Griffiths St FK1 ... 60 A2
Grigor Ave EH4 ... 92 B2
Grigor Dr EH4 ... 92 B2
Grigor Gdns EH4 ... 92 C2
Grindlay St EH3 ... 232 B2
Grindlay Street Ct EH3 ... 232 B2
Groathill Ave EH4 ... 92 B1
Groathill Gdns E **2** EH4 ... 92 B1
Groathill Gdns W **1** EH4 ... 92 B1
Groathill Loan EH4 ... 92 B1
Groathill Rd N EH4 ... 92 B1
Groathill Rd S EH4 ... 92 B1
Grodwell Dr FK12 ... 4 C4
Grosvenor Gdns EH12 ... 122 C4
Grosvenor St EH12 ... 232 A2
Grove End KY11 ... 47 A2
Grove Cres FK7 ... 39 A1
Grove End EH18 ... 182 A4
Grove St Denny FK6 ... 36 B1
 Edinburgh EH3 ... 232 A2
Grovemount FK7 ... 19 B4
Grundie's Well Rd EH17 ... 155 C3
Guardians Wood EH12 ... 122 B4
Guardwell Cres EH17 ... 155 B4
Guildhall St KY12 ... 29 A2
Guildie Howes Rd EH47 ... 207 C1
Guildhaugh Rdbt
 EH48 ... 145 B3
Guildry Gr KY12 ... 29 C2

Gullane Prim Sch EH31 ... 52 A1
Gunn Rd FK3 ... 61 B3
Gunner Rd FK3,EH51 ... 62 B4
Guthrie St EH1 ... 233 A2
Guttergates Rd KY11 ... 30 A3
Gyle Ave EH12 ... 120 C3
Gyle Park Gdns EH12 ... 121 A3
Gyle Rbdt EH12 ... 120 C3
Gyle Sh Ctr EH12 ... 121 A3
Gylemuir Prim Sch
 EH12 ... 121 B3
Gylemuir Rd EH12 ... 121 B3
Gylers Rd EH12 ... 53 A2

H

Haddington Inf Sch
 EH41 ... 132 A4
Haddington Pl EH7 ... 93 C1
Haddington Rd
 East Linton EH40 ... 103 B4
 Musselburgh EH21 ... 127 A3
 North Berwick EH39 ... 54 B3
 Tranent EH33 ... 128 C3
Haddington Station Ind Est
Haddon's Ct EH1 ... 131 C4
Haddow Gr KY3 ... 50 B4
Hadfast Rd EH22 ... 158 B3
Hadrian Way FK1 ... 64 A3
Haig Ave Kirkcaldy KY1 ... 17 B4
 Stirling FK8 ... 2 A2
Haig Cres Bathgate EH48 ... 145 B3
 Dunfermline KY12 ... 29 B3
Haig St FK3 ... 61 B3
Hailes App EH13 ... 153 A4
Hailes Ave EH13 ... 153 A4
Hailes Bank EH13 ... 153 A4
Hailes Castle* EH41 ... 103 A2
Hailes Cres EH13 ... 153 A4
Hailes Gdns EH13 ... 153 A4
Hailes Gr EH13 ... 153 A4
Hailes Loan EH41 ... 102 A2
Hailes Pk EH13 ... 152 C4
Hailes Pl KY12 ... 29 B2
Hailes St EH3 ... 232 B1
Hailesland Gdns EH14 ... 121 C1
Hailesland Gr EH14 ... 121 C1
Hailesland Pk EH14 ... 121 C1
Hailesland Pl EH14 ... 121 C1
Hailesland Prim Sch
 EH14 ... 152 C4
Hailesland Rd EH14 ... 121 C1
Hailstonegreen ML11 ... 215 A1
Hailstones Cres EH48 ... 143 C3
Hailstonespark FK10 ... 153 C3
Haining Gr KY12 ... 83 A3
Haining Pl
 Grangemouth FK3 ... 61 C4
 Livingston EH54 ... 147 A3
Haining Rd EH49 ... 84 B3
Haining Terr EH49 ... 83 C3
Haining Valley Steadings
 EH49 ... 83 C3
Hakness Cres EH33 ... 128 B3
Halbeath Dr KY11 ... 29 C3
Halbeath Pl KY11 ... 29 C3
Halbeath Rd
 Dunfermline KY11 ... 29 B3
 Halbeath KY11 ... 30 A3
Halbeath Ret Pk KY11 ... 30 A3
Haberts Cres FK7 ... 7 A1
Haldane Ave
 Bridge of A FK9 ... 2 A3
 Haddington EH41 ... 100 C1
Haldane Gr KY12 ... 26 B4
Haldane Sq EH54 ... 173 B3
Halket Cres FK7 ... 7 A1
Halketshall KY11 ... 45 B2
Halkett Cres EH31 ... 52 A1
Hall La KY5 ... 14 A4
Hall Rd EH54 ... 117 C3
Hall Row KY11 ... 45 A2
Hall St Cowdenbeath KY4 ... 14 A4
 Lochgelly KY5 ... 14 A4
Hall Terr EH48 ... 113 C3
Hallcraig Cres FK7 ... 19 B1
Hallcroft Cl EH28 ... 119 B1
Hallcroft Cres EH28 ... 119 B1
Hallcroft Gdns EH28 ... 119 B1
Hallcroft Grn EH28 ... 119 B1
Hallcroft Neuk EH28 ... 119 B1
Hallcroft Pk EH28 ... 119 B1
Hallcroft Rise EH28 ... 119 B1
Hallglen Prim Sch FK1 ... 60 A1
Hallglen Rd FK1 ... 60 A1
Hallglen Terr FK1 ... 60 A1
Hallhead Rd EH16 ... 123 C1
Hallhill EH42 ... 106 B4
Halliburton Terr EH39 ... 53 A2
Hallows The KY1 ... 17 C4
Hallyards Rd
 Newbridge EH29 ... 119 A4
 Ratho Sta EH28 ... 119 B3
Halmyre St EH6 ... 94 A2
Halyard Rise KY11 ... 47 C1
Halyard Terr KY12 ... 15 A1
Hamburgh Pl EH6 ... 93 C3
Hamilton Ave
 Linlithgow EH49 ... 84 C3
 Stenhousemuir FK5 ... 38 C2

Hamilton Cres
Gullane EH31 . . . . .52 A1
Maddiston FK2 . . . . .82 C3
Newtongrange EH22 . . . . .183 A3
Hamilton Dr
Edinburgh EH15 . . . . .124 C4
Falkirk FK1 . . . . .60 A2
Stirling FK9 . . . . .2 B2
Hamilton Dr W EH15 . .124 C4
Hamilton Gdns EH15 . . . .124 C4
Hamilton Gr EH15 . . . . .124 C4
Hamilton La
Bathgate EH48 . . . . .144 C4
Bo'ness EH51 . . . . .63 C4
Hamilton Pk
Edinburgh EH15 . . . . .124 C4
Linlithgow EH49 . . . . .84 C3
Hamilton Pl
Edinburgh EH3 . . . . .93 A1
Linlithgow EH49 . . . . .84 C3
Rosyth KY11 . . . . .46 C2
Hamilton Rd
Bathgate EH48 . . . . .144 C4
Grangemouth FK3 . . . . . . .61 C3
Gullane EH31 . . . . .52 A1
North Berwick EH39 . . . . . .54 A4
Stenhousemuir FK2, FK5 . . .38 B3
Hamilton Sq EH51 . . . . . .63 B3
Hamilton St Falkirk FK1 . . .59 B3
Lochgelly KY5 . . . . .14 A3
Hamilton Terr
Edinburgh EH15 . . . . .125 A4
High Valleyfield KY12 . . . . .26 A1
Inverkeithing KY11 . . . . . . .47 B1
Hamilton Way EH47 . . . .170 C3
Hamilton Wynd EH6 . . . . .93 C3
Hamiltons Folly Mews
EH8 . . . . .233 B1
Hammermen's Entry
EH8 . . . . .233 B3
Hampton Terr EH12 . . . .122 C4
Handax ML11 . . . . .215 A1
Haney's Way FK51 . . . . .64 A4
Hanion Gdns FK2 . . . . . .82 C4
Hanover Ct
Broxburn EH52 . . . . .117 C3
Livingston EH54 . . . . .147 A1
Hanover Grange FK3 . . . .61 A4
Hanover St EH2 . . . . . . .232 C4
Happy Valley Rd EH47 . .171 C4
Harbour Dr KY11 . . . . . . .47 C2
Harbour La EH30 . . . . . . .68 A1
Harbour Pl
Burntisland KY3 . . . . .50 C4
Dalgety Bay KY11 . . . . .47 C1
Edinburgh EH15 . . . . .95 A1
Inverkeithing KY11 . . . . . . .47 B1
Harbour Rd Bo'ness EH51 . .64 B4
Edinburgh EH15 . . . . .95 A1
Kinghorn KY3 . . . . .35 A1
Musselburgh EH21 . . . . . .126 A3
Harburn Ave EH54 . . . . .146 C3
Harburn Ave W EH54 . .146 C4
Harburn Dr EH55 . . . . . .172 C2
Harburn La EH55 . . . . . .172 C2
Harburn Rd EH55 . . . . . .172 C2
Harcourt Rd KY2 . . . . . . .17 A3
Harden Pl EH11 . . . . . . .122 C3
Hardengreen Bsns Ctr
EH22 . . . . .156 C1
Hardengreen Ind Est
EH22 . . . . .156 C1
Hardengreen Junc
EH22 . . . . .182 C4
Hardengreen La EH22 . .156 C1
Hardgate EH41 . . . . .101 A1
Hardgate Ct EH41 . . . . .101 A1
Hardhill Dr EH48 . . . . . .144 C3
Hardhill Pl EH48 . . . . . . .144 A3
Hardhill Rd EH48 . . . . . .144 C4
Hardhill Road Travelling Peoples Site EH48 . . .144 B3
Hardhill Terr EH48 . . . . .144 C3
Hardie Cres FK7 . . . . .8 B2
Hardie Ct FK7 . . . . .7 B2
Hardie Rd EH54 . . . . .146 B4
Hardie Terr EH40 . . . . . .103 B4
Hardwell Cl EH8 . . . . . . .233 B2
Hardy Gdns EH48 . . . . . .145 C3
Hareburn Ave FK1 . . . . .112 A3
Harelaw Rd EH13 . . . . . .153 A3
Hares Cl EH52 . . . . .97 B2
Harestanes Rd EH48 . . . .143 C2
Harewood Cres EH16 . . .124 C2
Harewood Dr EH16 . . . . .124 C2
Harewood Rd EH16 . . . . .124 C2
Harkenburn Gdns EH26 .203 B3
Harlands The FK10 . . . . . .9 C4
Harlaw Gait EH14 . . . . .151 B1
Harlaw Gr EH26 . . . . . . .203 B3
Harlaw Hill EH32 . . . . . . .96 C1
Harlaw March EH14 . . . .177 B4
Harlaw Rd Balerno EH14 .151 A1
Currie EH14 . . . . .152 A1
Harlawhill Gdns EH32 . . .97 A1
Harley Ct FK7 . . . . .60 A4
Harley St KY11 . . . . .47 A2
Harlington Pl FK2 . . . . . . .82 C4
Harlow Ave FK2 . . . . .61 B1
Harlow House Ranger Ctr*
EH14 . . . . .178 A4
Harlton Terr EH4 . . . . . .178 B4
Harmony Cres EH19 . . . .182 B4
Harmony Ct EH19 . . . . . .182 B4
Harmony St EH19 . . . . . .182 B4

Harmony Wlk EH19 . . . .182 B4
Harness Ct EH20 . . . . . . .181 B4
Harpendale Cres EH39 . . .53 B3
Harper's Brae EH26 . . . .204 A3
Harperdean Terr EH41 . .100 C1
Harriebrae Pk KY12 . . . . .28 C2
Harriet St KY1 . . . . .17 C3
Harris Ct FK10 . . . . .10 A3
Harris Dr KY2 . . . . .16 C4
Harris Pl Dunfermline KY11 .29 B1
Grangemouth FK3 . . . . . . .61 B3
Harrismith Pl FK7 . . . . .7 C1
Harrison Gdns EH11 . . . .122 C2
Harrison La EH11 . . . . . .122 C3
Harrison Pl
Edinburgh EH11 . . . . .122 C2
Falkirk FK1 . . . . .59 C3
Harrison Rd EH11 . . . . . .122 C3
Harrysmuir Cres EH53 . .148 A4
Harrysmuir N EH53 . . . . .148 A4
Harrysmuir Prim Sch
EH54 . . . . .148 A4
Harrysmuir Rd EH53 . . . .148 A4
Harrysmuir S EH53 . . . . .148 A4
Harrysmuir Terr EH53 . . .148 A4
Hart St EH1 . . . . .93 B1
Hart Street La EH1 . . . . . .93 B1
Hart Wynd FK7 . . . . .7 C1
Hartfield Terr ML7 . . . . . .212 A4
Harthill Ind Est ML7 . . . .168 B3
Harthill Prim Sch ML7 . .168 C3
Harthill Rd
Blackridge EH48 . . . . .142 B1
Fauldhouse EH47 . . . . . . .193 B3
Hartington Gdns EH10 . .123 A3
Hartington Pl EH10 . . . . .123 A3
Hartley Pl FK3 . . . . .61 A3
Hartwood Gdns ML7 . . . .191 A1
Hartwood Rd
West Calder EH55 . . . . . . .172 B1
Hartwood ML7 . . . . .191 A2
Hartwoodhill Hospl
ML7 . . . . .191 A2
Harvest Dr EH28 . . . . . . .119 A3
Harvest Rd EH28 . . . . . . .119 A3
Harvest St KY2 . . . . .16 B4
Harvesters Way EH14 . . .152 B4
Harvey Ave FK2 . . . . .61 C1
Harvey Wynd FK8 . . . . . . .2 A1
Harvieston Villas EH42 . .207 B4
Hatfield Pl [4] EH48 . . . .145 A4
Hatton Pl EH9 . . . . .123 B3
Haugh Gdns FK2 . . . . .39 A1
Haugh Pk EH14 . . . . .122 A1
Haugh Rd Burntisland KY3 .50 B4
Stirling FK9 . . . . .2 A1
Haugh St Edinburgh EH4 . .93 A1
Falkirk FK2 . . . . .39 A1
Haughs Way FK6 . . . . . . .36 C1
Haven Pk
Dalgety Bay KY11 . . . . .47 C1
South Alloa FK7 . . . . .9 C2
Haven's Edge KY12 . . . . .45 C2
Hawes Brae EH30 . . . . . . .68 B3
Hawk Brae EH54 . . . . . . .147 B3
Hawkcraig Rd KY3 . . . . . .49 A4
Hawkhead Cres EH16 . . .155 A4
Hawkhead Gr [3] EH16 . .155 A4
Hawkhill EH7 . . . . .94 A2
Hawkhill Ave EH7 . . . . . . .94 A2
Hawkhill Rd Alloa FK10 . .10 B3
Kincardine FK10 . . . . .23 B3
Hawkins Terr EH26 . . . . .204 A4
Hawksmuir [3] KY1 . . . . .17 B3
Hawkwood Terr ML11 . . .215 A1
Hawley Rd FK1 . . . . .60 B2
Hawthorn Bank
Carnock KY12 . . . . .27 B3
Cockenzie & Port Seton
EH32 . . . . .97 A2
Queensferry EH30 . . . . . . .68 A1
Seafield EH47 . . . . .172 A4
Hawthorn Cres
Cowdenbeath KY4 . . . . . . .12 C1
Easthouses EH22 . . . . . . .183 B4
Fallin FK7 . . . . .8 B3
Stirling FK8 . . . . .1 C1
Hawthorn Ct EH47 . . . . .172 A4
Hawthorn Dr Denny FK6 . .36 B2
Falkirk FK1 . . . . .59 C2
Fallin FK7 . . . . .8 B3
Harthill ML7 . . . . .168 C3
Shotts ML7 . . . . .159 B4
Hawthorn Gdns EH20 . . .155 A1
Hawthorn Pl
Edinburgh EH17 . . . . .155 C3
Ormiston EH35 . . . . .159 B4
Shotts ML7 . . . . .212 A4
Uphall EH52 . . . . .116 C2
Hawthorn St FK3 . . . . . . .61 B3
Hawthorn Terr EH32 . . . . .97 A2
Hawthornbank La EH4 . . .93 A1
Hawthornbank Pl EH6 . . .93 B3
Hawthornbank Rd EH41 .100 C1
Hawthornden Ave EH19 . .82 A3
Hawthornden Gdns
EH19 . . . . .182 A4
Hawthornden Pl EH6 . . . .93 C2
Hawthornden Prim Sch
EH19 . . . . .181 C3
Hawthorns Pl FK5 . . . . . . .38 B3
Hawthorns The EH31 . . . .52 A2
Hawthornvale EH6 . . . . . .93 B3
Hay Ave EH16 . . . . .124 C2
Hay Dr EH16 . . . . .125 A2
Hay Gdns EH16 . . . . .124 C3

Hay Gr KY11 . . . . .29 C1
Hay Pl EH16 . . . . .124 C2
Hay Rd EH16 . . . . .124 C2
Hay Terr EH16 . . . . .124 C2
Hayfield Edinburgh EH12 .121 A4
Falkirk FK2 . . . . .60 B4
Hayfield Ind Est KY2 . . . .17 A4
Hayfield Pl KY2 . . . . .17 A4
Hayfield Rd Falkirk FK2 . . .60 B4
Kirkcaldy KY1 . . . . .17 B4
Hayfield Terr FK6 . . . . . . .57 C4
Hayford Mills FK7 . . . . . . .6 B3
Hayford Pl FK7 . . . . .6 B3
Haygate Ave FK7 . . . . . . .82 C4
Haymarket EH12 . . . . . . .232 A2
Haymarket Cres EH54 . .147 A3
Haymarket Sta EH12 . . .232 A2
Haymarket Terr EH12 . . .122 C4
Haymarket Yds EH12 . . .122 C4
Haypark Bsns Ctr FK2 . . .61 C1
Haypark Rd FK6 . . . . .57 B3
Hays Com Bsns Ctr
EH16 . . . . .124 B2
Hayworth Ave FK2 . . . . . .61 A2
Hazel Ave KY2 . . . . .17 A3
Hazel Cres FK6 . . . . .36 B2
Hazel Ct EH42 . . . . .78 A1
Hazel Dr EH19 . . . . .182 A3
Hazel Gr
Dumfermline KY11 . . . . . . .46 C4
Falkirk FK2 . . . . .60 B4
Livingston EH54 . . . . .148 A3
Shotts ML7 . . . . .192 A2
Hazel La EH20 . . . . .180 C4
Hazel Rd FK3 . . . . .61 B3
Hazelbank Gdns FK8 . . . . .2 A1
Hazelbank Terr EH11 . . .122 C2
Hazeldean Ave EH51 . . . .63 B3
Hazeldean Terr EH16 . . .124 A1
Hazelhurst FK2 . . . . .82 C4
Hazelwood Gr EH16 . . . .124 B1
Head of Muir Prim Sch
FK6 . . . . .57 B3
Headlesscross Rd EH47 .192 C1
Headrig Rd EH17 . . . . . . .156 B2
Headrigg Row EH16 . . . .124 B1
Headwell Ave KY12 . . . . .29 A3
Headwell Ct KY12 . . . . . . .29 A3
Headwell Rd KY12 . . . . . .29 A3
Headwell Sch KY12 . . . . .29 A3
Heaney Ave EH53 . . . . . .148 A4
Heath Rd KY11 . . . . .46 C2
Heath Row FK4 . . . . .81 B3
Heather Gr
Dumfermline KY11 . . . . . . .46 C4
Maddiston FK2 . . . . .83 A3
Heather Pk EH47 . . . . . . .146 A1
Heatherbank EH54 . . . . .147 B3
Heatherdale Gdns FK6 . . .57 C4
Heatherfield Glade
EH54 . . . . .147 A3
Heathervale Wlk EH48 . .144 A3
Heatherwood Ind Est
EH47 . . . . .146 C4
Heathery The KY11 . . . . . .46 C4
Hedge Row EH20 . . . . . .180 C4
Hedges The FK1 . . . . .59 C3
Heggie's Wynd KY1 . . . . .17 A1
Heights Rd EH48 . . . . . . .142 B2
Helen La KY11 . . . . .46 C3
Helenslea Cotts [7]
EH48 . . . . .145 A3
Helmsdale Pk KY12 . . . . .28 C1
Henderland Rd EH12 . . . .122 B4
Henderson Ave FK10 . . . .10 A4
Henderson Cres EH52 . . .117 A3
Henderson Ct EH53 . . . . .148 C2
Henderson Gdns
Edinburgh EH6 . . . . .93 C3
Tranent EH33 . . . . .128 B3
Henderson Pl Alva FK12 . . .5 A4
Broxburn EH52 . . . . .117 A3
Edinburgh EH3 . . . . .93 B1
Henderson Place La EH3 .93 A1
Henderson Row EH3 . . . . .93 A1
Henderson St
Bridge of A FK9 . . . . .2 A4
Edinburgh EH6 . . . . .93 C3
Kingseat KY12 . . . . .12 A1
Lochgelly KY5 . . . . .14 A4
Henderson Terr EH11 . . .122 C3
Hendry Cres KY2 . . . . .17 A3
Hendry Rd KY2 . . . . .17 A3
Hendry St FK2 . . . . .60 B4
Henning Rd KY11 . . . . . . .17 A1
Hennings The FK10 . . . . . .5 B3
Henry Ross Pl EH30 . . . . .68 A1
Henry St Alva FK12 . . . . . . .5 A3
Bo'ness EH51 . . . . .64 A3
Henryson Rd KY11 . . . . . .29 C2
Hens Nest Rd EH47 . . . . .170 C3
Hepburn Dr EH22 . . . . . .157 B1
Hepburn Rd EH41 . . . . . .101 A1
Herald Rise EH54 . . . . . .147 B2
Herbertshire St FK6 . . . . .36 C1
Hercus Loan EH21 . . . . .126 A3
Herd Gn EH54 . . . . .147 A4
Herd Terr EH20 . . . . .181 A4
Herdmanflatt EH41 . . . . .101 A1
Herdmanflatt Hospl
EH41 . . . . .101 A1
Hershill Ave FK1 . . . . .81 B3
Heriot Bridge EH1 . . . . .232 C2
Heriot Gdns KY3 . . . . .33 C1
Heriot Hill Terr EH7 . . . . .93 B2
Heriot Pl EH3 . . . . .232 C2
Heriot Row EH3 . . . . .232 B4

Heriot St KY11 . . . . .47 B1
Heriot Way EH38 . . . . . .228 B1
Heriot-Watt Univ EH14 .151 C4
Heritage Dr FK2 . . . . .39 A2
Hermand Cres EH11 . . . .122 C2
Hermand Gdns EH55 . . .172 C2
Hermand St EH11 . . . . . .122 B2
Hermand Terr EH11 . . . .122 B2
Hermiston Gait Ret Pk
EH11 . . . . .121 A2
Hermiston House Rd
EH12,EH14 . . . . .120 C1
Hermiston Junc EH11,
EH12 . . . . .121 A1
Hermitage Dr EH10 . . . . .123 A1
Hermitage Gdns EH10 . .123 A1
Hermitage of Braid Visitor
Ctr* EH10 . . . . .123 B1
Hermitage Park Gr EH6 . .94 A2
Hermitage Park Lea EH6 .94 A2
Hermitage Park Prim Sch
EH6 . . . . .94 A2
Hermitage Pk EH6 . . . . . .94 A2
Hermitage Pk S EH6 . . . .94 A2
Hermitage Pl EH6 . . . . . . .94 A2
Hermitage Rd FK9 . . . . . . .2 A3
Hermitage Terr EH10 . . . .123 A1
Hermits Croft EH8 . . . . .233 C1
Heron Ind Complex
EH54 . . . . .146 B4
Heron Sq EH54 . . . . .146 B4
Hervey St FK10 . . . . .10 A4
Hetherington Dr FK10 . . .11 A2
Heugh Brae EH39 . . . . . . .54 C3
Heugh Rd EH39 . . . . .54 C3
Heugh St FK1 . . . . .60 A2
Heugh The
North Berwick EH39 . . . . . .54 C3
Tranent EH33 . . . . .128 B4
Hewitt Pl KY11 . . . . .49 B4
Higginson Loan EH22 . . .183 C3
High Academy Gr EH48 .143 C3
High Academy La EH48 .143 C3
High Beveridgewell
KY12 . . . . .28 C3
High Brae EH48 . . . . .113 C3
High Buckstone EH10 . . .154 B3
High Mdw ML8 . . . . .215 A1
High Mill Rd ML8 . . . . . .230 A1
High Park Rise EH26 . . . .203 C2
High Port EH49 . . . . .85 A4
High Rd Maddiston FK2 . . .83 A3
Roslin EH25 . . . . .204 C3
Spott EH42 . . . . .106 B2
High Riggs EH3 . . . . .232 B2
High School Wynd EH1 . .233 B2
High School Yds EH1 . . . .233 B2
High St Aberdour KY3 . . . .49 A4
Aberlady EH32 . . . . .71 B2
Airth FK2 . . . . .22 C4
Alloa FK10 . . . . .10 A3
Bathgate EH48 . . . . .145 A4
Bonnybridge FK4 . . . . .58 A3
Bonnyrigg & Lasswade
EH18 . . . . .156 A1
Bonnyrigg & Lasswade,
Broomieknowe EH19 . . . .182 A4
Burntisland KY3 . . . . .50 C4
Clackmannan FK10 . . . . . .10 C2
Cockenzie & Port Seton
EH32 . . . . .97 B2
Cowdenbeath KY4 . . . . . . .13 B2
Dalkeith EH22 . . . . .157 A2
Dunbar EH42 . . . . .78 B1
Dunbar, Belhaven EH42 . . .78 A1
Dunfermline KY12 . . . . . . .29 A2
Dysart KY1 . . . . .18 A4
East Linton EH40 . . . . . . .103 B4
Edinburgh EH1 . . . . .233 A3
Falkirk FK1 . . . . .60 A2
Gifford EH41 . . . . .163 C2
Haddington EH41 . . . . . . .132 A4
Inverkeithing KY11 . . . . . . .47 A1
Kincardine FK10 . . . . .23 B3
Kinghorn KY3 . . . . .34 C1
Kirkcaldy KY1 . . . . .17 B2
Kirkliston EH29 . . . . .89 A1
Linlithgow EH49 . . . . .85 A4
Loanhead EH20 . . . . .181 B4
Lochgelly KY5 . . . . .14 A4
Musselburgh EH21 . . . . . .126 B3
North Berwick EH39 . . . . . .54 B4
Ormiston EH35 . . . . .159 C4
Penicuik EH26 . . . . .203 C2
Prestonpans EH32 . . . . . . .96 C1
Queensferry EH30 . . . . . . .68 B1
Shotts ML7 . . . . .191 C2
Slamannan FK1 . . . . .110 A4
Tranent EH33 . . . . .128 B3
High Station Ct FK1 . . . . . .60 A2
High Station Rd FK1 . . . . .60 A2
High View Gr FK1 . . . . . . .81 B3
Highfield Livingston EH54 .147 A2
North Berwick EH39 . . . . . .54 A2
Highfield Ave EH49 . . . . . .84 C4
Highfield Cres EH49 . . . .144 C4
Highfield Rd EH39 . . . . . . .54 A3
Highland Dr FK5 . . . . .38 B2
Highland Dykes Cres
FK4 . . . . .58 A3
Highland Dykes Dr FK4 . . .58 A3
Highlea Circ EH14 . . . . . .177 A4
Highlea Gr EH14 . . . . . . .177 A4
Hill Cres EH48 . . . . .145 A4
Hill Ct KY12 . . . . .29 B3
Hill Gr KY12 . . . . .26 B4
Hill House Rd FK6 . . . . . . .57 C4

Hill of Beath Prim Sch
KY4 . . . . .12 C1
Hill of St Margaret KY12 . .29 C3
Hill Pk FK10 . . . . .10 A4
Hill Pl Alloa FK10 . . . . .10 A4
Edinburgh EH8 . . . . .233 B2
Inverkeithing KY11 . . . . . . .47 A1
Kirkcaldy KY1 . . . . .17 B2
Mayfield EH22 . . . . .183 C3
Shotts ML7 . . . . .191 C3
Hill Rd Gullane EH31 . . . . .51 C1
Harthill ML7 . . . . .168 B3
Pathhead EH37 . . . . .185 A3
Hill Sq EH8 . . . . .233 B2
Hill St Alloa FK10 . . . . .10 A4
Cowdenbeath KY4 . . . . . . .13 B2
Dunfermline KY12 . . . . . . .29 A2
Dysart KY1 . . . . .18 A4
Edinburgh EH2 . . . . .232 C4
Inverkeithing KY11 . . . . . . .47 A1
Kirkcaldy KY1 . . . . .17 A2
Stirling FK7 . . . . .7 A2
Hill Street La N EH2 . . . .232 C4
Hill Street La S EH2 . . . . .232 C4
Hillary Rd FK5 . . . . .38 C1
Hillbank KY11 . . . . .47 A2
Hillcoat Loan EH15 . . . . . .95 A1
Hillcoat Pl EH15 . . . . .95 A1
Hillcrest Bo'ness EH51 . . . .63 C3
Cowdenbeath KY4 . . . . . . .13 A2
Hillcrest Ave KY2 . . . . . . .16 C3
Hillcrest Dr FK10 . . . . .10 B3
Hillcrest Pl FK6 . . . . .57 B4
Hillcrest Rd FK1 . . . . .59 C1
Hillend Ind Pk KY11 . . . . . .48 B3
Hillend Rd KY11 . . . . .47 B2
Hillfield Cres KY11 . . . . . .47 A2
Hillfield Rd KY11 . . . . .47 A1
Hillfoot Terr ML8 . . . . . . .230 A1
Hillfoots Rd FK9 . . . . .2 C2
Hillhead EH9 . . . . .182 A4
Hillhead Ave ML8 . . . . . .230 A1
Hillhead Dr FK1 . . . . .59 C1
Hillhouse Ave EH48 . . . .144 B3
Hillhouse Cres EH27 . . . .149 C2
Hillhouse Rd EH4 . . . . . . .92 A1
Hillhouse Terr EH27 . . . .149 C2
Hillouseridge Rd ML7 . . .191 B3
Hillock Ave FK2 . . . . .61 B1
Hillpark Ave EH4 . . . . .91 C2
Hillpark Brae EH4 . . . . . . .91 C1
Hillpark Cres
Bannockburn FK7 . . . . .7 B1
Edinburgh EH4 . . . . .91 C1
Hillpark Ct EH4 . . . . .91 C2
Hillpark Dr
Bannockburn FK7 . . . . .7 B1
Edinburgh EH4 . . . . .91 C1
Hillpark Gdns EH4 . . . . . . .91 C1
Hillpark Gn EH4 . . . . .91 C1
Hillpark Gr EH4 . . . . .91 C1
Hillpark Loan EH4 . . . . . . .92 A1
Hillpark Rd EH4 . . . . .91 C1
Hillpark Terr EH4 . . . . . . .91 C1
Hillpark Way EH4 . . . . . . .92 A1
Hillpark Wood EH4 . . . . . .92 A1
Hillside FK10 . . . . .5 B1
Hillside Ave KY11 . . . . . . .48 A2
Hillside Camp Rd KY11 . .46 C1
Hillside Cotts
Linlithgow EH49 . . . . .85 B4
Cousland EH22 . . . . .158 B3
Hillside Cres EH7 . . . . . . .93 C1
Hillside Cres N EH23 . . . .207 B4
Hillside Cres S EH23 . . . .207 B4
Hillside Dr EH48 . . . . . . .144 B2
Hillside Rd EH51 . . . . .64 B3
Hillside Pl
Blackridge EH48 . . . . .142 B2
Longridge EH47 . . . . .90 B2
Hillside Sch KY3 . . . . .49 A4
Hillside St EH7 . . . . .93 C1
Hillside Terr Alloa FK10 . . .10 A4
Craigiehall EH30 . . . . .90 B3
Westquarter FK2 . . . . .61 A2
Hilltop EH49 . . . . .84 C4
Hillview Cowdenbeath KY4 .13 A2
Edinburgh EH4 . . . . .92 A1
Oakley KY12 . . . . .26 C4
Hillview Ave EH52 . . . . . .117 C3
Hillview Cotts EH22 . . . . .119 B1
Hillview Cres
Crossgates KY4 . . . . .30 C3
Edinburgh EH12 . . . . .121 B4
Hillview Dr Bridge of A FK9 .2 A3
Edinburgh EH12 . . . . .121 B4
Hillview La EH34 . . . . . . .173 C2
Hillview Pl
Broxburn EH52 . . . . .117 C3
Crossgates KY4 . . . . .30 C3
Fallin FK7 . . . . .8 B2
Hillview Rd Brightons FK2 . .82 B4
Edinburgh EH12 . . . . .121 B4
High Bonnybridge FK4 . . . .58 B2
Ormiston EH35 . . . . .159 C4
Stenhousemuir FK5 . . . . . .38 B2
Hillview Terr Alloa FK10 . . .10 B3
Edinburgh EH12 . . . . .121 A4
Hillview
Ratho Sta EH28 . . . . .119 B3
Hillwood Ave EH28 . . . . .119 B3
Hillwood Cres EH28 . . . .119 B3
Hillwood Gdns EH28 . . . .119 B3
Hillwood Pl EH30 . . . . . . .89 C1
Hillwood Prim Sch
EH28 . . . . .119 B3
Hillwood Rd EH28 . . . . . .119 B3
Hillwood Rise EH28 . . . . .119 B3
Hillwood Terr
Ratho Sta EH28 . . . . .119 B3

Hillwood Terr *continued*
Rosyth KY11 47 A2
Hilton FK7 20 C4
Hilton Cres FK10 10 B4
Hilton Ct EH41 132 A4
Hilton Farm Steadings KY11 46 A2
Hilton Rd Alloa FK10 10 B4
Cairneyhill KY12 27 C1
Rosyth KY11 46 B1
Hilton Terr FK7 8 B2
Hilton View KY4 13 C3
Hirst Cres FK7 8 B2
Hirst Ct FK7 8 B2
Hirst Gdns ML7 191 B3
Hirst Rd ML7 167 B2
Hirstrigg Cotts ML7 167 A2
Hoban Sq EH52 117 C3
Hobart St EH54 148 A3
Hodge St FK1 60 A2
Hogarth Ave EH23 183 B1
Hoggan Cres KY11 29 B1
Hoghill Ct EH53 148 C2
Hoghill Pl EH53 148 C2
Holborn Pl KY11 46 C3
Holbourne Pl FK11 4 A4
Holden Way KY11 48 A3
Holly Ave FK5 38 C2
Holly Bank EH22 183 C4
Holly Cres KY11 46 C4
Holly Pl KY1 17 B4
Holly Terr EH19 182 A3
Holly Wlk EH20 180 C4
Hollybank Pl EH53 148 C1
Hollybank Terr EH11 122 C2
Hollyhock Glade EH54 173 B4
Holmes Farm La EH52 117 A3
Holmes Rd EH52 117 A2
Holmlea Ave FK2 82 B4
Holton Cres FK10 5 B1
Holton Sq FK10 5 B1
Holy Cross RC Prim Sch EH6 93 B3
Holy Family RC Prim Sch EH52 87 C1
Holy Rood RC High Sch EH15 124 B3
Holy Trinity Episcopal Prim Sch FK8 7 A4
Holy Trinity Prim Sch FK8 7 A4
Holygate Pl EH52 117 B3
Holyrood Bsns Pk EH16 124 B2
Holyrood Park Rd EH16 233 C1
Holyrood Pl
Dunfermline KY12 29 A2
Stenhousemuir FK5 38 C2
Holyrood Rd EH8 233 C3
Home Farm Cotts FK6 57 C3
Home Pk KY3 49 B4
Home St EH3 232 B1
Homesteads The FK8 6 B4
Honeybank Cres ML8 230 A2
Honeyman Ct EH48 143 C4
Hood Pl KY11 46 C1
Hookney Terr FK6 36 B1
Hope Cotts EH51 64 B3
Hope Lane N EH15 125 A4
Hope Park Cres
Edinburgh EH8 233 B1
Haddington EH41 101 A1
Hope Park Gdns EH48 144 C3
Hope Park Sq EH8 233 B1
Hope Park Terr EH8 233 B1
Hope Pk EH41 101 A1
Hope Pl
Musselburgh EH21 126 C3
Tranent EH33 128 B4
Hope St Bo'ness EH51 63 C4
Carluke ML8 230 A1
Cowdenbeath KY4 13 C3
Edinburgh EH2 232 B3
Falkirk FK1 60 A3
Inverkeithing KY11 47 A1
Queensferry EH30 89 A4
Stirling FK8 1 C1
Hope Street La EH2 232 B3
Hope Terr EH9 123 B2
Hopefield Dr EH47 171 B4
Hopefield Pk EH19 182 A3
Hopefield Pl
Blackburn EH47 171 B4
Bonnyrigg & Lasswade EH19 182 A3
Hopefield Prim Sch EH19 182 A3
Hopefield Rd EH47 171 B4
Hopefield Terr
Bonnyrigg & Lasswade EH19 182 A3
Edinburgh EH6 93 C3
Hopelands Rd EH26 202 C3
Hopepark EH48 144 C3
Hopepark Terr FK4 57 C3
Hopetoun Cres EH7 93 C1
Hopetoun Dr
Bridge of A FK9 2 A4
Haddington EH41 100 C1
Hopetoun Ho* EH30 66 C1
Hopetoun La EH48 145 A3
Hopetoun Mews EH41 101 A1
Hopetoun Mon* EH39 100 C3
Hopetoun Pk EH31 52 A2
Hopetoun Pl KY2 16 B3
Hopetoun Rd EH30 68 A1
Hopetoun St
Bathgate EH48 145 A3
Edinburgh EH7 93 C2
Hopetoun Terr
Gullane EH31 52 A2
Ormiston EH35 159 C4
Hopetoun Trout Fishery* EH52 88 A3
Hopetoun View KY11 48 B2
Hopeward Ct KY11 48 B2
Hopeward Mews KY11 48 B1
Hoprig Pk TD13 140 C1
Hoprig Rd TD13 140 C1
Hornbeam Cres FK2 61 A2
Horne Terr EH11 232 A1
Horsburgh Bank EH14 151 B2
Horsburgh Gdns EH14 151 B2
Horsburgh Gr EH14 151 B2
Horse Wynd EH8 233 C3
Hoseason Gdns EH4 91 B1
Hosie Rigg EH15 125 A3
Hospital Cross Head KY11 29 B1
Hospital Hill KY11 29 A1
Hospital Intc EH54 147 B2
Hospital Rd EH41 100 C1
Hot Pot Wynd KY1 18 A3
Houldsworth Cres ML7 212 A4
Houldsworth St KY12 26 A4
Houliston Ave KY11 47 A2
House O' Muir Rd ML7 167 A2
House O'Hill Ave EH4 92 A2
House O'Hill Brae EH4 92 A2
House O'Hill Cres EH4 92 A2
House O'Hill Gdns EH4 92 A2
House O'Hill Gn EH4 92 A2
House O'Hill Gr EH4 92 A2
House O'Hill Pl EH4 92 A2
House O'Hill Rd EH4 92 A2
House O'Hill Row EH4 92 A2
House O'Hill Terr EH4 92 A1
House O'Muir EH26 179 C1
Houston Ct 1 KY12 28 C2
Houston Ind Est EH54 148 A4
Houston Rd
Livingston EH54 147 A3
Uphall Sta EH54 117 A1
Houston Terr EH54 117 A1
Houstoun Gdns EH52 116 C2
Houstoun Ind Est
Dechmont EH54 116 C1
Livingston EH54 147 C4
Houstoun Intc EH54 147 C4
Houstoun Rd EH54 147 C3
Houstoun Rd W EH54 146 C3
Howard Cres KY11 29 B1
Howard Pl Dysart KY1 18 A4
Edinburgh EH3 93 B2
Howard St Edinburgh EH3 93 B2
Falkirk FK1 59 C2
Howburn Cres ML7 168 C3
Howburn Rd ML7 168 B3
Howden E EH54 147 C2
Howden Hall Cres EH16 154 C3
Howden Hall Ct EH16 154 C3
Howden Hall Dr EH16 154 C3
Howden Hall Gdns EH16 155 A3
Howden Hall Loan EH16 154 C3
Howden Hall Pk EH16 154 C3
Howden Hall Rd EH16 155 A3
Howden Hall Way EH16 155 A3
Howden South Rd EH54 147 C2
Howden St EH8 233 B1
Howden St Andrew's RC Prim Sch EH54 147 C2
Howden W EH54 147 B2
Howe Pk EH10 153 C3
Howe St EH3 232 C4
Howetown FK10 5 B2
Howgate Prim Sch EH26 204 A1
Howgate Sh Ctr 7 FK1 60 A2
Howie's Pl FK1 59 A2
Howieson Ave EH51 63 C3
Howieson Gn EH52 116 C2
Howlands Rd FK7 7 A2
Howley Ave EH54 147 C2
Hudson Rd KY11 46 C2
Hugh Ave KY5 14 A4
Hugh Miller Pl EH3 93 A1
Hugh Pl KY5 14 A4
Hugh Russell Pl EH30 89 A4
Hughes Cres EH22 183 C3
Humbie Prim Sch EH36 187 A1
Humbie Rd EH29 89 A1
Humbie Terr KY3 49 B4
Hume Cres FK9 2 A3
Hume Ct FK9 2 A3
Hummel Rd EH31 51 C1
Hungerage Sq EH33 128 B3
Hunt Cl EH22 157 A2
Hunt Pl KY12 28 A1
Huntburn Ave EH49 85 B4
Hunter Ave EH20 181 B4
Hunter Ct EH20 181 B4
Hunter Gdns
Bonnybridge FK4 58 A3
Broxburn EH52 118 A3
Denny FK6 36 B1
Hunter Gr Bathgate EH48 145 C3
Whitburn EH47 169 C3
Hunter Pl
Dunfermline KY12 28 C3
Kirkcaldy KY1 17 A2
Shotts ML7 191 C3
Stenhousemuir FK2 39 A2
Hunter Rd EH54 147 B1
Hunter Sq Edinburgh EH1 233 A3
Gorebridge EH23 207 B4
Hunter St Kirkcaldy KY1 17 A2
Shotts ML7 191 B3
Hunter Terr
Bonnyrigg & Lasswade EH19 182 A4
Loanhead EH20 181 B4
Hunter's Cl EH1 232 C2
Hunter's La EH47 170 A3
Hunter's Tryst Prim Sch EH13 153 C4
Hunterfield Ct EH23 207 B4
Hunterfield Pk EH23 183 B1
Hunterfield Rd EH23 207 B4
Hunterfield Terr EH23 183 A1
Hunters Hill EH26 203 B3
Hunting Pk EH54 116 C1
Huntingdon Pl EH7 93 C1
Huntlaw Rd EH34 160 C3
Huntley Cres FK8 1 C1
Huntley House Mus* EH8 233 B3
Huntly Ave EH54 146 C3
Huntly Cres KY2 16 B4
Huntly St EH3 93 B2
Huntly Terr ML7 192 A2
Huron Ave EH54 147 C2
Hursted Ave EH22 183 B4
Hurworth St FK1 59 C2
Husband Pl KY11 29 C1
Hutchison Ave EH14 122 B2
Hutchison Cotts EH14 122 B2
Hutchison Crossway EH14 122 B2
Hutchison Gdns EH14 122 B2
Hutchison Gn KY11 29 A1
Hutchison Loan EH14 122 B2
Hutchison Medway EH14 122 B2
Hutchison Pk EH14 122 B2
Hutchison Pl EH14 122 B2
Hutchison Rd EH14 122 B2
Hutchison Terr EH14 122 B2
Hutchison View EH14 122 B2
Hutton Pk FK10 10 B4
Hutton Sq EH54 173 B3
Hyndford Ho EH39 54 A4
Hyndshaw Rd ML8 230 A2
Hyvot Ave EH17 155 B3
Hyvot Bank Ave EH17 155 C3
Hyvot Ct EH17 155 B3
Hyvot Gdns EH17 155 B3
Hyvot Gn EH17 155 B3
Hyvot Gr EH17 155 B3
Hyvot Loan EH17 155 B3
Hyvot Pk EH17 155 B3
Hyvot Terr EH17 155 B3
Hyvot View EH17 155 B3

I

Ibris Pl EH39 54 A4
Icehouse Brae FK2 61 A2
Implement Rd EH42 77 C1
Imrie Pl EH26 203 C3
Inch Ave KY3 49 A3
Inch Colm Ave FK5 38 B2
Inch Cres EH48 145 B3
Inch Garvie Terr FK5 38 B2
Inch View KY3 34 C1
Inchcolm Dr KY11 68 A3
Inchcolm Rd KY11 29 C2
Inchcolm Terr EH30 89 A4
Inchcorse Pl EH48 145 B1
Inchcross EH48 144 C2
Inchcross Ind Est EH48 144 C2
Inchcross Pk EH48 144 C1
Inchcross Steadings EH48 144 C1
Inches The KY11 48 A1
Inchgarvie Cres KY11 29 C2
Inchgarvie Pk EH30 68 A1
Inchgarvie Rd KY2 16 C4
Inchkeith Ave EH30 89 B4
Inchkeith Ct KY11 29 C2
Inchkeith Dr KY11 29 C2
Inchkeith Pl FK1 60 A1
Inchkeith Sch KY12 42 B4
Inchmickery Ave KY11 48 B3
Inchmickery Rd KY11 48 B3
Inchmuir Rd EH48 145 A1
Inchna FK11 4 A3
Inchview EH32 96 C1
Inchview Cres EH21 127 B3
Inchview Gdns KY11 48 A2
Inchview N EH32 96 C1
Inchview Prim Sch EH4 92 B2
Inchview Rd EH21 127 B3
Inchview Terr EH7 94 C1
Inchyra Pl FK3 61 C3
Inchyra Rd FK3 61 C3
India Pl EH3 232 B4
India St EH3 232 B4
Industrial Rd EH6 94 A2
Industry La EH6 93 C3
Infirmary St EH1 233 B2
Ingleston Ave FK6 36 B3
Inglewood Gdns FK10 10 A4
Inglewood Pl 7 EH16 155 A4
Inglewood Rd FK10 9 C4
Inglewood St EH54 147 C3
Inglis Ave EH32 97 B2
Inglis Cres KY3 34 C2
Inglis Dr FK2 39 B1
Inglis Farm EH32 97 B2
Inglis Gn Rd EH14 122 A1
Inglis Green Rigg EH14 122 A1
Inglis Pl FK2 82 C4
Inglis St KY12 29 A2
Inglis' Ct EH1 232 C2
Ingram Pl FK2 82 C3
Inkerman Ct EH26 204 A4
Inn Pl EH54 147 A1
Innellan Cres ML7 191 C3
Innerpeffray Dr FK2 39 A2
Innerwick Prim Sch EH42 108 A1
Innes Bldgs EH33 128 B3
Institution St KY1 17 C4
Inver Ct FK2 39 B1
Inverallan Ct FK9 1 C4
Inverallan Dr FK9 1 C4
Inverallan Rd FK9 1 C4
Inveralmond Com High Sch EH54 147 B3
Inveralmond Dr EH4 91 A3
Inveralmond Gdns EH4 91 A3
Inveralmond Gr EH4 91 A3
Inverary Dr FK5 38 C3
Inveravon Rd EH20 155 A1
Inveresk Rdbt EH51 62 B3
Inveravon Terr EH21 126 B3
Inverene Pl KY11 30 A1
Inveresk Brae EH21 126 B3
Inveresk Est The EH21 126 B2
Inveresk Gate EH21 126 B2
Inveresk Ind Est EH21 126 B3
Inveresk Lodge Gdn* EH21 126 B2
Inveresk Mills Ind Pk EH21 126 A3
Inveresk Rd EH21 126 B3
Inveresk Village Rd EH21 126 B2
Inverkeithing High Sch KY11 47 B2
Inverkeithing Mus* KY11 47 A1
Inverkeithing Prim Sch KY11 47 A2
Inverkeithing Rd
Aberdour KY3 49 A4
Crossgates KY4 30 C3
Inverkeithing Sta KY11 47 B2
Inverkip Dr ML7 191 C3
Inverleith Ave EH3 93 A2
Inverleith Ave S EH3 93 A2
Inverleith Gr EH3 92 C2
Inverleith Pl EH3 93 A2
Inverleith Place La EH3 93 A2
Inverleith Row EH3 93 A2
Inverleith Terr EH3 93 A2
Inverleith Terrace La EH3 93 B2
Invertiel Bank KY1 17 A1
Invertiel Rd KY1 35 A4
Invertiel Terr KY1 17 A1
Inzievar Prim Sch
Oakley KY12 26 C3
Oakley KY12 26 C4
Inzievar Terr KY12 27 A3
Iona Pl FK1 60 A1
Iona Rd KY11 29 C2
Iona St EH6 93 C2
Ireland Ave EH47 169 C3
Irene Terr FK1 82 C1
Ironmills Rd EH22 156 C2
Irvine Cres EH48 144 C3
Irvine Pl FK8 7 A4
Irving Ct FK1 59 C3
Islands Cres FK1 60 A1
Islay Ct FK3 61 B3
Islay Rd KY11 29 C1
Ivanhoe Cres EH16 124 A1
Ivanhoe Pl FK8 2 A1
Ivanhoe Rise EH54 148 A1
Ivy Gr KY11 46 C4
Ivy La KY1 18 A4
Ivy Terr EH11 122 C3
Ivybank Ct FK2 61 C1
Izatt Ave KY11 29 A1
Izatt St FK10 10 A4
Izatt Terr FK10 11 A2

J

Jacklin Gn EH54 147 A4
Jackson Ave FK3 61 B4
Jackson Pl EH54 147 B2
Jackson St EH26 203 C3
Jacob Pl FK1 60 A2
Jacobite Way EH32 97 A1
Jacobs Way EH23 207 B4
Jail Wynd FK8 7 A4
Jamaica Mews EH3 232 B4
Jamaica St EH3 232 B4
Jamaica St W EH3 232 B4
Jamaica Street North La EH3 232 B4
Jamaica Street South La EH3 232 B4
James Bank KY12 29 A2
James Cornwall Ct FK3 61 C3
James Croft Dr FK1 59 C1
James Ct KY4 13 B1
James Gillespie's High Sch EH9 123 B3
James Gillespie's Prim Sch EH9 123 B3
James Gr KY1 17 A1
James Hog Cres KY12 26 C3
James Lean Ave EH22 157 A2
James Leary Way EH19 182 B4
James Miller Rd KY11 46 C1
James Smith Ave FK2 82 C3
James St Alva FK12 5 A3
Armadale EH48 143 C3
Bannockburn FK7 7 B1
Cowdenbeath KY4 13 B1
Dunfermline KY12 29 A2
Edinburgh EH15 125 B4
Falkirk FK2 60 A3
Haggs FK4 57 A2
Laurieston FK2 60 C2
Musselburgh EH21 126 B3
Stenhousemuir FK5 38 B1
Stirling FK8 2 A1
James Street La EH15 125 B4
James Watt Ave EH51 64 A4
James Wilson Dr FK2 83 A3
James Young High Sch The EH54 147 C1
James' Park La KY3 33 C1
James' Pk KY3 33 C1
Jameson Pl EH6 93 C2
Jamieson Ave
Bo'ness EH51 63 C3
Stenhousemuir FK5 38 C2
Jamieson Gdns ML7 191 C3
Jane St EH6 93 C2
Jane Welsh Carlyle Mus* EH41 132 A4
Janefield EH17 155 A2
Jarnac Ct EH22 157 A2
Jarvey St EH48 145 A4
Jarvie Pl FK2 60 A4
Jasper Ave FK2 61 A2
Jawbanes Rd KY2 35 A4
Jean Armour Ave 6 EH16 124 A1
Jean Armour Dr EH22 157 B1
Jeffrey Ave EH4 92 A1
Jeffrey Bank EH51 63 C4
Jeffrey St EH1 233 B3
Jeffrey Terr FK2 61 C1
Jellyholm Rd FK10 10 C4
Jenks Loan EH22 183 A3
Jennie Rennie's Rd KY11 29 A1
Jessfield Pl EH51 63 C3
Jessfield Terr EH6 93 B3
Jewel & Esk Valley Coll
Dalkeith EH22 156 C1
Edinburgh EH15 125 B3
Jewel The EH15 125 A3
Jock's Hill Cres EH49 84 C4
John Bernard Way EH23 207 B3
John Brown Ct EH41 101 A1
John Connelly Ct 3 KY12 28 C3
John Cotton Bsns Ctr EH7 94 A1
John Cowane Row FK9 2 A2
John Cres EH33 128 B3
John Davidson Dr FK6 36 B2
John Humble St EH22 183 C3
John Knox Pl EH26 203 C3
John Knox Rd EH32 98 C3
John Mason Ct EH30 89 B4
John McDouall Stuart Mus* KY1 18 A4
John Muir Birthplace* EH42 78 B1
John Muir Cres EH42 106 B4
John Muir Ctry Pk* EH42 77 B2
John Muir Gdns EH42 106 B4
John Muir Pl EH42 106 B4
John Murray Dr FK9 2 A4
John Row Pl KY12 27 A4
John Rushforth Pl FK8 1 C1
John Smith Way ML7 191 B3
John St Dunfermline KY11 29 A1
Edinburgh EH15 125 B4
Falkirk FK2 60 A4
Haggs FK4 57 A2
Kincardine FK10 23 B2
Kirkcaldy KY2 17 A3
Penicuik EH26 203 C3
John Street La
Edinburgh EH15 125 B4
Penicuik EH26 203 C3
John Street La E EH15 125 B4
John Street La W EH15 125 B4
John Stuart Gait KY12 26 C3
John Woods Pl KY4 30 C4
John's La EH6 94 A3
John's Pl EH6 94 A3
Johnnie Cope's Rd EH33 128 A4
Johnsburn Gn EH14 151 A1
Johnsburn Haugh EH14 151 A1
Johnsburn Pk EH14 177 A4
Johnsburn Rd EH14 151 A1
Johnston Ave
Stenhousemuir FK5 38 C2
Stirling FK9 2 A2
Uphall EH52 116 C2
Johnston Cres
Dunfermline KY11 29 A1
Lochgelly KY5 14 A4
Johnston Ct EH52 116 C2
Johnston Pk
Cowdenbeath KY4 13 B3
Inverkeithing KY11 47 A1
Johnston Pl Denny FK6 36 B1
Penicuik EH26 203 C4
Johnston St FK7 7 B1

Johnston Terr
Cockenzie & Port Seton
EH32 ....97 B2
Edinburgh EH1 ....232 C2
Johnstone Ct FK12 ....5 A3
Johnstone La ML8 ....230 A1
Johnstone St Alva FK12 ...5 A3
Menstrie FK11 ....3 C3
Johny Moat Pl EH32 .....96 C1
Jones Ave FK5 ....59 B4
Jones Gn EH54 ....147 A4
Jones St KY12 ....12 A1
Joppa Gdns EH15 ....125 B4
Joppa Gr EH15 ....125 B4
Joppa Pk EH15 ....125 B4
Joppa Rd EH15 ....125 B4
Joppa Terr EH15 ....125 B4
Jordan La EH10 ....123 A2
Joseph Scott Gdns
EH52 ....117 C2
Jubilee Ave EH54 ....146 C3
Jubilee Cres EH23 ......183 B1
Jubilee Dr KY11 ....46 A1
Jubilee Rd Denny FK6 ...36 C2
Newbridge EH12 ....119 C4
Whitburn EH47 ....170 A3
Junction Pl EH6 ....93 C3
Junction Rd KY1 ....17 B4
Juner Pl EH23 ....183 B1
Juniper Ave EH14 ......152 B3
Juniper Gdns EH14 ....152 B3
Juniper Gr
Dunfermline KY11 ....46 B4
Edinburgh EH14 ....152 B3
Livingston EH54 ....148 A3
Juniper Green Prim Sch
EH14 ....152 B3
Juniper La EH14 ....152 B3
Juniper Park Rd EH14 .152 B3
Juniper Pl EH14 ....152 B3
Juniper Terr EH14 ......152 B3
Juniperlee EH14 ....152 B3
Jura EH54 ....146 C3
Jura Pl FK3 ....61 B3
Justinhaugh Dr EH49 ...84 B4

K

Kaemuir Ct EH48 ....112 C3
Kaim Cres EH48 ....145 B3
Kaimes Ave EH27 ......149 C2
Kaimes Cres EH27 ......149 C2
Kaimes Gdns EH27 .....149 C2
Kaimes Gr EH27 ....149 C2
Kaimes Pl EH27 ....149 C2
Kaimes Rd EH12 ....121 C4
Kaimes Specl Sch EH16 155 B3
Kaimes View EH27 .....156 A4
Kaimes Brae EH54 ......147 A1
Kaimes Ct EH54 ....147 A1
Kaimes Dr EH54 ....147 B1
Kaimes Gdns EH54 .....147 B1
Kaimes Gn EH54 ....147 B1
Kaimes Pl EH54 ....147 B1
Kaimes Wlk EH54 ......147 B1
Kames Pl KY12 ....29 B3
Kames Rd ML7 ....191 C3
Karries Ct FK6 ....57 A4
Katesmill Rd EH14 .....153 A4
Katherine St Kirkcaldy KY2 17 A3
Livingston EH54 ....148 A3
Katrine Cres KY2 ....16 C4
Katrine Ct FK10 ....10 B3
Katrine Dr KY12 ....28 A1
Katrine Pl FK6 ....57 B3
Katrine Rd Shotts ML7 .191 C3
Whitburn EH47 ....170 B4
Kay Gdns EH32 ....97 B2
Kay Rd KY12 ....43 B4
Keavil Pl KY12 ....28 A1
Kedslie Pl EH16 ....154 C4
Kedslie Rd EH16 ....154 C4
Keilarsbrae FK10 ....5 B1
Keir Ave FK8 ....2 A2
Keir Gdns FK9 ....2 A4
Keir Hardie Ave FK2 ....61 A2
Keir Hardie Dr FK12 ...183 C3
Keir Hardie Rd FK12 ....5 A4
Keir Hardie Terr KY11 ...29 C1
Keir St Bridge of a FK9 ...2 A4
Cowdenbeath KY4 ....13 A2
Edinburgh EH3 ....232 C2
Keirsbeath Ct KY12 .....12 A1
Keith Ave FK7 ....7 A4
Keith Cres FK6 ....92 A1
Keith Gdns EH52 ....117 B3
Keith Pl Dunfermline KY12 29 B2
Inverkeithing KY11 .....47 B2
Keith Rd KY1 ....46 B1
Keith Row EH4 ....152 B2
Keith St EH11? 92 A1
Kekewich Ave EH7 ......94 C1
Kellie Pl Alloa FK10 .....10 A4
Dunbar EH42 ....106 B4
Kellie Rd EH42 ....106 B4
Kelliebank FK10 ....9 C3
Kelly Ct FK8 ....7 A4
Kelly Dr FK6 ....36 C2
Kelly's La ML8 ....230 B3
Kellywood Cres FK10 ...23 C2
Kelso Dr ML8 ....230 A1
Kelso Pl KY2 ....17 A3
Kelso St EH52 ....117 A3

Kelty Ave EH51 ....64 A4
Kelvin Dr ML7 ....192 A2
Kelvin Sq EH54 ....148 A4
Kelvin St FK3 ....40 A1
Kemp's Cnr EH7 ....94 B1
Kemp Pl FK3 ....43 A1
Kemper Ave FK1 ....60 B2
Kempston Pl EH30 ......89 B4
Kendieshill Ave FK2 ....83 A3
Kenilworth Ct FK9 ....2 A4
Kenilworth Dr
Edinburgh EH16 ....155 A4
Laurieston FK2 ....60 C2
Kenilworth La FK3 ......61 B3
Kenilworth Rd FK9 ......2 A4
Kenilworth Rise EH54 ..147 C1
Kenilworth St FK3 ......61 B3
Kenmore Ave
Livingston EH54 ....146 C3
Polmont FK2 ....62 A1
Kenmore Terr KY2 ......16 C4
Kenmuir St FK1 ....59 A3
Kenmure Ave EH8 .....124 B4
Kenmure Pl
Dunfermline KY12 ....29 B3
Stenhousemuir FK5 .....38 C2
Kennard Rd FK2 ....82 B4
Kennard St Falkirk FK2 ..60 B3
Lochgelly KY5 ....14 A4
Kennedie Pk EH53 .....148 B2
Kennedy Cres
Dunfermline KY12 ....29 A3
Kirkcaldy KY2 ....17 A3
Tranent EH33 ....128 B4
Kennedy Ct EH41 ......131 C4
Kennedy Way FK2 ....22 C2
Kenneil Mus * EH51 ....63 B3
Kenningknowes Rd FK7 ..6 C3
Kennington Ave EH20 .181 A4
Kennington Terr EH20 .181 A4
Kent Rd Alloa FK10 ......9 C4
Stirling FK7 ....7 A3
Kent St KY12 ....29 B3
Kentigern Mall EH26 ..203 C2
Keppel Rd EH39 ....54 A3
Keppock Pl FK1 ....59 C0
Kepscaith Cres EH47 ..170 A3
Kepscaith Gr EH47 .....170 A3
Kepscaith Rd EH47 ....170 A3
Kerr Ave FK4 ....156 C1
Kerr Cres FK4 ....57 A2
Kerr Pl Denny FK6 ....36 B1
Dunfermline KY12 ....29 C1
Kerr Rd EH33 ....128 B3
Kerr St EH3 ....93 A1
Kerr Way EH33 ....128 B3
Kerr's Wynd EH21 .....126 B3
Kerrisk Dr KY11 ....29 C1
Kerse Gdns FK2 ....60 C3
Kerse Gn Rd FK10 ......10 C3
Kerse La FK1 ....60 B4
Kerse Pl FK1 ....60 B3
Kerse Rd Grangemouth FK3 61 B4
Stirling FK7 ....7 B3
Kersebonny Rd FK8 .....6 B4
Kersehill Cres FK2 ......60 B4
Kersie Rd FK7 ....9 C2
Kersie Terr FK7 ....9 C2
Kersiebank Ave FK3 ....61 C3
Kestrel Brae EH54 .....147 B3
Kestrel Dr FK2 ....82 C4
Kettil'stoun Cres EH49 .84 B3
Kettil'stoun Ct EH49 ....84 B3
Kettil'stoun Gr EH49 ....84 B3
Kettil'stoun Mains EH49 84 B3
Kettilstoun Rd EH49 ....84 B3
Keverkae FK10 ....9 C3
Kevock Rd EH18 ....181 C4
Kevock Vale Pk EH19 .182 A4
Kew Gdns EH48 ....145 A3
Kew Terr EH12 ....122 C4
Kidd St KY1 ....17 B4
Kier Ct FK9 ....2 A4
Kilbagie St FK10 ....23 B2
Kilbean Dr FK1 ....59 C1
Kilbirnie Terr FK6 ......36 B2
Kilbrennan Dr FK1 ......59 A2
Kilburn Rd KY12 ....28 A1
Kilchurn Ct EH12 ......121 A4
Kilcruik Rd KY3 ....34 C2
Kildean Hospl FK8 ....1 C1
Kildean Sch FK8 ....1 C1
Kildinny Gdns KY12 ....28 C1
Kildonan Pk KY12 ......28 C1
Kildrummy Ave FK5 ....38 C2
Kilduthie Pl FK10 ....23 B3
Kilfinan Rd ML7 ....191 B3
Kilgour Ave KY1 ....17 B4
Kilgraston Rd EH9 ....123 B2
Kilin Ct KY12 ....28 C1
Kilin Dr FK2 ....62 A1
Kilchochan Way KY12 ..29 B3
Kilmartin Way KY12 ....29 B3
Kilmaurs Rd EH16 ....124 A2
Kilmaurs Terr EH16 ...124 A2
Kilmory Ct FK1 ....59 B2
Kilmory Gdns ML8 ....230 A2
Kilmun Rd KY2 ....16 B4
Kilmundy Dr KY3 ....33 B1
Kincadzow Rd ML8 ...230 B3
Kilncraigs Ct FK10 .....10 B3
Kilncraigs Rd FK10 .....10 B3
Kilncroftside EH14 ....122 A1
Kilne Pl EH54 ....147 A2
Kilngate Brae EH17 ...155 B3
Kilns Pl FK2 ....59 C3
Kilns Rd FK2 ....60 A3
Kilpair St 6 EH41 .....132 A4

Kilpunt Gdns EH52 ....118 A3
Kilpunt Rdbt EH52 ....118 A3
Kilpunt View EH52 ....118 A3
Kilrie Cotts KY2 ....33 C4
Kilrymont ML11 ....215 A1
Kilspindie Ct EH32 ......71 B2
Kilsyth Rd FK4 ....57 A2
Kilwinning Pl EH21 ...126 B3
Kilwinning St EH21 ...126 B3
Kilwinning Terr EH21 .126 B3
Kincarnes Gr EH51 .....64 B4
Kincairne Ct FK10 ......23 C2
Kincardine Rd FK2 .....39 B2
Kincraig Pl KY12 ....28 C1
Kinellan Gdns EH12 ...122 B4
Kinellan Rd EH12 .....122 B4
King Cres EH55 ....182 B2
King Edwards Way EH29 89 A1
King James Dr EH22? ...
King James IV Rd KY11 .46 B1
King Malcolm Cl EH10 .154 B3
King O' Muirs Ave FK10 .4 C2
King O' Muirs Dr FK10 ..4 C2
King Robert Ct FK8 ......1 C1
King Sq EH55 ....172 B2
King St Armadale EH48 144 A3
Bathgate EH48 ....145 A3
Cowdenbeath KY4 ......13 A2
Edinburgh EH6 ....93 C3
Falkirk FK2 ....60 B3
Fallin FK7 ....8 B2
Inverkeithing KY11 .....47 B1
Kirkcaldy KY2 ....17 A3
Musselburgh EH21 ....126 B3
Shotts ML7 ....191 C2
Stenhousemuir FK5 ....38 C3
Stirling FK8 ....7 A4
King's Ave EH32 ....98 B2
King's Cramond EH4 ...91 A2
King's Cres Carluke ML8 230 A1
Rosyth KY11 ....46 C2
King's Ct EH32 ....98 B2
King's Dr KY3 ....34 C2
King's Gr EH32 ....98 B2
King's Knoll Gdns EH32 .54 B4
King's Mdw EH16 ......124 A2
King's Meadow Prim Sch
EH41 ....132 A4
King's Park Prim Sch
EH22 ....157 A1
King's Pk EH22 ....157 A1
King's Pk Rd FK8 ....6 C3
King's Rd Edinburgh EH15 95 A1
Longniddry EH32 ......98 B3
Rosyth KY11 ....46 C2
Tranent EH33 ....128 B3
King's Rd EH47 ....170 A3
King's Road Prim Sch
KY11 ....46 C2
King's Stables La EH1 .232 C2
King's Stables Rd EH1 .232 C2
King's Terr EH15 ....94 C1
Kingfisher Brae EH54 .147 B3
Kinghorn Pl EH6 ....93 B3
Kinghorn Prim Sch KY3 .34 C1
Kinghorn Rd
Burntisland KY3 ....34 A1
Kirkcaldy KY1, KY1 .....35 A4
Kirkcaldy Sta KY1 ......34 C1
Kinglass Ave EH51 .....64 A4
Kinglass Ct EH51 ....64 A4
Kinglass Dr EH51 ....64 A4
Kinglass Pk EH51 ......64 A4
Kings Ct Alloa FK10 .....10 A4
6 Falkirk FK1 ....60 A2
Kings Haugh EH16 .....124 B2
Kings Knot * FK8 ....6 C4
Kings Rd FK1 ....61 C4
Kingsburgh Ct EH40 ..103 B4
Kingsburgh Cres EH40 103 B4
Kingsburgh Rd EH12 ..122 B4
Kingseat Ave FK3 ......61 B3
Kingseat Pl FK3 ....61 C4
Kingseat Rd
Dunfermline KY12 ......29 B3
Halbeath KY11, KY12 ..30 A3
Kingsfield EH49 ....85 B4
Kingsgate KY12 ....29 A2
Kingshill Rd ML7 ......212 A4
Kingsinch Specl Sch
EH16 ....124 A1
Kingsknowe Ave EH14 122 A1
Kingsknowe Cres EH14 122 A1
Kingsknowe Ct EH14 ..121 C1
Kingsknowe Dr EH14 ..122 A1
Kingsknowe Gdns EH14 122 A1
Kingsknowe Gn EH14 ..121 C1
Kingsknowe Gr EH14 ..153 A4
Kingsknowe Pk EH14 ..121 C1
Kingsknowe Pl EH14 ..121 C1
Kingsknowe Rd N EH14 122 A1
Kingsknowe Rd S EH14 122 A1
Kingsknowe Sta EH14 .121 C1
Kingsknowe Terr EH14 122 A1
Kingslaw Ct EH33 .....128 B3
Kingslaw Farm Cotts
EH33 ....128 B3
Kingsley Ave FK5 ......38 C3
Kingsport Ave EH54 ...147 C2
Kingstables La FK8 ......7 A4
Kingston Ave EH16 ....124 B1
Kingston Cotts EH39 ...53 C1
Kingswell Pk FK10 .....10 B4
Kininmonth St KY1 .....17 A1
Kinleith Ind Est EH14 .152 A2

Kinloch Pl FK3 ....61 C3
Kinloss Ct KY12 ....26 A1
Kinnaird Ave FK2 ....39 A2
Kinnaird Dr FK5 ....38 C2
Kinnaird Park EH15 ...125 B2
Kinnaird Pl
Dunfermline KY12 ......29 B3
Kirkcaldy KY2 ....16 B2
Kinnear Rd EH3 ....93 A2
Kinneil Dr EH51 ....63 B3
Kinneil Prim Sch EH51 .63 C3
Kinneil Rd EH51 ....63 B4
Kinneil Sta* EH51 .....63 B4
Kinneil St EH3 ....63 B4
Kinnell Rd KY11 ....47 A1
Kinnis Ct KY12 ....28 C1
Kinnonmonth Ave KY3 .33 B1
Kintyre Pl FK1 ....59 B2
Kippielaw Dr EH22 ....157 B1
Kippielaw Gdns EH22 .157 B1
Kippielaw Medway
EH22 ....157 B1
Kippielaw Pk EH22 ....183 B4
Kippielaw Rd EH22 ....157 B1
Kippielaw Wlk EH22 ..157 B1
Kippithill EH36 ....187 A1
Kirk Ave FK5 ....38 C1
Kirk Brae
Edinburgh EH16 ....155 A4
Innerwick EH42 ....108 A1
Kincardine FK10 ....23 C3
Kirk Cramond EH4 ......91 B3
Kirk La EH54 ....147 A1
Kirk Loan EH12 ....121 C3
Kirk Path ML7 ....212 A4
Kirk Pk Dunbar EH42 ..78 A1
Kirk Ports EH39 ....54 B4
Kirk Rd Aberlady EH32 .71 B2
Bathgate EH48 ....145 B3
Shotts ML7 ....191 C2
Kirk St Culross KY12 ...25 B1
Edinburgh EH6 ....93 C2
Kincardine FK10 ....23 C2
Prestonpans EH32 ......96 C1
West Wemyss KY1 .....32 C3
Kirk Wynd
Clackmannan FK10 .....11 A3
2 Falkirk FK1 ....60 A2
Kirkcaldy KY1 ....17 B2
Stirling FK7 ....7 A2
Kirkbank Rd KY3 ....33 C1
Kirkbrae FK10 ....10 C2
Kirkbride Terr FK7 ......20 B2
Kirkburn FK1 ....110 A4
Kirkcaldy High Sch KY1 .17 A4
Kirkcaldy Mus & Art Gallery*
KY1 ....17 A2
Kirkcaldy Rd
Burntisland KY3 ....33 C1
Kinghorn KY3 ....35 A2
Kirkcaldy Sta KY1 ......17 B2
Kirkfield E EH54 ....147 A2
Kirkfield View EH54 ...147 B2
Kirkfield W EH54 ......147 A2
Kirkflat EH52 ....117 A2
Kirkford Ct KY4 ....13 A2
Kirkgate Alloa FK10 ...10 A3
Burntisland KY3 ....33 C1
Currie EH14 ....152 A2
10 Dunfermline KY12 ...28 C2
Edinburgh EH16 ....155 A4
Inverkeithing KY11 .....47 A1
Linlithgow EH49 ....85 A4
West Calder EH55 .....172 B2
Kirkhall Pl FK6 ....36 C2
Kirkhill Ct Broxburn EH52 117 B3
Fauldhouse EH47 ......191 B3
Gorebridge EH23 ......207 B4
Kirkhill Dr EH16 ....124 A2
Kirkhill Gdns
Edinburgh EH16 ....124 A3
Penicuik EH26 ....203 C3
Kirkhill Pk EH52 ....117 B3
Kirkhill Prim Sch EH52 117 B3
Kirkhill Rd
Broxburn EH52 ....117 B3
Edinburgh EH16 ....124 A3
Gorebridge EH23 ......183 A1
Kirkhill Way EH26 ....203 C3
Kirkland Dr FK6 ....36 A1
Kirklands
Dunfermline KY12 ......29 A1
Penicuik EH26 ....203 C2
Kirklands Park Cres
EH29 ....88 C1
Kirklands Park Gdns
EH29 ....88 C1
Kirklands Park Gr EH29 88 C1
Kirklands Park Rigg
EH29 ....88 C1
Kirklands Park St EH29 88 C1
Kirkliston Prim Sch
EH29 ....89 A1
Kirkliston Rd EH30 .....89 A4
Kirknewton Prim Sch
EH27 ....149 B2
Kirknewton Sta EH27 .149 A2
Kirkslap FK6 ....36 C1
Kirkstyle Gdns EH29 ..89 A1
Kirkton Ave EH48 .....145 B3
Kirkton Bank EH26 ....203 B3

Kirkton Bsns Ctr EH54 .147 A2
Kirkton N EH54 ....147 A2
Kirkton North Rd EH54 147 B2
Kirkton Pl
Cowdenbeath KY4 ......13 A3
Falkirk FK2 ....39 B2
Kirkton Rd KY3 ....33 C1
Kirkton South Rd EH54 147 B1
Kirkway FK2 ....22 B2
Kirkwood Ave FK2 .....61 B1
Kirkwood Cres KY12 ...28 A1
Kisimul Ct EH12 ....121 A4
Kitchener Cres EH32 ...98 C3
Kittle Yds EH9 ....123 C2
Klondyke St EH21 ......125 C2
Knaphill KY11 ....46 C4
Knights Way FK6 ....36 B2
Knightsbridge Ho EH54 147 B4
Knightsiaw Pl EH26 ...203 B3
Knightsridge Ct EH54 .147 B4
Knightsridge E EH54 ..147 B4
Knightsridge Prim Sch
EH54 ....147 B4
Knightsridge Rd EH52 .116 B1
Knightsridge Rdbt EH54 147 B4
Knightsridge W EH54 .147 B4
Knockenhair Rd EH42 .78 A1
Knockhill Cl KY5 ....14 A4
Knockhouse Farm Cotts
KY12 ....28 A2
Knockhouse Gdns KY12 28 A1
Knockhouse Rd KY12 ..28 A1
Knockhouse Terr KY12 .28 A1
Knoll Croft Rd ML7 ...192 A2
Knowe Park Rd EH47 .171 A1
Knowe The Alloa FK10 ...5 B1
Dalgety Bay KY11 ....48 B2
Knowefaulds Rd FK10 ..4 A2
Knowehead Rd FK2 ....61 B1
Knowepark Ct EH47 ...171 A1
Knowes Rd EH41 ......131 C4
Knowesley Pk EH41 ...131 B4
Knowetop EH54 ....173 B4
Knowetop Pl EH25 ....180 C2
Knowhead Rd KY12 ....28 A1
Knox Acad EH41 ......131 C4
Knox Pl EH41 ....132 A4
Komarom Pl EH22 ....157 B2
Kyle Ave FK7 ....20 C4
Kyle Pl EH7 ....233 C4
Kyles The KY1 ....17 C3

L

La Porte Prec FK3 ......61 B4
Labrador Ave EH54 ...147 C2
Laburnum Ave EH32 ...97 C2
Laburnum Dr KY1 ....17 B4
Laburnum Gr
Burntisland KY3 ....33 C1
Stirling FK8 ....6 C3
Laburnum Pl EH22 ....183 C3
Laburnum Rd
Dunfermline KY11 ......29 B1
Whitburn EH47 ....170 B3
Lade Braes KY11 ....48 A2
Lade Ct EH49 ....84 C4
Lade Dr FK5 ....59 B4
Lade Gn KY11 ....48 A2
Lade Mill FK7 ....8 B2
Lade Rd FK4 ....58 A3
Ladeside Ave EH47 ...177 B4
Ladeside Cres FK5 ....38 C1
Ladeside Dr EH47 .....171 B4
Ladeside Prim Sch EH47 171 A4
Ladeside Rd EH47 ....171 B4
Ladiemeadow EH12 ..121 C3
Lady Anne Ct KY4 ......30 C3
Lady Brae EH23 ....207 B4
Lady Brae Pl EH23 ....207 B4
Lady Ct EH47 ....170 C4
Lady Emily Way EH23 .207 B4
Lady Hall Rd TD13 ....140 C2
Lady Helen Cotts KY5 ..15 A4
Lady Helen St KY1 ......17 A1
Lady Jane Gdns EH39 .54 B3
Lady Jane Rd EH39 ....54 B3
Lady Lawson St EH3 ..232 C2
Lady Menzies Pl 3 EH7 .94 A1
Lady Nairne Cres EH8 124 B4
Lady Nairne Gr EH8 ..124 B4
Lady Nairne Loan EH8 124 B4
Lady Nairne Pl EH8 ...124 B4
Lady Pl EH54 ....147 A3
Lady Rd EH16 ....124 A2
Lady Road Pl EH22 ...183 A3
Lady Victoria Bsns Ctr
EH22 ....183 A2
Lady Wood Pl EH54 ..147 A3
Lady Wynd EH1 ....232 C2
Ladyburn Pl FK1 ....35 A2
Ladycroft EH14 ....151 B1
Ladysgate Ct FK2 ......39 A2
Ladysmill FK2 ....60 B3
Ladysmill Ind Est FK1 .60 B3
Ladysmith Rd EH9 ....123 C1
Ladysneuk Rd FK9 ......2 B1
Ladywell Ave EH12 ...121 B3
Ladywell Ct
Edinburgh EH12 ....121 B3

Ladywell Ct *continued*
Larbert FK5 ....**38** A2
Ladywell Dr FK10 ....**4** A2
Ladywell East Rd EH54 .**147** C3
Ladywell Gdns EH21 ....**121** B3
Ladywell Gr FK10 ....**11** A2
Ladywell Pl FK10 ....**4** A2
Ladywell Rd EH21 ....**121** B3
Ladywell View EH51 ....**63** B3
Ladywell Way EH21 ......**126** B3
Ladywell West Rd EH54 .**147** B3
Ladywood FK10 ....**11** B2
Ladywood Prim Sch
EH26 ....**204** A4
Lagan Rd ML8 ....**230** A1
Laggan Ave ML7 ....**192** A2
Laggan Path ML7 ....**191** C3
Laichfield EH14 ....**122** A2
Laichpark Pl EH14 ....**122** A2
Laichpark Rd EH14 ......**122** A2
Laing Gdns EH52 ....**117** B3
Laing Terr
Edinburgh EH15 ....**125** B4
Penicuik EH26 ....**203** C4
Laird Terr EH19 ....**182** B3
Laird's Entry EH37 ....**185** B2
Lakeside Rd KY2 ....**16** C2
Lamb's Ct EH48 ....**233** B1
Lamb's Pend EH26 ....**203** C2
Lambert Dr KY12 ....**29** B2
Lambert Terr FK10 ....**10** B4
Lamberton Ave FK7 ....**7** B2
Lamberton Ct EH34 ....**160** C3
Lambie St EH47 ....**170** A4
Lambs Ct EH6 ....**93** B4
Lamer St EH42 ....**78** C2
Lamington Rd EH33 ....**130** B4
Lammerlaws Rd KY3 ......**50** C4
Lammermoor Gdns
EH33 ....**128** A3
Lammermoor Terr
Edinburgh EH16 ....**124** B1
Tranent EH33 ....**128** A3
Lammermuir Cres
Dunbar EH42 ....**78** B1
Haddington EH41 ....**132** B4
Lammermuir Ct EH31 ....**52** A1
Lammermuir Pl KY2 ......**16** C3
Lammerview
Gladsmuir EH33 ....**130** B4
Tranent EH33 ....**128** B3
Lammerview Terr EH31 ..**52** A1
Lamond View FK5 ....**38** B1
Lamont Cres FK7 ....**7** B3
Lamont Way EH54 ....**147** B4
Lampacre Rd EH12 ......**121** C3
Lanark Ave EH54 ....**147** A3
Lanark Rd
Edinburgh, Kingsknowe
EH14 ....**122** A1
Edinburgh, Westerhailes
EH13, EH14 ....**152** C3
Landale Gdns KY3 ....**33** C1
Landale Pl KY3 ....**33** C1
Landale St KY5 ....**14** A4
Lane The EH21 ....**126** C1
Lang Loan EH17,EH20 ..**155** B2
Langfauld Gdns EH48 ..**144** C3
Langhill Pl FK6 ....**36** B1
Langlaw Prim Sch EH22 **183** B4
Langlaw Rd EH22 ....**183** B4
Langlees Prim Sch FK2 ..**60** A4
Langlees St FK2 ....**39** B1
Langriggs EH41 ....**132** A4
Langside EH40 ....**103** B4
Langside Cres EH55 ....**173** A3
Langside Dr EH48 ....**142** A2
Langside Gdns EH55 ....**173** A3
Langton Ave EH53 ....**148** C2
Langton Gdns EH53 ....**148** C2
Langton Rd
East Calder EH53 ....**148** C2
Edinburgh EH9 ....**123** C2
Westquarter FK2 ....**61** A2
Langton View EH54 ......**147** C4
Lanrigg Ave EH47 ....**193** C4
Lanrigg Ct EH47 ....**193** C4
Lanrigg Rd EH47 ....**193** C4
Lansbury Ct EH22 ....**157** A2
Lansbury St KY1 ....**17** C1
Lansdowne Cres
Edinburgh EH12 ....**232** A2
Kincardine FK10 ....**23** C2
Shotts ML7 ....**192** A2
Lapicide Pl EH6 ....**93** C3
Larbert Ave EH54 ....**147** A4
Larbert High Sch FK5 ....**38** C2
Larbert Rd FK4 ....**58** A3
Larbert Sta FK5 ....**38** B1
Larbert Village Prim Sch
FK5 ....**38** A1
Larbourfield EH11 ....**121** B1
Larch Cres EH22 ....**183** C3
Larch Dr EH47 ....**170** B3
Larch Gr
Dunfermline KY11 ....**46** B4
Stenhousemuir FK5 ....**38** C2
Larch St FK3 ....**61** B3
Larchbank EH54 ....**147** C3
Larchfield EH14 ....**151** B1
Larchfield Neuk EH14 ..**151** B1
Larchfield Path ML7 ....**192** A1
Largo Pl EH6 ....**93** C3
Larkfield Dr EH22 ....**156** C1
Larkfield Rd EH22 ....**156** C1
Lasswade Bank EH17 ..**155** B3
Lasswade Gr EH17 ....**155** B3

Lasswade High Sch
EH19 ....**182** A4
Lasswade High Sch Ctr
(Leisure Ctr)* EH19 ....**182** A4
Lasswade Prim Sch
EH19 ....**182** B4
Lasswade Rd
Bonnyrigg & Lasswade
EH18 ....**156** A1
Dalkeith EH22 ....**156** C1
Edinburgh EH16, EH17,
EH18 ....**155** B3
Loanhead EH20 ....**181** B4
Latch Pk EH13 ....**153** B4
Latch Rd EH42 ....**78** C1
Latch The KY12 ....**27** B1
Lathallan Dr FK2 ....**61** C1
Lauder Coll KY11 ....**30** A3
Lauder Loan EH9 ....**123** C2
Lauder Lodge EH22 ......**157** A2
Lauder Pl EH40 ....**103** C3
Lauder Rd Dalkeith EH22 **157** B1
Edinburgh EH9 ....**123** B2
Lauder St KY12 ....**27** B2
Lauderdale Cres EH42 ..**78** B1
Lauderdale St EH9 ......**123** B3
Laura Fergusson Ct
EH12 ....**91** A1
Laurel Bank EH22 ....**157** B1
Laurel Bank Pl EH22 ..**183** C3
Laurel Bank Rd EH22 ..**183** C3
Laurel Cres KY2 ....**17** A4
Laurel Ct Denny FK6 ......**36** B2
Falkirk FK1 ....**59** B3
Laurel Gr Bonnyrigg FK4 **57** C2
Westquarter FK2 ....**61** A1
Laurel Pl FK4 ....**57** C2
Laurel Rd KY11 ....**46** B3
Laurel Terr EH11 ....**122** C3
Laurelbank Ave FK4 ......**58** A2
Laurelbank Ct EH53 ....**148** C1
Laurelhill Gdns FK8 ....**6** C3
Laurelhill Pl FK8 ....**2** A1
Laurels The FK10 ....**4** A1
Laurencecroft Rd FK8 ....**2** A1
Laurie St EH6 ....**94** A2
Lauriston Prim Sch EH4 **61** A2
Lauriston Rd FK3 ....**61** A3
Lauriston Castle* EH4 ..**91** C3
Lauriston Dr KY12 ....**29** B3
Lauriston Farm Rd EH4 **91** C2
Lauriston Gdns EH3 ....**232** C1
Lauriston Pk EH3 ....**232** C1
Lauriston Pl EH3 ....**232** C2
Lauriston St EH3 ....**232** C2
Lauriston Terr EH3 ......**232** C2
Laurmont Ct FK2 ....**61** A2
Laverock Dr EH26 ......**203** B3
Laverock Pk EH49 ....**85** A3
Laverockbank Ave EH5 ..**93** B3
Laverockbank Cres EH5 **93** B3
Laverockbank Gdns EH5 **93** B3
Laverockbank Gr EH5 ....**93** B3
Laverockbank Rd EH5 ..**93** B3
Laverockbank Terr EH5 ..**93** B3
Laverockdale Cres
EH13 ....**153** A3
Laverockdale Loan
EH13 ....**153** A3
Laverockdale Pk EH13 ..**153** A3
Law Pl EH15 ....**95** A1
Law Prim Sch EH39 ....**54** B3
Law Rd Dunfermline KY11 **29** C2
North Berwick EH39 ....**54** B4
Lawers Cres FK2 ....**61** C3
Lawers Pl FK3 ....**61** C3
Lawers Sq EH26 ....**204** A4
Lawfield Rd EH22 ....**183** B4
Lawhead Cotts EH40 ....**75** C2
Lawhead Pl EH26 ....**203** B3
Lawhouse Toll EH15 ....**125** A2
Lawmarket EH1 ....**233** A3
Lawrence St EH41 ....**131** C4
Lawrie Dr EH26 ....**204** A3
Lawson Cres EH30 ....**89** B4
Lawson Ct EH42 ....**78** B1
Lawson Gdns KY1 ....**17** C1
Lawson Glade EH54 ....**173** B4
Lawson Pl Dunbar EH42 **78** B2
Maddiston FK2 ....**83** A3
Lawson St KY1 ....**17** C4
Lawswell FK10 ....**5** C2
Laxdale Dr FK6 ....**57** B4
Laxford Cres KY11 ....**48** A2
Leadburn Ave KY12 ......**29** A4
Leadervale Rd EH16 ....**154** C4
Leadervale Terr EH16 ..**154** C4
Leadside Cres KY12 ......**29** A4
Leamington Pl EH10 ....**123** A3
Leamington Rd EH3 ....**232** A1
Leamington Terr EH10 **123** A3
Learmonth Ave EH4 ......**92** C1
Learmonth Cres
Edinburgh EH4 ....**92** C1
West Calder EH55 ....**172** B2
Learmonth Ct EH4 ....**93** A1
Learmonth Gardens Mews [11]
EH4 ....**93** A1
Learmonth Gdns EH4 ....**92** C1
Learmonth Gr EH4 ....**92** C1
Learmonth Pk EH4 ....**92** C1
Learmonth Pl EH4 ....**92** C1
Learmonth St EH4 ....**232** A4
Learmonth Terr EH4 ......**92** C1
Learmonth Terr La
EH4 ....**232** A4
Ledi Ave FK10 ....**4** A1

Ledi Pl FK1 ....**81** C4
Ledi Terr EH26 ....**204** A4
Ledi View EH39 ....**2** A2
Ledmore Pl FK1 ....**60** C1
Lee Cres EH15 ....**125** A4
Legion Ct KY2 ....**17** A3
Leighton Cres EH22 ....**183** B4
Leighton St KY12 ....**26** A1
Leishman Ct EH48 ......**142** B2
Leith Acad EH6 ....**94** A2
Leith Ave KY3 ....**33** C1
Leith Pl FK6 ....**57** B4
Leith Prim Sch EH6 ......**94** A2
Leith St EH1 ....**233** A4
Leith Wlk Prim Sch EH7 **93** C1
Leith Wlk EH6,EH7 ....**93** C2
Lempockwells Rd EH34 **160** C3
Lendrick Ave FK1 ....**59** C1
Lennel Ave EH12 ....**122** B4
Lennox Ave FK7 ....**7** A2
Lennox Gdns EH49 ....**84** B4
Lennox Milne Ct EH41 ..**64** B2
Lennox Rd EH41 ....**132** B4
Lennox Row EH5 ....**93** A3
Lennox St EH4 ....**232** A4
Lennox Street La EH4 ..**232** A4
Lennox Terr FK3 ....**61** C2
Lennoxlove Acredales Cotts
EH41 ....**132** A4
Lennoxlove Ho* EH41 ..**132** A3
Lennyemuir EH12 ....**90** A1
Leny Pl KY12 ....**29** A3
Lenzie Ave EH54 ....**147** A4
Leopold Pl [2] EH7 ....**93** C1
Leslie Pl EH4 ....**93** A1
Leslie Rd KY11 ....**46** C3
Leslie St KY1 ....**35** A4
Lestrange Terr FK12 ....**5** A4
Letham Ave EH53 ....**148** A4
Letham Cotts FK2 ....**39** B4
Letham Cres EH53 ......**148** A4
Letham Dr EH41 ....**131** C4
Letham Gait KY11 ....**47** C2
Letham Gdns EH53 ......**148** A4
Letham Gr EH53 ....**148** A4
Letham Hill Ave KY11 ..**47** C2
Letham Mains Smallholdings
EH41 ....**131** B4
Letham Pk Dunbar EH42 **78** C1
Pumpherston EH53 ......**148** A4
Letham Pl Dunbar EH42 **78** B2
Pumpherston EH53 ......**148** A4
Letham Prim Sch EH54 **148** A3
Letham Rd Dunbar EH42 **78** B1
Livingston EH54 ....**148** A4
Letham Rise EH53 ....**148** A4
Letham Terrs FK2 ....**22** B1
Letham Way KY11 ....**47** C2
Leuchatsbeath Dr KY4 ..**13** A3
Leven Cl EH3 ....**232** B1
Leven Ct FK10 ....**10** B3
Leven Pl ML7 ....**191** C3
Leven St Edinburgh EH3 **232** B1
Falkirk FK2 ....**60** A4
Leven Terr EH3 ....**232** C1
Leven Wlk EH54 ....**148** A2
Levenseat Ind Est EH47 **193** C2
Levenhall KY4 ....**14** A2
Lewis Ct Alloa FK10 ....**10** A3
Falkirk FK1 ....**60** A1
Lewis Rd FK2 ....**61** C1
Lewis Terr EH11 ....**232** A2
Lewiswaie Ave EH21 ....**126** C3
Lewisvale Ct EH21 ....**126** C3
Leyden Pk EH19 ....**182** A4
Leyden Pl EH19 ....**182** A4
Leyden Rd EH27 ....**149** A1
Leys Park Rd KY12 ....**29** A2
Liberton Brae EH16 ......**155** A4
Liberton Dr EH16 ....**154** C4
Liberton Gdns EH16 ....**155** A3
Liberton High Sch EH17 **155** B4
Liberton Hospl EH16 ..**155** A4
Liberton Pl EH16 ....**155** A3
Liberton Prim Sch
EH16 ....**124** A1
Liberton Rd EH16 ....**155** A4
Library La FK3 ....**40** B1
Liddesdale Pl EH3 ....**93** A1
Liddle Dr EH51 ....**63** C3
Lidgate Shot EH28 ......**119** C1
Liggar's Pl KY12 ....**28** C1
Liggat Pl EH52 ....**117** C3
Liggat Syke EH52 ....**117** B3
Ligget Syke Pl EH52 ....**118** A3
Lighton Terr EH47 ......**171** A1
Lilac Ave EH22 ....**183** C3
Lilac Cres KY1 ....**17** B4
Lilac Gr KY11 ....**46** B4
Lilias La EH41 ....**163** C3
Lilly's La KY11 ....**29** A1
Lily Terr EH11 ....**122** C2
Lilybank Ct EH54 ....**146** C3
Lilyhill Terr EH8 ....**94** B3
Lime Ave EH30 ....**66** C1
Lime Gr Dunfermline KY11 **29** C1
Mayfield EH22 ....**183** C3
North Berwick EH39 ......**54** B4
Polmont FK2 ....**61** C1
Stenhousemuir FK5 ....**38** B1
Lime Pl EH19 ....**182** A3
Lime Rd FK1 ....**59** A2
Lime St EH6 ....**93** B3
Limebank Pk EH53 ......**148** C1
Limefield EH17 ....**155** C3
Limefield Ave EH55 ....**173** A3
Limefield Cres EH48 ..**145** C3

Limefield Gdns EH55 ..**173** A3
Limefield La EH48 ......**145** A3
Limefield Pl EH48 ......**145** B3
Limefield Rd
Bathgate EH48 ....**145** B4
West Calder EH55 ....**173** A3
Limekilns EH14 ....**161** A3
Limekilns Gr EH53 ......**148** A4
Limekilns Prim Sch KY11 **45** C2
Limekilns Rd KY12 ....**28** C1
Limerigg Prim Sch FK1 **110** B1
Limes The EH10 ....**123** A2
Limetree Wlk EH42 ......**76** B3
Limeylands Cres EH35 **159** B4
Limeylands Rd EH35 ....**159** B4
Lina St KY2 ....**17** A3
Linburn Gr KY11 ....**29** C2
Linburn Pk EH27 ....**150** A3
Linburn Pl KY11 ....**29** C2
Linburn Rd
Dunfermline KY11 ....**29** C2
Wilkieston EH27 ....**150** A3
Lindean Pl EH6 ....**94** A2
Lindean Terr EH27 ......**149** C3
Linden Ave Denny FK6 ..**36** B2
Stirling FK7 ....**7** B3
Linden Pl EH20 ....**181** B4
Lindores Dr Kirkcaldy KY2 **16** C4
Tranent EH33 ....**128** B3
Lindsay Dr FK9 ....**2** A2
Lindsay Gdns EH48 ....**145** B3
Lindsay Pl Edinburgh EH6 **93** C3
Lochgelly KY5 ....**14** A4
Lindsay Rd EH6 ....**93** C3
Lindsay Sq EH54 ....**146** B3
Lindsay St EH6 ....**93** C3
Lindsay Way EH54 ......**147** B4
Lindsay's Wynd KY12 ..**26** C3
Lingerwood Farm Cotts
EH22 ....**183** A2
Lingerwood Rd EH22 ..**183** A2
Lingerwood Wlk EH22 **183** A2
Linhouse Dr EH53 ......**148** C2
Linhouse Rd EH53 ......**148** C2
Link Rd Crombie KY12 ....**44** B3
Dalgety Bay KY11 ....**47** C2
Linkfield Ct EH21 ....**126** C3
Linkfield Rd EH21 ....**126** C3
Links Ave EH21 ....**126** A4
Links Ct Bo'ness EH51 ....**64** A4
Cockenzie & Port Seton
EH32 ....**97** C2
Links Dr KY12 ....**28** A1
Links Gardens La EH6 ..**94** A2
Links Gdns EH6 ....**94** A2
Links Pl Bo'ness EH51 ....**64** A4
Burntisland KY3 ....**50** C4
Cockenzie & Port Seton
EH32 ....**97** C2
Edinburgh EH6 ....**94** A3
Links Rd Bo'ness EH51 ..**63** B3
Cockenzie & Port Seton
EH32 ....**97** C2
Longniddry EH32 ....**98** C3
North Berwick EH39 ....**54** A4
Links St Kirkcaldy KY1 ..**17** A1
Musselburgh EH21 ......**126** B3
Links View
Cockenzie & Port Seton
EH32 ....**97** C2
Musselburgh EH21 ......**126** B4
Links Wlk EH32 ....**97** C2
Linlithgow Acad EH49 ..**84** B4
Linlithgow Bridge Prim Sch
EH49 ....**84** B4
Linlithgow Canal Ctr*
EH49 ....**85** A3
Linlithgow Pal* EH49 ....**85** A4
Linlithgow Pl EH52 ....**38** C2
Linlithgow Prim Sch
EH49 ....**85** A3
Linlithgow Prim Sch West
Port Annexe EH49 ....**84** C3
Linlithgow Sta EH49 ......**85** A3
Linlithgow Story Mus The*
EH49 ....**85** A4
Linlithgow Terr EH35 ..**159** B4
Linmill Rd FK1 ....**112** A3
Linn Dean Wildlife Reserve*
EH36 ....**211** B2
Linn Mill EH30 ....**67** C1
Linn Pl Airth FK2 ....**22** C2
Broxburn EH52 ....**117** C2
Linnet Brae EH54 ....**147** B3
Linsay Macdonald Ct
KY12 ....**29** B2
Lint Riggs FK1 ....**60** A3
Linton Ct KY3 ....**35** A2
Linton Gdns EH54 ......**146** C3
Linton La KY3 ....**35** A2
Linton Pl KY11 ....**46** C2
Lintview FK1 ....**110** A3
Linty La EH26 ....**203** B3
Linview La EH54 ....**173** C2
Linwell Ct FK3 ....**34** A1
Lion Well Wynd EH49 ..**84** C4
Lionthorn Rd FK1 ....**59** C1
Lipney FK11 ....**4** A3
Lismore Ave
Edinburgh EH8 ....**94** B3
Kirkcaldy KY2 ....**16** C4
Lismore Cres EH8 ....**94** A3
Lismore Pl KY2 ....**16** C4
Lismore Prim Sch EH15 **124** C3
Lister Ct FK9 ....**2** A3

Lister Rd EH54 ....**147** A1
Listloaning Pl EH49 ......**84** B4
Listloaning Rd EH49 ....**84** B4
Liston Dr EH29 ....**89** A1
Liston Pl EH29 ....**89** A1
Liston Rd EH29 ....**89** A1
Little Acre EH22 ....**183** B4
Little Carriden EH51 ......**64** B3
Little Cswy KY12 ....**42** B4
Little Denny Rd FK6 ......**36** B1
Little Footworn KY12 ....**44** C3
Little France Mills EH16 **124** B1
Little King St EH1 ....**233** A4
Little Rd EH16 ....**154** C4
Little Sandhaven KY12 ..**42** B4
Littlejohn Rd EH10 ......**153** C4
Livery St EH48 ....**145** A4
Livesay Rd KY11 ....**46** B1
Livesey Terr EH26 ......**204** A4
Livilands Ct FK8 ....**7** A3
Livilands Gate FK8 ....**7** A3
Livilands La FK8 ....**7** A3
Livingston North Sta
EH54 ....**147** A3
Livingston South Sta
EH54 ....**174** A4
Livingston Village Prim Sch
EH54 ....**147** A2
Livingstone Cres FK2 ..**60** C3
Livingstone Dr
Bo'ness EH51 ....**63** B3
Burntisland KY3 ....**33** C1
Laurieston FK2 ....**61** A1
Livingstone Rdbt
EH54 ....**116** B1
Livingstone La KY3 ....**49** B4
Livingstone Pl EH9 ......**123** B3
Livingstone Quadrant
ML7 ....**168** B2
Livingstone St EH55 ..**171** C1
Livingstone Terr FK2 ....**61** A1
Lixmount Ave EH5 ....**93** B3
Lixmount Gdns EH5 ......**93** B3
Lizzie Brice's Rdbt
EH54 ....**148** A1
Llynallan Rd ML7 ....**168** A3
Loan Pl ML7 ....**168** C3
Loan The Bo'ness EH51 ..**63** B3
Loanhead EH20 ....**181** B4
Pathhead EH37 ....**184** B4
Queensferry EH30 ....**68** A1
Torphichen EH48 ....**113** C3
Wallyford EH21 ....**127** A3
Loanburn EH26 ....**203** C3
Loanburn Ave EH26 ....**203** C3
Loanfoot Cres FK2 ......**117** A3
Loanfoot Gdns FK7 ......**20** B2
Loanfoot Rd EH52 ......**117** A2
Loanhead Ave
Bonnybridge FK4 ....**57** B3
Grangemouth FK3 ....**61** C3
Loanhead Hospl EH20 **181** B4
Loanhead Prim Sch
EH20 ....**181** B4
Loanhead Prim Sch (Annexe)
EH20 ....**181** B4
Loanhead Rd EH20 ......**155** A1
Loaning Cres EH7 ....**94** B1
Loaning Mills EH7 ....**94** B1
Loaninghill Pk EH52 ....**117** A2
Loaninghill Rd EH52 ....**117** A2
Loch Awe Way EH47 ..**170** B4
Loch Earn Way EH47 ..**170** B4
Loch Fyne Way EH47 ..**170** B4
Loch Linnhe Ct EH47 ..**170** B4
Loch Maree Way EH47 **170** B4
Loch Pl EH30 ....**68** A1
Loch Rd Edinburgh EH4 **92** A1
Queensferry EH30 ....**68** A1
Tranent EH33 ....**128** B3
Loch Sq EH33 ....**128** B3
Loch St KY12 ....**29** B4
Loch Trool Way EH47 ..**170** B4
Lochaber Cres ML7 ......**192** A2
Lochaber Dr FK5 ....**38** C2
Lochbank EH54 ....**147** C3
Lochbrae FK10 ....**5** B1
Lochbridge Rd EH39 ....**54** B3
Lochend Ave Dunbar EH42 **78** C1
Edinburgh EH7 ....**94** A2
Lochend Castle Barns
EH7 ....**94** A1
Lochend Cl EH8 ....**233** C3
Lochend Cres
Dunbar EH42 ....**78** B1
Edinburgh EH7 ....**94** B1
Lochend Dr EH7 ....**94** A1
Lochend Gdns EH7 ......**94** A1
Lochend Gr EH7 ....**94** B1
Lochend Pk EH7 ....**94** A2
Lochend Quadrant EH7 **94** B1
Lochend Rd Dunbar EH42 **78** C1
Edinburgh EH6, EH7 ......**94** A2
Ratho Sta EH28, EH29 ..**119** A4
Lochend Rd N EH21 ....**126** A1
Lochend Rd S
Edinburgh EH7 ....**94** A1
Musselburgh EH21 ......**126** A1
Lochend Sq EH7 ....**94** A1
Lochgelly High Sch KY5 **14** A4
Lochgelly Ind Pk KY5 ....**14** B4
Lochgelly Rd KY4 ....**13** B3

Lochgelly South Prim Sch KY5 .... 14 A4
Lochgelly West Prim Sch KY5 .... 14 A4
Lochgreen Rd FK1 .... 59 C1
Lochhead Ave FK6 .... 36 C1
Lochhead Ct KY12 .... 29 A3
Lochhill Cotts EH32 .... 99 C4
Lochies Rd
Burntisland KY3 .... 34 A1
Clackmannan FK10 .... 11 A2
Lochinvar Pl FK4 .... 58 B2
Lochinvar Rd KY11 .... 46 B1
Lochlands Ind Est FK5 .... 59 A4
Lochlea Gr KY2 .... 17 A4
Lochlea Terr KY2 .... 17 A4
Lochmaben Dr FK5 .... 38 C2
Lochpark Pl FK6 .... 36 C1
Lochridge Pl FK6 .... 36 B1
Lochrin Bldgs EH3 .... 232 B1
Lochrin Pl EH3 .... 232 B1
Lochrin Terr EH3 .... 232 B1
Lochshot Pl EH54 .... 147 A2
Lochside Ave EH12 .... 120 C2
Lochside Cres
Edinburgh EH12 .... 120 C2
Redding FK2 .... 61 A1
Lochside Ct EH12 .... 121 A2
Lochside Pl EH12 .... 121 A2
Lochside Rd FK1 .... 110 B1
Lochside View EH12 .... 120 C3
Lochwood Pk KY12 .... 12 A1
Lock Rd KY11 .... 67 A4
Lock Sixteen FK1 .... 59 B3
Lockerby Cotts EH16 .... 155 B3
Lockerby Cres EH16 .... 155 B3
Lockerby Gr EH16 .... 155 B3
Lockhart Terr EH25 .... 180 C2
Lockharton Ave EH14 .... 122 C1
Lockharton Cres EH14 .... 122 C1
Lockharton Gdns EH14 .... 122 C2
Lodge Dr FK5 .... 38 C1
Lodge St EH41 .... 132 A4
Logan St EH3 .... 93 B1
Logan Way EH54 .... 147 B4
Loganlea Ave EH7 .... 94 B1
Loganlea Cres EH55 .... 171 B1
Loganlea Dr EH7 .... 94 B1
Loganlea Gdns EH7 .... 94 B1
Loganlea Loan EH7 .... 94 B1
Loganlea Pl EH7 .... 94 B1
Loganlea Rd
Addiewell EH55 .... 171 B1
Edinburgh EH7 .... 94 B1
Loganlea Terr
Addiewell EH55 .... 171 B1
Edinburgh EH7 .... 94 B1
Logie Dr FK5 .... 38 A2
Logie Green Gdns EH7 .... 93 B2
Logie Green Loan EH7 .... 93 B2
Logie Green Rd EH7 .... 93 B2
Logie La FK9 .... 2 B4
Logie Mill EH7 .... 93 B2
Logie Pl KY12 .... 28 B3
Logie Rd FK9 .... 2 B2
Lomond Cres
Dunfermline KY11 .... 29 C1
Stenhousemuir FK5 .... 38 C2
Stirling FK9 .... 2 A2
Whitburn EH47 .... 170 A3
Lomond Ct FK10 .... 10 B3
Lomond Dr
Bannockburn FK7 .... 7 C1
Falkirk FK2 .... 39 B1
Lomond Gdns KY2 .... 16 C3
Lomond Rd Edinburgh EH5 .... 93 A3
Grangemouth FK3 .... 61 C3
Shotts ML7 .... 191 C3
Lomond St FK10 .... 4 C1
Lomond Vale EH26 .... 204 A4
Lomond View EH48 .... 112 C2
Lomond Way FK6 .... 57 B3
Lomond Wlk EH20 .... 155 A1
London Rd Dalkeith EH22 .... 157 A2
Edinburgh EH7, EH8 .... 94 A1
London St EH3 .... 93 B1
London Street Prim Sch EH7 .... 93 B1
Loney Cres FK6 .... 57 C4
Long Byres EH52 .... 117 C3
Long Craig Rigg EH5 .... 92 B4
Long Craig Wlk KY1 .... 35 A4
Long Craigs EH32 .... 97 C2
Long Craigs Terr KY3 .... 35 A2
Long Cram EH41 .... 131 C4
Long Crook EH30 .... 89 A4
Long Dalmahoy Rd
Currie EH14 .... 151 B3
Ratho EH27 .... 150 B2
Long Row Halbeath KY12 .... 30 A4
Menstrie FK11 .... 4 A4
Longannet Cotts FK10 .... 24 A1
Longbraes Gdns KY2 .... 16 B3
Longcroft Gdns EH49 .... 84 C4
Longcroft Holdings FK4 .... 57 A2
Longdales Ave FK2 .... 60 A4
Longdales Ct FK2 .... 60 A4
Longdales Pl FK2 .... 60 A4
Longdales Rd FK2 .... 60 A4
Longdyke Pl FK2 .... 39 B2
Longdykes Rd EH32 .... 97 A1
Longford ML11 .... 215 A1
Longformacus Rd EH16 .... 155 A4
Longhill Gdns KY11 .... 48 A2
Longniddry Farm Cotts EH32 .... 98 C3
Longniddry Prim Sch EH32 .... 98 C3
Longniddry Sta EH32 .... 98 C3
Longpark Pl EH54 .... 147 A2
Longridge Prim Sch EH47 .... 170 B1
Longridge Rd EH47 .... 170 A3
Longstone Ave
East Linton EH40 .... 103 B4
Edinburgh EH14 .... 122 A1
Longstone Cres EH14 .... 122 A2
Longstone Gdns EH14 .... 121 C2
Longstone Gr EH14 .... 122 A1
Longstone Pk EH14 .... 122 A1
Longstone Pl EH14 .... 122 A1
Longstone Prim Sch EH14 .... 122 A1
Longstone Rd EH14 .... 122 A1
Longstone St EH14 .... 122 A1
Longstone Terr EH14 .... 121 C2
Longstone View EH14 .... 121 C2
Lonsdale Cres KY3 .... 33 C1
Lonsdale Terr EH3 .... 232 C1
Lookaboutye Brae FK10 .... 11 A2
Loom Rd KY2 .... 17 A3
Lord President Rd EH39 .... 54 A4
Loretto Ct EH21 .... 126 A2
Loretto Jun Sch EH21 .... 126 B3
Loretto RC Prim Sch EH21 .... 126 B3
Loretto Schs EH21 .... 126 B3
Lorimar Pl FK2 .... 39 A1
Lorimer Gdns KY12 .... 29 B3
Lorimer View EH14 .... 152 C3
Lorne Gdns FK2 .... 60 C2
Lorne Gr EH20 .... 155 A1
Lorne Pl EH6 .... 93 C2
Lorne Prim Sch EH6 .... 93 C2
Lorne Rd FK5 .... 38 B1
Lorne Sq Edinburgh EH6 .... 93 C2
North Berwick EH39 .... 54 B4
Lorne St Edinburgh EH6 .... 93 C2
Kirkcaldy KY1 .... 17 C4
Lornshill Acad FK10 .... 4 C1
Lornshill Cres FK10 .... 9 C4
Losshill FK11 .... 4 A3
Lothian Bank EH22 .... 156 C1
Lothian Coll of Nursing & Midwifery EH3 .... 232 C2
Lothian Cres
Bo'ness EH51 .... 64 A3
Stirling FK9 .... 2 B2
Lothian Ct KY11 .... 47 B1
Lothian Dr EH22 .... 183 B4
Lothian Rd Dalkeith EH22 .... 157 A2
Edinburgh EH1 .... 232 B2
Lothian St
Bathgate EH48 .... 145 A4
Bo'ness EH51 .... 64 A3
Bonnyrigg & Lasswade EH19 .... 182 B4
Burntisland KY3 .... 50 C4
Dalkeith EH22 .... 157 A2
Edinburgh EH1 .... 233 A2
Rosewell EH24 .... 181 B1
Lothian Terr Kirkcaldy KY2 .... 17 A4
Newtongrange EH22 .... 183 A2
Lothians View KY11 .... 47 A1
Louburn EH48 .... 142 B2
Loudens Wlk FK6 .... 36 B3
Loughborough Rd KY1 .... 17 C4
Loughrigg KY11 .... 47 A4
Louisa Sq EH24 .... 181 B1
Louise St KY11 .... 29 B1
Louvain Gdns EH48 .... 143 C2
Lovedale Ave EH14 .... 151 A1
Lovedale Cres EH14 .... 151 A1
Lovedale Gdns EH14 .... 151 B1
Lovedale Gr EH14 .... 151 A1
Lovedale Rd EH14 .... 151 B1
Lovells Glen EH49 .... 84 B4
Lovers La EH30 .... 89 B4
Lovers Loan Alva FK12 .... 5 A4
Dunfermline KY12 .... 28 C1
Lovers Wlk FK8 .... 2 A1
Low Brae EH48 .... 113 C3
Low Causewayside
Culross KY12 .... 42 B4
Newmills KY12 .... 26 B1
Low Cswy Culross KY12 .... 25 C1
Torryburn KY12 .... 26 C1
Low Doors The EH27 .... 149 C1
Low Port Prim Sch EH49 .... 85 A4
Lower Alderston Rd EH41 .... 100 C1
Lower Bathville EH48 .... 144 A3
Lower Bridge St FK8 .... 2 A1
Lower Broomieknowe EH18 .... 182 A4
Lower Castlehill FK8 .... 2 A1
Lower Gilmore Pl EH3 .... 232 B1
Lower Glebe KY3 .... 49 B4
Lower Granton Rd EH5 .... 93 A3
Lower Joppa EH15 .... 125 B4
Lower London Rd EH7 .... 94 A1
Lower Valleyfield View EH26 .... 203 C2
Lower Wellheads KY11 .... 45 B2
Lowlands Crofts EH55 .... 196 B3
Lowrie Ave EH26 .... 203 B3
Lowry Pl KY11 .... 46 C2
Lt Sales Ave KY11 .... 47 C2
Ludgate FK10 .... 10 A3
Luffness Ct EH32 .... 71 B2
Luffness Gdns EH32 .... 71 B2
Luffness Mains Cotts EH39 .... 72 A2
Lugton Brae EH22 .... 156 C2
Lugton Specl Sch EH22 .... 156 C2
Lumley Ct FK3 .... 61 B4
Lumley Pl FK3 .... 61 B4
Lumley St FK3 .... 61 B4
Lumphinnans Prim Sch KY4 .... 13 B3
Lumphinnans Rd KY5 .... 14 A4
Lumsdaine Dr KY11 .... 48 A1
Lumsden Ct
Broxburn EH52 .... 117 B3
Ratho EH28 .... 119 B1
Lundin Rd KY12 .... 28 A2
Lussielaw Rd EH9 .... 123 C2
Lutton Court Bsns Ctr EH8 .... 233 B1
Lutton Pl EH8 .... 233 B1
Lyall Cres FK2 .... 61 C1
Lyars Rd EH32 .... 98 C3
Lyarthall EH52 .... 117 B3
Lychgate La EH52 .... 117 B3
Lychgate Rd FK10 .... 4 A1
Lydgait EH41 .... 101 A1
Lydgait Gdns EH41 .... 101 A1
Lyefield Pl EH54 .... 147 A2
Lygon Rd EH16 .... 123 C1
Lyle Gn EH54 .... 147 A4
Lynburn Prim Sch KY11 .... 29 C1
Lyne Gr KY12 .... 28 B1
Lyne St EH7 .... 94 A1
Lyne Terr EH26 .... 204 A4
Lynebank (Psychiatric) Hospl KY11 .... 30 A3
Lyneburn Cres KY11 .... 30 A3
Lynedoch Pl EH3 .... 232 A3
Lynedoch Place La EH3 .... 232 A3
Lyness Ct FK2 .... 61 C1
Lynn Lea Ave EH41 .... 132 B4
Lyon Cres FK9 .... 2 A3
Lyon Ct EH51 .... 63 B3
Lyon Dr EH54 .... 173 C3

M

Mac Cormick Terr EH26 .... 203 C4
Macadam Pl FK1 .... 59 B3
Macarthur Cres FK2 .... 82 C3
Macbeth Moir Rd EH21 .... 127 A3
Macbeth Rd KY11 .... 29 C2
Macdonald Ave EH48 .... 143 C3
Macdonald Dr FK7 .... 7 A2
Macdonald Pl KY3 .... 34 A1
Macdonald Sq KY11 .... 30 A3
Macdowall Rd EH9 .... 123 C2
Macduff Cres KY3 .... 34 C1
Mace Ct FK7 .... 7 B2
Macfarlane Cres FK1 .... 60 A3
Macfarlane Pl EH52 .... 116 C2
Machrie Ct FK1 .... 59 B2
Macindoe Cres KY1 .... 17 B4
Macintosh Pl FK1 .... 60 A1
Macintosh Rd EH54 .... 146 C1
Mackenzie Cres KY5 .... 14 B4
Mackenzie Pl EH3 .... 232 B4
Mackenzie Terr FK3 .... 61 B3
Mackie Pl KY11 .... 29 C1
Maclachlan Ave FK6 .... 36 B1
Maclardy Ct EH52 .... 116 C2
Maclaren Terr FK2 .... 39 A1
Maclean Cres FK12 .... 5 B4
Maclean Ct FK7 .... 7 B2
Maclean Gate KY11 .... 46 C4
Maclean Gdns KY11 .... 46 C4
Maclean Pl KY11 .... 46 C4
Maclean Terr EH48 .... 142 B2
Maclean Way KY11 .... 46 C4
Maclean Wlk KY11 .... 46 C4
Macmerry Ind Est EH33 .... 129 C3
Macmerry Prim Sch EH33 .... 129 B3
Macmillan Rd EH54 .... 147 B1
Macnair Ave EH39 .... 54 B3
Macpherson Pl FK1 .... 59 C1
Mactaggart Loan EH22 .... 183 A2
Madderfield Mews EH49 .... 85 A4
Maddiston Prim Sch FK2 .... 82 C3
Maddiston Rd FK2 .... 82 C4
Madeira Pl EH6 .... 93 C3
Madeira St EH6 .... 93 C3
Madill Pl FK5 .... 38 C2
Maesterton Pl EH22 .... 183 A2
Mag's Bank EH41 .... 133 A1
Magdala Cres EH12 .... 122 C4
Magdala Mews EH12 .... 122 C4
Magdalene Ave EH15 .... 125 A3
Magdalene Ct EH15 .... 125 A3
Magdalene Dr EH15 .... 125 A3
Magdalene Gdns EH15 .... 125 A3
Magdalene Loan EH15 .... 125 A3
Magdalene Medway EH15 .... 125 A3
Magdalene Pl EH15 .... 125 A3
Maggie Wood's Loan FK1 .... 59 C3
Magnus Rd EH51 .... 62 B3
Maid of the Forth* EH30 .... 68 B1
Maidencraig Cres EH4 .... 92 B1
Maidencraig Gr EH4 .... 92 B1
Maidenpark Pl EH51 .... 63 C3
Maidlands EH49 .... 85 B4
Main Point EH3 .... 232 C2
Main Rd Charlestown KY11 .... 45 A2
Crombie KY12 .... 44 C4
Grangemouth FK3 .... 62 A4
Macmerry EH33 .... 129 B3
Main St Aberdour KY3 .... 49 B4
Airth FK2 .... 22 B2
Alloa FK10 .... 5 B1
Auchtertool KY2 .... 15 A1
Avonbridge FK1 .... 112 A3
Balerno EH14 .... 151 B1
Bannockburn FK7 .... 7 B1
Bathgate EH48 .... 145 A4
Blackridge EH48 .... 142 B2
Bo'ness EH51 .... 64 A4
Bonnybridge FK4 .... 58 A3
Brightons FK2 .... 82 B4
Cairneyhill KY12 .... 27 B1
California FK1 .... 81 C3
Cambus FK10 .... 9 A4
Carnock KY12 .... 27 B4
Carrington EH23 .... 206 B3
Clackmannan FK10 .... 11 A2
Comrie KY12 .... 26 B4
Cowdenbeath, Hill of Beath KY4 .... 13 A1
Cowdenbeath, Lumphinnans KY4 .... 13 C3
Cowie FK7 .... 20 B4
Crossford KY12 .... 28 B1
Crossgates KY4 .... 30 C3
Dalmeny EH29, EH30 .... 89 C4
Dechmont EH52 .... 116 B1
East Calder EH53 .... 148 C2
East Saltoun EH34 .... 161 C2
East Whitburn EH47 .... 170 B4
Edinburgh, Davidsons Mains EH4 .... 91 C2
Elphinstone EH33 .... 128 A1
Falkirk FK1 .... 59 C3
Falkirk FK2 .... 39 B2
Falkirk, Bainsford FK2 .... 60 A4
Fallin FK7 .... 8 C2
Fauldhouse EH47 .... 193 B3
Forth ML11 .... 215 A1
Gifford EH41 .... 163 C3
Gorebridge EH23 .... 207 B4
Gullane EH31 .... 52 A1
Halbeath KY11 .... 30 A3
High Valleyfield KY12 .... 25 C1
Hillend KY11 .... 47 C2
Kirkliston EH29, EH30 .... 89 A1
Kirknewton EH27 .... 149 C1
Larbert FK5 .... 38 B1
Limekilns KY11 .... 45 B2
Linlithgow EH49 .... 84 B4
Livingston, Livingston Village EH54 .... 147 B1
Livingston,Deans EH54 .... 146 C3
Lochgelly KY5 .... 14 A4
Longniddry EH32 .... 98 C3
Longridge EH47 .... 170 B1
Maddiston FK2 .... 83 A3
Mid Calder EH53 .... 148 B2
Newton EH52 .... 88 A4
Newtongrange EH22 .... 183 A3
North Queensferry KY11 .... 68 B3
Ormiston EH35 .... 159 C4
Pathhead EH37 .... 185 A3
Pathhead, Dewartown EH37, EH23 .... 184 B3
Philpstoun EH49 .... 86 B4
Plean FK7 .... 20 B2
Polmont FK2 .... 61 C1
Ratho EH28 .... 119 B1
Redding FK2 .... 61 B1
Roslin EH25 .... 181 A2
Shieldhill FK1 .... 81 B3
Shotts ML7 .... 192 A2
Slamannan FK1 .... 110 A4
Stenhousemuir FK5 .... 38 C1
Stirling FK7 .... 6 B3
Stirling, St Ninians FK7 .... 7 A2
Stoneyburn EH47 .... 171 A1
Torryburn KY12 .... 26 B1
Townhill KY12 .... 29 B4
Tullibody FK10 .... 4 A1
Tyninghame EH42 .... 76 B2
West Calder EH55 .... 172 B2
Westfield EH48 .... 112 C3
Winchburgh EH52 .... 87 C2
Maddiston FK2 .... 82 C4
Main St E FK11 .... 4 A3
Main St W Hillend KY11 .... 47 C2
Menstrie FK11 .... 3 C3
Mains Of Craigmillar EH16 .... 124 B1
Mains Rd Harthill ML7 .... 168 C3
Linlithgow EH49 .... 84 C3
Maitland Ave
Bannockburn FK7 .... 7 B1
Musselburgh EH21 .... 126 A3
Maitland Cres FK7 .... 7 A2
Maitland Hog La EH29 .... 89 A1
Maitland Park Rd EH21 .... 126 A3
Maitland Rd
Kirkliston EH29 .... 89 A1
Rosyth KY11 .... 67 A4
Maitland St
Dunfermline KY12 .... 28 C2
Musselburgh EH21 .... 126 A3
Majors Loan FK1 .... 60 A2
Majors Pl FK1 .... 60 A2
Malbet Pk EH16 .... 155 A4
Malbet Wynd EH16 .... 155 A4
Malcolm Ct
Bathgate EH48 .... 144 C3
Dunfermline KY11 .... 29 A1
Malcolm Dr FK5 .... 38 C2
Malcolm St KY11 .... 29 A1
Mall Ave EH21 .... 126 B3
Mall The EH54 .... 148 A3
Mallard Brae EH54 .... 147 B3
Mallens Brae EH48 .... 114 A3
Malleny House Gdn* EH14 .... 151 B1
Malleny Millgate EH14 .... 177 B4
Malplaquet Ct ML8 .... 230 A1
Malta Gn EH4 .... 93 A1
Malta Terr EH4 .... 93 A1
Maltings The
Auchtertool KY2 .... 15 A1
Linlithgow EH49 .... 84 B3
Mamre Dr FK1 .... 81 C3
Man O' War Way EH51 .... 64 A4
Mandela Ave FK2 .... 60 B4
Manderston St EH6 .... 93 C2
Mandora Ct ML8 .... 230 A1
Manitoba Ave EH54 .... 147 C2
Mannan Dr FK10 .... 11 A2
Mannering Pl 9 EH16 .... 155 A4
Mannerston Holdings EH49 .... 65 B2
Mannfield Ave FK4 .... 57 C2
Manor Cres FK10 .... 4 A1
Manor Gdns EH42 .... 78 A1
Manor Loan FK9 .... 3 A3
Manor Pl EH3 .... 232 A3
Manor Powis Cotts FK9 .... 3 A2
Manor St FK1 .... 60 A2
Manor Wynd FK2 .... 83 A3
Manse Ave
Armadale EH48 .... 143 C3
Whitburn EH47 .... 170 A3
Manse Cres FK7 .... 7 A2
Manse Ct EH53 .... 148 C2
Manse Gr EH47 .... 171 B1
Manse La Burntisland KY3 .... 33 C1
Cockenzie & Port Seton EH32 .... 97 B2
Musselburgh EH21 .... 126 B3
Manse Pk EH52 .... 116 C3
Manse Pl Aberdour KY3 .... 49 A4
Bannockburn FK7 .... 7 C1
Bathgate EH48 .... 145 C3
Falkirk FK1 .... 60 A2
Inverkeithing KY11 .... 47 A1
Slamannan FK1 .... 110 A4
Manse Rd
Carrington EH23 .... 206 B3
Crossgates KY4 .... 30 C4
Dirleton EH39 .... 53 A3
Edinburgh EH12 .... 121 B3
Forth ML11 .... 215 A1
Inverkeithing KY11 .... 47 A1
Kincardine FK10 .... 23 C3
Kinghorn KY3 .... 34 C2
Kirkliston EH29 .... 89 A1
Linlithgow EH49 .... 85 A3
Roslin EH25 .... 181 A2
Shotts ML7 .... 192 A2
Torphichen EH48 .... 113 C3
Whitburn EH47 .... 170 A3
Manse St Aberdour KY3 .... 49 B4
Edinburgh EH12 .... 121 B3
Manse View
Armadale EH48 .... 143 C3
Innerwick EH42 .... 107 C1
Philpstoun EH49 .... 86 B4
Mansefield
Athelstaneford EH39 .... 101 C4
East Calder EH53 .... 148 C2
Mansefield Ct
2 Bathgate EH48 .... 145 A4
Livingston EH54 .... 147 B2
Mansefield Gr EH48 .... 145 A3
Mansefield St EH48 .... 145 A4
Mansewood Cres EH47 .... 170 A3
Mansfield Ave Alloa FK10 .... 5 B1
Musselburgh EH21 .... 126 B3
Newtongrange EH22 .... 183 A3
Mansfield Ct EH21 .... 126 B3
Mansfield Pl
Edinburgh EH3 .... 93 B1
Musselburgh EH21 .... 126 B3
Newtongrange EH22 .... 183 A3
Mansfield Rd
Balerno EH14 .... 177 B4
Musselburgh EH21 .... 126 B3
Newtongrange EH22 .... 183 A3
Mansionhouse Rd
Edinburgh EH9 .... 123 B3
Falkirk FK1 .... 59 B3
Manson Sq EH54 .... 146 B3
Manuel Rigg FK2 .... 82 C3
Manuel Terr EH49 .... 83 C3
Maple Ave FK5 .... 38 C2
Maple Ct 11 FK10 .... 10 A3
Maple Gr EH54 .... 148 A3
Maple Pl FK6 .... 36 B2
Maple St KY2 .... 17 A4
Mar Pl Alloa FK10 .... 10 A4
Alloa FK10 .... 5 B1
Stirling FK8 .... 7 A4
Mar St FK10 .... 10 A3
Mar Terr FK10 .... 11 A2
Maranatha Cres FK2 .... 82 B4
March Gait EH4 .... 91 C1
March Gr EH4 .... 92 A1
March Pines EH4 .... 91 C1
March Rd EH4 .... 92 A1
Marchbank Dr EH14 .... 177 B4
Marchbank Gdns EH14 .... 177 B4
Marchbank Gr EH14 .... 177 B4
Marchbank Pl EH14 .... 177 B4
Marchbank Way EH14 .... 151 B1
Marchburn Dr EH26 .... 203 B3
Marches Dr EH48 .... 144 A3
Marches The FK8 .... 7 A4
Marchfield Gr EH4 .... 92 A2
Marchfield Park La EH4 .... 91 C2

Marchfield Pk EH4 ....91 C2
Marchfield Terr EH4 ....92 A2
Marchglen FK13 ....5 C3
Marchhall Cres EH16 ...124 A3
Marchhall Pl EH16 ...124 A3
Marchhall Rd EH16 ...124 A3
Marchlands Ave EH51 .....64 A4
Marchlands La EH51 .....64 A4
Marchlands Terr EH51 .....64 A4
Marchmont Ave FK2 .....61 C1
Marchmont Cres EH9 ...123 B3
Marchmont Ct FK2 .....61 C1
Marchmont Mews FK2 .....61 C1
Marchmont Rd EH9 ...123 B3
Marchmont St FK10 ....5 B1
Marchside Ct FK10 ....5 B1
Marchwood Ave EH48 ..145 B3
Marchwood Cres EH48 ..145 B3
Marchwood Ct FK10 ...128 A1
Mardale Cres EH10 ...123 A2
Maree Ct FK10 ....10 B3
Maree Pl Crossford KY12 ...28 A1
Kirkcaldy KY2 ....16 C4
Maree Wlk EH54 ...148 A2
Margaret Ave
Bathgate EH48 ....145 C3
Haggs FK4 ....57 A2
Margaret Ct FK6 ....36 C1
Margaret Dr FK4 ....58 A3
Margaret Rd FK7 ....7 B2
Margaret Terr FK5 ....38 C2
Maria St KY1 ....17 B3
Marina Rd EH48 ...145 C3
Marine Dr EH4 ....92 A3
Marine Espl EH6 ....94 B3
Marine Par EH39 ....94 B3
Marine Rd Dunbar EH42 ..78 B2
Gullane EH31 ....52 A2
Marine Terr EH31 ....52 A2
Mariner Ave FK1 ....59 A3
Mariner Dr FK1 ....59 B3
Mariner Gdns FK1 ....59 B3
Mariner Rd FK1 ....59 A3
Mariner St FK1 ....59 B3
Mariners St KY2 ....17 A3
Mariners Wlk KY11 .....47 C2
Marion St KY1 ....17 A1
Marionville Ave EH7 .....94 B1
Marionville Cres EH7 .....94 B1
Marionville Dr EH7 .....94 B1
Marionville Gr EH7 .....94 B1
Marionville Pk EH7 .....94 A1
Marionville Rd EH7 .....94 B1
Marischal Dr EH16 ...124 C2
Marischal Pl 7 EH4 .....92 B1
Maritime La EH6 ....94 A3
Maritime St EH6 ....94 A3
Marjoribanks St EH48 ..145 A3
Mark La 8 EH41 ...132 A4
Market Ct EH41 ...101 A1
Market La EH49 ....85 A4
Market Pl
North Berwick EH39 .....54 B4
Whitburn EH47 ...170 A4
Market St Bo'ness EH51 ...63 C4
Dunfermline KY12 ....29 A2
Edinburgh EH1 ....233 A3
Haddington EH41 ...132 A4
Mid Calder EH53 ...148 B2
Musselburgh EH21 ...126 A3
Marketgate EH35 ...159 C4
Markfield Rd KY11 .....48 B2
Markle Steading EH40 ..103 A4
Marlborough Dr FK9 .....2 B2
Marlborough St EH15 ...125 A4
Marly Gn EH39 ....54 A3
Marly Rise EH39 ....54 A3
Marmion Ave EH25 ...180 C2
Marmion Cres
Edinburgh EH16 ...124 A2
North Berwick EH39 .....54 A4
Marmion Ct 8 EH39 .....54 A4
Marmion Rd
Bathgate EH48 ...145 A4
Grangemouth FK3 ....61 B3
North Berwick EH39 .....54 B4
Marmion St FK2 ....60 A4
Marquis Dr FK10 ....11 A2
Marrfield Rd EH54 ...117 A1
Marrfield Terr EH54 ...117 A1
Marschal Ct FK7 ....7 B2
Marshall Pl KY11 ....29 A1
Marshall Rd EH29 ....89 A1
Marshall St
Cockenzie & Port Seton
EH32 ....97 A2
Cowdenbeath KY4 ....13 B2
Edinburgh EH8 ...233 A2
Grangemouth FK3 ....61 B4
Marshall Terr FK3 ....61 B4
Marshall Way FK10 ....4 B2
Marshall's Ct EH1 ...233 B4
Marshill FK10 ....10 A3
Martin Brae EH54 ...147 B3
Martin Gr EH19 ...182 B4
Martin Pl EH22 ...156 C1
Martins La EH33 ...123 C2
Mary Erskine & Stewart's
Melville Jun Sch The
EH4 ....92 C1
Mary Erskine Sch The
EH4 ....92 A1
Mary Field EH15 ....95 A1
Mary Pl Clackmannan FK10 ...11 A3
Dunfermline KY11 ....29 A1
Mary Sq FK2 ....61 A2
Mary St KY2 ....60 C2
Mary Stevenson Dr FK10 ...10 A4

Mary Street Rdbt FK2 ...60 C2
Mary's Pl EH4 ....93 A1
Maryburn Rd EH22 ...183 B4
Maryfield 2 EH7 ....93 C1
Maryfield Pk EH53 ...148 B1
Maryfield Pl
Bonnyrigg & Lasswade
EH19 ...182 B4
2 Edinburgh EH7 ....93 C1
Falkirk FK1 ....59 A2
Maryflats Pl FK3 ....61 C4
Maryhall St KY1 ....17 B3
Marywell KY1 ....17 B3
Masefield Way EH12 .....90 A1
Mason Pl EH18 ...181 C3
Masserene Rd KY2 .....16 C3
Masterton Rd KY11 .....47 A4
Mather Terr FK2 ....60 C2
Mathers Ave EH47 ...169 C3
Mathie St FK3 ....61 B4
Mathieson Pl KY11 .....29 C1
Matthew St KY2 ....17 A3
Matthews Dr EH22 ...182 C2
Maukeshill Ct EH54 ...147 B1
Maule Terr EH31 ....52 A1
Maulsford Ave EH22 ...156 A4
Maurice Ave FK7 ....7 B2
Maurice Pl EH9 ...123 B1
Mauricewood Ave EH26 ..203 C4
Mauricewood Bank
EH26 ....203 C4
Mauricewood Gr EH26 ..203 C3
Mauricewood Pk EH26 ..203 C4
Mauricewood Prim Sch
EH26 ....204 A4
Mauricewood Rd EH26 ..203 C4
Mauricewood Rise
EH26 ....203 C4
Mavisbank EH20 ...181 B4
Mavisbank Ave FK1 .....81 B3
Mavisbank Pl EH18 ...181 C3
Maxton Cres FK12 ....5 B4
Maxton Ct EH22 ...157 A2
Maxton Pl KY11 ....46 C2
Maxwell Cres KY4 ....13 A1
Maxwell Pl FK7 ....7 B2
Maxwell Rd EH39 ....53 A2
Maxwell Sq EH54 ...173 B3
Maxwell St EH10 ...123 A2
May Terr EH39 ....54 A4
Maybank Villas EH12 ...121 B4
Mayburn Ave EH20 ...155 A1
Mayburn Bank EH20 ...181 A4
Mayburn Cres EH20 ...155 A1
Mayburn Ct EH20 ...181 A4
Mayburn Dr EH20 ...181 A4
Mayburn Gr EH20 ...181 A4
Mayburn Loan EH20 ...155 A1
Mayburn Terr EH20 ...155 A1
Mayburn Vale EH20 ...181 A4
Mayburn Wlk EH20 ...181 A4
Mayburry Rd EH12 ...121 A4
Mayfield Ave EH21 ...126 A2
Mayfield Cres
Clackmannan FK10 ....11 A3
Loanhead EH20 ...181 B4
Musselburgh EH21 ...126 A2
Mayfield Ct
Armadale EH48 ...143 C2
Loanhead EH20 ...181 B4
Stirling FK7 ....7 A2
Mayfield Dr
Armadale EH48 ...143 C3
Longcroft FK4 ....57 A2
Mayfield Gdns EH9 ...123 C2
Mayfield Gdns La EH9 ..123 C2
Mayfield Ind Est EH22 ..183 B3
Mayfield Mews FK1 .....59 C2
Mayfield Pl
Edinburgh EH12 ...121 B3
Mayfield FK2 ....183 B3
Musselburgh EH21 ...126 A2
Mayfield Prim Sch
EH22 ....183 B3
Mayfield Rd
Easthouses EH22 ...183 B4
Edinburgh EH9 ...123 C2
Redding FK2 ....61 B1
Mayfield St FK7 ....7 A2
Mayfield Terr EH9 ...123 C2
Mayflower St KY12 ...129 B4
Maygate KY1 ....29 A2
Mayne Ave FK9 ....2 A3
Mayshade Rd EH20 ...155 A1
Mayville Bank EH21 ...127 A3
Mayville Gdns EH5 .....93 B3
Mayville Gdns E EH5 ...93 B3
Mayville Pk EH42 ....78 B2
Mc Leod St EH52 ...117 C3
McAdam Sq EH54 ...173 B3
McAllister Ct FK7 ....7 B1
McCall Gdns EH40 ...103 B4
McCallum Ct EH48 ...143 C4
McCann Ave EH52 ...117 A3
McCathie Dr EH22 ...183 A1
McClelland Cres KY11 ...29 A1
McDiarmid Gr EH22 ...183 A2
McDonald Pl EH7 ....93 C2
McDonald Rd EH7 ....93 C2
McDonald St EH7 ....93 C2
McDouall Stuart Pl KY1 ...18 A4
McGahey Ct EH22 ...183 A2
McGhee Pl FK1 ....59 C1
McGinley Way EH48 ...84 B3
McGregor Ave KY5 .....14 A4
McGrigor Rd Rosyth KY11 ..46 C1

McGrigor Rd continued
Stirling FK7 ....7 A2
McIntosh Ct EH52 ...117 B3
Mackane Pl KY12 ....28 C1
McKay Dr KY11 ....29 C1
McKell Ct FK1 ....60 A2
McKenzie Pl FK1 ....60 A1
McKenzie St KY1 ....17 C4
McKinlay Cres EH10 ...180 B4
McKinnon Dr EH22 ...181 A4
McKinnon Dr EH22 ...183 C3
McKinnon Rd EH47 ...193 C4
McLachlan Ave FK7 ....7 A1
McLachlan St FK5 ....38 B1
McLaren Ave EH49 ....84 A3
McLaren Ct FK5 ....38 B1
McLaren Rd EH9 ...124 A2
McLaren Terr
Edinburgh EH11 ...232 A2
Stirling FK7 ....7 A2
McLauchlan Rise KY3 ...49 A4
McLauchlan View ML7 ..168 C3
McLean Pl
Bonnyrigg & Lasswade
EH18 ....181 C3
Gorebridge EH23 ...207 B4
McLean Prim Sch KY12 ..28 C2
McLean Wlk EH20 ...183 A2
McLeod Cres EH32 ....96 C1
McLeod St EH11 ...122 C3
McMartin Ct EH47 ...170 B4
McNab Gdns FK1 ....59 C1
McNeil Cres EH48 ...144 A3
McNeil Path EH33 ...128 B3
McNeil Way EH33 ...128 B3
McNeill St EH3 ...123 B3
McNeill Ave EH20 ...181 A4
McNeill Pl EH20 ...181 A4
McNeill St EH11 ...232 A1
McNeill Terr EH20 ...181 A4
McPhail Sq EH33 ...128 B3
McPherson Dr FK8 ....2 A1
McQuade St EH19 ...182 B4
McRae Cres KY3 ....33 C1
McVean Pl FK4 ....57 A2
Meadow Bank Sh Pk
EH8 ....94 A1
Meadow Cres EH47 ...193 C3
Meadow Cr
Burntisland KY3 ....33 C1
Carluke ML8 ....230 B1
Meadow Dr EH47 ...171 A1
Meadow Gn FK10 ....5 A1
Meadow La FK10 ....11 B2
Meadow La EH48 ...233 A1
Meadow Pk FK12 ....5 A3
Meadow Pl Bilston EH25 ..180 C2
Dunfermline KY12 ....29 C2
Edinburgh EH9 ...232 C1
Stirling FK8 ....2 A1
Stonehaven EH47 ...171 A1
Meadow Place Rd EH12 ..121 B3
Meadow Rd Currie EH14 ..151 C4
Stoneyburn EH47 ...171 A1
Meadow St FK1 ....60 B2
Meadowbank
Edinburgh EH8 ....94 A1
Livingston EH54 ...147 C3
Ormiston EH35 ....159 B4
Meadowbank Ave 15 EH8 ..94 A1
Meadowbank Cres
Edinburgh EH8 ....94 A1
Ormiston EH35 ....159 B4
Meadowbank Pl 15 EH8 ..94 A1
Meadowbank Rd
Kirknewton EH27 ...149 C2
Ormiston EH35 ...159 C4
Meadowbank Sports Ctr
EH7 ....94 A1
Meadowbank St FK2 .....61 B1
Meadowbank View
EH27 ....149 C2
Meadowend KY12 ....28 B1
Meadowfield
Burntisland KY3 ....33 C1
Cowdenbeath KY4 ....13 B3
Dalgety Bay KY11 ....48 A2
Meadowfield Ave EH8 ..124 C4
Meadowfield Ct EH8 ...124 B4
Meadowfield Dr EH8 ...124 C4
Meadowfield Ind Est KY3 ..33 C1
Meadowfield Rd EH12 ..120 C4
Meadowfield Terr EH8 ..124 B3
Meadowforth Rd FK7 .....7 B3
Meadowhead Cres
EH55 ....171 C1
Meadowhead Gdns
EH55 ....171 C1
Meadowhead Gr EH55 ..171 C1
Meadowhead Loan
EH55 ....171 C1
Meadowhead Pl EH55 ..171 B1
Meadowhead Terr EH55 ..171 B1
Meadowhouse Rd EH12 ..121 B3
Meadowpark KY9 ....2 A1
Meadowpark
Haddington EH41 ...132 A4
Seafield EH47 ...172 A4
Meadowpark Rd EH48 ..144 C3
Meadows The FK2 ....39 A1
Meadowside EH33 ...128 C3
Meadowside Pl EH27 ..149 C2
Meadowspot EH10 ...122 C1
Meadowview KY12 ....28 A1
Mearenside EH12 ...120 A4
Medwyn Pl FK10 ....9 C3

Meeks Rd FK2 ....60 A3
Meeting House Dr EH33 ..128 B3
Meggat Pl EH26 ...204 A4
Meggetland Terr EH14 ..122 C2
Meikle Rd EH54 ...147 B1
Meikle Sq KY1 ....18 A4
Melbourne Pl EH39 .....54 B4
Melbourne Rd
Broxburn EH51 ...117 C3
North Berwick EH39 .....54 B4
Melbourne St EH54 ...148 A3
Meldrum Cres KY3 ....33 B1
Meldrum Ct KY11 ....29 C1
Meldrum Prim Sch
EH54 ....146 C4
Meldrum Rd KY2 ....17 A3
Melford Rd ML7 ...192 A2
Melfort Dr FK7 ....7 A2
Melgund Pl KY5 ....14 A4
Melgund Terr EH7 ....93 B1
Mellerstain Rd KY2 .....16 B3
Mellock Gdns FK1 ....59 C1
Mellor Ct KY11 ....46 C2
Melrose Cres KY2 ....17 B3
Melrose Dr FK3 ....61 C3
Melrose Pl 10 FK1 ....60 A2
Melrose Prim Sch
EH18 ....181 C3
Melville Cotts EH18 ...156 B2
Melville Cres EH3 ...232 A3
Melville Dr EH9 ...233 A1
Melville Dykes Rd EH18 ..156 B1
Melville Dykes Road Rdbt
EH22 ....156 B1
Melville Gate EH22 ...156 B2
Melville Gate Rd EH22 ..156 C2
Melville Gdns KY3 ....50 B4
Melville Pl Bridge of A FK9 ..2 A4
Dunfermline KY12 ....29 A2
Kirkcaldy KY2 ....16 B3
Melville Rd EH22 ...156 C1
Melville St
Edinburgh EH3 ...232 A3
Falkirk FK1 ....60 A3
Lochgelly KY5 ....14 A4
Melville Street La EH3 ..232 A3
Melville Terr
2 Dalkeith EH22 ...156 C1
Edinburgh EH9 ...233 B1
Stirling FK8 ....7 A3
Melville View EH18 ...182 A4
Menstrie Bsns Ctr FK11 ...3 C3
Menstrie Castle* FK11 .....3 C3
Menstrie Pl FK11 ....4 A4
Menstrie Prim Sch FK11 ...4 A3
Menteith Ct FK10 ....10 B3
Menteith Dr KY11 ....29 C1
Menteith Rd FK9 ....2 A4
Mentone Ave EH15 ....95 A1
Mentone Gdns EH9 ...123 C2
Mentone Terr EH9 ...123 C2
Menzies Cres KY2 ....16 C3
Menzies Dr FK8 ....2 A1
Menzies Rd EH48 ...145 A3
Mercat La EH48 ...145 A3
Mercat Pl FK10 ....11 A2
Mercat The KY1 ....17 B2
Mercat Wynd 4 EH21 ...127 A3
Mercer St FK10 ....11 A1
Mercer St KY10 ....23 C2
Merchant St EH1 ...233 A2
Merchiston Ave
Edinburgh EH10 ...123 A3
Falkirk FK2 ....60 A4
Merchiston Bank Ave
EH10 ....123 A2
Merchiston Bank Gdns
EH10 ....123 A2
Merchiston Castle Sch
EH14 ....153 A4
Merchiston Cres EH10 ..123 A2
Merchiston Gdns
Edinburgh EH10 ...122 C2
Falkirk FK2 ....60 A4
Merchiston Gr EH11 ...122 C2
Merchiston Ind Est FK2 ..60 A4
Merchiston Mews EH10 ..123 A3
Merchiston Pk EH10 ...123 A3
Merchiston Rd
Falkirk FK2 ....60 A4
Falkirk, Grahamston FK2 ..60 A3
Merchiston Terr FK2 .....60 A3
Meredith Dr FK5 ....38 C2
Merker Terr EH49 ....84 C3
Merkland Cres KY11 .....48 A2
Merkland Dr FK7 ....60 C1
Merlin Way KY11 ....48 A1
Merlyon Way EH26 ...203 B4
Merrick Rd FK3 ....61 A3
Merrick Way FK3 ....61 C3
Merryfield Ave EH33 ...129 B3
Merrylees EH49 ....45 B4
Mertoun Pl EH11 ...122 C2
Merville Cres FK1 ....81 C3
Merville Terr FK1 ....81 C3
Methven Dr KY11 ....29 A3
Methven Pl KY11 ....17 A1
Methven Terr EH18 ...181 C3
Meuse La EH2 ....233 A3
Michaelson Sq EH54 ...147 B1
Mid Beveridgewell KY12 ..28 C3
Mid Brae 6 EH22 ....28 C3
Mid Calder Prim Sch
EH53 ....148 B2
Mid Cswy KY12 ....42 B4
Mid Gogarloch Syke
EH12 ....121 A3
Mid Liberton EH16 ...124 A1
Mid New Cultins EH11 ..121 A1

Mar – Mil 253
Mid Rd FK3 ....34 C2
Mid Road Ind Est EH32 ..127 C4
Mid St Bathgate EH48 ..145 A3
Kirkcaldy KY1 ....17 B3
Livingston EH54 ...146 C3
Lochgelly KY5 ....14 A4
Mid Steil EH10 ...122 C1
Middle Meadow Wlk
EH8 ....233 A1
Middle Street La FK3 ...40 B1
Middle Wlk KY12 ....29 A2
Middlebank St KY11 .....56 C2
Middleby Ct EH9 ...123 C2
Middleby St EH9 ...123 C2
Middlefield EH7 ....93 C2
Middlefield Ind Est FK2 ..60 C4
Middlefield Rd FK2 .....60 B3
Middleknowe EH14 ...152 B4
Middlemass Rd EH42 ..106 B4
Middlemass Ct FK2 .....60 A3
Middlemuir Rd FK4 .....57 A2
Middlepark EH14 ...152 B4
Middleshot EH14 ...152 B4
Middleshot Rd EH31 .....52 A2
Middleshot Sq EH32 .....97 A1
Middleton FK11 ....4 A3
Middleton Ave EH52 ...117 A2
Middleton Rd EH52 ...117 A2
Middlewood Pk EH54 ..146 C4
Midhope Pl FK2 ....88 A1
Midlothian Ski Ctr*
EH10 ....154 A1
Midmar Ave EH10 ...123 B1
Midmar Dr EH10 ...123 B1
Midmar Gdns EH10 ...123 A1
Midthorn Cres FK2 .....60 C3
Midtown FK11 ....4 A1
Milesmark Ct KY12 .....28 B3
Milesmark Prim Sch
KY12 ....28 B3
Mill Ct Bathgate EH48 ..145 A4
Falkirk FK2 ....39 A2
Mill Farm Rd KY3 ....49 A4
Mill Hill FK7 ....6 B3
Mill La Edinburgh EH6 ..93 C3
Kincardine FK10 ....23 C2
Mill Lade EH49 ....84 C4
Mill Of Airthrey Ct FK9 ...1 C4
Mill Rd Alloa FK10 ....10 C4
Armadale EH48 ...143 C3
Bathgate EH48 ...145 A4
Blackburn EH47 ...171 B4
Cambusbarron FK7 ....6 B3
Clackmannan FK10 ....11 A3
Dunfermline KY11 ....29 A3
Falkirk FK2 ....39 A2
Harthill ML7 ...168 C3
Linlithgow EH49 ....84 C4
Stenton EH42 ...104 B1
Mill Rdbt EH54 ...147 A2
Mill Road Ind Est EH49 ..84 C4
Mill St Alloa FK10 ....10 C4
Dunfermline KY12 ....28 C2
Kirkcaldy KY1 ....17 A1
Mill Wynd
East Linton EH40 ...103 C4
Haddington EH41 ...132 A4
Prestonpans EH32 ....96 C1
Millar Cres EH10 ...123 A2
Millar Pl Edinburgh EH10 ..123 A2
High Bonnybridge FK4 ..58 A2
Stenhousemuir FK2 .....39 A3
Millar Rd EH33 ...128 B3
Millar Place La EH10 ...123 A2
Millar Rd EH33 ...128 B3
Millars Wynd EH52 .....61 B1
Millbank EH14 ...151 B1
Millbank Cres FK10 .....11 A3
Millbank Gr EH23 ...207 B4
Millbank Pl EH52 ...116 C2
Millbank Sq EH47 ...170 A4
Millbank Terr FK2 ....82 C4
Millbrae EH53 ...148 B3
Millbrae Wynd EH14 ...122 B2
Millbrook Pl FK11 ....3 A3
Millburn Cres EH48 ...143 B3
Millburn Rd
Bathgate EH48 ...144 C3
Westfield EH48 ...112 C3
Millburn St FK2 ....60 B3
Milldean Gr KY12 ....29 B3
Miller Ave KY12 ....29 B3
Miller Cres EH51 ....64 B3
Miller Pl FK2 ....61 C1
Miller Pl Airth FK2 ....22 C2
Harthill ML7 ...168 C3
Miller Rd
Dunfermline KY12 ....28 C3
Grangemouth FK3 ....61 A3
Miller Row EH4 ...232 A3
Miller St Carluke ML8 ..230 A1
Harthill ML7 ...168 C3
Kirkcaldy KY1 ....17 C4
Millerfield EH49 ....84 B4
Millerfield Pl EH9 ...123 B3
Millerhill Rd
Dalkeith EH22 ...125 A1
Danderhall EH22 ...156 B4
Millers Ct EH33 ...128 A3
Millfield
Haddington EH41 ...132 A4
Livingston EH54 ...147 A1
Millfield Dr FK2 ....61 C1
Millflats St FK2 ....39 A1
Millgate EH52 ....87 C1

Millhall Rd FK7 ....7 A3
Millhaugh La EH48 .....145 A4
Millhill EH21 ....126 B3
Millhill La EH21 ....126 B3
Millhill St KY11 ....29 A1
Millhill Wynd EH21 ....126 B3
Millie St KY1 ....17 B3
Millway EH34 ....161 A3
Miln-acre EH6 ....93 B2
Milne Cres KY4 ....13 B2
Milne Rd KY11 ....46 C1
Milnepark Rd KY7 ....19 C4
Milsey Ct EH39 ....54 B4
Milton Brae FK7 ....7 A1
Milton Cl FK6 ....36 B2
Milton Cres
 Bannockburn FK7 ....7 B1
 Edinburgh EH15 ....125 A3
Milton Dr EH15 ....125 B4
Milton Gardens N EH15 .125 A3
Milton Gardens S EH15 .125 A3
Milton Gdns FK7 ....7 A1
Milton Glen EH15 ......125 C4
Milton Gn KY12 ....29 A1
Milton Gr Bannockburn FK7 .7 B1
 Edinburgh EH15 ....125 C4
Milton Link EH15 ......125 B3
Milton Pl KY2 ....19 A2
Milton Pl FK6 ....36 B2
Milton Rd Bannockburn FK7 .7 B1
 Edinburgh EH15 ....125 A3
 Kirkcaldy KY1 ....17 A1
Milton Rd W KY1 ....124 C3
Milton Road E EH15 ....125 B4
Milton Row FK6 ....36 C2
Milton St EH8 ....94 A1
Milton Terr
 Bannockburn FK7 ....7 A1
 Edinburgh EH15 ....125 C4
Minard Rd ML7 ....191 B3
Mine Rd FK9 ....2 A4
Miner's Terr EH21 ......127 A3
Mingle Pl EH51 ....64 A3
Minstrel Ct EH25 ......181 A2
Minthill Pl ML7 ....168 B3
Minto Ct FK12 ....5 A3
Minto Gdns FK12 ....5 A3
Minto Pl KY2 ....16 C2
Minto St Edinburgh EH9 .123 C2
 Lochgelly KY5 ....14 A4
Mission La 9 FK1 ......60 A2
Mitchell Cres Alloa FK10 ..9 C4
 Cowdenbeath KY4 ......13 A1
Mitchell Pl Falkirk FK1 ...59 C1
 5 Kirkcaldy KY1 ....17 B3
Mitchell Rd KY11 ....46 B1
Mitchell St
 Dalkeith EH22 ....156 C2
 Edinburgh EH6 ....94 A3
 Kirkcaldy KY1 ....17 B2
Mitchell Way EH33 .....128 B4
Mitchell Wlk KY11 ......46 C2
Mitchell's Cl 2 EH41 ..132 A4
Mitchellhall Brae EH41 .132 C3
Moat Dr EH14 ....122 B2
Moat Pl EH14 ....122 B2
Moat St EH14 ....122 B2
Moat Terr EH14 ....122 B2
Moat View EH25 ....180 C2
Mochrum Dr KY12 ......45 A4
Modan Rd FK7 ....7 A2
Moffat Ave
 Bonnyrigg & Lasswade
  EH19 ....182 A3
 Falkirk FK2 ....39 B3
Moffat Cres KY5 ....14 A4
Moffat Rd EH35 ....159 B3
Moidart Rd EH47 ....170 B4
Moir Ave EH21 ....127 A3
Moir Cres EH21 ....127 A3
Moir Ct KY4 ....12 C4
Moir Dr EH21 ....127 A3
Moir Pl EH21 ....127 A3
Moir St FK10 ....10 A4
Moir Terr EH21 ....127 A3
Moira Pk EH7 ....94 C1
Moira Terr EH7 ....94 C1
Moira Terrace La EH7 ..94 C1
Mollison Ave ML7 ......168 C3
Monar Ct KY11 ....48 A2
Monastery St KY12 .....29 A2
Moncks Rd FK1 ....60 B2
Moncreiff Terr EH9 ....123 C3
Moncrieff Way EH54 ...147 B4
Moncur St KY12 ....29 B4
Monkbarns Gdns 8
 EH16 ....155 A4
Monkland Rd EH48 ....144 C3
Monkmains Rd EH41 ...132 B4
Monkrigg Pl EH41 .....132 B4
Monksrig Rd EH26 .....203 B3
Monkswood Rd EH22 ..183 A2
Monktonhall Pl EH21 ..126 A2
Monktonhall Terr EH21 .126 A2
Monkwood Ct EH9 .....123 B2
Monmouth Terr EH3 ....93 A2
Montagu Terr EH3 ......93 A2
Montague St EH8 ......233 B1
Monteith Wlk ML7 .....191 C3
Montfort Pl FK1 ....60 A2
Montgomery Cres FK2 .39 A1
Montgomery Dr FK2 ...39 A1
Montgomery Pl FK2 ...39 A1
Montgomery St
 Edinburgh EH7 ....93 C1

Montgomery St continued
 Falkirk FK2 ....60 C3
Grangemouth FK3 ....61 B3
Kirkcaldy KY12 ....17 A3
Montgomery Street La
 EH7 ....93 C1
Montgomery Way FK9 ...2 A2
Montgomery Well FK2 ..39 A1
Montpelier EH10 ....123 A3
Montpelier Pk EH10 ...123 A3
Montpelier Terr EH10 ..123 A3
Montrose Rd Polmont FK2 .62 A1
 Stirling FK9 ....2 B1
Montrose Terr EH7 .....233 C4
Montrose Way FK4 .....57 B3
Monument View FK8 ....2 A1
Moodie St KY12 ....29 A2
Moor Rd Fala EH37 ....210 B3
 Pathhead EH37 ....185 B2
 Pencaitland EH35 .....206 B3
Moore Cotts EH52 .....117 B3
Moore House Sch EH48 .145 C3
Mooreland Gdns EH55 .171 B1
Moorelands EH55 ......171 B1
Moorfield Cotts EH22 ..156 B4
Moorfoot Ct EH19 .....182 A4
Moorfoot Pl
 Bonnyrigg & Lasswade
  EH19 ....182 A3
 Penicuik EH26 ....203 C3
Moorfoot View
 Bilston EH25 ....180 C3
 Bonnyrigg & Lasswade
  EH19 ....182 A3
Moorings The KY11 ....47 C1
Moorlands Pl EH55 ....171 B1
Moorside St ML8 ....230 A1
Morar Ct FK3 ....61 B3
Morar Dr FK2 ....39 B1
Morar Pl FK3 ....61 B3
Morar Rd KY12 ....28 A1
Moray Way ML7 ....192 A2
Moray Dr EH49 ....84 C3
Moray House Coll of Ed
 Edinburgh, Canongate EH8 .233 B3
 Edinburgh, Cramond EH4 .91 B3
Moray Park Terr EH7 ..94 A1
Moray Pk KY11 ....48 A2
Moray Pl Edinburgh EH3 .232 B4
 Grangemouth FK3 ......61 C4
Linlithgow EH49 ....84 C3
Moray Prim Sch FK3 ..61 C4
Moray Way N KY11 ....48 A1
Moray Way S KY11 ....48 A1
Morayvale KY3 ....49 B4
Moredun Dykes Rd
 EH17 ....155 C4
Moredun Park Ct EH17 .155 B4
Moredun Park Dr EH17 .155 B4
Moredun Park Gdns
 EH17 ....155 B4
Moredun Park Gn EH17 .155 C4
Moredun Park Gr EH17 .155 C4
Moredun Park Loan
 EH17 ....155 B4
Moredun Park Rd EH17 .155 C4
Moredun Park View
 EH17 ....155 C4
Moredun Park Way
 EH17 ....155 C4
Moredun Park Wlk
 EH17 ....155 C4
Moredun Prim Sch
 EH17 ....155 B4
Moredunvale Bank
 EH17 ....155 B4
Moredunvale Gn EH17 .155 B4
Moredunvale Loan
 EH17 ....155 B4
Moredunvale Pk EH17 .155 B4
Moredunvale Pl EH17 ..155 B4
Moredunvale Rd EH17 .155 B4
Moredunvale View
 EH17 ....155 B4
Moredunvale Way EH17 .155 B4
Morgan Ct FK7 ....7 B3
Morham Gait EH10 ....153 C4
Morham Lea EH10 .....153 C4
Morham Pk EH10 ......153 C4
Morham Village Houses
 EH41 ....133 B3
Morison Gdns EH30 ....68 A1
Morison Ct FK3 ....61 C2
Moriston Dr FK4 ....57 A2
Morley Cres FK7 ....7 A2
Morlich Cres KY11 .....48 A1
Morlich Ct KY11 ....48 A1
Morlich Gr KY11 ....48 A1
Morlich Pk KY11 ....48 A1
Morlich Pl KY11 ....48 A1
Morlich Rd KY11 ......48 A1
Morlich Wlk EH54 .....148 A2
Mornay Way ML7 ......191 B3
Morningside Ct EH10 ..123 A1
Morningside Dr EH10 ..123 A1
Morningside Gdns
 EH10 ....122 C1
Morningside Gr EH10 ..122 C1
Morningside Pk EH10 ..123 A2
Morningside Pl EH10 ..123 A2
Morningside Rd EH10 ..123 A2
Morningside Terr EH10 .123 A2
Morris Ct KY11 ....47 B1

Morris Rd EH22 ....183 B3
Morris Sq EH54 ....147 C1
Morris Terr FK8 ....7 A4
Morrison Ave
 Bonnyrigg & Lasswade
  EH19 ....57 C3
 Tranent EH33 ....128 C3
Morrison Cir EH3 ......232 A2
Morrison Ct EH3 ......232 A2
Morrison Dr
 Bannockburn FK7 ....7 B1
 Dumfermline KY11 .....46 C4
Morrison Link EH3 ....232 A2
Morrison St EH3 ......232 A2
Morrison Way EH54 ...147 B4
Mortimer Ct KY11 .....48 A1
Morton St EH15 ....125 A4
Mortonhall Gate EH16 .154 C3
Mortonhall Park Ave
 EH17 ....154 C3
Mortonhall Park Bank
 EH17 ....155 A3
Mortonhall Park Cres
 EH17 ....155 A3
Mortonhall Park Dr
 EH17 ....155 A3
Mortonhall Park Gdns
 EH17 ....154 C3
Mortonhall Park Gr
 EH17 ....155 A3
Mortonhall Park Pl
 EH17 ....155 A3
Mortonhall Park Terr
 EH17 ....155 A3
Mortonhall Park View
 EH17 ....154 C3
Mortonhall Park Way
 EH17 ....154 C3
Mortonhall Rd EH9 ...123 B2
Morven Dr FK1 ....60 B1
Morven Dr FK2 ....61 B1
Morven Gr EH54 ......147 C3
Morven Pl KY11 ....48 A2
Morven St EH4 ....91 B1
Morvenside EH14 .....152 B4
Morvenside Cl EH14 ..152 B4
Moss Intc EH40 ....147 B3
Moss Rd FK7 ....8 A2
Moss Way KY11 ....48 A3
Moss-side Rd KY4 .....13 A2
Mossband La ML7 .....191 C3
Mossbank
 Cowdenbeath KY4 .....13 A1
Livingston EH54 ......147 C3
 Rosyth KY11 ....46 C3
Mossburn Ave ML7 ...168 B3
Mosscastle Rd FK1 ...110 A4
Mossend EH55 ....172 B2
Mossend Terr KY4 ....13 A2
Mossgiel Ave Cowie FK7 .20 B4
 Stirling FK8 ....2 A1
Mossgiel Cotts EH54 .146 B4
Mossgiel Terr KY4 ....59 A3
Mossgiel Terr FK2 ....61 A1
Mossgiel Wlk 4 EH16 .124 A1
Mosshall Ind Est EH47 .171 A4
Mosshat Rd EH55 .....216 C2
Mosshouse FK7 ....6 A4
Mosside Ct EH47 ......171 B4
Mosside St EH47 ......145 B1
Mosside Rd EH47 .....171 B4
Moston Terr EH9 ......123 C2
Moston St KY5 ....14 A4
Moubray Gr EH30 .....39 B4
Moubray Rd KY11 ....48 B3
Moulin Way KY12 ....29 C3
Mound Pl EH1 ....232 C3
Mound The EH2 ......232 C3
Mount Alvernia EH16 ..155 A4
Mount Bartholomew FK4 .58 A3
Mount Grange EH9 ...123 B2
Mount Hooly Cres KY11 .68 B3
Mount Hope FK9 ....2 A4
Mount Lodge Pl EH15 .125 A4
Mount Oliphant FK7 ...20 B4
Mount Pleasant EH48 .143 C3
Mount Vernon Rd EH16 .155 A4
Mount William FK10 ...5 C2
Mountbatten Pl KY11 ..46 C2
Mountbatten St FK3 ..61 B3
Mountcastle Bank EH8 .124 C4
Mountcastle Cres EH8 .124 C4
Mountcastle Dr N EH15 .124 C4
Mountcastle Dr S EH15 .124 C3
Mountcastle Gdns EH8 .124 C4
Mountcastle Gn 1 EH8 .94 C1
Mountcastle Gr EH8 ..124 C4
Mountcastle Loan EH8 .124 C4
Mountcastle Pk 3 EH8 .94 C1
Mountcastle Pl 2 EH8 .94 C1
Mountcastle Terr EH8 .124 C4
Mountfair Gdns EH33 .129 B3
Mountfair Pl EH33 ....129 B3
Mountheoly Loan EH10 .154 B3
Mountjoy Terr EH21 ..126 B4
Mowbray Ct FK7 ....7 B2
Mowbray Gdns KY4 ..30 C3
Mowbray Rise EH54 ..147 C1
Muckle Hill Pk KY11 ..47 A1
Mucklets Ave EH21 ...126 A2
Mucklets Cres EH21 ..126 A2
Mucklets Ct EH21 ....126 A2
Mucklets Dr EH21 ....126 A2
Mucklets Pl EH21 ....126 A2
Mucklets Rd EH21 ....125 C2
Mudale Ct FK1 ....60 B1
Muir Ct KY4 ....30 C3
Muir Dr KY4 ....30 C3

Muir Pl KY12 ....29 B4
Muir Rd Bathgate EH48 .144 C4
 Livingston EH54 ......148 A4
 Townhill KY12 ....29 B4
Muir St FK5 ....38 B1
Muir Wood Cres EH14 .152 A3
Muir Wood Dr EH14 ..152 A3
Muir Wood Gr EH14 ..152 A3
Muir Wood Pl EH14 ..152 A3
Muir Wood Rd EH14 ..152 A3
Muir's Ct EH52 ....116 C2
Muiralehouse Rd FK7 ..19 C4
Muiravonside Ctry Pk*
 EH49 ....83 C2
Muirdale Terr EH4 ....91 C3
Muirdyke Ave FK2 ....39 B2
Muiredge & Jersy Rd
 ML7 ....191 A4
Muirend Ave EH14 ...152 C4
Muirend Ct EH51 .....64 A3
Muirend Gdns EH14 ..152 A1
Muirepark Ct EH51 ...64 A3
Muirfield Cres EH31 ..52 A1
Muirfield Ct EH40 ....103 C4
Muirfield Dr Gullane EH31 .52 A1
 Uphall EH52 ....116 C2
Muirfield Gdns EH20 ..181 B4
Muirfield Pk EH31 .....52 A2
Muirfield Rd FK5 ......38 C1
Muirfield Sta EH31 ....52 A1
Muirhall Steading EH52 .82 B2
Muirfield Terr EH12 ..122 B1
Muirfield Way EH54 ..146 C3
Muirhall Pl FK5 ....38 B2
Muirhall Rd FK5 ......38 B2
Muirhead Ave FK2 ....60 A4
Muirhead Pl Harthill ML7 .168 B2
 Penicuik EH26 ....203 C4
Muirhead Rd FK5 .....38 C2
Muirhouse Ave EH4 ..92 A2
Muirhouse Avenue N
 EH4 ....92 A3
Muirhouse Cl EH4 ....92 A2
Muirhouse Cres EH4 ..92 A3
Muirhouse Ct EH4 ....92 A3
Muirhouse Dr EH4 ....92 A3
Muirhouse Gdns EH4 ..92 A3
Muirhouse Gn EH4 ...92 A2
Muirhouse Gr EH4 ...92 A3
Muirhouse Loan EH4 .92 A3
Muirhouse Medway EH4 .92 A3
Muirhouse Parkway EH4 .92 A3
Muirhouse Pk EH4 ...92 A2
Muirhouse Pl E EH4 ..92 A2
Muirhouse Pl W EH4 .92 A2
Muirhouse Prim Sch
 EH4 ....92 A3
Muirhouse Terr EH4 ..92 A2
Muirhouse View EH4 .92 A3
Muirhouse Way EH4 ..92 A3
Muirhouses Ave EH51 .64 B3
Muirlaw ML11 ....215 A1
Muirlee Rd ML8 ......230 A4
Muirpark Ct EH33 ...128 C1
Muirpark Dr EH33 ...128 C3
Muirpark Gdns
 Tranent EH33 ....128 C3
 Tranent EH33 ....128 C3
Muirpark Gr EH33 ...128 C3
Muirpark Pl EH33 ...128 C3
Muirpark Rd EH33 ...128 C3
Muirpark Terr EH33 ..128 C3
Muirpark Wynd EH33 .128 C3
Muirs The FK10 ....4 B2
Muirside Ave EH10 ...4 A2
Muirside Dr EH33 ...128 B3
Muirside Gr EH33 ....27 B1
Muirside La KY12 ....44 B4
Muirside Rd KY10 ....4 B2
Muirton Rd FK7 ......7 C4
Muirton Way KY11 ...48 A3
Mulberry Dr KY11 ...29 C1
Mulberry Pl EH6 .....93 B3
Muldron Terr ML7 ...192 A1
Mull Ct Alloa FK10 ..10 A3
 Grangemouth FK3 ....61 B3
Multiplex Rdbt EH54 ..147 C1
Mumrills Rd FK2 .....61 B2
Mungal Ct EH33 ....128 A4
Mungalend Ct FK2 ..60 A4
Mungalhead Rd FK2 .60 A4
Mungle Pl EH55 .....172 B2
Mungle St EH55 .....172 B2
Munro Ave EH14 ....152 C4
Munro Dr EH19 .....182 B3
Munro Gdns FK2 ....60 C2
Munro Pl FK10 ......9 B2
Munro Rd FK7 ......7 C3
Munro St Kirkcaldy KY1 .17 A1
 Stenhousemuir FK5 ...38 B3
Munro Way EH54 ...147 B4
Murano Pl EH7 .....93 C1
Murderdean Rd EH22 .183 A3
Murdoch Terr EH11 ..232 A1
Murdostoun Cres ML7 .168 C3
Murieston Cres EH11 ..122 C3
Murieston Crescent La
 EH11 ....122 C3
Murieston E Rd
 EH54 ....174 A3
Murieston Gdns EH54 .174 A4

Murieston Gn EH54 ...173 C3
Murieston Gr EH54 ...174 A3
Murieston La EH11 ...122 C3
Murieston Mews EH11 .173 C3
Murieston Pk EH54 ...173 C3
Murieston Pk EH54 ...173 C3
Murieston Rd
 Edinburgh EH11 ......122 C3
 Livingston EH54 ......173 C2
Murieston Terr EH11 ..122 C3
Murieston Vale EH54 ..173 C2
Murieston Valley EH54 .173 C3
Murieston Way EH54 ..174 A4
Murieston West Rd
 EH54 ....173 C3
Murieston Wlk EH54 ..173 C3
Murnin Ct FK7 ....7 B2
Murnin Rd FK4 ....58 A2
Murnin Road Ind Est FK4 .58 A2
Murray Cotts EH12 ...121 B3
Murray Pl FK9 ....2 A3
Murray Cres KY2 ....83 A3
Murray Ct EH48 .....143 C3
Murray Pl
 Cambusbarron FK7 ....6 B3
 Stirling FK8 ....7 A4
Murray Way FK4 .....147 B4
Murray Wlk KY11 ....29 C2
Murrayburn App EH11 .121 B1
Murrayburn Dr EH11 ..121 B1
Murrayburn Gate EH14 .152 B4
Murrayburn Gdns EH11 .121 C1
Murrayburn Gn EH14 .121 C1
Murrayburn Gr EH14 ..121 C1
Murrayburn Junc EH14 .152 B4
Murrayburn Pk EH14 ..121 C1
Murrayburn Pl EH14 ..121 B1
Murrayburn Prim Sch
 EH11 ....121 C1
Murrayburn Rd EH11 ..121 C1
Murrayfield Ave EH12 .122 B4
Murrayfield Dr
 Blackburn EH47 ......171 B4
 Edinburgh EH12 ......122 B4
Murrayfield Gdns EH12 .122 B4
Murrayfield Hospl EH12 .122 A4
Murrayfield Pl
 Bannockburn FK7 ....7 B1
 Edinburgh EH12 ......122 B4
Murrayfield Prim Sch
 EH4 ....145 B1
Murrayfield Rd EH12 ..122 B4
Murrayfield Rugby Gd
 EH12 ....122 B3
Murrayfield Terr
 Bannockburn FK7 ....7 B1
 Edinburgh EH12 ......171 B4
Murrays Brae The EH17 .155 B2
Murrays The EH17 ....155 B2
Murraysgate Cres EH54 .169 C3
Murraysgate Ind Est
 FK7 ....169 C2
Murrayshall Rd FK2 ...61 B3
Murrel Rd KY3 ....49 B4
Murrel Terr KY3 ......49 B4
Mus of Childhood*
 EH1 ....233 C4
Mus of Fire* EH3 ....232 C2
Mus of Flight* EH39 .74 B1
Music Hall La KY12 ..29 A2
Musselburgh Burgh Prim Sch
 EH21 ....126 B3
Musselburgh Gram Sch
 EH21 ....126 B3
Musselburgh Sta
 Dalkeith EH22 ....157 A2
 Edinburgh EH15 ......125 C4
Musselburgh Sta EH21 .126 C2
Myers Ct KY12 ......39 B3
Myles Ho EH3 ....7 A4
Mylne Pl FK1 ....59 A3
Mylneburn Gdns KY11 .45 B2
Myothill Rd FK6 .....57 B4
Myre Cres KY3 ......35 A2
Myre Dale EH19 ....182 B3
Myreside Ct EH10 ...122 C1
Myreside Rd EH10 ..122 C2
Myreton FK7 ....19 C4
Myreton Motor Mus*
 EH32 ....72 A2
Myreton Rd FK3 .....61 B3
Myreton Way FK1 ...59 C2
Myretoungate FK12 ..5 A3
Myrtle Cres Bilston EH25 .180 C3
 Kirkcaldy KY2 ....17 A4
Myrtle Gr EH22 .....183 B4
Myrtle Terr EH11 ...122 C3

N

Nagle Rd KY12 ....12 A1
Nailer Rd Falkirk FK1 .59 C3
 Stirling FK7 ....7 A1
Nairn Ct FK1 ....60 B1
Nairn Rd EH54 .....146 C4
Nairn St KY1 ....17 B3
Naismith Ct KY3 ...40 C1
Nanayo Ave FK2 ...61 A3
Namur Rd EH26 ...204 A4
Nantwich Dr EH7 ..94 C2
Napier Ave EH48 ..145 B3
Napier Cotts FK7 ..60 A2
Napier Loan EH10 .123 A2
Napier Pl FK2 .....60 A4
Napier Rd EH10 ...123 A2

Napier Sq EH54 . . . . 148 A4
Napier St KY1 . . . . 17 C4
Napier Univ EH11 . . . . 121 B1
Napier Univ (Craighouse
Campus) EH10 . . . . 122 C1
Napier Univ (Craigleckhart
Campus) EH14 . . . . 122 B1
Napier Univ (Marchmont
Campus) EH9 . . . . 123 B3
Napier Univ (Merchiston
Campus) EH14 . . . . 123 A3
Nasmyth Ct EH54 . . . . 148 A3
Nasmyth Rd KY11 . . . . 46 A1
Nasmyth Sq EH54 . . . . 148 A3
Natal Pl KY4 . . . . 13 B2
National Flag Heritage Ctr *
EH39 . . . . 101 C4
National Gallery of
Scotland * EH2 . . . . 232 C3
National Lihy of Scotland *
EH1 . . . . 233 A3
National Portrait Gall *
EH2 . . . . 233 A4
Navar Ct ML7 . . . . 192 A2
Nebit The FK12 . . . . 4 C3
Neidpath Ct
Edinburgh EH12 . . . . 121 A4
Longniddry EH32 . . . . 98 C3
Neidpath Dr FK5 . . . . 38 C2
Neidpath Pl KY12 . . . . 29 B3
Neilson Gr KY3 . . . . 33 C1
Neilson Park Rd EH41 . . . . 132 A4
Neilson Sq EH54 . . . . 146 B3
Neilson St FK1 . . . . 60 A2
Nellburn EH54 . . . . 146 C3
Nellfield EH16 . . . . 155 A4
Nelson Ave EH54 . . . . 147 C2
Nelson Gdns KY3 . . . . 40 C1
Nelson Pl FK7 . . . . 7 B3
Nelson Rd FK1 . . . . 62 C3
Nelson St Edinburgh EH3 . 232 C4
Grangemouth FK3 . . . . 61 C4
Kirkcaldy KY2 . . . . 17 A3
Rosyth KY11 . . . . 46 C3
Ness The KY12 . . . . 26 C1
Nether Craigour EH17 . . . . 124 B1
Nether Craigwell EH13 . . . 152 A3
Nether Currie Cres
EH14 . . . . 152 A3
Nether Currie Pl EH14 . . . . 152 A3
Nether Currie Prim Sch
EH14 . . . . 152 A3
Nether Currie Rd EH14 . . . 152 A3
Nether Dechmont Cotts
EH54 . . . . 147 A4
Nether Liberton Ct
EH16 . . . . 124 A1
Nether St Dysart KY1 . . . . . . 18 A4
Kirkcaldy KY1 . . . . 17 B3
Netherbank EH16 . . . . 154 C3
Netherbank View EH16 . . . 154 C3
Netherbeath Rd KY4 . . . . . . 30 C4
Netherby Rd Airth FK2 . . . . . 22 B2
Edinburgh EH5 . . . . 93 A3
Netherfield Rd FK2 . . . . . . 121 B1
Nethergate KY3 . . . . 35 A1
Nethergate The FK12 . . . . 4 C2
Netherlaw EH39 . . . . 54 A3
Nethermains Prim Sch
FK6 . . . . 36 B1
Nethermains Rd FK6 . . . . . . 36 B1
Nethershot Rd EH32 . . . . . . 97 A1
Nethertoun Gr EH47 . . . . . 170 A2
Netherton Pl EH47 . . . . . . 170 A2
Netherton St ML7 . . . . 161 A1
Nethertown Broad St
KY12 . . . . 29 A1
Netherwood Pk EH54 . . . . . 147 A4
Nettlehill Dr EH54 . . . . 116 C1
Nettlehill Rd
Livingston EH54 . . . . 147 C4
Uphall Sta EH54 . . . . 117 A1
Neucks The FK1 . . . . 111 A3
Nevis Cres FK10 . . . . 10 A4
Nevis Dr EH54 . . . . 173 C3
Nevis Gdns EH26 . . . . 204 A4
Nevis Pl Falkirk FK1 . . . . 60 B1
Grangemouth FK3 . . . . 61 C3
Shotts ML7 . . . . 192 A2
New Arthur Pl EH8 . . . . . . 233 B2
New Bell's Ct EH6 . . . . 94 A3
New Broompark EH5 . . . . . . 92 C4
New Broughton 3 EH3 . . . . 93 B1
New Carron Rd FK5 . . . . 39 A2
New Century Dr ML7 . . . . . 161 C2
New Coll EH1 . . . . 232 C3
New Cut Rigg EH6 . . . . 93 B3
New Hallglen Rd FK1 . . . . . . 60 B1
New Holygate EH52 . . . . . . 117 B3
New Hos EH39 . . . . 75 A4
New Houses EH39 . . . . 74 B2
New Hunterfield EH23 . . . . 183 A1
New John's Pl EH8 . . . . 233 B1
New La EH6 . . . . 93 B3
New Lairdship Pl EH11 . . . 121 B2
New Lairdship Yards
EH11 . . . . 121 B2
New Line Rd FK7 . . . . 19 A4
New Liston Rd EH29 . . . . . . 89 A1
New Market Leisure Village
EH14 . . . . 122 B2
New Market Rd EH14 . . . . . 122 B2
New Mart Rd EH14 . . . . 122 A2
New Meadowspott
EH22 . . . . 174 B4
New Orchardfield EH6 . . . . . 93 C2
New Rd FK7 . . . . 7 B1

New Row
Dunfermline KY12 . . . . 29 A2
East Fortune EH39 . . . . 74 A2
Kincardine FK10 . . . . 24 A2
Tranent EH33 . . . . 128 B3
New Skinners Cl EH1 . . . . . 233 B3
New St Bridge of A FK9 . . . . . 1 C4
Cockenzie & Port Seton
EH32 . . . . 97 B2
Edinburgh EH8 . . . . 233 B3
Musselburgh EH21 . . . . . . 126 A3
Prestonpans EH32 . . . . 96 C1
Slamannan FK1 . . . . 110 A4
Tranent EH33 . . . . 128 B3
New Star Bank EH22 . . . . . 183 A3
New Swanston EH10 . . . . . 153 C3
New Tower Pl EH15 . . . . 95 A1
New Well Wynd EH49 . . . . . 84 C3
Newbattle Abbey Coll
EH22 . . . . 157 A1
Newbattle Abbey Cres
EH22 . . . . 182 C4
Newbattle Gdns EH22 . . . . 157 A1
Newbattle High Sch
EH22 . . . . 183 A4
Newbattle Terr EH10 . . . . . 123 A2
Newbiggin Cres FK10 . . . . . . 4 B1
Newbiggin Rd FK3 . . . . 61 C3
Newbigging
Auchtertool KY2 . . . . 15 B1
Musselburgh EH21 . . . . . . 126 B3
Newbigging Rd KY12 . . . . . . 27 B4
Newbigging Terr KY2 . . . . . . 15 B1
Newbridge Ind Est
EH28 . . . . 118 C3
Newbridge Rdbt EH28 . . . . 119 A3
Newburn Pl KY12 . . . . 29 B2
Newbyres Ave EH23 . . . . . . 183 B1
Newbyres Cres EH23 . . . . . 207 B4
Newbyres Gdns EH23 . . . . 207 B4
Newcarron Ct FK2 . . . . 60 A4
Newcraighall Bsns Pk
EH15 . . . . 125 A2
Newcraighall Dr EH21 . . . . 125 A2
Newcraighall Prim Sch
EH21 . . . . 125 C2
Newcraighall Rd EH15 . . . . 125 A2
Newcraighall Sta EH21 . . . 125 A2
Newhailes Ave EH21 . . . . . 126 A3
Newhailes Cres EH21 . . . . 126 A3
Newhailes Rd EH15 . . . . . . 125 C3
Newhall Rd EH6 . . . . 66 B1
Newhaven Heritage Mus *
EH6 . . . . 93 B4
Newhaven Main St EH6 . . . . 93 B4
Newhaven Pl EH6 . . . . 93 B4
Newhaven Rd EH6 . . . . 93 B3
Newhouse FK8 . . . . 7 A3
Newhouse Ave EH42 . . . . . . 78 B3
Newhouse Bsns Pk FK3 . . . 61 B4
Newhouse Dr FK1 . . . . 59 C1
Newhouse Pl FK3 . . . . 61 B4
Newhouse Terr EH42 . . . . . . 78 B3
Newhouses Rd EH52 . . . . . 118 A2
Newington La FK5 . . . . 37 B3
Newington Rd EH9 . . . . 123 C3
Newland Ave EH48 . . . . 145 A3
Newlands Pk
Dunfermline KY12 . . . . 29 A3
Edinburgh EH9 . . . . 123 C2
Newlands Pl FK10 . . . . 4 B2
Newlands Rd
Bannockburn FK7 . . . . 19 B4
Brightons FK2 . . . . 82 B4
Grangemouth FK3 . . . . 61 B3
Newliston Dr KY2 . . . . 16 B4
Newmains Farm La EH29 . . 89 A1
Newmains Rd EH29 . . . . 89 A1
Newmarket FK7 . . . . 7 C1
Newmarket Ctr FK1 . . . . 60 A3
Newmarket St FK1 . . . . 60 A3
Newmill & Canthill Rd
Shotts ML7 . . . . 167 A1
Shotts ML7 . . . . 191 A3
Newmills FK10 . . . . 4 A2
Newmills Ave EH14 . . . . . . 151 B2
Newmills Cres EH14 . . . . . 151 B2
Newmills Gr EH14 . . . . 151 B2
Newmills Rd Currie EH14 . 151 B2
Dalkeith EH22 . . . . 157 A2
Newmills Terr EH22 . . . . . . 157 A2
Newpark Cres FK7 . . . . 7 A1
Newpark Rd
Livingston EH54 . . . . 173 B3
Stirling FK7 . . . . 7 A1
Newpark Rdbt EH54 . . . . . 173 B4
Newtoft St EH17 . . . . 155 C3
Newton Ch Rd KY12 . . . . 27 C2
Newton Church Rd
EH22 . . . . 156 B4
Newton Cres KY11 . . . . 47 B2
Newton Pl KY11 . . . . 46 C2
Newton Port EH41 . . . . 101 A1
Newton Rd FK2,FK3 . . . . 40 A1
Newton St
Easthouses EH22 . . . . 183 B4
Edinburgh EH11 . . . . 122 C3
Newtongrange Prim Sch
EH22 . . . . 183 A3
Newtonloan St Andrew's
EH23 . . . . 183 A2
Newtonshaw FK10 . . . . 5 B1
Newtown EH51 . . . . 63 C4
Newtown Cotts EH51 . . . . . . 63 C3
Newtown St EH51 . . . . 63 C4

Newyearfield Bsns Pk
EH54 . . . . 147 B3
Newyearfield Rdbt
EH54 . . . . 147 B3
Nichollfield EH6 . . . . 93 B3
Nicholson Pl FK1 . . . . 59 C1
Nicholson Way EH54 . . . . . 147 B4
Nicklaus Gn EH54 . . . . 147 A4
Nicol Dr KY3 . . . . 34 A1
Nicol Pl EH52 . . . . 117 B3
Nicol Rd EH52 . . . . 117 B3
Nicol St KY1 . . . . 17 A2
Nicolson Sq EH8 . . . . 233 B2
Nicolson St EH8 . . . . 233 B2
Nicolton Ave FK2 . . . . 82 C4
Nicolton Ct FK2 . . . . 82 C4
Nicolton Rd FK2 . . . . 62 A1
Niddrie Farm Gr EH16 . . . . 124 C2
Niddrie House Ave 7
EH16 . . . . 124 C2
Niddrie House Dr EH16 . . . 125 A2
Niddrie House Gdns
EH16 . . . . 124 C2
Niddrie House Pk EH16 . . . 124 C2
Niddrie House Sq EH16 . . . 124 C2
Niddrie Mains Ct EH16 . . . 125 A2
Niddrie Mains Dr EH16 . . . 124 C2
Niddrie Mains Rd EH16 . . . 124 C2
Niddrie Mains Terr
EH16 . . . . 124 C2
Niddrie Marischal Cres
EH16 . . . . 125 A2
Niddrie Marischal Dr 5
EH16 . . . . 124 C2
Niddrie Marischal Gdns 3
EH16 . . . . 124 C2
Niddrie Marischal Gn 6
EH16 . . . . 124 C2
Niddrie Marischal Gr
EH16 . . . . 125 A2
Niddrie Marischal Loan 4
EH16 . . . . 124 C2
Niddrie Marischal Pl
EH16 . . . . 124 C2
Niddrie Marischal Rd
EH16 . . . . 125 A2
Niddrie Marischal St 2
EH16 . . . . 125 A2
Niddrie Mill Ave EH15 . . . . 125 A3
Niddrie Mill Cres EH15 . . . 125 A3
Niddrie Mill Dr EH15 . . . . . 125 A3
Niddrie Mill Gr EH15 . . . . . 125 A3
Niddrie Mill Pl EH15 . . . . . 125 A3
Niddrie Mill Prim Sch
EH15 . . . . 125 A2
Niddrie Mill Terr EH15 . . . . 125 A2
Niddry Dr EH52 . . . . 87 C1
Niddry Rd EH6 . . . . 233 A3
Niddry St S EH1 . . . . 233 B2
Niddry View EH52 . . . . 87 C1
Nidrie Cotts EH15 . . . . 125 B2
Nielson Ct EH47 . . . . 171 A4
Nigel Loan EH16 . . . . 155 A4
Nigel Rise EH54 . . . . 147 C1
Nile Gr EH10 . . . . 123 A2
Nile St KY2 . . . . 17 A3
Nimmo Ave EH32 . . . . 97 A1
Ninian Rd EH51 . . . . 62 C3
Ninth St EH22 . . . . 183 A3
Nisbet Dr FK6 . . . . 36 B1
Nisbet Rd EH11 . . . . 51 C1
Nith St KY11 . . . . 29 C1
Nithsdale St ML7 . . . . 191 B3
Niven Rd KY11 . . . . 47 B2
Niven's Knowe Rd EH20 . . 180 C4
Nivensknowe Pk EH20 . . . 180 C4
No 7 Pit Rd KY4 . . . . 13 B2
Nobel Pl EH25 . . . . 180 C2
Nobel View EH42 . . . . 82 A4
Noble Pl EH6 . . . . 94 A2
Norman Rise EH54 . . . . . . 147 C2
Normand Brae EH5 . . . . 18 A4
Normand Rd KY1 . . . . 18 A4
Normandy Pl KY11 . . . . 46 C1
North Approach Rd FK10 . . 23 C2
North Ave FK2 . . . . 83 A4
North Bank Rd EH32 . . . . . 127 C4
North Bank St EH1 . . . . 233 A3
North Berwick High Sch
EH39 . . . . 54 B4
North Berwick Mus *
EH39 . . . . 54 B4
North Berwick Sta EH39 . . . 54 A3
North Bridge EH1 . . . . 233 A3
North Bridge St
Bathgate EH48 . . . . 145 A3
Grangemouth FK3 . . . . 61 B4
North Broomage Rdbt
FK5 . . . . 38 A2
North Bughtlin Bank
EH12 . . . . 91 A1
North Bughtlin Brae
EH12 . . . . 91 A1
North Bughtlin Gate
EH12 . . . . 91 A1
North Bughtlin Neuk
EH12 . . . . 91 A1
North Bughtlin Pl EH12 . . . 91 A1
North Bughtlin Rd EH12 . . 91 A1
North Bughtlinfield EH12 . 91 A1
North Bughtlinrig EH12 . . . 91 A1
North Bughtlinside EH12 . . 91 A1
North Cairntow EH16 . . . . . 124 B3
North Castle St
Alloa FK10 . . . . 10 A3
Edinburgh EH2 . . . . 232 B4
North Charlotte St EH2 . . . 232 B3

North Clyde Street La
EH1 . . . . 233 A4
North Cres EH32 . . . . 97 A1
North East Circus Pl 13
EH3 . . . . 93 A1
North East Cumberland
Street La EH3 . . . . 93 B1
North East Thistle Street La
EH2 . . . . 232 C4
North Elphinstone Farm
Cotts EH33 . . . . 128 A1
North Esk Rd KY11 . . . . 46 B1
North Fort St EH6 . . . . 93 C3
North Gate EH48 . . . . 113 C3
North Grange Ave EH32 . . . 96 C1
North Grange Gr EH32 . . . . 96 C1
North Grange Rd EH32 . . . . 96 C1
North Green Dr FK2 . . . . 22 B2
North Greendykes Rd
EH52 . . . . 117 C4
North Greens EH15 . . . . . . 125 A3
North Gyle Ave EH12 . . . . . 121 A3
North Gyle Dr EH12 . . . . . . 121 A4
North Gyle Farm Ct
EH12 . . . . 121 A3
North Gyle Farm La
EH12 . . . . 121 A3
North Gyle Gr EH12 . . . . . . 121 A3
North Gyle Loan EH12 . . . . 121 A4
North Gyle Pk EH12 . . . . . . 121 A4
North Gyle Rd EH12 . . . . . . 121 A4
North Gyle Terr EH12 . . . . . 121 A3
North High St EH21 . . . . . . 126 A3
North Hillhousefield EH6 . 93 C3
North Junction St EH6 . . . . 93 C3
North Larches KY11 . . . . 29 C2
North Leith Sands EH6 . . . . 93 C3
North Loanhead KY11 . . . . . 45 C2
North Lorimer Pl EH32 . . . . 97 A2
North Main St FK2 . . . . 39 B2
North Meggetland
EH14 . . . . 122 C2
North Overgate KY3 . . . . . . 34 C2
North Park Terr EH4 . . . . . . 93 A1
North Peffer Pl EH16 . . . . . 124 B2
North Prim Sch KY2 . . . . . . 17 A3
North Queensferry Prim Sch
KY11 . . . . 68 B3
North Queensferry Sta
KY11 . . . . 68 B3
North Rd Dunbar EH42 . . . . 78 B2
Fauldhouse EH47 . . . . 193 C4
Inverkeithing KY11 . . . . 47 B3
North Reeves Pl EH47 . . . . 170 A3
North Roundall KY11 . . . . . . 45 C2
North Ronv KY11 . . . . 45 C2
North Seton Pk EH32 . . . . . 97 B2
North Shore Rd FK3 . . . . 40 C1
North St Alloa FK10 . . . . 10 A4
Bo'ness EH51 . . . . 64 A3
Clackmannan FK10 . . . . 11 A2
Dunbar EH42 . . . . 78 A1
Falkirk FK2 . . . . 60 A4
Lochgelly KY5 . . . . 14 A4
Ratho EH28 . . . . 119 B1
Stirling FK9 . . . . 2 B2
North St Andrew La
EH2 . . . . 233 A4
North St Andrew St
EH2 . . . . 233 A4
North St David St EH2 . . . . 233 A4
North View
Burntisland KY3 . . . . 50 C4
West Calder EH55 . . . . 172 B2
North View Cotts KY4 . . . . . 31 A4
North Way KY11 . . . . 68 B3
North Werber Pk EH4 . . . . . 92 C2
North Werber Pl EH4 . . . . . . 92 C2
North West Circus Pl
EH3 . . . . 93 A1
North West Cumberland
Street La EH3 . . . . 93 B1
North West Thistle Street La
EH2 . . . . 232 C4
North Wood Rd KY11 . . . . . . 46 C4
North Wynd EH22 . . . . 157 A2
Northbank Ct EH51 . . . . 64 A3
Northbank Dr EH51 . . . . 64 A3
Northbank Pk EH51 . . . . 63 C3
Northbank Rd KY12 . . . . 27 B1
Northbank Terr EH51 . . . . . 122 C2
Northcote St EH11 . . . . 122 C3
Northend FK7 . . . . 6 B3
Northfield
Cowdenbeath KY4 . . . . 13 B3
Tranent EH33 . . . . 128 C3
Northfield Ave
Edinburgh EH8 . . . . 124 B4
Shotts ML7 . . . . 192 A1
Northfield Broadway
EH8 . . . . 124 C4
Northfield Cir EH8 . . . . 124 C4
Northfield Cotts EH55 . . . . 172 B2
Northfield Cres
Edinburgh EH8 . . . . 124 C4
Longridge EH47 . . . . 170 B1
Northfield Dr EH8 . . . . 124 C4
Northfield E EH33 . . . . 128 C3
Northfield Farm Ave
EH8 . . . . 124 C4
Northfield Farm Rd
EH8 . . . . 124 C4
Northfield Gdns
Clackmannan FK10 . . . . 11 A2
Edinburgh EH8 . . . . 124 C4
Prestonpans EH32 . . . . . . 127 C4
Northfield Gr EH8 . . . . 124 C4

Northfield Mdws EH47 . . . 170 B1
Northfield Park Gr EH8 . . . 124 C4
Northfield Pk EH8 . . . . 124 C4
Northfield Rd Denny FK6 . . 36 B2
Edinburgh EH8 . . . . 124 B4
Northfield Sq EH8 . . . . 124 C4
Northfield Terr
Edinburgh EH8 . . . . 124 B4
Longridge EH47 . . . . 170 B1
Northflat Pl ML8 . . . . 230 B1
Northlawn Ct EH4 . . . . 91 C2
Northlawn Terr EH4 . . . . 91 C2
Northrig Cotts EH41 . . . . . 133 A4
Northumberland Place La
EH3 . . . . 232 C4
Northumberland St
EH3 . . . . 232 C4
Northumberland Street North
East La EH3 . . . . 93 B1
Northumberland Street North
West La EH3 . . . . 232 C4
Northumberland Street South
East La EH3 . . . . 232 C4
Northwood Pk EH54 . . . . . . 146 C4
Norton Pk EH7 . . . . 94 A1
Norton Pl KY11 . . . . 29 C1
Norton St FK12 . . . . 5 A4
Norval Pl KY11 . . . . 46 C2
Norwood Ave Alloa FK10 . . . 9 C4
Bonnybridge FK4 . . . . 58 A4
Whitburn EH47 . . . . 170 A3
Norwood Cres FK10 . . . . 9 C4
Norwood Ct
Bonnybridge FK4 . . . . 58 A4
Whitburn EH47 . . . . 170 A3
Norwood Gr FK10 . . . . 9 C4
Norwood Pl FK4 . . . . 58 A4
Nosirrom Terr EH49 . . . . 65 C3
Novar Cres KY11 . . . . 17 A1
Nungate Rd EH39 . . . . 54 A4
Nunraw Abbey * EH41 . . . 134 C1
Nursery Rd FK1 . . . . 59 C2

O

O'Hanlon Way FK8 . . . . 1 C1
Oak Ave EH20 . . . . 180 C4
Oak Bank FK2 . . . . 61 A1
Oak Cres Mayfield EH22 . . 183 C3
Plean FK7 . . . . 20 B2
Oak Dr Fallin FK7 . . . . 8 B2
Stenhousemuir FK5 . . . . 38 B1
Oak Gr Dumfermline KY11 . 46 C4
Livingston EH54 . . . . 148 A2
Oak La EH12 . . . . 91 C1
Oak Pl EH22 . . . . 183 C3
Oak St FK8 . . . . 1 C1
Oakbank Ave EH53 . . . . 148 C1
Oakbank Cotts EH55 . . . . . 172 B3
Oakbank Park Dr EH53 . . . 174 B4
Oakbank Park Way
EH54 . . . . 174 B4
Oakbank Pk EH54 . . . . 174 A4
Oakbank Pl EH52 . . . . 88 B1
Oakbank Rdbt EH53 . . . . . 148 C1
Oakfield Pl EH8 . . . . 233 B2
Oakfield St KY4 . . . . 12 C4
Oakfield Terr FK2 . . . . 83 A3
Oaklands Spec1 Sch
EH11 . . . . 121 C2
Oakley Ind Est KY12 . . . . . . 26 C4
Oaktree Ct KY1 . . . . 17 B4
Oaktree Junc EH41 . . . . . . 131 A4
Oaktree Sq KY1 . . . . 17 B4
Oakville Terr EH6 . . . . 94 A2
Oatlands Pk EH49 . . . . 85 A3
Oatridge Ag Coll EH52 . . . 116 C4
Oberon FK10 . . . . 9 C4
Observatory Gn EH9 . . . . . 123 C1
Observatory Rd EH9 . . . . . 123 C1
Ocean Dr EH6 . . . . 93 C4
Ocean Terminal Sh Ctr
EH6 . . . . 93 C4
Ochil Ave KY2 . . . . 16 C3
Ochil Cres FK8 . . . . 2 A4
Ochil Ct Queensferry EH30 . 89 B4
Tullibody FK10 . . . . 4 B2
Ochil Dr Maddiston FK2 . . . 83 A3
Shieldhill FK1 . . . . 108 A4
Ochil La EH47 . . . . 169 C3
Ochil Rd Alva FK12 . . . . 5 A4
Menstrie FK11 . . . . 4 A4
Stirling FK9 . . . . 2 B2
Ochil St Alloa FK10 . . . . 10 A4
Fallin FK7 . . . . 8 B2
Grangemouth FK3 . . . . 61 B4
Tullibody FK10 . . . . 4 B2
Ochil Terr
Cowdenbeath KY11 . . . . . . 29 C1
Falkirk FK2 . . . . 39 A1
Ochil View
Cowdenbeath KY4 . . . . 13 C3
Denny FK6 . . . . 57 B4
Kincardine FK10 . . . . 23 B2
Shieldhill FK1 . . . . 81 B4
Ochil View Ct FK5 . . . . 38 B3
Ochilmount FK7 . . . . 7 C4
Ochiltree Cres EH53 . . . . . 148 A1
Ochiltree Ct EH53 . . . . 148 A1
Ochiltree Dr EH53 . . . . 148 A1

Ochiltree Gdns EH16 ....124 B1
Ochiltree Terr FK1 ....59 A3
Ochilvale Terr FK10 ....5 B2
Ochilview Alva FK12 ....5 A4
Cowie FK7 ....20 C3
Ochilview Dr KY12 ....26 A1
Ochilview Pk (Stenhousemuir
FC) FK5 ....63 C3
Ochilview PI EH51 ....63 C3
Ochilview Rd EH51 ....63 C3
Ochilview Sq EH48 ....143 C3
Ochilview Terr EH51 ....63 C3
Ochre Cres FK7 ....20 B4
Octavia St KY2 ....17 A3
Ogilface Cres EH48 ....142 B1
Ogilvie PI KY3 ....2 A3
Ogilvie Rd FK8 ....7 A3
Ogilvie Terr EH11 ....122 C2
Ogilvie Way EH54 ....147 B4
Ogilvy Cres EH47 ....193 C3
Old Abbey Rd EH39 ....54 A4
Old Bellsdyke Rd FK5 ....38 A2
Old Bridge St B FK10 ....10 A3
Old Bridge Wynd FK9 ....2 A2
Old Broughton ◀ EH3 ....93 B1
Old Burdiehouse Rd
EH17 ....155 A2
Old Church La EH15 ....124 B3
Old Craighall Junc
EH21 ....126 A1
Old Craighall Rd EH21 ...156 C4
Old Dalkeith Rd EH22 .....156 B3
Old Dean Rd EH32 ....98 B2
Old Denny Rd FK5 ....38 A2
Old Drove Rd
Cambusbarron FK7 ....6 B3
West Linton EH46 ....219 A2
Old Eastfield St ML7 ....168 B3
Old Edinburgh Rd EH22 ..156 C2
Old Farm Ave EH13 ....153 B4
Old Farm Ct EH34 ....160 C3
Old Farm PI EH13 ....153 A4
Old Fishmarket Cl EH1 ...233 A3
Old Forge Gr KY12 ....26 C4
Old Glendevon Farm Cotts
EH52 ....87 B1
Old Golf Course Rd
EH48 ....144 A2
Old Hillview Rd KY4 ....30 C3
Old Kirk PI KY12 ....29 B2
Old Kirk Rd
Dunfermline KY12 ....29 B2
Edinburgh EH12 ....121 C4
North Queensferry KY11 ...68 A3
Old Linhurn Rd KY11 ....29 C2
Old Liston Rd EH28 ....119 A3
Old Mill Ct EH47 ....170 C4
Old Mill Ctyd The KY11 .....29 A1
Old Mill Ct EH47 ....170 C4
Old Mill La
Edinburgh EH16 ....124 A1
Gifford EH41 ....163 C3
Oakley KY12 ....26 C3
Old Mill Rd
Broxburn EH52 ....117 C3
Hartwood ML7 ....191 A1
Old Newmills Rd EH14 ....151 B2
Old Orch The KY11 ....45 B2
Old Perth Rd KY4 ....13 A2
Old Redding Rd FK2 ....60 C2
Old Refinery Rd FK3 ....62 A4
Old School Ct FK10 ....4 A1
Old Star Rd EH22 ....183 A3
Old Tolbooth Wynd EH8 ..233 B3
Old Town Bannockburn FK7 ..7 B1
Broxburn EH52 ....117 C3
Oldwalls PI FK3 ....61 C4
Oldwalls Rd FK3,EH51 .....62 B4
Oldwood PI EH54 ....147 A2
Oliphant Ct FK8 ....2 A4
Oliphant Gdns EH21 ......127 A3
Olive Bank Rd EH21 ......126 A3
Oliver Rd FK1 ....60 B2
Olivarton Ct KY1 ....17 A3
Olympia Arc KY1 ....7 B2
Onich PI ML7 ....192 A2
Onslow St EH54 ....148 A3
Orchard Bank EH4 ....92 C1
Orchard Brae EH4 ....92 C1
Orchard Brae Ave EH4 .....92 C1
Orchard Brae Gdns EH4 ...92 C1
EH4 ....92 C1
Orchard Brae Gdns W
EH4 ....92 C1
Orchard Brae W ◀ EH4 ...92 C1
Orchard Cres
Edinburgh EH4 ....92 B1
Prestonpans EH32 ....96 C1
Orchard Ct
East Linton EH40 ....103 C3
Kinghorn KY3 ....35 A2
Longniddry EH32 ....98 B2
Orchard Dr FK4 ....92 B1
Orchard Gdns KY3 ....35 A2
Orchard Gr Edinburgh EH4 ..92 C2
Kincardine FK10 ....101 A1
Polmont FK2 ....62 A1
Orchard House Hospl FK8 ..2 A1
Orchard La
Dunfermline KY11 ....29 B1
Dysart KY1 ....18 A4
Orchard Pk EH33 ....128 B4
Orchard PI Dysart KY1 .....18 A4
Edinburgh EH4 ....92 C1
Livingston EH54 ....147 A3

Orchard Rd Bridge of A FK9 ..2 A3
Edinburgh EH4 ....92 C1
Grangemouth FK3 ....62 B4
Kinghorn KY3 ....34 C2
Orchard Rd S EH4 ....92 B1
Orchard Sq KY11 ....45 B2
Orchard St Falkirk FK1 .....60 A3
Grangemouth FK3 ....61 B4
Orchard Terr
Clackmannan FK10 ....11 B1
Edinburgh EH4 ....92 C1
Kinghorn KY3 ....34 C2
Torryburn KY12 ....26 C1
Orchard The
Brightons FK2 ....82 B4
Crossford KY12 ....28 A1
Musselburgh EH21 ....126 A3
Ormiston EH35 ....159 C4
Tranent EH33 ....128 B4
Tullibody FK10 ....4 A1
Orchard Toll EH4 ....92 C1
Orchard View EH22 ....156 C1
Orchardcroft FK8 ....7 A4
Orchardfield EH40 ....103 B4
Orchardfield Ave EH12 ...121 B3
Orchardfield Terr ??? .150 A3
Orchardhead Loan
EH16 ....155 A4
Orchardhead Rd EH16 ....155 A4
Ordnance Rd KY12 ....44 B3
Oriel Cres KY7 ....17 A2
Oriel Rd KY2 ....16 C3
Orkney Ct FK10 ....10 A3
Orkney PI Falkirk FK1 ......60 A1
Kirkcaldy KY1 ....17 C4
Orlit Cotts EH49 ....85 B2
Ormelie Terr EH15 ....125 B4
Ormidale Terr EH12 ....122 B4
Ormiston Ave EH33 ....128 C3
Ormiston Cres E EH33 ...128 C3
Ormiston Cres W EH33 ..128 C3
Ormiston Cross* EH33 ...159 C4
Ormiston Dr Alloa FK10 ....4 C1
East Calder EH53 ....149 A2
Ormiston Farm Steadings
EH27 ....149 B1
Ormiston Pk KY12 ....29 B3
Ormiston Prim Sch
EH35 ....159 C4
Ormiston Rd
Pathhead EH37 ....185 A3
Tranent EH33 ....128 B3
Ormond Ct FK5 ....38 A2
Oronsay Ave FK2 ....82 C3
Orr Terr ML7 ....168 B2
Orrin Gr KY11 ....48 A2
Orrock Dr KY3 ....33 C1
Orrok Pk EH16 ....124 A1
Orwell PI
Dunfermline KY12 ....29 B2
Edinburgh EH11 ....122 C3
Orwell Prim Sch EH11 ...122 C3
Orwell Terr EH11 ....122 C3
Osborne Ct EH32 ....97 B2
Osborne Dr FK10 ....23 C2
Osborne Gdns FK1 ....59 C2
Osborne St FK1 ....59 C2
Osborne Terr
Cockenzie & Port Seton
EH32 ....97 B2
Edinburgh EH12 ....122 C3
Ossian Dr EH54 ....173 C3
Oswald Ave FK3 ....61 C4
Oswald Ct EH9 ....123 B2
Oswald Rd EH9 ....123 B2
Oswald Terr EH12 ....121 B3
Oswalds Wynd KY1 ....17 B2
Otterburn Pk EH14 ....153 A4
Otterston Gr KY11 ....48 A2
Otterston PI KY2 ....16 C4
Oudenarde Ct ML8 ....13 A4 ???
Our Lady of Lourdes RC Prim
Sch EH47 ....170 A3
Our Lady's RC Prim Sch
EH47 ....171 A1
Overhaven KY11 ....83 C4
Overton Cres Denny FK6 ..36 B1
East Calder EH53 ....149 A2
Redding FK2 ....61 A1
Overton Ct Kirkcaldy KY1 ..17 C4
Rosyth KY11 ....46 C4
Overton Mains KY1 ....17 C4
Overton Rd
Grangemouth, Bowhouse
FK3 ....62 A4
Grangemouth, Oil Refinery
FK3 ....62 B4
Kirkcaldy KY1 ....17 B4
Overton Terr FK6 ....36 B1
Owen sq EH54 ....147 C1
Oxcars Dr KY11 ....48 A2
Oxcraig St EH5 ....93 A3
Oxenfoord Ave EH37 ......185 A3
Oxenfoord Dr EH37 ....185 A3
Oxford St EH8 ....233 C1
Oxford Terr EH4 ....232 A4
Oxgang Rd FK5 ....38 A2
Oxgangs Ave EH13 ....153 C4
Oxgangs Bank EH13 ......153 C3
Oxgangs Brae EH13 ....153 C3
Oxgangs Broadway
EH13 ....153 C3
Oxgangs Cres EH13 ......153 C3
Oxgangs Dr EH13 ....153 C4
Oxgangs Farm Ave
EH13 ....153 C3

Oxgangs Farm Dr EH13 ..153 C3
Oxgangs Farm Gdns
EH13 ....153 C3
Oxgangs Farm Gr EH13 ..153 C3
Oxgangs Farm Loan
EH13 ....153 C3
Oxgangs Farm Terr
EH13 ....153 C3
Oxgangs Gdns EH13 ......153 C4
Oxgangs Gn EH13 ....153 C3
Oxgangs Gr EH13 ....153 C4
Oxgangs Hill EH13 ....153 C4
Oxgangs Ho EH13 ....153 C3
Oxgangs Loan EH13 ......153 C4
Oxgangs Medway EH13 ..153 C3
Oxgangs Path EH13 ......153 C3
Oxgangs Path E EH13 ....153 C3
Oxgangs Pk EH13 ....153 C3
Oxgangs Prim Sch
EH13 ....153 B4
Oxgangs Rd EH10 ....154 A3
Oxgangs Rd N EH13 ......153 C3
Oxgangs Rise EH13 ......153 C3
Oxgangs Row EH13 ....153 C3
Oxgangs St EH13 ....153 C3
Oxgangs Terr EH13 ....153 C3
Oxgangs View EH13 ......153 C3

P

Paddock The
Dirleton EH39 ....53 A3
Gullane EH31 ....52 A1
Musselburgh EH21 ....126 A4
North Berwick EH39 ....54 B3
Paddockhall Cotts EH49 ..65 B1
Paddockholm The EH12 ..121 C3
Page St KY5 ....14 A4
Paisley Ave EH8 ....124 B4
Paisley Cres EH8 ....124 B4
Paisley Dr EH8 ....124 B4
Paisley Gdns EH8 ....124 B4
Paisley Gr EH8 ....124 B4
Paisley Terr EH8 ....124 B4
Palmer Ct FK3 ....61 B4
Palmer PI Currie EH14 ...151 C2
Kingseat KY12 ....12 A1
Palmer Rd EH14 ....151 C2
Palmer Rise EH14 ....147 C1
Palmerston PI EH12 ......232 A3
Palmerston Place La
EH12 ....232 A2
Palmerston Rd EH9 ....123 B3
Pan Ha' KY1 ....18 A3
Panbrae Rd EH51 ....63 A4
Pankhurst Loan EH22 ....157 B2
Panmure PI EH3 ....232 C1
Pannie Rd KY11 ....17 B4
Panstead St FK3 ....61 C4
Panton Gn EH54 ....147 A4
Papana Cotts EH41 ....134 B1
Papple Farm Cotts
EH41 ....134 B3
Paradise La FK10 ....23 C2
Paradykes Prim Sch
EH20 ....181 A4
Pardovan Cres EH49 ....86 B4
Pardovan Holdings EH49 ..86 B4
Pardovan PI FK1 ....59 C3
Paris Ave FK6 ....36 C1
Paris St FK3 ....62 A4
Park Ave Bilston EH25 ....180 C3
Brightons FK2 ....82 B4
Cowdenbeath KY4 ....13 B2
Denny FK4 ....57 C3
Dunbar EH42 ....78 B2
Dunfermline KY12 ....29 A2
East Calder EH53 ....148 C2
Edinburgh EH15 ....125 A4
Gorebridge EH23 ....183 B1
Laurieston FK2 ....60 C2
Loanhead EH20 ....181 A4
Musselburgh EH21 ....126 C3
Stenhousemuir FK5 ....38 B1
Stirling FK8 ....7 B1
Park Cres Alloa FK10 ....7 A3
Bannockburn FK7 ....7 B1
Bonnyrigg & Lasswade
EH19 ....182 A4
Easthouses EH22 ....183 B4
Edinburgh EH16 ....155 A4
Gifford EH41 ....163 C3
Loanhead EH20 ....181 A4
Westquarter FK2 ....61 A2
Musselburgh EH21 ....126 C3
Shotts ML7 ....191 B2
Park Dr Bannockburn FK7 ..7 B1
Brightons FK2 ....82 B4
Cowdenbeath KY4 ....13 B2
West Calder EH55 ....173 A3
Park Gdns Bannockburn FK7 ..7 B1
Edinburgh EH16 ....155 A4
Musselburgh EH21 ....126 C3
Park Gr Broxburn EH52 ..117 C3
Edinburgh EH16 ....155 A4
Park Grove PI EH21 ....126 C3
Park Grove Terr EH21 ....126 C3
Park Hill EH23 ....183 A1
Park La Aberdour KY3 ....49 B4
Bo'ness EH51 ....64 A3
Edinburgh EH15 ....125 A4
Haddington EH41 ....131 C4
Musselburgh EH21 ....126 C3

Park La continued
Stirling FK8 ....7 A4
Park Lea KY11 ....47 A3
Park Par EH47 ....193 C3
Park PI Alloa FK10 ....10 B4
Clackmannan FK10 ....11 A2
Cowdenbeath KY4 ....30 C4
Dunfermline KY12 ....29 A2
Edinburgh EH6 ....93 B3
Kinghorn KY3 ....34 C1
Kirkcaldy KY1 ....17 A2
Livingston EH54 ....147 A3
Stirling FK7 ....6 C3
Park Prim Sch KY10 ....10 A3
Park Rd Blackridge EH48 ..142 C2
Bonnyrigg & Lasswade
EH19 ....182 A4
Broxburn EH52 ....117 C3
Cockenzie & Port Seton
EH32 ....97 B2
Dalkeith KY4 ....156 C1
Edinburgh EH6 ....93 B3
Falkirk FK2 ....39 A1
Gifford EH41 ....163 C2
Gorebridge EH23 ....183 B1
Grangemouth FK3 ....64 A4
Harthill ML7 ....169 A3
Kirkcaldy KY1 ....17 C4
Menstrie FK11 ....4 A3
Newtongrange EH22 .....183 A3
Ormiston EH35 ....159 B3
Rosyth KY11 ....46 C3
Shotts ML7 ....191 B3
Park Rd W KY11 ....46 B3
Park Road Prim Sch
KY11 ....47 A2
Park St Alloa FK10 ....5 A4
Cowdenbeath KY4 ....13 B2
Cowie FK7 ....20 C4
Falkirk FK1 ....60 A3
High Bonnybridge FK4 ...108 A3
Lochgelly KY5 ....14 A4
Park Terr Brightons FK2 ....82 B4
Broxburn EH52 ....117 A3
Kirknewton EH27 ....149 C1
Newcraighall EH21 ....125 C2
Stirling FK8 ....4 A1
Tullibody FK10 ....4 A1
Park View Brightons FK2 ..82 C4
Broxburn EH52 ....117 A3
Fauldhouse EH47 ....193 C4
Kirkcaldy KY2 ....16 C2
Loanhead EH20 ....181 A4
Musselburgh EH21 ....126 C3
Newcraighall EH21 ....125 C2
Pencaitland EH34 ....160 C4
Prestonpans EH32 ....96 C1
Stoneyburn EH47 ....171 B1
Westfield EH48 ....112 C2
Whitburn EH47 ....170 A4
Park View E EH4 ....59 C3
Park View E EH32 ....97 B2
Park-View EH32 ....98 C3
Parkandarroch Cres
ML8 ....230 A1
Parkend Cres FK1 ....81 B3
Parker Ave EH7 ....94 C1
Parker Rd EH7 ....94 C1
Parker Terr EH7 ....94 C1
Parkfoot Ct FK1 ....60 A1
Parkgate KY4 Alva FK12 .....4 C3
Rosyth KY11 ....46 C2
Parkgrove Ave EH4 ....91 B1
Parkgrove Bank EH4 ....91 B1
Parkgrove Cres EH4 ....91 B1
Parkgrove Dr EH4 ....91 B1
Parkgrove Gn EH4 ....91 B1
Parkgrove Loan EH4 ....91 B1
Parkgrove Neuk EH4 ....91 B1
Parkgrove Path EH4 ....91 B1
Parkgrove PI EH4 ....91 B1
Parkgrove Rd EH4 ....91 B1
Parkgrove Row EH4 ....91 B1
Parkgrove St EH4 ....91 B1
Parkgrove Terr EH4 ....91 B1
Parkgrove View EH4 ....91 B1
Parkhall Dr FK2 ....83 A3
Parkhead Ave EH11 ......121 C1
Parkhead Cotts EH55 ....172 C1
Parkhead Cres
Edinburgh EH11 ....121 C1
West Calder EH55 ....172 C2
Parkhead Ct EH11 ....121 C1
Parkhead Gdns
Edinburgh EH11 ....121 C1
West Calder EH55 ....172 C1
Parkhead Gr EH11 ....121 C1
Parkhead Loan EH11 .....121 C1
Parkhead PI
Easthouses EH22 ....183 B4
Edinburgh EH11 ....121 C1
Parkhead Rd Alloa FK10 ...10 B4
Linlithgow EH49 ....84 C4
Parkhead Smallholdings
EH49 ....64 A1
Parkhead St EH11 ....121 C1
Parkhead Terr EH11 ....121 C1
Parkhead View EH11 .....121 C1

Parkland Gr Comrie KY12 ..26 B4
Stoneyburn EH47 ....170 C1
Parklands EH52 ....117 B2
Parklands Cres KY11 ....48 A2
Parknuk Rd KY12 ....28 B3
Parkside EH28 ....119 A3
Parkside St
Dalkeith EH22 ....157 A2
Plean FK7 ....20 B2
Parkside PI EH22 ....157 A2
Parkside Rd ML7 ....191 B2
Parkside St KY2 ....47 A2
Parkside St
Edinburgh EH8 ....233 C1
Rosyth KY11 ....46 C2
Parkside Terr EH16 ....233 C1
Parkvale PI EH6 ....94 A2
Parkview Ave FK1 ....59 C1
Parkway FK10 ....10 A4
Parkwood Cres EH52 ......117 B3
Parkwood Gdns EH52 ....117 B3
Parliament Sq EH1 ....233 A3
Parliament St EH6 ....93 C3
Parrot La EH23 ....207 B4
Parrotshot EH15 ....125 A3
Parsonage The EH21 .....126 B3
Parsons Green Prim Sch
EH8 ....124 B4
Parsons Green Terr ◀
EH8 ....94 B1
Parsonspool
Bonnyrigg & Lasswade
EH19 ....182 B3
Dunbar EH42 ....78 B1
Paterson Dr FK1 ....81 B3
Paterson PI
Bonnybridge FK4 ....58 B3
Bridge of A FK9 ....2 A3
Paterson Way KY11 ....29 A1
Paterson's Ct EH52 ....117 C3
Path Brae EH29 ....89 A1
Path The Bannockburn FK7 ..7 B1
Kirkcaldy KY1 ....17 B2
Pathead Prim Sch KY11 ...17 B4
Pathfoot Ave FK9 ....2 B4
Pathfoot Dr FK9 ....2 B4
Pathfoot Rd FK9 ....2 B4
Pathhead Ct ◀ KY1 ....17 B3
Pathhead Prim Sch
EH37 ....185 A2
Patie's Rd EH14 ....153 B4
Paton St Alloa FK10 ....10 A4
Dunfermline KY12 ....29 B3
Patrick Dr FK1 ....81 C4
Patriothall ◀ EH3 ....93 A1
Patterson La KY4 ....13 B2
Patterson PI KY2 ....17 A3
Patterson St KY12 ....47 A3
Pattison St EH6 ....94 A3
Pattle Ct EH39 ....54 A4
Paul Dr FK2 ....22 C2
Paul PI KY4 ....13 B2
Paul St KY5 ....14 A3
Pavilion View FK10 ....9 C4
Pavilions The FK10 ....9 C4
Paxstone Cres ML7 ....168 C3
Paxstone Dr ML7 ....168 C3
Paxton Cres KY5 ....14 A4
Paxton PI KY5 ....14 A4
Peachdales EH14 ....131 C4
Peacock Ct EH19 ....182 C4
Peacock Ct EH6 ....93 B4
Peacock Parkway EH19 ..182 C3
Peacock PI EH19 ....182 B3
Peacocktail Cl EH15 ......125 A2
Pearce Ave EH12 ....121 B4
Pearce Gr EH12 ....121 B4
Pearce Rd EH12 ....121 B4
Pearson Ave FK4 ....57 B3
Pearson PI FK4 ....57 B3
Peathill Rd FK4 ....58 A3
Peatville Gdns EH14 ......122 A1
Peatville Terr EH14 ....122 A1
Peddie PI FK3 ....61 C4
Peden St ML7 ....168 B3
Peebles Rd EH26 ....203 C2
Peebles St KY1 ....35 A4
Peel Pentland Ctr EH20 ..155 A1
Peel Terr EH9 ....123 C2
Peel Rd EH54 ....147 B2
Peel Terr EH9 ....123 C2
Peffer Bank EH16 ....124 B2
Peffer Ind Est EH16 ......124 B2
Peffer PI EH16 ....124 B2
Peffer St EH16 ....124 B2
Peffer's PI EH41 ....132 A4
Peffermill Ind Est EH16 ..124 B2
Peffermill Prim Sch
EH16 ....124 B2
Peffermill Rd EH16 ....124 B2
Peggy's Mill Rd EH4 ....91 A2
Peirson Rd KY12 ....29 C2
Pelstream Ave FK7 ....7 A2
Pembroke PI FK12 ....4 C2
Pembroke St FK5 ....38 B2
Pencaitland Prim Sch
EH34 ....160 C3
Pencraig Brae EH40,
Pender Gdns FK2 ....83 A3
Penders La FK1 ....60 A3
Pendreich Ave EH19 ......182 B4
Pendreich Dr EH19 ....182 B4
Pendreich Gr EH19 ....182 B4
Pendreich Terr EH19 ......182 B4
Pendreich View EH19 .....182 B4
Pendreich Way FK9 ....2 B3

Pen – Que 257

Penicuik High Sch EH26 ..203 C3
Penicuik Rd EH25,EH26 ..180 C2
Pennelton Pl EH51 ..63 C3
Pennyschool Pl FK10 ..11 A2
Pennywell Ct EH4 ..92 A3
Pennywell Gdns EH4 ..92 A3
Pennywell Gr EH4 ..92 A3
Pennywell Medway EH4 ..92 A3
Pennywell Pl EH4 ..92 A3
Pennywell Rd EH4 ..92 A3
Pennywell Villas EH4 ..92 A3
Pentland
  Bathgate EH48 ..145 C3
  Currie EH14 ..151 C2
  Edinburgh EH13 ..153 A4
  Newton Grange EH23 ..183 A2
  Penicuik EH26 ..203 C3
Pentland Cres
  Edinburgh EH10 ..154 A4
  Rosewell EH24 ..181 B2
Pentland Ct Bilston EH25 ..180 C3
  Dalgety Bay KY11 ..48 B2
Pentland Dr
  Edinburgh EH10 ..153 C3
  Whitburn EH47 ..170 B3
Pentland Gait Off Pk
  EH11 ..121 A1
Pentland Gr EH10 ..154 A4
Pentland Hills Regional Pk
  EH14, FH26 ..201 B4
Pentland Ind Est EH20 ..181 A4
Pentland Pk
  Livingston EH54 ..148 A2
  Loanhead EH20 ..180 C4
Pentland Pl Currie EH14 ..151 C2
  Kirkcaldy KY2 ..16 C3
Pentland Rd
  Bonnyrigg & Lasswade
  EH19 ..182 A4
  Edinburgh EH13 ..153 A4
  Edinburgh, Old Pentland
  EH10 ..154 B1
Pentland Rise KY11 ..48 B3
Pentland Terr
  Dunfermline KY11 ..29 C1
  Edinburgh EH10 ..154 A4
  High Valleyfield KY12 ..26 A1
  Penicuik EH26 ..203 C3
Pentland View
  Currie EH14 ..151 C2
  Dalkeith EH22 ..157 B1
  Edinburgh EH10 ..154 A3
  Uphall EH52 ..117 A3
Pentland View Cres
  EH25 ..180 C2
Pentland View Ct
  Currie EH14 ..152 A2
  Livingston EH54 ..147 A3
Pentland View Pl EH25 ..180 C2
Pentland View Rd
  Kirkliston EH29 ..89 A1
  Penicuik EH26 ..180 C2
Pentland View Terr
  EH25 ..180 C2
Pentland Way FK3 ..61 C3
Pentland Wlk EH47 ..170 B3
Pentlandfield Bsns Pk
  EH25 ..180 B3
Pentlands Gdns EH10 ..154 A4
Pentlands Science Pk
  EH26 ..180 B2
Peoples Story Mus The *
  EH8 ..233 B3
Peppercraig Quarry Site
  EH41 ..100 C1
Percival St KY2 ..17 A3
Perdrixmove EH14 ..122 B1
Perth Rd KY4 ..13 B3
Perth St EH3 ..93 A1
Petershall Wildlife Reserve *
  EH48 ..145 B4
Petershill Gdns EH48 ..145 B4
Petersweil Brae FK7 ..7 C1
Pettigrew's Cl FK22 ..157 A2
Pettycur Bay KY3 ..34 C1
Pettycur Bay Holiday Pk
  KY3 ..34 B1
Pettycur Ho KY3 ..34 B1
Pettycur Rd KY3 ..34 C1
Peveril Rise EH54 ..173 C4
Peveril Terr EH16 ..155 A4
Phantassie Cotts EH40 ..103 C4
Phantassie Sq EH40 ..103 C4
Philip Ave Bathgate EH48 ..145 C3
  Linlithgow EH49 ..84 C4
Philip Dr FK5 ..38 B1
Philip Pl EH26 ..203 C4
Philip St FK2 ..60 A4
Philpingstone La EH51 ..64 B4
Philpingstone Rd EH51 ..64 B4
Phoenix Ind Est FK7 ..7 B4
Phoenix La KY12 ..28 C2
Picardy Pl EH1 ..233 A4
Pier Pl EH6 ..93 A4
Pier Rd EH51 ..64 B4
Pierhead Bldgs KY11 ..68 B3
Piersfield Gr EH8 ..94 B1
Piersfield Pl EH8 ..94 B1
Piersfield Terr EH8 ..94 B1
Piershill La ⬛ EH8 ..94 B1
Piershill Pl ⬛ EH8 ..94 B1
Piershill Sq E EH8 ..94 B1
Piershill Sq W EH8 ..94 B1
Piershill Specl Sch EH8 ..124 B4
Piershill Terr ⬛ EH8 ..94 B1
Pike Rd FK7 ..7 B2

Pilgrims Hill EH49 ..85 B4
Pilkham Ct KY4 ..13 B2
Pilmuir St KY12 ..29 A3
Pilrig Gdns EH6 ..93 C2
Pilrig House Cl EH6 ..93 C2
Pilrig Ind Est EH6 ..93 C2
Pilrig Park Specl Sch
  EH6 ..93 C2
Pilrig St EH6 ..93 C2
Pilton Ave EH5 ..92 C3
Pilton Cres EH5 ..92 C3
Pilton Dr EH5 ..92 C3
Pilton Dr N EH5 ..92 C3
Pilton Gdns EH5 ..92 C3
Pilton Loan EH5 ..92 C3
Pilton Pl EH5 ..92 C3
Pine Gn EH51 ..63 B2
Pine Gr Alloa FK10 ..10 B3
  Dumfermline KY11 ..46 C4
  Westquarter FK2 ..148 A3
Pine St EH42 ..78 A1
Pine Wlk EH5 ..22 B1
Pineapple The * FK2 ..22 A1
Pinebank EH14 ..147 C3
Pines The EH31 ..52 A2
Pinewood Dr KY11 ..46 C4
Pinewood Pk EH54 ..146 C4
Pinewood Pl EH22 ..183 C3
Pinewood Rd EH22 ..183 C3
Pinewood Sch EH47 ..171 C4
Pinewood View EH22 ..183 C3
Pinkerton Pl KY11 ..46 C3
Pinkhill EH12 ..122 A3
Pinkie Ave EH21 ..126 C3
Pinkie Dr EH21 ..126 C3
Pinkie Hill Cres EH21 ..126 C3
Pinkie Pl EH21 ..126 C3
Pinkie Rd EH21 ..126 C3
Pinkie St Peter's Prim Sch
  EH21 ..126 C3
Pinkie Terr EH21 ..126 C3
Pinkie Wlk EH33 ..128 B3
Pinnel Pl KY11 ..48 B2
Pipe La EH15 ..95 A1
Pipe St EH15 ..95 A1
Piper Cres KY3 ..33 B1
Pirig Cotts EH6 ..93 C2
Pirleyhill Dr FK1 ..81 B3
Pirleyhill Gdns FK1 ..60 A1
Pirnhall Rd FK7 ..19 B4
Pirniefield Bank EH6 ..94 B2
Pirniefield Gdns EH6 ..94 B2
Pirniefield Gr EH6 ..94 B2
Pirniefield Pl EH6 ..94 B2
Pirniefield Terr EH6 ..94 B2
Pirnie St EH6 ..93 C2
Pitbauchlie Bank KY11 ..29 B1
Pitcairn St KY11 ..29 B1
Pitcaple Gdns EH54 ..173 B3
Pitcorthie Dr KY11 ..46 C4
Pitcorthie Prim Sch
  KY11 ..29 C1
Pitcorthie Rd KY11 ..29 B1
Pitdinnie Pl KY12 ..27 B1
Pitdinnie Rd KY12 ..27 B1
Pitfairn Rd FK10 ..5 C2
Pitfirane Pk KY12 ..28 A1
Pitfour Pl KY2 ..16 B4
Pitlochry Pl ◢ EH7 ..94 A1
Pitmedden Rd KY11 ..30 A1
Pitreavie Bsns Pk KY11 ..46 B4
Pitreavie Cres KY11 ..46 B3
Pitreavie Dr KY11 ..46 B3
Pitreavie Ind Est KY11 ..46 B3
Pitreavie Prim Sch KY11 ..46 B4
Pitsligo Rd EH10 ..123 A2
Pitt St EH6 ..93 C3
Pitt Terr FK8 ..7 A3
Pittencrieff Ct EH12 ..126 C3
Pittencrieff House Mus *
  KY12 ..28 C2
Pittencrieff Prim Sch
  KY12 ..28 C2
Pittencrieff St KY12 ..28 C2
Pittville St EH15 ..125 B4
Pittville Street La EH15 ..125 B4
Place Charente EH22 ..157 B1
Plane Gr KY11 ..46 C4
Plane St EH42 ..78 A1
Plantation St KY5 ..14 A4
Player Dr KY12 ..12 A1
Player Gn EH54 ..147 A4
Players Rd FK7 ..7 B4
Plean Country Pk * FK7 ..20 A1
Plean Ind Est FK7 ..20 B1
Pleasance Edinburgh EH8 ..233 B2
  Falkirk FK1 ..60 A2
Pleasance Brae EH28 ..27 C1
Pleasance Ct
  ⬛ Falkirk FK2 ..60 A2
  Halbeath KY12 ..30 A4
Pleasance Gdns FK1 ..60 A2
Pleasance Rd
  Dumfermline KY11 ..29 C3
  Falkirk FK2 ..60 A2
Pleasance Row ML11 ..215 A2
Pleasance Sq ◢ FK1 ..60 A2
Pleasance The FK10 ..32 B2
Pleasures The FK10 ..9 C4
Plewlandcroft EH30 ..68 A1
Plewlands Ave EH10 ..122 C1
Plewlands Gdns EH10 ..122 C1
Plewlands Pl EH30 ..89 A4

Plewlands Terr EH10 ..122 C1
Pleydell Pl ⬛ EH16 ..155 A4
Plough La EH33 ..128 B3
Plover Brae EH54 ..147 B3
Plummer Ct EH22 ..157 A2
Pointgarry Rd EH39 ..54 A4
Polbeth Ave EH55 ..172 C3
Polbeth Cres EH55 ..172 C3
Polbeth Gdns EH55 ..172 C3
Polbeth Ind Est EH55 ..172 C3
Polbeth Pl EH55 ..172 C3
Polbeth Rd EH55 ..172 C3
Polbeth West Calder Ind Est
  EH55 ..172 C2
Poldrate EH41 ..132 A4
Polkemmet Bsns Ctr
  EH47 ..169 C3
Polkemmet Ctry Pk*
  EH47 ..169 A3
Polkemmet Dr ML7 ..169 A3
Polkemmet La ML7 ..169 A3
Polkemmet Prim Sch
  EH47 ..170 A3
Polkemmet Rd
  Harthill ML7 ..168 C3
  Whitburn EH47 ..169 C3
Pollard Glebe EH11 ..122 A2
Pollock Wlk KY12 ..28 A3
Polmaise Ave FK7 ..7 A2
Polmaise Cres FK7 ..3 B3
Polmaise Rd FK7,FK8 ..6 C2
Polmaise Terr FK7 ..3 A3
Polmont House Gdns
  FK2 ..61 C2
Polmont Pl FK2 ..61 C2
Polmont Rd FK2 ..61 A2
Polmont Sta FK2 ..61 C1
Polson Gdns EH33 ..128 A3
Polton Avenue Rd EH19 ..182 A2
Polton Bank EH18 ..181 C1
Polton Bank Terr EH18 ..181 C1
Polton Cotts EH18 ..181 B3
Polton Ct EH19 ..182 A4
Polton Dr EH19 ..182 A4
Polton Gdns EH18 ..182 A4
Polton Pl EH19 ..182 A4
Polton Rd
  Bonnyrigg & Lasswade
  EH18 ..182 A4
  Loanhead EH20, EH18 ..181 B4
Polton Rd W EH18 ..181 C3
Polton St EH19 ..182 A3
Polton Terr EH18 ..182 A4
Polwarth Ave FK2 ..82 B4
Polwarth Cres
  Edinburgh EH11 ..123 A3
  Prestonpans EH32 ..97 A1
Polwarth Gdns EH11 ..122 C3
Polwarth Gr EH11 ..122 C3
Polwarth Pk EH11 ..122 C3
Polwarth Pl EH11 ..122 C3
Polwarth Terr
  Edinburgh EH11 ..122 C2
  Prestonpans EH32 ..97 A1
Polworth Pl KY4 ..13 B2
Pomathorn Bank EH26 ..203 C2
Pomathorn Rd EH26 ..203 C2
Pompee Rd FK10 ..5 A1
Ponton St EH3 ..232 B1
Poolewe Dr FK2 ..61 A2
Poplar Cres KY2 ..17 A4
Poplar Gdns EH22 ..183 A2
Poplar La EH6 ..94 A3
Poplar Pk EH22 ..97 B2
Poplar St Dunbar EH42 ..78 A1
  Grangemouth FK3 ..61 B4
Poplar Terr EH19 ..182 A3
Poplars The FK10 ..9 A4
Port Buchan EH52 ..115 C2
Port Edgar Water Sports Ctr
  EH30 ..67 C1
Port Hamilton EH3 ..232 B2
Port Laing Wynd KY11 ..68 B4
Port St Clackmannan FK10 ..11 A2
  Stirling FK8 ..7 A1
Portal Rd FK3 ..61 B3
Portdownie FK1 ..59 B3
Porteous' Pend EH1 ..232 C2
Porterfield KY12 ..26 C4
Porterfield Rd EH4 ..92 C2
Portgower Pl EH4 ..93 A1
Portland Pl Edinburgh EH6 ..93 C3
  Fauldhouse EH47 ..193 B3
Portland St EH6 ..93 C3
Portobello High Sch
  EH15 ..124 C4
Portobello L Ctr* EH15 ..95 A1
Portobello Rd EH8 ..94 C1
Porterow Cres FK2 ..62 A1
Port Office La KY11 ..68 B3
Posthill KY11 ..6 B1
Potter Pl FK2 ..39 C2
Potterrow EH8 ..233 A2
Potters Path EH33 ..128 B3
Pottery St KY1 ..17 C4
Pottery The
  Edinburgh EH15 ..95 A1
  Prestonpans EH32 ..96 C1
Pottis Rd FK7 ..7 B2
Pottishaw Pl EH48 ..145 B1
Pottishaw Rd EH48 ..144 C1

Povert Rd EH19, EH23 ..182 C1
Powderhall Brae EH7 ..93 B2
Powderhall Rd EH7 ..93 B2
Powdermill Brae EH23 ..207 B3
Powdrake Rd FK3 ..61 C4
Pratt St KY1 ..17 A1
President Kennedy Dr
  FK7 ..20 B2
Preston Ave
  Linlithgow EH49 ..84 C3
  Prestonpans EH32 ..97 A1
Preston Cres
  Inverkeithing KY11 ..47 B1
  Linlithgow EH49 ..84 C3
  Prestonpans EH32 ..97 A1
Preston Cross Cotts
  EH32 ..97 A1
Preston Ct
  Linlithgow EH49 ..84 C3
  Prestonpans EH32 ..127 C3
Preston Grange Ind Mus
  EH32 ..127 B2
Preston Lodge High Sch
  EH32 ..97 A1
Preston Market Cross*
  EH32 ..97 A1
Preston Mill * EH40 ..103 C4
Preston Pk EH49 ..84 C3
Preston Pl EH37 ..185 A2
Preston Rd
  East Linton EH40 ..103 C4
  Linlithgow EH49 ..84 C3
  Prestonpans EH32 ..97 A1
Preston St
  High Valleyfield KY12 ..26 A1
  Rosewell EH24 ..181 B1
Preston Street Prim Sch
  EH8 ..233 C1
Preston Terr
  Inverkeithing KY11 ..47 B1
  Linlithgow EH49 ..84 C3
  Prestonpans EH32 ..97 A1
Preston Twr
  Prestonpans EH32 ..97 A1
  * Prestonpans EH32 ..97 A1
Prestonfield Ave EH16 ..124 A2
Prestonfield Bank EH16 ..124 A2
Prestonfield Cres EH16 ..124 A2
Prestonfield Gdns EH16 ..124 A2
Prestonfield Pk EH16 ..124 B2
Prestonfield Prim Sch
  EH16 ..124 A2
Prestonfield Rd EH16 ..124 A2
Prestonfield Terr EH16 ..124 A2
Prestongrange Rd EH32 ..127 C4
Prestongrange Terr
  EH32 ..96 C1
Prestonhall Cres EH24 ..181 B1
Prestonhall Rd EH24 ..181 B1
Prestonkirk Gdns EH40 ..103 C4
Prestonpans Inf Sch
  EH32 ..96 C1
Prestonpans Prim Sch
  EH32 ..128 A4
Prestonpans Sta EH32 ..128 A4
Pretoria Pl
  Cowdenbeath KY4 ..13 A2
  Polmont FK2 ..61 C1
Pretoria Rd FK5 ..38 A1
Priest Bank EH41 ..134 B1
Priestfield Ave EH16 ..124 A2
Priestfield Cres EH16 ..124 A2
Priestfield Gdns EH16 ..124 A2
Priestfield Gr EH16 ..124 A3
Priestfield Rd EH16 ..124 A3
Priestfield Rd N EH16 ..124 A3
Prime Gilt Box St KY2 ..17 A3
Primmer Pl KY4 ..13 B2
Primrose Ave
  Grangemouth FK3 ..61 A3
  Rosyth KY11 ..46 B3
Primrose Bank Rd EH5 ..93 A3
Primrose Cres EH22 ..157 B1
Primrose Ct
  Broxburn EH52 ..117 C3
  Rosyth KY11 ..46 B3
Primrose Dr EH30 ..90 B2
Primrose Gdns
  Carrington EH23 ..206 B3
  Queensferry EH30 ..89 B4
Primrose La
  Cowdenbeath KY4 ..13 B3
  Kincardine FK10 ..23 C2
  Rosyth KY11 ..46 B3
Primrose Pl Alloa FK10 ..10 A3
  Livingston EH54 ..147 A3
Primrose Rd KY11 ..46 B3
Primrose St Alloa FK10 ..10 A4
  Bonnybridge FK4 ..58 A3
  Edinburgh EH6 ..94 A2
Primrose Terr
  Dalkeith EH22 ..157 B1
  Edinburgh EH11 ..122 C3
Prince Regent St EH6 ..93 C3
Princes St California FK1 ..81 C3
  Edinburgh EH2 ..232 C3
  Falkirk FK1 ..60 A3
  Grangemouth FK3 ..61 C4
  Stirling FK8 ..7 A4
Princess Mall Sh Ctr
  ..233 A3
Princess Margaret Rose
  Hospl (Orthopaedic)
  EH10 ..154 B3
Princess Mary Pl EH41 ..101 A1
Princess Mary Rd EH41 ..101 A1
Princess St FK4 ..58 A3
Priors Grange EH48 ..113 C3

Priorscroft EH48 ..113 C3
Priorwood Dr KY11 ..30 A1
Priory Ct KY12 ..29 A2
Priory Gr EH30 ..89 A4
Priory La KY12 ..29 A2
Priory Rd Linlithgow EH49 ..84 C3
  Whitecross EH49 ..83 C3
Priory Sq FK10 ..23 C2
Priory Wlk EH41 ..132 B4
Priory Wynd EH39 ..54 A4
Promenade
  Edinburgh EH15 ..95 A1
  Limekilns KY11 ..45 B2
  Musselburgh EH21 ..126 A4
Promenade The EH42 ..97 B2
Prora Cotts EH39 ..73 B2
Prospect Bank Cres EH6 ..94 B2
Prospect Bank Gdns EH6 ..94 A2
Prospect Bank Gr EH6 ..94 B2
Prospect Bank Pl EH6 ..94 B2
Prospect Bank Rd EH6 ..94 B2
Prospect Bank Sch EH6 ..94 B2
Prospect Bank Specl Sch
  EH6 ..94 B2
Prospect Bank Terr EH6 ..94 B2
Prospect St
  Cowdenbeath KY4 ..13 A2
  Falkirk FK1 ..59 C3
Prospecthill Rd FK1 ..60 A1
Providence Brae EH51 ..63 C3
Provost Haugh EH14 ..152 B3
Provost Hunter Ave FK12 ..5 B4
Provost Kay Pk KY1 ..17 B3
Provost Milne Gr EH30 ..89 B4
Provost Rd Bo'ness EH51 ..63 B3
  Linlithgow EH49 ..85 A4
Pryde Ave EH19 ..182 A4
Pryde Terr EH19 ..182 A4
Puir Wife's Brae EH48 ..145 B3
Pullar Ave FK9 ..2 A3
Pullar Ct FK9 ..2 A3
Pumpherston Prim Sch
  EH53 ..148 A4
Pumpherston Rd EH54,
  EH53 ..148 B3
Pyothall Ct EH52 ..117 B3
Pyothall Rd EH52 ..117 B3
Pypers Wynd EH32 ..96 C1

Q

Quadrant EH39 ..54 B4
Quadrant La EH39 ..54 B4
Quadrant The EH26 ..203 C3
Quakerfield FK7 ..7 C1
Quality St Dysart KY1 ..18 A4
  Edinburgh EH4 ..91 C2
  North Berwick EH39 ..54 B4
Quality Street Junc EH4 ..91 C2
Quality Street La EH4 ..91 C2
Quarrolhall Cres FK2 ..39 A2
Quarry Brae Brightons FK2 ..82 C4
  Kirkcaldy KY1 ..17 A1
Quarry Cl EH8 ..233 B1
Quarry Cotts EH15 ..125 A2
Quarry Ct KY11 ..13 A2
Quarry Howe EH14 ..151 B1
Quarry Knowe FK7 ..19 C4
Quarry Pl Alloa FK10 ..10 A4
  Shotts ML7 ..191 B3
Quarry Rd
  Cambusbarron FK7 ..6 B3
  Fauldhouse EH47 ..193 C3
  Shotts ML7 ..191 B3
Quarry St ML7 ..191 B3
Quarrybank EH14 ..152 B4
Quarrybank Cl EH14 ..152 B4
Quarrybank Ct EH14 ..152 B4
Quarrybank End EH14 ..152 B4
Quarryfoot Gdns EH19 ..182 A4
Quarryfoot Gn EH19 ..182 A4
Quarryford Farm Cotts
  EH41 ..190 C4
Quarryknowes The EH51 ..63 C3
Quarryside Ct KY12 ..28 B3
Quarryview EH14 ..152 B4
Quayside Gr EH54 ..147 B2
Quayside St EH6 ..93 C3
Quebec Ave EH54 ..147 C2
Queen Anne Dr EH28 ..119 A3
Queen Anne High Sch
  KY12 ..29 A3
Queen Anne Pk EH28 ..119 A3
Queen Anne St KY12 ..29 A2
Queen Charlotte La EH6 ..94 A3
Queen Charlotte St EH6 ..94 A3
Queen Margaret Cl
  EH10 ..154 B3
Queen Margaret Coll
  EH12 ..121 B4
Queen Margaret Coll (Leith
  Campus) EH6 ..94 A2
Queen Margaret Dr EH30 ..89 B4
Queen Margaret Fauld
  KY12 ..
Queen Margaret Gdns
  KY12 ..29 A3
Queen Margaret Pk KY12 ..29 C3
Queen Margaret Rd KY3 ..34 C1
Queen Margaret's Pl
  KY11 ..68 B3
Queen St Alloa FK10 ..10 A4

Queen St continued
Alva FK12 .....5 A4
Bannockburn FK7 .....7 B1
Edinburgh EH2 .....232 C4
Falkirk FK2 .....60 B3
Fallin FK7 .....9 A2
Grangemouth FK3 .....61 C4
Inverkeithing KY11 .....47 A1
Stirling FK8 .....7 A4
Queen Street Gdns E
EH3 .....232 C4
Queen Street Gdns W
EH3 .....232 C4
Queen's Ave Bridge of A FK9 .....2 A3
Edinburgh EH4 .....92 A2
Queen's Ave S 🖪 EH4 .....92 B1
Queen's Bay Cres EH15 .....125 B4
Queen's Bldgs KY11 .....46 C3
Queen's Cres
Carluke ML8 .....230 A1
Edinburgh EH9 .....123 C2
Falkirk FK1 .....59 C3
Queen's Ct EH9 .....1 C4
Queen's Dr EH8 .....233 C2
Queen's Dr
Pencaitland EH34 .....160 C3
Shieldmuir FK5 .....38 B1
Queen's Gdns EH4 .....92 B1
Queen's La FK9 .....2 A4
Queen's Park Ave EH8 .....94 A1
Queen's Park Ct EH8 .....124 A3
Queen's Pl EH2 .....78 C1
Queen's Rd
Broxburn EH52 .....117 C2
Dunbar EH42 .....78 C1
Edinburgh EH4 .....92 B1
Stirling FK8 .....6 C4
Queen's St FK1 .....81 C3
Queen's Wlk EH16 .....124 C2
Queens Ave
Broxburn EH52 .....117 C2
Haddington EH41 .....100 C1
Queens Cres KY3 .....34 C1
Queens Ct FK5 .....38 B2
Queens Dr Denny FK6 .....36 C2
Falkirk FK1 .....59 C3
Queens Gdns EH53 .....148 C2
Queens Terr EH53 .....148 C2
Queens Way KY11 .....46 A1
Queensferry High Sch
EH30 .....89 B4
Queensferry Mus ★ EH30 .....68 B1
Queensferry Prim Sch
EH30 .....68 B1
Queensferry Rd
Dumfermline KY11 .....46 B4
Edinburgh, Braepark EH4 .....91 A2
Edinburgh, Orchard Brae
EH4 .....92 B1
Kirkliston EH29 .....89 A1
Rosyth KY11 .....46 C3
Queensferry St EH2 .....232 A3
Queensferry Street La
EH2 .....232 B3
Queensferry Terr EH4 .....92 A1
Queenshaugh KY12 .....27 B4
Queenshaugh Dr FK8 .....2 B1
Queensway EH26 .....203 C4
Quench Rd FK3 .....62 A3
Quentin Rise EH54 .....147 C1
Quidenham Ct EH39 .....54 A3
Quilts The EH6 .....93 C3
Quilts Wynd EH6 .....93 C3
Quoiters Ct EH47 .....171 B4

R

R L Stevenson's Birthplace &
Mus ★ EH3 .....93 B2
Race Rd EH48 .....144 C4
Rae Ct FK2 .....39 B2
Rae St Cowdenbeath KY4 .....13 B1
Stenhousemuir FK5 .....38 B2
Rae's Ct EH14 .....155 A3
Raeburn Cres
Kirkcaldy KY2 .....17 A2
Whitburn EH47 .....170 A3
Raeburn Mews EH4 .....93 A1
Raeburn Pl EH4 .....93 A1
Raeburn Rigg EH54 .....147 A3
Raeburn St EH4 .....93 A1
Raes Gdns EH19 .....182 B4
Rae Rd FK2 .....82 C3
Rainhill Ct FK2 .....82 C4
Raith Ave KY4 .....13 B2
Raith Cres KY2 .....17 A2
Raith Ctr KY4 .....13 B2
Raith Dr KY2 .....17 A2
Raith Gdns KY2 .....16 C2
Raleigh Ct FK1 .....59 C3
Ramage Rd ML8 .....230 A1
Ramillies Ct Carluke ML8 .....230 A1
Penicuik EH26 .....204 A4
Ramsay Ave FK2 .....61 A2
Ramsay Cotts EH19 .....182 C2
Ramsay Cres
Bathgate EH48 .....145 B3
Burntisland KY3 .....34 A1
Mayfield EH22 .....183 C3
Ramsay Ct EH54 .....148 B3
Ramsay La
Kincardine FK10 .....23 C2
Limekilns KY11 .....45 B2
Ramsay Pl Edinburgh EH15 .....95 A1

Ramsay Pl continued
Penicuik EH26 .....203 B3
Stirling FK8 .....2 A1
Ramsay Rd KY1 .....17 A1
Ramsay Terr EH18 .....181 C3
Ramsay Wlk EH22 .....183 C3
Ramsey Ct FK10 .....23 C2
Ramsey Gdn EH1 .....232 C3
Ramsey La EH1 .....232 C3
Ramsey Pl KY11 .....46 C2
Ramsey Tullis Ave FK10 .....4 B1
Ramsey Tullis Dr FK10 .....4 B1
Randolph Cliff EH3 .....232 A3
Randolph Cres
Bannockburn FK7 .....7 B1
Brightons EH3 .....82 B4
Dunbar EH42 .....106 B4
Edinburgh EH3 .....232 A3
Randolph Ct Kirkcaldy KY1 .....18 A4
Stirling FK8 .....7 A3
Randolph Gdns FK6 .....36 B1
Randolph Ind Est KY1 .....18 A4
Randolph La EH3 .....232 B3
Randolph Pl
Bannockburn FK7 .....7 B1
Edinburgh EH3 .....232 B3
Kirkcaldy KY1 .....18 A4
Randolph Rd FK8 .....7 A2
Randolph St
Cowdenbeath KY4 .....13 B2
Dumfermline KY12 .....29 A2
Randolph Terr FK7 .....7 A2
Randyford Rd FK2 .....60 B3
Randyford St FK2 .....60 C3
Range Rd EH51 .....62 B4
Rankeillor St EH8 .....233 B1
Rankin Ave EH9 .....123 C1
Rankin Cres FK4 .....57 B3
Rankin Dr EH9 .....123 C1
Rankin Rd EH9 .....123 C2
Rankine Sq EH54 .....146 B3
Rankine Wynd FK10 .....4 B1
Rannoch Ct EH16 .....10 B3
Rannoch Dr
Crossford KY12 .....28 A1
Whitburn EH47 .....170 B4
Rannoch Gr EH4 .....91 B1
Rannoch Pl Edinburgh EH4 .....91 B1
Shieldhill FK1 .....81 C4
Shotts ML7 .....191 C3
Stenhousemuir FK5 .....38 C2
Rannoch Rd
Edinburgh EH4 .....91 B1
Grangemouth FK3 .....61 C4
Kirkcaldy KY2 .....16 C4
Rosyth KY11 .....46 C1
Whitburn EH47 .....170 B4
Rannoch Terr EH4 .....91 B1
Rannoch Wlk
Livingston EH54 .....148 A2
Whitburn EH47 .....170 B4
Ransome Gdns EH4 .....91 B1
Raploch Prim Sch FK8 .....1 C1
Raploch Rd FK8 .....1 C1
Rashiehill Cres EH55 .....194 C3
Rashiehill Rd FK1 .....110 A3
Rashiehill Terr EH55 .....194 C3
Rashiehill ML11 .....215 A1
Rashierigg Pl EH47 .....170 A1
Ratcliffe Terr EH9 .....123 C2
Rathbone Pl EH15 .....95 A1
Ratho Park Rd EH28 .....119 B1
Ratho Pl KY12 .....29 B2
Ratho Prim Sch EH28 .....119 B1
Rattray Gdns EH47 .....171 C4
Rattray St EH51 .....64 A4
Rattray Terr KY5 .....14 B4
Ravelrig Gait EH14 .....151 A1
Ravelrig Hill EH14 .....151 A1
Ravelrig Pk EH14 .....151 A1
Ravelrig Rd EH14 .....151 A2
Ravelston Dykes EH12 .....122 B4
Ravelston Dykes La
EH4 .....122 A4
Ravelston Dykes Rd
EH4 .....122 A4
Ravelston Gdn EH4 .....122 B4
Ravelston House Gr 🔟
EH4 .....92 B1
Ravelston House Loan
EH4 .....92 B1
Ravelston House Pk EH4 .....92 B1
Ravelston House Rd EH4 .....92 B1
Ravelston Hts EH4 .....92 B1
Ravelston Pk EH4 .....122 C4
Ravelston Pl EH4 .....122 C4
Ravelston Rise EH4 .....122 B4
Ravelston Terr EH4 .....92 C1
Ravelsykes Rd EH26 .....203 B3
Ravendean Gdns EH26 .....203 B3
Ravens Craig 🔠 KY1 .....17 B3
Ravenscraig Castle ★
KY1 .....17 C3
Ravenscraig Park Nature
Trail ★ KY1 .....17 C3
Ravenscraig St KY1 .....17 C3
Ravenscroft Gdns EH17 .....155 C3
Ravenscroft Pl EH17 .....155 C3
Ravenscroft St EH17 .....155 C3
Ravenshaugh Cres
EH21 .....127 A3
Ravenshaugh Rd EH21 .....127 A4
Ravenswood Ave EH16 .....124 B1
Ravenswood Rise EH54 .....173 C4
Rectory La KY1 .....18 A4
Red Craigs KY2 .....16 B4
Red Fox Cres EH26 .....180 A1

Red Row KY11 .....45 B2
Redbrae Ave EH51 .....64 A3
Redbrae Rd EH51 .....59 B3
Redbraes Gr EH7 .....93 B2
Redbraes Pl EH7 .....93 B2
Redburn Rd
Blackridge EH48 .....142 A1
Prestonpans EH32 .....96 C1
Redburn Rd N EH32 .....96 C1
Redburn Wynd EH32 .....17 B2
Redcraig Rd EH53 .....148 C1
Redcroft Pl EH47 .....171 A1
Redcroft St EH22 .....156 A4
Redcroft Terr EH47 .....171 A1
Redding Ind Est EH47 .....61 A1
Redding Rd Brightons FK2 .....82 B4
Redding EH2 .....61 A1
Reddoch Rd FK2 .....62 A2
Redford Ave EH13 .....153 B3
Redford Bank EH13 .....153 B3
Redford Cres EH13 .....153 B3
Redford Dr EH13 .....153 A3
Redford Gdns EH13 .....153 B3
Redford Gr EH13 .....153 B3
Redford Loan EH13 .....153 B3
Redford Neuk EH13 .....153 B3
Redford Pl EH13 .....153 B3
Redford Rd EH13 .....153 B3
Redford Terr EH13 .....153 B3
Redford Wlk EH13 .....153 B3
Redgauntlet Terr EH16 .....124 B1
Redhall Ave EH14 .....122 A1
Redhall Bank Rd EH14 .....122 A1
Redhall Cres EH14 .....122 A1
Redhall Dr EH14 .....122 A1
Redhall Gdns EH14 .....122 A1
Redhall House Dr EH14 .....122 A1
Redhall Gr EH14 .....122 A1
Redhall Pl EH14 .....122 A1
Redhall Rd EH14 .....122 A1
Redhall View EH14 .....122 A1
Redhaws Rd ML7 .....192 A2
Redheugh Loan EH23 .....183 B1
Redheughs Ave EH12 .....121 A2
Redheughs Rigg EH12 .....121 A2
Redholm Pk EH39 .....54 C3
Redhouse Cotts EH49 .....86 C2
Redhouse Ct EH54 .....171 C4
Redhouse Est EH52 .....14 B2
Redhouse Pl EH47 .....145 B1
Redhouse Rd EH47 .....172 A4
Redlands Ct EH47 .....170 C4
Redlands Rd FK10 .....4 A2
Redmill Cotts EH47 .....170 C4
Redmill Ct EH47 .....170 C4
Redmill View EH47 .....170 C4
Redmire Cres ML7 .....212 A4
Redpath Dr FK2 .....39 A2
Redwell Pl FK10 .....9 C4
Redwing Brae EH54 .....147 B3
Redwood Gr EH22 .....182 C3
Redwood Wlk EH22 .....183 A3
Reed Dr EH22 .....183 A4
Reedlands Dr FK6 .....57 B2
Regal Gr ML7 .....191 C2
Regent Pl EH7 .....94 A1
Regent Rd EH7, EH8 .....233 B4
Regent Sq EH49 .....85 A4
Regent St
Edinburgh EH15 .....125 A4
Kincardine FK10 .....23 C2
Regent Street La EH15 .....125 A4
Regent Terr EH7 .....233 C4
Regent Terrace Mews
EH7 .....233 C4
Regents Way KY11 .....48 A2
Regis Ct EH4 .....91 A2
Register Pl EH2 .....233 A4
Register St EH51 .....63 C4
Reid Ave KY4 .....30 C3
Reid St Dumfermline KY12 .....29 A2
Lochgelly KY5 .....14 B4
Reid's Cl EH8 .....233 C3
Reid's Ct EH8 .....58 A2
Reilly Rd FK4 .....58 A2
Relugas Gdns EH9 .....123 C2
Relugas Pl EH9 .....123 C2
Relugas Rd EH9 .....123 C2
Rendall Gdns EH52 .....117 C3
Rennie Pl EH40 .....103 B4
Rennie Sq EH54 .....173 B3
Rennie St FK1 .....60 A2
Rennie's Isle EH6 .....93 C3
Research Ave N EH14 .....120 C1
Research Ave S EH14 .....151 C4
Restalrig Ave EH7 .....94 B1
Restalrig Cir EH7 .....94 B2
Restalrig Cres EH7 .....94 B1
Restalrig Dr EH7 .....94 B1
Restalrig Gdns EH7 .....94 B1
Restalrig Pk EH7 .....94 A2
Restalrig Rd EH6,EH7 .....94 A2
Restalrig Rd S EH7 .....94 B1
Restalrig Sq EH7 .....94 B2
Restalrig Terr EH6 .....94 A2
Retail Pk Rdbt EH54 .....147 C1
Reveston La EH47 .....170 A3
Reynard Gdns EH49 .....84 A3
Rhodders Gr FK12 .....5 A4
Rhodes Pk EH39 .....54 C3
Rhodes St KY1 .....29 A1
Riccarton Ave EH14 .....151 A1
Riccarton Cres EH14 .....152 A2
Riccarton Gr EH14 .....152 A3
Riccarton Mains Rd
EH14 .....152 A3

Riccarton Prim Sch
EH14 .....151 C2
Riccarton Rd EH49 .....84 C3
Richard Quinn St FK7 .....20 B4
Richmond Dr FK2 .....82 B4
Richmond La EH8 .....233 B2
Richmond Pl
Edinburgh EH8 .....233 B2
Lochgelly KY5 .....14 A4
Richmond Terr
Bo'ness EH51 .....63 C4
Edinburgh EH11 .....232 A2
Riddochhill Cres EH47 .....171 B4
Riddochhill Ct EH47 .....171 A4
Riddochhill Dr EH47 .....171 B4
Riddochhill Rd EH47 .....171 B4
Riddochhill View EH47 .....171 A4
Ridge Ct EH47 .....170 A1
Ridge Way KY11 .....48 A3
Riding Pk EH4 .....91 A2
Ridley Dr KY11 .....46 C2
Riego St EH3 .....232 B2
Rifle Rd EH51 .....62 B4
Rig Pl EH32 .....71 B2
Rig St EH32 .....71 B2
Rigg Pk EH42 .....78 B1
Riggs View KY12 .....27 C4
Rigley Terr EH32 .....127 C4
Rillbank Cres EH9 .....233 A1
Rillbank Terr EH9 .....123 B3
Rimmon Cres ML7 .....191 C3
Ring Rd FK10 .....10 A4
Ringwood Pl 🖪 EH16 .....155 A4
Rintoul Ave KY12 .....26 A4
Rintoul Pl Blairhall KY12 .....26 A4
Edinburgh EH3 .....93 A1
Riselaw Cres EH10 .....154 A4
Riselaw Pl EH10 .....154 A4
Riselaw Rd EH10 .....154 A4
Riselaw Terr EH10 .....154 A4
Ritchie Ct KY12 .....122 C3
Ritchie Pl Bo'ness EH51 .....64 A3
Rivaldsgreen Cres EH49 .....85 A3
River Gore Gr EH23 .....207 B4
River Gore Rd EH23 .....207 B4
River Gr EH23 .....207 B4
River St KY2 .....39 A1
River View KY11 .....48 A1
River Wlk KY11 .....48 A1
Riverbank View FK8 .....7 A4
Riverside Cres EH12 .....122 B4
Riverside Gr EH12 .....122 B4
Riverside Rd EH12 .....122 B4
Riverside Edinburgh EH4 .....91 A4
Newbridge EH28 .....118 C3
Riverside Ct
Linlithgow EH49 .....84 B4
Livingston EH54 .....147 B2
Riverside Dr
Haddington EH41 .....101 A1
Stirling FK8 .....2 B1
Riverside Gdns EH12 .....126 A3
Riverside Lea Crofts
EH47 .....171 C4
Riverside Pl EH41 .....101 B1
Riverside Prim Sch
Livingston EH54 .....148 A2
Stirling FK8 .....2 B1
Riverside Rd
Craigiehall EH30 .....90 C2
Grangemouth FK3 .....62 A3
Riverside Terr FK10 .....23 C2
Riverside View FK10 .....10 A2
Road 10 FK3 .....62 B3
Road 11 FK3 .....62 A3
Road 13 FK3 .....62 A3
Road 15 FK3 .....62 A3
Road 18 FK3 .....62 A3
Road 21 FK3 .....62 A3
Road 24 FK3 .....62 A3
Road 25 FK3 .....62 A3
Road 27 FK3 .....62 A3
Road 28 FK3 .....62 A3
Road 29 FK3 .....62 A3
Road 30b FK3 .....62 A3
Road 30c FK3 .....62 A3
Road 31 FK3 .....62 A3
Road 32 FK3 .....62 A3
Road 33 FK2,FK3 .....62 A3
Road 4a FK3 .....62 A4
Road 4b FK3 .....62 B4
Road 5a FK3 .....62 B4
Road 6 FK3 .....62 B3
Road 7 FK3 .....62 B4
Road 8 FK3 .....62 B4
Road 9 FK3 .....62 B4
Roanhead Terr FK10 .....23 C2
Roanshead Rd EH22 .....183 B4
Robb's Loan EH14 .....122 B2
Robb's Loan Gr EH14 .....122 B2
Robert Bruce Ct FK5 .....38 B1
Robert Burns Dr EH16 .....124 B1
Robert Burns Mews
EH22 .....157 B2
Robert Dick Ct FK10 .....4 B1
Robert Hardie Ct FK5 .....38 B1
Robert Kinmond Ave FK10 .....4 B1
Robert Knox Ave EH40 .....103 B4
Robert Smillie Ave EH22 .....183 C3
Robert Smith Ct KY4 .....13 C3
Robert Smith St ML7 .....191 C2
Roberts Ave FK1 .....17 C4
Robertson Ave
Bathgate EH48 .....144 C3

Robertson Ave continued
Bonnybridge FK4 .....58 A3
Edinburgh EH11 .....122 B3
Prestonpans EH32 .....97 A1
Tranent EH33 .....128 B3
Robertson Bank EH23 .....207 B3
Robertson Ct
Armadale EH48 .....143 C2
Stenhousemuir FK5 .....38 B1
Robertson Dr EH33 .....128 B4
Robertson Pl FK7 .....7 A2
Robertson Rd KY12 .....29 B3
Robertson St FK12 .....5 A4
Robertson Way EH54 .....147 B4
Robertson's Cl
Dalkeith EH22 .....157 A2
Edinburgh EH1 .....233 B2
Robertsons Bank EH23 .....207 B4
Robins Neuk EH33 .....129 B3
Rocheid Pk EH4 .....92 C2
Rochester Terr EH10 .....123 A4
Rocks Rd KY11 .....45 A2
Rockville Gr EH49 .....85 A3
Rockville Terr EH19 .....182 A4
Roddinglaw Rd EH12 .....120 B2
Rodel Dr FK2 .....61 C1
Rodney Pl EH7 .....93 B1
Rodney St Edinburgh EH7 .....93 B1
Grangemouth FK3 .....61 B3
Roebuck Pl EH51 .....63 B3
Rolland St KY12 .....29 A2
Roman Camp EH47 .....185 A2
Roman Camp Cotts
EH52 .....117 B1
Roman Camp Way
EH37 .....185 A2
Roman Cres ML7 .....192 A2
Roman Dr FK1 .....59 B3
Roman Rd
Bonnybridge FK4 .....58 A2
Inverkeithing KY11 .....47 A1
Roman Way EH51 .....63 B3
Romero Pl EH16 .....123 C3
Romyn Rd KY11 .....46 B1
Ronades Rd FK2 .....60 A4
Ronald Cres FK5 .....43 B4
Ronald Pl FK8 .....7 A4
Ronaldshay Cres FK3 .....61 C4
Ronaldson Gr KY12 .....29 B3
Rood Well Cotts EH42 .....104 C1
Roodlands General Hospl
EH41 .....100 C1
Roods Cres KY11 .....47 A1
Roods Rd KY11 .....47 A1
Roods Sq KY11 .....47 B2
Roomlin Gdns KY1 .....17 C4
Roosevelt Rd EH27 .....149 C2
Rope Wlk EH32 .....96 C1
Ropeway KY11 .....46 A1
Rosabelle Rd EH25 .....180 C2
Rosabelle St KY1 .....17 C4
Rose Ave EH19 .....182 B3
Rose Cotts EH19 .....182 B3
Rose Cres KY12 .....29 A2
Rose Ct EH4 .....91 C2
Rose Gdns
Bonnyrigg & Lasswade
EH19 .....182 B3
Carneyhill KY12 .....27 B1
Rose Gr EH19 .....182 B3
Rose La Lochgelly KY5 .....14 A4
Queensferry EH30 .....68 A1
Torryburn KY12 .....26 C1
Rose Neuk EH19 .....182 B3
Rose Pk
Bonnyrigg & Lasswade
EH19 .....182 B3
Edinburgh EH5 .....93 A3
Rose Pl EH19 .....182 B3
Rose St Alloa FK10 .....4 C1
Bonnybridge FK4 .....58 A3
Burntisland KY3 .....50 C4
Cowdenbeath KY4 .....13 B2
Dunfermline KY12 .....29 A2
Edinburgh EH2 .....232 C3
Rose Street North La
EH2 .....232 C3
Rose Street South La
EH2 .....232 C3
Rose Terr
Bonnyrigg & Lasswade
EH19 .....182 B3
Denny FK6 .....36 B1
Stenhousemuir FK5 .....38 C2
Rose Way EH19 .....182 B3
Rose's Wlk EH52 .....116 C2
Rosebank Alloa FK10 .....5 B1
Edinburgh EH4 .....91 C2
Dunfermline KY12 .....29 B1
Rosebank Ave FK1 .....59 C3
Rosebank Cotts EH22 .....232 A2
Rosebank Gdns
Alloa FK10 .....10 B4
Edinburgh EH5 .....93 A3
Kincardine FK10 .....23 C2
Rosebank Gr EH5 .....93 A3
Rosebank Rd EH5 .....59 C3
Rosebank Rd
Edinburgh EH5 .....93 A3
Livingston EH54 .....173 A4
Rosebank Roadside EH54 .....173 A4
Rosebank Way EH54 .....173 A4
Rosebay Glade EH54 .....173 B3
Roseberry Ave EH54 .....147 A3
Roseberry Pl EH54 .....147 A3
Rosebery Ave EH30 .....89 B4

Rosebery Cres
- **5** Bathgate EH48 ....**145** A3
- Edinburgh EH12 ....**122** C4
- Gorebridge EH23 ....**207** B3

Rosebery Crescent La
- EH12 ....**122** C4

Rosebery Ct
- Dalgety Bay KY11 ....**47** C1
- Kirkcaldy KY1 ....**17** A3

Rosebery Gr KY11 ......**47** C1

Rosebery Pl
- Dalgety Bay KY11 ....**47** C1
- Gullane EH31 ....**52** A1
- Stirling FK8 ....**7** A4

Rosebery Resr* HE23 ..**225** A3

Rosebery Terr KY1 ......**17** A3

Rosebery View KY11 .....**47** C1

Roseburn Ave EH12 ....**122** B4

Roseburn Cliff EH12 ....**122** C4

Roseburn Cres EH12 ...**122** B4

Roseburn Dr EH12 .....**122** B4

Roseburn Gdns EH12 ..**122** B4

Roseburn Maltings
- EH12 ....**122** C4

Roseburn Pl EH12 ......**122** B4

Roseburn Prim Sch
- EH12 ....**122** B3

Roseburn St EH12 ......**122** B3

Roseburn Terr EH12 ....**122** C4

Rosebush Cres KY11 ....**29** B2

Rosedale Ct EH24 ......**205** B4

Rosedale Gr EH24 ......**181** B1

Rosedale Neuk EH24 ...**181** B1

Rosefield Ave EH15 ....**125** A4

Rosefield Avenue La
- EH15 ....**125** A4

Rosefield La EH15 ......**125** A4

Rosefield Pl EH15 ......**125** A4

Rosefield St EH15 ......**125** A4

Rosehall EH41 ....**131** C4

Rosehall Ct EH41 ......**131** C4

Rosehall Pl EH41 ......**131** C4

Rosehall Rd ML7 ....**191** B2

Rosehall Terr KY1 ....**60** A2

Rosehill Pl EH54 ....**147** A2

Rosehill Terr EH30 ......**89** B4

Roselea Dr FK2 ....**82** C4

Rosemaeln Pl KY12 .....**29** B2

Rosemary Ct FK6 ....**36** B1

Rosemead Terr FK1 .....**81** C3

Rosemill Ct KY12 ....**26** B1

Rosemount Ave KY2 ....**17** A4

Rosemount Bldgs EH3 .**232** A2

Rosemount Ct EH48 ...**145** A3

Rosemount Dr EH52 ...**116** C2

Rosemount Gdns FK1 ...**81** B3

Roseneath Pl EH9 .....**123** B3

Roseneath St EH9 .....**123** B3

Roseneath Terr EH9 ....**123** B3

Rosetay Ct KY12 ....**29** B2

Rosethorn Wynd KY12 ..**29** B2

Rosevale Pl EH6 ....**94** A2

Rosevale Terr EH6 ......**94** A2

Roseville Gdns EH5 .....**93** B3

Rosewell Prim Sch
- EH24 ....**181** C1

Rosewell Rd EH24 .....**181** C1

Roslin Chapel* EH25 ..**181** A2

Roslin Glen Cntry Pk*
- EH25 ....**180** C1

Roslin Prim Sch EH25 ..**180** C2

Roslin Prim Sch (Bilston
- **Annexe)** EH25 .....**180** B3

Ross Ave KY11 ....**48** A1

Ross Gdns Falkirk FK1 ...**59** B3
- Tranent EH33 ....**128** B3

Ross Ct FK7 ....**7** C3

Ross Gdns Edinburgh EH9 .**123** C2
- Kirkcaldy KY1 ....**17** C4
- High Sch EH33 ......**128** B3

Ross La KY12 ....**29** B2

Ross Pl Edinburgh EH9 ..**123** C2
- Kinghorn KY3 ....**34** C1
- Newtongrange EH22 ..**183** A3

Ross Rd EH16 ....**123** C1

Ross St KY12 ....**29** A3

Ross Way EH54 ....**147** B4

Rossend Terr KY3 ......**50** B4

Rossie Pl EH7 ....**94** A1

Rossland Pl KY3 ....**34** C1

Rosslyn Cres EH6 ......**93** C2

Rosslyn St KY1 ....**17** C4

Rosslyn Terr EH6 ......**93** C2

Rosslynlee Hospl EH25 .**204** C3

Rossness Dr KY3 ....**34** C1

Rossvail Sch FK1 ....**59** B3

Rosyth Europarc
- North Queensferry KY11 ..**68** A4
- Rosyth KY11 ....**46** B1

Rosyth Sta KY11 ....**46** C3

Rothes Dr EH54 ....**173** C3

Rothesay Mews EH3 ..**122** C4

Rothesay Pl
- Edinburgh EH3 ....**232** A3
- Musselburgh EH21 ...**126** B3

Rothesay Terr EH3 ....**232** A3

Roughburn Rd EH9 ....**123** A2

Roughlands Cres FK2 ...**39** A2

Roughlands Dr FK2 .....**39** A2

Roull Gr EH12 ....**121** B3

Roull Pl EH12 ....**121** C3

Roull Rd EH12 ....**121** B3

Round The KY12 ....**29** B2

Roundel The FK2 ......**60** B4

Roundelwood FK10 .....**5** A1

Roundhouse FK7 ......**20** B4

Rowallan Ct EH12 ......**121** A4

Rowallan Dr FK7 ....**19** C4

Rowan Cres FK1 ....**59** A2

Rowan Ct Bannockburn FK7 .**7** C1
- Pathhead EH37 ....**185** A2

Rowan Dr EH47 ....**163** C2

Rowan Gdns EH19 ....**182** A3

Rowan Gr
- Dunfermline KY11 ......**29** B1
- Livingston EH54 ......**148** A3

Rowan La EH47 ....**145** B1

Rowan St Blackburn EH47 .**145** B1
- Dunbar EH42 ....**78** A1

Rowan Terr
- Blackburn EH47 ......**171** B4
- Cowdenbeath KY4 .....**13** B2

Rowanhill Cl EH32 ......**97** B2

Rowanhill Dr EH32 ......**97** B2

Rowanhill Pk EH32 ......**97** B2

Rowanhill Way EH32 ....**97** B2

Rowans The Alloa FK10 ...**5** B1
- Gullane EH31 ....**52** A2

Rowantree Ave EH14 ..**151** C2

Rowantree Gr EH14 ...**151** C2

Rowantree Rd EH22 ...**183** C4

Rowantree Wlk FK5 .....**38** B2

Roxburgh Pl
- Edinburgh EH8 ....**233** B2
- Stenhousemuir FK5 ....**38** C2

Roxburgh St
- Edinburgh EH8 ....**233** B2
- Grangemouth FK3 .....**61** C4

Roxburghe Pk EH24 .....**78** C1

Roxburghe Terr EH42 ...**78** C1

Roy Dr EH54 ....**173** C3

Royal (Dick) Veterinary Coll
- EH8 ....**233** B1

Royal Bank Sch The
- EH16 ....**123** C3

Royal Botanic Gdn* EH3 .**93** A2

Royal Cir EH3 ....**232** B4

Royal Coll of Physicians
- **232** C4

Royal Cres EH3 ....**93** B1

Royal Ct EH26 ....**203** B4

Royal Edinburgh Hospl
- EH10 ....**123** A2

Royal Gdns FK8 ....**7** A4

Royal High Prim Sch The
- EH8 ....**124** B4

Royal High Sch The EH4 .**91** B2

Royal Hospl for Sick Children
- EH9 ....**123** B3

Royal Infirmary of Edinburgh
- Edinburgh, Edmonstone
- EH16 ....**124** C1
- Edinburgh, West Meadow Park
- EH3 ....**233** A2

Royal Mile Prim Sch
- EH8 ....**233** C3

Royal Mus of Scotland*
- EH1 ....**233** A2

Royal Obsy* EH9 ......**123** B1

Royal Park Terr EH8 .....**94** A1

Royal Scot Ct EH48 ....**145** A3

Royal Scot Way KY12 ...**29** A3

Royal Scottish Acad*
- **232** C3

Royal Scottish National Hospl
- The FK5 ....**37** C2

Royal Terr Edinburgh EH7 .**233** B4
- Linlithgow EH49 ....**84** C3

Royal Victoria Hospl EH4 .**92** C1

Royal Yacht Britannia*
- EH6 ....**93** C4

Royston Mains Ave EH5 .**92** C3

Royston Mains Cl EH5 ...**92** C3

Royston Mains Cres EH5 .**92** B3

Royston Mains Gdns EH5 .**92** C3

Royston Mains Gn EH5 ...**92** C3

Royston Mains Pl EH5 ...**92** B3

Royston Mains Rd EH5 ...**92** B3

Royston Mains St EH5 ...**92** B3

Royston Prim Sch EH5 ...**92** C3

Royston Rd EH54 ......**146** C4

Royston Rdbt EH54 ....**146** B4

Royston Terr EH3 ....**93** A2

Rudolf Steiner Sch
- EH10 ....**122** C2

Rulley View FK6 ....**36** B2

Rullion Green Ave EH26 .**203** B4

Rullion Green Cres
- **203** B4

Rullion Green Gr EH26 ..**203** B4

Rullion Rd EH26 ....**203** B3

Rumblingwell KY12 ......**28** B3

Rumlie The FK1 ....**110** A3

Run The FK5 ....**64** B2

Rushbank EH54 ....**147** C3

Ruskie Rd EH4 ....**64** B2

Ruskin Pl EH22 ....**183** C3

Russel Ct KY5 ....**14** A4

Russel Pl EH5 ....**93** A3

Russel Rd EH11 ....**122** B3

Russell Ave EH48 ......**143** C4

Russell Ct KY11 ....**29** C1

Russell Gdns EH12 ....**122** C4

Russell Gr KY3 ....**33** B2

Russell Hill Ct FK5 ......**38** A4

Russell Pl Bonnybridge FK4 .**57** B3
- **1** Kirkcaldy KY1 ....**17** B3
- Oakley KY12 ....**26** C4

Russell Rd EH11 ......**122** C3

Russell St
- Cowdenbeath KY4 .....**13** A2
- Lochgelly KY5 ....**14** A4

Rutherford Ct
- Bridge of A FK9 ....**2** A4

Rutherford Ct continued
- Kirkcaldy KY1 ....**17** C4

Rutherford Dr EH16 ....**124** A1

Rutherford Sq EH54 ...**173** B3

Ruthven Pl EH16 ......**124** B1

Ruthven Rd EH39 ....**53** A2

Rutland Court La EH3 ..**232** B2

Rutland Sq EH1 ....**232** B3

Rutland St EH1 ....**232** B3

Ryebank EH54 ....**147** C3

Ryehill Ave EH6 ....**94** A2

Ryehill Gdns EH6 ....**94** A2

Ryehill La EH6 ....**94** A2

Ryehill Pl EH6 ....**94** A2

Ryehill Terr EH6 ....**94** A2

Rymalton KY1 ....**17** B3

S

Sacred Heart Prim Sch
- EH26 ....**203** C3

Sacred Heart RC Prim Sch
- FK3 ....**61** C3

Saddletree Loan EH16 ..**124** B1

Sailors' Wlk KY3 ....**50** B4

Sainford Cres FK2 ......**39** A1

Sainthill Ct EH39 ....**54** A4

St Alban's Rd EH9 .....**123** C2

St Andrew Pl EH6 ......**94** A2

St Andrew Sq EH2 .....**233** A4

St Andrew St
- Dalkeith EH22 ....**157** A2
- Dunfermline KY11 ......**29** B1
- North Berwick EH39 ...**54** B4

St Andrew's Ct FK5 .....**38** A2

St Andrew's Dr Airth FK2 .**22** A4
- Armadale EH48 ......**143** C4
- Uphall EH52 ....**116** C2

St Andrew's High Sch
- KY1 ....**17** B4

St Andrew's RC Prim Sch
- FK1 ....**60** C2

St Andrew's Way EH54 .**146** C3

St Andrews Pl **11** FK1 ...**60** A2

St Andrews Way Bsns Units
- EH54 ....**146** C3

St Ann's Ave EH18 ....**181** C3

St Ann's Path EH18 ...**181** C3

St Anne's Cres FK7 ......**7** C1

St Anne's Ct EH22 ....**183** A3

St Anthony La EH6 ......**93** C3

St Anthony Pl EH6 ......**93** C3

St Anthony's RC Prim Sch
- EH48 ....**143** C3

St Augustine's RC High Sch
- EH12 ....**121** B2

St Baldred's Cres EH39 ..**54** B3

St Baldred's Rd EH39 ...**54** B3

St Bernadette's RC Prim Sch
- FK10 ....**4** A1

St Bernard's Cres EH4 ...**93** A1

St Bernard's Row **5** EH4 .**93** A1

St Bride's RC Prim Sch
- KY4 ....**13** A2

St Bridget's Church*
- KY11 ....**48** B2

St Bridgets Brae KY11 ...**48** B2

St Brycedale Ave KY1 ...**17** A2

St Brycedale Rd KY1 ....**17** A2

St Catherine Ct EH52 ...**82** C4

St Catherine's Gdns
- EH12 ....**122** A3

St Catherine's Manor
- EH12 ....**122** A3

St Catherine's Pl EH9 ..**123** C3

St Catherine's RC Prim Sch
- EH16 ....**155** A3

St Catherine's Wynd
- KY12 ....**28** A3

St Catherines Cres ML7 .**191** C3

St Clair Ave EH6 ....**94** A2

St Clair Cres EH25 .....**181** A2

St Clair Pl EH6 ....**94** A2

St Clair Rd EH6 ....**94** A2

St Clair St Edinburgh EH6 .**94** A2

St Clair Terr EH10 .....**122** C1

St Clairs Entry KY3 ......**35** A1

St Clement's Cres EH21 .**127** A2

St Clement's Gdns N
- EH21 ....**127** A2

St Clement's Gdns S
- EH21 ....**127** A2

St Clement's Terr EH21 .**127** A2

St Colm's Abbey* KY3 ..**49** A1

St Colm's Ed Ctr & Coll
- EH3 ....**93** A3

St Colme Ave EH30 .....**89** B3

St Colme Cres EH5 .....**49** A4

St Colme Dr KY11 ......**48** B3

St Colme Rd KY11 ......**48** B2

St Colme St EH3 ......**232** B4

St Columba's High Sch
- KY11 ....**29** C2

St Columba's RC Prim Sch
- EH48 ....**145** C3

St Crispin's Pl FK1 ......**60** A2

St Crispin's Specl Sch
- EH16 ....**123** C2

St Cuthbert's RC Prim Sch
- EH14 ....**122** B2

St Cuthbert's Bsns Pk KY1 .**48** A2

St David's
- Dalgety Bay KY11 ......**48** A2
- Larbert FK5 ....**38** A1

St David's Pl EH3 .....**232** A2

St David's RC High Sch
- EH22 ....**157** A1

St David's RC Prim Sch
- Dalkeith EH22 ....**157** B1
- Edinburgh EH4 ....**92** B2

St David's Terr EH3 ....**232** A2

St Davids EH22 ......**183** A3

St Davids Dr KY11 ......**48** A2

St Fillan's Terr EH10 ...**123** A1

St Fillans Cres KY3 ......**49** B4

St Fillans Gr KY3 ....**49** B4

St Fillans Pl KY2 ....**16** B4

St Fillans Rd KY2 ....**16** B4

St Francis Xavier's RC Prim
- Sch FK2 ....**60** A3

St Francis's RC Prim Sch
- EH16 ....**124** C2

St Gabriel's RC Prim Sch
- EH32 ....**96** C1

St George's Ct FK5 ......**38** A1

St George's Sch for girls
- EH12 ....**122** C4

St Germains Terr EH33 .**129** B3

St Giles Sq FK1 ....**59** A3

St Giles St EH1 ....**233** A3

St Giles Way FK1 ......**59** A3

St Giles' Cath* EH1 ...**233** A3

St Helen's Pl EH48 ....**143** C3

St James Ctr EH1 .....**233** A4

St James Pl KY3 ....**35** A1

St James Sq EH1 .....**233** A4

St James' Orch FK7 ......**7** B1

St James' Pl EH1 .....**233** A4

St James's Gdns EH26 .**203** C2

St James's View EH26 ..**203** C2

St John Ogilvie RC Prim Sch
- EH54 ....**146** C3

St John St Edinburgh EH8 .**233** B3
- Spott EH42 ....**106** B2

St John's Rd KY3 ....**7** A4

St John's RC Prim Sch
- EH47 ....**193** C3

St John Vianney RC Prim Sch
- EH16 ....**124** A1

St John's Ave
- Edinburgh EH12 ......**121** C3
- Falkirk FK2 ....**60** B3
- Linlithgow EH49 ....**84** C3

St John's Cres EH12 ...**121** C3

St John's Ct KY11 ......**47** B2

St John's Dr KY12 ......**29** B2

St John's Gate FK6 ......**36** B1

St John's Gdns Denny FK6 .**36** B1
- Edinburgh EH12 ......**121** C3

St John's Gr FK6 ....**36** B1

St John's Hill EH8 .....**233** B2

St John's Pl EH48 .....**147** B2

St John's Pl KY12 ....**29** B2

St John's Prim Sch FK10 ..**9** C3

St John's RC Prim Sch
- Edinburgh EH15 .....**125** A4
- Rosyth KY11 ....**46** C2

St John's Rd
- Broxburn EH52 ......**117** C2
- Edinburgh EH12 ......**121** C3
- Edinburgh EH12 ......**121** C3

St John's Way EH51 ....**63** C3

St Johns Ct EH54 .....**147** C2

St Joseph's Prim Sch
- EH11 ....**121** C2

St Joseph's RC Prim Sch
- Bonnybridge FK4 ......**58** A2
- Linlithgow EH49 ....**84** C3

St Josephs RC Prim Sch
- EH47 ....**169** C3

St Katharine's Brae
- EH16 ....**155** A3

St Katharine's Cres
- EH16 ....**155** A3

St Katharine's Loan
- EH16 ....**155** A3

St Kentigern Rd EH26 ..**203** B3

St Kentigerns RC Acad
- EH47 ....**171** A4

St Kilda Cres KY2 ......**16** C4

St Laurence Cres FK1 ..**110** A3

St Lawrence St KY11 ....**29** B1

St Leonard's EH8 ......**123** C3

St Leonard's Bank EH8 .**233** C1

St Leonard's Crag EH8 ..**233** C1

St Leonard's Ct KY11 ...**29** B1

St Leonard's Hill EH8 ..**233** B1

St Leonard's La EH8 ...**233** B1

St Leonard's Pl
- Dunfermline KY11 ......**29** A1
- Kinghorn KY3 ....**34** C2

St Leonard's St
- Dunfermline KY11 ......**29** A1
- Edinburgh EH8 ......**233** B1

St Luke's Prim Sch EH22 .**183** B3

St Magdalene's Ave EH49 .**85** A4

St Margaret St KY12 ....**29** A2

St Margaret's Cres FK2 ..**61** C1

St Margaret's Dr EH48 .**143** C3

St Margaret's Pl EH9 ..**123** B2

St Margaret's RC Prim Sch
- Dunfermline KY11 ......**29** B2
- Loanhead EH20 ......**155** B1

St Margaret's Prim Sch
- FK2 ....**61** B1

St Margaret's RC Acad
- EH54 ....**147** B2

St Margaret's RC Prim Sch
- Cowie FK7 ....**20** B4
- Queensferry EH30 .....**68** B1

St Margaret's Rd
- Edinburgh EH9 ....**123** A2
- North Berwick EH39 ...**54** B4

St Margaret's Sch EH16 .**124** A2

St Margarets Ct KY12 ...**29** A2

St Margarets Gdns FK2 ..**61** B1

St Marie's RC Prim Sch
- KY2 ....**17** B4

St Mark's La EH15 .....**125** A4

St Mark's Pl EH15 .....**125** A4

St Mark's RC Prim Sch
- EH14 ....**121** A1

St Martin's La EH41 ....**132** B4

St Martin's Gate EH41 .**132** B4

St Martin's Pl EH41 ....**132** B4

St Martin's RC Prim Sch
- EH33 ....**128** B3

St Mary's (Leith) RC Prim Sch
- EH6 ....**94** A3

St Mary's Church*
- EH41 ....**132** A4

St Mary's Glebe KY1 ....**17** B3

St Mary's Music Sch
- EH12 ....**122** C4

St Mary's Pl
- Bathgate EH48 ......**145** B3
- Edinburgh EH15 .....**125** B4
- Kirkcaldy KY1 ....**17** B3

St Mary's Pleasance & Lady
- Kitty's Gdn* EH41 ...**132** B4

St Mary's Prim Sch
- EH19 ....**182** A3

St Mary's RC Cath*
- EH1 ....**233** A4

St Mary's RC Prim Sch
- Bannockburn FK7 ......**7** B1
- Bathgate EH48 ......**145** B3
- Bo'ness EH51 ....**64** A4
- Edinburgh EH1 ....**93** B1
- Haddington EH41 ....**132** A4
- Polbeth EH55 ....**172** C3
- Stirling FK8 ....**1** C1

St Mary's Rd KY1 ......**17** B3

St Mary's St EH1 .....**233** B3

St Mary's Wynd FK8 .....**7** A4

St Marys Pl FK3 ....**61** C4

St Matthew's Prim Sch
- EH24 ....**181** C1

St Michael's Ave EH21 .**126** B3

St Michael's Hospl EH49 .**85** A3

St Michael's Wynd EH49 .**85** A4

St Michaels La EH49 ....**85** A4

St Modan's High Sch FK7 .**7** A2

St Modans St EH54 .....**60** A2

St Mungo's High Sch
- FK3 ....**60** A3

St Mungo RC Prim Sch
- FK10 ....**10** B3

St Mungo's View EH26 .**203** C3

St Mungo's Wynd FK10 ..**10** A3

St Nicholas (Specl Sch)
- EH11 ....**122** B3

St Nicholas RC Prim Sch
- FK5 ....**117** B2

St Ninian's Ave EH49 ....**84** B3

St Ninian's Dr EH12 ....**121** B4

St Ninian's RC Prim Sch
- Edinburgh EH7 ....**94** B1
- Livingston EH54 .....**148** A1

St Ninian's Rd
- Edinburgh EH12 ......**121** B4
- Linlithgow EH49 ....**84** C4

St Ninian's Terr EH10 ..**122** C1

St Ninian's Way EH54 ...**24** A4

St Ninians Prim Sch FK7 ..**7** A2

St Ninians Rd
- Cambusbarron FK7 .....**6** C3
- Stirling FK8 ....**7** A3

St Ninians Row EH1 .....**93** B1

St Ninians Way
- Blackness EH49 ......**65** C2
- Musselburgh EH21 ...**127** A3

St Patrick Sq EH8 .....**233** B1

St Patrick St EH8 .....**233** B1

St Patrick's RC Prim Sch
- Denny FK6 ....**36** C2
- Shotts ML7 ....**191** C2

St Paul's Dr EH48 .....**144** A3

St Paul's RC Prim Sch
- EH15 ....**148** C2

St Peter's Bldgs EH11 .**232** A1

St Peter's Ct KY11 ......**47** B2

St Peter's Pl EH11 ....**232** A1

St Peter's RC Prim Sch
- Edinburgh EH10 .....**123** A2

St Ronan's Terr EH10 ..**123** A1

St Serf's Pl KY1 ....**17** B3

St Serf's Pl FK10 ....**4** A2

St Serf's Prim Sch FK10 ..**4** A2

St Serf's Rd FK10 ....**4** A2

St Serf's St EH54 .....**122** C4

St Serf's Wlk FK12 ....**4** C3

St Serfs Gr FK10 ....**11** A2

St Stephen Pl EH3 ......**93** A1

St Stephen St EH3 ......**93** A1

St Teresa Pl EH11 ....**122** C2

St Thomas of Aquin's High
- Sch EH3 ....**232** B1

St Thomas Rd EH9 ......123 C2
St Thomas's PI FK7 .....6 C3
St Thomas's Well FK6 ..6 B4
St Triduana's Chapel*
EH7 ......94 B1
St Valery Dr FK7 .....7 A2
St Vincent St EH3 .....93 A1
Salamanca Cres EH26 ..204 A4
Salamander PI EH6 ....94 A3
Salamander St EH6 ....94 A3
Salamander Yds EH6 ...94 B3
Salen Loan ML7 .....192 A2
Salisbury PI EH9 .....123 C3
Salisbury Rd EH16 ....123 C3
Salisbury St FK7 ......17 A3
Salisbury View EH22 ..183 B3
Salmon Dr FK1 .....59 C1
Salmon Inn Pk FK2 ....61 B1
Salmon Inn Rd FK2 ....61 B1
Salmond PI 6 EH7 .....94 A1
Salt Preston PI EH32 ..96 C1
Saltcoats Dr FK3 .....61 C4
Saltcoats Gdns EH14 ..173 C3
Saltcoats Rd
Grangemouth FK3 .....62 A4
Gullane EH31 .....42 A1
Salter's Rd Dalkeith EH22 157 B3
Wallyford EH21 .....127 A2
Salters' Gr EH22 .....122 C2
Salters' Rd Dalkeith EH22 157 B2
Pathhead EH37 .....186 A1
Salters' Terr EH22 .....157 B2
Saltire Gdns EH19 ....101 C4
Saltoun Prim Sch EH34 .161 C3
Saltpans KY11 .....45 A2
Savage Rd KY11 .....46 B1
Salvesen Cres EH4 ....92 A3
Salvesen Gdns EH4 ....92 A3
Salvesen Gr EH4 .....92 A3
Salvesen Terr EH4 ....92 A3
Samoa Terr EH26 .....204 A4
Samrt Village Bssns Campus
FK10 ......9 C4
Sand Port EH6 .....94 A3
Sand Port Trad Est EH6 .93 C3
Sandeman Ct FK10 ....23 C2
Sanderling Way KY11 ..30 A3
Sanderson Terr KY2 ...15 A1
Sanderson's Gr EH33 ..128 B4
Sanderson's Wynd EH33 128 A4
Sandford Gdns EH15 ..125 A4
Sandiland Dr EH53 ....148 A1
Sandilands KY11 .....45 B2
Sandpiper Dr KY11 ....30 B1
Sandport PI EH6 .....93 C3
Sandport St EH6 .....93 C3
Sands The EH41 .....132 A4
Sandy Loan Gullane EH31 .52 A1
Laurieston FK2 .....61 A2
Sandy Rd KY3 .....32 B3
Sandyford Ave EH49 ...84 A3
Sandyhill Ave ML7 ....192 A2
Sandyloan Cres FK2 ...61 A2
Sandyvale PI ML7 ....192 A2
Sang PI KY1 .....17 A2
Sang Rd KY1 .....17 A2
Sarazen Ct EH54 .....147 A4
Sarazen Gn EH54 .....147 A4
Sauchenbush Rd KY2 ..16 C3
Sauchie Ct FK7 .....7 A1
Sauchie Hospl FK10 ...10 B4
Sauchie St FK7 .....7 A1
Sauchiebank EH11 ....122 C3
Saughbank EH52 .....117 A3
Saughs The EH22 .....183 A2
Saughton Ave EH11 ...122 A3
Saughton Cres EH12 ..122 A3
Saughton Gdns EH12 ..122 A3
Saughton Gr EH12 ....122 A3
Saughton Loan EH12 ..122 A3
Saughton Mains Ave
EH11 ......121 C2
Saughton Mains Bank
EH11 ......122 A2
Saughton Mains Dr
EH11 ......121 C2
Saughton Mains Gdns
EH11 ......121 C2
Saughton Mains Gr
EH11 ......122 A2
Saughton Mains Loan
EH11 ......121 C2
Saughton Mains Pk
EH11 ......122 A2
Saughton Mains PI
EH11 ......121 C2
Saughton Mains St
Edinburgh EH11 .....122 A2
Edinburgh EH11 .....121 C2
Saughton Mains Terr
EH11 ......121 C2
Saughton Rd EH12 ....121 C2
Saughton Rd N EH12 ..121 C3
Saughtonhall Ave EH12 122 A3
Saughtonhall Ave W
EH12 ......122 A3
Saughtonhall Cir EH12 .122 B3
Saughtonhall Cres
EH12 ......122 A3
Saughtonhall Dr EH12 .122 A3
Saughtonhall Gdns
EH12 ......122 A3
Saughtonhall PI EH12 .122 B3

Saughtonhall Terr EH12 .122 B3
Saunders Ct KY1 .....17 A1
Saunders St
Edinburgh EH3 .....232 B4
Kirkcaldy KY1 .....17 A1
Savile PI EH9 .....123 C2
Savile Terr EH9 .....123 C2
Sawers Ave FK6 .....36 B1
Saxe Coburg PI EH3 ...93 A1
Saxe Coburg St EH3 ...93 A1
Scarlett Pk EH21 .....127 A3
Schaw Ct FK10 .....5 B1
Schaw Rd EH32 .....97 A1
Schawpark Ave FK10 ..5 B1
Schiltron Way FK7 ....7 B2
Scholars' Brae KY3 ...50 C4
School Brae Bo'ness EH51 .63 C4
Bonnyrigg & Lasswade
EH18 ......156 A1
Dysart KY1 .....18 A4
Edinburgh EH4 .....91 A3
West Barns EH42 .....105 C4
School Gn
Bonnyrigg & Lasswade
EH18 ......156 A1
Longniddry EH32 .....98 C3
School La Bathgate EH48 .145 A3
Cockenzie & Port Seton
EH32 ......97 B2
Hillend KY11 .....47 C2
Menstrie FK11 .....4 A4
Mid Calder EH53 .....148 B2
Shotts ML7 .....212 A4
School Mews FK11 ....4 A4
School PI EH51 .....116 C2
School Rd Aberlady EH32 .71 B2
Broxburn EH52 .....117 B3
East Linton EH40 ....103 C4
Lauriestoun FK2 .....61 A2
Longridge EH47 .....170 B1
North Berwick EH39 ..54 B4
Redding FK2 .....61 B1
Tullibody FK10 .....4 A1
School Row KY12 .....28 B3
School St
Cowdenbeath KY4 ....13 B2
Shotts ML7 .....191 C2
School View Bo'ness EH51 .64 A4
Redding FK2 .....61 B1
School Wlk FK5 .....38 B2
School Wynd KY1 .....17 A1
Schoolhouse Ind Est
EH55 ......171 C1
Schoolyard Ct EH25 ..181 A2
Sciennes EH9 .....123 C3
Sciennes Gdns EH9 ...123 C3
Sciennes Hill PI 4 EH9 .123 C3
Sciennes House PI 3
EH9 ......123 C3
Sciennes PI 1 EH9 ....123 C3
Sciennes Prim Sch EH9 123 B3
Sciennes Rd EH9 .....123 B3
Sclanderburn Rd FK6 ..57 B4
Scobie PI KY12 .....29 A2
Scollon Ave EH19 ....182 B4
Scone Gdns EH8 .....94 B1
Scotch Whisky Heritage Ctr
The* EH1 .....232 C2
Scotia PI FK2 .....60 C2
Scotland Dr KY12 ....29 C2
Scotland St EH3 .....93 B1
Scotlands Cl EH51 ....63 C4
Scotmill Way KY11 ....47 B2
Scots Mill PI KY11 ....47 C2
Scotstoun Ave EH30 ..89 B4
Scotstoun Gn EH30 ...89 A4
Scotstoun Pk EH30 ...89 B4
Scotstoun Rd FK7 ....20 C4
Scott Ave FK2 .....61 A1
Scott Cres FK10 .....10 A3
Scott Ct Alva FK12 ....5 A3
Livingston EH54 .....148 B3
Scott PI EH47 .....193 C3
Scott Rd EH26 .....203 C4
Scott St Dunfermline KY12 .28 C3
Grangemouth FK3 .....61 B3
Kirkcaldy KY1 .....17 A1
Stirling FK8 .....2 A2
Scott Terr EH48 .....145 B3
Scottish Ag Mus* EH28 119 C3
Scottish Ag Science Agency
EH12 ......121 A4
Scottish Korean War Meml
The* EH48 .....114 B3
Scottish Mining Mus*
EH22 ......183 A2
Scottish Nat Gall of Mod
Art* EH4 .....122 C4
Scottish Pol Coll FK10 .23 C3
Scottish Prison Service Coll
FK2 ......82 B4
Scottish Seabird Ctr*
EH39 ......54 B4
Sea Rd EH42 .....77 C1
Sea Wynd EH32 .....71 B3
Seabegs Cres FK4 ....58 A2
Seabegs PI FK4 .....57 C2
Seabegs Rd FK4 .....57 C2
Seacliff EH39 .....56 A3
Seacot EH6 .....94 B2
Seafield Ave EH6 .....94 B2
Seafield Cres
Bilston EH25 .....180 C3
Dunbar EH42 .....78 A1
Kirkcaldy KY1 .....35 A1
Seafield Ct FK1 .....59 C3
Seafield Gdns KY1 ....35 A4
Seafield Inf Sch EH54 .146 A1

Seafield Moor Rd EH25,
EH10 ......180 B3
Seafield PI
Dalgety Bay KY11 .....48 A1
Edinburgh EH6 .....94 B3
Seafield Rd Bilston EH25 180 C3
Blackburn EH47 .....171 C4
Edinburgh EH6 .....94 B2
Kirkcaldy KY1 .....35 A4
Seafield Rd E EH15 ...94 C2
Seafield Rows EH47 ..146 A1
Seafield St EH6 .....94 B2
Seafield View
Kinghorn KY3 .....35 A2
Kirkcaldy KY1 .....35 A4
Seafield Way EH15 ...94 C2
Seaforth Dr EH4 .....92 B1
Seaforth PI
Burntisland KY3 .....50 B4
Edinburgh EH6 .....93 C3
Stirling FK8 .....7 A4
Seaforth Rd FK2 .....39 B1
Seaforth Terr
Bonnyrigg & Lasswade
EH19 ......181 C3
4 Edinburgh EH5 ....92 C4
Sealcar St EH5 .....92 C4
Sealock Ct FK3 .....61 B3
Sealstrand KY11 .....48 B2
Seaport St EH6 .....94 A3
Seaside PI KY3 .....49 B4
Seaton PI FK1 .....60 A2
Seaview Cres EH15 ...125 C4
Seaview PI EH51 .....63 C4
Seaview Terr EH15 ...125 C4
Seco PI KY4 .....13 B2
Second Gait EH14 ....151 C4
Second St EH22 .....183 A2
Sedgebank EH54 .....147 C3
Seggarsdean Cres EH41 132 B4
Seggarsdean Ct EH41 .132 B4
Seggarsdean Pk EH41 .132 B4
Seggarsdean Terr EH41 132 B4
Selkirk Ave KY4 .....13 B1
Selkirk Rd KY11 .....67 A4
Selm Pk EH54 .....148 A2
Selvage PI KY11 .....47 A2
Selvage St KY11 .....47 A2
Semple St EH3 .....232 B2
Seton Chapel* EH32 ..97 C2
Seton Ct
Cockenzie & Port Seton
EH32 ......97 C2
Tranent EH33 .....128 B3
Seton Dr FK7 .....7 B2
Seton Mains EH32 ....98 A2
Seton PI
Cockenzie & Port Seton
EH32 ......97 B2
Dalgety Bay KY11 .....48 B3
Edinburgh EH9 .....123 C3
Kirkcaldy KY2 .....16 B4
Seton Sands Caravan Pk
EH32 ......97 C2
Seton Terr EH51 .....64 A4
Seton View EH32 .....97 C2
Seton Wynd EH32 ....97 C2
Seventh St EH22 .....183 A3
Shadepark Cres EH22 .157 A2
Shadepark Dr EH22 ...157 A2
Shadepark Gdns EH22 .157 A2
Shaftesbury Pk EH11 ..122 C2
Shaftesbury St FK10 ..10 A4
Shafto PI EH51 .....63 C3
Shamrock St KY12 ....29 A3
Shandon Cres EH11 ..122 C2
Shandon PI EH11 .....122 C2
Shandon Rd EH11 ....122 C2
Shandon St EH11 .....122 C2
Shandon Terr EH11 ...122 C2
Shandwick PI EH2 ....232 A3
Shanks Ave FK6 .....57 C4
Shanks Rd EH47 .....170 A4
Shannon Dr FK1 .....59 C2
Shanter Way 7 EH16 .124 A1
Sharp Terr FK3 .....61 B3
Sharpdale Loan EH16 .124 A2
Shaw Ave EH48 .....143 C3
Shaw Cres KY5 .....14 A4
Shaw PI Armadale EH48 .143 C2
Grangemouth FK3 .....61 B3
Mayfield EH22 .....183 B4
Shaw St KY11 .....29 B1
Shaw's Cres EH26 ....180 A1
Shaw's PI EH7 .....93 C2
Shaw's Sq EH1 .....93 C1
Shaw's St EH7 .....93 C2
Shaw's Terr EH7 .....93 C2
Shearer Sq KY11 .....29 C1
Sheephousehill EH47 ..193 C3
Sheperdlands Gr KY12 .26 B4
Shepherd Cres KY3 ...50 B4
Shepherds Loan KY11 .46 B2
Sheriff Bank EH6 .....93 C3
Sheriff Brae EH6 .....93 C3
Sheriff Pk EH6 .....93 C3
Sheriffhall Junc EH22 .156 B3
Sheriffmuir Rd FK9 ....2 A4
Sheriffmuirlands FK9 ..2 A2
Sheriffs Pk EH49 .....85 C4
Sherriff Hall Cotts EH39 .74 C4
Sherriff La KY5 .....38 C2
Sherwood Ave EH19 ..182 B3
Sherwood Cres EH19 .182 B3
Sherwood Ct EH19 ...182 B3
Sherwood Dr EH19 ...182 B3

Sherwood Gr EH19 ...182 B3
Sherwood Ind Est EH19 182 B4
Sherwood Loan EH19 .182 B3
Sherwood Pk EH19 ...182 B3
Sherwood PI EH19 ....182 B3
Sherwood Terr EH19 ..182 B3
Sherwood View EH19 .182 B3
Sherwood Way EH19 .182 B3
Sherwood Wlk EH19 ..182 B3
Shetland Ct FK10 .....10 A1
Shetland PI KY1 .....17 C4
Shiel Ct FK2 .....61 B2
Shiel Gdns Falkirk FK2 .39 B1
Shotts ML7 .....192 A2
Shiel Wlk EH54 .....148 A3
Shieldhill Prim Sch FK1 .81 B3
Shieldhill Rd FK2 .....82 A4
Shields Ct EH52 .....117 C3
Shields Rd KY11 .....29 C2
Shieling The KY12 ....27 C1
Shierlaw Gdns FK2 ...22 B2
Shillinghill FK10 .....10 A3
Shinwell PI KY11 .....46 C2
Shiphaugh PI FK8 ....2 B1
Shire Way FK10 .....9 C3
Shirra's Brae Rd FK7 ..7 A2
Shoestanes Rd EH38 .228 B1
Shoestanes Terr EH38 228 B1
Shore EH6 .....94 A3
Shore PI EH6 .....94 A3
Shore Rd Aberdour KY3 .49 B4
Airth FK2 .....22 C2
Dysart KY1 .....18 A3
Queensferry EH30 ....68 A1
Stirling FK8 .....7 B4
Shore St EH6 .....78 C2
Shore The FK10 .....10 A3
Shorthope St EH21 ...126 B3
Shotts Rd
Fauldhouse EH47 .....193 B2
Harthill ML7 .....167 C1
Shotts Sta ML7 .....191 C2
Shottsburn Rd ML7 ...167 A2
Shottskirk Rd ML7 ....191 B3
Shrub Mount EH15 ...95 A1
Shrub Place La EH7 ...93 C1
Sibbald PI EH54 .....147 A3
Sibbalds Brae EH48 ..143 A3
Sidegate EH41 .....132 A4
Sidegate Mews EH41 .132 A4
Sidehead Rd ML7 .....168 C3
Sidlaw PI FK3 .....61 B3
Sidlaw St KY2 .....16 C4
Sienna Gdns EH9 ....123 C3
Sighthill Ave EH11 ...121 C1
Sighthill Bank EH11 ..121 B1
Sighthill Cres EH11 ..121 B1
Sighthill Ct EH11 .....121 B1
Sighthill Dr EH11 ....121 B1
Sighthill Gdns EH11 ..121 B1
Sighthill Gn EH11 ....121 C1
Sighthill Gr EH11 ....121 C1
Sighthill Ind Est EH11 .121 A2
Sighthill Loan EH11 ..121 B1
Sighthill Neuk EH11 ..121 B1
Sighthill Pk EH11 ....121 B1
Sighthill Prim Sch EH11 121 B1
Sighthill Rd EH11 ....121 B1
Sighthill Rise EH11 ..121 B1
Sighthill St EH11 .....121 B1
Sighthill Terr EH11 ...121 B1
Sighthill View EH11 ..121 B1
Sighthill Wynd EH11 .121 B1
Silk Ho FK1 .....60 A3
Silver St Dunbar EH42 .78 B1
Kincardine FK10 .....23 C2
Silverbarton Terr KY3 .33 B1
Silverbirch Glade EH54 .173 B4
Silverburn Dr EH26 ..203 B3
Silverburn Gdns FK12 .5 B4
Silverdale Rd FK2 ....82 C4
Silverknowes Ave EH4 .91 C2
Silverknowes Bank EH4 91 C2
Silverknowes Brae EH4 92 A2
Silverknowes Cres EH4 91 C2
Silverknowes Ct EH4 ..91 C1
Silverknowes Dell EH4 .91 C2
Silverknowes Dr EH4 ..91 C2
Silverknowes Eastway
EH4 ......92 A2
Silverknowes Gdns EH4 92 A2
Silverknowes Gn EH4 .92 A1
Silverknowes Gr EH4 ..91 C3
Silverknowes Hill EH4 .91 C2
Silverknowes Loan EH4 91 C2
Silverknowes Midway
EH4 ......92 A1
Silverknowes Neuk EH4 92 A2
Silverknowes Parkway
EH4 ......91 C3
Silverknowes PI EH4 ..91 C3
Silverknowes Prim Sch
EH4 ......91 C2
Silverknowes Rd EH4 .91 C3
Silverknowes Rd E EH4 91 C2
Silverknowes Rd S EH4 91 C1
Silverknowes Southway
EH4 ......92 A2
Silverknowes Terr EH4 .91 C2
Silverknowes View EH4 92 A2
Silversands Nature Reserve*
KY3 ......49 B4
Simon Sq EH8 .....233 B2
Simpson Cres EH48 ..145 B3
Simpson Dr FK2 .....61 A1
Simpson Parkway EH54 147 A1
Simpson Rd EH52 ....118 A3

Simpson St FK1 .....59 C3
Simpson Wlk KY11 ...29 C1
Sinclair Cl EH11 .....122 C2
Sinclair Cres FK6 ....36 B1
Sinclair Ct Aberlady EH32 .71 B2
Bannockburn FK7 .....7 C1
Sinclair Dr
Cowdenbeath KY4 ....13 A1
Fallin FK7 .....8 B2
Sinclair Gdns
Dunfermline KY12 ....29 A2
Edinburgh EH11 .....122 C3
Sinclair PI
Edinburgh EH11 .....122 B3
Falkirk FK2 .....39 A1
Sinclair Way EH54 ...147 B3
Sinclairtown Prim Sch
KY1 ......17 C4
Sir George Bruce Rd
KY12 ......26 C4
Sir Harry Lauder Rd
EH15 ......125 A4
Sir James Black Gait
KY5 ......14 A4
Sir John Brown PI 46 C4
Sir John Graham Ct FK5 .38 A1
Sir Robert Maule PI
FK10 ......23 C2
Sir Walter Scott's Mon*
EH2 ......233 A3
Sir William Fraser Homes
EH13 ......153 A4
Sir William Wallace Ct
KY5 ......38 A2
Sivewright Ct FK10 ...23 C2
Sixth St EH22 .....183 A3
Skaithmuir Ave FK2 ..39 A2
Skaithmuir Cres FK2 ..39 A2
Skelmorlie PI FK5 ....38 C2
Skeltie Maur Ave EH19 .182 A3
Skene St EH54 .....58 A3
Skibo Ct KY12 .....29 A2
Skibo PI KY2 .....16 B3
Skye Ct FK3 .....61 B3
Skye Dr FK2 .....61 C1
Skye Rd KY11 .....29 C1
Skylaw Terr ML11 ....215 A1
Skythorn Way FK1 ...59 C1
Slaeside EH14 .....151 B1
Slamannan Prim Sch
FK1 ......110 A4
Slamannan Rd
Avonbridge FK1 .....112 A3
Falkirk FK1 .....60 A1
Slamannan FK1 .....110 A1
Slateford Gn EH14 ...122 B2
Slateford Rd EH14 ...122 B2
Slateford Sta EH14 ...122 B2
Sleigh Dr EH7 .....94 B1
Sleigh Gdns EH7 .....94 B1
Sligo St KY12 .....26 C4
Sloan St EH6 .....93 C2
Small St KY5 .....14 A3
Smallburn PI FK3 ....61 C3
Smeaton Gdns KY7 ...17 B3
Smeaton Gr EH21 ....126 B2
Smeaton Ind Site KY1 .17 B4
Smeaton Rd KY1 .....17 B3
Smiddy Brae FK2 .....61 C2
Smiddy Wynd Alva FK12 .5 A3
Newmills KY12 .....26 B1
Smileyknowes Ct EH39 .54 A3
Smith Art Gallery & Mus*
FK8 ......2 A1
Smith Ave KY4 .....13 A2
Smith PI FK6 .....36 B1
Smith St FK2 .....60 A4
Smith's PI EH6 .....93 C2
Smith's Terr 11 KY1 ...9 C3
Smithfield Loan FK10 ..5 B1
Smithfield St EH11 ...122 B3
Smithy Brae EH27 ....149 C1
Smithy Green Ave EH22 156 A4
Smithy Row EH39 ....74 A2
Snab Brae EH51 .....63 B4
Snab La EH51 .....63 B4
Snowden Sch Ltd FK8 .7 A4
Snowdon PI FK8 .....7 A3
Snowdon Place La FK7 .7 A3
Society La EH55 .....172 B2
Society PI EH55 .....172 B2
Society Rd EH30 .....67 C1
Solway Dr FK6 .....57 B4
Somers Pk EH33 .....128 B3
Somerset PI EH6 .....94 A2
Somerville Rd KY11 ...46 B1
Somerville St KY3 ....50 C4
Sommers Pk EH53 ...148 B1
Sommerville Gdns FK9 .2 A3
Somerfield Ave EH41 .131 C4
Somerfield Ct EH41 ..131 C4
Somerfield Gr EH41 ..131 C4
Somerfield PI EH41 ..131 C4
Souillac Dr FK6 .....36 B1
Souter Way FK5 .....38 B2
South Acres KY12 ....27 B1
South Approach Rd FK2 .23 A1
South Ave Blairhall KY12 .26 A4
South Bank FK10 .....5 B1
South Bantaskine Dr
FK1 ......60 A2
South Bantaskine Rd
FK1 ......60 A2

South Barnton Ave EH4 ....91 C2
South Beechwood EH12 .122 A3
South Brae FK2 ....83 A3
South Bridge EH1 ....233 A3
South Bridge St
　Bathgate EH48 ....145 A3
　Grangemouth FK3 ....40 B1
South Broomage Ave
　FK5 ....38 B1
South Castle Dr FK4 .....46 C3
South Charlotte St EH2 ..232 B3
South Clerk St EH8 ......233 B1
South College St EH8 ...233 A2
South Craigs Rd FK2 .....82 C4
South Cres
　East Saltoun EH34 ......161 C2
　Prestonpans EH32 ....97 A1
South Dewar St KY12 ......28 C2
South Doors EH32 ....97 B2
South Dr KY12 ....28 C2
South East Circus Pl
　EH3 ....232 B4
South East Cumberland
　Street La EH3 ....93 B1
South Elizabeth Street La
　EH2 ....232 C4
South Eliza Pl EH8 ......124 B4
South Ettrick Rd EH10 ..122 C2
South Fergus Pl KY1 .....17 A2
South Fort St EH6 ....93 C3
South Gait EH39 ....53 C4
South Gayfield La 🔢
　EH1 ....93 C1
South Gillsland Rd
　EH10 ....122 C2
South Grange Ave EH32 ..127 C4
South Gray St EH9 ......123 C2
South Gray's Cl EH1 ....233 B3
South Green Dr FK2 ......22 C2
South Groathill Ave FK4 .92 B1
South Gyle Access
　EH12 ....121 B2
South Gyle Broadway
　EH12 ....121 A2
South Gyle Cres EH12 ...121 A2
South Gyle Crescent La
　EH12 ....121 A3
South Gyle Ind Est
　EH12 ....121 A3
South Gyle Loan EH12 ...121 A3
South Gyle Mains EH12 ..121 A3
South Gyle Pk
　Edinburgh EH12 ....121 A2
　Edinburgh EH12 ....121 A3
South Gyle Rd EH12 .....121 A3
South Gyle Sta EH12 ....121 A3
South Gyle Wynd EH12 ...121 B2
South Hamilton Rd 🔢
　EH39 ....54 A4
South Hill St KY3 ....50 C4
South Hirst Rd ML7 .....167 B2
South Knowe KY4 ....30 C3
South Larch Rd KY11 .....29 C2
South Lauder Rd EH9 ...123 C2
South Laverockbank Ave
　EH5 ....93 C4
South Learmonth Ave 🔢
　EH4 ....92 C1
South Learmonth Gdns 🔢
　EH4 ....92 C1
South Loanhead KY11 ....45 C2
South Loch Pk EH48 ....145 A3
South Lodge Ave EH53 ..148 B1
South Lorimer Pl EH42 ..97 B2
South Lorne Pl 🔢 EH6 ..93 C2
South Lumley St FK3 .....61 B4
South Marshall St FK3 ...61 B4
South Maybury EH12 ....121 A3
South Mellis Pk EH8 ...124 C4
South Melville La FK4 ...60 A3
South Mid St EH48 .....145 A3
South Morningside Prim Sch
　EH10 ....123 A1
South Morton St EH15 ..125 B4
South Oswald Rd EH9 ..123 B2
South Overgate KY3 ......35 A2
South Oxford St EH8 ...123 C2
South Parrotshot EH15 ..125 A3
South Philipingstone La
　EH51 ....64 B4
South Pilmuir Rd FK10 ..11 A2
South Pk Armadale EH48 143 C2
　Edinburgh EH6 ....93 B3
South Pleasance Ave
　FK1 ....60 A2
South Rd
　Fauldhouse EH47 ....193 C4
　Grangemouth FK3 ....62 A3
South Roundall KY11 .....45 C2
South Row
　Charlestown KY11 ....45 A2
　Kirkcaldy KY1 ....17 C4
South Scottoun EH30 ....89 B4
South Seton Pk EH32 ....97 B2
South Shore Rd FK3 .....41 A1
South Sloan St EH6 .....93 C2
South St Armadale EH48 .143 C3
　Bo'ness EH51 ....63 C4
　Cambus FK10 ....9 C4
　Cowdenbeath KY4 ....13 B1
　Dalkeith EH22 ....157 A2
　Dunbar EH42 ....78 A1
　Musselburgh EH21 ......126 A3
　Stirling FK9 ....2 B1
South St Andrew St
　EH2 ....233 A4

South St David St EH2 ..233 A3
South Steil EH10 ....122 C1
South Trinity Rd EH5 ....93 A3
South View
　Burntisland KY3 ....50 C4
　Stenhousemuir FK5 ......38 B1
South Village EH53 .....148 B3
South West Cumberland
　Street La EH3 ....93 B1
South West Thistle Street La
　EH2 ....232 B3
Southbank EH4 ....91 C2
Southbank Ct EH4 ....91 C2
Southcroft FK12 ....4 C3
Southern Cres KY2 ......16 C2
Southerton Gdns KY2 ...16 C2
Southerton Rd KY2 .....16 C2
Southerton Terr KY2 ....16 C2
Southfield Ave ML7 ....192 A2
Southfield Bank EH15 ..124 C3
Southfield Cres
　Shotts ML7 ....192 A2
　Stirling FK8 ....7 A3
Southfield Ct EH42 ......78 A1
Southfield Dr FK1 ......110 A3
Southfield Farm Gr
　EH15 ....124 C4
Southfield Gdns E EH15 124 C4
Southfield Gdns W
　EH15 ....124 C3
Southfield Hospl EH17 .155 B4
Southfield Loan EH15 ..124 C3
Southfield Loan EH17 ..124 C3
Southfield Pl EH15 .....125 A4
Southfield Rd
　Cousland EH22 ....158 B3
　Shotts ML7 ....192 A2
Southfield Rd E EH15 ..124 C3
Southfield Rd W EH15 ..124 C3
Southfield Sq EH15 ....124 C3
Southfield Terr EH15 ..124 C3
Southhouse Ave EH17 ..155 A3
Southhouse Broadway
　EH17 ....155 A2
Southhouse Cres EH17 .155 B2
Southhouse Gdns EH17 155 B2
Southhouse Gr EH17 ...155 A2
Southhouse Loan EH17 155 A3
Southhouse Medway
　EH17 ....155 A2
Southhouse Rd EH17 ...155 A2
Southhouse Sq EH17 ...155 A3
Southhouse Terr EH17 .155 B3
Southlawn Ct EH4 ....91 C2
Soutra Aisle* EH37 ....211 A1
Sovereign Ct EH48 .....144 A3
Spa Pl EH15 ....95 A1
Spalding Cres EH7 .....157 A2
Speedwell Ave EH22 ...156 A4
Spence Ave KY3 ....33 C1
Spence St
　Bonnybridge FK4 ....58 A3
　Edinburgh EH16 ....123 C3
Spencer Pl Edinburgh EH5 93 A3
　Kirkcaldy KY1 ....17 A2
Spencerfield Rd KY11 ...47 B1
Spencerfield Steadings
　KY11 ....47 C2
Spens La KY11 ....46 B1
Spey Ct Grangemouth FK3 61 B3
　Stirling FK7 ....7 A3
Spey Dr EH54 ....148 A2
Spey St EH7 ....93 C2
Spey Street La EH7 ......93 C2
Spey Terr EH7 ....93 C2
Spier's Pl EH6 ....93 C3
Spilmersford View
　EH34 ....161 A3
Spinkhill FK2 ....60 C1
Spinnaker Way KY11 ....47 C1
Spinner's Ct KY12 ....27 B1
Spinney The FK7 ....155 B3
Spinneys The KY11 ......48 B2
Spittal Hill FK9 ....2 B2
Spittal St Edinburgh EH3 232 B2
　Stirling FK8 ....7 A4
Spittalfield Cres KY11 ..47 B1
Spittalfield Rd KY11 ....47 B1
Spott Ave EH42 ....106 B2
Spott Loan EH42 ....106 B2
Spott Rd EH42 ....78 C1
Spottiswoode Gdns
　EH53 ....148 B1
Spottiswoode Rd EH9 ..123 B3
Spottiswoode St EH9 ..123 B3
Sprig Way ML7 ....168 C3
Spring Gdns EH8 ....94 A1
Springbank Gdns FK2 ...60 B3
Springbank Rd
　Shotts ML7 ....191 B3
　Stirling FK7 ....7 B3
Springbank Terr KY12 ...29 A3
Springfield Edinburgh EH6 93 C2
　West Barns EH42 ....77 C2
Springfield Cres
　🔢 North Berwick EH39 ..54 A4
　Queensferry EH30 ....89 B4
Springfield Dr FK1 ......93 C2
Springfield Gdns 🔢
　EH39 ....54 A4
Springfield La 🔢 EH6 ...93 C2
Springfield Lea EH30 ....67 C1
Springfield Pl
　Gorebridge EH23 ....207 B4
　Queensferry EH30 ....67 C1
　Roslin EH25 ....181 A2

Springfield Prim Sch
　EH49 ....85 B4
Springfield Rd Alloa FK10 10 B4
　Denny FK6 ....36 C1
　Linlithgow EH49 ....85 B4
　Penicuik EH26 ....222 C3
　Queensferry EH30 ....67 C1
　Stirling FK7 ....7 A3
Springfield St EH6 ......93 C2
Springfield Terr
　Queensferry EH30 ....67 C1
　West Barns EH42 ....77 C1
Springfield View EH30 ..68 A1
Springhead Rd ML7 ....212 A4
Springhill & Leadloch Rd
　ML7,EH47 ....192 C1
Springhill Brae KY4 ....103 C4
Springhill Rd ML7 .....192 A2
Springhill View ML7 ...192 A2
Springkerse Ind Est FK7 .7 B3
Springkerse Rd FK7 ......7 B3
Springkerse Rdbt FK7 ...7 A3
Springvalley Gdns EH10 123 A2
Springvalley Terr EH10 .123 A2
Springwell Pl EH11 ....122 C3
Springwood Rosyth KY11 .47 A4
　Stirling FK7 ....7 A3
Springwood Ave EH16 ..155 A4
Springwood Pk EH16 ...155 A4
Sprinty Ave EH35 ......159 B4
Sprinty Dr EH35 ....159 B4
Sprotwell Terr FK10 .....5 B1
Spruce Dr EH47 ....170 B3
Spruce Gr
　Dumfermline KY11 ....46 B4
　Livingston EH54 ....148 A3
Spylaw Ave EH13 ......152 C4
Spylaw Bank Rd EH13 .153 A4
Spylaw Pk EH13 ....152 C4
Spylaw Rd EH10 ....122 C2
Spylaw St EH13 ....153 A4
Square The
　Cockburnspath TD13 ...140 C2
　Danderhall EH22 ....156 A4
　East Linton EH40 ......103 C4
　Fallin FK7 ....8 B2
　Gifford EH41 ....163 C3
　Newtongrange EH22 ....183 A3
　Spott EH42 ....106 B2
　Torphichen EH48 ....84 C3
Sraebouse Wynd ML8 ..202 A1
Stable La EH10 ....123 A2
Stable Rd ML7 ....192 A3
Stables Cl KY11 ....46 B1
Stables The EH22 ......183 A4
Staffa FK4 ....60 A1
Staffa Pl FK1 ....60 A1
Stafford St EH3 ....232 A3
Stair Pk Edinburgh EH12 122 B4
　North Berwick EH39 .....54 A3
　Tranent EH33 ....128 A4
Standalane EH10 ....123 A2
Standhill EH48 ....144 C2
Standhill Ct EH48 ......144 C2
Standing Stone Wlk
　KY11 ....29 C1
Standingstone Rd EH30 ..89 C3
Standrigg Rd FK1,FK2 ...82 A3
Stane Prim Sch ML7 ...192 A2
Stane Rd ML7 ....192 A1
Stanedykehead EH16 ..154 C3
Stanhope Pl EH12 .....122 C4
Stanhope St EH12 .....122 C4
Stanistone Rd ML8 ....230 A1
Stankards Rd EH52 ....116 C2
Stanley Ave EH55 .....180 C3
Stanley Dr Bridge of A FK9 .2 A4
　Newtongrange EH22 ......23 A1
Stanley Gdns FK2 ......82 C3
Stanley Pk KY11 ....47 A3
Stanley Pl Edinburgh EH7 94 A1
　Ormiston EH35 ....159 C4
Stanley Rd Edinburgh EH6 93 B3
　Gullane EH31 ....52 A3
　Harthill ML7 ....169 A3
Stanley St EH15 ....125 A4
Stanley Terr KY12 ......27 A3
Stanton Ave FK10 ....9 C3
Stanwell St EH6 ....93 C2
Stapeley Ave EH7 ....94 C1
Starbank Rd EH5 ....93 B3
Stark Ave FK1 ....59 A3
Stark's Brae EH5,ES1 ...64 A4
Stark's Park (Raith Rovers
　FC) KY1 ....17 A1
Starlaw Ave EH48 .....145 C3
Starlaw Bsns Pk EH54 .146 B2
Starlaw Cres EH48 ....145 C3
Starlaw Gdns EH48 ....145 C3
Starlaw Rd EH47,EH54 .146 B2
Starlaw Terr EH48 .....145 C3
Starlaw West Rdbt
　EH47 ....146 A2
Starlaw Wlk EH48 .....145 C3
Starley Hall Sch KY3 ....50 A4
Starryshaw Rd ML7 ....191 C3
Station Ave EH41 ......131 C4
Station Brae
　Edinburgh EH15 ....125 A4
　Kinghorn KY3 ....34 C1
Station Ct
　Addiewell EH55 ....171 C1
　Haddington EH41 ......131 C4
　North Berwick EH39 ....54 A4
Station Loan EH14 ....151 B2

Station Pl KY3 ....49 B4
Station Rd
　Addiewell EH55 ....171 C1
　Armadale EH48 ....143 C2
　Bannockburn FK7 ....7 C1
　Blackridge EH48 ....142 B1
　Bridge of A FK9 ....1 C4
　Brightons FK2 ....61 C1
　Broxburn EH52 ....117 C3
　Cambus FK10 ....4 A1
　Cowdenbeath KY4 ....13 B2
　Cowie FK7 ....20 B3
　Dalkeith EH22 ....156 C1
　Dirleton EH39 ....53 B2
　Dunbar EH42 ....78 C1
　Dysart KY1 ....18 A4
　East Linton EH40 ......103 C4
　Edinburgh EH12 ....121 C3
　Gifford EH41 ....163 C3
　Gorebridge EH23 ....207 B4
　Grangemouth FK3 ....40 B1
　Gullane EH31 ....52 A1
　Haddington EH41 ......132 A4
　Kincardine FK10 ....23 B2
　Kirkcaldy KY2 ....17 A2
　Kirkliston EH29 ....89 A1
　Kirknewton EH27 ......149 B2
　Linlithgow EH49 ....85 A4
　Loanhead EH20 ....181 B4
　Lochgelly KY5 ....14 A4
　Longcroft FK4 ....57 A2
　Musselburgh EH21 .....126 B3
　Newtongrange EH22 ....183 A3
　North Berwick EH39 ....54 A4
　Oakley KY12 ....26 C3
　Prestonpans EH32 .....128 A4
　Queensferry EH30 ....68 B1
　Ratho Sta EH28 ....119 B3
　Roslin EH25 ....181 A2
　Shotts ML7 ....191 C2
　Slamannan FK1 ....110 A3
Station Row
　Macmerry EH33 ....128 A2
　🔢 North Berwick EH39 ..54 A4
Station Terr EH29 ....89 A1
Station View EH30 ......89 B4
Station Yd KY3 ....35 A1
Staunton Rise EH54 ...173 B4
Steads Pl EH6 ....93 C2
Steading The EH22 ......98 B1
Steadings The EH42 .....84 A4
Steel Gr KY12 ....26 B4
Steel's Pl EH10 ....123 A2
Steelyard The 🔢 EH48 .145 A3
Steeple Cres KY11 ......48 A2
Steil Gr EH33 ....183 C3
Steils The EH10 ....122 C1
Stein Sq FK7 ....7 A3
Stein's Pl KY4 ....13 C3
Stenhouse Ave EH11 ...122 A2
Stenhouse Ave W EH11 122 A2
Stenhouse Cotts EH11 .122 A2
Stenhouse Cross EH11 .122 A2
Stenhouse Dr
　Burntisland KY3 ....33 B1
　Edinburgh EH11 ....122 A2
Stenhouse Gdns EH11 .122 A2
Stenhouse Gdns N
　EH11 ....122 A2
Stenhouse Gr EH11 ....122 A2
Stenhouse Mill Cres
　EH11 ....122 A2
Stenhouse Mill La EH11 122 A2
Stenhouse Mill Wynd
　EH11 ....122 A2
Stenhouse Pl E EH11 ..122 A2
Stenhouse Pl W EH11 ..122 A2
Stenhouse Prim Sch
　EH11 ....122 A2
Stenhouse Rd
　Edinburgh EH11 ....122 A2
　Stenhousemuir FK5 .....38 C1
Stenhouse St E EH11 ...13 A2
Stenhouse St W EH11 ..121 C2
Stenhouse Terr EH11 ..122 A2
Stenhousemuir Prim Sch
　FK5 ....38 C2
Stennis Gdns EH17 ....155 B4
Stenton Loan EH42 ....135 C4
Stenton Prim Sch EH42 104 C1
Stenton Rd EH42 ......105 C4
Stephen Pl KY5 ....14 A4
Stephen's Dr KY12 ......47 B2
Steps St FK5 ....38 C2
Sterling (annexe) YH*
　FK8 ....2 A3
Steuart Rd FK9 ....1 C4
Stevenlaw's Cl EH1 .....93 C1
Stevenson Ave FK11 ...122 B3
Stevenson Coll EH11 ...121 B2
Stevenson Ct
　Bridge of A FK9 ....2 A3
　Longniddry EH32 ....98 B2
Stevenson Dr EH11 ....122 A2
Stevenson La EH22 ....183 A2
Stevenson Rd EH22 .....98 B2
Stevenson Pl EH18 ....181 B3

Stevenson Rd
　Edinburgh EH11 ....122 B3
　Penicuik EH26 ....204 A4
Stevenson St FK3 ....61 B3
Stevenson Terr
　Bathgate EH48 ....145 B3
　Edinburgh EH11 ....122 B3
Stevenson Way EH32 ....98 B2
Stewart Ave Bo'ness EH51 63 C4
　Currie EH14 ....151 C2
　Falkirk FK2 ....39 A1
　Linlithgow EH49 ....84 C3
Stewart Clark Ave EH30 .89 B4
Stewart Cres
　Currie EH14 ....151 C2
　Lochgelly KY5 ....14 A4
Stewart Dr EH47 ....169 C4
Stewart Gdns EH14 ....151 C2
Stewart Gr
　Danderhall EH22 ......156 A4
　Harthill ML7 ....168 C3
Stewart Pl Currie EH14 .151 C2
　Kirkliston EH29 ....89 A1
Stewart Rd Currie EH14 151 C2
　Falkirk FK2 ....60 B3
Stewart Sq KY5 ....2 A1
Stewart St
　Bonnybridge FK4 ....57 C3
　Cambusbarron FK7 ....6 B3
　Dysart KY1 ....18 A4
　Townhill KY12 ....29 B4
　West Calder EH55 ......172 B1
Stewart Terr
　Edinburgh EH11 ....122 C3
　Queensferry EH30 ....68 A1
Stewart Way FK4 ......147 B3
Stewart's Melville Coll
　EH4 ....92 C1
Stewartfield EH6 ....93 B2
Stewartfield Cres EH52 117 C2
Stewartfield Rd EH52 ..117 C3
Stirling Bsns Ctr FK8 ....7 A3
Stirling Castle* FK8 .....1 C1
Stirling Ct FK7 ....7 B4
Stirling E Ed Ctr FK7 .....7 A3
Stirling High Sch FK8 ....7 A3
Stirling Pl FK7 ....20 B2
Stirling Rd Alloa FK10 ...9 C4
　Alva FK12 ....5 C4
　Edinburgh EH5 ....93 A3
　Falkirk FK1,FK5 ....59 B4
　Fallin FK7 ....8 B2
　Torwood FK5 ....5 A3
　Tullibody FK10 ....4 A2
Stirling Royal Infmy FK8 .7 A3
Stirling St Alva FK12 .....5 A4
　Denny FK6 ....36 B2
Stirling Sta FK8 ....7 A3
Stobhill Prim Sch EH23 207 B4
Stobhill Rd EH23 ......183 A2
Stobie Pl KY12 ....26 C4
Stobs Pl KY2 ....16 C4
Stockbridge Prim Sch
　EH3 ....93 A1
Stone Ave EH22 ....183 B3
Stone Cres EH22 ......183 B3
Stone Pl EH22 ....183 B3
Stonebank EH54 ......147 C3
Stonedyke Cres ML8 ..230 A2
Stonedyke Rd ML8 ....230 A2
Stonehaap Crofts EH47 194 C4
Stonelaws Cotts EH40 .75 A3
Stoneybank Ave EH21 ..126 A3
Stoneybank Cres EH21 126 A3
Stoneybank Ct EH21 ..126 A3
Stoneybank Dr EH21 ..126 A3
Stoneybank Gdns EH21 126 A3
Stoneybank Gdns N
　EH21 ....126 A3
Stoneybank Gdns S
　EH21 ....126 A3
Stoneybank Gr EH21 ..126 A3
Stoneybank Pl EH21 ..126 A3
Stoneybank Rd EH21 ..126 A3
Stoneybank Terr EH21 126 A3
Stoneyburn Prim Sch
　EH47 ....171 B2
Stoneycroft Rd EH30 ...68 B1
Stoneyflatts EH30 ......89 A4
Stoneyflatts Cres EH30 .89 A4
Stoneyflatts Pk EH30 ...89 A4
Stoneyhill Ave EH21 ..126 A3
Stoneyhill Cres EH21 ..126 A3
Stoneyhill Ct EH21 ....126 A3
Stoneyhill Dr EH21 ....126 A3
Stoneyhill Farm Rd
　EH21 ....126 A3
Stoneyhill Gr EH21 ....126 A3
Stoneyhill Pl EH21 ....126 A3
Stoneyhill Rd EH21 ....126 A3
Stoneyhill Terr EH21 ..126 A3
Stoneyhill Wynd 🔢
　EH21 ....126 A3
Stoneywood Pk FK6 .....36 A1
Stony Brae FK10 ....24 B1
Stories Pk EH40 ....103 C4
Strachan Ct EH51 ....63 B4
Strachan Gdns EH4 .....92 A1
Strachan Rd EH4 ....92 A1

Strachan St FK1 .....59 C2
Straiton Mains EH20 ...155 A1
Straiton Pk EH20 ....155 A1
Straiton Pl EH15 ....125 A4
Straiton Rd
 Loanhead EH20 .....180 C4
 Straiton EH20 ......155 A1
Strand Dr EH48 .....144 C1
Strang's Pl FK1 ....81 C3
Strathallan Ct FK4 ...2 A3
Strathallan Dr KY2 ...16 C3
Strathallan Rd FK4 ...9 B4
Strathalmond Ct EH4 ...90 C2
Strathalmond Gn EH4 ...90 C2
Strathalmond Pk EH4 ...90 C2
Strathalmond Rd EH4 ...90 C2
Strathavon Terr EH48 ..112 C3
Strathbeg Dr KY11 ...47 C2
Strathbrock Pl
 Broxburn EH52 .....117 C3
 Uphall EH52 ....116 C2
Strathearn Ct
 Grangemouth FK3 ...61 C4
 West Barns EH42 ...77 C1
Strathearn Pl EH9 ...123 A2
Strathearn Rd
 Edinburgh EH9 ....123 B2
 Kirkcaldy KY1 .....17 C4
 North Berwick EH39 ..53 C4
Strathesk Gr EH26 ...204 A3
Strathesk Pl EH26 ...204 A3
Strathfillan Rd EH9 ..123 B2
Strathkinnes Rd KY2 ..17 A2
Strathlachlan Ave ML8 .230 A1
Strathlogie EH48 ....112 C3
Strathmiglo Pl FK5 ...38 C2
Strathmore Cres FK9 ...46 B3
Strathmore Dr
 Dunfermline KY12 ...29 B3
 Stirling FK9 ....2 A2
Strathmore St KY3 ...34 C2
Strathyre Dr FK47 ...171 B1
Strawberry Bank
 Dalkeith EH22 .....156 C1
 Linlithgow EH49 ...85 A3
Streets Pl KY12 .....29 B4
Stripehead 🄿 FK10 ..10 A3
Striven Dr FK2 ......39 B1
Striven Pl KY2 ......16 C4
Stromness Gdns EH54 .173 B3
Strowan Rd FK3 .....61 C4
Strowan Sq EH54 ....61 C4
Struan Dr KY11 .....47 A2
Struan Pl KY11 .....47 A2
Strude Howe FK12 ...5 A4
Strude Mill FK12 ....5 A4
Strude St FK12 ......5 A4
Stuart Cres EH12 ...121 A4
Stuart Ct Bathgate EH48 .143 A4
 Edinburgh EH12 ...121 A4
Stuart Gn EH12 .....121 A4
Stuart Gr FK3 ....61 A3
Stuart Pk EH12 .....121 A4
Stuart Pl KY4 ....13 B3
Stuart Rd KY11 .....46 B1
Stuart Sq EH12 .....121 A4
Stuart Terr EH48 ...145 A3
Stuart Wynd EH12 ...121 A4
Styles Pl FK1 ....59 C1
Succoth Ave EH12 ...122 B4
Succoth Ct EH12 ....122 B4
Succoth Gdns EH12 ...122 B4
Succoth Pk EH12 ....122 B4
Succoth Pl EH12 ....122 B4
Suffolk Rd EH16 ....123 C2
Sugarhouse Cl EH8 ...233 B3
Suilven Hts FK2 ....61 A2
Summer Bank EH3 ...93 B1
Summer Pl FK43 .....4 A2
Summerfield Gdns EH6 .94 A2
Summerfield Pk EH42 ..78 A1
Summerfield Pl EH6 ...94 A2
Summerford FK1 ....59 B2
Summerford Gdns FK1 .59 B2
Summerford Rd FK1 ...59 B2
Summerhall EH8 ....233 B1
Summerhall Cres EH9 ..233 B1
Summerhall Pl EH9 ...233 B1
Summerhall Sq EH9 ...233 B1
Summerlee EH22 ....96 C1
Summerside Pl EH6 ...93 B3
Summerside St EH6 ...93 B3
Summertrees Ct EH16 ..124 A1
Summerville Ct EH54 ...148 A4
Suna Path ML7 .....192 A2
Sunart Pl FK3 ......61 B3
Sunbury Mews EH4 ...122 C4
Sunbury Pl EH4 ....122 C4
Sundew Glade EH54 ...173 B4
Sunningdale La KY12 ..28 B3
Sunnybank ML7 ....191 C3
Sunnybank Rd FK7 ...7 A2
Sunnybank Terr 🄿 EH7 .94 A1
Sunnybrae ML11 ...215 A1
Sunnydale Dr EH48 ...142 C2
Sunnydale Rd EH48 ...142 C2
Sunnylaw Pl FK1 ....59 C2
Sunnylaw Rd FK9 ....2 A4
Sunnyside Edinburgh EH7 .94 A1
 Stirling FK7 ....2 A2
 Stoneyburn EH47 ...171 A1
Sunnyside Ave EH48 ...94 C4
Sunnyside Cotts FK2 ...82 B4
Sunnyside Ct Alloa FK10 .10 B4

Sunnyside Ct continued
 Cowdenbeath KY4 ...13 B2
Sunnyside Pl KY5 ...14 A3
Sunnyside Prim Sch
 FK10 ....10 A4
Sunnyside Rd Alloa FK10 .10 A4
 Brightons FK2 .....82 B4
 Falkirk FK1 ....59 C3
Sunnyside St FK1 ...59 C3
Surcoat Loan FK7 ...7 C2
Sutherland Ave
 Alloa FK10 ....10 B4
 Stirling FK9 ....2 A2
Sutherland Cres EH48 ..145 A3
Sutherland Dr FK6 ...57 B4
Sutherland Pl KY1 ...17 C4
Sutherland St EH12 ..122 C4
Sutherland Way EH54 ..147 B3
Suttie Way FK9 .....1 C4
Suttieslea Cres EH22 ..183 B3
Suttieslea Dr EH22 ...183 B3
Suttieslea Pl EH22 ...183 B3
Suttieslea Rd EH22 ...183 B3
Suttieslea Wlk EH22 ..183 B3
Sutton Pk Cres FK5 ...38 C2
Sutton Pl FK2 ......60 B3
Swallow Craig KY11 ..42 A4
Swallowdrum Rd KY12 .28 B3
Swan Cres FK23 ....207 B4
Swan Pl FK3 ....61 B3
Swan Rd Kirkcaldy KY1 .60 C4
 Tranent EH33 .....128 B3
Swan Spring Ave EH10 .154 A4
Swanfield EH6 ......93 C3
Swanston Ave EH10 ...154 A3
Swanston Cres EH10 ..154 A3
Swanston Dr EH10 ...154 A2
Swanston Gdns EH10 ..154 A3
Swanston Gn EH10 ...154 A3
Swanston Gr EH10 ...154 A2
Swanston Loan EH10 ..154 A3
Swanston Muir EH10 ..153 C3
Swanston Pk EH10 ...154 A3
Swanston Pl EH10 ...154 A3
Swanston Rd EH10 ...154 A2
Swanston Row EH10 ..154 A3
Swanston Terr EH10 ..154 A3
Swanston Way EH10 ..154 A3
Swift Brae EH54 ....147 B3
Swinburne Dr FK10 ...5 A1
Swintons Pl KY4 ....12 C1
Sword's Way FK7 ....39 A1
Sycamore Ave
 Bo'ness EH51 ......63 B3
 Cockenzie & Port Seton
 EH32 ....97 B2
 Kirkcaldy KY1 .....17 B4
Sycamore Cres KY4 ...13 B3
Sycamore Dr EH47 ...170 B3
Sycamore Gdns EH12 ..121 C3
Sycamore Glade EH54 .173 B4
Sycamore Gr
 Dunfermline KY11 ...46 B4
 Winchburgh EH52 ...87 C1
Sycamore Pl FK8 ....6 C2
Sycamore Rd EH22 ...183 C3
Sycamore Wlk EH47 ..171 B4
Sycamores The FK10 ...4 A1
Sydney Pk EH7 .....94 C1
Sydney Pl EH7 .....94 C1
Sydney St EH54 ....148 A3
Sydney Terr EH7 ....94 C1
Sylvan Gr EH51 ....63 B3
Sylvan Pl EH9 .....123 A3
Sylvan Way EH48 ...144 C3
Syme Pl Edinburgh EH13 .153 C4
 Rosyth KY11 ......46 B3
Syme Rigg EH10 ....153 C4
Symington Pl FK2 ...39 A2

T

Ta-Verne La KY11 ...29 B1
Tailend Ind Pk EH54 ..146 B2
Tailend Rdbt EH54 ...146 B2
Tait Dr Larbert FK5 ...59 B4
 Penicuik EH26 .....203 C3
Tait St EH22 ....157 A2
Talbot St FK1 ......61 A3
Talisker FK10 ......4 A4
Talisman Pl EH16 ...124 A1
Talisman Rise EH54 ..173 B4
Talman Gdns FK2 ...61 C2
Tam O'Shanter Dr FK7 .22 A3
Tamfourhill Ave FK1 ..59 B2
Tamfourhill Ind Est FK1 .59 B2
Tamfourhill Rd FK1 ...59 B2
Tanera Ct FK1 .....60 A1
Tanhouse Brae KY12 ..42 B4
Tanners Rd FK1 ....60 A2
Tannery La FK8 ....2 A1
Tantallon Castle* EH39 .55 C4
Tantallon Dr FK2 ...39 A2
Tantallon Gdns EH54 .173 C3
Tantallon Pl EH9 ...123 A3
Tantallon Rd EH39 ...54 C3
Tantallon Terr EH39 ...54 C4
Tapitlaw Gr KY12 ...26 B4
Tappoch Pl FK5 ....38 A2
Taransay Dr FK2 ...61 C1
Tarbert Pl FK2 .....61 C1
Tarbert Terr FK10 ...23 C2
Tarbet Pl ML8 .....230 A1
Tarbrax Path ML7 ...192 A2
Tarbrax Rd EH55 ...217 C1
Tarduff Dr FK2 .....83 A3

Tarduff Pl FK6 .....36 A1
Targate Rd KY12 ...28 B3
Targe Wynd FK7 ...7 C2
Targe Rd FK3 ......62 B4
Tartraven Pl EH52 ...118 A3
Tarvit St EH3 ......232 C1
Tashieburn Rd ML11 ..215 C1
Tavern Cotts KY4 ....30 C4
Taxi Way KY11 .....48 B3
Tay Ct FK10 ....10 B3
Tay Pl ML7 ....191 C3
Tay St Edinburgh EH11 .122 C3
 Falkirk FK2 ....39 B1
 Grangemouth FK3 ...40 A1
Tay Terr KY11 .....29 C1
Tay Wlk EH54 .....148 A2
Taylor Ave KY4 ....13 B2
Taylor Ct Falkirk FK2 ..60 B4
 Grangemouth FK3 ...61 C4
Taylor Gdns EH6 ...93 C3
Taylor Gn EH54 ....147 B4
Taylor Pl Dalkeith EH22 .157 B1
 🄿 Edinburgh EH8 ...94 A1
Taylor Rd EH47 ....169 C3
Taylor's Rd FK5 ....38 B1
Taymouth Rd FK2 ...62 A1
Teal Pl KY11 ......30 A1
Tedder St FK1 .....61 B3
Telferton EH7 .....94 C1
Telford Coll (North Campus)
 EH5 ....92 C3
Telford Coll (South Campus)
 EH4 ....92 C1
Telford Ct FK2 .....39 A2
Telford Dr EH4 ....92 B2
Telford Gdns EH4 ...92 B2
Telford Pl Edinburgh EH4 .92 B2
 Linlithgow EH49 ...84 B4
Telford Rd EH4 ....92 B2
Telford Sq Falkirk FK1 .59 C3
 Livingston EH54 ...147 C4
Telford View EH49 ...84 B3
Telny Pl KY3 ......49 B4
Templar La EH1 ....233 A2
Templar Pl EH11 ....52 A1
Templar Rise EH54 ...173 B4
Templar's Cramond EH4 .91 A2
Templars Cres KY11 ..34 C2
Temple Denny Rd FK6 .36 B3
Temple Park Cres EH11 .122 C3
Temple Pk EH3 ....206 B1
Temple Prim Sch 206 B1
Templedean Pk EH41 .101 A1
Templehall Ave KY2 ..16 C4
Templeland Gr EH12 ..121 B4
Templeland Pl EH12 ..121 B4
Templeland Rd EH12 ..121 B4
Ten Acres EH10 ....5 A1
Tenacres Pl FK3 ....61 C3
Tenacres Rd EH54 ...61 C3
Tenant's March EH55 .172 B2
Tennant St EH6 ....93 C2
Tennent Pk EH53 ...148 B1
Tenth St EH22 .....183 A3
Tern Brae EH54 ....147 B3
Tern Rd KY11 .....30 A1
Terrace Rdbt EH54 ...147 C1
Terrace St KY1 .....18 A4
Terragles EH26 ....203 B3
Terrars Croft EH8 ...233 C1
Terris St KY4 ......13 B2
Teviot Gr EH26 ....203 C4
Teviot Pl EH1 .....233 A2
Teviot St FK1 ......59 C2
Teviotdale Pl EH3 ...93 A1
Thane St FK3 ......61 B3
Thimblehall Dr KY12 ..29 B2
Thimblehall Pl KY12 ..29 B2
Thimblehall Rd KY12 ..29 B2
Third Gait KY11 ....151 C4
Thirlestane Pl EH9 ...123 A3
Thirlestane La EH9 ...123 A3
Thirlestane Rd EH51 ..64 A4
Thirlestane Rd EH9 ...123 B3
Thirlfield Wynd EH54 ..146 C1
Thistle Ave Denny FK6 .36 B2
 Grangemouth FK3 ...61 A3
Thistle Ct KY4 .....30 C3
Thistle Ind Est
 Broxburn EH52 .....118 A3
 Cowdenbeath KY4 ...13 B3
 Stirling FK7 ....7 B3
Thistle Pl
 Edinburgh EH11 ...232 A1
 Stirling FK8 ....2 A1
Thistle St Alloa FK10 ..10 B3
 Burntisland KY3 ...50 C4
 Cowdenbeath KY4 ...13 B3
 Dunfermline KY12 ...29 A3
 Falkirk FK2 ....60 B2
 Kirkcaldy KY1 .....17 C4
Thompson Pl KY11 ...110 A2
Thomson Cres
 Cockenzie & Port Seton
 EH32 ....97 B2
 Currie EH14 ......152 A3
 Falkirk FK1 ....60 B2
Thomson Dr EH52 ...116 C2
Thomson Dr EH14 ...152 A3
Thomson Gn EH54 ...147 A4
Thomson Gr Currie EH14 .152 A3
 Uphall EH52 ......116 C2
Thomson Pl
 Cambusbarron FK7 ...6 B3
 Rosyth KY11 ......46 C2
Thomson Rd EH14 ...152 A3

Thomson Terr ML7 ...191 B3
Thorburn Gr EH13 ...153 B3
Thorburn Rd EH13 ...153 A3
Thorburn St KY12 ...46 C4
Thorn Tree FK2 ....26 C3
Thornbridge Gdns FK2 .60 C2
Thornbridge Pl FK2 ...60 C3
Thornbridge Rd FK2 ..60 C3
Thornbridge Sq FK2 ..60 C3
Thornburn Terr EH26 ..203 C2
Thorndale Gdns FK4 ..57 A1
Thorndene Ct FK1 ...59 C1
Thorndene Terr FK1 ..110 A4
Thorne Ct EH39 ....54 A4
Thorne Rd FK10 ...10 C3
Thornhill Dr KY2 ...17 A3
Thornhill Rd Falkirk FK2 .60 B3
 Kirkcaldy KY2 .....17 B3
Thornton Ave EH4 ...58 A1
Thornton Pl EH47 ...193 B3
Thornton Rd EH24 ...181 B1
Thorntree Cres EH32 ..97 A1
Thorntree St EH6 ...94 A2
Thorntreeside Ind Est
 EH6 ....94 A2
Thornville Terr EH6 ...94 A2
Thorny Bank FK3 ...157 B2
Thornybank Ind Est
 EH22 ....157 B2
Thornybauk EH3 ...232 B1
Thornyhall EH22 ...157 B2
Threave Loan KY11 ...30 A1
Threipmuir Ave EH14 .177 B4
Threipmuir Gdns EH14 .177 B4
Threipmuir Pl EH14 ..177 B4
Thrums The FK2 ....61 A2
Thurston Pl EH54 ...147 B3
Tibbies Loan FK7 ...20 B4
Timber Bush EH6 ...94 A3
Timmeryetts EH52 ...117 B3
Timmons Pk KY5 ...14 A4
Timmons Pl FK6 ....36 B1
Tinian Cres KY12 ...26 B1
Tinto Dr FK3 ......61 C3
Tinto Pl Dunfermline KY11 .29 C1
 Edinburgh EH6 ....93 C2
Tipperary Pl FK5 ...38 C1
Tipperlinn Rd EH10 ..123 A2
Tippet Knowes Ct EH52 .87 C2
Tippet Knowes Pk EH52 .87 C2
Tippet Knowes Rd EH52 .87 C1
Tippethill Hospl EH48 .144 A1
Tiree Cres FK2 .....61 B1
Tiree Pl Falkirk FK1 ...60 A1
 Kirkcaldy KY2 .....16 C4
Titania St EH54 ....116 C1
Toddshill Rd EH29 ...89 A1
Tolbooth St 🄿 Falkirk FK1 .60 A2
 Kirkcaldy KY1 .....17 B2
Tolbooth Wynd EH6 ..94 A3
Toll Rd FK10 ......23 C2
Toll Rdbt EH54 ....146 C2
Toll View TD13 ....140 C2
Tollcross EH3 .....232 B1
Tollcross Prim Sch EH3 .232 B1
Tollgate KY11 .....29 C1
Tolmount Cres KY12 ..29 B2
Tolmount Dr KY12 ...29 B2
Tolsta Cres FK2 ....61 C1
Tophill Entry FK1 ...59 C3
Toravon Dr FK2 ....83 A3
Torbain KY2 ......16 B4
Torbain Prim Sch KY2 ..16 B4
Torbain Rd KY2 ....16 A4
Torbane Ave EH47 ...170 C4
Torbane Dr EH47 ...170 C4
Torbeith Gdns KY4 ...12 C1
Torbothie Rd ML7 ...192 A2
Torbrex Farm Rd FK7 ..7 A3
Torbrex La FK7 ....7 A3
Torbrex Rd FK7 ....7 A3
Torburn Ave FK7 ...20 B2
Torduff Rd EH13 ...153 A2
Torlea Pl FK5 ......38 A3
Torness Power Sta Visitor
 Ctr* EH42 ....108 C2
Toronto Ave EH54 ...147 C2
Toronto Prim Sch EH54 .147 C2
Torosay Ave FK2 ...82 C3
Torphichen EH53 ...148 A1
Torphichen Pl EH3 ...232 A3
Torphichen Preceptory*
 EH48 ....113 C3
Torphichen Prim Sch
 EH48 ....113 C3
Torphichen St EH48 ..145 A4
 Edinburgh EH3 ....232 A2
Torphin Bank EH13 ..152 C3
Torphin Rd EH13 ...152 C3
Torrance Pk EH4 ...91 B1
Torridon Ave FK2 ...39 B1
Torridon Ct FK10 ...10 B4
Torridon Dr KY11 ...46 C1
Torridon La EH54 ...146 C4
Torridon Pl KY11 ...46 C1
Torridon Rd Kirkcaldy KY2 .16 C4
 Rosyth KY11 ......46 C1
Torridon Rd FK47 ...170 B4
Torridon Wlk EH54 ..148 A2
Torrin Loan ML7 ...192 A2
Torry Dr FK12 .....4 C4
Torryburn Prim Sch
 KY12 ....29 C1
Torsonce Rd EH22 ...156 C1
Torvean Pl KY11 ...29 B1
Torwood Ave
 Grangemouth FK3 ...61 C3

Torwood Ave continued
 Larbert FK5 ....38 A1
Torwood Pl KY12 ...29 B3
Torwood Sch FK5 ...37 C3
Tory Bay Ct KY12 ...26 B1
Touch Prim Sch KY11 ..29 C2
Touch Rd FK7,FK8 ...6 A3
Touch Wards KY12 ...29 C2
Touchhill Cres FK7 ...20 B2
Tovey Rd KY11 .....46 B1
Toward Ct EH12 ...121 A4
Tower Gdns The FK1 ..64 B4
Tower Pl
 Clackmannan FK10 ...10 C3
 Edinburgh EH6 ....94 A3
Tower Sq FK10 ....10 A3
Tower St Alloa FK10 ..10 A4
 Edinburgh EH6 ....94 A3
Tower Terr KY1 ....17 C4
Tower View FK10 ...5 C1
Towerbank Prim Sch
 EH15 ....95 A3
Towers Ct FK2 .....60 A3
Towers Pl FK2 .....2 B2
Town Burn FK7 ....6 C2
Town Head Mus KY12 .42 B4
Town House St FK6 ...36 C1
Townhall St KY11 ...47 B1
Townhead Dysart KY1 .18 B4
 Kinghorn KY3 .....34 C2
Townhead Gdns EH47 .170 B3
Townhill Ctry Pk* KY12 .29 B4
Townhill Rd KY12 ...29 B4
Townhill Rd KY12 ...29 B4
Townsend Cres KY1 ..17 B2
Townsend Pl KY1 ...17 B2
Trafalgar La EH6 ...93 C3
Trafalgar St EH6 ...93 C3
Trainers Brae EH39 ...54 A3
Tranent Inf Sch EH33 .128 B4
Tranent Prim Sch EH33 .128 A4
Tranent Rd EH33 ...128 A1
Transy Gr KY12 ....29 B2
Transy Pl KY12 ....29 B2
Traprain Cres EH48 ..144 C4
Traprain Terr
 Haddington EH41 ..101 A1
 Loanhead EH20 ...181 B4
Traquair Pk E EH12 ..121 C3
Traquair Pk W EH12 ..121 C3
Trelawney Terr EH26 ..204 A4
Tremayne Pl KY12 ...28 C3
Trench Knowe EH10 ..154 A3
Trenchard Pl KY12 ...28 C3
Tressilian Gdns 🄱
 EH16 ....124 A1
Trevelyan Cres EH34 .160 C3
Trevelyan Pl EH34 ...160 C3
Trinity Acad EH6 ...93 B3
Trinity Cres EH5 ...93 A3
Trinity Ct EH5 .....93 A3
Trinity Gr EH5 .....93 A3
Trinity Mains EH5 ...93 A3
Trinity Prim Sch EH6 .93 B3
Trinity Rd EH5 .....93 A3
Trinity Way KY5 ....93 A3
Tron Ct EH10 ......4 A1
Tron Sq EH1 ......233 A3
Trondheim Parkway
 KY11 ....29 C1
Trondheim Pl KY11 ...29 C1
Trongate KY3 .....35 A2
Trotter Haugh EH9 ..123 B2
Troup Ct FK3 .....61 B4
Trough Dyke EH10 ..153 C3
 Stenhousemuir FK5 ...38 B2
Tryst Rd FK5 ......38 B2
Tudor Ct FK2 ......60 A3
Tuke St KY12 ......29 A2
Tulliallan Pl FK3 ....39 A2
Tulliallan Prim Sch FK10 .23 C2
Tulliallan Terr FK10 ...23 C3
Tullibody Rd FK10 ...4 C1
Tulligarth Pk FK10 ...10 A4
Tulligarth Pk FK10 ...10 A4
Tulloch Ct KY4 ....13 B3
Tulloch Rd ML7 ....192 A2
Tummel Dr KY2 ....16 B4
Tummel Pl
 Grangemouth FK3 ...61 C2
 Stenhousemuir FK5 ...38 C2
Turf Pl EH47 ......171 B4
Turnbull Gr KY11 ...29 C1
Turnbull Way EH54 ..147 B3
Turner Ave EH14 ...151 B2
Turner Pk EH14 ...151 B2
Turner St EH48 ....145 A4
Turnhigh Rd EH47 ...170 A2
Turnhouse Farm Rd
 EH12 ....90 B1
Turnhouse Rd EH12 ..120 B4
Turnstone Rd KY11 ...30 A1
Turret Ct EH10 ....10 B3
Turret Dr FK2 .....62 A1
Turret Gdns EH32 ...127 C4
Turret Rd FK3 .....61 B4
Turriff Pl KY2 .....16 C4
Twain Ave FK5 .....39 A2
Tweed Ave KY11 ...17 C4
Tweed Dr EH54 ....148 A3
Tweed St
 Dunfermline KY11 ...29 C1
 Grangemouth FK3 ...40 A1
Tweeddale Ave EH41 .163 C3
Tweeddale Cres EH41 .163 C3
Tweeddale Ct EH11 ...233 B3
Tweeddale Gr KY11 ...29 C1
Tweeddale Gr EH41 ..163 C3

Tygetshaugh Ct FK6 ....36 B2
Tyhmebank EH54 ....147 C3
Tyler's Acre Ave EH12 .....121 C3
Tyler's Acre Gdns EH12 ....121 C3
Tyler's Acre Rd EH12 ......121 C3
Tyndrum PI FK7 ....2 A4
Tyne CI East Linton EH40 ...103 C4
  Haddington EH41 ....132 A4
Tyne Ct EH41 ....132 A4
Tyne Ho EH41 ....132 A4
Tyne Pk EH34 ....161 A3
Tynebank Rd EH41 ....132 A4
Tynecastle High Sch
  EH11 ....122 C3
Tynecastle La EH11 ....122 C3
Tynecastle Pk (Heart of
  Midlothian FC) EH11 .....122 C3
Tynecastle Terr EH11 ......122 C3
Tyneholm Cotts EH34 ......159 B3
Tynemount Ave EH35 ....159 B3
Tynemount Rd EH35 ....159 B4
Tyneview EH35 ....159 C4
Tyrwhitt PI KY11 ....46 C2
Tytler Gdns EH8 ....94 A1

U

Ugston Cotts EH41 ....100 B1
Ulg Way ML7 ....192 A2
Ulster Cres EH8 ....124 B4
Ulster Dr EH8 ....124 B4
Ulster Gdns EH8 ....124 B4
Ulster Gr EH8 ....124 B4
Ulster Terr EH8 ....124 B4
Underwood Cotts FK7 ....6 B3
Underwood Rd FK7 ....6 B3
Union Dr EH47 ....170 A3
Union Gdns FK1 ....59 B3
Union Pk EH19 ....182 A3
Union PI Brightons FK2 ......61 A1
  Edinburgh EH1 ....233 B4
  Larbert FK5 ....38 A1
Union Rd Bathgate EH48 ...145 A3
  Broxburn EH52 ....117 B3
  Falkirk FK1 ....59 B3
  Grangemouth FK3 ....40 B1
  Linlithgow EH49 ....84 C3
  Whitburn EH47 ....170 A3
Union Sq EH55 ....172 B2
Union St ⊞ Alloa FK10 .....10 A3
  Bo'ness EH51 ....63 C4
  Bo'ness EH51 ....64 A4
  Bridge of A FK9 ....2 A4
  Burntisland KY3 ....50 C4
  Cowdenbeath KY4 ....13 B2
  Edinburgh EH1 ....93 C1
  Falkirk FK2 ....60 A4
  Kirkcaldy KY1 ....17 C4
  Lochgelly KY5 ....14 A4
  Shotts ML7 ....191 B3
  Stenhousemuir FK5 ....38 C2
  Stirling FK8 ....2 A1
Unity Pk ML7 ....191 B2
Univ of Dundee Sch of
  Nursing & Midwifery Fife
  Campus KY2 ....17 A2
Univ of Edinburgh EH8 ....233 A2
Univ of Edinburgh (King's
  Buildings Campus)
  EH9 ....123 C1
Universal Rd FK2 ....60 C4
University Rd W FK9 ....2 B3
Uphall Prim Sch EH52 .....117 A3
Uphall Sta EH54 ....117 A1
Uphall Station Inf Sch
  EH54 ....117 A1
Uphall Station Rd EH53 ...148 A4
Upper Bathville EH48 ......143 C2
Upper Bow EH1 ....233 A3
Upper Broomieknowe
  EH18 ....182 A4
Upper Castlehill FK8 ....7 A4
Upper Coltbridge Terr
  EH12 ....122 C4
Upper Craigour FK17 ......155 C4
Upper Craigour Way
  EH17 ....124 B1
Upper Craigs FK8 ....7 A4
Upper Cramond Ct EH4 ....91 A2
Upper Dean Terr EH4 .....232 A4
Upper Gilmore PI EH3 .....232 B1
Upper Gilmore Terr
  EH3 ....232 B1
Upper Gray St EH9 ....123 C3
Upper Grove PI EH3 ....232 A1
Upper Hermitage EH6 ......94 A2
Upper Millhill St KY11 ......29 A2
Upper Newmarket St
  FK1 ....60 A3
Upper Wellheads KY11 .....45 C2
Ure Cres EH48 ....58 A3
Ure Ct FK3 ....61 B4
Urquhart Cres KY12 ....28 C2
Urquhart Ct KY1 ....16 B3
Urquhart Cut KY12 ....28 C2
Urquhart Farm Cotts
  KY12 ....28 B1

V

Vale Gr FK8 ....1 C3
Vale PI FK6 ....36 C2
Valeview FK5 ....38 A4
Valley Field View EH26 ...203 C2

Valley Gdns KY2 ....16 C3
Valley Gdns S KY2 ....16 C3
Valley Prim Sch KY2 ....17 A4
Valley View KY2 ....16 C3
Valleyfield Ave KY12 ....26 A1
Valleyfield PI
  Cowdenbeath KY4 ....13 B3
  Stirling FK7 ....7 B3
Valleyfield Rd EH26 ....203 C2
Valleyfield St EH3 ....232 C1
Valleyfield Woodland Pk
  High Valleyfield KY12 .....26 A1
  * High Valleyfield KY12 ...26 A2
Valleyview Dr FK2 ....60 A4
Valleyview PI FK2 ....60 A4
Vancouver Ave FK4 ....147 C2
Vandeleur Ave EH7 ....94 C1
Vandeleur Gr EH7 ....94 C1
Vandeleur PI EH7 ....94 C1
Vardon Gn EH54 ....147 B2
Vardon Rd EH31 ....52 A2
Vaucluse PI EH26 ....203 C2
Veere Pk KY12 ....25 C1
Veitch's Sq ⊞ EH4 ....93 A1
Vellore Rd FK1 ....83 A3
Venachar PI KY12 ....28 A1
Vennachar St ML7 ....191 C3
Vennel The Denny FK6 .....36 C1
  Dunbar EH42 ....78 C1
  Linlithgow EH49 ....85 A4
  Queensferry EH30 ....68 B1
Ventnor PI EH9 ....124 A2
Ventnor Terr EH9 ....123 C2
Venturefair Ave KY12 ......29 A3
Veronica Cres KY1 ....17 B4
Vetch Pk EH41 ....101 A1
Veterane Cotts EH48 .....145 B3
Vexhim Pk EH15 ....125 A3
Vicar St FK1 ....60 A3
Viceroy St KY1 ....17 B4
Victor Park Terr EH12 ....121 B4
Victoria Gdns
  Newcraighall EH21 ....17 A2
  Newtongrange EH22 ....182 C3
Victoria Hospl KY2 ....17 A1
Victoria Mills Ind Est
  EH51 ....64 B4
Victoria Pk
  Fauldhouse EH47 ....193 C4
  Haddington EH41 ....101 A1
Victoria PI Bo'ness EH51 ...64 A4
  Brightons FK2 ....61 B1
  Dunbar EH42 ....78 B2
  Stirling FK8 ....7 A4
Victoria Prim Sch
  EH6 ....93 B4
  Falkirk FK2 ....60 B3
Victoria Rd Falkirk FK2 .....60 B3
  Grangemouth FK3 ....61 C4
  Haddington EH41 ....132 A4
  Harthill ML7 ....168 C3
  Kirkcaldy KY1 ....17 B3
  Larbert FK5 ....38 A1
  Newtongrange EH22 ....182 C3
  North Berwick EH39 ......54 B4
  Stirling FK8 ....7 A4
Victoria Sq FK8 ....7 A4
Victoria St Alloa FK10 .....10 A4
  Dunbar EH42 ....78 B2
  Dunfermline KY12 ....29 A3
  Dysart KY1 ....18 A4
  Edinburgh EH1 ....233 A3
  Harthill ML7 ....168 C3
  Livingston EH54 ....148 A2
  Rosewell EH24 ....181 B1
Victoria Terr
  Dunfermline KY12 ....13 C3
  Edinburgh EH1 ....233 A3
  Haddington EH41 ....101 A1
  Menstrie FK11 ....4 A1
  Musselburgh EH21 ....126 C3
Viewbank Dr EH19 ....182 B4
Viewbank Rd EH19 ....182 B4
Viewbank View EH19 .....182 B4
Viewcraig Gdns EH8 ......233 B2
Viewcraig St EH8 ....233 B2
Viewfield EH19 ....182 A3
Viewfield Ave EH19 ......182 B4
Viewfield Dr FK12 ....4 A3
Viewfield Rd
  Kirkcaldy KY1 ....152 C4
  Tarbrax EH55 ....217 C2
Viewfield St Harthill ML7 ..168 C3
  Stirling FK8 ....7 A4
Viewfield Terr
  Cowdenbeath KY4 ....13 C3
  Dunfermline KY12 ....29 A2
Viewforth Bo'ness EH51 ....64 A4
Cockenzie & Port Seton
  EH32 ....97 B2
  Dunbar EH42 ....78 B1
  Edinburgh EH10 ....123 A3
  North Berwick EH39 ......54 B4
Viewforth Ave KY1 ....17 C4
Viewforth Ct KY3 ....34 C1
Viewforth Dr FK2 ....61 A2
Viewforth Gdns
  Edinburgh EH10 ....123 A3
  Kirkcaldy KY1 ....17 C4
Viewforth High Sch KY1 ...17 C4
Viewforth PI Kinghorn KY3 .34 C1
  Queensferry EH30 ....89 A4
Viewforth Rd EH30 ....89 A4
Viewforth Sq EH10 ....123 A3
Viewforth St KY1 ....17 C4

Viewforth Terr
  Edinburgh EH10 ....123 A3
  Kirkcaldy KY1 ....17 C4
  Tranent EH33 ....128 B3
Viewpark Gdns EH19 .....182 A4
Viking Way KY11 ....46 B1
Villa Bank FK6 ....36 C1
Villa Rd EH30 ....89 A4
Village La EH54 ....147 A2
Vinefields EH41 ....160 C3
Violet Bank ⊞ EH48 ......145 A3
Violet Terr EH11 ....122 C3
Vivian Terr EH4 ....92 A2
Vogrie Cres S EH23 ......207 B4
  Vogrie Ctry Pk* EH23 ...184 B2
Vogrie PI EH23 ....207 B4
Vogrie Rd EH23 ....207 B4
Voil Rd FK9 ....2 A2
Volunteer's Gn KY1 ....17 B2
Vorlich Cres EH26 ....204 A4
Vorlich Ct FK1 ....81 C4
Vorlich PI FK9 ....2 A2

W

W Parliament Sq EH1 .....233 A3
Waddell St FK7 ....7 A2
Wadingburn La EH18 .....155 C1
Wadingburn Rd EH18 ....181 C4
Waggon Rd Bo'ness EH51 ..63 C4
  Brightons FK2 ....82 B4
  Crossford KY11 ....45 B4
  Falkirk FK2 ....60 A4
  Inverkeithing KY11 ....47 B3
Wakefield Ave EH7 ....94 C1
Walden Dr EH41 ....163 C3
Walden PI EH41 ....163 C2
Walden Terr EH41 ....163 C2
Waldie Ave EH49 ....85 A3
Walk The Alloa FK10 ....10 A4
  Dysart KY1 ....18 A4
Walker Cres EH22 ....156 B1
Walker Dr
  Brightons FK4 ....57 B3
  Queensferry EH30 ....68 A1
Walker PI
  Bonnyrigg & Lasswade
  EH18 ....29 C1
  Cowdenbeath KY4 ....13 A2
Walker St
  East Linton EH40 ....103 B4
  Edinburgh EH3 ....232 A3
  Kincardine FK10 ....23 A2
  Kirkcaldy KY2 ....17 A3
  Lochgelly KY5 ....14 A4
Walkers Ct EH14 ....121 C1
Walkers Rig EH14 ....121 C1
Walkers Wynd EH14 .....121 C1
Wall Gdns FK1 ....59 B3
Wall St FK1 ....59 B3
Wallace Brae Ave FK2 .....82 B4
Wallace Brae Bank FK2 ...82 B4
Wallace Brae Dr FK2 ......82 B4
Wallace Brae Gr FK2 ......82 B4
Wallace Brae Rise FK2 ....82 B4
Wallace Cres
  Brightons FK2 ....61 B4
  Denny FK6 ....36 B1
  Plean FK7 ....20 B2
  Roslin EH25 ....181 A2
Wallace Ct
  Grangemouth FK3 ....61 B4
  Stirling FK8 ....2 A1
Wallace Gate FK8 ....7 A4
Wallace High Sch FK2 .....82 B4
Wallace Mill Gdns 148 B2
Wallace Monument* KY2 ..2 C2
Wallace PI
  Cambuskenneth FK7 ......6 B3
  Falkirk FK2 ....60 A4
  Kingseat KY12 ....12 A1
  Tranent EH33 ....128 B4
Wallace Rd EH48 ....145 B3
Wallace St Alloa FK10 .....10 B4
  Bannockburn FK7 ....7 C1
  Cowdenbeath KY4 ....13 B1
  Dunfermline KY11 ....29 B1
  Falkirk FK2 ....60 A4
Wallace View
  Bo'ness EH51 ....63 B3
  Shieldhill FK1 ....81 B2
  Stirling FK7 ....7 B1
Wallace Wlk EH47 ....171 A1
Wallacelea FK2 ....82 B4
Wallacestone Brae FK2 ....82 A4
Wallacestone Prim Sch
  FK2 ....82 B4
Walls PI KY11 ....29 C1
Wallsend Ct KY12 ....28 B3
Wallstale Rd FK7 ....6 C1
Wallyford Ind Est EH21 ..127 A2
Wallyford Prim Sch
  EH21 ....127 A3
Wallyford Sta EH21 ....127 A3
Walmer Dr KY12 ....28 A3
Walnut Gr KY11 ....46 B4
Walter Scott Ave EH16 ...124 A1

Wanless Ct EH21 ....126 B3
Ward Ave FK2 ....61 B1
Ward St FK5 ....147 A3
Wardie Ave EH5 ....93 A3
Wardie Ct EH5 ....93 A3
Wardie Dell EH5 ....93 A3
Wardie Gr EH5 ....92 C3
Wardie House La EH5 .....93 A3
Wardie Pk EH5 ....93 A3
Wardie Prim Sch EH5 .....93 A3
Wardie Rd EH5 ....93 A3
Wardie Sq EH5 ....93 A3
Wardieburn Dr EH5 ....92 C3
Wardieburn PI E EH5 .....92 C3
Wardieburn PI N EH5 .....92 C3
Wardieburn PI S EH5 .....92 C3
Wardieburn PI W EH5 .....92 C3
Wardieburn Rd EH5 ......92 C3
Wardieburn St E EH5 .....92 C3
Wardieburn St W EH5 ....92 C3
Wardieburn Terr EH5 .....92 C3
Wardiefield EH5 ....93 A3
Wardlaw Cres
  Dunfermline KY11 ....29 B1
  Oakley KY12 ....26 C4
Wardlaw PI
  Edinburgh EH11 ....122 C3
  Falkirk FK2 ....39 B1
Wardlaw St
  Cowdenbeath KY4 ....13 B2
  Edinburgh EH11 ....122 C3
Wardlaw Terr EH11 ......122 C3
Wardlaw Way KY12 ....26 C4
Wardrop Cres EH48 ......145 A4
Ware Rd Dirleton EH39 ....54 A4
  North Berwick EH39 ......54 A4
Warrender Cres EH42 .....78 C1
Warrender Ct EH39 ....54 A4
Warrender Park Cres
  EH9 ....123 B3
Warrender Park Rd
  EH9 ....123 A3
Warrender Park Terr
  EH9 ....123 B3
Warriston Ave EH3 ....93 B2
Warriston Cres EH3 ....93 B2
Warriston Dr EH3 ....93 A2
Warriston Farm Rd
  EH14 ....151 B3
Warriston Gdns EH3 ......93 B2
Warriston Gr EH3 ....93 B2
Warriston Rd EH3, EH7 ...93 B2
Warriston Terr EH3 ....93 A2
Washington La KY12 ......28 B3
Water Of Leith Visitor Ctr*
  EH14 ....122 B1
Water of Leith Walkway*
  EH14 ....151 B1
Water Ski Ctr* KY12 ......29 A4
Water St EH6 ....94 A3
Water Yett FK1 ....59 B3
Waterfall Wlk EH22 ....156 A1
Waterlands Gdns ML8 ....230 A2
Waterloo Bank EH26 .....203 C2
Waterloo PI
  Edinburgh EH1 ....233 A4
  Elphinstone EH33 ......128 A1
Waters End FK2 ....39 A1
Waters' Ct EH6 ....94 A3
Waterside
  ⊞ Haddington EH41 ....132 A4
  Linlithgow EH49 ....84 C3
Watertoun Rd EH9 ....123 C2
Watling Ave FK2 ....61 A2
Watling Dr FK1 ....59 B3
Watling Gdns FK1 ....59 B3
Watson Ave EH11 ....122 C3
Watson Cres EH11 ....122 C3
Watson Gn EH54 ....147 B4
Watson PI
  Armadale EH48 ....144 A3
  Dunfermline KY12 ....29 A3
Watson St
  Cowdenbeath KY4 ....13 B2
  Falkirk FK2 ....60 A4
  Penicuik EH26 ....203 C2
Watt Ave EH48 ....144 A3
Watt Gr EH22 ....183 A2
Watt Pk EH22 ....183 A2
Watt Rd KY11 ....46 A1
Watt St KY1 ....17 A3
Watt's CI EH21 ....126 A3
Watters Cres KY5 ....14 C4
Wauchope Ave EH16 ....124 C2
Wauchope Cres EH16 ...124 C2
Wauchope PI EH16 ......124 C2
Wauchope Rd EH16 .....124 C2
Wauchope Sq EH16 .....124 C2
Wauchope Terr EH16 ....124 C2
Waugh Path EH19 ....182 B4
Waughton Cotts EH40 ....74 C3
Waulkmill Dr EH26 ......204 A3
Waulkmill Loan EH14 ....120 A3
Waulkmill Rd EH26 ......203 C3
Waulkmill View EH26 ....204 A3
Wavell St FK3 ....39 C4
Waverley Bridge EH1 ....233 A3
Waverley Cres
  Bonnyrigg & Lasswade
  EH19 ....182 B4
  Grangemouth FK3 ....61 B3
  High Bonnybridge FK4 ....82 A4
  Livingston EH54 ....147 A3
Waverley Ct EH19 ....182 B4

Waverley Dr EH19 ....182 B4
Waverley Park Terr EH8 ...94 A1
Waverley Pk
  Bonnyrigg & Lasswade
  EH19 ....182 B4
  Edinburgh EH8 ....94 A1
  Mayfield EH22 ....183 B3
  Redding FK2 ....61 A1
Waverley PI EH7 ....94 A1
Waverley Rd
  Bonnyrigg & Lasswade
  EH19 ....182 B4
  Dalkeith EH22 ....156 C4
  Stenhousemuir FK5 ....38 B1
Waverley St
  Bathgate EH48 ....145 A4
  Falkirk FK2 ....60 A4
  Mayfield EH22 ....183 B3
Waverley St Ind Units ⊞
  EH48 ....145 A4
Waverley Stps EH1 ......233 A3
Waverley Terr
  Bonnyrigg & Lasswade
  EH19 ....182 B4
  Mayfield EH22 ....183 B3
  Stenhousemuir FK5 ....38 B1
Wayfarers Dr KY11 ....47 C2
Wayfarers Pk KY11 ....47 C2
Wayfarers Way KY11 .....47 C2
Weaver Row FK7 ....7 A2
Weaver's Knowe Cres
  EH14 ....151 C3
Weavers Cres KY2 ....17 A3
Weavers La EH47 ....170 A3
Weavers Wlk KY12 ....29 A1
Webster Ave FK2 ....39 A2
Webster Ct EH52 ....117 C3
Webster PI KY11 ....46 B3
Wedderburn Cres KY11 ...29 C1
Wedderburn PI KY11 ......29 B1
Wedderburn St KY11 .....29 B1
Wedderburn St KY2 ......16 B4
Wedderburn Terr EH21 ..126 B2
Wee Brae EH18 ....156 A1
Wee Row FK7 ....60 A3
Weir Ave EH14 ....156 C1
Weir Cres EH22 ....156 C1
Weir Dr FK7 ....82 B4
Weir St Falkirk FK1 ....60 B3
  Stirling FK8 ....1 C1
Weld Ct EH3 ....232 A3
Well Rd Bridge of A FK9 ...2 A4
  Lochgelly KY5 ....14 A4
Well Wynd EH33 ....128 B3
Wellflats Rd EH29 ....89 A1
Wellgate Dr FK9 ....2 A4
Wellgreen PI EH10 ....7 A3
Wellhead CI EH30 ....89 A4
Wellington PI EH6 ....94 A3
Wellington Sch EH26 ....222 C3
Wellington St EH7 ....93 C1
Wellmyre FK10 ....11 A2
Wellpark EH52 ....116 C4
Wellpark Cres FK7 ....6 C2
Wellpark Terr FK4 ....58 A3
Wellside EH41 ....131 C4
Wellside PI FK1 ....60 A3
Wellside PI FK1 ....60 A3
Wellview La EH54 ....173 C3
Wellwood Prim Sch
  KY12 ....29 A4
Welsh Gdns ⊞ 94 A3
Welsh Rd EH47 ....169 C3
Wemyss Ct KY11 ....46 C3
Wemyss Gdns EH11 .....127 B3
Wemyss PI
  Cowdenbeath KY4 ....13 B2
  Rosyth KY11 ....46 C3
Wemyss Terr EH32 ....97 B2
Wemyssfield KY1 ....17 A2
Werberside Mews EH4 ...92 C2
Wesley Cres EH19 ......182 B4
Wesley PI FK2 ....82 A4
West Adam St EH8 ......233 B2
West Annandale St EH7 ..93 B2
West Approach Rd
  EH3 EH11 ....232 A2
West Baldridge Rd KY12 ..28 C3
West Bankton PI EH54 ...173 C4
West Barns Prim Sch
  EH42 ....77 C1
West Bay Rd EH39 ....53 C4
West Benhar Rd ML7 ....168 A2
West Boreland Rd FK6 ....36 B1
West Bow EH1 ....233 A3
West Bowling Green St
  EH6 ....93 C3
West Bridge St FK1 ....60 A3
West Brighton Cres
  EH15 ....125 A4
West Broomhill Rd KY3 ..50 B1
West Bryson Rd EH11 ...122 C3

West Burnside EH52 ....117 C3
West Cairn Cres EH26 ...203 C3
West Caiystane Rd
EH10 ....154 A3
West Calder High Sch
EH55 ....173 A3
West Calder Sta EH55 ...172 B2
West Calder Workspace
EH55 ....172 B2
West Camus Rd EH14 ....154 A3
West Carmuirs Loan FK5 .58 C3
West Carnethy Ave
EH13 ....153 A3
West Castle Rd EH10 ...123 A3
West Catherine Pl EH12 .122 C4
West Cherrybank EH6 ....93 B3
West Church Dr FK3 .....40 A1
West Clifton Farm Cotts
EH53 ....149 B4
West Coates EH12 ....122 C4
West Colinton Ho EH13 .153 A3
West College St EH1 ...233 A2
West Craigs Ave EH12 ..120 C3
West Craigs Cres EH12 .120 C4
West Craigs Ind Est
EH12 ....120 C4
West Cres EH34 ....161 C2
West Croft EH28 ....119 C1
West Cromwell St EH6 ...93 C3
West Crosscauseway
EH8 ....233 B1
West Ct
Edinburgh, Niddrie Mains
EH16 ....124 C2
Edinburgh, Ravelston EH4 .92 B1
West Dr Dunfermline KY12 .29 A2
Stenhousemuir FK5 ......38 B1
West End
Cockburnspath TD13 .....140 C2
West Calder EH55 ....172 B1
West End Gdns FK10 ....10 A3
West End Pl EH11 ....122 C3
West Fenton Cotts EH32 .72 C4
West Fentoun Gait EH31 .52 B1
West Fergus Pl KY11 ....17 A2
West Ferryfield EH5 .....92 C3
West Garleton Holdings
EH41 ....100 C2
West Gate Rd EH14 ......62 A4
West Glen Ave EH54 ....146 C3
West Gorgie Pk EH14 ...122 B2
West Gorgie Pl EH14 ...122 B2
West Grange Gdns EH9 .123 B2
West Granton Access
EH4,EH5 ....92 B3
West Granton Rd EH5 ....92 B3
West Hall Rd EH52 .....117 C2
West Harbour Rd
Charlestown KY11 ....45 A2
Cockenzie & Port Seton
EH32 ....97 A2
Edinburgh EH5 ....92 C4
West Harwood Crofts
EH55 ....196 B3
West Holmes Gdns
EH21 ....126 A3
West Holmes Pl EH52 ...117 A2
West Holmes Rd EH52 ..117 A2
West James St FK12 .....5 A3
West Johnstone St FK12 ..5 A3
West La KY4 ....13 A1
West Leven St KY3 ......50 C4
West Link Rd EH9 ....2 B3
West Links Rd EH31 .....51 C1
West Loan EH32 ....96 C1
West Loan Ct EH32 .....127 C4
West Lodge Gdns FK10 ...9 C4
West Lorimer Pl EH32 ...97 A2
West Lothian Coll EH54 .147 B1
West Main St
Aberlady EH32 ....71 B2
Armadale EH48 ....143 C3
Blackburn EH47 ....171 B4
Broxburn EH52 ....117 A2
Harthill ML7 ....168 C3
Uphall EH52 ....116 C2
Whitburn EH47 ....169 C3
West Mains
West Mains St EH22 ......32 A2
West March St KY1 ......17 B4
West Mayfield EH9 .....123 C2
West Mill Bank EH13 ...153 A3
West Mill La EH4 ....232 A3
West Mill Rd EH13 .....152 C3
West Montgomery Pl [6]
EH7 ....93 C1
West Muir Rd EH55 .....172 B1
West Murrayfield FK7 ....7 B1
West Nethertown St
KY12 ....29 A1
West Newington Pl EH9 .123 C3
West Nicolson St EH8 ...233 B2
West Norton Pl EH7 ....233 C4
West Park Gr EH52 .....117 A3
West Park Pl EH11 .....122 C3
West Pilton Ave EH4 .....92 B2
West Pilton Bank EH4 ....92 B3
West Pilton Cres EH4 ....92 A3
West Pilton Crossway
EH4 ....92 B3

West Pilton Dr EH4 .....92 B3
West Pilton Gdns EH4 ...92 B3
West Pilton Gn EH4 .....92 B3
West Pilton Gr EH4 .....92 B3
West Pilton Loan EH4 ...92 B3
West Pilton March EH4 ..92 B3
West Pilton Pk EH4 .....92 B3
West Pilton Pl EH4 .....92 B3
West Pilton Rd EH4 .....92 B3
West Pilton Rise EH4 ...92 B3
West Pilton St EH4 .....92 B3
West Pilton Terr EH4 ...92 B3
West Pilton View EH4 ...92 B2
West Pk Carnock KY12 ....27 B3
Lochgelly KY5 ....14 A4
West Port Dunbar EH42 ..78 B1
Dysart KY1 ....18 A4
Edinburgh EH1 ....232 C2
Linlithgow EH49 ....8 A4
West Port Prt EH4 ....84 C3
West Powburn EH9 ......123 C2
West Preston St EH8 ...123 C3
West Prim Sch KY1 ......17 A1
West Quality St KY1 .....18 A4
West Rd Charlestown KY11 .45 A2
Haddington EH41 ....131 C4
Whitekirk EH42 ....75 C4
West Register St EH2 ...233 A4
West Register Street La
EH2 ....233 A4
West Relugas Rd EH9 ...123 B2
West Richmond St EH8 ..233 B2
West Sands KY11 ....68 B3
West Saville Rd EH16 ..123 C2
West Saville Terr EH9 ..123 C2
West Saville Gdns EH9 .123 C2
West Scotland Street La [1]
EH3 ....93 B1
West Seaside EH32 ......96 C1
West Shore Bsns Ctr EH5 .92 B4
West Shore Rd EH5 ......92 B4
West Shore Road Trad Est
EH5 ....92 B4
West Silvermills La EH3 ..93 A1
West St EH26 ....203 C2
West Stirling St FK12 ....4 C4
West Telferton EH7 .....94 C1
West Terr EH49 ....65 B2
West Tollcross EH3 .....232 B1
West Torbain KY2 ....16 B4
West Twinnigoul Gdns
EH33 ....128 B3
West Vennel [7] FK10 ...10 A3
West Way KY11 ....48 A3
West Werberside EH4 ....92 C2
West Windygoul EH33 ...128 A3
West Windygoul Gdns
EH33 ....128 A2
West Winnelstrae EH5 ...92 C2
West Woods EH4 ....92 C2
West Wynd [8] KY1 ......17 B3
Westbank Ct EH33 ......129 B3
Westbank Gdns EH33 ...129 B3
Westbank Loan EH15 .....95 A1
Westbank Pl EH15 ....95 A1
Westbank Rd EH33 .....129 B3
Westbank St EH15 ....95 A1
Westbank Terr EH33 ....129 B3
Westburn Ave
Cowdenbeath KY4 ....13 A1
Edinburgh EH14 ....152 B4
Falkirk FK1 ....59 C2
Westburn Gr EH14 .....152 B4
Westburn Middlefield
EH14 ....152 B4
Westburn Pk EH14 .....152 B4
Westburn Prim Sch
EH11 ....121 B1
Westcliffe Ct EH5 ....61 C3
Westcraigs Pk EH48 ....142 B2
Westcraigs Rd
Blackridge EH48 ....142 B2
Harthill ML7 ....168 C3
Westend Pl EH39 ....54 A4
Wester Bankton EH54 ..174 A4
Wester Bogie Rd KY2 ....16 A4
Wester Broom Ave
EH12 ....121 B3
Wester Broom Dr EH12 .121 B3
Wester Broom Gdns
EH12 ....121 B3
Wester Broom Gr EH12 .121 B3
Wester Broom Pl EH12 .121 B3
Wester Broom Terr
EH12 ....121 B3
Wester Cl EH6 ....93 B4
Wester Coates Ave
EH12 ....122 C4
Wester Coates Gdns
EH12 ....122 C4
Wester Coates Pl EH12 .122 C4
Wester Coates Rd EH12 .122 C4
Wester Coates Terr
EH12 ....122 C4
Wester Drylaw Ave EH4 ..92 A2
Wester Drylaw Dr EH4 ...92 A2
Wester Drylaw Pk EH4 ...92 B2
Wester Drylaw Pl EH4 ...92 A2
Wester Drylaw Row EH4 ..92 B1
Wester Hailes Ed Ctr
EH11 ....121 B1
Wester Hailes Pk EH14 .152 C4
Wester Hailes Rd EH14 .152 B4
Wester Hailes Sta EH14 .152 B4
Wester Hill EH10 ....153 C4
Wester Pencaitland Farm
Cotts EH34 ....160 B3

Wester Row EH14 ......120 C1
Wester Steil EH10 ......122 C1
Westerdunes Pk EH39 ....53 B4
Westerglen Rd FK1 ......60 A1
Westerlands Dr FK8 ......7 A3
Westerlea Ct FK9 ....2 A3
Westerlea Dr FK9 ....2 A3
Westerlea Sch EH12 ....122 B4
Westermains EH48 ......143 C3
Western Ave
Crossford KY12 ....28 A1
Falkirk FK2 ....60 A3
Western Gdns EH12 .....122 B4
Western General Hospl
EH4 ....92 B2
Western Pl EH12 ....122 B4
Western Terr EH12 .....122 B4
Westerton FK7 ....20 B4
Westerton Dr FK9 ....2 A4
Westerton Rd
Broxburn EH52 ....118 A3
Grangemouth FK3 ....61 C4
Westerton Terr FK2 ......39 B2
Westfield FK10 ....24 A2
Westfield Ave EH11 ....122 B3
Westfield Bank [8] EH22 .156 C1
Westfield Ct [4] EH22 ..156 C1
Westfield Dr [5] EH22 ..156 C1
Westfield Gr
Crossgates KY4 ....30 C3
Edinburgh EH11 ....122 C3
Westfield Pk EH22 .....156 C1
Westfield Pl FK6 ....36 C1
Westfield Prim Sch
EH48 ....112 C2
Westfield Rd EH11 .....122 B3
Westfield Rdbt FK2 ......60 C3
Westfield Specl Sch
EH22 ....157 A2
Westfield St
Edinburgh EH11 ....122 B3
Falkirk FK2 ....60 C3
Westfield Trad Est FK6 ..36 C1
Westgarth Ave EH13 ...153 A3
Westgate Dunbar EH42 ..78 B2
Mid Calder EH53 ....48 A2
North Berwick EH39 .....54 A4
Westgate Ct [9] EH39 ...54 A4
Westhall Cres KY12 .....27 B1
Westhall Gdns
Edinburgh EH10 ....123 A3
Uphall EH52 ....117 A2
Westhaugh Rd FK9 ....2 A2
Westhouse Ave EH22 ...183 C3
Westhouse Dr EH22 ....183 C3
Westhouse St EH22 ....183 C3
Westhouses Rd EH22 ...183 C3
Westland Cotts EH17 ...155 C3
Westmill Rd EH18 ......184 A4
Westmill Wynd EH18 ....182 A4
Westminster Pl EH5 .....38 C2
Westmost Cl EH6 ....93 B4
Westpoint EH42 ....78 B1
Westquarter Ave FK2 ....61 A1
Westquarter Prim Sch
FK2 ....61 A1
Westray Terr FK1 ....60 B1
Westside Plaza Sh Ctr
EH14 ....152 B4
Westview EH4 ....84 B4
Westview Cres FK10 ......4 B1
Westwater St KY5 ....14 A4
Westwood Ave KY1 ......17 C4
Westwood Pk EH54 .....146 C4
Westwood Pl KY11 ......29 C2
Westwood View EH55 ...172 B2
Wharry Rd FK12 ....4 C4
Wheatfield Gr EH20 ....181 A4
Wheatfield Loan EH20 ..155 A1
Wheatfield Pl EH11 .....122 B3
Wheatfield Rd EH11 ....122 B3
Wheatfield St EH11 ....122 B3
Wheatfield Terr EH11 ...122 B3
Wheatfield Wlk EH20 ...181 A4
Wheatlands Ave FK4 .....58 A3
Wheatsheaf La EH22 ...157 A2
Wheldale Rd EH11 ......54 B3
Whimbrel Pl KY11 ....30 B2
Whin Park Ind Est EH42 .97 A2
Whin Pk EH22 ....97 A2
Whinbank EH54 ....147 C3
Whinhill KY11 ....29 B2
Whinneyknowe KY11 ....68 A3
Whinniehill Terr KY12 ...27 B3
Whinny Hill Cres KY11 ..47 A1
Whinnyburn Pl KY11 ....46 B3
Whinrig EH52 ....117 B3
Whins of Milton Sch FK7 ..7 A2
Whins Pl EH15 ....95 A1
Whins Rd Alloa FK10 ....10 B4
Stirling FK7 ....7 A1
Whinwell Rd FK8 ....2 A1
Whirlbut Cres KY12 .....29 A1
Whirlbut St KY11 ....29 A1
Whitburn Acad EH47 ...170 B4
Whitburn Rd
Bathgate EH48 ....144 C2
Livingston EH54 ....147 B2
Whitdale Prim Sch
EH47 ....170 B3

White Castle Fort* ......

White Hart St EH22 ....157 A2
White Horse Cl EH8 ....233 C3
White Pk EH11 ....122 C3
White St EH47 ....170 A3
White's Cl EH22 ....157 A2
Whitecraig Cres EH21 ..126 C1

Whitecraig Cres EH21 ..126 C1
Whitecraig Gdns EH21 .126 C1
Whitecraig Gdns E
EH21 ....126 C1
Whitecraig Prim Sch
EH21 ....126 C1
Whitecraig Rd EH21 ....126 C1
Whitecraig Terr EH21 ..126 C1
Whitecross Prim Sch
EH49 ....83 C3
Whitedalehead Rd
EH47 ....170 B3
Whitedales EH10 ....154 B3
Whitefield Neuk KY12 ...29 C3
Whitefield Rd EH47 .....29 C3
Whitegates PI FK1 ......59 B2
Whitehall Ct EH4 ....92 A1
Whitehead Gr EH30 .....89 B4
Whitehill Ave EH21 ....126 A2
Whitehill Dr
Blackburn EH47 ....171 B4
Dalkeith EH22 ....157 B1
Whitehill Farm Rd
EH21 ....126 A2
Whitehill Gdns EH21 ...126 A2
Whitehill Gr EH22 .....157 B1
Whitehill Ind Est EH48 .145 B1
Whitehill Pl
Rosewell EH24 ....181 B1
Stirling FK8 ....7 A3
Whitehill Rd
Blackburn EH47 ....145 B1
Edinburgh EH15, EH21,
EH22 ....125 B2
Rosewell EH24 ....181 C1
Whitehill View EH47 ...171 B4
Whitehouse Loan EH9 ..123 B3
Whitehouse Rd
Edinburgh EH4 ....91 A2
Stirling FK8 ....7 A3
Whitehouse Terr EH9 ..123 B2
Whitelaw Cres KY11 .....29 B1
Whitelaw Dr EH48 ......145 C3
Whitelaw Pl KY11 ....29 B1
Whitelaw Rd KY11 ......29 B1
Whitelaw St EH48 ......142 B1
Whitelea Cres EH14 ....177 B4
Whitelea Rd EH14 .....177 B4
Whiteloch Rd EH33 ....129 B3
Whitemoss La EH27 ....149 C1
Whitemoss Rd EH27 ...149 C1
Whitemyre Ct KY12 .....28 B3
Whitequarries Ind Est
EH52 ....87 B4
Whites Quay KY11 ....47 C1
Whiteside EH48 ....144 C2
Whiteside Ind Est EH48 .144 C2
Whitesideloan FK2 ......82 C4
Whitestone Pl EH48 ....145 B1
Whitingford EH6 ....93 B3
Whitson Cres EH11 .....122 A3
Whitson Gr EH11 ......122 A3
Whitson Pl E EH11 .....122 A3
Whitson Pl W EH11 ....122 A3
Whitson Rd EH11 ......122 A3
Whitson Terr EH11 .....122 A3
Whitson Way EH11 .....122 A3
Whitson Wlk EH11 .....122 A3
Whitten La EH49 ....84 C4
Whittingehame Dr FK1 ..132 B4
Wholeflats Rd FK3 ......61 C3
Wholeflats Rdbt FK3 ....61 C3
Wholequarter Ave FK2 ..61 B1
Whyte Pl EH7 ....94 A1
Whyte Wlk KY11 ....29 C2
Whytehouse Ave KY1 ....17 A2
Whyteman's Brae KY1 ...17 B4
Whytemans Brae Hospl
KY1 ....17 A4
Whytescauseway KY1 ...17 A2
Whyteyetts KY1 ....5 B1
Wilderness Rdbt EH54 ..173 B3
Wilderness The FK2 .....22 B2
Wildridge Way KY5 ......14 A4
Wilfred Terr [3] EH8 .....94 B1
Wilkieston Rd EH28 ....119 B1
William Black Pl EH30 ...89 B4
William Booth Pl FK7 .....7 A2
William Jameson Pl
EH15 ....95 A1
William Sharp Pl KY11 ..13 B2
William St
Dunfermline KY12 ....28 C2
Edinburgh EH3 ....232 A3
Kirkcaldy KY1 ....17 A1
William Street NE La
EH3 ....232 A3
William Street NW La
EH3 ....232 A3
William Street SE La
EH3 ....232 A3
William Street SW La
EH3 ....232 A3
Williamfield Ave FK7 .....7 A2
Williamfield Sq [2]
EH15 ....125 A4
Williamson Ave FK2 .....39 A1
Williamson Pl FK2 ....60 B4
Williamson St FK1 ....60 A2
Williamson's Quay KY1 ..17 B2
Williamston Intc EH54 ..148 A1
Williamston Prim Sch
EH54 ....148 A1
Williamstone Ct EH39 ...54 A3
Willow Ave EH19 ......182 A3

Willow Brae EH47 ......193 C3
Willow Dell EH51 ....63 B3
Willow Dr KY1 ....17 A4
Willow Gr
Dunfermline KY11 ....46 C4
Fauldhouse EH47 ......193 C3
Livingston EH54 ....148 A3
Willow Grange FK2 ......61 B1
Willow Pk EH47 ....193 C3
Willow Rd EH22 ....183 C2
Willow Tree Pl EH14 ...151 B2
Willowbank EH54 ......147 C3
Willowbank Row EH6 ....93 B3
Willowbrae FK2 ....82 B4
Willowbrae Ave EH8 ...124 B4
Willowbrae Gdns EH8 .124 B4
Willowbrae Rd EH8 ....124 B4
Willowdean EH49 ....86 B2
Willowpark (Specl Sch)
EH11 ....122 B3
Willows The
Cairneyhill KY12 ....27 B1
Tullibody KY10 ....4 A1
Wilson Ave
Dalkeith EH22 ....157 B2
Denny FK6 ....36 B1
Falkirk FK1 ....59 B3
Kirkcaldy KY2 ....17 A3
Polmont FK2 ....61 C1
Prestonpans EH32 ......96 C1
Wilson Dr Bannockburn FK7 .7 B1
Falkirk FK1 ....59 B3
Wilson Gdns FK1 ....59 B3
Wilson Pl FK4 ....58 A2
Wilson Rd Falkirk FK1 ...59 B3
Gorebridge EH23 ....183 B1
Livingston EH54 ....146 C2
Shotts ML7 ....212 A4
Wilson St Blairhall KY12 .26 A4
Cowdenbeath KY4 ....13 B2
Grangemouth FK3 ....61 B3
Penicuik EH26 ....203 C3
Townhill KY12 ....29 B4
Wilson Terr
Broxburn EH52 ....117 A3
Stoneyburn EH47 ......171 A1
Wilson Way KY11 ....46 B3
Wilson Wlk EH33 ....128 B3
Wilson's Cl KY12 ....29 A2
Wilson's Pk EH15 ....95 A1
Wilsontown Rd ML11 ...215 B1
Wilton Rd
Edinburgh EH16 ....123 C2
Carluke ML8 ....230 A1
Winchburgh Cotts EH52 .87 C1
Winchburgh Prim Sch
EH52 ....87 C1
Winchester Ave FK6 .....36 C2
Winchester Avenue Ind Est
FK6 ....36 C2
Winchester Ct FK6 ......36 C2
Windlebrook KY11 ......47 A4
Windmill Gn KY1 ....17 C4
Windmill Knowe KY4 ....30 C3
Windmill La EH8 ....233 B1
Windmill Pl KY1 ....18 A4
Windmill Rd KY1 ....17 C4
Windmill St EH8 ....233 A1
Windsor Ave FK1 ....59 C2
Windsor Cres Falkirk FK1 .59 C2
Maddiston FK2 ....83 A3
Penicuik EH26 ....204 A3
Windsor Dr Denny FK6 ...36 B2
Falkirk FK1 ....59 C2
Penicuik EH26 ....204 A3
Windsor Gdns Alloa FK10 ..9 C2
Falkirk FK1 ....59 C2
Musselburgh EH21 .....126 C3
Windsor Park Dr EH21 ..126 C3
Windsor Park Pl EH21 ..126 C3
Windsor Park Terr
EH21 ....126 C3
Windsor Pl Musselburgh
EH21 ....126 C3
Windsor Pl
Edinburgh EH15 ....125 A4
Shotts ML7 ....191 C3
Stirling FK8 ....7 A4
Windsor Rd Falkirk FK1 ..59 C2
Penicuik EH26 ....204 A3
Windsor Sq EH26 ......204 A3
Windsor St Edinburgh EH7 .93 C1
Menstrie FK11 ....4 C3
Shotts ML7 ....191 C3
Windsor Street La EH7 ..93 C1
Windsor Terr EH26 .....204 A3
Wingate KY2 ....16 C1
Wingates Rd EH39 ....54 A3
Windygoul Cres EH33 ..128 C3
Windyknowe Cres EH48 .144 C3
Windyknowe Pk EH48 ..144 C3
Windyknowe Prim Sch
EH48 ....144 B3
Winelaw Pl EH23 ....174 A3
Winifred Cres KY2 ......17 A3
Winifred St KY2 ....17 A3
Winterfield Mains EH42 ..78 A1
Winterfield Pl EH42 .....78 A1
Winton La KY12 ....28 A3
Winton Ct EH33 ....128 C2
Winton Ct
Cockenzie & Port Seton
EH32 ....97 B2
Winton Gr Edinburgh EH10 ..
Tranent EH33 ....128 C2
Winton Dr EH10 ....154 B2
Winton Gdns EH10 .....154 B2

Winton Gr
Edinburgh EH10 ....154 A3
Tranent EH33 ....128 C2
Winton Ho* FK34 ....160 B4
Winton Loan
Edinburgh EH10 ....154 A2
Macmerry EH33 ....129 A3
Winton Pk
Cockenzie & Port Seton
EH32 ....97 B2
Edinburgh EH10 ....154 A2
Winton Pl EH33 ....128 B3
Winton Terr
Edinburgh EH10 ....154 A3
New Winton EH33 ....129 A2
Winton Way FK33 ....128 B2
Wishart Ave
Bonnyrigg & Lasswade
EH19 ....182 B4
North Berwick EH39 .....54 B3
Wishart Dr FK7 ....7 B2
Wishart Pl Dalkeith EH22 156 C1
Kirkcaldy KY1 ....17 C3
Wishaw Terr EH7 ....94 A1
Wisp Gn EH15 ....125 A2
Wisp The EH15,EH16 ..125 A2
Witchbrae KY12 ....29 A2
Wolfe Rd FK1 ....60 B2
Wolfstar Farm Cotts
EH35 ....159 C3
Wolrige Rd EH16 ......155 A4
Wolseley Cres EH8 ....94 B1
Wolseley Pl EH8 ......94 B1
Wolsey Ave EH19 .....182 B3
Wood Avens FK10 ....4 B1
Wood Dr EH47 ....169 C3
Wood Lea FK10 ....23 C3
Wood Pl Livingston EH54 .147 B2
Rosyth KY11 ....46 C3
Wood Rd KY11 ....46 B1
Wood St FK3 ....61 B4
Wood Terr EH48 ....144 A3
Wood's Ct EH19 ....182 A4
Woodbank KY4 ....13 A1
Woodbank Crofts EH48 .112 C1
Woodbank Gr KY12 .....26 B4
Woodbine Gdns EH32 ...96 C1
Woodbine Terr EH6 .....94 A2
Woodburn Ave
Dalkeith EH22 ....157 B1
Redding FK2 ....61 A1
Woodburn Bank EH22 ..157 B2
Woodburn Cres
Bonnybridge FK4 ....57 C2
Oakley KY12 ....26 C4
Redding FK2 ....61 A1
Woodburn Dr Alloa FK10 ...4 C1
Dalkeith EH22 ....157 A2

Woodburn Gdns
Dalkeith EH22 ....157 B2
Falkirk FK2 ....60 C3
Woodburn Gr EH22 .....157 B1
Woodburn Loan EH22 ..157 B2
Woodburn Medway
EH22 ....157 B2
Woodburn Pk EH22 ....157 B2
Woodburn Pl EH22 ....157 B2
Woodburn Prim Sch
EH22 ....157 B2
Woodburn Rd
Dalkeith EH22 ....157 B2
Falkirk FK2 ....60 B3
Woodburn St
Dalkeith EH22 ....157 B2
Falkirk FK2 ....60 C3
Woodburn Terr
Dalkeith EH22 ....157 B2
Edinburgh EH10 ....123 A2
Woodburn View EH22 ..157 B2
Woodburn Way FK12 .....5 A3
Woodbush EH42 ....78 C1
Woodbush Brae EH42 ..78 C1
Woodbush Ct EH42 .....78 C1
Woodbush Pl EH42 .....78 C1
Woodend Gdns KY11 ....47 C3
Woodend Ind Est KY4 ...13 A1
Woodend Pk EH25 .....180 C2
Woodend Pl KY4 ....13 A1
Woodend Rd ML8 ......230 A1
Woodend Wlk EH48 ....143 C3
Woodfield Ave EH13 ..152 C3
Woodfield Pk
Bilston EH25 ....180 B3
Edinburgh EH13 ....152 C3
Woodhall Ave EH14 ....152 B3
Woodhall Bank EH13 ..152 C3
Woodhall Dr EH14 .....152 B3
Woodhall Gr EH13 .....152 C3
Woodhall Millbrae
EH14 ....152 C3
Woodhall Pl EH34 .....160 C3
Woodhall Rd EH34 ....160 B3
Woodhall Terr EH14 ...152 B3
Woodhead Farm Rd
KY12 ....25 C1
Woodhead Gr EH48 ....143 B3
Woodhead Pl EH48 ....144 C3
Woodhead St KY12 .....26 A1
Woodhill Ct FK3 ....28 A1
Woodhill Gr KY12 ....28 A1
Woodhill Rd EH48 .....142 A2
Woodland Park Nature
Reserve* FK12 ....5 B4
Woodland Pk* FK12 .....5 B4
Woodland Way FK6 .....57 B4
Woodlands FK10 ....5 C1

Woodlands Bank KY11 ..48 A2
Woodlands Cotts EH48 ..144 A3
Woodlands Cres FK1 ....60 A2
Woodlands Dr
Bo'ness EH51 ....63 B3
Brightons FK2 ....82 C4
Crossford KY12 ....28 A1
Woodlands Gr
Armadale EH48 ....144 A3
Edinburgh EH15 ....124 C3
Townhill KY12 ....29 B4
Woodlands Pk EH54 ...146 C4
Woodlands Rd KY2 ......16 B3
Woodlands Terr KY12 ...26 A4
Woodlands The KY11 ....46 C3
Woodlea Cotts EH49 ....65 A2
Woodlea Gdns Alloa FK10 ..5 A1
Bonnybridge FK4 ....57 C3
Woodlea Pk FK10 ....10 A4
Woodmill Cres KY11 .....29 B2
Woodmill High Sch KY11 .29 C2
Woodmill Pl KY11 ....29 C2
Woodmill Rd KY11 ......29 B2
Woodmill St KY11 ......29 A2
Woodmill Terr KY11 .....29 A2
Woodmuir Pl EH55 ....194 C3
Woodmuir Prim Sch
EH55 ....194 C3
Woodmuir Rd
Breich EH55 ....194 C3
Whitburn EH47 ....170 B3
Woodrow EH23 ....183 B1
Woodside KY4 ....13 B2
Woodside Ave KY11 .....46 C3
Woodside Ct
Cambusbarron FK7 ....6 B3
Falkirk FK1 ....60 A2
Woodside Dr EH26 .....203 C3
Woodside Gdns
Brightons FK2 ....82 C4
Musselburgh EH21 .....126 C3
Woodside Gr FK5 ....59 B4
Woodside Pl
Bridgend EH49 ....86 B2
Fallin FK7 ....8 B2
Woodside Rd Alloa FK10 ...4 C1
Forrestfield ML6 ....141 A2
Stirling FK8 ....2 A2
Tullibody FK10 ....4 A1
Woodside St KY11 ......46 C3
Woodside Terr
Bridgend EH49 ....86 B2
Clackmannan FK10 ......10 C2
Edinburgh EH15 ....125 B4
Falkirk FK1 ....60 A2
Tarbrax EH55 ....217 C2
Woodstock Pl EH16 ....124 A1
Woodville Ct EH52 ....117 B2

Woodville Terr EH6 .....94 B2
Wooer St [4] FK1 ....60 A2
Woolfords Cotts EH55 ..217 A4
Woolmet Cres EH22 ....156 A4
Wordie Rd FK7 ....6 C2
Wotherspoon Cres
EH48 ....143 C3
Wotherspoon Dr EH51 ...63 B3
Wright Pl Kirkcaldy KY1 ...17 B4
Lochgelly KY5 ....14 A4
Wright St FK2 ....60 A3
Writers Ct EH42 ....78 B2
Writers Mus* EH1 .....233 A3
Wymet Ct KY12 ....29 A2
Wymet Ho KY12 ....29 A2
Wynd The Alva FK12 .....5 A4
Dalgety Bay KY11 ....48 B2
Gifford EH41 ....163 C3
Ormiston EH35 ....159 C4
Wyndford Ave EH52 ...117 A3
Wyndford Pl EH52 .....117 A3
Wyre Hayes Cotts KY4 ..30 C4
Wyvern Pk EH9 ....123 B2
Wyvis Pk EH26 ....204 A4
Wyvis Pl ML7 ....192 A2

Y

Yardheads EH6 ....93 C3
Yardley Pl FK2 ....39 A1
Yarrow Ct EH26 ....204 A4
Yarrow Pl FK3 ....61 C3
Yeaman La EH11 ....122 C3
Yeaman Pl EH11 ....122 C3
Yellowcraig Trail* EH39 ..53 A4
Yester Pl EH41 ....100 C1
Yester Prim Sch EH41 ..163 C2
Yetholm Pk KY12 ....28 C1
Yetts The FK7 ....6 B3
Yew Gr EH54 ....148 A3
Yew Terr FK2 ....61 A1
Yewlands Cres EH16 ...155 A4
Yewlands Gdns EH16 ..155 A4
Yieldshields Rd ML8 ...231 B2
York Arc FK3 ....40 B1
York Dr FK2 ....60 B3
York La Edinburgh EH1 ..233 A4
Grangemouth FK3 ....40 B1
York Pl Dunfermline KY12 ..29 B3
Edinburgh EH1 ....233 A4
Kirkcaldy KY1 ....17 C4
York Rd Edinburgh EH5 ...93 B3
North Berwick EH39 .....54 A4
York Sq FK3 ....40 B1
York St FK2 ....60 B3
Young Ave EH33 ......128 B3
Young Cres EH48 ......144 C3

Young Ct KY4 ....13 B2
Young Sq EH54 ....173 B3
Young St Edinburgh EH2 ..232 B3
West Calder EH55 ......172 B1
Young Street La N EH2 ..232 B3
Young Street La S EH2 ..232 B3
Young Terr KY4 ....13 A2
Young's Terr [2] KY1 ....17 B3
Youngs Rd EH52 ......118 A3
Yule Pl EH47 ....145 B1
Yule Terr EH47 ....171 B4

Z

Zealandia Rd KY11 ......46 A1
Zetland Dr
Grangemouth FK3 ....61 A4
Laurieston FK2 ....61 A2
Zetland Pl Edinburgh EH5 ..93 A3
Lochgelly KY5 ....14 A4
Skinflats FK2 ....39 C2
Zetland St FK10 ....11 A2
Zetland Terr FK2 ....61 C1

Any feature in this atlas can be given a unique reference to help you find the same feature on other Ordnance Survey maps of the area, or to help someone else locate you if they do not have a Street Atlas.

The grid squares in this atlas match the Ordnance Survey National Grid and are at 1 kilometre intervals. The small figures at the bottom and sides of every other grid line are the National Grid kilometre values (**00** to **99** km) and are repeated across the country every 100 km (see left).

To give a unique National Grid reference you need to locate where in the country you are. The country is divided into 100 km squares with each square given a unique two-letter reference. Use the administrative map to determine in which 100 km square a particular page of this atlas falls.

The bold letters and numbers between each grid line (**A** to **C**, **1** to **4**) are for use within a specific Street Atlas only, and when used with the page number, are a convenient way of referencing these grid squares.

Example The railway bridge over DARLEY GREEN RD in grid square A1

Step 1: Identify the two-letter reference, in this example the page is in **SP**

Step 2: Identify the 1 km square in which the railway bridge falls. Use the figures in the southwest corner of this square: Eastings **17**, Northings **74**. This gives a unique reference: **SP 17 74**, accurate to 1 km.

Step 3: To give a more precise reference accurate to 100 m you need to estimate how many tenths along and how many tenths up this 1 km square the feature is. This makes the bridge about **8** tenths along and about **1** tenth up from the southwest corner.

This gives a unique reference: **SP 178 741**, accurate to 100 m.

Eastings (read from left to right along the bottom) come before Northings (read from bottom to top). If you have trouble remembering say to yourself "Along the hall, THEN up the stairs"!

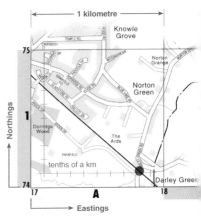

Name and Address	Telephone	Page	Grid reference

Addresses

Name and Address	Telephone	Page	Grid reference